BANKS, LIABILITY AND RISK

SECOND EDITION

BANKS, LIABILITY AND RISK

EDITED BY

ROSS CRANSTON

Cassel Professor of Commercial Law,
London School of Economics

SECOND EDITION

PUBLISHED JOINTLY WITH
THE CENTRE FOR COMMERCIAL LAW STUDIES AND
THE CHARTERED INSTITUTE OF BANKERS

LONDON   NEW YORK   HAMBURG   HONG KONG
LLOYD'S OF LONDON PRESS LTD
1995

Lloyd's of London Press Ltd.
Legal & Business Publishing Division
27 Swinton Street
London WC1X 9NW
Great Britain

USA AND CANADA
Lloyd's of London Press Ltd.
Suite 308, 611 Broadway,
New York, NY 10012, USA

GERMANY
Lloyd's of London Press GmbH
59 Ehrenbergstrasse, 2000 Hamburg 50
Germany

SOUTH-EAST ASIA
Lloyd's of London Press (Far East) Ltd.
Room 1101, Hollywood Centre,
233 Hollywood Road
Hong Kong

First published 1991
Second edition 1995

British Library Cataloguing in Publication Data
A catalogue record
for this book is available
from the British Library
ISBN 1-85044-552-4

Text set in 10 on 12pt Sabon by
Mendip Communications Ltd.
Frome, Somerset
Printed in Great Britain by
WBC Print Ltd.,
Bridgend, Mid-Glamorgan

PREFACE

There is no need to underline the risks and liabilities facing banks at present. Even the most cursory glance at the financial press reveals the strains imposed on banks worldwide, sometimes to breaking point. It was therefore appropriate that the publishers should have thought it ripe to publish a second edition of a book on lender liability.

I am grateful to the contributors, who have revised their original chapters, sometimes substantially. In preparing this new edition I have taken the opportunity to include new chapters from Germany, the Nordic countries and Canada. There is also a new chapter on environmental liability, mentioning United States, but focusing on United Kingdom law. Thanks to Professor Wymeersch and his publishers, Kluwer, there is again included a chapter on the situation in continental Europe. In producing this volume, I owe much to my research assistant, Sonali Abeyratne and to James McCaughey of the legal department at National Westminster Bank. The royalties again go to the Centre for Commercial Law Studies, which continues its splendid work in bringing together the academic and the professional in the study of the subject.

ROSS CRANSTON

CONTENTS

CHAPTER 12 LENDER LIABILITY IN THE UNITED STATES: A DECADE IN PERSPECTIVE *Joseph Jude Norton* 329

CONTRIBUTORS

ARI HUHTAMÄKI: Attorney, Finland; Ass. Professor, Åbo Akademi University

ROSS CRANSTON: Cassel Professor of Commercial Law, London School of Economics

MICHAEL FORDHAM: Barrister, London

ROY GOODE: Norton Rose Professor of English Law, University of Oxford

GREGORY HILL: Barrister, London

ANNIE HOCKADAY: Barrister, London

PARKER HOOD: Solicitor; Faculty of Law, University of Edinburgh

JOHN JARVIS: Q.C., London

JAN KLEINEMAN: Professor of Private Law, University of Stockholm

PETER NANKIVELL: Solicitor, Barker Gosling, Melbourne

J. J. NORTON: Sir John Lubbock Professor of Banking Law, Centre for Commercial Law Studies, London

M. H. OGILVIE: Professor of Law, Carleton University, Ottawa, Canada

RICHARD SALTER: Barrister, London

DIRK SCHLIMM: Rechtsassessor, Dr. iur., Germany; Director Corporate Affairs, Husky Injection Molding Systems Ltd., Canada

DAVID WOLFSON: Barrister, London

EDDY WYMEERSCH: Professor of Law, University of Ghent, Belgium

TABLE OF CASES

AUSTRALIA

BELGIUM

CANADA

FINLAND

FRANCE

GERMANY

Reichsgericht

Bundesgerichtshof

Oberlandesgericht

HONG KONG

MALAYSIA

NETHERLANDS

NEW ZEALAND

NORWAY

TABLE OF LEGISLATION

CHAPTER 1

BANKS, LIABILITY AND RISK

Banks face risk in a variety of situations. The most serious risk is that of going out of business. That is not a risk which confronts bankers outside the United States on a regular basis, but it is not something unknown in Europe in recent times. The law has an obvious relevance to that process, and better provision needs to be made for that eventuality. A more frequent risk for banks is of default by a borrower. That risk ranges from what is compendiously described as the Third World debt crisis to home mortgage and credit card default. Law and lawyers have a role in responding to these situations. Rescheduling agreements, legal action on behalf of banks which have abandoned hope of a negotiated repayment, and counterclaims on behalf of defaulting borrowers all feature.

This book addresses some of these more frequent risks. The term sometimes used these days to describe its subject matter is "lender liability". "Lender liability" is an elastic term, but is generally taken to cover situations in which lenders may be liable to borrowers, potential borrowers, the shareholders, directors, creditors and guarantors of borrowers and potential borrowers, and even to other lenders. Institutional and cultural features of the legal system in the United States—jury trial for civil cases, contingent fees, the propensity to litigate and so on—have spawned a variety of claims falling within this description, including claims for negligence in processing a loan application, failing to negotiate in good faith following a commitment letter, refusing to lend, negligently administering a loan, and improperly calling payment of a demand loan or accelerating and cancelling a facility.[1] While there has not been the same range of claims in other jurisdictions, there has been some recent notable litigation against lenders, in particular the Swiss Franc litigation in Australia.[2] As Professor Wymeersch explains in his chapter, the drive behind much of this litigation is to find a deep pocket when borrowers fail.

Case law in recent years provides some guidance as to the fate of lender liability claims. There is no specific head of lender liability but in particular instances traditional legal doctrines have been mobilised. The present chapter

1. See *infra*, Chapter 12.
2. *Infra*, Chapter 11.

1

examines the broad trend of these decisions. In some jurisdictions, of course, scholarly contributions are influential. I write as a common lawyer, and with no theoretical pretensions. Some of the matters discussed here recur in the following chapters. Chapters 2, 10 and 11, on England, Canada and Australia, remind us that, even in Commonwealth jurisdictions, the trend is far from uniform. Some, but not all, Commonwealth courts are invoking notions of reasonable expectations, and in isolated cases, commercial morality, which could extend the liability of banks.

For the purposes of exposition, and because it enables us to see better some points of practical guidance, this chapter examines lender liability across the life cycle of a loan, in other words, how lenders might incur liability during negotiations for a loan, once the loan has been entered into and is on foot, and if the loan turns sour and is terminated. The doctrinal basis of liability sometimes cuts across some of these categories, but in some respects falls rather neatly into them. This chapter is not concerned with the liability the lender may face as a result of indigenous statutory provisions.

I. THE PRELIMINARY STAGES

Agency, authority and *vires*

There are no obligations on a lender to provide money, but once it has discussions with a potential borrower there is the possibility of liability as a result of what is said (or not said) or done (or not done). At the outset, one must decide what a lender has said or how it has acted. One must look to the actions of its officials, its managers and employees. The law of agency determines whether they had actual or apparent authority to bind the lender in purporting, say, to approve a loan.[3] This involves scrutiny of officials' actual authority to approve loans, for example, the written limitations on their authority. In particular circumstances, the lender may be estopped from denying the authority of the persons who gave a commitment letter to the potential borrower or entered into a loan transaction on its behalf. The legal lesson is that to protect against liability being sheeted home for what officials might say or do, lenders should have clear written authorisation procedures, internal controls to prevent undisciplined practices, and possibly standard clauses for letters and documents to put borrowers on notice about how a loan application will be approved.

Conversely, lenders must make similar checks on those in the borrower organisation with whom they are dealing. So, too, must they make checks on the *vires* of organisations to whom they lend. The "swaps litigation" in Britain brought this point home sharply to international financial markets. It will be recalled that there it was ultimately held that local authority swaps transactions

---

3. *Banbury* v. *The Bank of Montreal* [1918] A.C. 626 is an old case, but illustrates the principle.

were *ultra vires* under the relevant legislation.[4] A further wave of litigation held that the banks could recover on restitutionary principles[5]—but with hindsight a more cautionary approach would have obviated the problem the banks faced.

Arrangers of bank syndicates

Various jurisdictions have recognised the potential liability of an arranger (lead) bank in a bank syndicate to other members of the syndicate for loss suffered by the syndicate as a whole. In the United States liability has been largely placed on the basis of the fiduciary duties which the arranger might owe the syndicate.[6] In the Netherlands the *ABN Amro*[7] case suggests a foundation for liability in the new Civil Code. There the arranger was held liable to bondholders for the borrower's prospectus, because the code makes unlawful the act of a person who "causes the publication of a [misleading] statement relating to ... services which are offered by himself or a person for whom he acts in the course of a profession ...". Would an incorrect information memorandum sent out to syndicate members fall within this article? In England syndicate members might be able to claim against an arranger for its failure to use reasonable care in the valuation of the borrower's property.[8]

Commitment letters

To what extent will the lender incur liability under commitment letters, even though a facility letter or loan agreement has not been completed? Whether a commitment letter is binding depends on the nature of the particular commitment letter. In England a commitment letter "subject to contract" will generally not be regarded as binding, but the same is not the case with one "subject to documentation". Otherwise the following circumstances seem to be relevant in determining whether a commitment letter is intended to be binding, how the document is described, whether it contains a reasonably complete statement of the proposed terms, and the steps preceding, and subsequent to, the completion of the commitment letter. It may be that although there is no right to demand financing from a bank, so that a commitment letter is not binding in that sense, it will give rise to limited contractual obligations, in particular the payment of commitment fees.

The practical advice which comes from this is that lenders must decide whether or not they want their commitment letters to be legally binding. If not,

---

4. *Hazell* v. *Hammersmith and Fulham LBC* [1992] 2 A.C. 1.
5. E.g., *Westdeutsche Landesbank Girozentrale* v. *Islington LBC* [1994] 1 W.L.R. 938 (on appeal).
6. *Credit Français International, SA* v. *Sociedad Financiera de Comercio, SA*, 490 N.Y.S. 2d 670 (1985).
7. *Association of Bondholders Coopag Finance BV* v. *ABN Amro Bank NV*, on appeal noted [1993] 11 J.I.B.L. N–214 (F. Schlingmann).
8. *Banque Bruxelles Lambert SA* v. *Eagle Star Insurance Co. Ltd.*, *The Times*, 7 March 1994.

the easiest method of preventing it is to use formulary language such as "subject to contract". If they are to be binding, then the language should suggest that they are binding (for instance, say so and have the lender sign its "acceptance" of the terms) and the terms in the letter must be clearly indicative of the final terms.

Duty to advise

Generally speaking, a lender will be under no obligation to advise a potential borrower about the nature of the borrowing, its prudence or other features. For there to be a legal duty to advise, there must be special aspects. (In English law negotiations for a commercial contract of lending do not, of course, demand good faith.) The first is if there is a misrepresentation—a failure to speak or act can constitute conduct which misleads. Conduct capable of giving rise to an estoppel might found a claim for misrepresentation. Reliance is essential to such a claim, however, and a plaintiff may be unable to show that it was led to believe that a representation was being made and that it relied on the representation.

Second, there can be liability for a failure to disclose in precontractual negotiations, if there has been a voluntary assumption of responsibility to disclose and reliance on that assumption.[9] In some cases, having regard to the special circumstances and the relationship between the parties, a voluntary assumption of responsibility might be deemed to have been made. Ordinarily this would not occur in precontractual negotiations between a lender and a borrower, even if there were an established business relationship, or a banker–customer relationship, between the two. There is a decision in one of the Australian Swiss franc loan cases to the effect that negligent misstatement covers omissions as well as statements.[10]

Thirdly, if a relationship is fiduciary in character, then disclosure is necessary if a person is to avoid liability for putting interest above duty or duty to one above that to another. *Woods* v. *Martins Bank Ltd.*[11] is the oft cited authority which might found a fiduciary relationship between lender and borrower, but there is much wrong with that case, not least that predating *Hedley Byrne* it was necessary for the judge to find a fiduciary relationship if liability was to be imposed for negligent advice. However, the Canadian courts have taken it up in the leading case, *Standard Investments Ltd.* v. *Canadian Imperial Bank of Commerce.*[12] The Ontario Court of Appeal said that a fiduciary relationship existed between a bank and a company which approached its president for financial and other assistance in effecting the takeover of another company. Breach of that duty occurred because the bank was, through the agency of its chairman, attempting to thwart the takeover. In fact, it is difficult to see how in

---

9. The *Hedley Byrne* principle in English law: [1964] A.C. 465.
10. *Davkot Pty. Ltd.* v. *Custom Credit Corp. Ltd.*, 1988, unreported, p. 304 below.
11. [1959] Q.B. 55.
12. (1985) 22 D.L.R. (4th) 410.

the ordinary case there can be a fiduciary relationship between a lender and borrower. After all, a lender is not undertaking to prefer the borrower's interest to its own. Of course the situation may be different if the lender has positively assumed the role of financial advisor or promoter of a particular financial scheme. Moreover, if a borrower is able to establish a fiduciary relationship, it needs also to establish breach of duty. The situation giving rise to a breach in the *Standard Investments* case was exceptional.

In *Cornish* v. *Midland Bank plc* Kerr L.J. said, *obiter*:

"I think that I would be inclined to the view that in the circumstances of this case, the Bank owed a duty to the plaintiff, as the Bank's customer, to proffer to her some adequate explanation of the nature and the effect of the document which she had come to sign. If expert evidence had been called as to the standard practices of banks in situations such as the present, I think that this would have supported the conclusion that bankers themselves recognize that their proper professional standards would not be consistent with mere silence on their part in such situations."[13]

The context of this remark was whether advice should be given to a potential guarantor. At common law a bank which takes a guarantee is bound to disclose unusual features in the transaction which has been guaranteed. That the lender is unhappy with the borrower's credit and that the borrower is in grave financial difficulties and consistently exceeding its overdraft limit have been held not to be unnatural features requiring disclosure.[14] Much more needs to be disclosed under other systems of law.

In fact, Kerr L.J.'s remark may extend beyond the area of guarantees. In situations "such as the present" he seems to be saying that if it is the practice of bankers not to remain silent, the law will impose an obligation to advise. (What the bank's manual provided proved important in the court's decision.) Terms can be implied in contracts on the basis of custom and usage, which seems to be the basis for Kerr L.J.'s suggestion. If this is the case there would need to be a contract between the lender and potential borrower, into which such a term could be implied, such as that between banker and customer.

Negligent advice

If advice is given in precontractual negotiations, and it proves to be wrong, then the borrower or potential borrower may have an action in contract or tort. Liability in tort on the basis of *Hedley Byrne* depends importantly on a sufficient proximate relationship between the lender and the borrower (or potential borrower) and on there being reliance on the statement. It will be easier to establish proximity when a professional lender advises an unsophisticated member of the public. There have been several common law cases now where the

---

13. [1985] 3 All E.R. 513, 522–523.
14. See *Commercial Bank of Australia* v. *Amadio* (1983) 151 C.L.R. 447, 454–457.

courts have held that a bank was liable in negligence when its bank manager failed to explain clearly to a wife the effect of a charge taken over joint property to secure a husband's borrowings.

It was really the factual issue of what responsibility the bank had assumed that split the Privy Council in the West Indian case, *Royal Bank Trust Company (Trinidad) Ltd.* v. *Pampellonne.*[15] Lord Goff, writing for the majority, relied on the finding of the trial judge that the bank had been prepared to do no more than pass on such information it had. Lord Templeman and Sir Robin Cooke seem to have drawn the inference that there was an assumption of responsibility by the bank, and hence proximity, because of the serious business purposes associated with the plaintiffs' visits to the bank and their trust in the bank to exercise a degree of care in relation to the accuracy of the information passed on. At the least, they concluded, the banks could have warned the plaintiffs not to rely on the information without further investigation.

Once a lender enters upon the task of advising a potential borrower, it is obliged to explain fully and properly about the nature of the borrowing. Fulfilling the duty of care may thus demand a full account of the attendant risks and the disadvantages of the particular borrowing. In several Australian decisions this principle has been applied.[16]

The potential borrower who never enters a contract can, of course, only sue in tort. The potential borrower who becomes a borrower might also have an action in contract, at least for innocent misrepresentation, although the action in tort survives. What happens, though, if the contract has express provisions—not uncommon in commercial contracts—about the effect of precontractual representations? In particular, what of an attempt in the contract to exclude liability for misrepresentation or negligent misstatement? Exclusions of liability for misrepresentation and negligence are now subject to statutory control in many jurisdictions. In any event courts are unlikely to countenance any but the clearest attempt to excuse negligent action or other duties.[17]

Undue influence, unconscionability and duress

At common law a loan or its attendant security may be rendered unenforceable by undue influence, unconscionability or duress.

Undue influence can be actual or presumed. There are established categories where undue influence is presumed—parent and child, solicitor and client, trustee and beneficiary, but not husband and wife, and certainly not lender and borrower. One area that has given rise to litigation is the extent to which a lender can be liable for the undue influence exercised by a third party, such as a

---

15. [1987] 1 Lloyd's Rep. 218.
16. E.g., *Chiarabaglio* v. *Westpac Banking Corporation* (1989) 11 A.T.P.R. 50–602; (1991) A.T.P.R. (Digest) 46–067.
17. Notably *Tai Hing Cotton Mill Ltd.* v. *Liu Chong Hing Bank* [1986] A.C. 80.

husband exerting undue influence over his wife to have her give security over the matrimonial home for his business debts. The House of Lords has said that a lender will be tainted by that undue influence if the third party is the agent of the lender (a rare occurrence) or if the lender has constructive notice of a vitiating factor. A lender will be deemed to have constructive notice in the example mentioned if the lender fails to indicate to the wife (in the absence of the husband) the risks involved or that she should take independent advice.[18]

There is an overlap between undue influence and unconscionable dealing. The requirements for the latter are that there be circumstances of special disadvantage which affect a person's ability to judge their own self interest, and that the lender take advantage of that situation unfairly and unconscientiously. The onus is then on the lender to demonstrate that what occurred was not unconscionable because, for example, the weaker party took, or was recommended to take, adequate advice, or that a full explanation was given as to the implications of the transaction, or that the terms of the arrangement, viewed objectively, were reasonable. *Commercial Bank of Australia Ltd.* v. *Amadio*[19] is the leading Commonwealth case.

Economic duress is unlikely to lead to the vitiation of a lending agreement. The prerequisites for economic duress are pressure to induce the victim to enter into the contract, and that the pressure is illegitimate. The illegitimate pressure need not be the sole reason for the entry into the contract. It was the absence of causation which led the New South Wales Court of Appeal to hold in one case that economic duress was not made out. There the bank refused to hand over monies unless the security document was signed. Although the court regarded the pressure which the bank applied as being unlawful, it concluded that it had played no part in the execution of the mortgage, which had occurred before the pressure was applied.[20]

II. THE LIFETIME OF THE LOAN

During the lifetime of the loan, its terms will obviously determine much of the relationship between the lender and the borrower. Courts will imply only reluctantly additional duties in contracts, unless the relationship falls into an established category. So, if the relationship is also a banker–customer relationship, certain terms might be implied by law into the contract between the parties.

Although there will be general reluctance on the part of courts to imply terms as against a lender, this does not mean that the words of the written loan agreement are the only repository of a lender's obligations during its lifetime.

18. *Barclays Bank plc* v. *O'Brien* [1994] 1 A.C. 180.
19. (1983) 151 C.L.R. 447.
20. *Crescendo Management Pty. Ltd.* v. *Westpac Banking Corp.* (1988) 19 N.S.W.L.R. 41.

First, the contract may be partly oral and partly written, or there may be a side letter; secondly, the words must be construed; thirdly, the bank may be under a duty to exercise due care and skill in effecting some of its contractual obligations; and fourthly, the bank is under a duty not to make mis-representations or to proffer negligent advice.

Terms of the loan

What the terms mean is a matter of construction, although clauses relating to matters such as representations and warranties, covenants and default must be construed in the light of relevant case law. A lender may waive any term for its benefit (for example, a stipulation for so many days notice to draw down).

Duty of care and skill

The duty to exercise care and skill may arise in the performance of the terms of the loan. It has proved a fertile field for liability in the United States, as we see in Chapter 12. Much depends, however, on the particular terms involved and on what the lender has undertaken to do (if anything). For example, has the lender assumed a responsibility to respond immediately to any enquiry, or has it undertaken only to give more general views about market trends, if asked?

The duty to exercise care and skill is imposed on anyone performing a service in the course of a business. For example, the lender should exercise care and skill in paying over money on draw-down: if it executes the request for draw-down knowing that it is dishonestly given by, for example, fraudulent directors of the borrowing company, shutting its eyes to the obvious fact of dishonesty, or acting recklessly in failure to make such enquiries as an honest and reasonable lender would make, it will be liable.

The duty of care and skill arose in several of the Australian Swiss franc cases in relation to advising on and managing the loan. For example, in *Lloyd* v. *Citicorp Australia Ltd.*,[21] Rogers J. had regard to the volatility and uncertainties of the foreign exchange market in deciding on the standard expected of the lender in that case. (There was no question but that the lender had taken on the role of adviser in that case.) Moreover, the nature and extent of advice

"will vary with the known commercial experience of the client. It seems to me likely that the advice to be given to the treasurer of a multinational corporation in relation to dealing in foreign currencies will be minimal compared to that required to be given to a farmer in western New South Wales who, to the knowledge of the adviser, is entering the foreign exchange market for the first time."[22]

In the exercise of any management functions with such loans, and delivering advice as to the taking of decisions relevant to the borrower's foreign exchange

21. (1986) 11 N.S.W.L.R. 286.
22. At p. 288.

exposure, a bank would owe a duty of care to use skill and diligence which a reasonably competent and careful foreign exchange manager would exercise. In measuring this standard, the volatility and unpredictability of the foreign exchange market would need to be taken into account. The advice or information required would vary from one situation to another, depending on the circumstances in which it was sought and given.

What more precisely is the standard of care and skill required in such cases? It is easy enough to state in theory: the duty is to exercise the care and skill of an ordinary lender in exercising that particular activity. Certainly the law does not impose liability for what turns out to be an error of judgement, unless the error was such that no reasonably well informed and competent lender would have made it. Moreover: "Two reasonable persons can perfectly reasonably come to opposite conclusions on the same set of facts without forfeiting their title to be regarded as reasonable ... Not every reasonable exercise of judgement is right, and not every mistake in exercise of judgement is unreasonable."[23]

Sometimes it will be obvious that a lender is in breach of duty. For example, the manager of a bank acting as agent for an insurance company will be in breach of duty in advising in relation to a proposal for insurance for a personal loan that a medical condition need not be disclosed. In more complex cases much will depend on the evidence, in particular the expert evidence as to what should have been done by the lender in the particular circumstances. As with liability for negligent advice, exemption clauses become important.

Negligence

Negligent advice has already been discussed as has the duty to exercise care and skill. In a straightforward loan, there seem to be few other possibilities. In relation to third parties, there would seem to be no duty on a lender to refuse draw-down or to accelerate so as to prevent loss to, say, a guarantor of the borrower. The lender's business is to lend; it is not unnatural if it terminates on default. The guarantor is not in the ordinary course in a sufficiently proximate relationship to be the beneficiary of such a duty.

Constructive trusts

To avoid liability, or to obtain money paid out on a loan, lenders may attempt to invoke this branch of common law. Thus a fraudulent officer in a borrowing company may have managed to divert money which has been drawn down for a loan. Or a lender may seek to impose a constructive trust on property which has been bought with monies lent to, but not repaid by, a fraudulent borrower.[24]

---

23. *Re W (an infant)* [1971] A.C. 682, 700.
24. See Chapter 2 *infra*.

Confidentiality

The problem of confidentiality arises in various ways for lenders. To what extent may the lead manager divulge to other members of the syndicate information which it has obtained from the borrower? May a lender disclose information it has about a borrower to potential buyers of the loan? How much information about the borrower must a lender disclose to a guarantor?

The duty of confidentiality of banks is well established. That obligation applies to lenders generally since on general principle it arises whenever a person (a borrower) imparts to another (a lender) private or secret matters (about the borrower's financial affairs) on the express or implied understanding that the communication is for a restricted purpose. Developments in this area are statutory, as bankers and lenders are increasingly exempted from the duty of confidentiality, or obliged (with statutory protection) to breach it, in relation to information they have about a customer's or borrower's wrongdoing or suspected wrongdoing.

III. TERMINATION

Courts in some jurisdictions have imposed liability on lenders for failure to give a borrower a reasonable time to pay before security was enforced; and so on. Other courts have not gone as far.

Duty to continue lending?

In the oft quoted United States decision, *KMC Co. Inc.* v. *Irving Trust Co.*,[25] the sixth circuit Court of Appeals held that the implied obligation of good faith might impose on lenders the duty to give notice to a borrower before refusing to advance further funds under a financial agreement. A Canadian court has applied a reasonableness test (seven days in that case) to termination of a line of credit.[26] There is no such duty in English law,[27] although in particular circumstances a lender may be estopped from withdrawing credit without reasonable notice.

As Dr Schlimm explains in Chapter 8, termination has been the focus of attention in German lender liability cases. Termination of the lending contract—as with continuous contracts generally—requires the lender to show cause. Objectively banks must show that there has been an impairment of the loan or a material deterioration of assets. Moreover, the demands of good faith and fair dealing also have an impact here. There is some recognition of the principle by the Bundesgerichtshof and some appeal courts that lenders might

---

25. 757 F.2d 752 (1985).
26. *Whonnock Industries Ltd.* v. *National Bank of Canada* (1987) 42 D.L.R. (4th) 1.
27. *Re L.H.F. Woods Ltd.* [1970] 1 Ch. 27.

have become so involved with a borrower that they owe a duty of loyalty to stand by them during temporary financial difficulties.[28]

Default

There is no concept in English law of a reasonable time to pay. The authority is *Bank of Baroda* v. *Panessar*.[29] There Walton J. held that a debtor required to pay money on demand was allowed only such time as was necessary to implement the mechanics needed to discharge the debt before being in default and that in view of modern methods of communication and the transfer of money the available time needed was exceptionally short. The New Zealand Court of Appeal has reached the same conclusion. In *Gibson* v. *ANZ Banking Group (N.Z.) Ltd.*,[30] it was held that a two-hour notice was reasonable as a condition precedent to the appointment of a receiver, given that the companies were insolvent and could not have paid the demand from their own resources. There is an older decision of the English Court of Appeal, which established that equity will not interfere to give relief against acceleration of a loan, although default on the part of the borrower was because of a mistake or error in the borrower's office about the date of payment.[31] The case is consistent with more recent decisions on forfeiture.

By contrast other common law jurisdictions such as the United States, Canada and Australia generally oblige lenders to give a reasonable period within which to meet a demand for repayment.[32] Reasonable time depends on the circumstances, but at its most generous might involve sufficient time for the borrower to take some action such as refinancing. So too in civil law jurisdictions. Thus in Germany the Bundesgerichtshof has held that although there is no general rule, in particular circumstances the principles of good faith and fair dealing demand a warning in certain circumstances, for example, a bank cannot contradict the reasonably generated expectations that it will give advance notice.

Workout

A workout is characterised by legal uncertainty. Since the lender has not yet invoked the formal default mechanisms, its actions in a workout do not enjoy the protection of the express provisions in the loan agreement. Some sort of workout agreement is necessary. Even then a lender might still be exposed to the

---

28. pp. 227 *et seq.* below.
29. [1987] Ch. 335.
30. [1986] 1 N.Z.L.R. 556.
31. *TC Trustees Ltd.* v. *J.S. Darwen (Successors) Ltd.* [1969] Q.B. 295.
32. *KMC Co. Inc.* v. *Irving Trust Co.* 757 F.2d 752 (1985); *Ronald Elwyn Lister Ltd.* v. *Dunlop Canada Ltd.* (1982) 135 (3rd) D.L.R. 1; *Bunbury Foods Pty. Ltd.* v. *National Bank of Australasia Ltd.* (1984) 51 A.L.R. 609.

risks of liability to persons other than the borrower, particularly to creditors and potential creditors of the borrower, and perhaps even in some circumstances, to its shareholders. The *Central States Stamping* decision in the United States is an example (below p. 355).

To what extent will non-statutory duties be imposed on lenders in a workout because of their active intervention in the borrower's affairs? The argument was considered by the English Court of Appeal in the *Pinios* case.[33] In that case, the bank instead of calling default entered into a tripartite agreement with Pinios and a manager, whereby the manager was appointed as sole and exclusive agent to manage and conduct the activities of the vessel whose construction was being financed. The manager was obliged to manage and conduct the activities of the vessel in the best interests of Pinios and the bank, but failed to insure adequately. The vessel was lost. After failing to obtain payment from the manager, despite a successful judgment of the House of Lords, Pinios now counterclaimed against the bank, arguing that it was under a duty to see that the manager did not underinsure the vessel. The Court of Appeal refused to imply such a term into the contract as against the bank.

An additional argument was that the bank owned Pinios a duty of care because it actively intervened in the procuring of the insurance. The authorities cited for this proposition are the well known ones that a debenture holder is responsible for what a receiver does if it gives the receiver directions or interferes with his conduct on the realisation. In the result, the Court of Appeal was prepared to accept the proposition but held that Pinios could not succeed on the facts: although entitled to do so under the workout agreement, the bank had not directed and interfered with the manager's activities.

There is also the possibility in some jurisdictions of statutory liability being imposed on banks in a workout. An example discussed in Chapter 2 is whether banks can be "shadow directors" of insolvent companies.[34] The lesson for a lender of all this is the more it interferes in a workout, the greater the risk of it being liable if things go wrong. In addition, the lender in a workout situation must be careful to document any extension of time and reserve the right to accelerate and terminate. Otherwise, it may be held to have waived its rights under the loan agreement to a greater extent than intended.

Enforcing security

The duty to the borrower required of a holder of security in exercising a power of sale in English law is that the holder of security must obtain a proper price for the property being sold. Liability for loss at an undervalue is otherwise imposed.[35] The duty of the holder of security in obtaining a proper price is also

---

33. [1989] 3 W.L.R. 185. This aspect was not dealt with on appeal: [1990] A.C. 637.
34. See also Chapter 12, pp. 358–359 below (the "instrumentality theory").
35. See Chapters 2, pp. 75–79; and 4, pp. 152–153 below.

owed to a guarantor of the borrower. *Bishop* v. *Bonham* addressed the issue of whether liability can be avoided by the terms of a security. The Court of Appeal held that the holder of the security was not exempted by a clause permitting it to sell as it "may think fit", nor by a clause which provided that it would not be liable for "any loss howsoever arising in connection with such sale".[36]

Environmental liability

Lender liability for environmental damage might be imposed as a result of statute, as with the Superfund legislation in the United States, or at least the way the courts have interpreted it. In the famous *United States* v. *Fleet Factors Corporation*[37] the 11th circuit Court of Appeals held that a secured lender might be liable under the legislation if it had the capacity to influence the borrower's treatment of waste. Mere monitoring of the borrower's business or giving specific advice would not be sufficient, but further involvement could trigger liability.[38] So far environmental liability outside the United States has been a fear, rather than a reality. Lenders are most vulnerable if they exercise their rights to security and occupy or foreclose against polluted land or a polluting facility. However, they must generally be on guard and take steps such as obliging environmental audits of potential borrowers, contacting relevant regulatory authorities direct, and including environmental covenants in the loan documentation.[39]

IV. CONCLUSION

In many ways this chapter is a collection of single instances. The description "lender liability" is precisely that, a description, not a concept known in law. Moreover, in many jurisdictions nothing about the *extension* of liability should be read into the term (by contrast with the connotation of "lender liability" in the United States). What can be said is that whatever the courts might do, banks themselves will continue to attempt to minimise the risk of liability in the way their rights and borrowers' liabilities are formulated in loan and security documentation. As Professors Huhtamäki and Kleineman remind us in Chapter 9, many lender liability claims arose in the 1980s as government deregulated and banks relaxed controls and aggressively pursued business. The worldwide financial recession towards the end of the decade meant banks called loans and failing enterpreneurs sought deeper pockets than their own. The shift away from the political and financial excesses of the 1980s means that once the litigation

36. [1988] 1 W.L.R. 742.
37. 901 F.2d 1550 (1990).
38. In later proceedings in the case the lender was held to be liable for its actions in foreclosing against the borrower: 819 F. Supp. 1079 (1993).
39. *Infra*, Chapter 5.

generated in that decade works its way through the system, we shall return to quieter times. Experience suggests, however, that once lawyers get the bit between their teeth they are very reluctant to let go.

ROSS CRANSTON

CHAPTER 2

LENDER LIABILITY UNDER ENGLISH LAW

"Neither a borrower nor a lender be: for loan oft loses both self and friend ..."[1]

INTRODUCTION

Lender liability is a somewhat amorphous concept.[2] In speaking of it in its literal sense, it is necessary to distinguish between: (i) a situation in which a lender is liable to a borrower for loss caused to the borrower by the lender's (wrongful) conduct; and (ii) one where the borrower is seeking to avoid liability or its obligations under a loan or security documentation, so that the lender suffers a loss through not being able to recover its debt, rather than having to compensate the borrower—that is to say, there are vitiating factors affecting the validity of the documentation. It is the former situation which is truly one of "lender liability"[3] and with which this chapter is primarily concerned, although, in accounting terms, both scenarios impact on a lender's profitability, and so, where relevant, the other side of lender liability, involving risk to the lender, will be looked at.[4]

Lender liability, in its primary sense, involves more than "acting wrongfully" towards a borrower (in a moral, if not, legal connection): actual loss to the borrower must result from the lender's conduct, and the lender must be liable to compensate the borrower as a consequence.[5] This view is reflected in the decision of the Privy Council in *China and South Sea Bank Ltd.* v. *Tan Soon Gin, George (alias George Tan)*,[6] where a guarantor tried to evade liability under a

---

1. Shakespeare, W., *Hamlet* I, 3, 1600–1601.
2. Professor R. Cranston, "Lender Liability—Parts I and III" [1990] A.L.J. 653, at 790, refers to lender liability as "an elastic term" and as "a description, not a concept known in law".
3. Nicolaides refers to it as situations where "courts have found lenders liable—to their customers and their customers' other creditors—for acting 'wrongfully' to their customers": see C.M. Nicolaides, "A Survey of Lender liability in the United States" J.I.B.L. 160. See also the definition of Cranston, *supra*, at p. 653.
4. Cf. J. Jarvis Q.C. and M. Fordham, *Lender Liability: environmental risk and debt* (1993) Cameron May, ("Jarvis and Fordham") Ch. 1, at p. 3, who refer to liability in an environmental sense of direct liability, but also indirect liability regarding the commercially vital concerns of increased exposure or vulnerability through environmental law.
5. A similar view is taken by Nicolaides, *supra*, at p. 168.
6. *China and South Sea Bank Ltd.* v. *Tan Soon Gin, George (alias George Tan)* [1990] 1 A.C. 536 (P.C.).

15

guarantee to a lender on the basis that shares in the principal debtor, which were mortgaged to the lender to secure the guarantee, had become worthless; and that the creditor, with knowledge of the decline in the shares' value, should have sold them before they became worthless. In delivering the Board's advice, Lord Templeman said[7]:

"No creditor could carry on the business of lending if he could become liable to a mortgagee and to a surety or to either of them for a decline in the value of mortgage part property, *unless the creditor was personally responsible for the decline.*" (Emphasis added.)

In the United States, until recently, the main "weapon" of borrowers in lender liability actions has been the covenants of "good faith" and "fair dealing", which the courts have "incorporated" into loan agreements or security documents—both at common law (by implication) and under statute.[8] At common law, there was a tendency, which has now been substantially reversed, to imply these covenants into agreements, where the lender's conduct was "immoral"[9] or "irregular"[10]; this was in addition to the parties' contractual rights under them and the more extensive tortious duties imposed in the United States. The requirement for implying such covenant was whether it could be said there was a "special relationship" between the parties. Such a "special relationship" is akin to a fiduciary relationship[11] or undue influence—as opposed to a *Hedley Byrne & Co. Ltd.* v. *Heller and Partners Ltd.*[12] "special relationship", giving rise to liability in tort for negligent misstatement. The result was that, where a lender had not dealt in "good faith" or "fairly" with a borrower—even though the lender may have acted strictly within its rights— damages awarded by juries (and upheld on appeal) had a strong punitive element. This mixture of co-existent tort and contract liability, called "contorts", has been an important area of the lender liability debate in the United States.

---

7. Per Lord Templeman, at p. 545. See also *Federal Deposit Insurance Corporation* v. *Coleman* No. C–8272, 33 Tex. Sup. Ct. J. 557 (1990).

8. Under sections 1.203 and 1.208 of the Uniform Commercial Code ("UCC"), of which there is no English equivalent. Section 1.203 imposes duties of good faith and fair dealing in the performance and enforcement of contracts. Section 1.208 provides that where a lender seeks to accelerate a debt, it must believe in good faith that its chances of payment are impaired; but the section does not apply to a demand debt. See also section 205 of the *Restatement (Second) of Contracts*, which says that "every contract imposes upon each party a duty of good faith and fair dealing in its performance and its enforcement". And see *K.M.C. Co. Inc.* v. *Irving Trust Co.* 757 F.2d 752 (6th circuit 1985).

9. Cf. May L.J. in *Bank of Nova Scotia* v. *Hellenic Mutual War Risks Association (Bermuda) Ltd. (The Good Luck)* [1990] 1 Q.B. 818, at p. 897, who said that "immorality of conduct does not of itself provide a basis for implying a term in a contract. It serves only as an incentive to the court to imply the term if, on principle, it is possible to do so."

10. See Robert Goff L.J. (as he then was) in *Bank of India* v. *Transcontinental Commodity Merchants Ltd.* [1983] 2 Lloyd's Rep. 298, at p. 302.

11. See *Standard Wire and Cable Company* v. *Ameritrust* 697 F. Supp. 368 (C.D. Cal. 1988) and *Arnold* v. *National County Mutual Fire Insurance* (1987) 725 S.W. 2d. 165 (Tex.).

12. [1964] A.C. 465 (H.L.(E.)). See the origin of the special relationship in the speech of Lord Devlin in *Hedley Byrne & Co. Ltd.* v. *Heller & Partners Ltd.* [1964] A.C. 465 (H.L.(E.)) and the discussion of the fiduciary relationship cases therein.

These concepts of "good faith" and "fair dealing" are "equitable" remedies, imposed on a lender for unconscionable dealing. However, whilst English courts of equity are courts of conscience, they do not attempt to rewrite the parties' contract. Rather, they may set aside a contract where there has been unconscionable conduct,[13] equitable fraud, or undue influence, or they may restore to the person so affected the benefits he has lost. If a contract has not been performed in accordance with its terms, then, if appropriate, damages for breach will be awarded.

English courts—which have dealt with only one major all-embracing lender liability action, and this was resolved in the lender's favour[14]—have a rather different approach to their United States counterparts. They will look at any contract between the parties—in this case, a lender and borrower—and the primary obligations the parties have sought to impose upon each other under that contract; and they will be very reluctant to imply terms, unless they are a matter of "necessity", since the parties are free to determine their obligations. Covenants of "good faith" and "fair dealing" will not fall within a test of "necessity". Moreover, under English law, there is no statutory requirement of "good faith" and "fair dealing" per se in freely negotiated contracts.[15] Also, English courts whilst not imposing greater liability in tort than in contract, when there is a contract between the parties giving rise to liability,[16] are now more ready to allow concurrent liability, provided the imposition of liability in tort is not excluded by the contractual structure[16a] but will rarely award punitive damages: which are tortious, and not contractual.

Nonetheless, this is not to say that a lender, under English law, does not have responsibilities towards a borrower. A lender must use reasonable skill and care

13. As to unconscionability: see *Burmah Oil Co. Ltd.* v. *The Governor of the Bank of England, The Times,* 4 July 1981, where, in a rescue situation, shares in BP were sold to the lender at a price below the Stock Exchange price. This was held not to be unconscionable or against the lender's duty of fair dealing. Equity would not give relief for an unfair bargain—it has to be an unconscionable one, the terms of which showed conduct shocking the conscience of the court. There, but for the lender's interference, a liquidation would have occurred.

14. *Williams & Glyn's Bank Ltd.* v. *Barnes,* a 706 page judgment of Ralph Gibson J. (as he then was), delivered on 26 March 1980, reported, in part, in [1981] Com. L.R. 205.

15. Nicolaides, *supra,* who states, at p. 161, that, "... one well-recognised principle of UK banking law is that a bank owes it customer a duty of skill and reasonable care—a standard very similar to the duty of good faith and fair dealing and one frequently found breached by US Courts in holding lenders liable for damages to their customers". Note section 138 of the Consumer Credit Act 1974 and section 244 of the Insolvency Act 1986 (discussed later in the text), which speak of a credit agreement being extortionate if it is contrary to the principles of "fair dealing"; and section 238(5) of the Insolvency Act 1986, which provides a defence to having a transaction set aside for being at an undervalue if the transmission was, *inter alia,* in "good faith". Cf. Bingham L.J. (as he then was) in *Interfoto Picture Library Ltd.* v. *Stiletto Visual Programmes Ltd.* [1989] Q.B. 433, at p. 439.

16. See *Tai Hing Cotton Mill Ltd.* v. *Liu Chong Hing Bank Ltd.* [1986] A.C. 80 (P.C.). Cf. *Henderson* v. *Merrett Syndicates Ltd.* [1994] 3 W.L.R. 761 (H.L.(E.)); noted by Mulcahy, L.-A., (1994) 15 *The Company Lawyer* 246.

16a. See *Henderson* v. *Merrett Syndicates Ltd.* [1994] 3 W.L.R. 761 (H.L.(E.)) and *Spring* v. *Guardian Assurance Plc* [1994] 3 W.L.R. 354 (H.L.(E.)).

when dealing with a borrower, and can be liable to a borrower for loss arising from a failure to exercise such care. For example, where a mortgagee sells a property at less than the current market value, the mortgagee is liable for the difference between the proper price[17] of the property and the price obtained; or, where a borrower, upon being told by an officer of a lender that approval by the lender's credit committee was a mere formality (only to find out later that approval was not given and was never likely to be), wrote cheques in reliance upon the officer's statement, it was held that the lender was liable in negligence for the loss suffered as a consequence by the borrower, who had relied upon the officer's prediction, which was given without reasonable care.[18]

The following discussion is in the context of a commercial loan, where the parties are at arm's length. Questions of undue influence[19] and inequality of bargaining power and the need to obtain independent advice will not be examined.

NATURE OF BANK AND CUSTOMER RELATIONSHIP

As in the United States,[20] the relationship between lender and customer, under English law, is one of a debtor and creditor,[21] in respect of deposits made by a customer with a lender, which changes to one of creditor and debtor when a loan is made.[22] It is not, normally, a fiduciary relationship[23]—although it can be in very limited situations discussed later—but is, essentially, one of contract.[24]

17. *Downsview Nominees Ltd.* v. *First City Corporation Ltd.* [1993] A.C. 295 (P.C.).

18. *Box* v. *Midland Bank Ltd.* [1979] 2 Lloyd's Rep. 391. See also *First Energy (UK) Ltd.* v. *Hungarian International Bank Ltd.* [1993] 2 Lloyd's Rep. 194 (C.A.), concerned with the question of whether a senior manager, due to his position, had ostensible authority—even though he did not have actual authority—to bind the lender to provide credit facilities to the borrower ("HIB"), where the manager confirmed to HIB that head office approval had been given, when it had not been and was subsequently refused. This refusal left the borrower without finance for three projects. In an action by HIB that the lender was bound by the manager's statements, it was held that the manager had ostensible authority to bind the lender due to his position, and there was nothing to indicate he did not have actual authority. Cf. the Bank of Scotland, whose advertisements state that the local manager makes the decisions.

19. On this question: see *Barclays Bank plc* v. *O'Brien* [1994] 1 A.C. 180 (H.L.(E.)) and *C.I.B.C. Mortgages plc* v. *Pitt* [1994] 1 A.C. 200, and the article by A. Berg, "Wives' Guarantees—Constructive Knowledge and Undue Influence" [1994] L.M.C.L.Q. 34.

20. *Smith's Cash Store* v. *First National Bank* 149 Cal. 32, 84 p. 663 (1906) and *Bank of Martin* v. *England* 385 U.S. 99 101 (1966). See the discussion by K. Curtis, "The Fiduciary Controversy: Injection of Fiduciary Principles Into The Banker Depositor & Banker–Borrower Relationship" (1987) *Loyola L.A. Law Review* 795.

21. *Foley* v. *Hill* (1842) 2 H.L. Cas. 28 and *Lipkin Gorman* v. *Karpnale Ltd.* [1991] A.C. 548, at pp. 573–574, per Lord Goff of Chieveley.

22. *Foley* v. *Hill* (1842) 2 H.L. Cas. 28 and *Lipkin Gorman* v. *Karpnale Ltd.* [1991] A.C. 548 at pp. 573–574, per Lord Goff of Chieveley.

23. *Morrison* v. *Bank of New Zealand* [1991] 3 N.Z.L.R. 291, at p. 295; *Burmah Oil Ltd.* v. *Governor of the Bank of England* (1981) 125 S.J. 528, *The Times*, 4 July 1981; *James* v. *Australia and New Zealand Banking Group Ltd.* (1986) 64 A.L.R. 347; and *Waryk* v. *Bank of Montreal* (1991) 85 D.L.R. (4th) 514.

24. *Joachimson* v. *Swiss Bank Corporation* [1921] 3 K.B. 110 (C.A.), approved by the Privy Council in *Tai Hing Cotton Mill Ltd.* v. *Liu Chong Hing Bank Ltd.* [1986] A.C. 80. A lender has a

Ordinarily, the terms of the contract between the lender and borrower will be unwritten and implied[25]; but, in the context of a commercial loan, with which this chapter is concerned, the terms will be set out in loan and security documentation which governs the rights and obligations of the parties, and so will be express and in writing.

Banker's references: the duty of confidentiality

Part of the duty a lender owes to its customer is to keep the customer's affairs confidential. This duty of confidentiality arises under the implied contract[26] between the lender and its customer, and may also arise in equity.[27] With regard to third parties relying on lenders for credit references as to the financial soundness of a lender's customer, liability may arise in negligence under *Hedley Byrne* principles,[28] subject to the validity of any disclaimer, which would now be subject to the reasonableness requirements[29] of the Unfair Contract Terms Act 1977 ("UCTA").[30]

Information will be considered confidential if it satisfies three characteristics[31]:

(i) the information transferred was not in the public domain;

(ii) the circumstances of the transfer are such that the recipient is under a duty to the confider with respect to the information; and

---

duty to act with reasonable skill and care: see *Selangor United Rubber Estates Ltd.* v. *Cradock (No. 3)* [1968] 1 W.L.R. 1555.

25. *Joachimson* v. *Swiss Bank Corporation* [1921] 3 K.B. 110 (C.A.).

26. *Tournier* v. *National Provincial and Union Bank of England* [1924] 1 K.B. 461 (C.A.). On the question of lender's secrecy: see J.McI. Walter and N. Ehrlich, "Confidences—Bankers and Customers: Powers of Banks to Maintain Secrecy and Confidentiality" (1989) 63 A.L.J. 404 and *Paget's Law of Banking* (1989) 10th edn. (M. Hapgood, ed.), at pp. 257–264. See also J.L. McDougall Q.C., "The Relationship of Confidence": Ch. 8 in *Equity, Fiduciaries and Trusts* (1993) Carswell (D.M.W. Waters Q.C., ed.). The duty could also be set out in any express contract between the parties.

27. *Seager* v. *Copydex Ltd.* [1967] 1 W.L.R. 923, at p. 931, per Lord Denning M.R. and *Attorney-General* v. *Guardian Newspapers Ltd. (No. 2) ("Spycatcher")* [1990] 1 A.C. 109 (H.L.(E.)).

28. Such as in the Canadian case of *Vita Health Co. (1985) Ltd.* v. *Toronto Dominion Bank* 51 C.P.R. (3d) 72 (Man. Q.B. 1993), noted in [1994] J.I.B.L., at N–73. Cf. *Spring* v. *Guardian Assurance Plc* [1994] 3 W.L.R. 354 (H.L.(E.)).

29. See section 11 of UCTA.

30. See *Smith* v. *Eric S. Bush* [1990] 1 A.C. 831 (H.L.(E.)), which considered a disclaimer by a surveyor under UCTA.

31. *Coco* v. *A.N. Clark (Engineers) Ltd.* [1969] R.P.C. 41, at p. 47, per Megarry J. (as he then was). Approved in *LAC Minerals Ltd.* v. *International Corona Resources Ltd.* (1989) 61 D.L.R. (4th) 14 and *Hospital Products Ltd.* v. *United States Surgical Corp.* (1984) 156 C.L.R. 41. See also Megarry V.C. in *Thomas Marshall (Exports) Ltd.* v. *Guinle* [1979] 1 Ch. 227, at p. 248E–G; and Lord Goff of Chieveley in *Spycatcher, supra,* at p. 281B, who said ". . . a duty of confidence arises when confidential information comes to the knowledge of a person (the confidant) in circumstances where he has notice, or is held to have agreed, that the information is confidential, with the effect that it would be just in all the circumstances that he should be precluded from disclosing the information to others." For a discussion of *Spycatcher*: see Professor G. Jones, "Breach of Confidence—after *Spycatcher*" (1989) C.L.P. 49.

(iii) the information has been used for a purpose other than that for which it was intended.

Thus, financial information about a customer would come within this definition. This rule of confidentiality relating to lenders is not absolute. There are four exceptions to it[32]:

(i) where there is a duty under compulsion of law[33];
(ii) where there is a public duty to disclose[34];
(iii) where the interests of the lender require it[35]; and
(iv) where disclosure is made with the express or implied consent of the customer.

It is this last category, which is most relevant to lender's references, particularly when a reference is given without the express consent of the customer. In view of the recently updated Code of Practice for lenders, entitled "Good Banking",[36] which says that, before there is disclosure of a customer's details, the customer's

---

32. *Tournier* v. *National Provincial and Union Bank of England* [1924] 1 K.B. 461, at p. 473, per Bankes L.J.

33. See, for example, the Companies Act 1985 (as amended); Bankers Book Evidence Act 1879; Drug Trafficking Offences Act 1986, *Barclays Bank plc* v. *Taylor* [1989] 1 W.L.R. 1666 and case note on it (1990) 106 L.Q.R. 204; section 39 of the Banking Act 1987; and *Robertson* v. *Canadian Imperial Bank of Commerce* [1994] 1 W.L.R. 1493 (P.C.) (concerning a subpoena duces tecum).

34. See, for example, *Price Waterhouse* v. *Bank of Credit and Commerce International Holdings, The Times*, 30 October 1991; and *Canadian Imperial Bank of Commerce* v. *Sayori*, 83 B.C.L.R. (2d) 167 (BCCA), noted [1994] J.I.B.L., at N–98 (concerning fraud).

35. See *Sutherland* v. *Barclays Bank Ltd.* (1938) 5 *Legal Decisions Affecting Bankers* 163; *The Times*, 24 & 25 November 1938. See also *Bank of Tokyo Ltd.* v. *Karoon* [1987] 1 A.C. 45 (H.L.(E.)), in which a subsidiary of the main lender passed on information to its parent about K, who was a customer, and this was held to be a breach of confidence. As Walter and Ehrlich observe, the case raises a problem for a lender who obtains confidential information in his capacity as a lender about a company of which he is a director: see "Confidences—Bankers and Customers: Powers of Banks to Maintain Secrecy and Confidentiality" (1989) 63 A.L.J. 404, at p. 417. The problem also arises in relation to the lead lender in a syndicate, where it is also lending to one of its customers and the lead lender obtains information about its customer. There, the lender has a conflict of interests, as it has a duty to preserve the customer's confidentiality and also has a duty of disclosure to the other syndicate members. In such a case, the decision of Donaldson J. (as he then was) in *North and South Trust Co.* v. *Berkeley* [1971] 1 W.L.R. 470, at pp. 484–486 may be of some assistance, as it provides that a fiduciary will not be compelled to disclose confidential information to B if it would mean the fiduciary would be breaching his duty to A, whom the fiduciary had acted for in the first place and whom B knew the fiduciary acted for: see discussion of it by Professor P. Finn, "Fiduciary Law and the Modern Commercial World": Ch. 1 in *Commercial Aspects of Trusts and Fiduciary Obligations* (1992) Clarendon Press (E. McKendrick ed.), at 25 and case note by M. Kay and D. Yates, "An Unremedied Breach of a Fiduciary Duty" (1972) M.L.R. 78. Cf. *Spector* v. *Ageda* [1973] Ch. 30, at p. 48, per Megarry V.C., who said that an adviser is required to put both his skill and knowledge at his client's disposal and if the adviser is not prepared to divulge relevant knowledge, then he should not act for the client. Recent cases on solicitors and conflicts of interest have adopted a hard line and indicated that even "Chinese walls" are not acceptable: see *Supasave Retail Ltd.* v. *Coward Chance* [1991] Ch. 259 and *Re a firm of Solicitors* [1992] Q.B. 959 (C.A.); and case notes by C. Boxer, "Chinese Walls: no longer impenetrable", *The Lawyer*, 15 September 1992, at p. 8. See also Arden J. in *Mortgage Express Ltd.* v. *Bowerman & Partners (a firm), The Times*, 19 May 1994; and *Kelly* v. *Cooper* [1993] A.C. 205 (P.C.).

36. Second edition, March 1994, at para. 9.1 Status Enquiries (Banker's References) and the meaning of "Status Enquiries" in the Definition section.

consent should be obtained, the scope for lender liability in this area should be reduced. But, where the lender does make an unauthorised disclosure, the customer has a cause of action for damages or compensation in equity (or a constructive trust or an account of profits) against the lender for any loss suffered.

In England, a recent newspaper report[37] indicates that two British businesses are threatening to sue the Union Bank of Switzerland after it was alleged that one of the lender's branch managers gave a reference stating that a customer was good for "£18m". However, it is argued that, in Switzerland, the "m" refers not to millions, but to "mille" (thousands).[38] The dispute arose out of the sale of property in Spain. The lender is denying liability.

Fiduciary duty

Despite the general creditor/debtor nature of the lender and borrower relationship, in which each party deals at arm's length and looks after its own interests, there are circumstances when this will not be so, and the lender will be under a fiduciary duty. By fiduciary duty it is meant that there is a reasonable expectation on the part of one party (the borrower) that the other party (the lender) will put the first party's (the borrower's) interests ahead of its own.[39] It is a standard of loyalty,[40] in which the borrower "has relaxed, or is justified in believing he can relax, his self-interested vigilance or independent judgement because, in the circumstances of the relationship, he reasonably believes or is entitled to assume that the other is acting or will act in his (or their) joint interests".[41] The key question relates to the role that the alleged fiduciary has taken with regard to the beneficiary's affairs.[42] Thus, a person may be a fiduciary in relation to some of his activities, but not others,[43] which can well be the position with lenders. Also, for a person to be liable as a fiduciary, with the higher standard of responsibility involved, it is necessary for a person to either

---

37. *Financial Times*, 21 March 1994.

38. It is stated that in Switzerland, "mio" means millions.

39. *LAC Minerals Ltd.* v. *International Corona Resources Ltd.* (1989) 61 D.L.R. (4th) 14, at p. 40; *DHL International (NZ) Ltd.* v. *Richmond Ltd.* [1993] N.Z.L.R. 10, at p. 23; *Hospital Products Ltd.* v. *United States Surgical Corp.* (1984) 156 C.L.R. 41; Professor P.D. Finn, "The Fiduciary Principle": Ch. 1 in *Equity, Fiduciaries and Trusts* (1989) Carswell (T.G. Youdan, ed.) ("The Fiduciary Principle"), at pp. 46–47, cited with approval in *LAC Minerals, supra*, at p. 29, and "Contract and the Fiduciary Principle" (1989) 12 U.N.S.W.L.J. 76, at p. 93; and the Hon. Mr Justice J.R.M. Gautreau, "Demystifying The Fiduciary Mystique" [1989] 68 *Canadian Bar Review* 1, at p. 7. See also case note on the *DHL* case by P. Hood, "Fiduciary obligations in a contractual/ commercial context: *DHL International (NZ) Ltd.* v. *Richmond Ltd.* [1994] J.B.L. 285.

40. Professor P.D. Finn, "The Fiduciary Principle", *supra* at p. 28 and "Contract and the Fiduciary Principle", *supra*, at p. 83.

41. Professor P.D. Finn, "Contract and the Fiduciary Principle", *supra*, at p. 94.

42. See Professor R.P. Austin, "Commerce and Equity—Fiduciary Duty and Constructive Trust" (1986) O.J.L.S. 444, at p. 446.

43. *N.Z. Netherlands Society "Oranje" Inc.* v. *Kuys* [1973] 1 W.L.R. 1126, at p. 1130, per Lord Wilberforce (P.C.).

knowingly accept to be a fiduciary or accept a position, such as trustee, agent or company director, in which the law imposes a fiduciary obligation.[44] Hence, in *Bowkett* v. *Action Finance Ltd.*,[45] when a legal executive, who was acting for the lender in relation to the execution of loan documentation by an elderly couple, made it clear to them orally that she was not acting for them, obtained a written acknowledgement of this from the couple and advised them to take independent legal advice, it was held the lender was not to be under a fiduciary obligation to the couple.

Care, however, must be taken in examining a relationship to see if it is fiduciary in character. Terms such as "reliance", "vulnerability", "trust and confidence" and "ascendancy" are "characteristics"[46] and not explanations of a fiduciary relationship, and are apt to mislead, as they are prevalent in other types of legal relationships, such as a contract or tort. For example, in an executory contract for the sale of goods where the seller has provided goods to the buyer on credit (without the benefit of a retention of title clause), the seller is reliant on the buyer to pay the price, and is vulnerable until he has been paid; moreover, he may have trusted the buyer to pay him and has confidence[47] that he will.[48]

However, in a normal arm's length commercial transaction, like a loan, a fiduciary relationship will be rare.[49] A lender will not be acting in the interests of another (the borrower) rather than its own. Moreover, there is a "judicial reluctance" to find such a relationship, except where the application of this "blunt tool of equity" is really necessary.[50] The reason why it is rare is clearly explained by Kennedy J. (of the Supreme Court of Western Australia), in a passage cited by Sopinka J. in the Supreme Court of Canada[51]:

"It would seem that part of the reluctance to find a fiduciary duty within an arm's length

44. *Committee on Children's Television Inc.* v. *General Food Corp.* 673 P. 2d 660 (1983).

45. [1992] 1 N.Z.L.R. 449.

46. Gautreau, "Demystifying The Fiduciary Mystique", *supra*, at p. 5.

47. See Gibbs C.J. in *Hospital Products Ltd.* v. *United States Surgical Corp.* (1984) 156 C.L.R. 41, at p. 69.

48. For an excellent discussion of the fiduciary concept and its characteristics: see Finn, "The Fiduciary Principle", *supra*, and "Contract and the Fiduciary Principle", *supra*; Gautreau, "Demystifying The Fiduciary Mystique", *supra*; and Professor D. Waters, "Banks, Fiduciary Obligations and Unconscionable Transactions" [1986] 65 *Canadian Bar Review* 37.

49. *LAC Minerals Ltd.* v. *International Corona Resources Ltd.* (1989) 61 D.L.R. (4th) 14, at p. 61, per Sopinka J. See also *Hospital Products Pty. Ltd.* v. *United States Surgical Corp.* (1984) 156 C.L.R. 41, where the High Court of Australia refused to find a fiduciary relationship in a commercial relationship; see the note on this case by Professor R.P. Austin, "Commerce and Equity—Fiduciary Duty and Constructive Trust" (1986) O.J.L.S. 444.

50. *LAC Minerals Ltd.* v. *International Corona Resources Ltd.* (1989) 61 D.L.R. (4th) 14, at p. 61, per Sopinka J. (with whom McIntyre J. concurred and Lamer J. agreed). See comments on this case by Professor D. Waters, "*LAC Minerals Ltd.* v. *International Corona Resources Ltd.*" [1990] 69 *Canadian Bar Review* 455; and G. Hammond, "Equity and Abortive Commercial Transactions" [1990] 106 L.Q.R. 207.

51. *LAC Minerals Ltd.* v. *International Corona Resources Ltd.* (1989) 61 D.L.R. (4th) 14, at p. 61, citing The Hon. Mr Justice G.A. Kennedy, "Equity in a Commercial Context" in *Equity and Commercial Relationships* (1987), The Law Book Company (P.D. Finn ed.)

commercial transaction is due to the fact that the parties in that situation have an adequate opportunity to prescribe their own mutual obligations, and that the contractual remedies available to them to obtain compensation for any breach of those obligations should be sufficient. Although the relief granted in the case of a breach of a fiduciary duty will be moulded by the equity of the particular transaction, an offending fiduciary will still be exposed to a variety of available remedies, many of which go beyond mere compensation for the loss suffered by the person to whom the duty was owed, equity, unlike the ordinary law of contract, having regard to the gain obtained by the wrongdoer, and not simply to the need to compensate the injured party."

A similar view has been expressed by Dawson J. in *Hospital Products Pty. Ltd. v. United States Surgical Corporation*[52] and by the New Zealand Court of Appeal in *DHL Ltd. v. Richmond.*[53]

Furthermore, the imposition of a fiduciary relationship where the parties are in a contractual relationship must not be inconsistent with the express terms of that contract,[54] as it is not for the court to rewrite the parties' bargain and impose a higher standard than that contracted for. This requirement of consistency with the contract is similar to the implication of terms. In the context of lender and borrower, the relevant contracts will generally be loan and security documentation.

When then will a lender be under a fiduciary obligation? The most likely situation is when the lender takes on the role of an adviser to the borrower, and is in a position where it has a conflict of interests as a result. It is trite law that a fiduciary is not allowed to have a conflict of interests,[55] and that the fiduciary must make a full disclosure of material facts to its principal.[56]

Common instances of this scenario are as follows:

(i) where it is clear that the borrower is relying on the lender for guidance—this will often be so where the customer is one of longstanding. The position is well put by the Federal Court of Australia, who said[57]:

"A lender may be expected to act in its own interests in ensuring the security of its position as lender to its customer but it may have created in the customer the expectation that nevertheless it will advise in the customer's interests as to the

---

52. (1984) 156 C.L.R. 41, at p. 147.

53. [1993] N.Z.L.R. 10. See case note on this by P. Hood, "Fiduciary obligations in a contractual/commercial context: *DHL International (NZ) Ltd. v. Richmond Ltd.*" (1994) J.B.L. 285.

54. *Cooper* v. *Kelly* [1993] A.C. 205 (P.C.); *Hospital Products Pty. Ltd.* v. *United States Surgical Corp.* (1984) 156 C.L.R. 41; *Raymond Harrison & Co's. Trustee* v. *North West Securities* 1989 S.L.T. 718, at p. 722G–I; and *In Re Gold Corp. Exchange Ltd. (In Receivership)* [1994] 3 W.L.R. 199 (P.C.).

55. *Aberdeen Railways Ltd.* v. *Blaikie Bros.* (1854) 1 Macq. 461, at p. 471, per Lord Cranworth L.C. (H.L.(Sc)).

56. *Brickenden* v. *London Loan & Savings Co.* [1934] 3 D.L.R. 465, at p. 469, per Lord Thankerton (P.C.). It is not relevant that the disclosure of material information would not have altered the principal's action. As to the lender's duty of disclosure: see R. Cranston, "The Bank's Duty of Disclosure" [1990] J.B.L. 163, especially at p. 164.

57. *Commonwealth Bank of Australia* v. *Smith* (1991) 102 A.L.R. 453, at p. 476.

wisdom of a proposed investment. This may be the case where the customer may fairly take it that to a significant extent his interest is consistent with that of the lender in financing the customer for a prudent business venture. In such a way the lender may become a fiduciary and occupy the position of ... 'an investment adviser'[58] ..."

(ii) where the lender acts for both the vendor and purchaser in a sale transaction or has them as customers, leading to a conflict of interests, particularly when the vendor has an overdraft with the lender.[59]

(iii) where the lender fails to disclose material facts to the borrower/advisee—this is related to (ii) above. For example, in *Standard Investments Ltd.* v. *Canadian Imperial Bank of Commerce*,[60] the lender failed to disclose to the predator, whom it was acting for in a takeover, after it found out, that another part of the lender was helping the target, and that some directors of the lender had bought a stake in the target to protect it. A fiduciary duty was held to exist as the predators had relied on the lender for advice and guidance (which the lender said it would give) and it "had a duty to disclose any conflict of interests to deal fairly with" the[61] predators, which it did not do; rather, the lender had "practised secrecy and non disclosure while pursuing its own interests".[62]

Similarly, in *Commonwealth Bank of Australia* v. *Smith*,[63] customers of long standing (21 years) sought a loan to help purchase the leasehold of an hotel. The lender's manager took on the role of self-appointed adviser to the borrowers. He recommended that they purchase a different hotel from the one they wanted—this hotel was being sold by a borrower of the lender (although there was no pressure on the vendor from the lender to reduce its overdraft); told the borrowers not to consult an accountant or hotel broker as he would advise them and this would save costs; told the borrowers that the transaction was a good one, and there was no point in seeking to reduce the sale price when the

---

58. See *Catt* v. *Marac Aust Ltd.* (1986) 9 N.S.W.L.R. 639.

59. See for example, *Woods* v. *Martin Bank Ltd.* [1959] Q.B. 55; *Hayward* v. *Bank of Nova Scotia* (1985) 19 D.L.R. (4th) 758; and *McBean* v. *Bank of Nova Scotia* (1981) 15 B.L.R. 296 (aff'd on appeal), where the same lender manager advised customers of long standing to invest in the business of another customer who bred exotic cows and who was substantially indebted to the lender, and was held to be in breach of his fiduciary duties—see discussion by M.H. Ogilvie, "Banks, Advice-Giving and Fiduciary Obligations" (1985) 17 Ottawa L. Rev. 263; *Commonwealth Bank of Australia* v. *Smith* (1991) 102 A.L.R. 453 (Federal Court of Australia); and *Standard Investments Ltd.* v. *Canadian Imperial Bank of Commerce* (1985) 22 D.L.R. (4th) 410—see article by Professor D. Waters, "Banks, Fiduciary Obligations and Unconscionable Transactions" (1986) 65 *Canadian Bar Review* 37; and *Guertin* v. *Royal Bank of Canada* (1984) 1 D.L.R. (4th) 68, where a lender's manager used confidential information obtained from his customer/borrower to assist a company owned by the manager's wife to outbid the customer/borrower for a snack bar in a shopping centre. The manager was held to be under a duty to disclose his interest.

60. (1985) 22 D.L.R. (4th) 410.

61. *Ibid.*, at p. 443.

62. *Ibid.*, at p. 443.

63. (1991) 102 A.L.R. 453 (Federal Court of Australia).

borrowers queried whether it was not too high; and failed to disclose the lender's valuation which suggested the borrowers were paying too much for the hotel, although the value of the hotel was sufficient to cover the lender's security.[64] A valuation obtained a year after the purchase revealed that the property was worth substantially less than the purchase price.

In an action for, *inter alia,* breach of fiduciary duty, the court held that the lender was under a fiduciary duty as the customers had "looked to [the manager] as their guide in the matter. They evinced complete faith in him and they relied on him",[65] and he had breached that duty. The lender had a clear conflict of interests; and although the manager had mentioned that he acted for the vendor and might not be able to disclose some information to the purchasers, this did not amount to obtaining fully informed consent, which is a question of fact in the circumstances and for which no precise formula exists. Moreover, there had been a clear failure to disclose material facts—in this case, relating to the valuation.

Two final matters need to be mentioned. First, where the borrower exercises its own independent judgement on a matter, the lender will not be liable as a fiduciary.[66] Secondly, there is a distinction between a lender providing information and giving advice.[67] It is only in the second situation that a lender will be liable as a fiduciary.

Where a lender has breached a fiduciary duty, resulting in (economic) loss to the borrower, the most likely equitable remedy is compensation. Compensation is designed to put the beneficiary (the borrower) "in as good a position pecuniarily as that in which he was before the injury".[68] Whilst it looks to the

---

64. There was also an internal memorandum from the manager to his head office, indicating that the existing lease had four and a half years to run; that the landlord of the hotel indicated that he would renegotiate the lease, but, as this was unlikely to happen before the settlement, the repayments of the loan would be set within the existing lease. However, prior to completion, the landlord indicated that he would consider renewing the lease at the expiration of the old one, but the manager did not discover whether the extension had been granted. Thus, the lender's valuation was based on the mistaken view that the lease was for a longer period.

65. *Ibid.,* at p. 474.

66. Professor P. Finn, "The Fiduciary Principle", at p. 50. See also the American case of *Steinberg v. Northwestern National Bank*, 307 Minn. 487, 238 N.W. 2d. 218.

67. *James* v. *Australia and New Zealand Banking Group Ltd.* (1986) 64 A.L.R. 347, at p. 369, per Toohey J. See also *Royal Bank Trust Co. (Trinidad) Ltd.* v. *Pampellonne* [1987] 1 Lloyd's Rep. 218 (P.C.), where merely providing pamphlets on a particular subject was not enough to impose liability (in this case, for negligent misrepresentation).

68. *Nocton* v. *Lord Ashburton* [1914] A.C. 923, at p. 952, per Lord Haldane. See also *Brickenden v. London Loan & Savings Co.* [1934] 3 D.L.R. 465 (P.C.); *McKenzie v. McDonald* [1927] V.L.R. 134; *Day* v. *Mead* [1987] 2 N.Z.L.R. 443; *Canson Enterprises Ltd.* v. *Boughton & Co.* (1991) 85 D.L.R. (4th) 129; *Catt* v. *Marac Australia Ltd.* (1986) 9 N.S.W.L.R. 639; *Hill* v. *Rose* [1990] V.L.R. 125; and *Bennett* v. *Minister of Community Welfare* (1992) 66 A.L.J.R. 550. See also the following articles: I.E. Davidson, "The Equitable Remedy of Compensation" (1982) 13 M.U.L.R. 349; the Hon. Mr Justice Gummow, "Compensation for Breach of Fiduciary Duty": Ch. 2 in *Equity, Trusts and Fiduciaries* (1989) Carswell (T.G. Youdan, ed.); L. Aitken, "Developments in Equitable Compensation: Opportunity or Danger?" (1993) 67 A.L.J. 596; and J.D. Davies, "Equitable Compensation: 'Causation, Foreseeability and Remoteness' ": Ch. 14 in *Equity, Trusts and Fiduciaries* (1993) Carswell (D.M.W. Waters, ed.).

loss to the beneficiary, and so is similar to the tortious measure for damages, the two are not always the same.[69] Compensation looks at whether the loss would have resulted if no breach had occurred[70]—it does not ask whether the loss was caused or flowed from the breach,[71] and is not concerned so much with concepts of "remoteness" and "foreseeability" or "causation",[72] being of "a more absolute nature than the common law obligation to pay damages for tort or breach of contract".[73] Moreover, there is no requirement to mitigate loss, although "losses resulting from clearly unreasonable behaviour on the part of the plaintiff will be adjudged to flow from that behaviour, and not from the breach".[74] Nonetheless, "the loss resulting from breach of the relevant duty"[75] needs to be ascertained, because compensation is not unlimited.[76]

Hence, the borrower should be able to recover all he has lost due to the breach, whether or not it was foreseeable or remote. This means that the actual loss due to the breach will be assessed with the benefit of hindsight, namely the value at the date of the trial, rather than the date of the breach, as in tort and contract.[77]

THE NATURE OF THE LOAN AGREEMENT: CONTRACTUAL CONSTRUCTION

When a contract has been negotiated, English courts have been reluctant to go outside the "four corners" of the contract (or loan documentation) and admit extrinsic evidence. This is in contrast to the United States, where lender liability theories permit a borrower to go beyond the "four corners" of the loan or security document; in this regard, "a course of conduct" may be critical.[78]

---

69. *Canson Enterprises Ltd.* v. *Boughton & Co.* (1991) 85 D.L.R. (4th) 129. Here, the Supreme Court of Canada, by majority, held that, with the fusion of law and equity, the measure for compensation in equity should be the same as the measure of damages for tort. With respect, whilst on many occasions the result might be the same, such an analysis, as McLachlin J. observed in *Canson*, ignores the difference that the law attaches to a tortfeasor and a fiduciary (of whom a much higher standard is expected). A similar view is taken by Meagher, Gummow and Lehane, in their classic work, *Equity: Doctrines and Remedies* (1992) 3rd edn., at para. 263.

70. *Re Dawson (Dec'd)* [1966] 2 N.S.W.L.R. 211, at p. 215, per Street J. (as he then was).

71. *Re Dawson (Dec'd)* [1966] 2 N.S.W.L.R. 211, at p. 215.

72. *Hill* v. *Rose, supra,* at p. 144. See also the view of McHugh J. in *Bennett* v. *Minister of Community Welfare* (1992) 66 A.L.J.R., at pp. 557–558, who considers the two actions of negligence and compensation as being fundamentally different.

73. *Commonwealth Bank Ltd.* v. *Smith, supra,* at p. 480.

74. *Canson, supra,* at p. 163, per McLachlin J. However, La Forrest J., at p. 148, says that mitigation in equity is based on fairness and justice, which it is submitted is correct.

75. *Nocton* v. *Lord Ashburton, supra,* per Lord Haldane.

76. *Canson, supra,* at p. 160.

77. *Canson, supra,* at pp. 160–161 and 162.

78. See Joseph Jude Norton "Lender Liability in the United States: A Decade in Perspective", in Chapter 12 hereof ("Norton") for a discussion of the position in the United States.

The House of Lords has held that evidence of negotiations relating to the parties' intentions should not be received in evidence.[79] Evidence should be restricted to the factual background known to the parties before the date of the contract, including evidence of the genesis and, objectively, the aim of the transaction.[80] Moreover, their Lordships have said that post-contractual behaviour is not admissible to show the parties' intention.[81] Also, it is common in most loan agreements and security documents for there to be a provision to the effect that the contract in question constitutes the entire agreement between the parties (i.e. an "entire contract" clause), that it supersedes all previous agreements and can only be altered by an instrument in writing between the parties.[82]

Exceptions

(a) Course of dealing and prior agreement

However, to these general rules, there are two exceptions. First, evidence is admitted to prove a custom or trade usage.[83] Terms which do not appear on the face of the document, but which alone give it the meaning the parties wished it to have, may be relevant where there is a history of dealing between them.[84] This may be particularly so in a commercial loan between a lender and a borrower of longstanding concerning repayment of a loan.[85] Although each case will depend on its facts, in *Morrison* v. *Bank of New Zealand*[86] it was held that the clear

---

79. *Prenn* v. *Simmonds* [1971] 1 W.L.R. 1381, at p. 1385, per Lord Wilberforce. See also the cases on deletions referred to in *NZI Capital Corporation Pty. Ltd.* v. *Child* (1991) 23 N.S.W.L.R. 481.

80. *Prenn* v. *Simmonds* [1971] 1 W.L.R. 1381, at p. 1385, per Lord Wilberforce. See also Robert Goff J. (as he then was) in *Ets. Soules & Cie.* v. *International Trade Development Co. Ltd.* [1979] 2 Lloyd's Rep. 122, at p. 133.

81. See *Whitworth Street Estates (Manchester) Ltd.* v. *James Miller & Partners Ltd.* [1970] A.C. 583 (H.L.(E.)), and *Schuler A.G.* v. *Wickman Machine Tools Sales Ltd.* [1974] A.C. 235 (H.L.(E.)). Cf. *Hide & Skin Trading Pty. Ltd.* v. *Oceanic Meat Traders Ltd.* (1990) 20 N.S.W.L.R. 310 and case note by L. Jones, "Construction—Admissibility of Evidence of Post-Contract Conduct" (1991) 4 *Journal of Contract Law* ("J.C.L.") 163. See also S. Charles Q.C., "Interpretation of Ambiguous Contracts by Reference to 'Subsequent Conduct'" (1991) J.C.L. 16. Where, however, post-contractual behaviour is used to show what was agreed, and not as an aid to interpretation, this does not breach the rule: see *National Bank of New Zealand Ltd.* v. *Murland* [1991] 3 N.Z.L.R., 86, at p. 93, citing *Chitty on Contracts, General Principles* (1989) 26th edn. ("*Chitty*").

82. See *Boyd & Forrest* v. *Glasgow & South Western Railway Co.* 1915 S.C. (H.L.) 20; and see also *Johnson Matthey Ltd.* v. *A.C. Rochester Overseas Corp.* (1990) 23 N.S.W.L.R. 190, and the cases cited therein on p. 196.

83. See Professor G.H. Treitel, *The Law of Contract* (1991) 8th edn., at pp. 180–183.

84. For a discussion of course of dealing contracts: see J. Swanton, "Incorporation of Contractual terms by a Course of Dealing" (1993) 6 J.C.L. 223.

85. Cf. *CIP Line* v. *Toronto Dominion Bank* (1988) 55 D.L.R. (4th) 308, where a lender had continued a line of credit for several months although the customer was not complying with certain loan requirements, but then reduced the credit without notice. It was held that no course of dealing had arisen between the parties by which the lender was required to give the customer notice.

86. [1991] 3 N.Z.L.R. 291, at pp. 294–295. Cf. *Henry Kendall & Sons* v. *Williams Lillico & Sons Ltd.* [1969] 2 A.C. 31.

words of a mortgage could not be modified by a course of dealing. Secondly, whilst, *prima facie*, a loan document purports to be a valid record of the parties' intention, it may have been previously agreed[87] to postpone its operation until the occurrence of a future event, such as the approval of a third party, which has yet to take place.

(b) Waiver, variation and estoppel

Furthermore, there may well be oral or written representations made before or after a contract has been executed which alter the parties' obligations under it. In this respect, three situations are common: waiver, variation and estoppel.

(i) Waiver A waiver occurs when one party to an agreement (in this case, it will be the lender) by his conduct or words, either expressly or impliedly, represents clearly to the other party that it does not insist upon its strict legal rights. The representation—usually by way of a forbearance—is unsupported by consideration and is acted upon by the other party with the result that the first party, having made the representation, cannot seek to enforce its strict legal rights.[88] Thus, there is no mutuality.[89] For example, a lender may dispense with the borrower's need to comply with certain conditions precedent in a loan agreement; or not insist upon a particular payment on the specified date, but allow a borrower to pay it later. To try to avoid any problems with a possible waiver, there is normally a clause in a loan agreement preserving a lender's rights in relation to any waiver it may give, so that its future rights are not extinguished, even though a waiver does not irrevocably alter the parties' rights.

(ii) Variation A variation is to be distinguished from a waiver in that there is mutuality between the parties and consideration. The parties agree to change a loan agreement or security document. The agreement is altered in a manner that may prejudice or benefit either party—this detriment or benefit provides consideration for each party's promise.[90] For example, there may be a variation of the security documentation required under a facility letter—instead of taking a director's guarantee, in addition to a mortgage over an asset of the borrower, the lender may take a mortgage over another asset of the borrower. Because of the element of mutuality, there can be no variation if the alteration is for one party's benefit only.[91] A variation is reconcilable with the prohibition on extrinsic evidence not being admitted to affect an agreement's terms, as the rule

87. For example, by a side letter.

88. *Charles Rickards Ltd.* v. *Oppenheim* [1950] 1 K.B. 616, at p. 622, per Denning L.J. (as he then was); *Neylon* v. *Dickens* [1978] 2 N.Z.L.R. 35 (P.C.); *W.J. Alan & Co. Ltd.* v. *El Nasr Export and Import Co.* [1972] 2 Q.B. 189 at p. 213, per Lord Denning M.R. See also recent decisions of the House of Lords in *Motor Oil Hellas (Corinth Refineries) S.A.* v. *Shipping Corporation of India (The Kanchenjunga)* [1990] 1 Lloyd's Rep. 391; and the High Court of Australia in *Commonwealth of Australia* v. *Verwayen* (1990) 170 C.L.R. 394.

89. *Chitty*, at paras. 207, 208 and 1605–1608.

90. See *Chitty*, at para. 206; and Professor G.H. Treitel, *The Law of Contract* (1991), 8th edn., at p. 96 and the cases cited therein.

91. *Chitty*, at paras. 206 and 1599.

concerns the parties' original intention, not a later alteration. As a matter of prudence—whether or not an agreement is required to be in writing[92]—all variations should be in writing and acknowledged by the parties, and if there is doubt about the question of consideration, the variation should be by way of deed.

(iii) Estoppel The third exception in this group is estoppel. Two types of estoppel are relevant here: estoppel by representation (or estoppel *in pais*) and promissory estoppel[93] (a form of estoppel made famous by Lord Denning,[94] which is similar to waiver). The elements of an estoppel by representation[95] are that: (a) there is a representation by the lender to the borrower either in words or by acts or by conduct, or, where there is a duty to speak, by silence or inaction; and (b) the representation is made with the intention (actual or presumptive), and has the result, of inducing the borrower, on the strength of the representation, to alter his (the borrower's) position to his detriment. Thus, there is reliance and detriment in relation to a representation, and there is a permanent alteration of the parties' rights. However, estoppel by representation does not of itself provide a cause of action.

Promissory estoppel, under English law, is "fundamentally" different[96] from the United States form which "developed partly in response to the limiting effects of the adoption of the bargain theory of consideration" and is not part of English jurisprudence.[97] Before discussing this doctrine in detail, one obvious difference to note is that in the United States, promissory estoppel founds a cause of action; in England, it does not.

There are generally considered to be five elements of promissory estoppel under English law.[98] First, there needs to be a clear and unequivocal

92. *Chitty*, at para. 1600.
93. *Central London Property Trust Ltd.* v. *High Trees House Ltd.* [1947] K.B. 130. The literature on promissory estoppel is voluminous. In particular, see Lord Denning, *The Discipline of Law* (1979), Butterworths; *Chitty*, at paras. 209–243; and the Hon. Mr Justice G.A. Kennedy, "Equitable Estoppel" (1984) 58 A.L.J. 573, which contains a comprehensive review of the authorities up to 1984.
94. *Ibid.*
95. Spencer Bower and Turner, *Estoppel by Representation* (1977) 3rd edn., Ch. 1.
96. Kennedy, "Equitable Estoppel" (1984) 58 A.L.J. 573, at p. 578.
97. *Waltons Stores (Interstate) Ltd.* v. *Maher* (1988) 164 C.L.R. 387, at p. 402, per Mason C.J. and Wilson J.
98. See Meagher, Gummow and Lehane, *Equity: Doctrines and Remedies* (1988) 2nd edn., at para. 1706 (the third edition (1992) has been altered to reflect the Australian position more fully); Kennedy, "Equitable Estoppel" (1984) 58 A.L.J. 573; *Halsbury's Laws of England*, 4th edn., Vol. 16, at para. 1071, which lists three factors; and E.M. Heenan, *Estoppel; General Principles* (1984), Law Society of Western Australia Seminar on Equitable Remedies and Estoppel. See also the judgment of Brennan J. in *Waltons Stores (Interstate) Ltd.* v. *Maher* (1988) 164 C.L.R. 387, at pp. 428–429, who outlined six components in equitable estoppel, thus: "[I]t is necessary for the plaintiff to prove that (1) the plaintiff assumed that a particular legal relationship then existed between the plaintiff and the defendant or expected that a particular legal relationship would exist between them and, in the latter case, that the defendant would not be free to withdraw from the expected legal relationship; (2) the defendant has induced the plaintiff to adopt that assumption or expectation; (3) the plaintiff acts or abstains from acting in reliance on the assumption or expectation; (4) the defendant knew or intended him to do so; (5) the plaintiff's action or inaction

representation or assurance in the form of a promise, which is voluntary, from the promisor to the promisee. This assurance is given with the intention, or in the knowledge, that the promisee will alter his legal position in reliance on it. Unlike estoppel *in pais* (or estoppel by representation), this promise relates to future conduct, and does not have to relate to an existing fact.

Secondly, there must be existing legal relations (usually contractual) between the parties. However, the Privy Council, in *Bank Negara Indonesia* v. *Hoalim*,[99] has indicated that it is sufficient if legal rights or relations came into existence upon the promisee changing his position due to the promisor's promise.[100] In the leading case of *Combe* v. *Combe*,[101] the relationship was not contractual, nor was it a pre-existing relationship or obligation.[102]

Thirdly, there must be action or reliance upon the promise or assurance. In contrast to estoppel *in pais*, there does not have to be detriment; it is sufficient if the promisee alters his position in reliance on the assurance[103]—this can amount to the promisee being given an extension of time.[104] Equity intervenes because it would be unconscionable for the promisor to resile from his position, not because of the action of the promisee in reliance upon the assurance.[105] Thus, it is the withdrawal of the promise, not the acting upon it.[106]

Fourthly, like waiver, promissory estoppel is temporary in its effect. The promisor may resile from this promise by giving the promisee sufficient notice that he intends to resume his former position. However, when the promisee has gone too far in reliance upon the assurance, and cannot resume its former position, the estoppel becomes permanent,[107] although such a situation is, arguably, a variation supported by consideration.[108]

Lastly, promissory estoppel is "a shield not a sword"[109]: it does create a cause of action.[110] But this does not mean that promissory estoppel cannot be used as

---

will occasion detriment if the assumption or expectation is not fulfilled; and (6) the defendant has failed to act to avoid that detriment whether by fulfilling the assumption or expectation or otherwise."

99. [1973] M.L.J. 3.

100. See also *Evenden* v. *Guildford City Association Football Club Ltd.* [1975] 2 All E.R. 269 and *Durham Fancy Goods Ltd.* v. *Michael Jackson (Fancy Goods) Ltd.* [1968] 2 Q.B. 839, for cases where the relationship was not contractual.

101. [1951] 2 K.B. 215 (C.A.).

102. See Kennedy, "Equitable Estoppel" (1984) 58 A.L.J. 573, at p. 587.

103. See *Central London Property Trust Ltd.* v. *High Trees House Ltd.* [1947] K.B. 130, at pp. 134–135, per Denning J. (as he then was) and *Combe* v. *Combe* [1951] 2 K.B. 215, at pp. 220–221, per Denning L.J. (as he then was).

104. Meagher, Gummow and Lehane, *Equity Doctrines and Remedies* (1988) 2nd edn., at para. 1706.

105. Kennedy, "Equitable Estoppel" (1984) 58 A.L.J. 573, at p. 587.

106. *Ibid.*

107. *Ajayi* v. *R T Briscoe (Nigeria) Ltd.* [1964] 1 W.L.R. 1326. This is similar to the change of position defence in restitution: see *Lipkin Gorman* v. *Karpnale Ltd.* [1991] A.C. 548 (H.L.(E.)).

108. See Heenan, *supra*, at p. 27.

109. Per Birkett L.J. in *Combe* v. *Combe* [1951] 2 K.B. 215, at p. 224.

110. Per Denning L.J. (as he then was) in *Combe* v. *Combe* [1951] 2 K.B. 215, at p. 221.

part of an action by a plaintiff, or by a defendant on a counterclaim.[111] For example, in *Birmingham and District Land Co.* v. *Land and North Western Railway Co.*,[112] the plaintiff sought an injunction and declaration concerning its interest in land which was subject to a previous agreement and succeeded in obtaining the declaration. The doctrine was also used in an attacking fashion in *Hughes* v. *Metropolitan Railway Co.*,[113] where a lessee sought to defeat an action for ejectment.[114]

Whilst it has been a popular plea, promissory estoppel has rarely succeeded.[115] Nonetheless, estoppel may be relevant if a lender brings an action against a borrower for non-payment of a loan, and there has been an oral statement by a representative of the lender that the borrower does not have to repay it till a later date, which the borrower relies on to his detriment. For example, the borrower may alter his position by using the sum that would have been repayable for another purpose, such as paying another creditor or using it to purchase equipment or an item of stock. The borrower may be able to raise promissory estoppel as a defence to a claim for the sum in question and to counterclaim for damages for breach of contract.[116] Also, it may be relevant where the lender has said it would lend money to the borrower, who, in reliance on this representation, proceeds to purchase items for its business only to find the lender later refusing the loan. In such a situation—depending on the nature of the representation—the lender may be estopped from refusing the loan.[117]

As a matter of prudence, any representation which may give rise to an estoppel, waiver or variation should be in writing—even if this amounts to a confirmatory letter—so that there can be no dispute about it. A common

111. Meagher, Gummow & Lehane, *Equitable Doctrines and Remedies* (1988) 2nd edn., at para. 1707.

112. (1888) 40 Ch. D. 268 (C.A.).

113. (1877) 2 App. Cas. 439 (H.L.(E.)).

114. See also *Combe* v. *Combe* [1951] 2 K.B. 215 and *Argy Trading Development* Co. Ltd. v. *Lapid Developments Ltd.* [1977] 1 W.L.R. 444. D.J.M. Bennett Q.C. argues that equitable estoppel could be used as a sword by the simple device of suing upon the state of facts created by the estoppel and then seeking to strike out the denial: see "Equitable Estoppel and Related Estoppels" (1987) 61 A.L.J. 540, at p. 545. Thus, it is submitted that it may be a question of who sues first. See also recent Commonwealth authority: *Legione* v. *Hately* (1983) 152 C.L.R. 406 (High Court of Aust.); *Waltons Stores (Interstate) Ltd.* v. *Maher* (1988) 164 C.L.R. 387; *Foran* v. *Wright* (1989) C.L.R. 385; (1990) A.L.R. 413 and *Commonwealth* v. *Verwayen* (1990) 170 C.L.R. 394; and *Burbery Mortgage Finance & Savings Ltd.* v. *Hindsbank Bank Holdings Ltd.* [1989] 1 N.Z.L.R. 356 (C.A.) in which case it was stated promissory estoppel is not limited to dealings between parties having prior contractual relations.

115. Kennedy, "Equitable Estoppel" (1984) 58 A.L.J. 573, at p. 579. A plea of waiver and estoppel was unsuccessful in *Williams & Glyn, supra*; see especially at pp. 303 and 308–311 of the transcript.

116. See also the Court of Appeal decision in *Lombard North Central plc* v. *Stobart, The Times*, 2 February 1990, where a finance company was held to be barred by its undervaluation of a motor car and was estopped from enforcing its strict legal rights against the purchaser, who had acted upon the finance company's unequivocal representations.

117. Cf. *Winterton Constructions Pty. Ltd.* v. *Hambros Australia Ltd.* (1993) 111 A.L.R. 649. Cf. also *First Energy (UK) Ltd.* v. *Hungarian International Bank Ltd.* [1993] 2 Lloyd's Rep. 194 (C.A.).

example of an estoppel or waiver arises in guarantees, where the lender seeks to set up an estoppel or waiver of rights against the guarantor by a provision in the guarantee document stating that the guarantee was not entered into on the basis of any representation from the lender or its agents.

(c) Implied terms

As stated previously, English courts have shown a strong reluctance to imply terms in a contract. The sorts of factors (which may overlap)[118] that a court will look at in implying a term into a contract are that:

> (i) the term must be reasonable and equitable;
> (ii) the term must be necessary to give business efficacy to the contract, so that no term will be implied if the contract is effective without it;
> (iii) it must be so obvious that "it goes without saying"[119];
> (iv) it must be capable of clear expression; and
> (v) it must not contradict an express term of the contract.[120]

The test most frequently used is that laid down by Lord Wilberforce in *Liverpool City Council* v. *Irwin*,[121] in which his Lordship said that terms should only be implied by law "as the nature of the contract itself implicitly requires, no more, no less: a test, in other words, of necessity".[122] This test has been held to be appropriate to both the implication of terms in fact and the implications of terms in law.[123] The former refers to "an implied term necessary to give business efficacy to a particular contract"[124]; the latter refers to the implication of a term "as a necessary incident of a definable category of contractual relationship",[125]

118. See *BP Refinery (Westernport) Pty. Ltd.* v. *Shire of Hastings* (1982) 149 C.L.R. 337 at p. 347 (P.C.), approved by the High Court of Australia in *Codelfa Construction Pty. Ltd.* v. *State Rail Authority of New South Wales* (1981–1982) 149 C.L.R. 337 and *Khoury* v. *Government Insurance Office of New South Wales* (1983–1984) 165 C.L.R. 622.

119. It can also be expressed by saying that the both parties would have agreed to it without hesitation: see Lord Cross of Chelsea in *Liverpool City Council* v. *Irwin* [1977] A.C. 239, at p. 258.

120. See the recent decision of the Court of Appeal in *Johnstone* v. *Bloomsbury Health Authority* [1992] Q.B. 333. Note the discussion by A. Phang, "Implied Terms in English Law—Some Recent Developments" [1993] J.B.L. 394 and E. MacDonald, "Express and Implied Terms and Exemptions" (1991) 107 L.Q.R. 555.

121. [1977] A.C. 239 (H.L.(E.)); see also Bowen L.J. in *The Moorcock* (1889) 14 P.D. 64 (C.A.). As to implied terms generally: see *Chitty*, at paras. 901 *et seq.*

122. At p. 254F. Cf. Lord Salmon in the same case, at p. 262, who referred to a transaction becoming "inefficacious, futile and absurd"; and Lord Cross of Chelsea, at p. 258.

123. See Lord Bridge of Harwich in *Scally* v. *Southern Health and Social Services Board* [1992] 1 A.C. 294, at p. 307—an employment contract case. See also Ralph Gibson L.J. in *Reid* v. *Rush & Tompkins Group plc* [1990] 1 W.L.R. 212, at p. 220, a non-lending case where there was a refusal to imply a term in a contract of employment that an employer should insure an employee against the risk of injury by third parties caused to him while acting in the course of employment. In that case, his Lordship (who delivered the leading judgment) said that such a term could not be implied under the test of necessity as being applicable to all such contracts of employment, nor could it be implied as a term which the parties must have agreed.

124. *Scally* v. *Southern Health and Social Services Board* [1992] 1 A.C. 294, at p. 307.

125. *Ibid.*

and is based on "wider considerations".[126] Nonetheless, the criterion justifying implication of the second kind "is necessity not reasonableness".[127] Moreover, it is suggested that any implementation in loan documentation will be an implication of fact: not law, as a loan contract is a commercial contract to be construed according to its terms.[128]

Clearly, vague notions of "good faith" and "fair dealing" do not fall within any of the five criteria listed above and terms cannot be said to be "necessary" on this basis. Examples of the courts' reluctance to imply terms into a loan agreement are to be found in *Williams & Glyn's Bank Ltd.* v. *Barnes*,[129] the only comprehensive English case on lender liability.

Briefly stated, the facts were that Mr Barnes ("Barnes"), the defendant, was the chairman, managing director and majority shareholder in Northern Development Holdings ("NDH"). NDH was involved in property development. Prior to 1973, NDH had been very profitable. The plaintiff lender ("the lender") had become the principal clearing lender for NDH from 1965, although NDH had also borrowed very substantial sums from numerous other sources. In July of 1972, at Barnes' request, the lender raised NDH's overdraft from £2.5m to £6.5m. Whilst the lender felt that NDH's financial needs should be met by an increase in equity, rather than an increase in borrowings, the lender did not insist upon this or advise NDH to undertake any additional equity financing.

In October 1972, Barnes was granted a personal loan of £1m by the lender for 12 months to allow him to buy more shares in NDH. This loan was secured by a share charge in favour of the lender over Barnes' shares in NDH. It was anticipated by both parties that the loan would be repaid by Barnes out of monies owed to him, or to other companies which he controlled, by NDH. The lender did not want to be repaid out of the sale proceeds of the shares, because it considered that adverse publicity would result if Barnes sold a large parcel of NDH shares.

The building boom collapsed in 1973, causing NDH great difficulties. In August of that year, Barnes sought to increase NDH's overdraft from £6.5m to £14m. The lender refused, although from 1966 it had increased NDH's overdraft, upon Barnes' request, from £20,000 to £6.5m in 1972. A further difficulty was created in that, since 1971, NDH had also raised money under a complex system of revolving credits with a secondary lender. This secondary lender collapsed in December 1973 and NDH found itself liable to repay £3m on the bills of exchange which it had drawn down or accepted, though it had only borrowed £1.5m on them. The lender agreed to lend NDH £3m to meet the bills on the terms of a facility letter, dated 14 January 1974 (the "January facility

---

126. *Ibid.*
127. *Ibid.*, at p. 307.
128. *Williams & Glyn's Bank Ltd.* v. *Barnes* [1981] Com. L.R. 205, at p. 209.
129. [1981] Com. L.R. 205.

letter"). Under the January facility letter, NDH's total borrowings from the lender were increased to £11m on a temporary basis.

By June 1974, NDH was unable to pay the interest due on its loan from the lender. In July 1974, the lender and the other main lenders to NDH entered into a moratorium agreement under which interest "was rolled up". The lender issued a new facility letter to NDH in August 1974 (the "August facility letter"), which expressly made the lender's loans to NDH repayable "on demand". New security arrangements were also introduced. A further £100,000 was lent personally to Barnes by the lender in September 1974 to enable him to meet pressing financial difficulties.

A new moratorium agreement, entitled "the Heads of Agreement", was entered into in November 1974. Pursuant to the Heads of Agreement, any five or more parties, who were together owed more than £10m, could terminate the moratorium. In June 1974, the parties to the Heads of Agreement made demands on NDH and appointed a receiver. On 30 May 1975, the parties to the Heads of Agreement decided to bring the moratorium to an end.

The lender sued Barnes for the sum of £1.1m plus interest. Barnes admitted the loans were due, subject to various defences and counterclaims. Interestingly, NDH was not a party to the action, as Barnes could not convince the directors to become involved.

On the basis of these facts, four attempts were made to imply terms into the various loan documents agreements. The first related to an application of the principle in the House of Lords' decision in *Southern Foundries (1926) Ltd.* v. *Shirlaw*[130] in which it was said that, where a party ("X") enters into an arrangement which can only take effect by the continuance of an existing state of circumstances, there is an implied agreement that X shall not do anything to alter that state of affairs. Barnes argued that repayment of the £1m lent to him was to be out of monies NDH owed him and that it was an implied term that repayment should not be made impossible by the lender's breaches of its duty to, and contract with, NDH.

Ralph Gibson J. (as he then was) held that, in the absence of an express provision in the loan agreement with Barnes that the lender would be repaid out of monies owed to Barnes by NDH, justice did not require such a term to be implied.[131] There was no evidence that Barnes had entered into an arrangement that only took effect due to a particular state of affairs continuing, namely, the fund as a source of repayment. If it was shown that the lender's wrongful acts to NDH had destroyed the fund, Barnes' defence would have succeeded.[132]

The second issue[133] relating to implied terms, concerned the position of the lender as chargee of Barnes' shares in NDH and whether a duty of care was owed to Barnes by the lender when the shares significantly decreased in value. In

---

130. [1940] A.C. 701 (H.L.(E.)).
131. [1981] Com. L.R. 205, at p. 206, and especially at pp. 285–286 of the transcript.
132. [1981] Com. L.R. 205, at p. 206.
133. [1981] Com. L.R. 205, at p. 208.

holding this was an action which NDH alone could bring, Ralph Gibson J. said Barnes could only sue for damages for alleged negligence and breach of contract by the lender to NDH if there was an implied term to this effect in the loan contract or under a rule of law. There was no such rule and no material upon which a term could be implied.[134]

The third issue was whether, through a course of dealing, the lender was obliged to increase NDH's overdraft on request, or to give 12 months' notice of refusal.[135] It was held that such terms could not be implied for two reasons. First, such terms were inconsistent with the express terms of the facility letter of July 1972; and, secondly, they were not "necessary".[136] A contract between a lender and its customer is an ordinary commercial contract to be construed according to its terms and in accordance with the basic principle that parties are free to determine their primary obligations.[137]

The fourth issue concerning implied terms related to the implication of a term that a period of reasonable notice should be given for the repayment of NDH overdrafts. As to this contention, Ralph Gibson J. said, first[138]:

"... that in the absence of any express agreement providing for the duration of the facility, or for the date of repayment, the court must consider whether, according to the ordinary rules for implication of terms into commercial contracts, any term controlling the duration of the facility or the date of repayment is to be implied. If no such term must be implied, then money lent under the facility is no more than money lent and is, therefore, repayable on demand."

His Lordship then rejected a contention that knowledge on the part of a lender that a borrower intended to spend all or part of the money in a business venture which would take a long period to develop, could give rise to an implied term requiring a period of notice for repayment to be calculated by reference to the probable duration of that business venture.[139] Clearly, such a contention would be folly if the venture suddenly collapsed or looked like collapsing.

But, in construing the January facility letter (which was silent as to duration and spoke of the "usual banking conditions"), his Lordship said that the express words in it required that, in order to give "business efficacy" to that facility letter, the lending thereby agreed was not repayable "on demand", and the January facility could not be cancelled by the lender when it chose.[140] Accordingly, a period of reasonable notice had to be given, which Ralph Gibson

---

134. *Ibid.*, and at pp. 361 and 364 of the transcript.

135. [1981] Com. L.R. 205, at p. 209, and at pp. 491 and 493 of the transcript.

136. See *Liverpool City Council* v. *Irwin* [1977] A.C. 239 (H.L.(E.)) and *The Moorcock* (1889) 14 P.D. 64.

137. See also Lord Diplock in *Photo Production Ltd.* v. *Securicor Transport Ltd.* [1980] A.C. 827, at p. 848.

138. [1981] Com. L.R. 205, at p. 210. Cf. *Cryne* v. *Barclays Bank plc* [1987] B.C.L.C. 548 (C.A.). See also the case recently brought against Barclays Bank plc by the administrators of a company called Crimpfil, noted in *The Independent*, 30 April 1994, on p. 17, *The Daily Telegraph*, 21 April 1994, and noted in [1994] J.I.B.L., at N–151.

139. [1981] Com. L.R. 205, at p. 210.

140. [1981] Com. L.R. 205, at p. 210, and especially at pp. 605, 608 and 609 of the transcript.

J. concluded would have been unlikely to exceed one month.[141] His Lordship stated that this was part of the general rule that "money lent is repayable without demand, or at latest on demand, unless the lender expressly or impliedly agrees otherwise".[142] In this case, it had been agreed otherwise.

The principle of the *Liverpool City Council* case has also been applied by the Court of Appeal in another lending case. In *National Bank of Greece SA* v. *Pinios Shipping Company (No. 1) (The Maira (No. 3))*,[143] the court, in a "one-off" transaction, refused to imply a term that the lender was under a duty of care to the borrower to ensure that a third party did not underinsure a vessel being built by the borrower for which the lender was giving guarantees secured by a mortgage. This was a specific transaction, and it was not necessary to imply such a term, which should have been expressly included.

Rationale of general rules

The rationale for these rules and, in particular, the refusal to imply terms, appears in the House of Lords' decision in *Photo Production Ltd.* v. *Securicor Transport Ltd.*[144] In that case, Lord Wilberforce said: "At the stage of negotiation as to the consequences of a breach, there is everything to be said for allowing the parties to estimate their respective claims according to the contractual provisions they have made themselves ..."[145]

Lord Diplock, in his classic speech in the same case, said: "A basic principle of the common law of contract is that the parties are free to determine for themselves what primary obligations they will accept." His Lordship went on to distinguish secondary obligations, such as the payment of damages for non-performance of a primary obligation[146] (which is a breach of contract).

GOOD FAITH AND FAIR DEALING: LIABILITY IN TORT AND CONTRACT

Unlike the United States, where courts imply duties of "good faith" and "fair dealing" in contracts and readily find liability in tort, English courts have in the

141. [1981] Com. L.R. 205, at p. 210.
142. *Ibid.*
143. [1990] A.C. 637, at p. 646, per Lloyd L.J. (as he then was); see case note by D.A. Kingsford Smith, "Implied Terms in the Banker and Customer Relationship (The Maira (No. 3))" [1989] L.M.C.L.Q. 40. This case went on appeal to the House of Lords solely on the question of whether a lender can claim compound interest once the borrower's account has been closed. The Court of Appeal was reversed on this point, the House of Lords stating that the lender can claim compound interest: see [1990] A.C. 637 (H.L.(E.)).
144. [1980] A.C. 827 (H.L.(E.)).
145. *Ibid.*, at p. 843.
146. *Ibid.*, at p. 848; see also B. Dickson, "The Contribution of Lord Diplock to the General Law of Contract" (1989) 9 O.J.L.S. 451, at p. 463, where it is noted that there are no fewer than 18 cases in which Lord Diplock sat as a judge containing a reference to the distinction between primary and secondary obligations.

last decade, emphasised that liability in tort and contract (the two most fruitful sources of liability) are separate and distinct. This does not mean that there cannot be overlapping liability: one possible area of overlap is negligent misrepresentation, particularly in a precontractual situation.[147] But, if there is a contract between the parties, a party's liability in tort cannot be greater than its liability in contract. The reason that a contractual analysis has been preferred is that, in contract, the parties have agreed to regulate their obligations and liabilities to each other, whereas in tort, duties may be owed to the world at large.[148]

This approach is best summarised in the statement of the Privy Council in *Tai Hing Cotton Mill Ltd.* v. *Liu Chong Hing Bank Ltd.*,[149] where Lord Scarman sounded the following warning:

"Their Lordships do not believe that there is anything to the advantage of the law's development in searching for a liability in tort where the parties are in a contractual relationship. *This is particularly so in a commercial relationship. Though it is possible as a matter of legal semantics to conduct an analysis of the rights and duties inherent in some contractual relationships including that of banker and customer* either as a matter of contract law ... or as a matter of tort law ... their Lordships believe it to be correct in principle and necessary for the avoidance of confusion in the law to adhere to the contract analysis: on principle because it is a relationship in which the parties have, subject to a few exceptions, the right to determine their obligations to each other, and for the avoidance of confusion because different consequences do follow according to whether the liability arises from contract or tort ..." (Emphasis added.)

A similar view, regarding the delineation of liability in tort and contract, was expressed by Lord Bridge of Harwich in *D. & F. Estates Ltd.* v. *Church Commissioners for England*.[150]

This approach has subsequently been reconsidered by the House of Lords,[150a] which has said that, where there is an assumption of responsibility under *Hedley Byrne* which is not inconsistent with, or excluded by, an existing

---

147. See *Esso Petroleum Co. Ltd.* v. *Mardon* [1976] Q.B. 801 (C.A.) cited without disapproval by the House of Lords in *Banque Keyser Ullmann S.A.* v. *Skandia (UK) Insurance Co. Ltd.* [1991] 2 A.C. 249, at p. 275. See also Oliver J. (as he then was) in *Midland Bank Trust Co. Ltd.* v. *Hett Stubbs and Kemp* [1979] Ch. 384, the Court of Appeal in *Howard Marine and Dredging Co. Ltd.* v. *A. Ogden & Sons (Excavations) Ltd.* [1978] Q.B. 574 (C.A.), and the House of Lords in *Henderson* v. *Merrett Syndicates Ltd.* [1994] 3 W.L.R. 761, which approved the *Midland Bank Trust Co.* case, *supra*.

148. See Lord Reid in *Koufos* v. *Czarnikow Ltd.* (*The Heron II*) [1969] 1 A.C. 350, at p. 386 (H.L.(E.)) who said: "In contract, if one party wishes to protect himself against a risk which to the other party would appear unusual, he can direct the other party's attention to it before the contract is made ... But in tort there is no opportunity for the injured party to protect himself in that way."

149. [1986] A.C. 80, at p. 107.

150. [1989] A.C. 177, at p. 206 (H.L.(E.)). Cf. the American case of *Foley* v. *Interactive Data Corporation*, 765 P.2d 373 (Cal. 1988), where the court distinguished between *ex delicto* and *ex contractu* remedies and held there was no cause of action in relation to an implied covenant of "good faith", albeit in an employment contract, which marked a departure from previous case law.

150a. *Henderson* v. *Merrett Syndicates Ltd.* [1994] 3 W.L.R. 761 (H.L.(E.)), per Lord Goff of Chieveley, with Lords Keith of Kinkel, Browne-Wilkinson, Mustill and Nolan agreeing.

contractual chain or structure between the parties,[150b] there can be concurrent liability in contract and tort, so that the plaintiff may choose the best remedy for him[150c]; *Tai Hing Cotton* it was observed was a case about whether there could be a tortious duty of care which was more extensive than the duty of care provided for in the parties' contract[150d]: not whether there could be concurrent liability.

Consistently with the rise of freedom of contract,[151] there has been a narrowing of the duty of care in negligence, which is no longer based upon reasonable foreseeability under the two-tiered formula of Lord Wilberforce in *Anns* v. *Merton London Borough Council.*[152] In *Peabody Donation Fund (Governors)* v. *Sir Lindsay Parkinson & Company Ltd.,*[153] Lord Keith of Kinkel emphasised that *Anns* should not be treated as being of a definitive character and that there needed to be a relationship of proximity between the parties in Lord Atkin's sense[154] of a "close and direct relationship". Also, that it must be "just and reasonable" in all the circumstances to impose a duty of care—mere foreseeability alone is insufficient.[155] These views were repeated and expanded upon in *Yuen Kun-yeu* v. *Attorney-General of Hong Kong,*[156] where the Commissioner for deposit-taking companies in Hong Kong was held not to be liable in negligence to an investor in one such company (who lost money when

150b. An example of an inconsistent standard contractual structure in a construction matter is where the sub-contractor has not assumed any responsibility to the building owner, only to the main contractor under his contract with him: see Lord Goff, at p. 790D–H.

150c. Per Lord Goff, at pp. 778–789. See also Lord Browne-Wilkinson, at pp. 798–800.

150d. Per Lord Goff, at p. 790D–H, agreeing with Sir Thomas Bingham M.R. in the Court of Appeal below.

151. As is emphasised in the speech of Lord Diplock in *Photo Production Ltd.* v. *Securicor Transport Ltd.* [1980] A.C. 827, at p. 848.

152. [1978] A.C. 728, at pp. 751–752. An interpretation which, it is submitted, is erroneous; see also Gibbs C.J. in *Sutherland Shire Council* v. *Heyman* (1985) 157 C.L.R. 424, at p. 441 and Lord Keith of Kinkel in *Yuen Kun-yeu* v. *Attorney-General of Hong Kong* [1988] A.C. 175, at p. 191. *Anns* was recently overruled by the House of Lords in *Murphy* v. *Brentwood District Council* [1991] 1 A.C. 398.

153. [1985] A.C. 210, at p. 240; see case note by S. Todd, "The Liability of Public Authorities: Divergence in the Common Law" (1986) 102 L.Q.R. 370.

154. [1932] A.C. 562, at p. 580.

155. See Lord Wilberforce in *McLoughlin* v. *O'Brian* [1983] 1 A.C. 410 (H.L.(E.)), who thought it clear that "foreseeability does not of itself, and automatically, lead to a duty of care".

156. [1988] A.C. 175, at pp. 190–194. See P. Cane, "Economic Loss in Tort: Is the Pendulum out of Control" (1988) 52 M.L.R. 200. See also *Minories Finance Ltd.* v. *Arthur Young* [1989] 2 All E.R. 105, in which it was held that the Bank of England owed no duty of care to the commercial lenders it regulated in the United Kingdom. It was neither just nor fair and reasonable to make the lender assume or share any commercial responsibilities which private lenders owed to themselves to conduct their commercial dealings prudently and with care so as to make profits and avoid making losses. Also, the Banking Act 1987, designed to protect depositors, meant the importation of a duty of care was unsustainable. See the comments thereon by G.A. Penn, in *Banking Supervision* (1989) Butterworths, at pp. 20–22; and see also *Davis* v. *Radcliffe* [1990] 1 W.L.R. 821 (P.C.). The recent case law is well reviewed in the following articles: see the Rt. Hon. Sir Robin Cooke, "An Impossible Distinction" (1991) 107 L.Q.R. 46; Professor J. Fleming, "Requiem For *Anns*" (1990) 106 L.Q.R. 525; I. Duncan-Wallace, Q.C., "*Anns* Beyond Repair" (1991) 107 L.Q.R. 228; and J. Stapleton, "Duty of Care and Economic Loss" (1991) 107 L.Q.R. 249.

the company collapsed through fraud), because there was a lack of proximity between the parties.

Moreover, as recently noted by the House of Lords in *Caparo Industries plc* v. *Dickman*,[157] there has been a recognition of "the inability of any single general principle to provide a practical test which can be applied to every situation to determine whether a duty of care is owed and, if so, what is its scope". Concepts of "proximity" and "reasonableness", which are in addition to foreseeability, are "little more than convenient labels" and not susceptible to precise definition. Rather, there is a trend towards looking "to the more traditional categorisation of distinct and recognisable situations as guides to the existence, the scope and the limits of the varied duties of care which the law imposes".[158] Novel categories of negligence should be developed incrementally and by analogy with established categories, as opposed to large extensions of the duty of care.[159] Finally, in *Murphy* v. *Brentwood District Council*,[160] the House of Lords overruled their decision in *Anns* as being inconsistent with the above principles.

Other examples of the more restrictive approach to questions of a duty of care are found in several recent cases. In *Huxford* v. *Stoy Hayward & Company (a firm)*,[161] Popplewell J. held there was no duty of care owed in tort to a company's directors and shareholders, owing to a lack of proximity, where the company, at the specific request of its lenders, instructed accountants to undertake an investigation into the company's financial affairs and report to the directors, with copies of the report to the lenders. The resulting contract was between the advisers and the lenders alone, such that the advisers owed no contractual duty of care to the company or its directors or shareholders or guarantors. In *Al Saudi Banque* v. *Clarke Pixley (a firm)*[162]—which was approved by the House of Lords in *Caparo*[163]—Millett J. held that certain lenders who lent money to a company were owed no duty of care by the company's auditors for negligently audited accounts which had failed to show the company was insolvent.[164]

In *Williams & Glyn*, the question of whether the lender owed a duty to Barnes

157. [1990] 2 A.C. 605 (H.L.(E.)). See case note (1990) 106 L.Q.R. 349.
158. Per Lord Bridge of Harwich, at p. 618.
159. See Brennan J. in *Sutherland Shire Council* v. *Heyman* (1985) 157 C.L.R. 424, at p. 481, cited with approval in *Caparo* by Lord Bridge of Harwich, at p. 618 and Lord Oliver of Aylmerton, at p. 633. See also Lord Brandon of Oakbrook in *Leigh and Sillivan Ltd.* v. *Aliakmon Shipping Co. Ltd. (The Aliakmon)* [1986] A.C. 785, at p. 815, who stated that a duty of care should not be imposed in cases where it has been repeatedly held there is no duty of care; and that *Anns* was a case applying to novel situations.
160. [1991] 1 A.C. 398 (H.L.(E.)).
161. [1989] 5 B.C.C. 421.
162. [1990] 1 Ch. 313.
163. See Lord Bridge of Harwich at p. 623; Lord Oliver of Aylmerton at p. 641; and Lord Jauncey of Tullichettle at p. 662.
164. See also *Pacific Associates Inc.* v. *Baxter* [1990] 1 Q.B. 993 (C.A.); *Norwich City Council* v. *Harvey* [1989] 1 W.L.R. 828 (C.A.); *Reid* v. *Rush and Tompkins Group plc* [1990] 1 W.L.R. 212 at p. 235 (C.A.); and *Marc Rich & Co. A.G.* v. *Bishop Rock Marine Co. Ltd. (The Nicholas H)* [1994] 1 W.L.R. 1071 (C.A.).

as a shareholder of the borrower (NDH) was answered in the negative. Ralph Gibson J. held[165] that no duty of care was owed by the lender to Barnes, in his capacity as shareholder in NDH, not to breach duties which the lender owed to NDH. (Had NDH been a party, then the lender may have been liable to NDH.) The only allegations of negligence against the lender could be for giving, or failing to give, advice, as Barnes did not otherwise fall within the principle in *Donoghue* v. *Stevenson*.[166] However, whilst the lender advised NDH as its customer, it had not asked to advise the shareholders or procure any benefit for them in their actions for NDH. The lender had no reason to suppose that the shareholders were relying upon them to advise NDH in the shareholders' interests, and liability did not arise in tort under the principle in *Hedley Byrne*[167] of an assumption of responsibility and reliance.

Also, the shareholders were not closely and directly affected by the lender's act, and it would be neither "fair nor just" in the circumstances to impose a duty of care upon the lender—in fact, there was much to the contrary. Furthermore, under the rule in *Salomon* v. *Salomon & Company Ltd.*,[168] the shareholders were separate legal entities from NDH and it was said that a lender's decision would be made difficult if a shareholder could claim against it on the basis of a duty owed to a borrowing company.[169] This reasoning is very similar to that adopted a decade later in *Caparo*.

Allied with the change in attitude towards the duty of care under *Anns*, the decision in *Junior Books Ltd.* v. *Veitchi Company Ltd.*[170] has been eroded. In that case, their Lordships, on special facts, allowed recovery for pure economic loss on the basis that the relationship between the pursuer and a sub-contractor was very close: being akin to contract, except for the absence of privity. But, in a line of cases[171] culminating in *Murphy* v. *Brentwood District Council*,[172] there

165. [1981] Com. L.R. 205, at p. 209, and especially at pp. 332–335 of the transcript. As to the liability of lenders for giving advice: see the paper by A. Malik, "Giving Advice", delivered at a seminar by the Legal Studies and Services Group Ltd., entitled "Legal Responsibilities and Liabilities of Banks", on 27 September 1988, London.

166. [1932] A.C. 562 (H.L.(Sc.)).

167. [1964] A.C. 465 (H.L.(E.)). See also *Henderson* v. *Merrett Syndicates Ltd.* [1994] 3 W.L.R. 761 (H.L.(E.)).

168. [1897] A.C. 22 (H.L.(E.)).

169. See pp. 335–336 of the transcript. Cf. the recent decision of Mervyn Davies J. in *Al-Nakib Investments (Jersey) Ltd.* v. *Longcroft* [1990] 1 W.L.R. 1390, in which it was held that the duty of care which the directors of a company owed to the company's shareholders regarding a prospectus issued by the company for a rights issue did not extend to a situation where reliance was placed on the prospectus by the shareholders for the purpose of buying the shares in the market.

170. [1983] 1 A.C. 520 (H.L.(Sc.)).

171. *Tate & Lyle Industries Ltd.* v. *Greater London Council* [1983] 2 A.C. 509, at p. 530 (H.L.(E.)) per Lord Templeman; *Muirhead* v. *Industrial Specialties Tank Ltd.* [1986] Q.B. 507 (C.A.); *Simaan General Contracting Co.* v. *Pilkington Glass Ltd. (No. 2)* [1988] Q.B. 758 (C.A.); *Greater Nottingham Co-operative Society Ltd.* v. *Cementation Piling and Foundations Ltd.* [1989] Q.B. 71 (C.A.); *D. & F. Estates Ltd.* v. *Church Commissioners for England* [1989] A.C. 177 (H.L.(F.)); and see also *Candlewood Navigation Corporation Ltd.* v. *Mitsui O.S.K. Ltd. (The Mineral Transporter)* [1986] A.C. 1, at p. 25 (P.C.), per Lord Fraser of Tullybelton; and *Leigh and Sillivan Ltd.* v. *Aliakmon Shipping Co. Ltd. (The Aliakmon)* [1986] A.C. 785 (H.L.(E)).

172. [1991] 1 A.C. 398 (H.L.(E.)).

has been a rejection of the opening up of liability for pure economic loss in tort[173] and a marginalising of *Junior Books*. Recovery for pure economic loss is now to be based upon the *Hedley Byrne* principle.

Negligent misstatement

Hedley Byrne was re-evaluated by the House of Lords in two cases, *Smith* v. *Eric S. Bush*[174] and *Caparo*.[175] In *Bush*, there was a negligent valuation of a house, which the valuer knew would be relied on by the mortgagor, and probably by the mortgagee. In holding the valuer to be under a duty of care to the mortgagor, their Lordships re-examined the concept of voluntary assumption of responsibility in the speech of Lord Devlin in *Hedley Byrne*.[176]

Lord Griffiths, who delivered the leading speech, said that voluntary assumption of responsibility is not a helpful or realistic test for liability and that "assumption of responsibility" is only meaningful if it refers to circumstances in which the law deems the maker of a statement to have assumed responsibility to the person who acts upon the former's advice.[177] Echoing Lord Keith of Kinkel in *Peabody* and *Yuen Kun-yeu* (where, ironically, *Hedley Byrne* was said to be a case of voluntary assumption of responsibility), Lord Griffiths stated[178] that a person is said to have assumed responsibility (i.e. an adviser owes the recipient of advice a duty of care) if it is foreseeable that, if the advice is negligent, it is likely to cause the recipient to suffer damage; that there is a sufficient relationship of proximity between the parties; and that it is just and reasonable to impose liability. This approach is similar to the approach taken in Australia, where the High Court has applied the "neighbourhood principle" to negligent misrepresentations and, in particular, has emphasised the need for proximity.[179]

The question whether, on Lord Griffiths' test, a lender has assumed responsibility (as in *Hedley Byrne* or *Box* v. *Midland Bank Ltd.*[180]) will be one of fact. In *Royal Bank Trust Company (Trinidad) Ltd.* v. *Pampellonne*,[181] the Privy Council said that a lender was not under a duty of care to a borrower when it provided the borrower with printed information, but not advice, about certain investments. It is suggested, however, that the dissent of Lord Templeman and

173. Recovery of pure economic loss is still recoverable in contract.

174. [1990] 1 A.C. 831 (H.L.(E.)). See case note by D. Allen, "Hedley Byrne Revalued" (1989) 105 L.Q.R. 508.

175. [1990] 2 A.C. 605 (H.L.(E.)). Cf. *AWA Ltd.* v. *Daniels (trading as Deloitte Haskins & Sells)* (1992) 7 A.C.S.R. 759 (on the question of the contributory negligence by a company in an action against its auditors).

176. [1964] A.C. 831, at p. 529. Cf. Lord Denning M.R. in *McInerney* v. *Lloyds Bank Ltd.* [1974] 1 Lloyd's Rep. 246, at p. 253.

177. At p. 862. See also Lord Roskill in *Caparo Industries plc* v. *Dickman* [1990] 2 A.C. 605, at p. 628, who expressed agreement with this statement.

178. At pp. 864–865.

179. *San Sebastian Pty. Ltd.* v. *Minister Administering the Environmental Planning & Assessment Act 1979* (1986) 61 C.L.R. 340, at p. 355.

180. [1979] 2 Lloyd's Rep. 391.

181. [1987] 1 Lloyd's Rep. 218 (P.C.).

Sir Robin Cooke is more compelling. The result in this case is similar to that reached by Toohey J. in the Federal Court of Australia in *ANZ* v. *James*,[182] who drew a distinction between a lender giving advice and merely passing on information.

Liability for negligent misstatement was further reviewed by the House of Lords in *Caparo*, where Lord Bridge of Harwich said[183]:

"The damage which may be caused by the negligently spoken or written word will normally be confined to economic loss sustained by those who rely on the accuracy of the information or advice they receive as a basis for action. The question what, if any, duty is owed by the maker of a statement to exercise due care to ensure its accuracy arises typically in relation to statements made by a person in the exercise of his calling or profession. In advising the client who employs him the professional man owes a duty to exercise that standard of skill and care appropriate to his professional status and will be liable both in contract and in tort for all losses which his client may suffer by reason of any breach of that duty."

After examining the authorities on negligent misrepresentation, which was regarded as "a relatively narrow corner of the field" of negligence (including *Bush's* case, and the "masterly analysis" of the relevant principles by Denning L.J. (as he then was) in *Candler* v. *Crane, Christmas & Co.*[184] which required little, if any, modification or amplification), his Lordship concluded[185]:

"The salient feature of all these cases is that the defendant giving advice or information was fully aware of the nature of the transaction which the plaintiff had in contemplation, knew that the advice or information would be communicated to him directly or indirectly and knew that it was very likely that the plaintiff would rely on that advice or information in deciding whether or not to engage in the transaction in contemplation. In these circumstances the defendant could clearly be expected, subject always to the effect of any disclaimer of responsibility, specifically to anticipate that the plaintiff would rely on the advice or information given by the defendant for the very purpose for which he did in the event rely on it. So also the plaintiff, subject again to the effect of any disclaimer, would in that situation reasonably suppose that he was entitled to rely on the advice or information communicated to him for the very purpose for which he required it."

However, it is an entirely different matter when a statement is put into general circulation and it might "foreseeably be relied upon by strangers to the maker of the statement for any one of a variety of reasons which the maker of the statement had no specific reason to anticipate".[186] Consequently, there is a need for a limit or control mechanism, because it would be quite unwarranted to confer on the world at large an entitlement to use the benefit of expert knowledge or professional expertise which can be attributable to the maker of the statement. His Lordship noted that, for negligent misrepresentation, an essential ingredient of proximity is that the defendant knew his statement would be communicated to the plaintiff, either as an individual or a member of an

182. (1986) 64 A.L.R. 347.
183. [1990] 2 A.C. 605, at p. 619.
184. [1951] 2 K.B. 164, at pp. 179–184.
185. [1990] 2 A.C. 605, at pp. 620–621.
186. *Supra*, at p. 621.

identifiable class, with regard to a particular transaction or type of transaction, and that the plaintiff would be very likely to rely on it for the purpose of deciding whether or not to enter into that transaction or type of transaction.[187]

These remarks have particular significance for lenders as there will be very close proximity between them and a borrower. Normally, a borrower will rely upon the statements of the lender in relation to a particular transaction. Moreover, it is reasonable that they do so.[188]

Lord Oliver of Aylmerton considered that four factors[189] were relevant— although not conclusive or exclusive—in determining a "special relationship":

(a) the advice is needed for a purpose, which the adviser is aware of;
(b) the adviser knows his advice will be communicated to the advisee, as an individual or as a member of an identifiable class, so that it will be used by the advisee for the purpose required;
(c) it is known the advice is likely to be acted on by the advisee; and
(d) the advisee acts upon the advice to his detriment.

His Lordship, whilst stating *Smith* v. *Eric S. Bush* had gone further than any other decision of the House of Lords, felt, like Lord Bridge of Harwich, that there was need for a control mechanism and said there were "powerful reasons" against extending liability to find a relationship of proximity between an adviser and third parties who may come across the adviser's advice, although this is strictly unrelated either to the intended recipient or to the purpose for which the advice is given.[190] Lord Oliver went on to conclude that there was nothing in the statutory duties[191] of a company auditor giving rise to a special relationship.

Since those cases, there have been four important decisions of the Court of Appeal (of which two are discussed below),[192] an interesting decision, factually, by Lord Osborne in the Court of Session in Scotland,[193] and two decisions of the House of Lords.[193a]

In *James McNaughton Paper Group Ltd.* v. *Hicks Anderson & Co.*,[194] the issue concerned the liability of the defendants, a firm of accountants, for: (i) negligence and breach of duty in the preparation of "final draft" accounts of their client, a group of companies ("the group"), which the plaintiffs wished to take over where it was known that the plaintiffs would rely on the accounts in

187. *Ibid.*
188. *Ibid.*
189. *Supra*, at p. 638.
190. *Supra*, at p. 642.
191. See sections 221, 227, 235, 236, 237, 240, and 241 and 245 of the Companies Act 1985 (as amended).
192. *James McNaughton Paper Group Ltd.* v. *Hicks Anderson & Co.* [1991] 2 Q.B. 113, and *Morgan Crucible Co. plc* v. *Hill Samuel & Co. Ltd.* [1991] 2 W.L.R. 655 are the two main cases, but see also *Galoo Ltd. (In Liquidation)* v. *Bright Grahame Murray (A Firm)* [1994] 1 W.L.R. 1560 (C.A.) (on causation) and *Marc Rich*, *supra*.
193. *Bank of Scotland* v. *3i plc* [1993] B.C.L.C. 968, a decision delivered on 29 November 1991.
193a. *Spring* v. *Guardian Assurance Plc* [1994] 3 W.L.R. 354 (H.L.(E.)), and *Henderson* v. *Merrett Syndicates Ltd.* [1994] 3 W.L.R. 761 (H.L.(E.)).
194. [1991] 2 Q.B. 113 (C.A.).

deciding whether to acquire shares in the group and at what price; and (ii) an erroneous statement concerning the group's accounts from a member of the defendants, in response to a question from the plaintiffs during negotiations. The defendants were held not liable in negligence, as there was insufficient proximity between them and the plaintiffs; the defendants could not foresee the loss the plaintiffs claimed they suffered due to their reliance on the draft accounts and the answer to the question; furthermore, it was not fair, just and reasonable to impose a duty of care.

In reaching his decision, Neill L.J., who delivered the leading judgment,[195] outlined six factors which should be considered in deciding whether a duty of care should be imposed for negligence[196]:

(1) the purpose for which the statement was made;
(2) the purpose for which the statement was communicated;
(3) the relationship between the adviser, the advisee and any relevant third party;
(4) the size of any class to which the advisee belongs[197];
(5) the state of knowledge of the adviser; and
(6) reliance by the adviser.

These six factors were considered helpful by a strong Court of Appeal[198] in *Morgan Crucible Co. plc* v. *Hill Samuel & Co. Ltd.*,[199] in which *Caparo* was distinguished on the facts of the case. *Morgan Crucible*, like *James McNaughton*, concerned a takeover, although the takeover was contested. Allegations of negligence were made against the defendants (the well-known merchant bank) who acted as advisers to the company taken over by the plaintiffs ("the target"), the accountants, and the directors of the target. These allegations related to financial statements made when the plaintiffs were identified as a bidder. It was claimed these statements were inaccurate and constituted "continuous representations", as they had not been withdrawn or corrected. The Court of Appeal allowed the plaintiff's application to amend their pleadings to include these allegations, as the claim, if it went to trial, was not bound to fail; there was reliance on the statements, which was intended; and there was sufficient proximity.

In the Scottish case of *Bank of Scotland* v. *3i plc*,[200] the issue was what was the meaning of the term "commitment" in the context of a venture capital transaction, where the pursuers continued to lend money to a company on the basis of a "representation" from the defender that it had firm commitments for funds. The facts, which are lengthy, can be stated as follows.

The lender ("BS") provided facilities to a company ("IPS") which

195. With which Nourse and Balcombe L.JJ. agreed.
196. At pp. 125F–126G.
197. There is a suggestion of the floodgates argument here.
198. Comprising Slade L.J., Mustill L.J. (as he then was), and Nicholls L.J. (as he then was).
199. [1991] 2 W.L.R. 655 at p. 674G.
200. [1993] B.C.L.C. 968.

manufactured semiconductors. 3i led a syndicate who were to provide equity and loan stock to IPS. In 1987, negotiations took place between IPS and 3i regarding the issuing of convertible loan stock, which was considered necessary before IPS's share capital could be sold; security for this was to be taken over IPS's intellectual property.

BS became concerned at the amount IPS was borrowing from it. Also, the lender had departed from certain conditions on which it had previously agreed IPS's overdraft. Consequently, there was a series of letters and meetings between 3i and others, and BS. One of the managers of BS, M, wrote to 3i on 20 August 1987, saying that M understood 3i were looking for "firm commitments" from the next week, and M asked that 3i keep M informed. On 1 September, W, from 3i, telephoned M and said 3i had commitments of up to £1.155m, and that if there was no increase, 3i would make up the difference.

But, in September, difficulties arose in relation to the taking of security over IPS's intellectual property, which was important in the context of the loan stock, as a lender with a floating charge refused to consent to the security. BS were not aware of this, but, it was held, they were not entitled to assume that these matters had been resolved.

On 1 October, another manager of BS was advised by another executive of 3i that 3i were having problems regarding the arranging of loan stock and that the lender should watch its exposure. As a result of the stock market crash later that month, 3i and the other potential investors did not subscribe for the loan stock. Subsequently, the lender was invited by IPS to appoint a receiver.

However, in between this time, BS had lent IPS £1.34m from 1 September until the receiver being appointed, doing so on the basis of its interpretation of the conversation of 1 September concerning "commitment", which it interpreted as meaning the syndicate was under a binding legal obligation to subscribe for the loan stock. The lender sued for negligent misrepresentation on three grounds:

(i) 3i owed BS a duty of care regarding the call of 1 September and the use of the word "commitment";

(ii) that that duty had been breached by 3i using the word "commitment", which signified a legally binding obligation; and

(iii) that the misrepresentation about the commitment had led to the lender suffering loss, as it had relied on it to advance further funds to IPS.

It was held, applying *Caparo* and *James McNaughton*, that:

(i) no duty of care was owed, due to a lack of proximity;

(ii) no breach of duty had occurred anyway; and

(iii) the call on 1 October operated as a *novus actus interveniens*, and broke the chain of causation between that call and the subsequent advances by the lender.

With regard to the question of a lack of proximity, Lord Osborne highlighted three factors. First, that 3i were entitled to conclude that they were dealing with a lender which was not seeking to enforce its strict lending policy. Secondly, that BS never made it clear to 3i that the end of August was the lender's deadline for new funds. And thirdly, that on 1 September M and W were at cross purposes. W was merely satisfying M's request for further information, and was not, as BS contended, telling BS that the funds were committed (in the sense of being legally bound), thus inducing BS to alter its position. Also, his Lordship felt it would not be fair, just and reasonable to impose a duty of care.

As to the second matter, of breach of any duty of care, if one had been found to be owing, Lord Osborne said that this had not been breached by the conversation on 1 September. In his view, 3i's evidence that amongst venture capitalists "commitment" did not mean a legally enforceable obligation was correct.

The case emphasises four matters, although it was one lending institution versus another, and not borrower versus lender. First, the approach to the duty of care question, as with *James McNaughton* and *Morgan Crucible*, is based on that of Lord Griffiths in *Smith* v. *Eric S. Bush*[201] and Lord Keith of Kinkel in *Yuen Kun-yeu* v. *Attorney-General of Hong Kong*,[202] which is not entirely consistent with the incremental approach in *Caparo* (although a lack of proximity is crucial). Secondly, the strictness of the requirement of proximity is emphasised, although it is likely that a borrower will be sufficiently proximate. Thirdly, it shows the value of seeking written confirmation of something as important as commitments to a project. A letter from BS, seeking to confirm that there were firm (binding) commitments, would have emphasised to 3i that they were dealing to cross purposes. The problem seems to have really been that the lender had made an internal decision about lending, which coloured its judgement, but had not communicated it to 3i. Also, it would seem self-evident that "commitment" or even "firm commitment" does not mean binding commitment, as someone can be committed to something, but events can occur—as here—which, before they bind themselves, cause them to change their mind. Lastly, the case confirms other authority[203] that it is not appropriate to rely on a telephone conversation in seeking to establish a duty of care.

The position as to pure economic loss (for negligent misstatement) has, however, been very recently re-appraised by Lord Goff of Chieveley in two cases: *Spring* v. *Guardian Assurance Plc*,[203a] and *Henderson* v. *Merrett Syndicates Ltd*.[203b] (in which case his Lordship delivered the leading speech).

201. [1990] 1 A.C. 831 (H.L.(E.)).

202. [1988] A.C. 175, at pp. 190–194.

203. *L. Shaddock and Associates Pty. Ltd.* v. *Paramatta City Council* (1981) 150 C.L.R. 225; and *Howard Marine & Dredging Co. Ltd.* v. *Ogden & Sons (Excavations) Ltd.* [1978] Q.B. 574 (C.A.).

203a. [1994] 3 W.L.R. 354 (H.L.(E.)), concerning a negligent reference. Lord Lowry agreed with Lord Goff, whilst Lords Slynn of Hadley and Woolf followed the foreseeability, proximity and fair, just and reasonable test; Lord Keith of Kinkel held no duty of care arose.

203b. [1994] 3 W.L.R. 761 (H.L.(E.)), relating to claims by Lloyd's names against underwriting agents they did not have a contract with. Lords Keith of Kinkel, Browne-Wilkinson, Mustill and Nolan agreed with Lord Goff.

In his speeches, Lord Goff goes back to *Hedley Byrne* and analyses what that case actually decided and upon what basis recovery for pure economic loss was, for the first time, allowed. His Lordship concludes that for there to be liability, there needs to be: (i) an assumption of responsibility[203c]; and (ii) reliance on the exercise of reasonable skill and care by the defendant[203d]; he also refers to "special skill", which is to be interpreted widely to include knowledge.[203e] Lord Goff acknowledges the incremental approach that the House of Lords has adopted, but said it was always clear that recovery was allowable under *Hedley Byrne*[203f]; and his Lordship said also that liability could be imposed under the *Hedley Byrne* principle using the analogy approach or, as he favoured, by the application of the broad principle. Lord Goff further said that once there has been an assumption of responsibility, there is no need to enquire whether it is "fair, just and reasonable" to impose liability for pure economic loss.[203g] The emphasis is now on the relationship between the parties and not how it arose.[203h]

The implications of the negligence cases for lenders are, thus, threefold. First, where there is liability in tort and contract, a lender's liability in tort cannot be greater than its liability in contract and the matter will be governed by contract, although liability in negligence may still arise for negligent misstatement where this is not inconsistent with the contractual matrix. Secondly, unless there is an effective disclaimer, a lender is likely to fall within *Hedley Byrne* (as re-examined) for any negligent advice it gives to a borrower, since there will be an assumption of responsibility and reliance is intended. Thirdly, a lender, generally, will not be liable to the individual shareholders of a corporate borrower for a negligent misstatement, since there will be no assumption of responsibility to them, only one to the company.

Standard of care

In seeing whether there has been a breach of any duty of care, one has to have regard to the standard of care that is exercised by a lender.[204] The test in this

---

203c. *Spring*, at p. 369; *Henderson*, at pp. 775H and 782A.

203d. *Spring*, at p. 369; *Henderson*, at pp. 776C and 782A.

203e. *Spring*, at p. 369; *Henderson*, at p. 776C.

203f. *Henderson*, at p. 778.

203g. *Henderson*, at p.776H.

203h. See Oliver J. (as he then was) in *Midland Bank Trust Co. Ltd.* v. *Hett Stubbs & Kemp* [1979] Ch. 348, approved by Lord Goff in *Henderson* v. *Merrett Syndicates Ltd.* [1994] 3 W.L.R. 761, at pp. 783–787. See also Lord Oliver in *Murphy* v. *Brentwood District Council* [1991] 1 A.C. 398, at p. 486A, who spoke of the relationship of the parties (which he also said was called proximity).

204. See, for example, Lord Bridge of Harwich in *Caparo Industries plc* v. *Dickman* [1990] 2 A.C. 605, at p. 619.

The plaintiffs could have undertaken their own due diligence to check the position of the group, which would have been the prudent thing to do—obtain independent advice.

context is that a professional person is required to exercise the reasonable skill and care of a person of that calling[205]: thus, the notion of "the reasonable banker" referred to by the Court of Appeal in *Lipkin Gorman* v. *Karpnale Ltd.*[206] This concept of the standard of care is becoming increasingly important and is a factor in not allowing recovery for pure economic loss, which is what a lender's claim will be for.[207]

Lending practice: imprudence of borrowing

A corollary of the relationship between lender and borrower, being one of creditor and debtor, is that the lender is not under a duty to advise the borrower of the prudence of any transaction which the borrower is entering into and for which the lender is providing finance.[208] For liability to arise, there would need to be an express or implied contract; or a relationship giving rise to liability for negligent misstatement; or a fiduciary duty. In *Williams & Glyn*,[209] it was held that no duty of care fell upon a lender either to consider the prudence of lending from a customer's point of view, or to advise with respect to it. The "neighbourhood principle"[210] could not be extended to a lending transaction where the lender lent money as requested. The lender merely did what it was asked: it lent the money. As neither NDH nor Barnes were required to borrow money, it was impossible to sustain the view that the lender, which was dealing with a competent businessman, without its advice being sought, would assume responsibility or must consider the prudence of borrowing from the customer's point of view. As it was stated by the learned judge, when giving his abridged reasons for judgment in open court: "Banks and their customers are entitled to take commercial risks; indeed, they must do so."[211]

This question of advising customers on the commercial wisdom of

---

205. *Bolam* v. *Friern Hospital Management Committee* [1957] 1 W.L.R. 582, at p. 586, per McNair J., approved by the House of Lords in *Sidaway* v. *The Board of Governors of Bethlem Royal Hospital* [1985] A.C. 871 (H.L.(E.)).

206. [1989] 1 W.L.R. 1340. This notion was not overturned on appeal: see [1991] 2 A.C. 548 (H.L.(E.)).

207. See the dissenting speech of Lord Brandon of Oakbrook in *Junior Books Ltd.* v. *Veitchi Company Ltd.* [1983] 1 A.C. 520 (H.L.(Sc.)), and the majority speech of Lord Fraser of Tullybelton in the same case. See also Sir John Donaldson M.R. (as he then was) in *Leigh and Sillivan Ltd.* v. *Aliakmon Shipping Co. Ltd. (The Aliakmon)* [1985] Q.B. 350, at p. 368, approved by the House of Lords [1986] A.C. 785, at p. 818; and see also *Littlewoods Organisation Ltd.* v. *Maloco* [1987] A.C. 241 (H.L.(Sc.)).

208. [1981] Com. L.R. 205, at pp. 207–208, and at pp. 351–353 of the transcript. See also May L.J. in *Lipkin Gorman* v. *Karpnale Ltd.* [1989] 1 W.L.R. 1340, at p. 1356, who said: "There is nothing [in the contract between lender and customer], express or implied, *which could require a lender to consider the commercial wisdom or otherwise of the particular transaction.*" (Emphasis added). See also *Redman* v. *Allied Irish Bank plc* [1987] 3 F.T.L.R. 264, at p. 266 per Saville J. (as he then was); *Weitzman* v. *Hendon* (1989) 61 D.L.R. (4th) 525, at p. 547, per Robins J.A.

209. [1981] Com. L.R. 205.

210. See *Donoghue* v. *Stevenson* [1932] A.C. 562 (H.L.(Sc.)).

211. At p. 8 of the Lexis transcript of the abridged reasons for judgment, delivered in open court, on 26 March 1980.

transactions was recently considered by the Court of Appeal in *Lloyds Bank plc* v. *Cobb*,[212] where the position is well summed up by Scott L.J., who said:

"The ordinary business of a High Street bank is to hold on current account terms the funds of its customers, to make arrangements for overdrafts on current accounts and to make loans to customers. The ordinary business of a High Street bank does not include giving advice to customers on the wisdom of commercial projects for the purposes of which the bank is asked to lend money.

In my judgment, the ordinary relationship of bankers and customers does not place on the bank any contractual or tortious duty to advise the customers on the wisdom of commercial projects for the purpose of which the bank is asked to lend money. If the bank is to be placed under such a duty, there must be a request from the customer, accepted by the bank, or some arrangement between the customer and the bank, under which the advice is to be given.

If a customer applies to the bank for a loan for the purposes of some commercial project, and the bank examines the details of the project for the purpose of deciding whether or not to make the loan, the bank does not thereby assume any duty to the customer. It conducts the examination of the project for its own prudent purposes as lender and not for the benefit of the proposed borrower. If the borrower chooses to draw comfort from the bank's agreement to make the loan, that is the borrower's affair. In order to place the bank under a duty of care to the borrower the borrower must, in my opinion, make clear to the bank that its advice is being sought. The mere request for a loan, coupled with the supply to the bank of the details of the commercial project for whose purposes the loan is sought, does not suffice to make clear to the bank that its advice is being sought ..."

After rejecting the plaintiff's claim, on the evidence, his Lordship continued:

"People who engage in speculative commercial ventures must accept the consequences of the failure of their ventures just as they will enjoy the consequences of their success. They cannot be allowed to transfer the burden of the failure of their ventures on to the shoulders of a bank lender which was never asked to and never assumed to give advice on the wisdom of the venture."

To this general rule there is a possible caveat. Ralph Gibson L.J. suggested in *Williams & Glyn's Bank Ltd*. v. *Barnes*[213] that if it can be shown that a lender knew of the imprudence of the borrowing, what the money was to be used for, and the likelihood of damage to the borrower, then it may be possible to say that there is an implied representation by the lender that it was a safe venture and that it was reasonable for the borrower to rely on it, having regard to the type of advertisement lenders use.[214] It is suggested though that the facts would need to be very specific, and that this caveat is one of limited application.

Foreign exchange contracts

In Australia recently, borrowers have sought to sue lenders where the borrower has entered into futures contracts and has lost money. They have argued that the

212. Unreported decision, delivered on 18 December 1991. Noted in [1992] J.B.L. 419.
213. At p. 353 of the transcript.
214. At p. 353 of transcript in *Williams & Glyn's Bank* v. *Barnes*, per Ralph Gibson L.J. See also Brightman J. (as he then was) in *Bartlett* v. *Barclays Bank Trust Co. Ltd.* [1980] Ch. 515, at p. 534 in relation to lender advertisements and holding out; and also E. Andrew, "Customer Care and Banking Law" [1989] J.I.B.L. 101, at p. 104.

lender should have explained the risk involved to them and advised them to have "hedging contracts". In most cases,[215] the borrowers have been unable to recover their losses because the nature of the contract was speculative, and because they were commercial men, who knew, or ought to have known, of the risk involved.[216]

OTHER TORTIOUS REMEDIES

In this section, it is proposed to look at tortious remedies—apart from a claim in negligence—available to a borrower, most notably the economic torts in which the claim is for pure economic loss, due to damage or harm caused to the borrower's economic interests.

(1) Fraud/deceit

In *Derry* v. *Peek*,[217] the House of Lords outlined a three-pronged test for fraud. In a well-known passage, Lord Herschell said[218]: "fraud is proved when it is shown that a false representation has been made (1) knowingly, or (2) without belief in its truth, or (3) recklessly, careless whether it be true or false." The measure of damages under English law for fraud or deceit is a tortious measure, that is to say, it is reliance based and seeks to put the victim of the fraud (the borrower) in the position he would have been in if the fraudulent representation had not have been made[219]: not in the position he would have been if the representation had been proved.[220]

215. Cf. *Foti* v. *Banque Nationale de Paris* (1990) Aust. Torts Reports 67, 835—a case decided on special facts. The plaintiffs, who were Italian migrants, wanted a loan denominated in Swiss francs to purchase a shopping centre. It was held that the lender was liable. (Claims are also being brought under the Australian Trade Practices Act 1974 for deceptive and misleading conduct.) The position is discussed more fully by P. Nankivell, in Chapter 11 hereof. See also J. Nestell, "Bank's Liability to Foreign Currency Borrowers" (1990) 64 A.L.J. 776, and *Lloyd* v. *Citicorp Australia Ltd.* (1986) 11 N.S.W.L.R. 286.

216. E.P. Ellinger, "Banker's liability for advice respecting currency transactions: the Australian experience" (1989) J.B.L. 499.

217. (1889) 14 App. Cas. 337 (H.L.(E.)). This is similar to the position in the United States: see *National Bank of El Paso* v. *Farah Manufacturing Company Inc.* 678 S.W. 2d 661, at p. 681 (Tex. App. 1984)—a case with bizarre facts.

218. *Ibid.* at p. 374, per Lord Herschell.

219. *Doyle* v. *Olby (Ironmongers) Ltd.* [1969] 2 Q.B. 158 (C.A.), at p. 167 per Lord Denning M.R.; at p. 168, per Winn L.J. and per Sachs L.J., at p. 171; this case was cited with approval by the Court of Appeal in *Smith Kline & French Laboratories Ltd.* v. *Long* [1989] 1 W.L.R. 1, and *East* v. *Maurier* [1991] 1 W.L.R. 461, at pp. 464–465 (in which a loss of profits element was included as flowing from the deceit); this latter case is noted by J. Marks, "Loss of Profits in Damages for Deceit" (1992) 108 L.Q.R. 386; *Royscott Trust Ltd.* v. *Rogerson* [1991] 2 Q.B. 297, at pp. 305 and 309, noted (1991) 107 L.Q.R. 547; see S. Evans, "Two Cases on Damages in Deceit" (1993) 5 J.C.L. 73. See also *Smith New Court Securities Ltd.* v. *Scrimgeour Vickers (Asset Management) Ltd.* [1994] 1 W.L.R. 1271 (C.A.).

220. This is the same measure as for negligent misrepresentation: both at common law for tort and under section 2(1) of the Misrepresentation Act 1967 (with its fiction of fraud in respect of contracts entered into on the basis of misrepresentation).

Whilst the elements are clear, difficulty arises with regard to statements of intention by a lender (such as stating an intention to make a company insolvent and padlocking its doors, as in *National Bank of El Paso* v. *Farah Manufacturing Company Inc.*[221]). Under English law, a representation must be a statement of fact, past or present, as distinct from a statement of opinion or intention. But, as Bowen L.J. said in *Edgington* v. *Fitzmaurice*[222]:

"There must be a misstatement of an existing fact: but the state of a man's mind is as much a fact as the state of his digestion. It is true that it is very difficult to prove what the state of a man's mind at a particular time is, but if it can be ascertained it is as much a fact as anything else. A misrepresentation as to the state of a man's mind is, therefore, a misstatement of fact."

Thus, if the state of a person's mind can be ascertained, and that state indicates an intention to make a false statement, fraud may be proved.[223] A statement of intention may be one of fact if the statement is false, so that the person expressing an opinion did not hold it, or, on his knowledge of the facts, could not have honestly held the opinion.[224] For example, a statement by a lender ("X") as to one of its customers ("Y"), in response to an enquiry by another lender ("Z") on behalf of one of its customers, that Y was "a good credit risk" or "would be a most satisfactory person to do business with", when, in fact, Y was overdrawn and in difficulty, may be regarded as a false statement of fact and would entitle Z to relief against X if, as result of that statement, Z contracted with Y and suffered loss.[225]

In *Farah's* case[226] the lenders stated ambiguously (although falsely, as it later turned out) to the board of directors of the borrower that reinstating a former officer of the borrower would breach a management change default clause in the loan agreement (which permitted the loan to be accelerated if a management change occurred), resulting in the lenders accelerating the loan and making the company insolvent.

In addition to intention, it is also necessary to show that the misrepresentation was material and that it induced the recipient to enter into the contract.[227] For example, a statement by a lender, as chargee of shares, to a potential purchaser, that there were other parties interested in purchasing the shares, when there were not, induced the potential purchaser to buy the shares and suffer loss due to an unrelated fraud by another party.[228]

---

221. 678 S.W. 2d 661, at p. 682 (Tex. App. 1984).
222. (1885) 29 Ch. D. 459, at p. 483.
223. Pleading fraud is something counsel must not do lightly.
224. *Chitty*, at para. 414.
225. *Ibid.*
226. 678 S.W. 2d. 661.
227. See *Smith* v. *Chadwick* (1884) 9 App. Cas. 187 at p. 190, per Lord Selbourne; Oliver J. (as he then was) in *Nautamix BV* v. *Jenkins of Retford Ltd.* [1975] F.S.R. 385, at p. 394, citing *Spencer Bower and Turner's Actionable Misrepresentation* (1974) 3rd edn., at paras. 99 and 115 on pp. 118 and 132; and Millett J. (as he then was) in *London plc* v. *Fayed (No. 2)* [1992] 1 W.L.R. 1, at p. 6.
228. See *Smith New Court Securities Ltd.* v. *Scrimgeour Vickers (Asset Management) Ltd.* [1994] 1 W.L.R. 1271 (C.A.). The false statement of the lender was unrelated to a subsequent fraud and fall

Moreover, in certain circumstances, this representation, inducing a contract, does not have to be a positive one: it can be by silence. In the Canadian Case of *Sugar* v. *Peat Marwick Ltd.*,[229] S had invested money in DF, which purchased the assets of DFD and continued to trade. DF failed and S sued Canadian Investment Banking Corporation ("C.I.B.C.") and its agents, Peat Marwick Ltd. ("Peats"), whom the lender appointed as receivers of DFD, on the basis that they knew of substantial falsification of the records of DFD, by its then owners (the Ks), concerning accounts receivable and had not warned her husband, SS, a person experienced in turning companies around. It was not until after the purchase by S that SS discovered the fraud, although the lender (which had financed the paper part of the purchase) had known about this a month earlier.[230] Moreover, all the documentation was not available to SS, and even if it had been, it was not up to date and not accurate. SS did have accounts receivable on which, it was found, SS relied on documents from Peats and the lender regarding validity of the accounts receivable when deciding to purchase DFD.

The judge found that the lender was aware of the falsification over a month before the sale and the amount of the falsification may have been up to $200,000; that the lender did not inform either Peats or the Ss (its customer), although it knew it was not mistaken about the falsification; and S relied on documents from Peats and the lender regarding validity of the accounts receivable when deciding to purchase DFD. Accordingly, it was held that C.I.B.C. was liable for fraudulent misrepresentation[231] to the Ss through Peats, its agents.[232]

The lender knew that the documents provided and the oral statements made by their agents, Peats, whilst accurate as far as they went, did not disclose the full position; the lender thus made a representation of fact, which it was intended the Ss would act on, which they did.

(2) Economic duress

Under English law, there are two bases for economic duress: one is the coercion

---

in share price of the company concerned (Ferranti International Signal plc). In that case, the lender, which was chargee of shares in a company it had made a loan to, wished (and needed) to sell the shares at a certain price. It had a standby facility with a broking subsidiary to help it realise the security at a certain price.

229. (1989) 66 O.R. (2d.) 766; noted by M.H. Ogilvie, "How Banks Engage in Fraudulent Misrepresentations: *Sugar* v. *Peat Marwick Ltd.*" Case and Comment (1989–90) 5 B.F.L.R. 88.

230. As a matter of prudence, a lender should be concerned that the purchase price is not too high, as it will mean its loan will be repaid more easily.

231. A finding that the lender did not owe Mr and Mrs S a fiduciary duty is open to question, as it would appear that the Ss had a reasonable expectation the lender would act in their interests and make full disclosure.

232. It was not relevant, owing to the lender's fraud, that Mr and Mrs S may have been negligent in not making a full disclosure; Mr and Mrs S were not estopped due to their delay in telling the lender of the false entries in the accounts—they were correct to try to redeem the situation by seeking to revive DF; and the lender, by giving further credit, took a similar approach. Cf. *Redgrave* v. *Hurd* (1881) 20 Ch. D. 1. (C.A.).

of the will of the victim and the other is the application of illegitimate pressure.[233] The first theory found acceptance due to two opinions of Lord Scarman. In *Pao On* v. *Lau Yiu Long*[234]—a case involving non-performance of an agreement to purchase shares, when the price had decreased, instead of increasing—his Lordship, in delivering the advice of the Privy Council, stated,[235] "there is nothing contrary to principle in recognising economic duress as a factor which may render a contract voidable, provided always that the basis of such recognition is that it must amount to *coercion of the will*, which *vitiates consent*. It must be shown that the payment made or the contract entered into was not a *voluntary act*." And in *Universe Tankships Inc. of Monrovia* v. *International Transport Workers' Federation (The Universe Sentinel)*,[236] a case of industrial blackmail, before the House of Lords, Lord Scarman said: "there must be pressure, the practical effect of which is compulsion or the absence of choice ... The classic case of duress is, however ... the victim's intentional submission arising from the realisation that there is no practical choice open to him."[237]

The other theory surrounding economic duress, which is gaining support, is that of illegitimate pressure. The House of Lords recently doubted the validity of the coercion of will theory[238] and referred, *obiter*, to illegitimate pressure constituting a significant cause inducing the victim to enter into a contract; and in *Enimont Overseas AG* v. *RO Jugotanker Zadar (The Olib)*,[239] Webster J. did not apply the coercion of will theory. The illegitimate pressure theory is found in the minority advice in *Barton* v. *Armstrong*.[240] There, a strong minority, comprising Lord Wilberforce and Lord Simon of Glaisdale, said the basis of economic duress is that there is no true consent in that consent is not voluntary.[241] Absence of choice does not negate consent, because in life, including commerce and finance, acts are done under great pressure, so that the person who did them can be said to have no choice.[242] Economic duress will not necessarily be present in normal commercial contractual situations where the

233. Cf. the position in the United States in *Farah*'s case 678 S.W. 2d. 661, at p. 684.
234. [1980] A.C. 614 (P.C.)
235. *Ibid.*, at p. 636.
236. [1983] 1 A.C. 366, at p. 400 (H.L.(E.)). See also *Barton* v. *Armstrong* [1976] A.C. 104 (P.C.).
237. [1983] A.C. 366, at p. 400. Interestingly, in the same case, Lord Diplock (at p. 384) said of economic duress: "the rationale is that his apparent consent was induced by pressure exercised on [the victim] by that other party which the law does not regard as legitimate ..."
238. *Dimskal Shipping Co. SA* v. *International Transport Workers Federation (The Evia Luck)* [1991] 1 A.C. 152, at pp. 165G–166B, citing with approval the decision of the New South Wales Court of Appeal in *Crescendo Management Pty. Ltd.* v. *Westpac Banking Corporation* (1988) 19 N.S.W.L.R. 41, and the minority advice in *Barton* v. *Armstrong* [1976] A.C. 104 (P.C.). The overborne will theory is contrary to the House of Lords' decision in *DPP for Northern Ireland* v. *Lynch* [1975] A.C. 653 (a criminal duress case).
239. [1991] 2 Lloyd's Rep. 108. See discussion by A. Phang, "Economic Duress—Uncertainty Confirmed" (1991) 4 J.C.L. 147.
240. [1976] A.C. 104. Although it is agreed that the minority and majority reached the same conclusions on the law, but differed on the facts: see *Pao On* v. *Lau Yiu Lang* [1980] A.C. 614, at p. 635, per Lord Scarman.
241. [1976] A.C. 104, at p. 121.
242. *Ibid.*

parties are seeking to obtain the best deal for themselves, as commercial pressure, by itself, is not enough. This is because where one party is in a stronger bargaining position than another (and this may often be the case with a lender) there will always be commercial pressure.[243] What needs to be established is pressure which is not regarded as legitimate.[244] This involves showing two things:

> (i) the use of some illegitimate means of persuasion; and
> (ii) a relationship between the illegitimate means and the course of action followed.[245]

It was accepted that duress does not need to be "*the* reason, nor the *predominant* reason nor the clinching reason" why the victim acted as he did: duress can be *a* reason. Once it is established pressure was exerted, the onus is on the person applying it to show it did not contribute to the victim contracting.[246]

With regard to the overborne will theory,[247] the will is not destroyed, but deflected,[248] and a person "subject to duress usually knows only too well what he is doing", however, he decides "to submit to the demand or pressure rather than take an alternative course of action".[249]

The most likely form of duress to confront a borrower is where a lender refuses to enter into, or renegotiate, a loan facility which is critical to the borrower, except on certain terms favourable to it or very onerous ones to the borrower, rather than the lender threatening not to perform an existing contractual obligation. This, of course, is to be distinguished from a bad bargain, where the lender obtains favourable terms through strong negotiation (or a change of circumstances). It may be, as Ralph Gibson J. pointed out,

---

243. Per Lord Diplock in *Universe Tankships Inc. of Monrovia* v. *International Transport Workers' Federation (The Universe Sentinel)* [1983] 1 A.C. 366, at p. 384.

244. *Barton* v. *Armstrong, supra*, at p. 121, per Lords Wilberforce and Simon of Glaisdale.

245. *Ibid.* See the test, in similar terms, of McHugh J. (delivering the leading judgment) in *Crescendo Management Pty. Ltd.* v. *Westpac Banking Corporation* (1988) 19 N.S.W.L.R. 41, at p. 46A, who said there were two questions to ask: (i) whether any pressure induced the victim to contract, and (ii) whether the pressure went beyond what the law regards as legitimate; pressure was illegitimate if it involved unlawful threats or unconscionable conduct. Noted by Professor P. Birks, "The Travails of Duress" [1990] L.M.C.L.Q. 342; and P. Ridge, "Duress and Undue influence: Recent cases" (1989) 63 A.L.J. 504. See also the three point formulation of Webster J. in *The Olib* [1991] 2 Lloyd's Rep. 108, at p. 114 col. 2: (i) commercial pressure was exercised on the victim; (ii) the pressure was not legitimate; and (iii) the victim "was coerced by that pressure into doing something because he had no practical alternative than that of submission to the pressure so that he is to be regarded as not having given his true consent to that act".

246. *Crescendo Management Pty. Ltd.* v. *Westpac Banking Corporation* (1988) 19 N.S.W.L.R. 41, at p. 46D–E, per McHugh J.

247. *Crescendo Management Pty. Ltd.* v. *Westpac Banking Corporation* (1988) 19 N.S.W.L.R. 41, at p. 46D–E, per McHugh J.

248. Citing *DPP for Northern Ireland* v. *Lynch* [1975] A.C. 653. See P.S. Atiyah, "Economic Duress and The Overborne Will" (1982) 98 L.Q.R. 197; and see also D. Tiplady, "Concepts of Duress" (1983) 99 L.Q.R. 188 and P.S. Atiyah, "Duress and the Overborne Will Again" (1983) 99 L.Q.R. 353.

249. (1988) 19 N.S.W.L.R. 41, at pp. 45–46.

perfectly valid to impose onerous conditions on a borrower in view of the economic climate and the state of the borrower.[250]

A lender must be careful that statements imposing conditions in rescheduling do not amount to blackmail—being "an unwarranted demand with menaces" with a view to gain.[251] To escape liability, a lender would need to show either that there were reasonable grounds for the demand—and it is arguable that repeated failures to pay may be regarded as reasonable—or that the use of any "menaces" was valid in the circumstances. This is a subjective question. Blackmail is an indictable offence with a maximum penalty of 14 years; if the lender is not liable, an individual manager may be.[252]

A customer with an overdraft from one lender can, of course, if he is able to obtain better terms from another lender, change lenders and repay the first loan in full. But, if the company's financial state is such that it is unable to borrow from another lender, the "difficulty of the company [is] likely to be shared by the [first] lender. The expense and risks of a receivership [are] clear, and the lender [will] frequently be forced to continue to support a customer from which it would like to escape."[253]

In *Williams & Glyn*, this happened after December 1973; and when the loan agreement expired the parties were forced to negotiate the best terms they could.

An interesting example of the problems that may arise occurred in *Crescendo Management Pty. Ltd. v. Westpac Banking Corp.*[254] where, as a way of procuring certain financial arrangements, the lender (Westpac) threatened to withhold money the borrower (Crescendo) was entitled to. However, a claim by Crescendo that the pressure of withholding the money induced it to execute a mortgage was unsuccessful, as the mortgage had preceded the pressure. The pressure had not affected the decision to execute the mortgage, although the pressure could be regarded as illegitimate.[255]

In determining whether there has been economic duress, the court will look at the following factors, which are not exclusive[256]:

    (i) a vigorous protest by the borrower;
    (ii) the inadequacies of another remedy which suggests there is no realistic alternative but to submit;

---

250. *Williams & Glyn's Bank Ltd.* v. *Barnes* [1981] Com. L.R. 205, at p. 209. See, for example, *Pao On* v. *Lau Yiu Long* [1980] A.C. 614 (P.C.).

251. Section 21(1) of the Theft Act 1968.

252. *Tesco Supermarkets Ltd.* v. *Nattras* [1972] A.C. 153 (H.L.(E.)). See also Penn, Shea and Arora, *The Law Relating to Domestic Banking* (1987), at para. 19.06.

253. [1981] Com. L.R. 205, at p. 209.

254. (1988) 19 N.S.W.L.R. 41. See also *Shivas* v. *Bank of New Zealand* [1990] 2 N.Z.L.R. 327, where allegations of duress in a "rescue" or refinancing involving directors' guarantees were rejected, although there was some degree of commercial pressure by the lender. Also, no complaint was made until two years later.

255. See Birks, "The Travails of Duress" [1990] L.C.M.L.Q. 342, at p. 343.

256. Per Lord Scarman in *Pao On* v. *Lau Yiu Long* [1980] A.C. 614, at pp. 635–636; and Goff and Jones, *The Law of Restitution* (1993) 4th edn., at p. 267.

(iii) the lender is aware of the borrower's personal financial circumstances (which will most certainly be the case); and

(iv) a prompt repudiation of the transaction by the borrower once the threat is removed.

The most relevant of these are the "no alternative test",[257] which the courts have interpreted to mean that there should be no "reasonable alternative",[258] and prompt repudiation. In their classic work, The Law of Restitution, Lord Goff of Chieveley and Professor Jones state that, as the law currently stands, an English court may not regard it as "legitimate" that a person (a lender), in making a threat (amounting to duress) believed that it was commercially reasonable to make a new demand (on the borrower).[259]

In a series of recent cases, the courts have set contracts aside for economic duress where there has been "no reasonable alternative". Examples of this have included a refusal to carry goods by road, unless payment was increased[260]; the payment of additional expenses concerning cargo being shipped under a bill of lading owing to fear that the cargo might be delayed or dumped and as the cargo was needed urgently[261]; and a refusal to erect stands for a very important "one off" exhibition, unless there were very favourable redundancy terms.[262]

Hence, where there has been an element of "commercial blackmail", the courts have accepted that the weaker party had "no practical alternative" and have set aside the agreement. The correct basis for doing so is that there was lack of true consent.[263] Therefore, in the renegotiation of a loan a lender must be careful, and act reasonably, in dealing with borrowers, so that the borrower has

---

257. See Atlas Express Ltd. v. Kafco (Importers and Distributors) Ltd. [1989] Q.B. 833 and case note by P.A. Chandler, "Economic Duress: Clarity or Confusion" [1989] L.M.C.L.Q. 270. Also see Universe Tankships Inc. of Monrovia v. International Transport Workers' Federation (The Universe Sentinel) [1983] 1 A.C. 366 (H.L.(E.)). Cf. North Ocean Shipping Co. Ltd. v. Hyundai Construction Co. Ltd. (The Atlantic Baron) [1979] Q.B. 705; and see the case note on this in (1979) 95 L.Q.R. 475.

258. B & S Contracts and Design Ltd. v. Victor Green Publications Ltd. [1984] I.C.R. 419, at p. 428 per Kerr L.J.; see also North Ocean Shipping Co. Ltd. v. Hyundai Construction Co. Ltd. (The Atlantic Baron) [1979] Q.B. 705; and Hobhouse J. in Vantage Navigation Corporation v. Suhail & Saud Bahwan Building Materials LLC (The Alev) [1989] 1 Lloyd's Rep. 138, at pp. 150–151; and see case note by P.A. Chandler, supra.

259. Goff and Jones, The Law of Restitution (1993) 4th edn., at p. 267.

260. Atlas Express Ltd. v. Kafco (Importers and Distributors) Ltd. [1989] Q.B. 833. Noted by A. Phang, "Whither Economic Duress? Reflections on Two Recent Cases" [1990] 53 M.L.R. 107; J.G. Starke Q.C., in "Recent Cases" (1989) A.L.J. 791; and P.A. Chandler, "Economic Duress: Clarity or Confusion" [1989] L.M.C.L.Q. 270. For a discussion of the law of economic duress: see E. MacDonald, "Duress Threatened by Breach of Contract" (1990) J.B.L. 460; and C. Battersby, "Economic Duress" (1989) 133 Solicitors' Journal 1424.

261. Vantage Navigation Corporation v. Suhail & Saud Bahwan Building Materials LLC (The Alev) [1989] 1 Lloyd's Rep. 138. See comments by A. Phang, "Whither Economic Duress? Reflections on Two Recent Cases" [1990] 53 M.L.R. 107.

262. B & S Contracts and Design Ltd. v. Victor Green Publications Ltd. [1984] I.C.R. 419.

263. See, for example, Webster J. in The Òlib, supra, at p. 114 col. 2.

no recourse against the lender by saying that he had "no reasonable alternative" but to accept the loan, or renegotiate the loan on very onerous terms.[264] If something goes wrong and the borrower defaults and seeks to avoid liability, it is likely that the plea of economic duress will only be raised when there are difficulties with repayment, and not shortly afterwards, therefore failing to satisfy the fourth criterion outlined above.

This will be particularly so, for example, in the circumstances envisaged by Ralph Gibson J. (as he then was) in *Williams & Glyn*,[265] where the borrower is in economic difficulties and is unable to seek alternative finance. In these circumstances, it is not unreasonable for a lender to insist upon stricter security arrangements, as they are the only source from which the borrower will be able to obtain funds. In *Williams & Glyn*, it was held that there was no economic duress in relation to discounting of bills of exchange where the borrower proceeded on a misunderstanding of the system by which money was raised.[266]

Moreover, courts will be reluctant to set aside a contract which has been allowed to continue and only later, when it has become disadvantageous to the borrower, has there been a protest. In *Alec Lobb (Garages) Ltd.* v. *Total Oil Circuit Britain Ltd.*,[267] Millett Q.C. (as he then was), sitting as a deputy High Court judge, refused to set aside a lease to the defendants and lease-back to the plaintiffs of the plaintiffs' garage, the purpose of which was to assist the plaintiffs who were in financial difficulty, where the period between signing the lease and objecting was 10 years.

Similarly, in the unreported Western Australian case of *Westfarmers* v. *Duffy*,[268] Duffy had sought to set aside various security documents relating to renegotiated loans for his farming operations well after the event, and Kennedy J., in a carefully reasoned judgment (of approximately 400 pages), held that there was no economic duress. This was because, at the time of the contracts, Duffy's financial plight (like that in *Alec Lobb*) was of his own making; Duffy had taken legal advice and had threatened proceedings; the agreements had been signed without protest; no complaint was raised till several months later and only when things had once again started to go wrong; and Duffy acted as if the agreement was valid for a long period of time and took the benefit of the contract.[269]

---

264. See, for example, *Crescendo Management Pty. Ltd.* v. *Westpac Banking Corporation* (1988) 19 N.S.W.L.R. 41, and *Shivas* v. *Bank of New Zealand* [1990] 2 N.Z.L.R. 327.

265. [1981] Com. L.R. 205, at p. 209.

266. See especially at pp. 514, 515 and 575 of the transcript, where it was said no threat was made to Barnes when the lender explained to him the effect of not paying the bills of exchange from the secondary lender.

267. [1983] 1 W.L.R. 89, revs'd in part [1985] 1 All E.R. 944 (C.A.).

268. Judgment was delivered in the Supreme Court of Western Australia on 6 February 1984. For a summary of this case: see the paper by T.E. O'Connor, in *Equitable Remedies and Estoppel Law* (1984) Law Society of Western Australia.

269. As to affirmation of the contract once the threat has been removed: see *Occidental Worldwide Investment Corporation* v. *Skibs A/S Avanti (The Siboen and the Sibotre)* [1976] 1 Lloyd's Rep. 293.

These cases emphasise that a borrower cannot blame his own financial incompetence or misfortune on a lender, who merely wishes to protect its position, where the only other alternative is insolvency and the borrower is aware of this. In *Duffy* and *Alec Lobb*, the "solutions" came from the borrower.

Economic duress is now an established part of English law, although actions to set aside contracts for it are not common, nonetheless, it may be that a borrower will use it as one method of vitiating a loan agreement—perhaps on a counterclaim.

(3) Tortious interference with contract

Like economic duress, this tort involves the application of commercial pressure by a lender upon a borrower. In *Edwin Hill & Partners* v. *First National Corporation plc*,[270] Stuart-Smith L.J. outlined the following five elements of this tort[271]:

  (i) a direct interference with a contract (contract B) between the borrower and a third party by the lender;
  (ii) a sufficient knowledge on the lender's part that the lender's conduct will interfere with contract B;
  (iii) an intention to bring contract B to an end;
  (iv) the lender's interference caused damage to the borrower; and
  (v) the interference must not have been justified.

Where liability is made out, the damages are the same as for unlawful interference with business and conspiracy—being damages at large (by which it is, apparently, meant that no proof of special damage is required).[272] But the measure of damages in interference with contract cases is not always the amount which the victim "might have recovered for breach of contract", although, in many cases, the plaintiff can be compensated properly by giving him the amount he "might have recovered from the contract breaker".[273]

---

270. [1989] 1 W.L.R. 255 (C.A.). For a discussion of this case and the defence of justification: see R. O'Dair, "Justifying an Interference with Contractual Rights" (1991) 11 O.J.L.S. 277.

271. *Ibid.*, at pp. 227–228. Cf. Hoffman L.J. in *Law Debenture Trust Corp. plc* v. *Ural Caspian Oil Corp. Ltd.* [1993] 1 W.L.R. 138, at p. 150G, who said there were "three elements to the tort: (1) a right to the plaintiff (2) violated by an actionable wrong (3) procured by the defendant"; and the position in the United States, where a valid contract known to the defendant and an unjustified and intentional interference contract resulting in damage to the plaintiff need to be shown: see *In re Quality Processing Inc.* 9 F.3d. 1360 (8th Cir. 1993).

272. See Brooking J. in *Ansett Transport Industries (Operations) Pty. Ltd.* v. *Australian Federation of Air Pilots (No. 2)* [1991] 2 V.R. 636, at pp. 645–646 and the cases cited there.

273. *Ansett (No. 2)*, *supra*, at p. 646.

In *Edwin Hill*, the lender—who was a mortgagee—interfered with the borrower's contractual rights with a third party (architects) since it sought to make the borrower's change their architects for a building project to one considered more prestigious. The court held, applying the above criteria, that the interference was justified, as the lender (as mortgagee) had an equal or superior right[274] upon the borrower's default.

However, in the Canadian decision of *Thermo King Corporation* v. *Provincial Bank of Canada*,[275] a lender wrongfully refused to issue a draft on its customer's instructions, knowing that the failure to issue the draft would cause the customer to breach a contract with the intended payee of the draft. In these circumstances, the lender was held liable for inducing breach of contract and the loss caused to the intended payee. The court said that a lender may only put its interests ahead of its customers if it has a right to do so—here, it did not.

As to what constitutes justification is unclear[276]; although the authorities indicate that where the interference is by unlawful means, the defence is not applicable.[277] Ultimately, it will depend on the facts (including the parties' conduct) so that, for example, an attempt merely to increase profits may not be justified.[278] Nonetheless, from a lender's point of view, *Edwin Hill* provides useful guidance in the context of enforcing security.[279]

Apart from the enforcement of its security, a lender will be concerned to preserve the priority of its security, which it will seek to do by means of a negative pledge clause in the security documentation prohibiting the creation of further security without that lender's consent[280]; it may also include a further assurance clause, under which the debtor agrees to execute such further

274. See also *Read* v. *Friendly Society of Operative Stonemasons of England, Ireland and Wales* [1902] 2 K.B. 732; and *Smithies* v. *National Association of Operative Plasterers* [1909] 1 K.B. 310 on this point. See also *Dellabarca* v. *Northern Storemen and Packers Union* [1989] 2 N.Z.L.R. 734 at p. 753, per Smellie J.

275. (1981) 130 D.L.R. (3d) 256. See also O'Dair, *supra*. The most commonly cited statement of justification is that of Romer L.J. in *Glamorgan Coal Co. Ltd.* v. *South Wales Miners Federation* [1903] 2 K.B. 545, at pp. 573–574, who said regard might be had to the following factors: the nature of the contract broken; the position of the contractual parties; the grounds for the breach; what was used to procure the breach; the relationship of the tortfeasor to the contract breaker; and the aim of the person in procuring the breach.

276. See *Clerk & Lindsell on Torts* [1989], 16th edn., at para. 15–12.

277. *Read* v. *Friendly Society of Operative Stonemasons* [1902] 2 K.B. 732; and *Ansett Transport Industries (Operations) Pty. Ltd.* v. *Australian Federation of Air Pilots (No. 1)* [1991] 1 V.R. 635, at p. 677, per Brooking J. See also *Building Workers' Industrial Union of Australia* v. *Odco Pty. Ltd.* (1991) A.L.R. 735, at p. 771, per Full Court of Federal Court of Australia.

278. See Nourse L.J. in *Edwin Hill*, *supra*, at p. 235.

279. Cf. *The Myrto* [1977] 2 Lloyd's Rep. 243 and the case of *Banco do Brasil SA* v. *The Alexandros G. Tsavliris* [1992] 3 FC 735, where, in a shipping context, a lender held a mortgage over a ship and the shipowner (the mortgagor), who had time-chartered the ship to a third party, had defaulted under the mortgage; it was held that the lender's conduct was justified, and that *The Myrto* did not form part of Canadian law. See also *Port Line Ltd.* v. *Benline Steamers Ltd.* [1958] 2 Q.B. 146; and *Swiss Bank* v. *Lloyds Bank* [1979] Ch. 548.

280. It is the practice to refer to a negative pledge on the Form M395, relating to registration of Charges.

documentation as is (reasonably) required. It is not uncommon for a borrower to seek funds from several sources, each of which will probably require security. Therefore, if a debtor has granted security over an asset to lender A and there is a negative pledge in the security documentation, and the borrower later seeks further finance from another source, lender B, who wants security, then, if lender B demands security from the borrower in breach of lender A's negative pledge, lender B is likely to be liable for inducing breach of contract,[281] as it is very likely to have sufficient knowledge of the pledge (and will have, as a matter of prudence, done a company search).[282] In such a case, there would, it is submitted, be no justification: as there is no equal or superior right—it is a simple case of breach and should be actionable.

Another scenario which could entail liability is as follows. Lender A is granted security over an asset of the borrower's with a negative pledge and further assurance clause; but, lender A subsequently consents to lender B taking security over the same asset, which is not to rank ahead of its own,[283] and lender B has a negative pledge to protect its position. Lender A now requires further security over more of the borrower's assets, some of which lender B has taken security over. Before executing the additional security, the borrower points out lender B's negative pledge. Nonetheless, lender A insists on execution and lender B sues for inducing breach of contract—this will be particularly important if the borrower becomes insolvent. In such a situation, it is suggested that lender A is protected for two reasons. First, on the basis that, arguably, it has an equal or superior right by virtue of its further assurance clause. Secondly, Buckley L.J. in *Smithies* v. *National Association of Plasterers*[284] regarded it as sufficient justification if a defendant (lender A) was doing no more than requiring performance of another contract made with the party to both contracts (the borrower), albeit that this contract is inconsistent with the one being breached. Nonetheless, prudence would dictate that lender A should first seek to obtain lender B's consent to avoid any difficulties.

(4) Unlawful interference with trade or business

Whilst this tort—concerned with an intention to directly or indirectly harm or have an "adverse impact"[285] on another's business or commercial interests, unlawfully or wrongfully, outside the bounds of normal competition—has been popular in the United States, it is still a developing one, of "uncertain ambit", in

---

281. For an excellent discussion of this issue: see J.B. Stone, "Negative Pledges and the Tort of Interference with Contractual Relations" [1991] J.B.L. 310.

282. Even though commercial law is opposed to constructive notice, sufficient knowledge would seem to indicate some type of constructive, as opposed to actual, knowledge. It would appear to encompass up to category (4) of Sir Peter Gibson's list of types of knowledge: see section on Constructive Trusts.

283. See Stone, *supra*, at pp. 318–319.

284. [1909] 1 K.B. 310, at p. 337.

285. J.K. Bertil, "Improper Interference With Another's Business" [1993] J.B.L. 519, at p. 523.

the United Kingdom,[286] although its existence is not in doubt after the decision of the Court of Appeal in *Lonrho plc* v. *Fayed*.[287]

This is a significant case, from a lender's point of view, arising out of the takeover battle for the House of Fraser plc (including Harrods department store) between the Fayed brothers and Lonrho plc. The significant aspect is that Lonrho plc sued not only the Fayed brothers, but also the Fayeds' merchant bank and one of its former directors for, *inter alia*, conspiracy and unlawful interference with their business, alleging that they (Lonrho plc) had consequently lost a chance of bidding for the House of Fraser plc.

It was alleged that the defendants had made fraudulent misrepresentations about the commercial standing and worth of the Fayeds to the Secretary of State, which had influenced him not to refer their bid to the Monopolies and Mergers Commission. It was not alleged that the lender or its former director knew that the facts told to them by the Fayeds were, allegedly, false. Rather, it was pleaded that they had a duty to satisfy themselves as to their truth, and this they failed to do. Accordingly, it was to be inferred that the advisers had acted recklessly or carelessly as to whether what they were told was true or false and, therefore, had acted fraudulently in that sense. Interestingly, and significantly, no distinction was made as to the position of the Fayeds and the bank and its former director.

The Court of Appeal, in discussing the striking out application, said that, in order to establish the tort of wrongful interference with trade or business, it is not necessary to prove a predominant purpose to injure the plaintiff—which is now like conspiracy, where the competitors use unlawful means to harm the victim.[288] A predominant purpose is not required when there is wrongful interference with a third party's contract with the victim, or where a third party is instrumental in the victim's destruction, and it should not be required where there is fraud on a third party, aimed at the victim. Nor is it necessary that there is a complete tort between the tortfeasor and the third party against whom the tort is committed. However, the unlawful act (in this case, the alleged fraudulent misrepresentation) has to be directed against the plaintiffs, or be intended to harm the plaintiffs.[289]

---

286. *Lonrho plc* v. *Fayed* [1990] 2 Q.B. 479, at p. 491, per Dillon L.J.; at p. 491, per Ralph Gibson L.J.; and at p. 493, per Woolf L.J.

287. [1990] 2 Q.B. 479 (C.A.) and see the cases referred to by the court. The matter went on appeal to the House of Lords on the issue of conspiracy. Conspiracy (and the question of predominant motive) was the main focus of the appeal before the Law Lords. However, it was said that the two issues—of unlawful interference with business and conspiracy—stood to fall together: see *Lonrho plc* v. *Fayed* [1992] 1 A.C. 448, at p. 470, per Lord Bridge of Harwich delivering the majority speech (Lords Brandon of Oakbrook, Goff of Chieveley and Jauncey of Tullichettle agreeing). Cf. Lord Templeman (at p. 471) who felt that "the ambit and ingredients of the torts of conspiracy and unlawful interference might ... require further analysis and reconsideration by the courts."

288. [1990] 2 Q.B. 479, at p. 489, per Dillon L.J. (Ralph Gibson and Woolf L.JJ. agreeing. This is now the position with conspiracy: see *Lonrho plc* v. *Fayed* [1991] 3 W.L.R. 188 (H.L.(E.)).

289. Per Dillon L.J., at p. 489, with whom Ralph Gibson and Woolf L.JJ. expressed agreement.

The court, nonetheless, stressed that it was not deciding the merits of the case, which were properly to be decided at trial on the evidence led. Woolf L.J. (as he then was), who agreed the claim should not be struck out, nevertheless expressed two reservations as to whether the fraud was sufficiently direct to amount to interference with Lonrho's business. First, that the alleged fraud related to the virtues of the Fayeds: and not Lonrho plc's deficiencies. Secondly, that the Secretary of State was, allegedly, influenced not to take action against the Fayeds, rather than take, or not take, action against Lonrho, and hence it was arguable whether the business asset supposedly damaged was capable of being a business interest for the purposes of this tort.[290]

Unlawful interference with business is a comparatively new tort, the boundaries of which are to be determined on a case-by-case basis, and, it is submitted, is not one likely to occur frequently, in the absence of, for example, a personality clash[291] or fraud. However, in determining those boundaries, the factors[292] to be considered will include: first, the nature of the intention needed to satisfy the requirement that the conduct be directed against the victim—especially where there is a fraudulent misrepresentation by X about himself to Y to cause Y to act in a manner in which X obtains or maintains a commercial advantage over Z or deprives Z of a commercial advantage[293]; secondly, the nature of the business interests, with respect to which the victim has to show he has suffered damage; thirdly, whether a sufficient nexus or directness of impact and consequence exists between the unlawful means used and the alleged damage causing the effect on the victim; and, fourthly, whether there is sufficient damage for there to be a cause of action.[294]

Normally, a lender's conduct will not be directed towards harming a borrower's business, since it is in the lender's interest that the borrower's business continues so as to service the loan. Furthermore, if a lender acts prudently, and in accordance with the terms of its loan and security documents, there is little likelihood that this tort (and, indeed, many other remedies) will be available to a borrower (or even a third party). Difficulties may arise where the party claiming to have been harmed is not the borrower, but a rival of the borrower, such as was alleged in the *Lonrho* case. As to what constitutes unlawful conduct is not clear—certainly intimidation, interfering with a contract, making fraudulent statements about a rival, are included; beyond that, the terrain is uncharted, although Dillon L.J. did suggest that merely breaching a statutory prohibition might not be enough, and that the complainant would have to show the breach "gave rise to a civil remedy".[295]

---

290. *Ibid.*
291. *K.M.C. Co. Inc.* v. *Irving Trust Company*, 757 F.2d. 752 (6th Cir. 1985).
292. Per Ralph Gibson L.J. at p. 492.
293. It would, arguably, be different and a clearer case if, in the example in the text, the fraudulent statements by X were about Z: see Ralph Gibson L.J., at p. 492, and Bertil, *supra*, at p. 531.
294. Per Ralph Gibson L.J., at p. 492.
295. [1990] 2 Q.B. 479, at p. 488.

The significance of the *Lonrho* case is that a lender, acting as a "merchant bank and adviser",[296] was identified with its client's alleged act. What this means is that, in general, lenders must, as in the case of liability as a constructive trustee for knowing assistance discussed below, be careful in assessing the actions of their clients, although no view either way is expressed on the *Lonrho* case.

(5) Conspiracy

It has now been settled by the House of Lords[297] that there are two types of conspiracy:

> (i) where lawful means are used, but the aim is an unlawful end; and
> (ii) where unlawful means are used.[298]

And that in the second type (where the means used are themselves illegal) it is not necessary, unlike the first type, to have the predominant motive of hurting the plaintiff.[299]

In the ordinary course of events, it is unlikely that a lender will be liable in damages for conspiracy, which are damages at large,[300] as its prime concern will be to get its loan repaid,[301] and it will not be interested in harming the borrower. However, there may be circumstances where a lender is very closely associated with a "Napoleonic figure", who is the major shareholder in private and public companies which have accounts with the lender, and this figure misappropriates money from the public companies into his own private companies, and the lender is regarded as having conspired with him. This seems to have been the situation in the Canadian case of *Claiborne Industries Ltd.* v. *National Bank of Canada*,[302] where the lender was found to have conspired with its customer ("B") in approving transfers from the plaintiff (a public company, which had several subsidiaries) to B's private companies without proper authority from the public companies; these transfers were for the benefit of B and the lender, and to the detriment of the public companies. Also, the release by the lender of security to the plaintiff, which was subsequently taken by B via his private companies, was entwined with the general conspiracy; as was the later acquisition of undervalued security in the plaintiff by the lender, which gave it a controlling interest in the plaintiff.

---

296. Per Dillon L.J., at p. 486.

297. *Lonrho plc* v. *Fayed* [1992] 1 A.C. 448. See article on it by H. Cohen, "Conspiracy, Intentional Harm and Economic Loss" [1991] J.I.B.L. 478.

298. At p. 464, per Lord Bridge of Harwich, citing Lord Devlin in *Rookes* v. *Barnard* [1964] A.C. 1129, at p. 1204 (H.L.(E.)).

299. At pp. 465–466.

300. *Lonrho plc* v. *Fayed (No. 5)* [1994] 1 All E.R. 188 (C.A.).

301. In the much publicised Laker litigation, an allegation of conspiracy was raised against various lenders, but the Court of Appeal refused to permit an English liquidator to bring proceedings in the United States under their anti-trust laws, as it would have been unconscionable to do so: see *Midland Bank plc* v. *Laker Airways Ltd.* [1986] Q.B. 689.

302. (1989) 59 D.L.R. (4th) 533. The possibility of the lender being liable as a constructive trustee was not considered after the finding of conspiracy.

Whilst the test used in Canada is slightly different to England—being engagement in a common design to commit an unlawful act which the participants should have known was likely to injure the plaintiff and it did—the circumstances, albeit briefly sketched, do show the dangers of trying to please charismatic borrowers and becoming too involved in their affairs, rather than retaining the traditional debtor/creditor relationship.

(6) Prima facie tort theory: intentional harm

Under this theory in United States law, four factors are required:

> (i) a lawful act by the defendant;
> (ii) an intent to cause injury to a plaintiff;
> (iii) injury to the plaintiff; and
> (iv) the absence of any justification for the defendant's action.[303]

This involves a process of balancing: (i) the nature and seriousness of the harm; (ii) the interest promoted by the perpetrator's conduct; (iii) the character of the means used by the perpetrator; and (iv) the perpetrator's motive. Whilst there are elements of the economic torts, discussed above, present[304] and English law does recognise damage for intentional physical harm to person, land and goods,[305] Clerk and Lindsell[306] conclude, after an examination of the relatively few cases on this subject, that there are no signs of adopting a general principle of liability for intention to injure. With these views it is respectfully agreed, and it is submitted that the *prima facie* tort theory is not part of English law. Also, in a lender liability situation, the loss will be purely economic—as no physical or property damage is involved—which is generally difficult to recover for under English law.[307]

---

303. *Bronfman* v. *Centerre Banks of Kansas City*, 705 S.W. 2d 42 (Mo. App. 1985).

304. See *Rookes* v. *Barnard* [1964] A.C. 1129 (H.L.(E.)).

305. *Wilkinson* v. *Downton* [1897] 2 Q.B. 57, a case of physical harm caused by a practical joke, where Wright J. (as he then was) said at pp. 58–59: "The defendant has ... wilfully done an act calculated to cause harm to the plaintiff—that is to say, to infringe her legal right to personal safety, and has in fact thereby caused physical harm to her. That proposition without more appears to me to state a good cause of action; there being no justification alleged for the act." See also *Janvier* v. *Sweeney* [1919] 2 K.B. 316; *Bunyan* v. *Jordan* (1937) 57 C.L.R. 1; *Street on Torts* (1988) 18th edn., Chapters 2 to 5; *Winfield & Jolowicz* (1989) 13th edn., at pp. 68–71; and *Clerk & Lindsell on Torts* (1989) 16th edn., at para. 1–76, who state that no general principle has been laid down and it would seem there is a reluctance to do so.

306. *Clerk & Lindsell on Torts* (1989) 16th edn., at para. 1–76.

307. *Candlewood Navigation Corporation Ltd.* v. *Mitsui O.S.K. Lines Ltd. (The Mineral Transporter)* [1986] A.C. 1 (P.C.); *Leigh and Sillivan Ltd.* v. *Aliakmon Shipping Co. Ltd. (The Aliakmon)* [1986] A.C. 785 (H.L.(E.)); *D. & F. Estates* v. *Church Commissioners for England* [1989] A.C. 177 (H.L.(E.)); *Murphy* v. *Brentwood District Council* [1991] 1 A.C. 398 (H.L.(E.)); and *Department of the Environment* v. *Thomas Bates and Sons Ltd.* [1991] 1 A.C. 499 (H.L.(E.)). Cf. *Spring* v. *Guardian Assurance Plc* [1994] 3 W.L.R. 354 (H.L.(E.)) and *Henderson* v. *Merrett Syndicates Ltd.* [1994] 3 W.L.R. 761 (H.L.(E.)), allowing recovery for pure economic loss under the *Hedley Byrne* principle.

THE LENDER AS A CONSTRUCTIVE TRUSTEE: KNOWING ASSISTANCE & KNOWING RECEIPT

In its ordinary business of paying and collecting cheques, and *a fortiori* of the debtor/creditor relationship with its customer, a lender will not be too concerned at the source of its customer's funds or to whom cheques are made out.[308] Thus, it will not be under any fiduciary obligation as a trustee to its customer or any third party. But there are circumstances where there has been *mala fides* by, for example, a lender's customer, and the lender is sufficiently aware of it or connected with it, such that the lender may be liable to the victim of this conduct, as a constructive trustee, for the loss suffered by a third party. These circumstances are set out in the judgment of Lord Selborne in *Barnes* v. *Addy*,[309] where his Lordship, in a well-known passage, says, in the context of agency, that strangers to a trust:

"... are not to be made constructive trustees merely because they act as the agents of trustees in transactions within their legal powers, transactions perhaps of which a Court of Equity may disapprove, unless those agents receive and become chargeable with some part of the trust property, or unless they assist with the knowledge in a dishonest and fraudulent design on the part of the trustees."

There are thus two types of liability,[310] as defined by Lord Selborne, although care needs to be taken not to read his Lordship's pronouncement as if it was an Act of Parliament[311]:

(a) agents (i.e. lenders) who receive and become chargeable with some part of the trust property—this is called "knowing receipt", and is receipt based liability[312]; and

(b) agents (i.e. lenders) who assist with knowledge in a dishonest and fraudulent design on the part of the trustees—this is called "knowing assistance", and is fault based.[313]

308. There are exceptions for lenders, where they suspect money is drugs related. See also Part V of the new Criminal Justice Act 1993, concerning money laundering.

309. (1874) L.R. 9 Ch. App. 244, at p. 251 (Court of Appeal in Chancery). James and Mellish L.JJ. concurred.

310. Thomas J. in *Powell* v. *Thompson* [1991] 1 N.Z.L.R. 597.

311. A similar view is expressed by Peter Gibson J. (as he then was) in *Baden Delvaux and Lecuit* v. *Société Générale pour Favoriser le Développement du Commerce et de l'Industrie en France S.A. ("Baden")* [1983] B.C.L.C. 325, at p. 404, also reported subsequently in [1992] 4 All E.R. 161, at p. 232; Professor P.B.H. Birks, "Trusts in the Recovery of Misapplied Assets: Tracing, Trusts and Restitution" (Misapplied Assets"): Ch. 8 in *Commercial Aspects of Trusts and Fiduciary Obligations* (1992) (E. McKendrick, ed.), at p. 152; and C. Harpum, "The Stranger As Constructive Trustee" (Part I) (1986) 102 L.Q.R. 114 ("Harpum Part I"), at p. 145.

312. *Agip (Africa) Ltd.* v. *Jackson* [1990] 1 Ch. 265, at p. 292, per Millett J. (as he then was); this case, at first instance, is noted by C. Harpum, "Liability For Money Laundering" [1990] C.L.J. 217 and by Professor P.B.H. Birks, "Misdirected Funds Again" (1989) 105 L.Q.R. 528. Similar views are expressed by Sir Peter Millett, writing extra-judicially, in "Tracing the Proceeds of Fraud" (1991) L.Q.R. 71, at pp. 72 and 80–81. An appeal against the decision of Millett J. was dismissed: see [1991] Ch. 547. The appeal was concerned, *inter alia*, with dishonesty in knowing assistance and adds little to the decision at first instance.

313. The Hon. Mr Justice Millett, "Tracing the Proceeds of Fraud" (1991) L.Q.R. 71, at pp. 72 and 83.

An example of the former is where a lender receives money from a customer, which it knows has been obtained by the customer in breach of trust, but the lender uses the money to reduce the customer's overdraft.[314] An example of the latter is where there is a breach of section 151 of the Companies Act 1985 (as amended), relating to financial assistance, by a customer, and the lender *qua* lender has a sufficient degree of knowledge of this breach to be regarded as having knowingly assisted by lending money for this acquisition of shares by the customer.[315]

Liability is, generally, personal,[316] as it will be a claim for the value received by the lender because the money will not, subject to the rules of tracing,[317] be identifiable; where it is still in the possession of the lender, then a proprietorial claim is available.[318] The guiding principle is that, where there is a breach of trust, the trustee is required to put the trust in the same position it would have been in had there been no such breach, i.e. a liability to compensate the trust.[319] Consequently, an intermeddler in a trust (a lender) is required to "either relinquish an improper gain that he has made in his self-assumed fiduciary capacity role, or to make good a loss suffered as a result of his actions".[320] The lender is to compensate the victim for the loss it (the lender) helped to inflict through its conduct.

It is proposed to look at the two types of liability separately, commencing with "knowing assistance".

(a) Knowing assistance

There are three common scenarios for knowing assistance:

    (i) where it is claimed that the lender has assisted a trustee to commit a breach of trust, such as honouring a cheque drawn on a trust account or transferring money[321];

---

314. *Thomson* v. *Clydesdale Bank* [1893] A.C. 282 (H.L.(Sc.)), 1893 20 R. (H.L.) 59, where the vital element of knowledge was absent; and *Westpac Banking Corporation* v. *Savin* [1985] 2 N.Z.L.R. 41, where it was not.

315. *Selangor United Rubber Estates Ltd.* v. *Cradock (No. 3)* [1968] 1 W.L.R. 1555; and *Belmont Finance Corporation Ltd.* v. *Williams Furniture Ltd. (No. 1)* [1979] Ch. 250.

316. *Paget's Law of Banking* (1989) 10th edn., at p. 232. Scott L.J. in *Polly Peck International plc* v. *Nadir* [1992] 2 Lloyd's Rep. 238, at p. 247 col. 1.

317. See A. Burrows, *The Law of Restitution* (1993), at pp. 57–76; Goff and Jones, *The Law of Restitution* (1993) 4th edn., at pp. 75–93.

318. See Professor P.B.H. Birks, "Misdirected funds: restitution from the recipient" [1989] L.M.C.L.Q. 296, at pp. 297–298 and 311–312; and T.G. Youdan, "The Fiduciary Principle: The Applicability of Proprietary Remedies": Ch. 3 in *Equity, Fiduciaries and Trusts* (1989) Carswell, (T.G. Youdan, ed.).

319. Birks, "Trusts in the Recovery of Misapplied Assets: Tracing, Trust, and Restitution": Ch. 8 in *Commercial Aspects of Trusts and Fiduciary Obligations* (1992) (E. McKendrick, ed.), at p. 154; and *Paget*, at p. 232.

320. Harpum, "The Stranger As Constructive Trustee" (Part I) (1986) 102 L.Q.R. 114, at p. 118.

321. Harpum, "The Stranger As Constructive Trustee" (Part I) (1986) 102 L.Q.R. 114, at p. 148. See the provisions of the Criminal Justice Act 1993 on this.

(ii) where the lender provides finance for the acquisition by the company of its own shares in contravention of section 151 of the Companies Act 1985 (as amended)[322]; and

(iii) the emerging area of money laundering.[323]

The basis of liability, under this head, is "nothing more than a formula for equitable relief ... [through which] a court of equity says that [the lender] shall be liable in equity, *as though he were a constructive trustee*.[324] [The lender] is made liable in equity as trustee by the imposition or construction of the court of equity. This is done because in accordance with equitable principles applied by the court of equity it is equitable that he should be held liable as though he were a trustee."[325]

The constituent elements for liability for knowing assistance are as follows[326]:

(i) The existence of a trust—although it is enough if there is a fiduciary relationship[327]; and it is not necessary for the trust property to have been received.

(ii) A dishonest and fraudulent design on the part of the trustee. There is no real difference[328] between the words "dishonest" and "fraudulent", which are to be given their normal meaning[329]—being more than "morally reprehensible" conduct.[330] However, mere negligence or

322. *Ibid.*, at p. 150.

323. See, for example, *Agip (Africa) Ltd.* v. *Jackson* [1990] 1 Ch. 265; and on appeal, [1991] Ch. 547 (C.A.); *Baden Delvaux and Lecuit* v. *Société Générale pour Favoriser le Développement du Commerce et de l'Industrie en France S.A. ("Baden")* [1983] B.C.L.C. 325, also reported subsequently in [1992] 4 All E.R. 161.

324. Cf. the views of Sir Peter Millett and Professor Birks, who argue that the accessory (the lender) is not a trustee, and his personal liability does not depend on there being any trust; also, the accessory will hold nothing which can be described as trust property: see, respectively, Introduction to *Commercial Aspects of Trusts and Fiduciary Obligations*, *supra*, and "Tracing the Proceeds of Fraud", *supra*, at p. 83; and "Trusts in the Recovery of Misapplied Assets: Tracing, Trusts, and Restitution", *supra*. With respect to two such distinguished jurists, their comments appear not to give sufficient weight to the fact that, in knowing assistance cases, the money is obtained in breach of fiduciary duty, e.g. where a director has misapplied company money, or see the facts of the *Agip* case—and the law, rightly, it is submitted, treats such money differently from that not obtained in breach of fiduciary duty owing to the special nature of a fiduciary and the high standards expected of him; added to this, the accessory (the lender) has by his conduct implicated himself in the fraud. The critical point is not what happens when the accessory is solvent, but what happens when he becomes insolvent. If there is a constructive trust, then the defrauded beneficiary will be paid in priority to the ordinary body of creditors: see on this *A.G. for Hong Kong* v. *Reid* [1994] 1 A.C. 324, at p. 331, per Lord Templeman. But if it is merely a personal claim in restitution, as this would be, then the beneficiary will not receive any priority. As the money has been taken in breach of fiduciary duty, it seems fair that the true owner of that money should receive priority over the general body of creditors.

325. *Selangor United Rubber Estates Ltd.* v. *Cradock* [1968] 2 All E.R. 1073, at p. 1097H–I.

326. *Baden, supra*, at p. 232j, cited with approval in *Re Montagu's Settlement Trust* [1987] Ch. 264, and in *Lipkin Gorman* v. *Karpnale Ltd.* [1989] 1 W.L.R. 1340 (C.A.).

327. *Baden, supra*, at p. 233; and *Agip (Africa) Ltd.* v. *Jackson* [1990] 1 Ch. 265.

328. *Belmont Finance Corp.* v. *Williams Furniture Ltd. (No. 1)* [1979] 1 Ch. 250, at 267D–E and *Baden, supra*, at p. 234c–d.

329. Harpum Part I, *supra*, at p. 146 fn. 7, and *Paget*, at p. 233.

330. *Baden*, at p. 234g–h.

carelessness is not sufficient to constitute liability,[331] although it was once thought it was.[332]

(iii) Assistance by the stranger or accessory to the trust (the lender) in the dishonest and fraudulent design. There must be actual participation, with knowledge, by the accessory,[333] so that the fraudulent design can be imputed to him,[334] i.e. the accessory must be implicated in the trustee's fraud[335]; if there is not, then the accessory (the lender) will not be liable. In the end, it is a question of fact as to whether the accessory has assisted or not.[336] The phrase "want of probity"[337] has been used as a touchstone in some cases. Its usefulness is questionable, as it is submitted that the real test, as suggested by Millett J. in his penetrating analysis of knowing assistance (both judicially[338] and extra-judicially[339]), is whether there has been a lack of honesty by the lender.

(iv) The accessory (i.e. lender) must have knowledge of the three matters listed above, as fraud and dishonesty involve questions of intention. As to the type of knowledge—either actual or constructive—there has been a debate, but for knowing assistance, as opposed to knowing receipt, the knowledge required is actual knowledge,[340] of which there are varying degrees.

The types of knowledge applicable in both knowing assistance and knowing receipt are helpfully set out by Peter Gibson J. in *Baden Delvaux and Lecuit* v. *Société Générale pour Favoriser le Développement du Commerce et de l'Industrie en France S.A. ("Baden"),*[341] although these categories are not

331. See Millett J. in *Agip (Africa) Ltd.* v. *Jackson* [1990] 1 Ch. 265, at p. 293; and Tipping J. in *Marshall Futures Ltd.* v. *Marshall* [1992] 1 N.Z.L.R. 316, at p. 326.

332. See, for example, *Selangor United Rubber Estates Ltd.* v. *Cradock (No. 3)* [1968] 1 W.L.R. 1555; *Karak Rubber Co. Ltd.* v. *Burden (No. 2)* [1972] 1 W.L.R. 602; and *Rowlandson* v. *National Westminster Bank Ltd.* [1978] 1 W.L.R. 798.

333. See Jacobs P. (as he then was) in *D.P.C. Estates Pty. Ltd.* v. *Grey* [1974] 1 N.S.W.L.R. 443, at p. 458.

334. See Vinelott J. in *Eagle Trust plc* v. *SBC Securities Ltd.* [1991] B.C.L.C. 438, at p. 449. This view was approved by the Court of Appeal in *Polly Peck International plc* v. *Nadir* [1992] 2 Lloyd's Rep. 238, at p. 243.

335. Harpum Part I, *supra*, at p. 116.

336. The Hon. Sir Peter Millett, "Tracing the Proceeds of Fraud" (1991) L.Q.R. 71, at p. 84.

337. Per Edmund-Davies L.J. (as he then was) in *Carl Zeiss Stiftung* v. *Herbert Smith & Co.* [1969] 1 Ch. D. 296, at p. 301; this was used in *Re Montagu's Settlement Trust, supra*, and *Lipkin Gorman* v. *Karpnale* [1989] 1 W.L.R. 1340 (C.A.).

338. *Agip (Africa) Ltd.* v. *Jackson* [1990] 1 Ch. 265, at p. 293.

339. "Tracing the Proceeds of Fraud", *supra*, at p. 84. Cf. *Paget*, at p. 233.

340. *Belmont Finance Corpn. Ltd.* v. *Williams Furniture Ltd. (No. 1)* [1979] 1 Ch. 250 (C.A.); *Lipkin Gorman* v. *Karpnale Ltd.* [1989] 1 W.L.R. 1340; *Agip (Africa) Ltd.* v. *Jackson* [1990] 1 Ch. 265.

341. [1983] B.C.L.C. 325, at p. 407. Also reported subsequently in [1992] 4 All E.R. 161, at p. 235.

"necessarily comprehensive"[342] nor rigid.[343] There, his Lordship outlined five types of knowledge, namely, that the lender:

(i) has actual knowledge; or
(ii) wilfully shuts its eyes to the obvious; or
(iii) wilfully and recklessly fails to make such enquiries as an honest and reasonable man would make; or
(iv) has knowledge of circumstances which would indicate the facts to an honest and reasonable man; or
(v) has knowledge of circumstances which would put an honest and reasonable man on enquiry.

Of these types of knowledge, the first three constitute actual knowledge and the last two constitute constructive knowledge.[344] In cases such as *Selangor United Rubber Estates Ltd.* v. *Cradock (No. 3)*[345] and *Karak Rubber Company Ltd.* v. *Burden (No. 2)*,[346] constructive knowledge was held to be sufficient and, on this basis, negligence, rather than dishonesty, by the accessories (i.e. the lenders) resulted in them being held liable. However, in more recent authority,[347] the courts have declined to impute constructive knowledge to an accessory and consequentially have refused to uphold claims where the accessory was negligent, rather than fraudulent. This is because if negligence was sufficient to constitute a fraudulent and dishonest design, then a lower standard would be required of the accessory than the offending trustee[348] (who was the perpetrator of the original breach of trust, and who, as a trustee, is subject to very high

---

342. Fox L.J. in *Agip (Africa) Ltd.* v. *Jackson* [1991] Ch. 547, at p. 567 (with whom Butler-Sloss and Beldam L.JJ. agreed), who regarded the list as "an explanation of the general principle".

343. Scott L.J., delivering the leading judgment in *Polly Peck International plc* v. *Nadir* [1992] 2 Lloyd's Rep. 238, at p. 243 col. 2, who felt that one category may merge into another.

344. See D. Petkovic, "The Banker as Constructive Trustee" [1989] J.I.B.L. 88, at p. 89. See also Millett J. in *Agip (Africa) Ltd.* v. *Jackson* [1990] 1 Ch. 265, and his Lordship's article, "Tracing the Proceeds of Fraud" (1991) L.Q.R. 71.

345. [1968] 1 W.L.R. 1555.

346. [1972] 1 W.L.R. 602.

347. *Carl Zeiss Stiftung* v. *Herbert Smith & Co. (No. 2)* [1969] Ch. 276 (C.A.); Slade L.J. in *Nihill* v. *Nihill*, unreported, 22 June 1983 (Court of Appeal (Civil Division)), cited with approval in *Lipkin Gorman* v. *Karpnale Ltd.* [1989] 1 W.L.R. 1340 (C.A.); Millett J. (as he then was) in *Agip (Africa) Ltd.* v. *Williams Furniture Ltd. (No. 1)* [1979] 1 Ch. 250 (C.A.); *Belmont Finance Corpn. Ltd.* v. *Williams Furniture Ltd. (No. 2)* [1980] 1 All E.R. 393; *Re Montagu's Settlement Trusts* [1987] Ch. 264; *Westpac Banking Corpn.* v. *Savin* [1985] 2 N.Z.L.R. 41; *Barclays Bank plc* v. *Quincecare* [1992] 4 All E.R. 363 (decision delivered on 24 February 1988); *Cowan de Groot Properties Ltd.* v. *Eagle Trust plc* [1991] B.C.L.C. 1045; *Eagle Trust Ltd.* v. *Eagle Trust plc* [1991] B.C.L.C. 438; *Polly Peck International plc* v. *Nadir* [1992] 2 Lloyd's Rep. 238; and *Equiticorp Industries Group Ltd.* v. *Hawkins* [1991] 3 N.Z.L.R. 700.

348. H. Norman, "Knowing assistance—a plea for help" (1992) Vol. 12 *Legal Studies* 322, at p. 334. See also Edmund-Davies L.J. in *Carl Zeiss Stiftung* v. *Herbert Smith & Co. (No. 2)* [1969] 2 Ch. 276, at p. 301.

standards of conduct[349]); also, one can be negligent but not dishonest,[350] and it is the dishonesty which is the critical thing and the accessory's knowing participation in it. The position is well put by Harpum,[351] who says that "the fraudulent design assisted and the stranger's knowledge of it must be integrally connected. The stranger is made liable because he is implicated in that fraud. If constructive notice of the design sufficed, the moral quality of the trustee's act would be irrelevant."

Added to this, English courts have narrowed the duty of care for liability in negligence and pure economic loss,[352] which is what a claim against an accessory would be; and are disentangling law and equity. If an accessory has merely been negligent—and not dishonest—he should be sued as a tortfeasor in negligence,[353] and not as a constructive trustee.

A further factor taken into account in rejecting constructive knowledge is the commercial effect that it would have on lenders who are paying and collecting a tremendous number of cheques each day.[354] Lenders are not required to play the "amateur detective",[355] and it would be both undesirable and "commercially impracticable".[356] The courts have also warned against the "unjustified wisdom of hindsight"[357] and imposing liability simply on the basis of "the sheer scale of payments"[358] made by the trustee. If at the time the lender has no reason to

349. See the judgment of McLachlin J. in the Supreme Court of Canada in *Canson Enterprises Ltd.* v. *Boughton and Co.* (1991) 84 D.L.R. (4th) 129, where, in the context of equitable compensation, the differences between liability for breach of fiduciary duty and negligence are referred to and the different standard of conduct required of a fiduciary and a tortfeasor noted.

350. A similar view is expressed by Millett J. in *Agip (Africa) Ltd.* v. *Jackson* [1990] 1 Ch. 265, at p. 293; and Tipping J. in *Marshall Futures Ltd.* v. *Marshall* [1992] 1 N.Z.L.R. 316, at p. 326.

351. Harpum Part I, *supra*, at p. 147.

352. See the discussion in the section on negligence. Note also the approach of the Privy Council in *China and South Sea Bank Ltd.* v. *Tan* [1990] 1 A.C. 536 and *Downsview Nominees Ltd.* v. *First City Corporation Ltd.* [1993] A.C. 295, which rejected trying to bring claims in negligence which properly belong in equity.

353. Cf. the Scottish case of *Weir* v. *National Westminster Bank plc* [1994] S.L.T. 1251, where the lender, who had cashed cheques for a dishonest agent of W, was sued in negligence and the claim was not struck out.

354. May L.J. in *Lipkin Gorman* v. *Karpnale Ltd.* [1989] 1 W.L.R. 1340, at p. 1356E–H. His Lordship felt that it was only when circumstances were such that any reasonable cashier would refuse to pay a cheque immediately and refer it to his superior that a cheque should not be paid upon presentation. And it would be rare for a manager to instruct staff to refer all cheques of a customer to him before paying them.

355. Alliott J. in *Lipkin Gorman* v. *Karpnale Ltd.* [1987] 1 W.L.R. 987, at p. 1006; Peter Gibson J. (as he then was) in *Baden, supra*, at p. 245; and Wylie J. in *Equiticorp Industries Group Ltd.* v. *Hawkins* [1991] 3 N.Z.L.R. 700, at p. 739. See also Millett J., at first instance, in *El Ajou* v. *Dollar Holdings plc* [1993] B.C.L.C. 735, at p. 758i, who said, in the context of knowing receipt, that a recipient of misapplied assets "is not expected to be unduly suspicious".

356. Dunn L.J. in *Nihill* v. *Nihill* [1983], unreported decision of the Court of Appeal C.A. transcript 276; and see Wallace J. in *Lankshear* v. *A.N.Z. Banking Group (New Zealand) Ltd.* [1993] 1 N.Z.L.R. 489, at p. 495.

357. *Polly Peck International plc* v. *Nadir* [1992] 2 Lloyd's Rep. 238, at p. 244, per Scott L.J.

358. *Ibid.* In that case, the scale of payments was 127 transfers of funds in the sum of £44.9 million from one lender through another. The group's annual turnover in the years 1987–1990 (first half) was, respectively: £380m, £967m, £1,162m, and £880m, with pre-tax profits of £84m, £144m, £160m, and £160m for the said period.

suspect any misapplication of funds or to be wary of the trustee, then, if events later turn out to indicate that the trustee has allegedly misapplied funds, the lender cannot be liable, particularly where the beneficiary was a successful business. Mere curiosity is not sufficient to satisfy the test of putting the honest and reasonable banker on enquiry[359]; neither is a mere possibility of wrongdoing: it must be at least "a serious or real possibility, albeit not amounting to a probability"[360] of the lender's customer being defrauded.[361]

Lastly, the relationship between the lender and its trustee customer is one of contract under which the lender agrees to honour (and collect) the customer's cheques, and it is not, generally, for the lender to consider the nature of the transaction involved—its role is largely mechanical, and, save in exceptional circumstances, the cheque should be honoured.[362] One such exception is when payment of the cheque would expose the lender to liability as a constructive trustee.[363]

Consequently, as a result of this contractual relationship, a lender could not be liable as a constructive trustee, unless it was also liable for breach of mandate for failure to perform its duty to pay cheques, subject to the qualification that this must be done without negligence.[364] The Court of Appeal has recently observed that the distinction between liability of a lender as a constructive trustee and for breach of mandate is "frequently blurred or unconsidered".[365]

359. *Polly Peck International* v. *Nadir, supra*, at p. 244 col. 2. See also *Parker L.J.* in *Lipkin Gorman* v. *Karpnale Ltd.* [1989] 1 W.L.R. 1340, at p. 1378.

360. *Lipkin Gorman* v. *Karpnale Ltd.* [1989] 1 W.L.R. 1340, at p. 1378, per Parker L.J. Cf. Slade L.J. in *Nihill* v. *Nihill, supra*, who referred to the probability of fraudulent breaches of trust being committed.

361. *Lipkin Gorman* v. *Karpnale Ltd.* [1989] 1 W.L.R. 1340, at p. 1378, per Parker L.J.

362. *Lipkin Gorman* v. *Karpnale Ltd.* [1989] 1 W.L.R. 1340, at p. 1356A–C, per May L.J. See also: *Barclays Bank plc* v. *Quincecare* [1992] 4 All E.R. 363, at pp. 375–376, per Steyn J. (as he then was), judgment delivered on 24 February 1988; *Gray* v. *Johnston* (1868) L.R. 3 H.L. 1, at p. 1; and Alliott J., at first instance in *Lipkin Gorman* v. *Karpnale Ltd.* [1987] 1 W.L.R. 987, at p. 1006, cited with approval in *Quincecare*.

363. *Manus Asia Co. Inc.* v. *Standard Chartered Bank*, a decision of Crudden D.J. of the Supreme Court of Hong Kong, delivered on 22 September 1988. The case is noted by Professor E.P. Ellinger, "New Cases on the Bank as Constructive Trustee" [1989] J.B.L. 255, at pp. 257–259, and by N. Clayton, "An Update on Banks as Constructive Trustees" [1990] J.B.L. 125. In this case, the lender had to balance competing claims for the same money. On the one hand, the US Securities and Exchange Commission ("SEC") had obtained judgment for a certain sum against L for insider dealing and was demanding this sum, being the proceeds of L's illegal activities; on the other hand, L was demanding payment of the sum to his lawyers in Hong Kong. The money was shown as a credit in L's account with the lender in Hong Kong, but was held in the lender's nostro account in New York. It was reluctantly paid to the SEC. There was a danger the lender may have had to pay out twice. An argument that payment of the sum in the Hong Kong account would expose the lender to liability as a constructive trustee to L's creditors was successful. It is suggested that if the lender had been required to pay out to L also, L would have been unjustly enriched and would have benefited from his own wrongdoing. See also *Finers (a firm)* v. *Miro* [1991] 1 W.L.R. 35 (C.A.).

364. *Lipkin Gorman* v. *Karpnale Ltd.* [1989] 1 W.L.R. 1340, at p. 1376, per Parker L.J.

365. *Ibid.*, at p. 1373.

Furthermore, there is a distinction between knowledge and notice of a fact or matter.[366] Thus, a person may have seen a document, and so have notice of it, but no knowledge of it, as it has not been read thoroughly; or, he may have read it, but forgotten what it is about.[367] Consequently, in the ordinary course of business, a lender will have notice of cheques paid in and honoured, but, in most cases, it will have no knowledge of what they relate to, so there will be no knowledge of, or participation in, a dishonest scheme. Moreover, the general prohibition on constructive notice in commercial matters[368] has been applied to knowing assistance[369]; and it would be inconsistent with the requirement of actual knowledge to impose liability based on constructive notice; mere notice would not be appropriate in knowing receipt cases.

Ultimately, despite what terminology is used, the real question is whether the lender has been honest or dishonest.[370] A failure to make an enquiry does not, of itself, result in liability: it is a failure to act honestly which imposes liability, i.e. misapplying funds.[371] But, a failure to make enquiries which honest men would have made does impose liability, as this goes to the question of honesty.[372]

In summary, unless a lender pays a cheque actually knowing that it represents misapplied trust property it will not be liable. The courts have realised the task facing lenders in policing every cheque drawn on a trust (or other) account, and that contractually, the lender is obliged to honour (or collect) its customer's cheques, except in rare circumstances. Thus, in the absence of clear participation in the fraud, a lender should not be held liable, as it was the trustee—not the lender—who perpetrated the original fraud.

(b) Knowing receipt

This head of liability is based on unjust enrichment,[373] being receipt based liability.[374] As with knowing assistance, knowledge is critical to founding

---

366. Sir Robert Megarry in *Re Montagu's Settlement Trusts* [1987] Ch. 264, at pp. 271–272, 276–277 and 285. See also Vinelott J. in *Eagle Trust plc* v. *S.B.C. Securities Ltd.* [1991] B.C.L.C. 438, at p. 447.

367. As with the will in *Re Montagu's Settlement Trusts, supra.*

368. Per Lindley L.J. (as he then was) in *Manchester Trust* v. *Furness* [1895] 2 Q.B. 539, at p. 545.

369. Vinelott J. in *Eagle Trust plc* v. *S.B.C. Securities Ltd.* [1991] B.C.L.C. 438, at p. 459. See also Millett J. in *El Ajou* v. *Dollar Land Holdings plc* [1993] B.C.L.C. 735, at p. 758g, who felt it inappropriate, in a knowing receipt case, to base liability on constructive notice in a "conveyancing sense ... where it is not the custom and practice to make inquiry".

370. Millett J. in *Agip (Africa) Ltd.* v. *Jackson* [1990] 1 Ch. 265, at p. 293. This view was not disagreed with on appeal: see [1991] Ch. 547, at pp. 569–570. It was cited with approval in *Eagle Trust plc* v. *S.B.C. Securities Ltd.* [1991] B.C.L.C. 438, at p. 446.

371. Millett J. in *Agip (Africa) Ltd.* v. *Jackson* [1990] 1 Ch. 265, at p. 295G–H.

372. *Ibid.*

373. *Gray* v. *Johnston* (1868) L.R. 3 H.L. 1, at p. 14, per Lord Westbury; see also, Thomas J. in *Powell* v. *Thompson* [1991] 1 N.Z.L.R. 597, at pp. 606–607; and Wallace J. in *Lankshear* v. *ANZ Banking Group (New Zealand) Ltd.* [1993] 1 N.Z.L.R. 489, at p. 496.

374. Millett J. in *Agip (Africa) Ltd.* v. *Jackson* [1990] 1 Ch. 265, at p. 292, and in "Tracing the Proceeds of Fraud" (1991) L.Q.R. 71, at pp. 72 and 80–81.

liability,[375] although, in knowing receipt, knowledge can be either constructive or actual,[376] as dishonesty is not an essential element of liability—the breach of trust can be fraudulent or innocent.[377] Knowing receipt is not a single category, and the different situations, of which the two main ones are as follows, need to be distinguished.[378]

First, where a person receives trust property for his own benefit, which has been transferred in breach of trust, with actual or constructive knowledge that the property is trust property and has been transferred to him in breach of trust—or, where the property is received without knowledge of such a breach, but the breach is subsequently discovered—the recipient is liable to account as a constructive trustee from the time of receipt in the first instance and the time of knowledge of breach in the second.[379]

Secondly, where a person (usually a trustee's agent) lawfully receives trust property—not for his own benefit—and subsequently misappropriates the trust property, or deals with it in a manner inconsistent with the trust,[380] such a recipient will be "liable to account as a constructive trustee",[381] provided he knows the property is trust property, even if he was not aware of the trust's precise terms.[382]

The key to the first class of case is that there is beneficial receipt by the accessory, in the sense of using the trust property for his own benefit by setting up title to it.[383] In a lending context, the most common situation will occur when the lender (mis)uses the trust property (money) to reduce the indebtedness of the trustee (who is a customer) to the lender by applying the trust property in reduction of the trustee's overdraft. Thus, a lender will not be liable for knowing receipt merely by paying or collecting cheques: as it will not be setting up title to

---

375. *Thomson* v. *Clydesdale Bank Ltd.* [1893] A.C. 282 (H.L. (Sc.)), 1893, 20 R. (H.L.) 59.

376. Millett J. in *Agip (Africa) Ltd.* v. *Jackson* [1990] 1 Ch. 265, at pp. 292–293, argues that as the basis of liability of knowing receipt and knowing assistance is different, then so should be the types of knowledge. Cf. the more "restrained" approach of his Lordship in *El Ajou* v. *Dollar Land Holdings plc* [1993] B.C.L.C. 735, at p. 758i.

377. Millett J. in *Agip (Africa) Ltd.* v. *Jackson* [1990] 1 Ch. 265, at p. 291, and in "Tracing the Proceeds of Fraud" (1991) L.Q.R. 71, at p. 80; see also Harpum Part I, at p. 116 and Vinelott J. in *Eagle Trust plc* v. *S.B.C. Securities Ltd.* [1991] B.C.L.C. 438, at p. 451. It could be argued that the receipt of trust property in the circumstances set out in this section amounts to dishonesty. Cf. *Westpac Banking Corporation* v. *Savin* [1985] 2 N.Z.L.R. 41, where it was said that the receipt and misappropriation almost amounted to fraud.

378. Millett J. in *Agip (Africa) Ltd.* v. *Jackson* [1990] 1 Ch. 265, at p. 291.

379. Millett J. in *Agip (Africa) Ltd.* v. *Jackson* [1990] 1 Ch. 265, at p. 291; see also "Tracing the Proceeds of Fraud" (1991) L.Q.R. 71, at p. 80.

380. *Agip (Africa) Ltd.* v. *Jackson* [1990] 1 Ch. 265, at p. 291, per Millet J.; *Baden* [1992] 4 All E.R. 161, at p. 231; *Polly Peck International plc* v. *Nadir* [1992] 2 Lloyd's Rep. 238, at p. 243 col. 2, per Scott L.J.; and *Eagle Trust, supra*, at p. 451, per Vinelott J.

381. Millett J. in *Agip (Africa) Ltd.* v. *Jackson* [1990] 1 Ch. 265, at p. 291.

382. *Ibid.*

383. *Westpac Banking Corporation* v. *Savin* [1985] 2 N.Z.L.R. 41; *Agip (Africa) Ltd.* v. *Jackson* [1990] 1 Ch. 265, at pp. 291–292; and "Tracing the Proceeds of Fraud" (1991) L.Q.R. 71,

the money, but merely acting as its customer's agent.[384] Also, a lender will not be liable for knowing receipt where it merely acts as a conduit or agent for its customer and passes on the trust property to its customer, even if it had knowledge of the breach of trust—the receipt in this instance is ministerial,[385] with the agent merely acting in accordance with his instructions; however, although it is arguable that the receipt and the loss are not related, the agent could be liable for knowing assistance.[386]

From a lender's point of view, its concern is paying out twice: once to the recalcitrant trustee (who will have absconded or be insolvent or both and from whom there is little chance of recovering its money); and also to the beneficiary, who will be seeking to sue the lender because it is unlikely to recover from the trustee. In this situation, the lender will be paying out the beneficiary from the lender's own profits, and not from the money in the trustee's account. Thus, it becomes a situation of lender liability.

From the beneficiary's perspective, in knowing receipt (and knowing assistance) cases, it will be trying to find a nexus by which it can make the lender, with whom it has no relationship in relation to the misappropriated trust money, liable for its loss. Ordinarily, as agent (i.e. the lender) will be liable to its principal (the rogue trustee), and not the *cestui que trust*[387] composed of the beneficiaries. Any beneficiary will only have a personal claim against the trustee for breach of trust (although the trustee would have an action against the agent).

---

at pp. 82–83. *Barnes* v. *Addy* (1874) L.R. 9 Ch. App. 244 also supports this. See also Hoffmann L.J. in *El Ajou* v. *Dollar Holdings plc* [1994] B.C.L.C. 464, at p. 478b (C.A.), who outlines three elements in knowing receipt: (i) a disposal of the beneficiary's assets in breach of fiduciary duty; (2) beneficial receipt of the assets by the accessory which are traceable as representing the beneficiary's assets; (3) knowledge by the accessory that the assets received are traceable to a breach of fiduciary duty.

384. Millett J. in *Agip, supra*, at p. 292, and "Tracing the Proceeds of Fraud", *supra*, at p. 83.

385. See Brightman J. (as he then was) in *Karak Rubber Co. Ltd.* v. *Burden (No. 2)* [1972] 1 W.L.R. 602, at pp. 632–633, and Birks, "Misdirected Funds", *supra*, at pp. 303–304.

386. See Birks, "Misdirected Funds", *supra*, at p. 304. This view of ministerial receipt and the requirement of beneficial use is disagreed with by Y.L. Tan, "Agent's liability for knowing receipt" [1991] L.M.C.L.Q. 357. He argues cogently that setting up title to property as determining receipt is against authority and is only recent. With respect, this is not so: see *Barnes* v. *Addy* (1874) 9 Ch. App. 244, at pp. 254–255 and the reference there to the defendant Duffield not using money for his own benefit; *Gray* v. *Johnston* (1868) L.R. 3 H.L. 1, at p. 14, per Lord Westbury (cf. Lord Cairns L.C., at p. 11); *Thomson* v. *Clydesdale Bank plc* [1893] A.C. 282, at pp. 292–293 (H.L.)(Sc)); 1893, 20 R. (H.L.) 59, at p. 63, per Lord Shand; *Coleman* v. *Bucks and Oxon Union Bank* [1897] 2 Ch. 243, at p. 254, per Byrne J.; and the more recent cases of *Belmont Finance Corpn. Ltd.* v. *Williams Furniture Ltd. (No. 2)* [1980] 1 All E.R. 393, at p. 407, per Goff L.J., who said becoming chargeable with the trust property means "receiving trust funds in such a way as to become accountable for them"; and *El Ajou* v. *Dollar Holdings plc* [1993] B.C.L.C. 735 at p. 757, per Millett J. and on appeal by Hoffmann L.J.: see *El Ajou* v. *Dollar Holdings plc* [1994] B.C.L.C. 464, at p. 478b.

387. See Y.L. Tan, "Agent's liability for knowing receipt" [1991] L.M.C.L.Q. 357, at pp. 361 and 363.

This nexus between a beneficiary and the agent (the lender) will occur when the latter ceases to act as its principal's agent by setting up his own title to the trust property, i.e. the agent goes beyond its agency and so has a greater connection with the misdirected trust property: by receiving trust property and becoming chargeable with it (or, by participating in a dishonest and fraudulent scheme with the trustee in relation to it and becoming linked with the principal's fraud[388]).

DUTY OF LENDER AS MORTGAGEE TO BORROWER/ MORTGAGOR

It has recently been reaffirmed that, under English law, when a mortgagee exercises his power of sale with regard to the mortgaged property in order to satisfy the debt owed to him, the mortgagee must do so in good faith[389] (by which it is meant that the mortgagee is not to "fraudulently or wilfully or recklessly to sacrifice the property of the mortgagor",[390] who has an equity of redemption) and for the purpose of repayment. This duty of the mortgagee to the mortgagor arises in equity, due to the relationship of the parties, and not in tort.[391] If it arose in tort, the claim would be for pure economic loss, which, on the current state of the authorities, would not be permitted.[392] The same duty of good faith in equity is owed to a subsequent encumbrancer, who is entitled to any balance of the proceeds of sale after the mortgagee's debt has been satisfied[393]; and, with regard to a guarantor, the mortgagee owes him a duty in equity too.[394]

Although the mortgagor has a right of redemption, the mortgagee is not a trustee of the power of sale. If there is a decline in value of the mortgaged property (due to market forces) and the mortgagee delays in foreclosing, the mortgagee is, generally, not liable to the mortgagor or a subsequent encumbrancer or a guarantor.

---

388. Cf. Conspiracy.

389. *Downsview Nominees Ltd.* v. *First City Corporation* [1993] A.C. 295 (P.C.); and see A. Berg, "Duties of a Mortgagee and a Receiver" [1993] J.B.L. 213.

390. *Kennedy* v. *De Trafford* [1897] A.C. 180, at p. 185, per Lord Herschell.

391. See *Parker-Tweedale* v. *Dunbar Bank Plc* [1991] Ch. 12 (C.A.), where the Court of Appeal rejected expressing the duties owed by a mortgagee to a mortgagor in terms of negligence. Rather, the duty was recognised by equity as arising out of the particular relationship between them. Any duty owed to a surety arose in the same way: see *China and South Sea Bank Ltd.* v. *Tan Soon Gin, George (alias George Tan)* [1990] 1 A.C. 536 (P.C.).

392. See section on Negligence.

393. *Downsview Nominees Ltd.* v. *First City Corporation* [1993] A.C. 295, at pp. 311–312, per Lord Templeman.

394. *China and South Sea Bank Ltd.* v. *Tan* [1990] 1 A.C. 536 (P.C.), at pp. 544–545, per Lord Templeman (P.C.).

In the *South China Sea* case[395] and in *Parker-Tweedale* v. *Dunbar Bank plc*,[396] delays in foreclosing in similar circumstances did not result in liability.[397] Also, in *Williams & Glyn*,[398] Ralph Gibson J. held that the lender owed no duty to Barnes, in his capacity as chargee of his shares in NDH, not to reduce their value by breaches of duty owed to NDH. The shares had not been lost or destroyed and the share certificates were always available for return to Barnes upon repayment of the loan. Barnes could not bring an action as pledger of the shares, as any such action regarding the loan could only be brought by NDH. In such situations the mortgagor has not, physically, lost anything. He has his property or his shares: they are now worth less, but may increase to be worth more than before. His loss is thus purely economic.

The above comments, concerning the timing of selling, now need to be read in the light of the recent Court of Appeal decision in *Palk* v. *Mortgage Services Funding plc*,[399] in which it was held that a mortgagor could apply to the court for an order, under section 91 of the Law of Property Act 1925, that the mortgaged property be sold, even though the mortgagee did not want to sell.

Whilst it has been said that as a result of the duty of good faith there can be a sale at a lower price than might have been reached, nonetheless, it is clear on the authorities[400] that a mortgagee owes the mortgagor a duty to obtain a proper price when selling the mortgaged property as a result of a foreclosure. If the mortgagee does not obtain such a price, then he is liable for the difference between the price obtained and what is the proper price of the property.[401]

Three other issues arise in this context. First, when a lender employs competent agents, such as real estate agents, to sell the mortgaged property on his behalf, and the agent breaches its duty to the mortgagee or makes "a serious blunder"[402] by, for example, misdescribing the property for sale in an advertisement,[403] with the result that the property did not sell, or did not sell for

---

395. [1990] 1 A.C. 536 (P.C.).

396. [1990] 2 All E.R. 877 (C.A.).

397. 762 S.W. 2d 243 (Tex. App. El Paso 1988).

398. [1981] Com. L.R. 205, at p. 208, and pp. 361, 364, 368 and 369 of the transcript. See also *Bank of Cyprus (London) Ltd.* v. *Gill* [1980] 2 Lloyd's Rep. 51 (C.A.).

399. [1993] Ch. 331.

400. See *Warner* v. *Jacobs* (1882) 20 Ch. D. 220, at p. 224, per Kay J.; *Kennedy* v. *De Trafford* [1896] 1 Ch. 762, at p. 762, per Lindley L.J. and [1897] A.C. 180, at p. 185, per Lord Herschell; *Farrars* v. *Farrars Ltd.* (1889) 40 Ch. D. 395, at pp. 410–411, per Lindley L.J.; *McHugh* v. *Union Bank of Canada* [1913] A.C. 229 (P.C.); and *Tomlin* v. *Luce* (1889) 41 Ch. D. 573, not reversed on appeal: see (1889) 43 Ch. D. 191. Indeed, it may be that the reference to good faith is merely a way of asserting that the mortgagee's duty to the mortgagor arises in equity: and not in negligence.

401. See, for example, *Cuckmere Brick Co. Ltd.* v. *Mutual Finance Ltd.* [1971] Ch. 949 (C.A.). See also *Parker-Tweedale* v. *Dunbar Bank plc* [1991] Ch. 12 (C.A.) and *Downsview Nominees Ltd.* v. *First City Corporation* [1993] A.C. 295 (P.C.).

402. Kekewich J. in *Tomlin* v. *Luce* (1889) 41 Ch. 573, at pp. 575–576; and see on appeal (1889) 43 Ch. D. 191, at p. 194 (C.A.). This phrase was cited by *Halsbury's Laws of England* (4th edn.), vol. 32, "Mortgages", at para. 729. The lender/mortgagee is not liable for errors of detail by the agents not affecting the sale or price realised: see *Halsbury, supra.*

403. See, for example, *Tomlin* v. *Luce, supra,* and *Commercial and General Acceptance Ltd.* v. *Nixon* (1982) 152 C.L.R. 491 (High Court of Australia).

as much as it should have, and loss resulted to the mortgagor or, indeed, a subsequent chargee, the mortgagee is liable, although he would have a cause of action against the agent.[404] Where, however, the failure to obtain the proper price is the fault of the mortgagee, and not the agents, then the mortgagee's action against the agents will be unsuccessful.[405]

Secondly, if the mortgagor seeks to halt the proposed sale of its mortgaged property or have it set aside, as he has a monetary counterclaim against the mortgagee for a debt—as opposed to challenging the validity of the mortgage[406]—then, before such an action can be brought, the position of the mortgagee needs to be safeguarded by the mortgagor either paying off the amount due and owing in relation to the mortgaged property or paying into court an amount that would meet the mortgagee's debt.[407] The rationale for this rule is that until the debt secured by the mortgage is satisfied, the mortgage and the debt remain valid, despite any claim the mortgagor may have (which claim may be successful or unsuccessful); the courts take the view that it would not be just or convenient to allow, in effect, a unilateral discharge of the mortgage and appropriation of the underlying debt without payment.[408]

Thirdly, if a mortgagee seeks to exclude liability for itself and any receiver it may wish to appoint, the position is unclear with regard to the application of the Unfair Contract Term Acts 1977 ("UCTA").[409]

In such situations, the attempt to exclude liability or breach of duty will need to be in clear and unambiguous language. This was a problem in *Bishop* v. *Bonham*,[410] where there was a mortgage of shares containing a provision which allowed the mortgagee to sell the shares as "he thought fit", and said he would not be liable for any loss howsoever arising. In an action on the basis that the shares were sold at an undervalue, the Court of Appeal held that the provision did not specifically exclude negligence; consequently, the mortgagee was still liable for the undervalue.

---

404. *Riverstone Meat Co. Pty. Ltd.* v. *Lancashire Shipping Co. Ltd (The Muncmaster Castle)* [1961] A.C. 807 (H.L.(E.)). If the mortgagee became insolvent, then the mortgagor could proceed against the agent personally, rather than against the mortgagee vicariously.

405. See *Predeth Castle* v. *Phillips Finance Co. Ltd.* [1986] 2 E.G.L.R. 144 (C.A.), where the mortgagee asked a surveyor to do a "crash sale valuation" of the mortgaged property, which the surveyor interpreted as meaning a more rapid sale than a forced sale valuation. The Court of Appeal upheld this interpretation and the mortgagee only had himself to blame when he sought to sell the property to a Miss Keeping, who sold it a few months later for nearly twice the price she paid for it. Fox L.J. opined "the hard fact is that Mr Phillips wanted to sell quickly and wanted to sell to Miss Keeping, he wanted to sell at a price which would enable Miss Keeping to make a quick profit." The mortgagee's problems were of his own making, not the result of the surveyor's advice.

406. *Cunningham* v. *National Australia Bank* (1987) 77 A.L.R. 632.

407. *Samuel Keller (Holdings) Ltd.* v. *Martins Bank Ltd.* [1971] 1 W.L.R. 43 (C.A.); *Barclays Bank plc* v. *Tennet* (unreported decision of the Court of Appeal, delivered on 6 June 1984); and *Inglis* v. *Commonwealth Trading Bank of Australia* (1972) 126 C.L.R. 161 (High Court of Australia).

408. *Samuel Keller, supra*, at p. 48A–C.

409. For examples of such a clause: see J.R. Lingard, *Bank Security Documents* (1993) 3rd edn., Specimen Documents, Document 1, clause 7.05, and Document 2, clause 8.05.

410. [1988] 1 W.L.R. 742 (C.A.).

The difficulty with the case is that there was no reference to UCTA, which would impose a test of reasonableness; and the duty of a mortgagee and receiver is now based in equity, and not negligence.[411]

If it was sought to defeat the exemption clause using UCTA, then it has been argued that, under Schedule 1, a mortgage of land and shares would be excluded from the Act's ambit.[412] The relevant provisions provide:

"1(b) any contract so far as it relates to the creation or transfer of an interest in land, or to the termination of such an interest, whether by extinction, merger, surrender, forfeiture or otherwise ...; and

1(e) any contract so far as it relates to the creation or transfer of securities or any right or interest in securities."[413]

With this view it is agreed. Taking security over land or shares would amount to the creation or transferring of an interest in either of them. Consequently, a mortgagee may well be able to exclude a breach of duty.

Receiver's duties

Like a mortgagee, a receiver[414] is under duty of good faith to a mortgagor (or a subsequent encumbrancer).[415] Thus, if a receiver sells the secured assets at lower than a proper price, he may be sued for an account in equity. (However, this is to be distinguished from a mortgagee's right to exercise his contractual rights to appoint a receiver, which is only challengeable on the ground of bad faith.[416])

By statute,[417] and under both the common law[418] and the instrument appointing him,[419] a receiver is made the agent of the mortgagor company. The receiver's agency, which is the key to the lender being liable, has been described as the only non-fiduciary agency[420]; and the receiver has been likened to the Roman god Janus,[421] who faces two ways, as a receiver owes duties to both the

---

411. *Downsview Nominees, supra.*

412. M. Lawson, "The Rights and Remedies of Mortgagees" [1988] J.I.B.L. 251, at p. 257. Cf. Berg, *supra*, at pp. 233–234.

413. Lingard rather ambiguously writes that UCTA "applies to contracts of guarantee though not to 'contracts relating to securities' ": see *Bank Security Documents, supra*, at para. 13.57 on p. 249. This seems to suggest that the reference to securities is the plural of security, i.e. mortgage or charge. If this is so, then, with respect, it appears to be inconsistent with the scheme of the Schedule; see also Penn, Shea and Arora, *The Law Relating to Domestic Banking* (1987), at para. 15.16 on p. 165.

414. By receiver it is meant an administrative receiver, who is normally appointed by a debenture, or floating charge, holder. Section 29(2) of the Insolvency Act 1986 defines an administrative receiver as a receiver over all, or substantially all, of the debtor's assets.

415. See *Downsview Nominees, supra*; and Berg, *supra*. See also Dr S. Robinson, "Lenders' (and Receivers') Liability when Selling: The Need to Resort to Basic Principles" (1994) 68 A.L.J. 206.

416. *Shamji* v. *Johnson Matthey Bankers Ltd.* [1986] B.C.L.C. 278.

417. Section 45 of the Insolvency Act 1986.

418. *Gosling* v. *Gaskell* [1897] A.C. 575 (H.L.(E.)).

419. See, for example, J.R. Lingard, *Bank Security Documents, supra*, Specimen Documents, clause 7 in Document 1 and clause 8 in Document 2.

420. Meagher, Gummow and Lehane, *Equity: Doctrines and Remedies* (1992) 3rd edn., at para. 2845 on p. 709.

421. Professor R.M. Goode Q.C., *Principles of Corporate Insolvency* (1990), at p. 82.

mortgagor company and the debenture holder appointing him. But this agency is something of a fiction in order to protect the debenture holder, as the courts have repeatedly held that the receiver's prime duty is to pay off the debt owed to the debenture holder.[422]

By the receiver being the agent of the company, it is the company in receivership which is liable for the acts and omissions of the receiver, not the debenture holder which appointed him. However, where the debenture holder interferes with the nature or conduct of the receivership, then the debenture holder is liable for the acts of the receiver (which can include a claim by guarantors)—for example, that the receiver sold the company's assets at an undervalue and called their guarantee into operation.[423] Liability is imposed on the debenture holder (the lender) on the basis that,[424] where the debenture holder interferes with the conduct of the receivership and issues instructions to the receiver, then, if the receiver acts in accordance with those instructions, he ceases to be the agent of the company in receivership and becomes the agent of the debenture holder, who, as principal, becomes liable for the acts of its agent.[425]

422. *Downsview Nominees Ltd.* v. *First City Corporation* [1993] 2 A.C. 295 (P.C.); *Gomba Holdings UK Ltd.* v. *Homan* [1986] 1 W.L.R. 1301, at p. 1305, per Hoffmann J.; and *Gomba Holdings UK Ltd.* v. *Minories Ltd.* [1988] 1 W.L.R. 1231, at p. 1233E–H, per Fox L.J.

423. *Standard Chartered Bank Ltd.* v. *Walker* [1982] 1 W.L.R. 1410 (C.A.); and *American Express International Banking Corp.* v. *Hurley* [1985] 3 All E.R. 564.

424. See *American Express International Banking Corp.* v. *Hurley* [1985] 3 All E.R. 564, at p. 571g, per Mann J. (as he then was). This was a curious case involving a company being put into receivership and subsequently going into voluntary liquidation with the receiver continuing to act after the liquidator was appointed. A claim was brought by a guarantor (who was also a director of the company) that the receiver had sold the company's assets at an undervalue. It was also sought to make the lender liable on the basis that it had constituted the receiver as its agent from the liquidation. In one part, the learned judge says, "there was constant communication between the bank and the receiver and the latter sought the former's approval to such actions as he proposed to take", although there is no real evidence in the judgment to support this: see at p. 568; but later (at p. 572), his Lordship found "that at no time either before or after the liquidation of the company did the bank direct or interfere with the receiver's activities. As [the receiver] put it, the bank 'trusted me to get on with it'." These two statements are somewhat difficult to reconcile with the view of the judge that the lender constituted the receiver as its agent after the liquidation (a matter which is not elaborated on).

425. In this situation, the lender, as debenture holder, would be unable to claim under the indemnity in the debenture, as this relates to acts and omissions done in "exercise or purported exercise of the powers contained [in the receivers' clause in the debenture]", i.e. in the ordinary course of the receivership: not where this agency arrangement has been breached. For an example of such a clause: see Lingard, *Bank Security Documents*, *supra*, Document 1, at clause 7.06 and Document 2, at clause 8.06. Cf. Berg, *supra*, at p. 234, who says that if a receiver is considered to be an officer of the company, then, in view of section 310 of the Companies Act 1985 (as amended), any indemnity to the receiver from the company's assets may be struck down. However, where the debenture holder has constituted the receiver as its agent, the debenture holder may have a claim against the receiver for an indemnity under an implied term of the agency agreement: see *American Express International Banking Corp.* v. *Hurley* [1985] 3 All E.R. 564, at p. 571h, per Mann J. (as he then was).

WRONGFUL TRADING—SHADOW DIRECTORS

In United States law, a lender may be liable under what is called the "Instrumentality Theory",[426] where his control and dominance over a borrower is so substantial as to indicate that effective control of the borrower's affairs rests with the lender, such that the dominance causes harm to the borrower or its other creditors through misuse of the lender's control. A related concept is found in English insolvency law under section 214 of the Insolvency Act 1986 concerning wrongful trading, which says that a director may be liable to make "such contribution (if any) to [a] company's assets as the court thinks proper" where a company continues to trade whilst it is insolvent.

In this context, a director includes a "shadow director", who is "... a person in accordance with whose directions or instructions the directors of the company are accustomed to act (but so that a person is not deemed a shadow director by reason only that the directors act on advice given by him in a professional capacity)".[427] The definition of shadow director (which will be discussed below) is of potential concern to lenders, as it may apply where they seek to have input into the management of a borrower in difficulty. An application for wrongful trading may be brought by a liquidator on a winding up if, under section 214(2), the following criteria are fulfilled:

(a) the company has gone into insolvent liquidation (by which it is meant that the company's assets are insufficient to pay its debts, liabilities and the expenses of the liquidation, not that it is unable to pay its debts[428]);

(b) the person, at some time prior to the winding up, knew, or ought to have known, that there was no reasonable prospect that the company would avoid going into insolvent liquidation; and

(c) the person was a director of the company at the time.

What the court is concerned with when making a wrongful trading order is to ensure that any depletion in a company's assets, which are attributable to the period after the moment when its directors knew, or ought to have known, there was no reasonable prospect of avoiding insolvent liquidation—namely, while the company's business is being carried out at the creditors' risk—"is made good".[429]

However, under subsection (3), if it can be shown that, at the relevant time, the person "took every step with a view to minimising the potential loss to the company's creditors as (assuming him to have known that there was no reasonable prospect that the company would avoid going into insolvent liquidation) he ought to have taken", then that person will be excused.

---

426. See *In re Clark Pipe & Supply Co. Inc.* 893 F.2d. (5th Cir. 1990), for example.
427. Section 251 of the Insolvency Act 1986.
428. Section 214(6) of the Insolvency Act 1986.
429. *Re Purpoint Ltd.* [1991] B.C.C. 121, at p. 128H, per Vinelott J.

If the words of section 251 are applied literally, it is possible that a lender, in seeking to protect its position under various security arrangements, may fall within the definition of a "shadow director". It is suggested that the proviso in the definition of "shadow director" would exclude professional advisers acting in that capacity, but does not exclude lenders.[430] Moreover, a lender with security who has, for example, appointed one of its officers as its nominee on the board of the borrower, may find it difficult to come within section 214(3); in addition, the officer is very likely to have a conflict of interests.[431]

For a case of shadow directorship to succeed, four things have to be established: (i) who the company's directors were (whether *de facto* or *de jure*); (ii) that the defendant directed those directors how to act in relation to the company; (iii) the directors did act as directed; and (iv) the directors "were accustomed so to act".[431a] Thus, there needs to be "first, a board of directors claiming and purporting to act as such; and secondly, a pattern of behaviour in which the board did not exercise any discretion or judgment of its own, but acted in accordance with the directions of others."[431b]

In the first case on section 214, *Re A Company (Number 005009 of 1987); ex parte Copp*,[432] which subsequently became *Re M.C. Bacon Ltd.*,[433] Knox J., in a striking out application under Order 18, rule 19 of the Rules of the Supreme Court, held that the claim by the borrower's liquidator, that the steps taken by M.C. Bacon Ltd. to implement the recommendations of its lender in the lender's report on the company made the lender a shadow director of the company, was not "obviously unsustainable", although his Lordship expressed no definite opinion on the matter. Nonetheless, the significant factor is that the claim was not rejected.[434] But, at the trial before Millett J., this argument was held to be "rightly abandoned" after six days.[435] It had been anticipated that, in addition to affidavits, there would be oral evidence supporting the company's case that the

---

430. See Penn, Shea and Arora, *The Law Relating to Domestic Banking* (1987), at para. 28.42; and Totty and Jordan, *Insolvency*, at B3.14.

431. This might expose him to an action for breach of fiduciary duty for failure to make a full disclosure, unless some form of consent is agreed at the time of his appointment. If found liable, the officer may then seek an indemnity from his principal (the lender) but this would depend on the circumstances.

431a. *Re Hydrodam (Corby) Ltd. (in liquidation)* [1994] 2 B.C.L.C. 180, at p. 183d–e; noted by Turing, D., "Lender Liability, Shadow Directors and the case of Re Hydrodam (Corby) Ltd." [1994] J.I.B.L. 244. The difference between a shadow director and a *de facto* director is explained by Millett J.: see *Re Hydrodam (Corby) Ltd. (in liquidation)*, *supra*, at p. 183.

431b. *Re Hydrodam (Corby) Ltd. (in liquidation)* [1994] 2 B.C.L.C. 180, at p. 183d–e, per Millett J. For examples of the classic shadow director: see Sir Peter Millett, "Shadow Directorship—A Real or Imagined Threat to Banks", *Insolvency Practitioner*, Jan. 1991, cited by Fidler, P., "Banks as Shadow Directors" [1992] J.I.B.L. 97.

432. [1989] B.C.L.C. 13.

433. [1990] B.C.C. 78.

434. Knox J., at p. 21, specifically declined to give reasons so as not to embarrass the trial judge.

435. *Re M.C. Bacon Ltd.* [1990] B.C.C. 78, at p. 79.

lender was acting as a shadow director. This did not occur, and costs were awarded against the company on this and other points.[436]

The wrongful trading provision was introduced into the Insolvency Act 1986 as a result of the Cork Committee Report[437]—which had as a member, P.J. Millett Q.C. (as he then was)—because it was difficult to prove a fraudulent intent in an action for "fraudulent trading".[438] The Cork Committee said that wrongful trading will not "attach to anyone unless that person is actually *party* to the company carrying on the offending business. It will not be sufficient that he is merely *privy* to it."[439] But, where a lender is actively involved in the management of a borrower company in order to protect its (the lender's) position, it may be liable—the critical factor is the degree of involvement in management.[440]

Section 214 of the Insolvency Act 1986 has, however, as referred to previously, been considered primarily in a non-lending context by Knox J. in *Re Produce Marketing Consortium Ltd.*[441] and *Re Produce Marketing Consortium Ltd. (No. 2).*[442] These decisions have provided guidance for subsequent cases.[443]

The facts were that Produce Marketing Consortium Ltd. ("the company") carried on business as agents with regard to the importation of fruit. Whilst the business was initially successful, the number of directors, its turnover and its profitability subsequently diminished. By 1981, there were only two directors: a Mr David and a Mr Murphy.

Owing to a failure to keep up-to-date accounts and to check their books to ascertain the extent of trading losses sustained, coupled with an unfounded belief in the prospect of an imminent turnaround of the company's fortunes, Messrs David and Murphy did not—but should have—realised that by July 1986 there was no reasonable prospect of the company avoiding insolvency. Nevertheless, they allowed the company to continue trading with a foreign firm called "Ramona", and to exceed its overdraft with the company's lender. This overdraft was guaranteed by Mr David up to £50,000.

In February 1987, a warning from the company's auditor that the directors might be liable for fraudulent or wrongful trading under the Insolvency Act 1986 was ignored.[444] Ultimately, in October 1987, the company went into a

---

436. *Re M.C. Bacon Ltd.*, *supra*, at p. 79.

437. Cmnd. 8558, June 1982.

438. Then under section 332 of the Companies Act 1948—now under section 213 of the Insolvency Act 1986. An action for fraudulent trading by Barnes in *Williams & Glyn* [1980] Com. L.R. 205—at a time when there was no "wrongful trading"—was unsuccessful on the evidence.

439. Cmnd. 8558, June 1982, at para. 1787.

440. See, for example, *Re Tasbian Ltd. (No. 3)* [1992] B.C.C. 358, where a company doctor involved in signing company cheques and a tax scheme was held to be a "shadow director".

441. [1989] B.C.L.C. 513; also called *Halls* v. *David and Murphy*, *The Times*, 18 February 1989.

442. [1989] B.C.L.C. 520.

443. *Re DKG Contractors Ltd.* [1990] B.C.C. 903; *Re Purpoint Ltd.* [1991] B.C.C. 121; and *Re Tasbian Ltd. (No. 3)* [1992] B.C.C. 358, and see case note by G. Syrota, "Insolvent Trading: Hidden Risks for Accountants and Banks Participating in 'Workouts' " [1993] U.W.A.L.R. 329.

444. Such a warning is normally critical, and a failure to heed it, fatal (as it was for Messrs David and Murphy).

creditors' voluntary liquidation and a liquidator was appointed. The liquidator wrote to the directors seeking an explanation as to why the company had continued to trade whilst insolvent, and applied, under section 214, for an order requiring the directors to contribute the sum of approximately £108,000 to the assets of the company on the ground of wrongful trading.

In the first action, the directors sought to avoid liability on the basis of section 727(1) of the Companies Act 1985, which purports to excuse negligence, default breach of duty or trust where an officer of a company "has acted honestly and reasonably, and that having regard to all the circumstances of the case ought fairly to be excused", either in whole or in part.

This plea was unsuccessful, and the section was held[445] inapplicable since sections 214(2)(b), (3) and (4) of the Insolvency Act 1986 are objective, whereas section 727 of the Companies Act 1985 imposes a subjective test. Consequently, it was difficult to see how the two could be intended to operate together. Also, it was "virtually impossible" to look at all the circumstances of a case and see whether a director has acted honestly and reasonably in deciding whether that director ought to be fairly excused and, at the same time, to impute to him some general knowledge, skill and experience, which he may well not have: this being a different test.

Moreover, it is suggested that section 214 specifically relates to wrongful trading and *a fortiori* is intended to cover the field in this area, whereas section 727, on its wording, makes no reference to wrongful trading. Section 727 would appear to apply to situations other than wrongful trading, which is consistent with Parliament having included a specific defence in section 214; if the test was that in section 727 of the Companies Act 1985 (as amended), then section 214(3) of the Insolvency Act 1986 would be irrelevant. The exemption from liability in each section reflects these differences in ambit and intention of the sections. But, even if section 727 was applicable, it could not be said that the directors, in this case, had acted reasonably, and that, in all the circumstances, they "ought fairly to be excused".

Having disposed of this preliminary defence, the main issue, of the construction of section 214, was heard in *Re Produce Marketing Consortium Ltd. (No. 2).*[446] It was held that the test to be applied by the court is one under which "the director in question is to be judged by the standards of what can reasonably be expected of a person fulfilling his functions, and showing

---

445. [1989] B.C.L.C. 513, at p. 518.

446. [1989] B.C.L.C. 520. For a discussion of section 214 and wrongful trading: see S. Gillespie, "Wrongful Trading Policy and Practice" [1989] J.I.B.L. 269; J. Bannister, "Wrongful Trading: the Courts Speak" (1989) *Insolvency Law & Practice* 30; E. Jacobs, "Putting Flesh on Wrongful Trading" [1989] *International Banking Law* 22; B. Mitchell, "Wrongful Trading Implications for Bankers" (1989) *Butterworth's Journal of International Banking and Financial Law*, June 1989, 251; S. Rajani, "Adjustment of Prior Transactions and Malpractice" (1989) *Insolvency Law & Practice* 38; and A. Hicks, "Advising on Wrongful Trading Parts 1 and 2 (1993) 14 *The Company Lawyer* 16 and 55.

reasonable diligence in doing so".[447] Thus, a lower standard is to be expected from a small company than a larger, more sophisticated one.[448] However, the Companies Act 1985 (as amended) sets out certain minimum standards, including an obligation to keep accounting records and to prepare a profit and loss account for a balance sheet, as well as to present copies of the accounts for that year ended to the company in general meeting and to deliver a copy of the accounts to the Registrar of Companies within 10 months.[449] Also, different standards of skill are to be expected of different directors, so that a higher standard in questions of wrongful trading will be required of a lender (or the finance director) than of a director with less financial acumen—"the man on the Clapham omnibus".

The director's knowledge—either actual or constructive—that there is no reasonable prospect of the company not going into insolvent liquidation is not limited to the documentary material available at the relevant time. The reference in section 214(4) of the Insolvency Act 1986 to facts which a director of a company not only ought to know, but also ought to ascertain—such wording does not appear in subsection (2)(b)—indicates that not only is information actually present to be included, but also information which, given reasonable diligence and an appropriate level of general knowledge, skill and experience, is ascertainable by the directors.[450]

Consequently, on the evidence, it was held Messrs Murphy and David knew that the year prior to January 1987 had been a very bad one. They had a close and intimate knowledge of the business and knew when turnover was up or down. A large decline in turnover meant a substantial loss, and hence a substantial increase in the deficit of assets over liabilities. This was the directors' actual knowledge. With regard to the knowledge and matters they should have ascertained, Knox J. concluded that, once the loss in the year ending 30 September 1985 was incurred, the company was in an irreversible decline and the directors ought to have concluded at the end of July 1986 that there was no reasonable prospect of the company avoiding insolvent liquidation, and that the question of minimising loss was inapplicable.

From a lender's perspective, requests for management accounts and other financial data under a loan agreement amount to constructive (if not actual) knowledge of a company's financial status where a lender is taking a more than passive interest in a borrower's business so as to protect its loan, and has undertaken an active management role by having its own representatives on the borrower's board.

---

447. At p. 550—this is with respect to subsection 214(4)(a).
448. At p. 550.
449. At p. 550; see sections 221(1) and (2)(a), 227(1) and (3), 241(1) and (3) and section 242(1) and (2) of the Companies Act 1985 (as amended).
450. At p. 550.

Section 214[451] of the Insolvency Act 1986 is a compensatory, rather than penal, provision.[452] A director is liable for "the amount by which the company's assets can be discerned to have been depleted by the director's conduct".[453] The "very wide words of discretion" chosen by Parliament meant, in Knox J.'s view, it was not desirable to spell out the limits of such discretion, although, in determining a director's contribution, it is not wrong to take into account that there has been no fraudulent intent.[454]

In exercising his discretion under section 214(1), Knox J., in *Re Produce Marketing*, considered the following factors relevant:

(a) this was a case of failure to appreciate what should have been clear, rather than of deliberate wrongdoing;

(b) that where statements of fact are made which are positively untrue, this is to be held against the maker;

(c) the ignoring of the auditor's warning in early February 1987;

(d) that Mr David had given a guarantee to the lender, limited to £50,000. The lender had a charge over anything which Mr David or Mr Murphy contributed, pursuant to the order of the court. *Pro tanto*, this would relieve Mr David from his guarantee liability;

(e) the lender was substantially, if not fully, secured. If the jurisdiction of the court is to be exercised, then it needs to be exercised in a way that will be of benefit to unsecured creditors; and

(f) there was unclear evidence regarding the disappearance of debtors from the statement of affairs.[455]

Taking all these matters into account, the two directors were ordered to contribute £75,000.

Various commentators have questioned whether any contributions recovered are "pooled" for the benefit of all creditors, or whether they are subject to any floating charges (which is the traditional rule).[456] At one point, Knox J. appears to accept secured creditors have priority, as he takes into account Mr David's £50,000 guarantee liability to the lender and says the lender held a charge over everything Messrs David and Murphy contributed to the company's assets, with a consequential reduction in the former's guarantee liability. However, his Lordship went on to state that, if the jurisdiction under section 214 is to be exercised, "it needs to be exercised in a way which will benefit unsecured creditors".[457] It is to be hoped this potential uncertainty will be clarified in subsequent decisions, as it is possible for a lender to be both a shadow director

451. At p. 553.
452. See also *Re DKG Contractors Ltd.* [1990] B.C.C. 903.
453. *Ibid.*
454. At p. 553f.
455. At pp. 553–554.
456. See Bannister, *supra*, at p. 32, and Mitchell, *supra*, at pp. 251–252.
457. At p. 554.

and a secured creditor, with a resultant contribution and distribution.[458] It would seem that the debenture holder's interests would prevail under the normal order of priorities. Nonetheless, it would be unusual for a liquidator, who is the only person who can bring such a claim, and who acts on behalf of the unsecured creditors, to bring an action for the benefit of the floating charge holder, bearing in mind the question of cost of such an action. It is more consistent with the nature and duties of the liquidator for such an action to be brought for the benefit of the general body of creditors, rather than a secured creditor, whose claim to priority of payment (including those under a floating charge) a liquidator often seeks to defeat.[459]

The approach of Knox J. in *Re Produce Marketing Consortium*,[460] of equating wrongful trading with misfeasance, is, with respect, open to doubt,[461] as section 214 of the Insolvency Act 1986, unlike section 212, does not refer to breach of duty, but looks at "any potential loss to the company's creditors[462]; in misfeasance actions, it has been held that proceeds from such an action must be applied against the amount owing to the debenture holder.[463] Wheeler[464] argues that a wrongful trading action is more akin to a preference action (in which it has been held[465] that proceeds of recovery go to the general body of creditors), as both are only triggered by liquidation and only apply to liquidators.

This is also consistent with the view of Vinelott J. in *Re Purpoint*[466] that the purpose of wrongful trading is to recoup any loss to the company in order to benefit the creditors as a whole, and that the court cannot direct payment to one class of creditors in preference to another.

Since *Re Produce Marketing*,[467] and the dismissal of the shadow directorship claim in *Re M.C. Bacon*,[468] there has been judicial support for the view that it is very unlikely that lenders will be shadow directors.

First, Sir Peter Millett, writing extra-judicially,[469] has said the possibility of a lender being a shadow director is very remote and the lender would have to go outside the normal lender/customer relationship. His Lordship distinguished between monitoring a financially troubled borrower's business, which is permissible, and interfering in its management or seeking to manage it, which is

---

458. *Quaere*: whether this might not be a case of the lender benefiting from its own wrongdoing?
459. See sections 238, 239, and 245 of the Insolvency Act 1986, for example.
460. [1989] 5 B.C.C. 399.
461. See S. Wheeler, "Swelling the Assets for Distribution in Corporate Insolvency" [1993] J.B.L. 256, at p. 265.
462. Which should be interpreted to mean all creditors.
463. *Re Anglo-Austrian Printing* [1985] 2 Ch. 891.
464. *Supra*, at pp. 265–266.
465. *Re Yagerphone* [1920] 1 Ch. 392.
466. [1991] B.C.C. 121.
467. [1989] B.C.L.C. 520.
468. [1990] B.C.C. 78.
469. "Shadow Directorship—A Real or Imagined Threat to Banks", *The Insolvency Practitioner*, Jan. 1991, noted by P. Fidler, "Banks as Shadow Directors" [1992] J.I.B.L. 97, at pp. 98–99. It has been said this article was the judgment Millett J. wanted to write in *M.C. Bacon Ltd.*, *supra*, where the point was abandoned: see Fidler, *supra*, at p. 98.

not. The concept of shadow directorship relates to the situation where the board as a whole abandons its decision-making role and becomes accustomed to following a third party's orders; it does not refer to the situation where one person is on the board to do what someone else wants him to do. The shadow director is consciously controlling the mind of the company via board decisions.[469a] It is not enough for the lender to be constituted a shadow director for it to attach conditions to continued financial support—e.g. further security, a reduction in the borrower's overdraft, the sending in of an investigation team, a call for (further) financial information and advice on strengthening capital—which conditions may be commercially sensible and leave the customer with no option if it wishes to continue trading. The critical point is that it is the company's directors—and not the lender—who make the decision regarding whether the company continues to trade. If the lender makes the decision, then it has stepped out of the lender/customer relationship to take on a management role, and so is responsible as a shadow director. It was the participation in the management of a borrower company by a "company doctor", who signed cheques and devised a scheme involving company employees to lessen the company's tax, that led to him being found liable as a shadow director in *Re Tasbian Ltd. (No. 3)*.[470] The difficult line between being a watchdog imposed by an outside investor and a shadow director[471] had been crossed.

The second development is the advice of the Privy Council in *Kuwait Asia Bank E.C.* v. *National Mutual Life Nominees Ltd.*,[472] where their Lordships considered the position of two lender nominee directors of a company in the context of, *inter alia*, section 2(1) of the New Zealand Companies Act 1955 (as amended) which is similar to section 251 of the Insolvency Act 1986 and defined "director" as: "A person in accordance with whose directions or instructions the persons occupying the position of directors of a company are accustomed to act."

The facts of the case were that a lender was beneficially interested in a company (AICS) which carried on the business of a money broker. The company had five directors—two of whom, A and H, were employees of the lender and were nominated by the lender to AICS's board. Under a trust deed, the plaintiff was appointed the depositors' trustee and AICS agreed to provide the plaintiff with monthly and quarterly certificates on behalf of the directors. Certificates were furnished, but these were inaccurate. This resulted in AICS going into liquidation, and the plaintiff settled actions brought against it by the unsecured creditors. The plaintiff then sought to sue, *inter alia*, the lender (as well as the directors A and H personally for breach of duty) for a contribution.

Their Lordships advised that the lender was not vicariously liable for the acts

469a. See Millett J. in *Re Hydrodam (Corby) Ltd. (in liquidation)* [1994] 2 B.C.L.C. 180, at p. 183d–e.
470. [1992] B.C.C. 358 (C.A.).
471. See Vinelott J., at first instance [1991] B.C.L.C. 792, at p. 802.
472. [1991] 1 A.C. 187 (P.C.).

and omissions of A and H, as those appointing directors owe no duty (in the absence of bad faith or fraud) to see they discharge their duties, although self-interest may dictate that the appointer checks to see that the directors carry out their duties properly; and that any breach of duty by A and H was done in their personal capacity as directors (agents) of AICS, and not as agents of the lender.[473]

On the main issue in this context, whether the lender was a "shadow director" under the New Zealand equivalent of the Insolvency Act 1986, the Judicial Committee dismissed this claim too. Their Lordships opined that A and H constituted two out of the five directors (the others being appointed by the other major shareholder in AICS); and there was no allegation (which was inherently unlikely) "that the directors in these circumstances were accustomed to act on the direction or instruction of the [lender]".[474] Consequently, no claim arose.

The position is well summarised in the following passage:

"In the absence of fraud or bad faith on the part of the [lender], no liability attached to the [lender] in favour of the plaintiff for any instruction or advice given by the [lender] to [H] and [A]. Of course, it was in the interests of the [lender] to give good advice and see that [H] and [A] conscientiously and competently performed their duties both under the trust deed and as directors of A.I.C.S. But such advice is not attributable to any duty owed by the [lender] to the plaintiff, which was only entitled to the protection which the trust deed provided, namely quarterly certificates furnished on behalf of all the directors of A.I.C.S. By the trust deed the directors of A.I.C.S. accepted and assumed responsibility for the quarterly certificates, and the directors did not include the [lender]. The Companies Act 1955 [for which one may read the Insolvency Act 1986 (UK)] can not alter the construction of the trust deed or impose on the [lender] a duty assumed by [H] and [A] but never assumed by the [lender]."[475]

It will be seen that, as a result of the views of Millett J. and the Privy Council, the great fear of lenders of liability as shadow directors when acting, normally, in either of two scenarios[476]—setting down conditions for continued lending facilities or appointing nominees to the board of the borrower—is now much more remote. It would seem that, whilst personal liability might arise for the nominee directors, the lender will not be vicariously liable unless it seeks to obtain "an improper advantage" for itself or causes the borrower harm or interferes with the borrower; or, when simply imposing conditions on a borrower, the lender goes beyond monitoring the company and starts to be involved in the management of the company.

One possible side effect of lenders being held to be shadow directors is that it may inhibit rescue attempts of companies in difficulties who, ironically, will seek and need a lender's assistance. Ironically, this would be against the spirit and intent of the Cork Committee and the Insolvency Act 1986.

473. At pp. 222–223.
474. At p. 223G. This is similar to Millett J.'s view.
475. At p. 224A–C.
476. Cf. the position in the USA, in the context of environmental liability, where the lender goes beyond enforcing its security and becomes involved in management.

To avoid being regarded as giving directions or instructions, prudent lenders should couch all discussions as advice. But the danger remains that a director may say on oath that he felt he was being told what to do by the lender.[477]

PREFERENCES: SECTION 239 OF THE INSOLVENCY ACT 1986

The provision in the United States' Federal Bankruptcy Laws stating that a 90-day preference may be extended to one year where a person has "insider status", is similar to the extension of a preference period from six months to two years under section 239 and section 240(1)(a) of the Insolvency Act 1986, where a preference is given to a "connected person". A person is "connected with a company" if he is a director[478] or shadow director[479] or an associate[480] of the company. It is being connected with a company as shadow director which is of most relevance and concern to lenders, as mentioned above. Section 239, relating to preferences—which also applies when a transaction is at an undervalue, pursuant to section 238 of the Insolvency Act 1986—was originally considered in *Re M.C. Bacon Ltd.*[481] (as was section 238). In a very carefully reasoned judgment, Millett J. examined the meaning of "preference", as defined in section 239(4) of the Insolvency Act 1986. That section provides:

"For the purposes of this section and section 241, a company gives a preference to a person if—
    (a)   that person is one of the company's creditors or a surety or guarantor for any of the company's debts or other liabilities, and
    (b)   the company does anything or suffers anything to be done which (in either case) has the effect of putting that person into a position which, in the event of the company going into insolvent liquidation, will be better than the position he would have been in if that thing had not been done."

Subsection (5) goes on to state that the company which gave the preference had to be "influenced in deciding to give it by a desire to produce in relation to that person the effect mentioned in subsection (4)(b)".

Millett J. noted that this was the first case under the new section and attempted to provide some guidance.[482] His Lordship was "emphatically" against the citation of cases under the previous legislation, as the language of the

---

477. Penn, Shea and Arora, *The Law Relating to Domestic Banking* (1987), at para. 28.42. In a striking out application before Knox J. in *Re A Company (No. 005009 of 1987); ex parte Copp* [1989] B.C.L.C. 13, it was hoped oral evidence would provide the key to a claim that the lender was a shadow director (although this proved not to be the case: see *Re M.C. Bacon Ltd., supra*, at p. 79).

478. Section 249 of the Insolvency Act 1986.

479. Section 251 of the Insolvency Act 1986.

480. Section 435 of the Insolvency Act 1986.

481. [1990] B.C.C. 78. See case notes by M. Taylor, "Bacon—Well Done" (1990) B.J.I.B.F.L. 212; and Professor I.F. Fletcher, Insolvency Section [1990] J.B.L. 70.

482. At p. 87A.

statute had "been so completely and deliberately changed".[483] Under the new legislation, the court is to enquire whether the company's decision was "influenced by a desire to produce the effect mentioned in subsection (4)(b)", not whether there was "a dominant intention" to prefer a creditor. This is a "completely different test" involving "at least two radical departures". First, "a dominant intention to prefer" does not have to be established—it is "sufficient that the decision was influenced by the requisite desire"[484] to improve a creditor's position in an insolvent liquidation. Secondly, there has to be a desire to produce the effect mentioned in subsection (4)(b), rather than an intention to prefer.[485] This is a subjective test,[486] whereas the previous test was objective,[487] and, it is suggested, entails a higher threshold as far as the lender is concerned. In the case of a connected person, the burden of proof is shifted so it rests on the connected person.[488]

Hence, a transaction will only be set aside under the new legislation if "the company positively wished to improve the creditor's position in the event of its own insolvent liquidation".[489] Evidence of this does not have to be direct, it can be inferred. Nonetheless, the requisite desire alone is not enough. The desire has to be influenced by the decision to enter into the transaction. This desire will only be one of the factors operating on directors' minds—it does not have to be the sole, or even the decisive, factor. If it were, then this would be too high a test.[490]

On the facts of the case, Millett J. found that the director of the company who was dealing with the lender was "not actuated by desire to improve the [lender's] position as a creditor in the event of the company's liquidation".[491] The director was responsible for ensuring the company did what he told the lender it would do, namely, give the lender a debenture[492] (which, of itself, involves more stringent security than a mortgage, and the power to appoint an administrative receiver).

---

483. At p. 87D. See also *Re Beacon Leisure Ltd.* [1991] B.C.C. 213, at p. 215, per Robert Wright Q.C. (sitting as a deputy High Court judge) and Mummery J. in *Re Fairway Magazines Ltd.* [1992] B.C.C. 924, at p. 927H.

484. *Ibid.*, at p. 87E.

485. *Ibid.* See also [1991] B.C.C. 213, at p. 216B.

486. In *Re Maxwell Communications Corp. plc (No. 2)* [1992] B.C.C. 757, at p. 760H, Hoffmann J. (as he was), whose judgment was approved on appeal (see same reference), said liability for a preference depended on "the subjective intentions of the person who made the payment" and cited *Re M.C. Bacon Ltd.* [1990] B.C.C. 78.

487. At p. 87F. This distinction between an intention (which is objective) and a desire to influence (which is subjective), made by Millett J. in *Re M.C. Bacon, supra*, was said by Robert Wright Q.C. (sitting as a deputy High Court judge) in *Re Beacon Leisure, supra*, at p. 216C, to be a distinction which might be small in many cases.

488. Section 239(6) of the Insolvency Act 1986; and see *Re Fairway Magazines Ltd.* [1992] B.C.C. 924, at p. 929E and *Re Beacon Leisure Ltd.* [1991] B.C.C. 213.

489. At p. 88A.

490. At p. 88C.

491. At p. 91G.

492. At p. 91F.

Since *Re M.C. Bacon Ltd.*, two other cases have come before the courts[493] and in both instances it was decided that there was no intention to prefer. In the second of these cases, *Re Fairway Magazines Ltd.*,[494] the facts were not untypical. A company in financial trouble was given a loan by one of its directors. In return, the company granted a debenture. The loan was to be repaid in instalments to its lender in reduction of the company's overdraft with the lender; this overdraft was guaranteed by the director, who increased the limit of this guarantee. The company made two payments to the lender, the effect of which was to reduce the director's exposure under his guarantee.

Five months later, the company went into voluntary liquidation and the debenture was challenged by the liquidator.

Mummery J. held that the presumption of an intention to prefer under section 239(6) of the Insolvency Act 1986 had been rebutted, as the company's purpose in granting the debenture was a commercial one so it could raise money from a source other than its lender, who was wanting the overdraft repaid, so that the company could keep trading.

His Lordship, after reviewing the authorities,[495] laid out the following propositions[496]:

(1) The new test under section 239 of the Insolvency Act 1986 is whether the decision to give security was influenced by a desire to improve the position of the creditor in an insolvent liquidation, and is "completely different" from the previous position.

(2) This desire is subjective and, thus, there may be "no direct evidence" of the giver's state of mind, although it may be inferred from the circumstances.

(3) If security is granted for "proper commercial considerations" and not by a "positive wish" to improve the position of a creditor in an insolvent liquidation, the security is valid. But, that such a wish is sufficient to invalidate the security because the intention to prefer "does not have to be the sole or decisive influence on the decision".

(4) The relevant time is not the date of execution of the security, but the time when the decision to grant it was made (i.e. at a board meeting) or in negotiations.

What is now clear is that, when a lender takes a debenture from a borrower in a

---

493. *Re Beacon Leisure Ltd.* [1991] B.C.C. 213, and *Re Fairway Magazines Ltd.* [1992] B.C.C. 924. See also *National Bank of Kuwait* v. *Menzies* [1994] 2 B.C.L.C. 306, at p. 319, per Balcombe L.J.
494. [1992] B.C.C. 924.
495. *Re M.C. Bacon, supra,* and *Re Beacon Leisure Ltd., supra.*
496. At pp. 929G–930A.

rescue situation, the lender's security is unlikely to be successfully challenged, and the lender will not be exposed to the risk of being unsecured.

TRANSACTIONS AT UNDERVALUE: SECTION 238 OF THE INSOLVENCY ACT 1986

Under section 238(4) of the Insolvency Act 1986, a transaction is at undervalue—and can be set aside under section 241—if:

"(a) the company makes a gift to [a] person or otherwise enters into a transaction with that person on terms that provide for the company to receive no consideration, or

(b) the company enters into a transaction with that person for a consideration the value of which, in money or money's worth, is significantly less than the value, in money or money's worth, of the consideration provided by the company."

To come within the section, six requirements need to be fulfilled:

(i) the transaction was entered into by the company;
(ii) for a consideration;
(iii) the value of which measured in money or money's worth;
(iv) is significantly less than the value;
(v) also measured in money or money's worth;
(vi) of the consideration provided by the company.[497]

Thus, there must be a comparison between the value the company obtained for the transaction and the value of the consideration the company provided. These values have to be measurable in "money or money's worth" and are to be regarded from the company's point of view.[498]

Applying this criteria to the facts of *Re M.C. Bacon Ltd.*, Millett J. held that granting a debenture was not a gift and it was not without consideration: the consideration being the lender's forbearance from calling in the overdraft and its honouring cheques and making fresh advances to the company during the period of the lender's facility.[499] Creating a security over a company's assets does not deplete them or diminish their value and does not fall within section 238(4).[500]

The charging of assets appropriates them to meet liabilities agreed to the other secured creditors and adversely affects the rights of other creditors in a winding up. The right to redeem and to sell or remortgage the charged assets is retained. What the company loses is its ability to apply the proceeds for a purpose

497. At p. 92C–D.
498. At p. 92E.
499. *Ibid.*
500. At p. 92E. Cf. the view of N. Segal, "Rehabilitation and Approaches Other Than Formal Insolvency": ch. 8 in *Banks and Remedies* (R. Cranston, ed.) (Lloyd's of London Press Ltd., 1992), at p. 157.

otherwise than satisfying the secured debt. It is not something capable of valuation in monetary terms and is not usually disposed of for value.[501]

Upon this basis, Millett J. concluded that no loss was suffered as a result of granting the debenture. Rather, once the debenture was demanded, the company was not able to sell or charge its assets without applying the proceeds in reduction of its overdraft. If it had tried to do so, then it would have called in the overdraft. By granting the security, "the company parted with nothing of value, and the value of the consideration which it received in return was incapable of being measured in money or money's worth".[502]

As the transaction did not fall within subsection (4), it was unnecessary to consider the defence in subsection (5)[503] of entering into the transaction in good faith and believing it would benefit the company, which, it is submitted, would apply to most lenders.

The decision, on both sections 238 and 239, will be welcomed by lenders because merely taking a debenture will not, on a liquidation, mean that the lender will have its security set aside or dealt with under section 241 of the Insolvency Act 1986. For borrowers, it means that a lender will be more likely to lend them money since it can be secured, and the fear of a security going back for a period of two years being set aside under section 240 is reduced.

One matter not addressed in the *M.C. Bacon* case, which still has to be tested judicially under section 238, is the question of "upstream guarantees" (where a subsidiary guarantees its parent's obligations).

INADVERTENT PARTNERSHIPS

It is less likely that there will be an unwitting partnership between a borrower and a lender under English law than under United States law, as the terms of a loan facility letter will normally clearly express the relationship between the parties as being lender and borrower—sometimes containing a provision stating that there is no partnership between the parties, though this is not conclusive. They will not be two or more persons carrying on business with a view to profit, as outlined in section 1(1) of the Partnership Act 1890 and the case law.[504] There is no mutuality between the parties. Also, unlike partners, they will not be in a fiduciary relationship. Moreover, even if there is a loan to a business to be repaid out of profits, this does not give rise to a partnership, and is expressly exempted

---

501. At p. 92F.
502. At p. 92G.
503. At p. 92H.
504. See also *Cox* v. *Hickman* (1860) 8 H.L. Cases 268; and *Davis* v. *Davis* [1894] Ch. 393. See also the High Court of Australia in *Canny Gabriel Castle Jackson Advertising Pty. Ltd.* v. *Volume Sales (Finance) Pty. Ltd.* (1974) 131 C.L.R. 321.

by section 2(3)(d) of the Partnership Act 1890. Consequently, the lender will not be jointly liable for the borrower's debts under section 9 of the Partnership Act 1890.

EXTORTIONATE CREDIT BARGAINS/EXCLUSION CLAUSES

There are two matters to be discussed here briefly: (1) extortionate credit bargains and (2) the Unfair Contract Terms Act 1977, as they may affect a lender's liability or position in relation to a borrower.

(1) Extortionate credit bargains: section 138 of the Consumer Credit Act 1974 and section 244 of the Insolvency Act 1986

Under the Consumer Credit Act 1974 ("CCA"), if a credit bargain is extortionate, the credit agreement may be reopened.[505] However, a commercial loan is unlikely to be affected, as the CAA only applies to transactions up to £15,000, and does not apply to companies. A credit bargain is extortionate, under section 138(1) of the CCA, if it: (i) is grossly exorbitant; or (ii) otherwise grossly contravenes the ordinary principles of fair dealing.

In assessing whether a credit bargain is extortionate, a court will look at factors such as the prevailing interest rate in the marketplace; the amount of credit sought; the term of the loan; the equity available; the speed with which the loan is required; the availability of other sources of finance; and the personal financial circumstances of a borrower (an individual).[506]

But, sums are not "grossly exorbitant" merely because they are greater than what the court would regard as "fairly due and reasonable".[507] And, just because a transaction is unwise or imprudent, does not mean it is extortionate.[508]

Cases falling within section 138 would be those approaching undue influence.[509] In *Coldunell Ltd.* v. *Gallon*,[510] the Court of Appeal held—in a claim for equitable relief by way of avoidance of a charge where a son had exercised an influence over his parents—that, as there was nothing unusual about the loan because the rate (20 per cent) was not unreasonable and the lender had acted in the way an ordinary commercial lender would be expected to act, the lender had discharged the burden of proof and the agreement was not extortionate within the meaning of section 138(1)(b) of the CCA.

---

505. As defined in section 9 of the CCA; see L. Bentley, and G.G. Howells, "Judicial Treatment of Extortionate Credit Bargains" [1989] *The Conveyancer* 164 and 234.

506. Section 138(2)–(5) of the CCA. On this area: see generally, Professor R. Goode, *Consumer Credit Law* (1989), Ch. 32.

507. *First National Securities Ltd.* v. *Bertrand* (1978), unreported decision of the County Court.

508. *Willis* v. *Wood*, The Times, 24 March 1984.

509. See Lord Denning M.R. in *Avon Finance Company Ltd.* v. *Bridger* [1985] 2 All E.R. 281, at p. 286.

510. [1986] Q.B. 1184 (C.A.).

A similar, and more relevant, provision in the context of a commercial loan is section 244 of the Insolvency Act 1986—although the case law on the CCA should be used as a guide. Pursuant to subsection (3), a transaction is extortionate if either it: (a) requires "grossly exorbitant payments to be made"; or (b) "otherwise grossly contravene[s] ordinary principles of fair dealing". The section goes on to say there is a presumption that the transaction is extortionate, if an application is made. The section applies when the party to a transaction is involved in the provision of credit to a company.[511] The court may make an order with respect to a transaction if the transaction is exorbitant, and may go back for a period of three years from the date of an administration order or liquidation.[512] This will have serious repercussions for a lender. An order under this section may include setting aside the transaction[513]; varying the terms of the transaction or any security[514]; and repayment of any sums paid.[515]

As to what will constitute an extortionate rate is not fully clear, as it is to be decided on a case by case basis. In cases under section 138 of the CCA, rates of 42 per cent per annum secured and 25.78 per cent per annum secured have been held not to be extortionate.[516] Also, Sir Gordon Borrie Q.C., when he was the Director General of the Office of Fair Trading, said that he was not in favour of capping interest rates in credit transactions, so that rates of 100 per cent or more should not be outlawed, provided they were freely entered into.[517]

(2) Unfair Contract Terms Act 1977

Its basic thrust concerns attempts by one party to a contract to exclude or limit its liability for negligence or breach of contract to the other party. There is a requirement of "reasonableness" which any limitation or exclusion must meet.[518] The Act would apply to disclaimers by lenders (such as the one in *Hedley Byrne*) for customer references[519]; or where a lender is advising a client and seeks to exclude or limit its liability—this will be particularly so in large transactions.

In *Smith* v. *Eric S. Bush*,[520] the House of Lords considered the effect of a disclaimer clause in relation to a negligent valuation of a property by a surveyor. Lord Griffiths[521] listed four factors which should be considered in determining

511. Section 244(1) of the Insolvency Act 1986.
512. Section 244(2) of the Insolvency Act 1986.
513. Section 244(2)(a) of the Insolvency Act 1986.
514. Section 244(2)(b) of the Insolvency Act 1986.
515. Section 244(2)(c) of the Insolvency Act 1986.
516. See *Woodstead Finance Ltd.* v. *Petrou*, *The Times*, 23 January 1986; and *Davies* v. *Directloans Ltd.* [1986] 1 W.L.R. 823, respectively.
517. *The Times*, 28 September 1991.
518. See sections 2, 3, 5, 6, 7 and 11; and see section 11 regarding reasonableness. For a full treatment of this Act: see *Chitty*, at paras. 982–1029.
519. A lender must be careful not to defame a customer.
520. [1990] 1 A.C. 831 (H.L.(E.)).
521. [1990] 1 A.C. 831, at p. 858.

whether a disclaimer is reasonable, although these are not exhaustive. First, whether the parties are of equal bargaining power. If it is a "one-off" situation between parties of equal bargaining power (such as a lender and a large public limited company), the requirement of reasonableness will be more easily discharged than where the borrower has no effective power to object. Secondly, whether it is reasonably practicable to obtain advice from an alternative source, taking into account considerations of cost and time. Thirdly, the difficulty of the task to be undertaken for which it is sought to exclude liability. If the undertaking involved is very difficult or dangerous, with a high risk of failure, this is an indication of the reasonableness of excluding, or limiting, liability as a condition of doing the work. Thus, work at the lower end of a person's professional expertise is less likely to be excluded. Fourthly, the practical consequences of the decision on the question of reasonableness. This involves the sums of money potentially at stake and the ability of the parties to bear the loss involved through insurance. Normally, professional men insure themselves and so the availability and cost of insurance is a relevant factor in considering which of the two parties should bear the risk of the loss.

Lord Griffiths did not believe that it would be unreasonable in all circumstances for professional men to exclude or limit their liability for negligence. Where a transaction involves "breathtaking sums of money",[522] which may turn upon professional advice for which it would be impossible to obtain adequate insurance cover and which would ruin the adviser if held personally liable, it may be reasonable to give advice on a no-liability basis or to limit liability to the extent of the adviser's insurance cover.[523]

The last observation will be particularly relevant to lenders advising on, for example, takeovers, mergers or flotations, where "breathtaking sums of money" are involved.

ENVIRONMENTAL LIABILITY

The primary concern for English and Welsh lenders who have taken security over the borrower's land, is being made liable for an environmental clean-up, owing to the land being contaminated, when they seek to enforce their security and become a mortgagee in possession after the borrower has defaulted. This concern is based on the situation in the United States under the Comprehensive Environmental Response Compensation and Liability Act 1980 ("CERCLA" or the "Superfund legislation"), which was resulted in environmental clean-up liability for lenders.[524]

522. At p. 859.
523. *Ibid.*
524. Environment in this context means any of the medium of land, air and the sea: see section 1 of the Environmental Protection Act 1990.

United States position

In the United States, under the Superfund, liability is retrospective and is not dependent on guilt; it is joint and several and applies to persons who are owners or operators of contaminated sites; and is guided by the polluter pays principle. However, there is an exemption—known as the "secured creditors' exemption"—for those who hold the "indicia of ownership",[525] but do not participate in management of the debtor.[526] Thus, secured creditors who are seeking to enforce their security are exempt.

The United States Environmental Protection Agency ("USEPA") has a fund for the purposes of clean-ups estimated at approximately US$1.8bn, but seeks to recover a contribution from "potentially responsible parties", i.e. owners and operators (which includes lenders), particularly as the cost of clean-ups is estimated to be approximately US$31m for each site.[527]

The main problems in the United States have occurred when a lender has gone outside the normal loan monitoring process and either has sought to participate in the management of the borrower or has tried to purchase the property it had security over.[528] The lender is thus acquiring an asset: not enforcing its security.

Case law has indicated that where a lender merely monitors a borrower's financial progress, it is not participating in the borrower's management, and comes within the exemption.[529] However, the decision in the celebrated case of *U.S.* v. *Fleet Factors Corp.*,[530] in which the court applied a test, in relation to participating in management, of the "capacity to influence", caused consternation in lending ranks.[531] Thus, a lender could be liable if its

---

525. This phrase refers to "evidence of interest in real or personal property held as security for a loan or other obligation, including title to real or personal property acquired incident to foreclosure or its equivalent", and includes: mortgages, liens, hypothecs, conditional sales, trust receipt transactions, factoring agreements, certain assignments, which are regarded as *bona fide* security interests: see United States Environmental Protection Agency Rule on the interpretation of CERCLA, 57 Fed. Reg. 18,334 (29 April 1992).

526. Section 101(20)(A).

527. *Financial Times*, 13 April 1994, at p. 22.

528. Such a case is *US* v. *Maryland Bank & Trust* Co. 632 F. Supp. 573 (D. Mid. 1986). This is highly questionable under English law, which requires that an auction has to be an independent bargain, in good faith and one in which reasonable precautions have been taken: see *Tse Kwong Lam* v. *Wong Chit Sen* [1983] 1 W.L.R. 1349 (P.C.) and the High Court of Australia in *ANZ Banking Group Ltd.* v. *Bangadilly Pastoral Co. Pty. Ltd.* (1976–77) 139 C.L.R. 195.

529. See *US* v. *Mirabile* 15 Envtl L. Rep. (Envtl L. Inst) 20,992 WL 97 (E.D. Pa. Sept. 6, 1985), in which a distinction was drawn between: (i) limiting participation to financial aspects of management; and (ii) participating in the "nuts and bolts, day to day production aspects of the business"—the latter being outside the statute, the former being within it; and *Guidice* v. *BFG Electroplating and Manufacturing* Co. 732 F. Supp. 556 (W.D. Pa. 1989).

530. 901 F.2D 1550 (11th Cir. 1990). See the discussion of this case in "Cleaning up the Debris after Fleet Factors: Lender Liability and CERCLA's Security Interest Exemption" (1991) Notes section, 104 *Harvard Law Review* 1249; and P. Shively, "An Alternative Analysis of Lender Liability and The Fleet Factors Decision: Practical Policy or Pariah?" (1991) *Wisconsin Law Review* 743.

531. *Ibid.*, at p. 1557.

involvement with the debtor/borrower was "sufficiently broad to support the inference that it could affect hazardous waste disposal decisions if it so chose".[532] Whilst the decision to impose liability was correct on the case's facts—there was a factoring agreement which allowed Fleet Factors to approve the goods which were shipped and set their price; also, it could supervise office administration, taxation forms and redundancy, as well as control access to the loan facility—the wide test used by the court had potential problems for the lending community.

The position was later rectified somewhat in Re Bergsoe Metal Corp.,[533] where the court said it was what the lender actually did which was important: not what it could do. Thus, investigating a borrower prior to granting a loan facility and retaining a right to re-enter the borrower's premises and foreclose upon default, were held to be essential steps in normal lending practice; it was said that the secured lender exemption would be meaningless if these steps were considered "participating in management". But, when Fleet Factors went on appeal to the Supreme Court, the court let it stand.[534]

The USEPA, aware of these difficulties, has issued a Rule,[535] which whilst not having judicial or legislative effect, may control the threshold question of the number.[536] The Rule seeks to clarify what is regarded as monitoring a loan's progress and participation in management, as well as setting a timetable for selling secured property so that a distinction can be drawn between lenders who hang on to property awaiting a pick up in the market and those who are seeking to acquire the property.

The other issue that the USEPA raised was the question of unjust enrichment[537] when the lender has the benefit of a cleaned-up property, although the lender is not guilty of any polluting, and the result is that the property is likely to have increased saleability and at a higher price. The amount of the enrichment is not spelt out, but it is submitted that the correct measure

532. Ibid., at pp. 1557–1558.
533. 910 F.2d. 668 (9th Cir. 1990).
534. Cert. denied 111 S. Ct. 752 (1991).
535. 57 Fed. Reg. 18,344 (29 April 1992) ("USEPA Rule"). For a discussion of this rule: see A.K. Obermann and R. Arnold, "Environmental Regulation—EPA Proposed Rule Clarifying Lender Liability" [1991] J.I.B.L. 371; W.R. Buck and M.M. Drough, "United States Environmental Protection Agency's Secured Lender Rule: Limitations to Superfund Exposure for Financial Institutions" [1992] J.I.B.L. 262; S.M. Campbell and F.J. Quinn, "Lender Liability in the US for Hazardous Waste Cleanup: New Proposed Rule Concerning Secured Creditor Exemption" International Business Lawyer Oct. 1991, 448; L.S. Zimmerman, J.B. Ruhl and J.L. McQuaid, "The US EPA Moves to Protect Financial Institutions from Superfund Liability" UKELA Journal Winter 1992–93, 53; and S.M. Taber, "Lender Liability Rules" International Business Lawyer Jan. 1993, 19.
536. In Kelly and Chemical Manufacturers Association v. E.P.A., the District of Columbia Court of Appeals held that the USEPA Rule was not binding on the courts, who were responsible for statutory interpretation: judgment delivered on 4 February 1994; noted [1994] J.I.B.L. N-116. See other cases and comments referred to in [1994] J.I.B.L. N-116.
537. Ibid., at p. 1116. See also US v. Maryland Bank & Trust Co. 632 F. Supp. 573 (D. Md. 1986).

is the difference between the price of the property before clean-up and the price after.

The Superfund legislation and its cost—particularly for lenders and insurers—has been criticised and there are proposals for reform.[538]

English law

With this in mind, the British Parliament has not brought into force section 61 of the Environmental Protection Act 1990 ("EPA") imposing liability to pay the costs of an environmental clean-up on "the owner for the time being" of contaminated land; it has also commissioned Consultation Papers by the Department of the Environment in England and Wales entitled, "Paying For Our Past",[539] and a separate, but parallel, review by the Scottish Office, called, "Contaminated Land Clean-up & Control", both of which reported in March 1994.[540]

Section 61 of the EPA

With regard to section 61 of the EPA, the perceived difficulty was that the key concept of "owner for the time being" was not defined, in contrast to the predecessor Act,[541] in which "owner" had been defined in terms of someone who would be entitled to receive the rack rent for the property either on their own behalf or for another person.[542] There was, therefore, uncertainty whether "owner" was to be a wider concept[543] than before, and whether it would include a mortgagee in possession (which it is felt it would do).[544]

This problem seems to have been recognised in "Paying For Our Past".[545] The

538. See *Financial Times*, 4 May 1994, at p. 21 and *The Economist*, 21 May 1994, at pp. 107–108.

539. This paper has been commented upon in *Financial Times*, 9 March 1994, and 4 May 1994 on p. 21. See also *The Economist*, 21 May 1994, pp. 107–108.

540. For a fuller discussion of environmental law: see W. Jarvis Q.C., M. Fordham and D. Wolfson, *infra*, Ch. 10 hereof, Jarvis Q.C. and Fordham, *Lender Liability: environmental risk and debt* (1993, Cameron May), Chapter 5; S. Troman, "The Relevance of Environmental Law for Banks" [1990] J.I.B.L. 433; A. Bryce, "Environmental Liability: Practical Issues for Lenders" [1992] J.I.B.L. 131; and M. Redman, "Environmental Law for Bankers and Insolvency Practitioners" [1993] J.I.B.L. 85. For a lender's perspective: see E. Welch and A. Parker, "A Bank's View of Lender Liability in Environmental Legislation" [1993] J.I.B.L. 217.

541. The Control of Pollution Act 1974. See also the Water Act 1990.

542. As Bryce notes, this is a common definition in Planning and Public Health Acts: see A. Bryce, "Environmental Liability: Practical Issues for Lenders" [1992] J.I.B.L. 131, at p. 134.

543. See Jarvis Q.C. and Fordham, *supra*, at Ch. 9.

544. See Jarvis Q.C. and Fordham, *supra*, at p. 143; A. Bryce, "Environmental Liability: Practical Issues for Lenders" [1992] J.I.B.L. 131, at p. 134; and M. Redman, "Environmental Law for Bankers and Insolvency Practitioners" [1993] J.I.B.L. 85, at p. 87.

545. At para. 3.21, but note that there is reference to "a similar, long established term" in section 81(4) of the EPA. In the Scottish Review, at para. 92, it is stated that section 61 of the EPA required amendment and a transfer of responsibilities and should not become law until this was done. See also para. 88.

Government has said that it does not want to have the problems of the Superfund,[546] but feels that there will be circumstances when it will be appropriate for the lender to contribute to the cost of clean-ups. However, not surprisingly, in view of the Consultation Papers, this view has yet to be spelt out. An indication of the Government's thinking is to be found in paras 4B 23–25 of "Paying For Our Past", where it is stated that those responsible for pollution, even if indirectly, should pay towards the cost of clean-up—there is a specific reference to lenders and financial institutions. It is also stated that liability should not be based on financial resources, as this would not be fair and would be damaging if lenders were made to pay an amount disproportionate to their loan; and that any limitations would need to be practical and be considered with regard to their effect on public finances. The idea of proportionality, referred to in the Consultation Paper,[547] appears to be part of Government thinking,[548] and seems to be a reference to the so-called "deep pockets" syndrome sometimes associated with the Superfund legislation—a consequence of which has been that lenders have turned down applications for loans from certain types of companies which are considered risky environmentally.[549] The Government is also in favour of the land being put into a state where it is "suitable for use", rather than into a pristine one.[550] And the polluter pays principle will be at the heart of the environmental regime.

In the meantime, whilst the legislation on clean-ups is being considered, there are certain things that lenders can do to try to protect themselves, as it seems clear that there will be some form of legislation imposing environmental liability (which may or may not include a secured lender exemption, such as that in the United States). For example, there should be a provision in new loan documentation stipulating that if there is a potential environmental problem, then, the loan becomes repayable immediately,[551] and covenants relating to the environment. In the case of both old and new loans in situations where the borrower might be an environmental risk, the lender should seek regular environmental information. With new loans, the lender should commission an environmental audit prior to lending.[552]

---

546. See the statement of the then Environment Minister, Mr Tim Yeo, in October 1993, cited in *Journal of Environment Policy and Law* 24/1 [1994] February, 34.

547. At para. 49.

548. See the statement of the then Environment Minister, Mr Tim Yeo, in October 1993, cited in *Journal of Environment Policy and Law* 24/1 [1994] February, 34.

549. See the statement of the British Bankers' Association, cited in *Journal of Environment Policy and Law*, 24/1 [1994] February, 34, who observed that in the United States companies in risky industries environmentally, such as chemical companies, are being refused loans.

550. At para. 2.12.

551. See, for example, J.R. Lingard, *Bank Security Documents* (1993) 3rd edn., Specimen Documents, Document 2, at clauses 1.01 and 2.03.

552. See the useful suggestions by Jarvis Q.C. and Fordham, *Lender liability: environmental risk and debt* (1993, Cameron May), Ch. 10, "Safe Lending", at pp. 169ff.

Duty of care: section 34 of EPA

This section places upon a person who "imports, produces, carries, keeps, treats or disposes of controlled waste or, as a broker, has control of such waste", a four part duty, which carries a criminal sanction, to take all reasonable steps to make sure that:

   (i) section 33 of the EPA is not breached by a third party,[553] i.e. where waste is being treated, kept or disposed of, that it is not being done so without, or in contravention of, a management licence, or that it is being done in a manner likely to harm humans or the environment[554];
   (ii) that waste does not escape from the person's control[555];
   (iii) where waste is being transferred, it is transferred "to an authorised person" or "a person authorised for transport", as defined in subsections (3) and (4)[556];
   (iv) the written description of waste which is being transferred is sufficient to allow the person receiving the waste to avoid breaching section 33 of the EPA and to comply with the requirement above regarding the escape of waste.[557]

   The penalty for breach of these duties is criminal and not civil, with a maximum fine of £20,000 on indictment for a summary conviction and an unlimited fine on an indictment.[558] However, the penalty does not just apply to the company, and officers (which would include a shadow director) and managers of the company can be liable also.[559]

   The difficulty that a lender faces with this duty of care is if it enters into possession under a mortgage over land on which waste is being produced or disposed of, and there is an inadvertent breach of the duty.

   To assist persons in the performance of their duties, a Code of Practice[560] has been published[561] which is admissible in evidence[562]; and regulations[563] have been published in relation to transfer notes, so guidance is at hand.

---

553. Section 34(1)(a) of the EPA. See also the helpful guidance in the joint circular from the Department of the Environment, the Scottish Office and the Welsh Office, "Environmental Protection Act Section 34, The Duty of Care", especially at p. 2.

554. "Environmental Protection Act Section 34, The Duty of Care", at p. 2.

555. Section 34(1)(b) of the EPA.

556. Section 34(1)(c)(i) of the EPA.

557. Section 34(1)(c)(ii) of the EPA.

558. Section 34(6) of the EPA. See also R. Harris, "The Environmental Protection Act 1990—Penalising the Polluter" [1992] J.P.L. 515, at p. 516.

559. Section 157 of the EPA.

560. *Waste Management: The Duty of Care*, a code of practice issued by HMSO, December 1991.

561. Pursuant to section 34(7) of the EPA.

562. Section 34(10) of the EPA.

563. The Environmental Protection (Duty of Care) Regulations 1991.

Environmental liability other than under the EPA

Whilst the EPA is, at present,[564] the main source of environmental law in the United Kingdom, the Water Resources Act 1991 ("WRA") provides[565] that the National Rivers Authority ("NRA") (at present) is able to recover clean-up costs from a person who "caused or knowingly permitted" noxious or polluting matter to be present at a place, which, in the NRA's opinion, is likely to enter any controlled waters or who "caused or knowingly permitted" the matter in question to be present in any controlled waters.[565a] In this regard, if a lender has, for example, exercised its security rights and moved into possession of an industrial factory, and noxious substances are flowing from the factory into controlled water, which the lender knows about but does nothing to stop, then the lender may be liable for clean-up costs. The question to be answered by the courts is whether the knowledge required is actual or constructive knowledge. It is suggested, on the wording of the section and the reference to "caused", that the knowledge required will be actual knowledge.

Under the common law, the decision of the House of Lords in *Cambridge Water Company* v. *Eastern Counties Leather*,[566] in which Lord Goff of Chieveley delivered the leading speech, held that the doctrine of *Rylands* v. *Fletcher*[567] did not apply in relation to a chemical solvent which had seeped into a neighbour's water supply.

DAMAGES IN CONTRACT AND TORT

The last matter to be discussed in this chapter—and, in practical terms, the most significant one once a lender's liability has been established—is the question of the measure of damages that may be recovered by a borrower against a lender in contract and tort. It is proposed to look at the measure of damages for breach of

---

564. It is likely that the European Union will play a role in this area and issue a directive or directives: see, for example, the Directive for Civil Liability for Damage Caused by Waste (Com (91) 219).

565. Section 163 of the WRA. See also section 161 of the Act. A criminal offence exists on the same basis under section 85: see *National Rivers Authority* v. *Alfred McAlpine Homes East Ltd.* [1994] 4 All E.R. 286.

565a. As to the meaning of "caused" and "knowingly permitted": see *Alphacell Ltd.* v. *Woodward* [1972] A.C. 824 (H.L.(E.)); and *Wychavon District Council* v. *N.R.A.* [1993] 2 All E.R. 440 (D.C.).

566. [1994] 2 W.L.R. 53 (H.L.(E.)). See case note by Professor R.F.V. Heuston, "The Return of *Rylands* v. *Fletcher*" (1994) 110 L.Q.R. 185.

567. (1868) L.R. 3 H.L. 330.

contract, contributory negligence, and punitive damages in tort, which have been so prevalent (and large) in United States cases. The measure of tortious damages, which has been discussed elsewhere in this chapter, is reliance based and is aimed at placing the victim of the tort in the position he would have been in had the tort not been committed. Contractual damages are more complex and require further examination since they will be a borrower's prime source of damages, unless there is liability under *Hedley Byrne*. The basic measure of damages for breach of contract is an expectation loss for lost profits,[568] and it seeks to place the injured party in the position he would have been in, so far as money can, if the contract had not been breached.[569]

(a) Contractual damages

If a lender refuses to lend money to a borrower after notice of draw-down, and the borrower suffers damage due to the lender's breach of a loan agreement, the borrower will be able to sue the lender for breach of contract. For example, in a very recent case,[570] the administrators of a borrower brought an action against a lender who had provided the borrower with an overdraft of £2m for 12 months; this arrangement being formalised in a facility letter. The difficulty was that the letter did not contain the usual provision that the overdraft was repayable on demand, so the overdraft was, effectively, a term loan. The lender, erroneously, called in the overdraft after six months after one of the borrower's major markets had collapsed. The learned judge dealing with the matter held that the lender had been instrumental in the borrower's demise. It is expected that damages will be fixed at £4.56m; the £1.3m still outstanding on the loan will be deducted from the final award. But an interim payment of £1.3m was made, being half the proposed award, with costs payable forthwith. A refusal to lend prior to notice of draw-down, in the absence of a breach by the borrower of the loan agreement, will be an anticipatory breach[571] of the agreement. Unless the borrower is unable to comply with the terms and conditions of the loan agreement, when the loan is refused, the borrower will have an election either to rescind and sue for breach, or to wait until just before the expiry date for draw-down and to issue the draw-down notice and sue for breach.

---

568. The victim may, however, seek merely to recover expenditure outlaid, which is a reliance loss: see later.

569. *Robinson* v. *Harman* (1848) 1 Ex. 850, at p. 855, per Parke B., 154 E.R. 363.

570. *Crimpfil plc (In Administration)* v. *Barclays Bank Plc, The Independent*, 30 April 1994, at p. 17; *The Daily Telegraph*, 21 April 1994; and noted [1994] J.I.B.L., at N–151.

571. *Hochester* v. *De la Tour* (1853) 2 E. & B. 678, which decided that the party not in breach has an election either to accept the breach and sue for damages, or not to accept the breach and to wait till the contract is due to be performed and then to sue damages for breach of contract. See also *Johnson* v. *Agnew* [1980] A.C. 367 (H.L.(E.)).

(i) Remoteness

In order to substantiate its claim for breach of contract, a borrower must prove that its loss is not too remote. A loss is considered not too remote if it:

(a) may fairly and reasonably be considered as arising naturally, i.e. according to the usual course of things from such breach of contract itself, or

(b) may reasonably be supposed to have been in the contemplation of both parties, at the time they made the contract, as the probable result of the breach of the contract.[572]

Where there are special circumstances which will affect the measure of damages, these should be communicated to the other party, so that they are within that party's contemplation. For example, if the loan is for a special purpose, or it has consequences for the borrower with third parties.

The principles in *Hadley* v. *Baxendale*, set out above, particularly the second limb, have been considered in several cases, although they have, arguably, received comparatively little judicial examination by the higher courts.[573] The effect of these decisions on the second limb may be synthesised into the proposition that, in order to substantiate its claim, a borrower must prove that its loss, as a result of a breach of contract by a lender, is not too remote, in that "if, at the time of contracting (and on the assumption that the parties actually foresaw the breach in question), [the loss] was within [the parties'] reasonable contemplation as a not unlikely result of that breach".[574]

An important recent decision by the House of Lords, on the first limb, arose in the Scottish case of *Balfour Beatty Construction (Scotland) Ltd.* v. *Scottish*

---

572. *Hadley* v. *Baxendale* (1854) 9 Exch. 341, at pp. 354–355, per Alderson B.

573. See *A/B Karlshamns Oljefabriker* v. *Monarch Steamship Co.* 1949 S.C. (H.L.) 1; *Victoria Laundry (Windsor) Ltd.* v. *Newman Industries Ltd.* [1949] 2 K.B. 528 (C.A.); *Koufos* v. *C. Czarnikow Ltd. (The Heron II)* [1969] 1 A.C. 350 (H.L.(E.)); and *Parsons (H) (Livestock) Ltd.* v. *Uttley Ingham & Co. Ltd.* [1978] Q.B. 791 (C.A.). See also the decision of Hobhouse J. in *The Forum Craftsman* [1991] 1 Lloyd's Rep. 81, at p. 85, where his Lordship says: "Remoteness of damage in contract cases is not to be decided on an all or nothing basis. The contemplation that some loss of profit might result from a breach of contract did not require that all profits lost must necessarily be recoverable. The liability in damages for breach of contract was a contractually assumed liability. The first and second rules in *Hadley* v. *Baxendale* limited the extent of that liability having regard to what was or must be taken to have been in the contemplation of the contracting parties that made the contract, and to the natural and probable consequences of a breach of a contract."

See also the recent decision of the House of Lords in the Scottish case of *Balfour Beatty Construction (Scotland) Ltd.* v. *Scottish Power plc*, 1994 S.L.T. 807.

574. (1854) 9 Exch. 341.

Power plc.[575] That case concerned damage to a concrete pour for a concrete aquaduct, which had to be abandoned and recommenced; the cause of the damage was the rupturing of fuses provided by the defender in their electricity supply system. The pursuer, who was the main contractor for the construction of a major road works in Edinburgh, entered into an agreement for the temporary supply of electricity with the defender. Pursuant to that contract, the pursuer sought to recover the cost of the demolition and reconstruction of the concrete pour. It was held that there could be no recovery under the first limb of *Hadley* v. *Baxendale*,[576] and so the claim failed. The leading speech was delivered by Lord Jauncey of Tullichettle,[577] and is notable for several things:

(1) His Lordship's citing without disapproval of the statement as to the first limb of *Hadley* v. *Baxendale* by the Lord Ordinary, Lord Clyde,[578] who said:

"I am content to leave the quantification [of the damages] as being limited to the loss which the defenders might reasonably have contemplated at the time of the contract, subject to the explanation that it is sufficient that the type of loss be of a type which might have been so contemplated. That it was actually of an unforseeable scale is not relevant."

Lord Clyde went on to hold that the defenders should only have anticipated the kind of damage flowing naturally from the breach (i.e. under the first limb), and that the damage claimed went beyond that.

(2) Lord Jauncey felt the critical finding was that the defenders were not aware of the need to preserve a continuous pour for the construction of the aqueduct, and consequently the Inner House (Second Division) were not correct to impute to the defenders, at the time of entry into the contract, technical knowledge of the details of concrete construction which the pursuer had not provided.

(3) Whilst Lord Wright had said in *A/B Karlshamns Oljefabriker* v. *Monarch Steamship Co.*[579] that the court assumes that the parties as businessmen will have a reasonable acquaintance with each other's business, this was not a general rule that in all cases contracting parties will be presumed to have knowledge of each other's business.

(4) But when the pursuer's activities involved complicated construction or manufacturing techniques, there was no reason why the defender, who supplied a commodity for use by the pursuer in those techniques, should be aware of all the techniques undertaken by the pursuer and the effect of any failure of, or deficiency in, the commodity merely because of the order for the commodity.

Thus, it is submitted, in the current context of lender and borrower, that a

---

575. 1994 S.L.T. 807. The reference to "defender" in the text is a reference to Scottish Power plc's predecessor, South of Scotland Electricity Board ("SSEB"), whose liabilities Scottish Power succeeded to.

576. *Chitty* at para. 1793. See also Sir Robin Cooke, "Remoteness of Damages and Judicial Discretion" [1978] C.L.J. 288.

577. Lords Keith of Kinkel, Bridge of Harwich, Browne-Wilkinson and Nolan, agreeing.

578. 1992 S.L.T. 811, at p. 813A. Lord Jauncey also cited, for the purposes of the appeal, the dictum of Lord Reid in *The Heron II* [1969] 1 A.C. 350, at p. 388E, that an event has to be "not unlikely to occur".

579. 1949 S.C.(H.L.) 1, at pp. 19 and 21.

lender will not be presumed to have a specialised knowledge of its clients' business necessarily, although, as a matter of prudence, it should have some knowledge or understanding of a borrower's business anyway so that it is able to make reasonably well informed lending decisions. For example, if a lender decides to lend a borrower money for a particular construction project, but certain special circumstances or expectations concerning third parties are not revealed to the lender, then it is likely that the lender would not be liable for anything other than nominal damages in this regard.[580]

One situation where it is arguable that a lender ("X") would be liable for damages occurs where there is a cross default clause in a loan agreement ("loan B") between the borrower and another lender ("Y"), and X, knowing that the borrower has other loan facilities containing cross default clauses (or very likely to contain them), wrongly accelerates its loan with the borrower ("loan A"), leading to loan B being accelerated as well. Also, it would not be open to benefit from its wrongful acceleration of loan A.[581]

As to the measure of damages recoverable by a borrower because of a lender's failure to lend when it agreed to, the borrower is put to an election whether to recover the profits lost (an expectation loss) or wasted expenditure (a reliance loss).[582] The rationale of this rule is that the borrower should not be in a better financial position as a result of the breach of contract by the lender than it would have been if the contract had been performed.[583] The important consideration is the nature of the loss suffered. If the borrower[584]—who is under a duty to mitigate any loss by going into the marketplace and trying to obtain alternative funding[585]—is able to obtain another loan more cheaply because interest rates fall, then the borrower will be claiming for any wasted expenditure, and not for an expectation loss, unless there are "special circumstances". However, if interest rates rise in the meantime, the borrower will be able to obtain the difference between the price of the old loan and the price of the new loan. If the borrower is unable to procure new funds because, for example, it has an unfavourable credit rating or its share price has fallen, the lender may, arguably,

---

580. Although the borrower may be in breach of its loan agreement for non-disclosure.

581. See *New Zealand Shipping Company Ltd.* v. *Société des Ateliers et Chantiers de France* [1919] A.C. 1 (H.L.(E.)), stating that a party to a contract cannot take advantage of its own wrongdoing: see Lord Finlay at p. 6; Lord Atkinson, at p. 9; Lord Shaw of Dumfermline, at p. 12; and Lord Wrenbury, at p. 14; and *Alghussein Establishment* v. *Eton College* [1988] 1 W.L.R. 587 (H.L.(E.)), noted by J.G. Starke, Recent Cases (1988) 62 A.L.J. 732.

582. *Anglia Television Ltd.* v. *Reed* [1972] 1 Q.B. 60 (C.A.) and *C.C.C. Films (London) Ltd.* v. *Impact Quadrant Films Ltd.* [1985] Q.B. 16 (C.A.).

583. *MacGregor on Damages* (1987) 15th edn. at para. 50, citing the much criticised case of *Cullinane* v. *British Reme Manufacturers Co. Ltd.* [1954] 1 Q.B. 292 (C.A.). See MacLeod [1970] J.B.L. 19 and Stoljar [1975] 91 L.Q.R. 68. Cf. the High Court of Australia in *Industrial (T.C.) Plant Pty. Ltd.* v. *Robert's (Queensland) Pty. Ltd.* [1964] A.L.R. 1083; and see their recent decision in *The Commonwealth* v. *Amann Aviation Pty. Ltd.* (1992) A.L.J.R. 223; noted by Professor G.H. Treitel Q.C., "Damages for Breach of Contracts in the High Court of Australia" [1992] 108 L.Q.R. 226; and J. Swanton (1992) 66 A.L.J. 460.

584. See Ackner L.J. (as he then was) in *C. & P. Haulage* v. *Middleton* [1983] 1 W.L.R. 1461.

585. See, for example, *Payzu Ltd.* v. *Saunders* [1919] 2 K.B. 581 (C.A.).

be liable for all the consequences flowing from the decision not to lend, which may be breach of contract with third parties (assuming these are known) and the resulting economic loss (which is not recoverable in tort), although the lender will use the fact that other lenders will not lend to the borrower as part of its defence and will construe the terms of the loan agreement very closely.

Moreover, unlike the United States, a borrower under a commercial contract cannot claim damages for emotional distress caused by a breach. English courts have distinguished between contracts involving comfort or pleasure, for which damages for emotional distress can be recovered in certain circumstances,[586] and contracts for profit (i.e. purely commercial contracts) for which they cannot.[587] Similarly, in tort, the law will compensate for nervous shock, but not for emotional distress.[588] Hence, a borrower may only recover in contract his economic loss—either as lost profits or as wasted expenditure—but not damages for any stress he may have suffered as a result of the lender's breach.

(ii) Contributory negligence in contract

One way in which a lender might seek to reduce his liability for breach of contract, is to claim that the borrower was contributorily negligent and thus have damages apportioned under the Law Reform (Contributory Negligence) Act 1945 (the "1945 Act"). For a long time there was doubt whether this Act applied to breaches of contract. But the law was finally settled by the Court of Appeal in *Forsikringsaktieselskapet Vesta* v. *Butcher*,[589] where it was held, in relation to a reinsurance contract, that, where liability in tort and contract are the same, the Act can apply. This decision was reaffirmed and applied by the

---

586. See, for example, *Jarvis* v. *Swan Tours Ltd.* [1973] Q.B. 233; see *Jackson* v. *Horizon Holidays Ltd.* [1975] 1 W.L.R. 1468. Cf. *Perry* v. *Sydney Phillips & Son* [1982] 1 W.L.R. 1287 and *Watts* v. *Morrow* [1991] 4 All E.R. 937, concerning damages for distress caused by negligent valuations; later case noted by Professor M. Furmston (1992) J.C.L. 64. Cf. *Branchett* v. *Beaney*, *The Times*, 14 February 1992.

587. *Hayes* v. *James & Charles Dodd (A Firm)* [1990] 2 All E.R. 815, at p. 824, per Staughton L.J.; noted by R. Halson, "Contract Damages: Expectation, Reliance and Mental Distress" [1991] C.L.J. 31. See also *Firsteel Cold Rolled Products Ltd.* v. *Anaco Precision Pressings Ltd.*, *The Times*, 21 November 1994; *Rae* v. *Yorkshire Bank plc* [1988] F.L.R. 1 (a case of wrongful dishonour of cheques); *Bliss* v. *South East Thames Regional Health Authority* [1987] I.C.R. 700 (C.A.); and *Box* v. *Midland Bank Ltd.* [1979] 2 Lloyd's Rep. 391, where a claim for anxiety and distress brought about by the negligence of the lender was rejected. For a discussion of the cases: see A. Burrows, "Mental Distress Damages for Breach of Contract" (1990) N.L.J. 596. See also the High Court of Australia in *Baltic Shipping Co.* v. *Dillon (The Mikhail Lermontov)* (1992–93) 176 C.L.R. 344. In that case, Mason C.J. (at p. 365), after saying that "the innocent party's disappointment and distress are seldom so significant as to attract an award of damages", continued: "For that reason, if for no other, it is preferable to adopt the rule that damages for disappointment and distress are not recoverable unless they proceed from physical inconvenience caused by the breach or unless the contract is one that the object of which is to provide enjoyment, relaxation or freedom from molestation". Noted S. Hetherington, "Passengers' Damages For Disappointment and Distress" [1993] L.M.C.L.Q. 289; and J. Swanton (1992) 67 A.L.J. 379.

588. *McLoughlin* v. *O'Brian* [1981] 1 A.C. 410 (H.L.(E.)). See also *Hill* v. *Chief Constable of West Yorkshire* [1989] A.C. 53 (H.L.(E.)).

589. [1989] A.C. 852 (H.L.).

Court of Appeal in *Lipkin Gorman*,[590] where a claim of contributory negligence against the plaintiffs was upheld, as the plaintiffs' senior partner knew C had been dishonest about certain travel expenses. However, it is inapplicable to a case of fraud—either personally or vicariously—being an intentional tort.[591]

Similarly, the Court of Appeal[592] has recently, and sensibly, sought to limit the application of the 1945 Act by holding it does not apply "where a party's liability arose from breach of a contractual provision which did not depend on a failure to take reasonable care".[593] In such a situation, contributory negligence cannot be a partial defence.[594] Thus, contributory negligence is not a defence for a damages claim based on breach of a strict contractual obligation. In the case in question, the contract and obligation undertaken did not impose on the plaintiff any duty in their own interest to prevent the defendant from committing breaches of the contract.[595] Where there is a breach of a strict contractual obligation, the only breaches available are release, waiver, or forbearance. It was never the intention that the 1945 Act is "to obtrude the defence of contributory negligence into an area of the law where it had no business to be".[596]

Thus, the gap opened in *Vesta* v. *Butcher* is beginning to be closed. Its ambit can only ever have been intended to be limited, bearing in mind the advice in *Tai Hing Cotton Mill Ltd.* v. *Liu Chong Hing Bank Ltd.*,[597] and so a lender seeking to apportion blame, in part, to a borrower for the lender's breach of loan or security documents, in which there is no requirement to take reasonable care, is unlikely to be unsuccessful.

(b) Tort punitive damages

One clear point of distinction between United States law and English law, with regard to lender liability, is that in the United States juries award very high levels of damages—especially punitive damages.[598] This is particularly so where the conduct of the lender has been viewed as reprehensible and has made a poor

---

590. [1988] 1 Lloyd's Rep. 19.

591. *Alliance & Leicester Building Society* v. *Edgestrop Ltd.* [1993] 1 W.L.R. 1462.

592. *Barclays Bank Plc* v. *Fairclough Building Ltd.* [1994] 3 W.L.R. 1057 (C.A.), relating to a building contract (Nourse and Beldam L.JJ. and Simon Brown P.).

593. *Barclays Bank Plc* v. *Fairclough Building Ltd.* [1994] 3 W.L.R. 1057 (C.A.), per Beldam L.J., Nourse L.J. and Simon Brown P. agreeing.

594. Beldam L.J., *supra*. See, for example, *Bank of Nova Scotia* v. *Hellenic Mutual War Risks Association (Bermuda) Ltd.* [1990] 1 Q.B. 818, at p. 904.

595. See Beldam and Nourse L.JJ., *supra*.

596. Per Nourse L.J., *supra*.

597. [1986] A.C. 80. (P.C.).

598. See, for example, *Commercial Cotton Co.* v. *United California Bank*, 163 Cal. App. 3d 511 (1985), where US$4,000 were awarded for wrongful debiting of an account and US$100,000 punitive damages for breach of the implied covenants of "good faith" and "fair trading"; and *Kruse/Jewell* v. *Bank of America*, 201 Cal. App. 3d. 354 (1988), where US$61 million were awarded as part of a US$6m judgment. A report in the *Financial Times*, 10 May 1994, p. 11, indicates that the United States Supreme Court will be reviewing high awards of punitive damages.

impression upon the jury, and it is sought to award damages against the lender in excess of the normal measure.

In England, punitive damages—which are tortious and not contractual[599]— will very rarely be awarded[600] (and usually only in defamation cases).[601] Moreover, lending cases are conducted before a single judge—and not a jury—in the High Court of Justice.

To obtain punitive damages, a borrower must show that a lender's conduct has been calculated to make a profit for the lender which may well exceed the compensation payable to the borrower.[602] Punitive damages are to "teach a wrongdoer that tort does not pay". By awarding punitive damages, the court is admitting into the civil law a principle which logically belongs to the criminal law.[603]

It is highly unlikely, except where the conduct of a lender is reprehensible—as in *Farah's* case, concerned with fraud and economic duress—that punitive damages will be awarded in a lending case. A borrower will usually only recover damages for his actual loss.

Whether a borrower can sue for punitive damages for deceit by a lender is rather doubtful. In *Archer* v. *Brown*,[604] Peter Pain J. (as he then was) held that, *inter alia*, the plaintiff—who was the victim of fraud concerning the sale of shares in a company, which had already been sold—was not entitled to punitive damages (even though they could be awarded in deceit) because of the principle that a person must not be punished twice for the same offence. It would be wrong to award punitive damages when the defendant had already been in prison. However, as a matter of general principle, his Lordship appeared to have no objection about awarding punitive damages for deceit.[605]

---

599. *Addison* v. *Gramophone Co. Ltd.* [1909] A.C. 488 (H.L.(E.)), where the House of Lords held that punitive damages could not be awarded in contract.

600. This view is also expressed by Neill L.J., at p. 519, in *Bradford City Metropolitan Council* v. *Arora* [1991] 2 Q.B. 507, Russell and Farquharson L.JJ. agreeing. (It would seem that the result in this case was treated as *per incuriam* by Stuart-Smith L.J. in *A.B.* v. *South West Water Services Ltd.* [1993] 2 W.L.R. 507, although the point concerning the rarity of such cases remains valid.)

601. For example, *State National Bank of El Paso* v. *Farah Manufacturing Co.*, 678 S.W. 2d 661 (Tex. App. 1984). See also A.L. Fey, "Punitive Damages in the United States" [1992] J.I.B.L. 198; and B. Feldthusen, in Notes of Cases (*Voris* v. *Insurance Corporation of British Columbia*) [1990] *Canadian Bar Review* 169, at p. 172 fn. 13, who says that research of punitive damages awards in the United States shows that awards of $1 million or more, whilst "by no means typical, are far from uncommon". Cf. recent English jury libel awards, e.g., Mr Jeffrey Archer, £500,000, and Lord Aldington, £1 million.

602. *Rookes* v. *Barnard* [1964] A.C. 1129, at pp. 1226–1227, per Lord Devlin, as explained by the House of Lords in *Cassell & Co. Ltd.* v. *Broome* [1972] A.C. 1027 (H.L.(E.)).

603. *Rookes* v. *Barnard* [1964] A.C. 1129 (H.L.(E.)).

604. [1985] Q.B. 401. Cf. *Metall und Rohstoff A.G.* v. *ACLI Metals (London) Ltd.* [1984] 1 Lloyd's Rep. 598 (C.A.) and Sachs L.J. in *Mafo* v. *Adams* [1970] 1 Q.B. 548.

605. See the Canadian Case of *Claiborne Industries Ltd.* v. *National Bank of Canada* (1989) 59 D.L.R. (4th) 533, where Can.$5 million (approx.) were awarded against a lender which was involved in fraud and conspiracy by the major shareholder of the plaintiff, although this is really an application of restitutionary principles.

Further doubt about the awarding of punitive damages for deceit has been caused by the decision of the Court of Appeal in *Gibbons* v. *South West Water Services Ltd.*,[606] following dicta in *Broome* v. *Cassell & Co. Ltd.*,[607] that before there can be an award of punitive damages, the tort for which such an award was sought to be made must have been one in which such an award was made prior to 1964. With respect, such an arbitrary cut-off point—the date of the decision in *Rookes* v. *Barnard*—is hard to support logically and is against the notion of a dynamic common law,[608] but it is welcome news to lenders, whose conduct normally would not warrant punitive damages anyway.

CONCLUSIONS

1. Under English law, liability will primarily be governed by the terms and conditions of any loan agreement negotiated between the parties: the courts will not imply terms favourable to either party, particularly the borrower, as the parties are deemed to have negotiated their primary obligations.

2. However, there can now be concurrent liability in tort, except where this is inconsistent with the obligations negotiated between the parties.

3. The main area where a lender is likely to be sued by a borrower is where the borrower has suffered loss when a transaction has failed, and the borrower feels he had been badly advised or misled by the lender. This will involve questions of the nature of the parties' relationship, what was said or written and what were the parties' expectations—this can lead to liability in negligence and/or for breach of fiduciary duty.

4. Where there is a diminution in the value of a security, due to a delay by the lender (or a receiver) in realising it or to market forces, this will not usually result in liability. This is because, ordinarily, the lender may sell the secured property when he likes, subject to the Law of Property Act 1925.

5. Lenders should—despite the absence of notions of "good faith" and "fair dealing"—act reasonably towards a borrower at all times and exercise reasonable care, as they are required to do, even to the extent of slightly favouring the borrower so that there is no recourse against them by the borrower in the courts, with the resultant publicity and cost. This is so where there may be circumstances giving rise to insolvent liquidation and the spectre of the lender being liable as a

---

606. [1993] 2 W.L.R. 507. This was a case of public nuisance; noted by A. Burrows, "The Scope of Exemplary Damages" (1993) 109 L.Q.R. 359; and R.G. Lee, "Exemplary awards and environmental law" [1992] J.B.L. 287; and G.S. Pipe, "Exemplary Damages After Camelford" (1993) 57 M.L.R. 91.

607. [1972] A.C. 1027, at p. 1076, per Lord Hailsham of St Marylebone L.C.; at p. 1036, per Lord Reid; at p. 1114, per Lord Wilberforce; and at pp. 1130–1131, per Lord Diplock.

608. A similar view is shared by Lee, *supra*, and Pipe, *supra*. Cf. Burrows, *supra*.

shadow director arises (although this is not so great a fear as it once was); or, when the lender is enforcing its security by a sale, it should obtain a "proper price": not just a price that will pay off the debt owed to it.

6. Allied to this, problems may arise where lenders seek to go beyond the provisions of loan and security documentation and the creditor/debtor relationship, and seek to have a management or advisory, rather than a monitoring, role; they start to increase the risk that they will be associated with the borrower and its failings.

7. It is extremely unlikely that there will be any punitive element in the damages awarded and a lender will only be liable to a borrower for loss the lender actually caused.

8. *Williams & Glyn* still remains the major case, under English law, on lender liability and covers all the major issues. However, it did to some extent turn upon its facts, as NDH, who was the lender's customer and the proper plaintiff, was not a party to the proceedings; also, the decision was not tested on appeal. Nonetheless, the case is indicative of the attitude of the courts to implying terms and imposing tortious duties of care on lenders who—in the absence of a vitiating factor such as economic duress—are seeking to protect their loans by imposing on a borrower more onerous conditions in a rescheduling than before. In *Williams & Glyn*, these matters were decided in the lender's favour.[609]

PARKER HOOD

---

609. Except for the question of reasonable notice in relation to the January facility letter—although it was held that, in principle, all loans are repayable on demand.

CHAPTER 3

BANKS AND RISK: HOME LENDING

SAFE AS HOUSES?

Compared to the building societies, the enthusiasm of banks for the home loans market is of recent origin. As recently as 1987, a major new textbook on banking law[1] could dismiss the whole subject to home lending by banks with the sentence: "One province in which the banks have not been traditionally active is that of loans for the purchase of private dwellings."[2] However, having come in to the market, the banks have competed for business with a will. The following tables[3] illustrate the banks' progress and the fight back of the building societies against erosion of their market share over the last five years.

It is easy even for a lawyer to understand the enthusiasm which the banks have shown for the home loans market. The provision of home loans enables the banks to keep within their own sphere of influence those customers and potential customers who would otherwise have become customers of a building society. This helps the banks to maintain their customer base, at a time when the building societies are competing even more effectively in the provision of traditional "bank" products such as chequeing accounts. Administrative costs of home lending are low: and modern techniques of securitisation enable those banks that wish to do so readily to convert the long term cash-flow of the loan repayments into an immediate capital asset.

Home loan rates of interest are not usually high by comparison with the cost to the banks of the money lent. But the risks inherent in home lending are also low. In order to keep the roof over their own and their families' heads, people will make efforts to keep up the repayments on their home loan which they might scorn to do to keep a car or a stereo system. If, despite their efforts, they

---

1. *Modern Banking Law*, by Professor E.P. Ellinger (1st ed., 1987).
2. *Op. cit.*, at p. 489. Other leading textbooks (e.g., *The Encyclopedia of Banking Law* by Cresswell, Blair, Hill and Wood, *The Law Relating to Domestic Banking* by Penn, Shea and Arora (1st Edn., 1987), *Paget's Law of Banking* (10th Edn., 1989)) have sections on land as security, but none has a section dealing with the special problems of the home loans market.
3. Source: *CSO Financial Statistics* (No. 388, August 1994), Table 3.2C: all figures in millions of pounds. The effect of the recession on new advances is obvious.

Year	Total loans outstanding secured on dwellings	Of which: Building Societies	Banks
1989	£258,003	£152,542	£79,192
1990	£295,038	£176,682	£85,677
1991	£320,814	£197,609	£90,372
1992	£339,054	£211,329	£96,436
1993	£357,688	£221,142	£108,447

Year	Total net advances secured on dwellings	Of which: Building Societies	Banks
1989	£33,823	£24,002	£7,108
1990	£33,211	£24,120	£6,394
1991	£25,525	£20,607	£4,776
1992	£17,528	£13,057	£6,301
1993	£14,148	£7,581	£9,712

are unable to keep up the payments mortgage protection insurance or the state[4] may make some or all of the payments for them.

If all else fails, the loan will be fully secured on the property.[5] Furthermore, in setting up the transaction, the lending bank will usually have employed solicitors to ensure that the mortgagor obtained and effectively mortgaged to the bank a good marketable title to the property, and will usually have relied upon a surveyor to confirm to it that the value of the property provided sufficient security for the loan. Both the solicitor and the surveyor are likely to be insured against claims for professional negligence. If the title or charge proves defective, or the property proves not to be worth sufficient to pay off the loan, the bank may be able to re-claim its losses from them. So the lending bank has three potential sources of repayment for its home lending—the borrower, the property and the professionals—each of which is likely to prove good for the money.

Against that background, it may seem a little eccentric to include an examination of home lending in a survey entitled "Banks and Risk". Even the combination of high real interest rates, falling property prices and the prospect of a period of economic recession is unlikely to turn home lending into high risk business. However, the economic conditions which make repayments more difficult to keep up and which increase the number of re-possessions are likely to act as a spur to the legal advisers of borrowers to devise new legal methods of

4. Interest payments (but not payments of capital or payments of insurance premiums under an endowment policy) in respect of a loan for the purchase of a dwelling occupied as a home by the claimant or a member of his family may be added to the applicable amount; of income support payable under section 20 of the Social Security Act 1986, provided that the claimant is treated as responsible for those payments. Where the claimant (and partner, if any) is under 60, for the first 16 weeks of income support only 50% of the interest repayments are treated as an assessable housing cost.

5. "Land ... is an excellent form of security, even where most of the security value resides in buildings on the land, for buildings can be insured and the whole tends to increase in value": Penn, Shea and Arora, op. cit., at para. 24.01.

ensuring that the consequences fall on the banks and not on the borrowers. Moreover, there has been[6] a substantial increase in the amount of fraud related to home lending—encouraged, perhaps, because the very "ordinariness" and apparent safety of the business makes lending institutions less wary in this area than in others.

In this chapter I intend to discuss some of the legal arguments upon which home loan borrowers have relied to avoid their liability to repay the bank (either personally or through sale of their home) and to speculate upon some possible developments. After a comment upon some of the problems of the relationship between the banks and their solicitors and surveyors, I shall mention some of the more frequent mortgage frauds: by husbands on wives and mistresses, by children on elderly parents, by strangers on each other—and by all of them on the lending institution. Finally, I shall look at the future and at what banks may do to lessen the risk of their home lending.

THE USER-FRIENDLY BANK

The power of advertising

Many banks now offer prospective home buyers more than just a loan. Barclays "Complete Mortgage Service" is a good example of the type of products on offer:

"Over the years, we've helped many first time and experienced buyers get the home of their dreams. Our Complete Mortgage Service has been developed to make home buying a little less worrying and a good deal easier.

All the details you need are available in our special ... Brochure ... a handy budget planner to work out how much you can comfortably afford to borrow ... a simple and clear explanation of the different types of mortgage ... valuations and surveys ... and a Home Buyers Guide ..."[7]

By such offers to provide the customer with comprehensive service and advice, banks may be taking on some onerous (and, perhaps, unexpected) duties.

An indirect warranty of the value of the property?

The Building Societies Act 1986 repealed section 30 of the Building Societies Act 1962, by virtue of which the fact of making an advance to a member was deemed to be a warranty by the building society that the purchase price was reasonable. Even before the repeal, enforceable warranties were few in number because it

6. If newspaper reports such as the "Insight" Report published in the *Sunday Times* for 6 March 1988 are to be believed. According to that article, "national mortgage fraud statistics do not exist, largely because of the reluctance of financial institutions to discuss the problem from fear of adverse publicity".

7. Leaflet: *Mortgages, A fast efficient way to buy your home.*

was standard practice to give the statutory notice excluding any such warranty.[8] No such statutory provision has ever applied to banks making home loans.

However, it may not be entirely fanciful to suggest that a hard-pressed borrower, faced with a house which has declined to a value less than the amount of the loan taken to buy it, may before long seek to argue that his bank owed him a duty (which, of course, it broke) to warn him not to borrow so much to buy his house.

The case usually cited as authority for the proposition that a bank has no duty to consider the prudence of its lending from the customer's point of view is *Williams & Glyn's Bank Ltd*. v. *Barnes*.[9] In that case, Gibson J. rejected Mr Barnes' claim that his bank owed him a duty to advise him on the prudence of his £1m borrowing for the purchase of shares.[10] But, as the judge pointed out, Mr Barnes was "a businessman of full age and competence", who did not claim to have relied upon any advertising material put out by the bank in any material respect. Gibson J. went on to observe that:

"It may be that, if it could be shown that the bank in fact knew of the imprudence of the borrowing, and of the application of the money intended, and the likelihood of damage to the borrower, it might be possible to prove a case of implied representation, and reliance, having regard to the terms of advertisements frequently used by banks."[11]

The case of the unworldly borrower who has taken the banks' advertising at its face value is yet to come before the courts. When it does, the advertisers' arguments may (as Gibson J. foreshadowed) meet the same fate as those deployed one hundred years ago against the influenza-struck Mrs Carlill.[12]

Moreover, the social and economic position enjoyed by bankers gives rise to high public and judicial expectations as to their standards of conduct.[13] Much bank advertising—with its talk of "listening",[14] of "backing business, not holding business back",[15] of "liking to say yes"[16]—sets out to encourage these expectations. So, even where the customer has not relied upon any specific

---

8. *Emmett On Title* (19th Edn.) para. 10.074.
9. [1981] Com. L.R. 205.
10. Transcript, pp. 350–353.
11. *Ibid.*, p. 353, para. 12.13.
12. *Carlill* v. *Carbolic Smoke Ball Co.* [1893] 1 Q.B. 256, affirming [1892] 2 Q.B. 484.
13. See, for example, the comments of Woolf L.J. in *Lloyds Bank* v. *Waterhouse* [1993] 2 F.L.R. 97; [1991] Fam. Law 23. "... the Bank's internal rules ... now provide that an intending guarantor *must* receive independent legal advice from a solicitor before executing the relevant document. *This is what I would expect of a responsible financial institution such as Lloyds Bank* ..." (my emphasis). These expectations are the other side of the judicial trust in the reliability of bankers, shown in dicta such as that of Lord Denning M.R. in *Bache & Co.* v. *Banque Vernes* [1973] 2 Lloyd's Rep. 437 at p. 440: "... this commercial practice (of inserting conclusive evidence clauses) is only acceptable because the bankers ... who insert them are known to be honest and reliable men of business who are most unlikely to make a mistake. Their standing is so high that their word is to be trusted ...".
14. Midland Bank Plc.
15. Barclays Bank Plc.
16. TSB England & Wales Plc.

advertisement, he (or she) may be able to rely upon these general expectations[17] as giving rise to an implied obligation[18] upon the bank to look after him in the most important financial transaction of his life, the purchase of his home.

Once start to explain ...

Bank advertisements offering a comprehensive home-buying package may, by offering *some* advice, oblige the banks to give *full and proper* advice throughout the transaction.

Banking lawyers may still debate whether it is the law, as Kerr L.J.'s *obiter* dictum in *Cornish* v. *Midland Bank*[19] suggests, that a bank owes its customers a duty "to proffer to [them] some adequate explanation of the nature and effect of" any security documentation they are asked by the bank to sign.[20] However,

---

17. As Sir Robin Cooke pointed out in his speech to the Ninth Commonwealth Law Conference in Auckland in April 1990, a guiding principle in many recent New Zealand developments, including some in contract and tort, has been "the need to give effect to reasonable expectations": see, for example, *Allied Finance and Investments* v. *Haddow & Co.* [1983] N.Z.L.R. 22, *Day* v. *Mead* [1987] 2 N.Z.L.R. 443, *Gillies* v. *Keogh* [1989] 2 N.Z.L.R. 327, *Elders Pastoral* v. *Bank of New Zealand* [1989] 2 N.Z.L.R. 180. In another New Zealand case, *Brown* v. *Heathcote County Council* [1987] 1 N.Z.L.R. 720, Lord Templeman in the Privy Council said at p. 726 that the Drainage Board's known practice of checking flood levels when building permit applications were referred to it was the equivalent of an express assumption of a duty of care to do so. On that basis, why should not the banks' known (and sometime advertised) standards of best practice be treated as equivalent to an express assumption of a duty of care to conform to those standards?

18. Even after *Tai Hing* [1986] A.C. 80, terms may still be implied into the contract between banker and customer on the basis that they are so obvious that they go without saying, or because the agreement is incomplete, provided that the term is one which must necessarily have been intended by both of them: see *Chitty* (27th Edn.) paras. 13–004—13–007. It would be difficult for a bank to argue that it did not intend a term consistent with its advertising. Until there is a contract between the parties, there is still the usual duty of care between those negotiating: *Esso* v. *Mardon* [1976] Q.B. 801. See also *Henderson* v. *Merrett Syndicates Ltd.* [1994] 3 W.L.R. 761. Once there is a contract, there will in any event be an implied term that the bank will carry out its banking services with reasonable care and skill: Supply of Goods and Services Act 1982, section 13. What a court will regard as reasonable care and skill on the part of the bank may be influenced by the expectations that the banks have encouraged by their advertising.

19. [1985] 3 All E.R. 513, at pp. 522–523; not followed in *Barclays Bank Plc* v. *Khaira* [1992] 1 W.L.R. 623. See also *Small* v. *Currie* (1853) 2 Drew. 102 at pp. 114–115, *per* Kindersley V-C; *Chetwynd-Talbot* v. *Midland Bank Ltd.* (1982) 132 N.L.J. 901; and *O'Hara* v. *Allied Irish Bank Limited* [1985] B.C.L.C. 52.

20. Most major financial institutions in the United Kingdom now subscribe to *Good Banking*— the code of banking practice issued jointly by the British Bankers' Association, the Building Societies Association and the Association for Payment Clearing Services (2nd ed., March 1994). This states (in para 14.1) that banks and building societies will advise private individuals proposing to give them a guarantee or other security for another person's liabilities (a) that by giving the guarantee or other security he or she might become liable instead of or as well as that other person, (b) whether the guarantee or security will be unlimited as to amount or, if this is not the case, what the limit of the liability will be, and (c) that he or she should seek independent legal advice before entering into that guarantee or security. It is likely that a court would be prepared to treat this stipulation as a term of the contract between a subscribing bank and its customer, or at least as providing evidence of what the bank ought to have done in pursuance of its implied obligation (see fn. 18, *supra*) to provide its services with reasonable care and skill. *Midland Bank* v. *Davey* (Court of Appeal, 13 October 1986) suggests that the principle is not to be extended from securities to mandates.

Glidewell L.J.'s formulation in that same case of the extent of the duty arising from the mere fact that the bank had attempted a brief explanation to Mrs Cornish has provoked no similar controversy. According to Glidewell L.J.: "... it is clear that, when Mr Park [the Grade 3 clerk deputed to deal with the execution of the charge] gave the Plaintiff an explanation, he undertook to explain fully and properly on the bank's behalf".[21]

It must be arguable, by analogy with Glidewell L.J.'s reasoning, that once a bank gives *any* advice to a prospective home buyer upon his home loan, it undertakes a duty to advise fully and properly: and it would follow that those banks which begin their advice to their customers in their advertising literature will be subject to this duty throughout the transaction.

Furthermore, once a bank has taken on in this way the responsibility of advertising, it must be unlikely that a court would allow any subsequent disclaimer of responsibility to exempt the bank from its onerous continuing duty.[22]

Low interest, high risk

In cases where banks are subject to the duties I have discussed above, particular situations are likely to call for special care.

A bank offering a "low-start" mortgage is likely to be under a duty to advise the prospective borrower fully and properly as to the problems he may face when the time to repay the rolled-up interest arrives.

Similarly, banks offering house purchase loans in currencies other than sterling will be under a duty to ensure that their customer fully appreciates the risks involved,[23] and is fully aware of the methods by which he can minimise those risks.

Failure to give a full and proper explanation of those aspects of the loans was one of the matters relied upon by Foster J. in holding in the Federal Court of Australia that the bank had been actionably negligent in the case of *Chiarabaglio* v. *Westpac Banking Corporation*.[24] In that case, which concerned

21. [1985] 3 All E.R. 513 at p. 520g–h.

22. Cf. *Smith* v. *Eric S. Bush* [1990] A.C. 831. The chief interest of this case to banking lawyers is that it confirms (by implication) that the standard form disclaimer on banks' status opinions will be ineffective to protect the banks by preventing any duty from arising, unless the disclaimer satisfies the requirement of reasonableness.

23. Under the Consumer Credit (Advertisements) Regulations 1989, all intermediate and full credit advertisements for credit to be secured on the debtor's home must contain the warning that "Your home is at risk if you do not keep up repayments on a mortgage or other loan secured on it", (*ibid.*, reg. 2 and Sched. 1, Part II para. 2 and Part III para. 2). In addition, intermediate and full advertisements for foreign currency mortgages must contain the statement "The sterling equivalent of your liability under a foreign currency mortgage may be increased by exchange rate movements", (*ibid.*, reg. 2 and Sched. 1, Part II para. 9 and Part III para. 16). However, a court would be unlikely to regard any of these brief compulsory warnings as a full and proper explanation of the risks involved.

24. (1989) A.T.P.R. 40–971; affirmed on appeal A.T.P.R. (Digest) 46–067.

a foreign currency loan to a wealthy couple for business purposes, Foster J. indicated that, in his view, an explanation of the nature and effect of the transaction which was adequate in all the circumstances:

"... would, quite clearly, require that there be put before the intending borrower in foreign currencies all matters reasonably envisaged as being relevant to the borrower's decision whether or not to enter into the loan ... It might well be thought that, at the present time, with the disastrous history of such loans now well known, a prudent adviser would not fulfil his duty unless he made reference to such loans in terms similar to those employed by Rogers J. in *Lloyd's* case, where His Honour said that 'venturing into the foreign exchange market ... disqualifies the activity from having any relationship with any accepted notion of prudence ... it is a gamble because unpredictable factors may have immediate and violent repercussions ... As in every true gamble, returns can be very high but so can losses'."

Further advances

Perhaps the most common situation calling for particular care is where a bank uses its standard "all monies" charge form to secure a home loan, and then subsequently makes a further advance[25] in reliance upon the same security. One of the principal differences between the practice of the building societies and that of some banks is this use, even for home loans, of the "all monies" charge form.[26] It was the bank's misstatement that the second charge form, signed by Mrs Cornish[27] to secure a small loan for the renovation of her and her husband's farmhouse home, was "like a building society mortgage" that led to the trouble in that case. In fact, it was an "all monies" charge, and was relied upon by the bank in making further loans to the husband.

Further advances may also give rise to complex Consumer Credit Act 1974 problems for banks. In 1987 the automatic statutory exemption for building society home lending was abolished[28] and replaced with a partial exemption. Banks,[29] whose home lending (within the financial limits) had previously been fully regulated under the 1974 Act, were for the first time given a similar privileged status.[30] The effect was "to put banks and other authorised deposit taking institutions on the same footing as building societies, though starting from opposite ends of the exemption spectrum".[31]

Professor Goode devotes 15 paragraphs of the Introduction to his *Consumer*

---

25. Especially for a purpose unrelated to the purpose of the original loan.

26. In *Lloyds Bank* v. *Waterhouse* [1993] 2 F.L.R. 97; [1991] Fam. Law 23, the Court of Appeal held that the difference between an "all monies" guarantee and a guarantee for a specific transaction was sufficiently fundamental to fulfil the *Gallie* v. *Lee* [1971] A.C. 1004 requirement for the defence of *non est factum*. A similar result would be likely if the documents under consideration were an "all monies" charge and a limited charge.

27. In *Cornish* v. *Midland Bank* [1985] 3 All E.R. 513.

28. Building Societies Act 1986, s. 120 and Sched. 18, para. 10.

29. Strictly speaking, institutions authorised under the Banking Act 1987 and wholly owned subsidiaries of such institutions.

30. Banking Act 1987, s. 88.

31. Goode, *Consumer Credit Legislation*, para. I [631.3].

Credit Legislation[32] to the problems caused by the "unfortunately extremely complex" effects of the 1974 Act[33] on further advances made by building societies on or after 1 January 1987. A discussion of the comparable problems for banks of the reverse process would take nearly as long, and I shall not attempt it here. It is enough to point out that where the original agreement (with any modifications made prior to the further advance in question) was wholly regulated, the modifying agreement created by a further advance by way of fixed sum credit will be wholly regulated by virtue of section 82(3) of the 1974 Act, even though it would have been exempt[34] as to the further advance if the latter had stood on its own.

The customer's remedies

In the preceding paragraphs, I have attempted to indicate those situations in which the duty to explain or advise may arise in connection with banks' home lending activities, and the possible extent of that duty. I now turn to the consequences if that duty does arise, and is broken.

If a bank breaks its duty to explain or to advise, the customer may, of course, recover the amount of any loss caused to him by the breach, provided that that loss is not too remote. Proof of loss will usually require the customer to satisfy the court that, had he been given a proper explanation and proper advice, he would have acted in a different way. Until recently, it could be said with confidence that such proof would be difficult in the case of an ordinary home loan, uncomplicated by further advances or the like. Customers, anxious to buy their own homes in a rapidly rising property market, might be expected to accept the lender's terms unless they were egregiously onerous. However, in today's highly competitive mortgage market, it may be much easier for a customer to persuade a court that, had he been properly advised, he would have accepted the better deal on offer from a competing financial institution.

More worryingly, the disgruntled (or desperate) customer may seek to rely upon the bank's breach of duty in order to seek to set aside the bank's security over the property. The well known (and much cited) case of *National Westminster Bank* v. *Morgan*[35] was, of course, a case involving home lending. The loan there was a bridging loan to refinance a building society loan that had fallen into arrears. The Order of the Court of Appeal,[36] which set aside the

32. Paras. I [2420] *et seq.*

33. Principally of ss. 18 and 82, which deal respectively with multiple agreements and modifying agreements.

34. The current statutory instrument prescribing the conditions for exemption is the Consumer Credit (Exempt Agreements) Order 1989, S.I. 1989 No. 869 (as amended).

35. [1985] A.C. 686.

36. [1983] 3 All E.R. 85.

bank's charge over the legal estate and over the wife's beneficial interest, would have prevented the bank obtaining possession of the property unless and until it subsequently obtained an Order for sale under section 30 of the Law of Property Act 1925, would have prevented the bank from claiming any payment from either Mr or Mrs Morgan for their occupation until sale, and would have preserved for Mr and Mrs Morgan the benefit of Mrs Morgan's share of the proceeds of any such sale.

In *Morgan* the House of Lords held (reversing the Court of Appeal) that, on the facts of that case, the relationship between the bank and the Morgans had never gone beyond the ordinary relationship of banker and customer. There was no general presumption of influence by a banker on his customer. However, Lord Scarman expressly approved[37] the passage from the judgment of Sir Eric Sachs in *Lloyds Bank* v. *Bundy*[38] in which he said "When ... a bank ... goes further and advises on more general matters germane to the wisdom of the transaction, that indicates that it may—not necessarily must—be crossing the line into the area of confidentiality".[39]

Where, as I have indicated, a bank offers its clients a full home lending service, including advice on the commercial wisdom of the transaction, there will be "no substitute ... for a meticulous examination of the facts"[40] to determine whether the bank has crossed the line; and, accordingly, no summary orders for possession without a full and expensive trial.

In *Morgan*, the House of Lords also held that a transaction must be shown to be "manifestly disadvantageous" to the person alleged to have been the subject of undue influence, before it will be set aside. Doubt is cast on that requirement in *CIBC Mortgages* v. *Pitt*.[41] It is extremely unlikely that a straightforward home loan secured by a charge on the property purchased with the money lent could be shown to constitute such a disadvantage. However, if the home loan is connected with some other transaction—for example, an arrangement under which money from the sale of a previous jointly owned home is released to pay off a husband's business indebtedness to the bank, and the new home brought with a fresh loan—or if a building society charge over the old property is replaced by an "all monies" charge over the new, taken in order to secure future business lending to the husband, it is possible to envisage circumstances in which this test of disadvantage could be held to be satisfied.

Another route to avoidance of the bank's security may be the

37. *Ibid.*, at pp. 708–709.

38. [1975] Q.B. 326 at p. 347.

39. Although Lord Scarman indicated that he "would prefer to avoid the term confidentiality as a description of the relationship which has to be proved".

40. Per Lord Scarman, at [1985] A.C. 709C, quoting a remark of Sir Eric Sachs later in the passage already cited. The latest (10th) edition of *Paget's Law of Banking* observes that: "In view of the fact that the position of financial adviser to a customer is one to which many banks properly aspire, it may not be infrequent that a bank has such a relationship of influence with its customer": *ibid.*, p. 485.

41. [1994] 1 A.C. 200.

Misrepresentation Act 1967. If the bank, prior to taking the security, makes a misrepresentation of fact to the mortgagor, the mortgagor, on discovering the true position, has a *prima facie* right to rescind the mortgage. So, in *Barclays Bank* v. *Waterson*[42] the mortgagors claimed that the bank had made misrepresentations to them concerning the condition and value of the premises they were to buy with the mortgage loan. His Honour Judge Ivor Taylor Q.C. held that these alleged misrepresentations gave rise to an arguable claim for rescission and therefore (unlike a claim merely for damages[43]) provided an arguable defence to the bank's claim for immediate possession.

One crumb of comfort for lenders may be the finding of the Court of Appeal in *Banque Keyser Ullmann SA* v. *Skandia (UK) Insurance*[44] that the words of section 2(1) of the Misrepresentation Act 1967 (which speak of a "misrepresentation...made") would "...on the ordinary meaning of words be inapt to refer to a misrepresentation which had not been made in fact but was (at most) merely deemed by the common law to have been made". This suggests that mere failures to explain or advise cannot, by being pleaded as misrepresentations by silence, be turned into grounds of defence to possession claims by lenders under their mortgage securities.

SOLICITORS AND SURVEYORS

Acting for both sides

Banks, in their home lending, tend to follow the pattern set by the building societies, and use the purchaser/mortgagor's solicitor to act also for the bank, provided that the firm is on the bank's panel of recognised solicitors. Despite the obvious possibilities of a conflict of interest between the solicitor's two clients, the bank and its customer, this arrangement usually saves costs.[44a]

One problem which may arise from the arrangement, however, is that it opens up the possibility that the customer may try to blame the bank for the solicitor's (real or alleged) mistakes. *Prima facie*, a solicitor is an independent contractor, for whose torts the bank should not be liable. However, if the bank has a contractual duty to advise the customer, and the solicitor is the bank's solicitor as well as that of the customer, why should he not be regarded as discharging the bank's duty rather than as acting independently for the customer in his own right, when explaining and advising the customer? Similarly, if the solicitor is

---

42. Noted at [1989] C.L.Y. 2505.

43. See *Barclays Bank* v. *Tennet* (unreported, Court of Appeal 6 June 1984); *Citibank Ltd.* v. *Ayivor* [1987] 1 W.L.R. 1157; *National Westminster Bank Plc* v. *Skelton* [1993] 1 W.L.R. 72; *Ashley Guarantee Plc* v. *Zacaria* [1993] 1 W.L.R. 62.

44. [1990] Q.B. 665, at p. 760C–E (affd. on different grounds [1991] 2 A.C. 249).

44a. A solicitor can properly act in a transaction for two parties with conflicting interests provided that he has obtained the informal consent of both parties: *Clark Boyce* v. *Monar* [1994] 1 A.C. 428.

incompetent, could the bank be made liable for having expressly or impliedly approved him as suitable?[45] In both cases, the customer would have a right of action against the solicitor. But he might prefer to pursue his remedy against the bank, in order to reduce or to deter the bank's claim against him.

Valuation is an art ...

Some building societies have their own teams of staff valuers,[46] and some banks may follow suit. If a bank does use a valuer who is in its own employ, it is likely to be held vicariously liable for any negligence he may commit. Also, the bank may feel inhibited from pursuing any remedies it may have against its own employee, even if the bank suffers loss through his negligent valuation.

If the bank obtains an independent valuation, and discloses that valuation to the mortgagor, it will not by that act alone assume liability to the mortgagor for the valuation.[47] However, it *will* be liable to the borrower/mortgagor if it has chosen the valuer (or possibly approved the borrower's choice) but has failed to take reasonable care to select a reasonably competent valuer.[48] It *may* also be liable to the mortgagor if it adopts the valuer's report as its own, for example by referring to it as "our valuer's report".[49]

For its own protection, the bank ought either to obtain its own report from the valuer, or obtain an acceptance by the valuer of responsibility to the bank. Unless the surveyor knows that his report is likely to be shown to the bank in connection with the specific transaction, he may owe them no duty of care.[50] If, as is frequently the case, the valuer has included a clause in his report disclaiming

45. Cf. the views of Lord Griffiths in *Smith* v. *Eric S. Bush* [1990] A.C. 831 at p. 865F–G concerning the mortgagee's liability to the mortgagor for selection of a competent surveyor.

46. See, e.g., *Stevenson* v. *Nationwide Building Society* (1984) 272 E.G. 665, where the building society would have been held vicariously liable for the negligence of their staff valuer but for a disclaimer which John Willmers Q.C. (sitting as a deputy Q.B. judge) held to be reasonable. Local authorities also use their own employed valuers: see, e.g., *Westlake* v. *Bracknell D.C.* (1987) 282 E.G. 868, and *Harris* v. *Wyre Forrest D.C.* [1990] A.C. 831.

47. *Odder* v. *Westbourne Park Building Society* (1955) 165 E.G. 261; *Curran* v. *Northern Ireland Co-ownership Housing Association Limited* (1986) 8 N.I.J.B. 1, reversed on another point at [1987] A.C. 718 but approved on this narrow issue in *Smith* v. *Eric S. Bush* [1990] A.C. 831, at pp. 840D, 840E, 847C, 865F.

48. Per Lord Griffiths, at [1990] A.C., at p. 865E–G.

49. See *Beresforde* v. *Chesterfield Borough Council and Woolwich Equitable Building Society* [1989] 2 E.G.L.R. 149. In that case, the report of the independent valuer was passed to the mortgagor on the society's headed standard form, and described the valuer as "the Society's valuer". The Court of Appeal refused to strike out a claim against the society based on its "adoption" of the negligent report.

50. Cf. the restrictions placed by the House of Lords on the liability of auditors in *Caparo* v. *Dickman* [1990] 2 A.C. 605, the decision of Phillips J. in *Mariola Marine Corp.* v. *Lloyd's Register of Shipping (The Morning Watch)* [1990] 1 Lloyd's Rep. 547 that a surveyor carrying out a routine survey for Lloyd's Register owes no duty of care to a prospective purchaser even though he knows that the prospective purchaser will rely upon his report, and the decision of the Court of Appeal in *Marc Rich & Co. A.G.* v. *Bishop Rock Marine Co. Ltd.* [1994] 1 Lloyd's Rep. 492 that a classification society's surveyor owed no duty of care to the owners of cargo subsequently shipped on board the vessel.

liability to anyone other than his client, a bank may find it substantially more difficult than an individual purchaser of a "dwelling house of modest value"[51] to argue that that disclaimer should not be given effect.

FRAUD UNRAVELS ALL

Wives, parents, and others

There are three common ways in which husbands defraud the banks and their wives or mistresses in connection with house purchase loans. The first is by ignoring or concealing their partner's interest entirely when purchasing or charging the property. The second is by procuring the woman's signature to the charge by misrepresentation, undue influence or duress. The third is by forgery, often with the assistance of the partner's intended replacement. Similar frauds are committed by children on their aged parents and by others in as close a relationship. In all these cases, the bank is not usually able to recover its losses from the husband or child, or from its solicitors or valuers. The contest resolves itself into a dispute between the bank and the innocent wife or parents, as to which of them should suffer for the fraud of the husband.

Ignoring the wife's (or parent's) interest

Where a wife or parent contributes to the purchase price of, or is promised a home for life in, a property to be legally owned by their husband or grown-up child, they will usually have an equitable interest in that property, binding upon the legal owner.[52]

If the legal owner then creates a legal charge over the property without the consent[53] of the non-owning party, the rights of the non-owning party will be

51. "... this is a decision in respect of a dwelling house of modest value ... I expressly reserve my position in respect of valuations of quite different types of property for mortgage purposes. In such cases it may well be that the general expectation of the behaviour of the purchaser is quite different": per Lord Griffiths in *Smith* v. *Eric S. Bush* [1990] A.C. 831, at p. 859G–H.

52. A married (or engaged) claimant may be able to claim an interest founded on contributions to improvements under section 37 of the Matrimonial Proceedings & Property Act 1970 (and in the case of engaged couples, section 2(1) of the Law Reform (Miscellaneous Provisions) Act 1970: see *Bernard* v. *Josephs* [1982] Ch. 391). Otherwise, to establish an interest the claimant must show a contractual licence (*Tanner* v. *Tanner* [1975] 1 W.L.R. 1346), a proprietary estoppel (*Pascoe* v. *Turner* [1979] 1 W.L.R. 431, *Coombes* v. *Smith* [1986] 1 W.L.R. 808: cf. *Re Basham Dec'd* [1986] 1 W.L.R. 1498), or a common intention acted upon in such a way as to give rise to an implied, resulting or constructive trust. There are three illuminating analyses of the legal principles relating to interests arising from common intention in the judgments of the Court of Appeal in *Grant* v. *Edwards* [1986] Ch. 638. See also the comments of Lord Bridge in *Lloyds Bank* v. *Rosset* [1991] 1 A.C. 107 at pp. 132B–133A.

53. The consent, in practice, may amount to no more than a knowledge that some part (however small) of the purchase price is to be raised by the mortgage loan (however large that loan eventually is): see *Paddington Building Society* v. *Mendelsohn* (1985) 50 P. & C.R. 244 and *Bristol & West Building Society* v. *Henning* [1985] 1 W.L.R. 778. This principle, that "... where a wife or other

subordinated to the rights of the chargee unless *(a)* the chargee has notice[54] of those rights, if the land is unregistered,[55] or *(b)* the non-owning party is in actual occupation of the property, if the land is registered.[56]

This type of fraud, where the legal owner raises money on the security of his property, ignoring or concealing the rights of a non-owning but occuping spouse or parent, was described by Lord Oliver in *Abbey National Building Society* v. *Cann*[57] as "... a familiar hazard for banks and building societies advancing money on the security of real property ...".[58]

However, the decisions in *Cann* and in the case heard immediately after it in the House of Lords, *Lloyds Bank Plc* v. *Rosset*,[59] have significantly reduced the risk of this type of fraud to banks. These two cases mark a notable shift of policy in favour of banks and other lending institutions, and against deserted wives and mistresses and defrauded parents.

The facts of *Cann* make sad reading. Mrs Cann had been helped by her son Geroge to buy her home as sitting tenant at a discounted valuation. That first property was bought in the joint names of Mrs Cann and George, with the aid of an endowment mortgage for the whole of the price. George promised his mother that she would have a roof over her head for the rest of her life. When it was sold, however, its successor was bought in Geroge's sole name, again with a mortgage which he alone paid. Eventually George bought his own home, then got into financial difficulties which meant that he could not afford to pay both mortgages. He agreed with his mother than he would sell the second property and buy a third, smaller, less expensive, one for her with the aid of a smaller mortgage. Unfortunately, when he came to buy the third property, he secretly approached the Abbey National for a substantial loan and fraudulently declared that the property was for his own sole occupation. The Abbey National mortgage released £21,000 of the equity from the previous properties for the son's own use. The son defaulted on the mortgage and did not contest the Abbey National's possession claim. Mrs Cann, however, asserted that she had an equitable interest in the property, which was an overriding interest taking

---

occupant claiming a beneficial interest knows that part of the price is being obtained by a mortgage loan, ... the Court will impute to the parties the intention that the rights of the wife are to be subject to the rights of the bank ..." (per Nicholls L.J. in *Lloyds Bank* v. *Rosset* [1988] 3 W.L.R. 1301 at p. 1325) was applied by the Court of Appeal and approved by the House of Lords in *Abbey National Building Society* v. *Cann* [1991] 1 A.C. 56, discussed below.

54. There are three kinds of notice: (1) actual notice; (2) constructive notice—where proper enquiry would have revealed the encumbrance—and (3) imputed notice—where agents such as solicitors or surveyors employed by the purchaser have actual or constructive notice: see *The Law of Real Property* by Megarry and Wade (6th edn.).

55. Where the chargee has notice of the non-owner's equitable interest, the chargee does not qualify as "equity's darling", the bona fide purchaser of a legal estate without notice. See, for example, *Kingsnorth Finance* v. *Tizard* [1986] 1 W.L.R. 783.

56. Land Registration Act 1925, s. 70(1)(g); *Williams & Glyn's Bank* v. *Boland* [1981] A.C. 487.

57. [1991] 1 A.C. 56.

58. [1991] 1 A.C., at p. 76G.

59. [1991] 1 A.C. 107.

priority over the charge by virtue of her actual occupation. By the time the appeal was heard, the amount due under the charge and costs amounted to some £45,000, well beyond the elderly Mrs Cann's means to repay.

The Court of Appeal found in favour of the Abbey National, primarily on the ground that by leaving it to the son to find the small balance of the purchase price of the property, Mrs Cann had subordinated her equity to the mortgage.[60] The Court of Appeal also held that the crucial time for establishing an overriding interest by actual occupation was the time of completion and (Dillon L.J. dissenting on this point) that Mrs Cann had not, on the facts,[61] been in actual occupation at that time.

The House of Lords affirmed the decision of the Court of Appeal, but (while approving the majority reasoning in the Court of Appeal) gave a more fundamental and far-reaching reason of their own why Mrs Cann's claim should fail.

The House of Lords in *Cann* held[62] that where a purchaser relies on a bank or building society loan for the completion of his purchase, the transactions of acquiring the legal estate and granting the charge are one indivisible transaction,[63] at least where there has been a prior agreement to grant the charge on the legal estate when obtained. The purchaser, in those circumstances, never acquires anything but an equity of redemption. It follows that no estoppel or trust binding the purchaser can take priority over the charge, for the purchaser never has the unencumbered legal estate to which that estoppel or trust can attach. The lending institution's charge will always have priority over the claims of the borrower's wife, parent or child: for their claims can only bite on the borrower's own interest, which from the moment of its creation is subject to the prior claim of the lending institution.

The decision in *Cann* could spell the end of *Boland*[64] problems for those lending on mortgage for the acquisition of property. The charges which were considered in *Boland* and *Brown*[65] were both second charges taken *after* the acquisition of the property to secure lending to the husband's businesses.[66] It

---

60. Applying *Paddington Building Society* v. *Mendelsohn* (1985) 50 P. & C.R. 244 and *Bristol & West Building Society* v. *Henning* [1985] 1 W.L.R. 778, discussed above.

61. The man who subsequently became Mrs Cann's husband had started to move in with Mrs Cann's furniture and a carpet layer to lay her carpets 25 minutes before completion, although she herself did not return from holiday until five days later.

62. Applying *Re Connolly Brothers Ltd. (No. 2)* [1912] 2 Ch. 25 and *Security Trust Co.* v. *Royal Bank of Canada* [1976] A.C. 503, and overruling *Church of England Building Society* v. *Piskor* [1954] Ch. 553.

63. The conveyancing problems which this concept of "one indivisible transaction" (per Lord Oliver at [1991] 1 A.C., at p. 92E may bring, for example with the usual wording of the Certificate of Value and with priorities where there is also a simultaneous second mortgage, are touched upon in an article by John Greed at (1990) N.L.J. 816.

64. *Williams & Glyn's Bank* v. *Boland* [1981] A.C. 487.

65. *Williams & Glyn's Bank* v. *Brown*, decided and reported with *Boland*.

66. See the facts set out by Lord Denning M.R. in the Court of Appeal, at [1979] Ch. 326C to 328B.

may also spell the end of such problems for those lending to pay off an existing first mortgage—and thus of the Law Commission's proposals[67] to overturn the decision in *City of London Building Society* v. *Flegg*.[68]

The decision in *Cann*, by establishing the principle of the single indivisible transaction and affirming the principles that the crucial time for establishing an overriding interest by actual occupation is the time of completion (when occupation is unlikely, if the loan is a loan of the purchase price), not the time of registration, and that someone who consents to the raising of money on a charge cannot complain against the lender that too much was fraudulently raised, has made the task of non-owning parties seeking to defend their interests against those of lending institutions markedly more difficult. The decision in *Lloyds Bank Plc* v. *Rosset*[69] will make it more difficult for them even to show that they have an interest to defend.

The bank's charge in *Rosset* was a first charge granted at the time of purchase: but it was given to secure an overdraft allowed to Mr Rosset to cover the cost of renovation of the property (which was semi-derelict) and not to secure the purchase price. That came from the husband's family trust in Switzerland, which insisted that the house be bought in the husband's sole name.

The trial judge held that Mrs Rosset was entitled, as against her husband, to an equitable interest on the basis of her work in the "joint venture" of renovating what was to be the family home, but held that her defence failed because she was not in actual occupation at the date of completion. The Court of Appeal (by a majority) held that she had been in actual occupation, through the builders which she and her husband were employing to renovate the house (by permission of the vendor, between contract and completion) and through her own regular visits to supervise them.

The House of Lords allowed the bank's appeal, and held that Mrs Rosset had no beneficial interest. Lord Bridge (with whose speech the other Law Lords agreed) laid stress upon the insistence of the Swiss Trustees that the house should be in the husband's sole name. He also stressed the distinction between cases such as *Eves* v. *Eves*[70] and *Grant* v. *Edwards*[71]—where the intention that the partner who is not the legal owner should have an interest in the property can be shown by evidence of express discussions—and those such as *Pettitt* v. *Pettitt*,[72] *Gissing* v. *Gissing*[73] and *Rosset* itself, where

"... there is no evidence to support a finding of an agreement or arrangement to share, however reasonable it might have been for the parties to reach such an arrangement if

67. Report No. 188 (December 1989).
68. [1988] A.C. 54. See the further article by John Greed at (1990) N.L.J. 867.
69. [1991] 1 A.C. 107.
70. [1975] 1 W.L.R. 1338.
71. [1986] Ch. 638.
72. [1970] A.C. 777.
73. [1971] A.C. 886.

they had applied their minds to the question, and where the court must rely entirely on the conduct of the parties both as the basis from which to infer a common intention to share the property beneficially and as the conduct relied on to give rise to a constructive trust. *In this situation direct contributions to the purchase price by the partner who is not the legal owner, whether initially or by payment of mortgage instalments, will readily justify the inference necessary to the creation of a constructive trust. But, as I read the authorities, it is at least extremely doubtful whether anything less will do ...*"[74]

The distinction between direct evidence of intention and inferred common intention derives from the speech of Lord Diplock in *Gissing* v. *Gissing*,[75] and has been discussed in many subsequent cases.[76] But the emphasis now laid upon it shows a restrictive tendency. Cases in the first class, where direct evidence of intention is available, are rare.[77]

In the second, much more common, class of case the question of what conduct will suffice to establish an interest has been the subject of some judicial and academic controversy. Where expenditure is concerned, the court will always look for expenditure "referrable to the acquisition of the house".[78] However, most previous statements of principle have not entirely ruled out the possibility that something other than expenditure might do[79]: and Lord Bridge's restatement of his "extreme" doubt that anything other than *direct* contributions to the purchase price will do seems narrower even than the classic formulation by Fox L.J. in *Burns* v. *Burns*[80] of what this much used[81] expression means:

"... a payment could be said to be referrable to the acquistion of the house if, for example, the payer either (a) pays part of the purchase price or (b) contributes regularly to the mortgage instalments or (c) pays off part of the mortgage or (d) *makes a substantial financial contribution to the family expenses so as to enable the mortgage instalments to be paid ...*"[82]

---

74. [1991] 1 A.C., at 132H (my emphasis).

75. [1971] A.C. 886.

76. See, for a recent example, the analyses in *Grant* v. *Edwards* [1986] Ch. 638, per Nourse L.J. at p. 647B–D, per Mustill L.J. at p. 652B–D, and per Sir Nicholas Browne-Wilkinson V.C. at p. 654F–H.

77. Per Nourse L.J. [1986] Ch. 638 at p. 647C.

78. Per Lord Diplock in *Gissing* v. *Gissing* [1971] A.C. 886 at p. 909.

79. For example, "... the necessary common intention, being something which can only be inferred from the conduct of the parties, *almost always* from the expenditure incurred by them respectively ...": per Nourse L.J. in *Grant* v. *Edwards* [1986] Ch. 638 at p. 647B; and "... the judge, in addition to considering the existence or not of an alleged express agreement or understanding, also went on to consider whether or not a common intention could be inferred that the Defendant should have an interest in the house, *even though he did not contribute anything to the cost of its acquisition.* Having regard to the principles established by cases such as *Pettitt* v. *Pettitt*, she was in my view quite right to do this ...": per Slade L.J. in *Thomas* v. *Fuller-Brown* [1988] 1 F.L.R. 245 (my emphasis).

80. [1984] Ch. 317.

81. "over-used", according to Lord Denning M.R. in *Hazell* v. *Hazell* [1972] 1 W.L.R. 301 at p. 304.

82. Explaining and applying *Falconer* v. *Falconer* [1970] 1 W.L.R. 1333 and *Hazell* v. *Hazell* [1972] 1 W.L.R. 301. Cf. May L.J.'s explanation (at [1974] Ch. 317, p. 342H–343A) that the decision in *Hall* v. *Hall* (1982) 3 F.L.R. 379 might be justified on the basis "... that the woman had

Perhaps the most interesting aspects of *Rosset* are the unanswered questions posed (expressly and by implication) by Lord Bridge at the end of his speech.[83] If Mrs Rosset had been able to establish that she had a beneficial interest, would the House of Lords have used a variant of the *Cann* principle to defeat her claim—perhaps on the basis that the prior agreement to grant the charge to secure the renovation overdraft had been perfected by the small contribution to the purchase price that the bank had made as an initial instalment of that overdraft in order to complete the transaction? Or would their Lordships have held that her visits to supervise the builders over a period of six weeks did not have the necessary "degree of permanence and continuity"[84] to amount to actual occupation?

For banks and other lending institutions, *Cann* at last brings some common-sense to the application of the principle[85] enshrined in section 70(1)(g) of the Land Registration Act 1925. This section "... is based upon the notion that the purchaser could, if he made proper enquiries and/or inspection of the property, discover the presence of a person in actual occupation or indications of that occupation which would at least put him on enquiry ...".[86] For the principle to work in practice, the choice of the time of completion rather than the time of registration as the time for establishing an overriding interest by occupation was essential. What use is an inspection after the transaction has already been completed?

Similarly, the rejection in *Cann* of the idea that "mere fleeting presence" by consent of the vendor between contract and completion can amount to actual occupation is to be welcomed. How could a pre-completion inspection in a typical "chain" transaction of domestic purchases and sales reveal the likely presence of someone who might only arrive at the property for the first time that very morning? In a rational system of law matters like this should not be left to be decided by the chance of whether the removal van gets to the property before or after the telegraphic transfer reaches the vendor's solicitors' bank.

It is, however, still open to debate whether such matters should be decided by the strict rules of conveyancing at all. Banks and other lending institutions will argue that the economic health of the country depends on the ability of small businessmen to unlock the capital tied up in their homes in order to invest in their businesses, and that banks will not lend if they cannot be certain of their security. But, in deciding which of two innocent parties—the deserted wife and

---

been working and had been applying substantially all her earnings towards the housekeeping. In those circumstances, it may have been argued that the woman had made an actual financial contribution to the acquisition of the family home, in that her pooled earnings had at the least made it easier for the man to pay the mortgage instalments".

83. [1991] 1 A.C. 107, at pp. 133H–134C.

84. Per Lord Oliver, in *Cann* [1991] 1 A.C. 56, 93G.

85. Cf. the unregistered land concept of notice, for which section 70(1)(g) of the Land Registration Act 1925 is the statutory substitute: see *Kingsnorth Finance* v. *Tizard* [1986] 1 W.L.R. 783.

86. Per Ralph Gibson L.J. in the Court of Appeal in *Cann* (1989) 57 P. & C.R. 381.

children or the bank—should suffer for the deserting husband's debts, considerations of self-interest as well as of social policy might suggest that the bank should bear the loss, because it is better able to. After all, if the deserted wife is evicted to pay the bank, it will be the state—our taxes—which in many cases will have to pay to rehouse her.[87]

Where there is no pre-existing charge, but a creditor seeks a charging order over the deserting husband's interest in the former matrimonial home, the courts will normally transfer the application to the Family Division, where the competing claims of creditors, wife and children can be balanced.[88] If there is no charge, but the husband is made bankrupt by his creditors, the Insolvency Act 1986[89] gives the bankruptcy court discretion to make "such order ... as it thinks just and reasonable having regard to ... all the circumstances of the case other than the needs of the bankrupt" with regard to the matrimonial home. There is a statutory presumption in favour of the family for one year and, thereafter, in favour of the creditors. But this presumption can be displaced where the circumstances of the case are exceptional.[90]

A similar statutory regime dealing with the rights of families in matrimonial homes charged by deserting husbands would have much to commend it. In practice, most banks will be reluctant to evict the very young or elderly victims of third party fraud from their homes. But some lenders still do not appreciate the force of the words of Lord Denning M.R. in *Boland*:

"... if a bank is to do its duty in the society in which we live, it should recognise the integrity of the matrimonial home. It should not destroy it by disregarding the wife's interest in it—simply to ensure that it is paid the husband's debt in full—with the high interest rate now prevailing. We should not give monied might priority over social justice ...".[91]

Misrepresentation, undue influence and duress

A mortgagee will only be affected by the mortgagor husband's mis-representations to, or by the undue influence of a mortgagor husband over,

---

87. Similar considerations would, of course, apply to the situation of elderly parents who have been defrauded by their children.

88. See *Harman* v. *Glencross* [1986] Fam. 81, and *Austin-Fell* v. *Austin-Fell* [1989] 2 F.L.R. 497.

89. Section 336.

90. It seems unlikely that the courts will adopt a less narrow and inflexible approach than that taken under the pre-1986 law, where hardship to creditors has been regarded as the determining factor in deciding whether to postpone sale, irrespective of the hardship to wives and children: see *Re Citro* [1991] Ch. 142, and *Lloyds Bank Plc* v. *Byrne and Byrne* [1993] Fam. Law 183.

91. [1979] Ch. 312 at pp. 332–333. Marc Beaumont, junior counsel for Mrs Cann, has written impassioned articles on the social and legal implications of the decisions of the Court of Appeal (at (1989) Conv. 158) and the House of Lords (at (1990) 87/19 L.S.G. 24). In this second article he comments that "... after *Cann* the banks have won this contest for all time ... the change in this field of the law which this case heralds inclines as far as it can in favour of the moneyed might lobby and away from the protection of the innocent, unenlightened and trusting (possibly aged) victim of mortgage fraud. This money-oriented trend may not be held to be legally defensible by the Courts, nor in time by the Law Commission and Parliament to be entirely morally supportable".

his wife if either (a) the mortgagee had given the husband actual or ostensible authority to exercise the influence or to make representations concerning the guarantee, or (b) the mortgagee had actual or constructive notice of the wrongdoing at the time it took the guarantee.[92]

Where the mortgage is a third-party charge and the mortgagor/guarantor and the principal debtor are living together, the possibility that one may influence the other is so strong that a creditor who knows of the fact of cohabitation will be fixed with constructive notice of any wrongdoing by the principal debtor unless he shows that he has taken reasonable steps to satisfy himself that the surety entered into the obligation freely and in knowledge of the true facts.[93] Unless there are special exceptional circumstances, a creditor will have taken such reasonable steps to avoid being fixed with constructive notice if the creditor warns the guarantor (at a meeting not attended by the principal debtor) of the amount of her potential liability and of the risks involved and advises the guarantor to take independent legal advice.[94]

The best protection against claims of undue influence is to insist that the borrowers take independent legal advice[95] and execute the charge in the presence of a solicitor who endorses his attestation with his confirmation that such explanation and advice has been given. The common practice by virtue of which both bank and borrower use the same solicitor may cause difficulties in this area. To be an effective protection to the bank, the advice ought to be given by a solicitor who is not also acting for the bank.[96] The better (if not always

---

92. *Barclays Bank Plc* v. *O'Brien* [1994] 1 A.C. 180 at p. 195E–G, per Lord Browne-Wilkinson.

93. *Barclays Bank Plc* v. *O'Brien* [1994] 1 A.C. 180 at pp. 198G–199B, per Lord Browne-Wilkinson. In *CIBC Mortgages* v. *Pitt* [1994] 1 A.C. 200, the House of Lords drew a sharp distinction between cases where a wife charges her share of jointly-owned property to secure her husband's liability to repay a loan made to him alone, and cases where the loan is to the husband and wife jointly. "What distinguishes the case of the joint advance from the surety case is that, in the latter, there is not only the possibility of undue influence having been exercised but also the increased risk of it having in fact been exercised because, at least on its face, the guarantee by a wife of her husband's debts is not for her financial benefit": [1994] 1 A.C. 200 at pp. 211G–H.

94. *Barclays Bank Plc* v. *O'Brien* [1994] 1 A.C. 180 at pp. 198G–199B, per Lord Browne-Wilkinson. This apparently simple formula has, unfortunately, given rise to a substantial volume of litigation. See, for example, the following cases: *Midland Bank* v. *Greene* (12 November 1993, Judge Rich QC, Ch.D.); *Allied Irish Bank* v. *Byrne* (1 February 1994, Ferris J.); *Bank Melli Iran* v. *Samadi-Rad* (9 February 1994, Robert Walker QC, Ch.D.); *Home Bridging Plc* v. *Berwin* (24 February 1994, C.A.); *Midland Bank* v. *Serter* (3 March 1994, D. Young QC, Ch.D.); *Midland Bank* v. *Massey* [1994] 2 F.L.R. 342, [1994] Fam. Law 562 (C.A.); *Shams* v. *United Bank Ltd.* (24 May 1994, Judge Bromley QC, Ch.D.); *Nottingham Building Society* v. *Colman* (26 May 1994, C.A.); *Barclays Bank Plc* v. *Boorman* (30 June 1994, C.A.).

95. "All that is necessary is that some independent person free from any taint of the relationship, or of the consideration of interest which would affect the act, should put clearly before the person what are the nature and consequences of the act. It is for adult persons of competent mind to decide whether they will do an act, and I do not think that independent and competent advice means independent and competent approval. It simply means that the advice shall be removed entirely from the suspected atmosphere; and that from the clear language of an independent mind, they should know precisely what they are doing.": per Fletcher Moulton L.J. in *Re Coomber* [1911] 1 Ch. 723 at p. 730.

96. See, e.g., *Lancashire Loans* v. *Black* [1934] 1 K.B. 380.

practical) course is to insist that the wife is represented by a different solicitor to her husband, preferably chosen by her and not by the bank for her.[97] Where the bank has any reason to believe that wrongdoing by the husband is a real possibility, even separate representation may not save the transaction.

Forgery

Banks compete for the business in the home lending market of people who are not otherwise their customers. They are therefore particularly vulnerable in this area to frauds by forgery, since they may have no means to knowing the persons with whom they are dealing outside the transaction itself.[98]

Avoidance of disposition

A bank which has notice of a husband's intention to make a disposition with the intention of defeating his wife's claim for financial relief against him in matrimonial proceedings is vulnerable to a claim by the defrauded wife to set aside the disposition under section 37 of the Matrimonial Causes Act 1973.[99] Such notice may be actual or constructive, and is not limited in the case of registered land to the statutory substitute for notice in the Land Registration Act 1925.[100] Where the husband is a customer of the bank, the bank's knowledge of his affairs may be held to put it on enquiry as to his motives, and so to establish the necessary knowledge to make the transaction a reviewable disposition.

Frauds which need complicity

In the summer of 1987 the press[101] reported the setting up by several banks active in the home loans market of an association[102] to combat the growing problem of home loan frauds. An unnamed banker was quoted as saying: "If you can think of a way of cheating on a mortgage application, the chances are someone has already tried it."

Certainly, home loan frauds take many forms. An honest valuer may be tricked into agreeing an artificially high valuation: or a dishonest one may deliberately put an excessive valuation on a property to release excess funds. A compliant employer may inflate the income information he provides to the lender, in order to assist his employee to obtain a larger mortgage than he can

97. Cf. *Bank of Baroda* v. *Shah* [1988] 3 All E.R. 24.
98. Cf. the facts of *First National Securities* v. *Hegerty* [1985] Q.B. 850.
99. See, e.g., *Perez-Adamson* v. *Perez-Rivas* [1987] Fam. 89, where the bank had failed to make a search at the Land Charges Registry and the wife's claim to set aside the charge in favour of the bank securing a "bridging" loan (with the proceeds of which the husband had fled the jurisdiction) succeeded.
100. *Kemmis* v. *Kemmis* [1988] 1 W.L.R. 1307.
101. See, for example, David Lascelles' article in the *Financial Times* for 22 June 1989, and Peter Gartland's article in *The Times* for 18 July 1987.
102. The Association of Mortgage Lenders.

reasonably afford. The mortgagee may declare that the property is to be for his own sole occupation, and then sub-let to family or on a commercial basis.

But the most serious frauds require the complicity of a solicitor (and often others). The classic mortgage fraud involves obtaining several loans from different lenders on the same property. With mortgage funds readily available from so many sources, perhaps 10 or a dozen loans each perhaps of £50,000 may be obtained with the help of a compliant solicitor, valuer and employer. If this £500,000 fraud is repeated, the conspirators will soon realise enough money to make it worth their while to leave the jurisdiction. The delay in providing title deeds to the lenders can readily be blamed on the Land Registry.

Avoiding such frauds requires care in lending and more thorough investigation of the applicant as well as of the property. The lender relies upon his solicitor and valuer for his protection. So one suggestion for overcoming the problem has been that lenders should maintain panels of solicitors and valuers whose honesty and competence they regularly check, and should refuse to allow anyone not on those panels to act for them. A less draconian suggestion is that this restriction should apply only to sole practitioners.

THE FUTURE

In this chapter, I have tried to draw attention to some of the principal risks that are involved for banks in their home lending activities. I have not touched upon the complications of insurance or pensions linked home loans, upon the problems which may be encountered if the bank attempts to enforce its security, or the complications which may arise if the customer is or becomes insolvent.

In the post-Jack,[103] post-Legal Services Act world the risks to banks engaged in home lending are likely to increase. One-stop shopping for the customer may involve banks in more extensive liability for the valuation and conveyancing aspects of the transaction. The chance of conflicts of interest will increase; and if the present trend of bank advertising continues, customers are increasingly likely to regard the bank as an insurer of the wisdom of the transaction.

Most banks make great efforts to live up to their advertising. The standards of best practice[104] mean little change for them: and for them, the element of risk may remain low. But for some banks, the adoption of these standards will require extensive revision of their procedures.

The most unpredictable feature of the future of home lending by banks is, of course, the state of the property market.

RICHARD SALTER

103. *Banking Services: Law and Practice Report by the Review Committee* (Cmnd. 622, 1989).
104. In the Code of Banking Practice.

CHAPTER 4

RISKS IN SECURED LENDING

This chapter is concerned with some of the things that can go wrong with secured lending, and with the precautions which can be taken, when the security is granted, to ensure that it can be realised (if necessary) with as little delay and expense as possible. Inevitably such precautions are an exercise in assuming the worst, and—it is to be hoped—in the vast majority of cases there will be no need ever to rely on the security, or on any special provisions of the documentation inserted to meet particular risks. But if security is taken at all, it should be framed on the basis that it may have to be enforced, and the draftsman should therefore assume, it is suggested, that the mortgagor will be insolvent and unwilling (or unavailable) to co-operate in realising the security, and that, because of arrears of interest or otherwise, there will be no margin of value in the property, so that it will be undesirable to incur any avoidable costs.

Although in fact the borrower is commonly insolvent when questions of relying on security arise, this chapter does not deal with the effect of the law of insolvency on the validity or the enforcement of mortgages, charges and debentures, and it is not suggested that everything that can go wrong has been identified: the problems of mortgage conveyancing seem to be infinite in their variety. What follows is a discussion of ways in which various principles of the general law can adversely affect security interests in property, and in particular such interests in land. There is no factor common to all types of risk: some of the relevant rules apply to all forms of dealing with property; some, most obviously those governing realisation, but also some of the priority rules, relate specifically to security. The following pages consider a selection of the "risks in secured lending" in approximately the order in which steps can be taken to deal with them.

RISKS ARISING FROM THE CHARACTER OF THE PROPERTY

It is fundamental to transactions of lending "new money" on security that the property should be worth what is lent (with a margin); should be likely to retain its value; and should be capable of being sold under the security quickly and conveniently, without any more applications to the court than are absolutely necessary. (A common example of an essential application is one to obtain vacant possession where the mortgagor is a residential occupier.) As regards valuation, a lawyer's function is to make sure that the valuer knows of any legal burdens which may affect the property's worth: an obvious example would be a restrictive covenant which (if enforceable) might prevent development or some other beneficial use. A slightly less obvious example might be an express grant of a right of way, or of some other essential easement, in restricted terms, such that it would not be exercisable in connection with some changed use of the property; alternatively, it might be that a property otherwise ripe for development in conjunction with an adjoining parcel should not be valued on that basis because of the principle that an easement appurtenant to Blackacre (adjoining) may not be exercised substantially for the benefit of Whiteacre (mortgaged). (*Harris* v. *Flower* (1904) 74 L.J. Ch. 127.)

It is also fundamental, and obvious, that the form of security should be appropriate to the property over which it is taken: thus where the value of the property derives from a business, for instance mineral extraction, the security should be such as will enable the creditor to realise that business, including both the land and the equipment, as a going concern: in practical terms, working gravelpits or similar properties should be charged by way of floating rather than fixed security. (Hotels, restaurants and public houses raise the same point, with the additional complication that in any realisation it will also be necessary to protect and preserve the liquor licence.) If security over industrial premises takes the form of a charge over the land but does not specifically include essential machinery, there will be a question whether any, or how much, of that machinery is a fixture, and therefore included in the charge; such questions are best avoided. Appropriate security in all such cases can only be taken from a company: a floating charge by an individual would be ineffective (except in the special case of a charge by a farmer to a bank), and a fixed charge of movable chattels would be registrable as a bill of sale, which would adversely affect the borrower's credit. The inclusion in the security of provisions appropriate to the special character of the property is desirable, to deal with conveyancing technicalities, in (at least) two other situations: where a block of flats may have to be realised by the grant of long leases, and where land is (or may become) cut off from access and services by other, uncharged, land belonging to the borrower.

Flats

It is arguably not open to a mortgagee of a block of flats to adopt the ordinary course of granting long leases of empty units at a premium, reserving only a ground rent and service charge, if the security confers no more than the statutory powers of sale and leasing. The Law of Property Act power of leasing only authorises the grant of a 50-year term, and requires the lease to reserve the best rent reasonably obtainable "without any fine being taken" (see section 99(3)(i) and (6)), so it cannot be used to grant a lease for 99 or 125 years in consideration of a capital sum and a small ground rent. The writer's personal view is that the power of *sale* does in fact justify the grant of such leases, because as a matter of conveyancing practice that is the normal way of realising such an asset: in *Re Judd and Poland and Skelcher's Contract* [1906] 1 Ch. 684, C.A., it was held that trustees might exercise a power of sale over leasehold property, in terms similar to a mortgagee's power under section 101(1)(i) of the 1925 Act, by dividing the property into lots and granting sub-leases. But it is understood that the Land Registry does not accept this reasoning; so the safe course must be to insert a power to grant leases, at a premium and for terms of up to perhaps 150 years, when taking a mortgage either of an unlet block of flats, or of a let block where voids may be expected on the termination of protected, or short-term, lettings.

"Island" sites

It is not unknown for there to be a mortgage of a piece of land which is cut off from any highway and will need, if realised, access and service easements over other land of the borrower: such a situation can be created directly, and can also arise as a result of arrangements for the phased release of completed parts of a development from a financier's security. It is understood that some practitioners do not regard this as creating any difficulty. However, in the present writer's view there is a potential technical problem (created by the abolition in 1926 of the possibility of *assigning* land by way of mortgage) in that the mortgagor remains the freeholder of both the dominant and the servient land, and cannot have rights in fee-simple, appurtenant to the dominant mortgaged land, against himself as owner of the servient land; and although appropriate easements could be granted to the mortgagee, by the mortgage, there seems to be a risk that they would only be appurtenant to the security interest, and would be extinguished with it on the power of sale being exercised. (See *Beddington* v. *Atlee* (1887) 35 Ch. D. 317 at 323–324, and Law of Property Act 1925, section 88(1)(b).) Nor, it is thought, would it be wholly safe to rely on the general law of implied grant of easements to create the appropriate rights on any exercise of the mortgagee's power of sale: if the mortgagor had previously disposed of the uncharged servient land, he might well have retained no more than "easements of necessity" appurtenant to his freehold interest, which is the interest that would be the subject of the mortgagee's sale. The safe course (in the absence of any decision that something simpler is effective) seems to be to adopt variants of the conveyancing mechanisms used for the realisation of equitable security. First, the mortgage can constitute the mortgagor a trustee of the freehold of the mortgaged land together with appropriate easements, and there are dicta in *Ecclesiastical Commissioners* v. *Kino* (1880) 14 Ch. D. 213, which suggest that trusteeship of the dominant land prevents unity of possession and allows fee-simple easements to exist. Secondly, the mortgage can contain a covenant by the mortgagor to grant appropriate easements over the neighbouring land in favour of any purchaser under the power of sale: *Rymer* v. *McIlroy* [1897] 1 Ch. 528, indicates that a covenant can create easements commensurate with whatever interest the covenantee or his successors may have or later acquire. (Such a covenant operates in equity and should be registered.) Thirdly, the mortgage can confer on the mortgagee a security power of attorney to give effect to the mortgagor's obligations in a realisation. Where the problem of an "island" site does not exist when the security is granted, but may arise later because of arrangements for the phased release of security, on partial discharge of the secured obligations as a development proceeds, it is also possible (and, it is suggested, advisable) to include in the security documentation a provision making it a condition of the right to a release that appropriate fee-simple easements are then created over the land released, for the benefit of that remaining in mortgage: if the released land is simultaneously transferred to a third party, there will be no conveyancing difficulty in complying with such a condition, and it will be for the mortgagor's benefit as well as for that of the mortgagee to ensure that the retained land has proper access and services.

OTHER PARTIES' INTERESTS EXISTING AT CREATION OF SECURITY

Pre-existing third party rights are mentioned above as being relevant to valuation. Such rights are not necessarily detrimental to lenders: a lease of a commercial property at a full rent to a reliable tenant may well be positively desirable. It is important for a lender to find out what rights there may be: that is the purpose of searches and inspections—and the corollary is the registration of the security when taken, so that it can be discovered by, and will be binding on, subsequent mortgagees, purchasers and tenants. It is not proposed to deal in this chapter with the routine of searches and registration: those are very important procedures, but they appear to work reasonably smoothly in practice. Additional precautions are necessary in relation to those interests in land which do not need to be registered and are discoverable by inspection, but which may in practice be missed if the lender does not inspect, or may attach to the land in the interval of time between the making of an inspection and completion of the security: if the mortgagee does not discover such interests when the security is created, but only on a question of enforcement arising, it will be too late to put matters right. Unregistrable interests commonly belong to persons in occupation, and risks arise if the mortgagor either does not obtain vacant possession, or enters into occupation before the security is completed; in the latter case the lender may lose priority to an occupier whom the mortgagor lets in before his own purchase is completed, but the House of Lords' decision in *Abbey National B.S.* v. *Cann* [1991] 1 A.C. 56, has significantly reduced the risk a lender runs in ordinary circumstances. The cases decided before *Cann* show such problems arising in relation to tenancies created before the mortgage, and in relation to beneficial interests under resulting or constructive trusts— typically in favour of the mortgagor's spouse.

Tenancies

If a prospective purchaser P is let into possession by the vendor V before completion, purports to grant a tenancy to T, and subsequently takes a conveyance from V and simultaneously mortgages the property to M, T has a "tenancy by estoppel" as against P, who cannot be heard (as between himself and T) to deny his own grant, and can be required by T to give effect to the tenancy—the estoppel is "fed"—when he acquires an interest out of which it could be created. But where the mortgage to M is made under a previous binding agreement by P to grant that security on completion, the purchase and mortgage are to be regarded as a single, indivisible transaction: see *Abbey National B.S.* v. *Cann* [1991] 1 A.C. 56 at 89A–93C and 101G–102C, H.L., overruling *Church of England B.S.* v. *Piskor* [1954] Ch. 553, C.A. The result appears to be that the relative priority of T and M is governed by the rule that as between competing equitable interests, the first in time prevails: their interests are both equitable before actual completion of the purchase. T will therefore be postponed to M if the agreement between P and M to create a mortgage on completion was made before P let T in as tenant: see *Cann, loc. cit.*, per Lord Jauncey of Tullichettle at 101B. If this be right, it is submitted that if the agreement between P and M is to preserve M's priority where the transaction is after 27 September 1989, it must comply with section 2 of the Law of Property (Miscellaneous Provisions) Act 1989, and in particular must be signed by or on behalf of both parties: compare pages 145–147 below. The extent of the disadvantage to M, if priority is lost, depends on the length of T's tenancy, and on whether T has any form of statutory security of tenure after it expires: when the *Piskor* case was decided, the Rent Acts considerably extended T's right to remain (if the letting was unfurnished). If T's tenancy is, for instance, a "shorthold" under the recent housing legislation, there is much less security of tenure, and so less risk to M: even if P lets T remain after the original tenancy expires, M has priority to any new tenancy P then grants to T. But if money is being lent on the basis of a vacant possession valuation, M will normally prefer to make sure that there is never a T whose interest has priority or may be argued to have priority to the mortgage; and that raises the question of what precautions should be taken at completion. It is understood that Sir Nicolas Browne-Wilkinson V-C has held (in an unreported decision at first instance) that a solicitor, who acted on a purchase for both the purchaser and the building society mortgagee, was not liable in negligence to the society where (to the solicitor's but not the society's knowledge) the property was occupied by a protected tenant of the vendor, and the solicitor released the advance at completion in reliance on the purchaser's false statement that the tenant had gone; the purchaser absconded, the security was deficient, and as between the solicitor and the lender the latter bore the loss, because the solicitor had no reason to suppose the purchaser was fraudulent and untrustworthy, and was under no duty, it was held, to tell the society there was a tenant in the premises. If it is decided to take precautions against mortgage frauds of this nature, it is thought that complete protection will only be obtained by someone inspecting the property on the lender's behalf on the day of completion, before the release of the advance is authorised; and it seems that in order to identify some of the cases in which it is desirable to have such an inspection, the lender's instructions to its solicitors and valuers should contain an express requirement to report the presence of a tenant (unless the mortgage is specifically agreed to be subject to that tenancy), and also to report if the borrower obtains possession before completion.

Resulting, etc., trusts

This is the familiar *Boland* problem (*Williams & Glyn's Bank Ltd.* v. *Boland* [1981] A.C. 487): typically, husband and wife live in a house which is registered in the husband's sole name; both work; both contribute directly or indirectly to paying for the property (for instance by keeping down instalments on a building society mortgage); the wife therefore has an interest in the property by way of resulting or constructive trust; she is in "actual occupation" within section 70(1)(g) of the Land Registration Act 1925; and therefore her interest is an "overriding interest" which is binding on a mortgagee who lends to the husband. The greatest risk to a lender arises from a loan to the registered proprietor for purposes not connected with the house: if the mortgage is essential to the acquisition of the property, the result will often be that the wife is found to have known that fact, and is held to have intended the mortgage to have priority. (Compare *Bristol and West B.S.* v. *Henning* [1985] 1 W.L.R. 778.) A similar argument may be available where the transaction is a re-mortgage, and the original mortgagee is calling in a loan which itself has priority over the beneficiary's interest. (Compare the facts of *NWB* v. *Morgan* [1985] A.C. 686.) It has even been held that a re-mortgage of which the occupying beneficiary is ignorant is nevertheless good against him or her up to the amount secured by the original mortgage. (*Equity & Law Home Loans Ltd.* v. *Prestidge* [1992] 1 W.L.R. 137: it is suggested—compare *loc. cit.* at 145D—that the beneficiary's interest is to be regarded as subsisting only in the part of the property, or of its proceeds, which represents its value in excess of the amount secured by the original mortgage.) Further, where the mortgage finances the initial acquisition of the property, on the most recent authority the beneficiary must be "in actual occupation" at the time of completion (i.e., when the purchase price is paid to the seller and the mortgage deed is unconditionally delivered to the lender), in order to obtain priority; the House of Lords has approved the decision of the Court of Appeal that it is not sufficient to go into occupation between completion and the effective date of registration, even though it is only on the latter date that the proprietor and the lender obtain legal estates in the property: see *Abbey National B.S.* v. *Cann* [1991] 1 A.C. 56, approving *Lloyds Bank* v. *Rosset* [1989] Ch. 350. In *Cann*, the court investigated in some detail whether the legal formalities were completed, and payment was made, before or after anything amounting to "occupation" was taken on behalf of the party claiming a beneficial interest; and it seems that in other similar cases it may equally be necessary to enquire whether the conveyancing formalities, and in particular the grant of the mortgage, were completed before or after the beneficiary arrived at the new house with the furniture van.

"Waivers"

The arguments outlined above may enable a mortgagee to assert priority; but it is desirable in all cases, especially where the lending is not related to the acquisition of the property, expressly to protect the mortgage's priority when it is created. Lenders appear, in practice, not to investigate exactly what interest an occupier may have, but rather to try to ensure that the mortgage has priority to the occupier's interest (if any), whatever it may be. The commonest course is to ask each adult occupier or proposed occupier to sign a document agreeing not to assert against the mortgagee any rights he or she may have, and acknowledging that the mortgage may if necessary be enforced against the entire interest in the property. There are numerous different forms of such waiver documents in use; it is suggested, however, that the only safe course is to treat any such form as a third party security: that is what it will in fact be if the occupier does have a beneficial share of the property but the mortgagee is to be entitled to take (if necessary) the entire proceeds of realisation. (Some precautions appropriate to the taking of third party security are outlined in the next section of this chapter.)

Trust for sale

An occupier's interest most commonly takes the form of a beneficial share in the house and its proceeds of sale, so that under the general law the registered proprietor technically holds the property on trust for sale. In some circumstances it is possible for the mortgage to be granted by two or more trustees for sale, and to overreach all the beneficial interests under the general law. (See *City of London B.S.* v. *Flegg* [1988] A.C. 54; Trustee Act 1925, s. 17; Law of Property Act 1925, s. 27.) That result is most likely to be produced where (as in the *Flegg* case) there is a properly constituted, or apparently properly constituted, trust for sale in existence before the proposal to mortgage the property is made, and the advance is for purposes authorised by the trust— which effectively means, in relation to registered land, purposes not forbidden by any restriction entered on the Register of Title. However, it does not follow that a sole proprietor who appoints a second trustee for sale, and purports to give the trustees wider powers of mortgaging than they would have under the general law, will succeed in overreaching an occupier's interest: as against an occupier with an interest under a resulting or constructive trust, the original proprietor and a new co-trustee have only the powers of mortgaging conferred by law—which do not include power to give security for money previously lent, or for money lent to one trustee in his private capacity, or even for money lent to enable the property to be bought. (See *Re Suenson-Taylor's Settlement* [1974] 1 W.L.R. 1280.) It is thought that if a sole proprietor executed a transfer to himself and another as trustees for sale, purporting to confer wide powers of mortgaging, a solicitor acting in the transaction might have difficulty in presenting the transfer for registration on the basis that there was to be no restriction of the trustees' powers of mortgaging to those conferred by the general law, if in fact (and to the solicitor's knowledge) there was a pre-existing trust for sale under which the trustees had only limited powers of mortgaging as against a third party occupier who was beneficially interested, and the object of the transaction was to defeat the third party's rights. If the transfer were nevertheless registered without any such restriction, the court might still find that the lender actually knew the second trustee had been appointed for the purpose of overreaching the occupier's interest, by a mortgage for an unauthorised purpose; and, it is thought, it would be at least arguable in those circumstances *either* that the occupier's interest was an "overriding" interest in relation to a mortgage which the trustees had no power, as against him, to grant, *or* even that the lender was not entitled to the protection conferred by the Land Registration Act 1925 on a purchaser "in good faith".

MORTGAGE DOCUMENTS: VITIATING FACTORS

Individuals

A contention that a mortgage is for some reason not binding, or ought to be rectified against the lender, is usually raised by someone who has given security for money lent to another: a borrower who has actually received a loan (and spent it) is not in a position to avoid liability by attacking the security. Special care is therefore needed when taking a third party security, including a guarantee, to ensure that the obligor cannot later claim to have been misinformed about the transaction, or to have entered into it under the undue influence of the principal borrower. An allegation of misinformation appears to be raised most frequently in relation to the "all monies" nature of banks' standard form documents: a guarantor or third party mortgagor will often say he thought, or that the lender told him, that the guarantee or security covered only the particular loan to the principal debtor which was contemplated when the document was executed, and that it therefore should not include further advances made later without reference to the guarantor/mortgagor. See *Lloyds Bank* v. *Ellis-Fewster* [1983] 1 W.L.R. 559, where it was contended that the instrument ought to be rectified so that it did not apply to further advances, and the defendant obtained leave to defend in Order 14 proceedings. It seems to be desirable, therefore, that any explanation of such a security which the lender may give, should specifically refer to the fact that it will cover future advances as well as the present one.

"Undue influence"

The relationships in which the existence of influence is traditionally presumed— priest and penitent, doctor and patient, solicitor and client, parent and unemancipated child—have so far proved less important in the field of securities than the relationships of husband and wife, worldly-wise son and elderly parent, and banker as his customer's trusted financial adviser, in which influence is not presumed but may be possible to show in fact. A transaction may be set aside for undue influence if the relationship between grantor and "influencer" is presumed or proved to have been such that the grantor's act was not the result of an exercise of free and independent judgement, though where undue influence is presumed but express influence is not specifically proved (see *C.I.B.C. Mortgages Ltd.* v. *Pitt* [1994] A.C. 200 at 209B–E) it must also be shown that the transaction was manifestly disadvantageous to the grantor. This requirement of "manifest disadvantage" was emphasised, and was important to the result, in *NWB* v. *Morgan* [1985] A.C. 686, where the mortgage procured by the bank's alleged "influence" secured money lent in order to redeem a prior building society mortgage which was in arrear, and which the society was threatening to realise: in effect Mrs Morgan was no worse off with the property charged to the bank than she had been whilst the prior mortgage existed. The decision is also important because it stresses that although a fiduciary relationship giving rise to a presumption of undue influence can exist between banker and customer (as was found in *Lloyds Bank* v. *Bundy* [1975] Q.B. 326), that is not the normal situation, and such a relationship does not arise merely from the fact of the banker explaining the effect of the transaction, without proffering advice on whether it is a wise one. Where the grantor's relationship with the principal debtor is within one of the traditional classes of presumed undue influence, or is shown (as will ordinarily be the case as regards the debtor's wife or cohabitee) to be such that there is a substantial risk of the debtor having exercised undue influence over, or misrepresented the effect of a guarantee or third party mortgage to, the grantor, and the transaction is on its face not to the grantor's advantage, the lender will be held to have constructive notice of any such influence (actual or presumed) or misrepresentation, and will be unable to rely on the guarantee or mortgage, *unless* he has taken reasonable steps to satisfy himself that the grantor's agreement to enter into the transaction was properly obtained: *Barclays Bank Plc* v. *O'Brien* [1994] A.C. 180 at

196D–F. The House of Lords has indicated (*ibid.* at 196G–197B) that in order to avoid being fixed with constructive notice in such circumstances, the lender should at least require to see the grantor personally in the absence of the principal debtor, and should at that meeting explain the extent of the grantor's liability under the proposed transaction, warn of the risk run, and urge the taking of independent legal advice. It is understood that in practice many banks and other lenders now go further, and insist on independent legal advice being taken in all such cases. The Court of Appeal has held that such advice complies with the substance of the House of Lords' guidance even if there is no meeting with the grantor alone, and that the lender is not concerned with the nature and extent of the advice given by the independent solicitor: *Midland Bank Plc* v. *Massey*, 18 March 1994 (reported in *The Times*, 23 March 1994).

A transaction procured by undue influence is voidable, not void: it is very rare for a document to be a complete nullity under the plea of *non est factum*. But since an "equity" to have a transaction set aside is capable of being enforced against third parties who have notice of it, the Court has held, in relation to registered land, that an occupier's right to have a transfer rectified is capable of being an "overriding interest" within the Land Registration Act 1925, s. 70(1)(g): *Blacklocks* v. *J.B. Developments* [1982] Ch. 183. The argument can therefore be advanced that a right to set a conveyance aside for undue influence is also an "overriding interest" if the grantor remains in occupation, and it follows that particular care is necessary when taking a "waiver of rights" from someone who has recently conveyed the property to the mortgagor, if the relationship between them is one in which there is a risk of undue influence having been exercised.

Companies

The *ultra vires* principle has become of less and less practical importance over recent years at least in relation to companies registered under the Companies Act, as opposed to bodies incorporated by special statutes. (Compare *Rosemary Simmons Memorial Housing Association Ltd.* v. *United Dominions Trust Ltd.* [1986] 1 W.L.R. 1440, applying strict common-law principles of *ultra vires* to a housing association incorporated under the Industrial & Provident Societies Act 1965.) With effect from 4 February 1991, Companies Act 1985, sections 35 to 35B and 322A (inserted by Companies Act 1989, sections 108 and 109) effectively abolish *ultra vires* in relation to Companies Act companies, so that direct lending, at least, will not be vitiated because the money is to be used for a purpose not covered by the objects clause in the memorandum of association. But, in relation particularly to third party security, it seems possible that a transaction may still be unenforceable if the directors act in excess of their authority, and in breach of their fiduciary duties, in causing the company to enter into it, if the other party knows of the wrongdoing or of facts which put him on enquiry. The decision in *Rolled Steel* v. *British Steel* [1986] Ch. 246, remains good law under the amended legislation: although new section 35B of the 1985 Act provides that a party to a transaction is "not bound to enquire" as to any limitation on the directors' powers, nevertheless the section does not protect such a party who does in fact know of such a limitation and that it is being exceeded. It is therefore suggested that, for the avoidance of disputes as to the existence of such knowledge, it is still a wise precaution to establish that there is a commercial justification for the giving of "upstream" or "cross" guarantees or securities by one company in favour of its holding or co-subsidiary companies.

Equitable securities over land: lender's signature

Section 2 of the Law of Property (Miscellaneous Provisions) Act 1989, which came into force on 27 September 1989, provides by subsection (1) that "a contract for the sale or other disposition of an interest in land can only be made in writing and only by incorporating all the terms which the parties have expressly agreed in one document or, where contracts are exchanged, in each", and by subsection (3) that "the document incorporating the terms or, where contracts are exchanged, one of the documents incorporating them (but not necessarily the same one) must be signed by or on behalf of each party to the contract". The section gives effect to Law Commission recommendations, and is designed to get rid of the complexities of section 40 of the Law of Property Act 1925, now repealed, and to abolish the doctrine of part performance. But the new section has its own problems. The difficulties relevant to this chapter arise *first* because ordinary agreements to lend on security—facility letters and offers of advance—may be subject to the section if they create obligations to grant mortgages, and *secondly*, because in the past—for other purposes—the courts have also analysed equitable securities over land as contracts to grant legal mortgages.

It is submitted that the common form of facility letter or offer of advance, whereby a lender agrees that a loan will be available on security being completed before or simultaneously with draw-down, is *not* a "contract to dispose of an interest in land" within section 2, because the borrower is never under any executory obligation to grant security: he can normally proceed or not, as he chooses (even if there is an unsecured obligation to pay an arrangement fee, or the lender's costs, in any event). Further, any defect in the initial arrangements will have no continuing adverse effect on the terms of the loan, or on the security, if in fact the transaction proceeds as contemplated: even if, immediately before completion and draw-down, there is a "contract" for secured lending avoided by section 2, that section will have no further application when the loan has been made and the security granted: compare *Tootal Clothing Ltd.* v. *Guinea Properties Management Ltd.* (1992) 64 P. & C.R. 452. Nevertheless, it is possible that a problem will arise if a lender allows the money to be drawn down before the mortgage has actually been executed; and until the position has been clarified there will also be at least a risk of a borrower defeating an application for summary judgment, in what should be a straightforward case, by arguing that the section raises a triable issue. (The possible priority advantage of having an enforceable agreement for a security has already been mentioned: page 139 above.) It is understood that at least some institutional lenders are adopting the practice of requiring all facility letters and offers of advance, and all variations made to them, to comply with the strictest interpretation of section 2: it is doubtful whether the usual letter signed by the lender by way of offer, with a copy countersigned by the borrower as acceptance, is an "exchange of contracts" within the section (compare *Commission for New Towns* v. *Cooper (Great Britain)* [1993] N.P.C. 115), and therefore the copy for counter-signature, it is thought, should for the sake of safety also be signed by the lender or on his behalf.

As regards equitable securities, a deposit of title deeds, where the deposit rather than any accompanying memorandum is the principal security, has been said to be both evidence, and part performance (by both borrower and lender), of a contract for a mortgage: see *Birch* v. *Ellames* (1794) 2 Anstruther 427. A "charge" of whatever land the borrower may, at some unspecified future date, acquire, has also been held to be effective because it is a specifically enforceable contract—although neither at law nor in equity can it operate as an immediate alienation of non-existent property: see *Holroyd* v. *Marshall* (1862) 10 H.L.C. 191; *Re Clarke* (1887) 36 Ch. D. 348. There are even statements applying a contractual analysis to an instrument framed as an immediate equitable charge: compare *Palmer* v. *Carey* [1926] A.C. 703. It has been held at first instance, in *United Bank of Kuwait plc* v. *Sahib & others*, 24 June 1994, per Chadwick J. (reported in *The Times*, 7 July 1994), that an agreement to grant a mortgage of land and a deposit of the land certificate for the purpose of security were both contractual arrangements which had to satisfy the requirements of section 2; the court specifically rejected the contention that a security by deposit is something distinct from an equitable charge arising by agreement. Unless and until an appellate court decides these issues in the opposite sense, it follows that a lender cannot rely on a deposit of title deeds (or of a land certificate) alone as creating security, and that documents creating equitable security—including documents primarily creating legal mortgages but with additional equitable charges of, for instance, any other interest in the land the borrower may acquire—must now be signed by the lender, as well as executed by the borrower, contrary to what was the normal practice before section 2 came into force. It remains arguable in the appellate courts, and at first instance in relation to the immediate equitable charge of land already belonging to the borrower (not expressed as an executory agreement for a charge), that despite the authorities mentioned and others to similar effect, section 2 of the 1989 Act does not apply to established forms of equitable security. First, it can be said that such securities, although they may have developed out of mere contractual relationships, should now be accepted as distinct legal institutions, and are not "contracts" for the purposes of section

2. Alternatively, it can be said that the principles of "proprietary estoppel" apply where a borrower has been paid money on the footing that the lender is to have security for its repayment; but proprietary estoppel is a notoriously unreliable weapon: it gives the court a discretion to do whatever is fair in all the circumstances as they appear at the end of the trial; it may be that the lender will have difficulty in establishing that it is appropriate on this basis to give full effect to a security which was taken in respect of "old" monies, if all the borrower received in exchange for the security was a few days or weeks of forbearance; and it may be held that the court should not re-introduce part performance "by the back door" in order to assist a lender who omitted to sign the security documents—to do so, it will be suggested, is an obvious and simple precaution. So, subject to the effect of future judicial decisions, the safe course will be always to take equitable security over land by means of a document, rather than by deposit of deeds or certificate as the operative security; and for someone to sign the document on the lender's behalf. (The agency should be such as can readily be proved, which means that as a practical matter the agent should be appointed in writing, even though that is not one of the requirements of section 2.) All this applies to equitable securities over specified land; to securities in general terms over after-acquired land, including debentures creating floating charges which will apply to such land; and to immediate equitable charges of "all the borrower's land". It probably also follows that a "waiver of rights", taken from an occupier who may have an interest in property, is capable of being analysed as a contractual dealing with the occupier's equitable interest, and should for safety's sake be signed on the lender's behalf: section 2 expressly defines an "interest in land" as including an interest in proceeds of sale.

MATTERS SUBSEQUENT TO CREATION OF SECURITY

Further advances

It is well established that a mortgage securing an overdraft or other running account may lose its priority to a subsequent incumbrance, if the mortgagee has notice of it, through the operation of the "rule in *Clayton*'s case" that credits and debits to a running account are set against one another in date order: even if the total amount of the overdraft does not increase, payments in are appropriated to the earliest indebtedness and extinguish it, whilst payments out create new debt, for which the security ranks below any incumbrance of which the lender then has notice. This is a risk of which lenders are well aware, and the practice is to "rule off" the borrower's account as soon as notice of an incumbrance is received (thus preserving the priority of the security for the debt as at that time), and to pass subsequent credits and debits through a separate account which has to remain in credit. Some lenders insert provisions in their security documents deeming the account to be "broken" in this way, without any action on the lender's part, on receipt of such notice: such a clause in a guarantee was held effective in *Westminster Bank* v. *Cond* (1940) 46 Com. Cas. 60, and it is submitted that a similar clause in a mortgage is equally effective.

The position is less straightforward, and it is submitted that the statutory protection apparently given to lenders is less complete than at first it appears, in relation to mortgages securing further advances which the mortgagee is obliged to make. One such transaction is a loan to finance a development project, made available on terms that it is to be drawn down in tranches to meet the sums payable by borrower to builder on successive certificates under the building contract. Another example—of particular relevance in times of high interest rates—is a "low start" or "reduced payment" facility under a residential mortgage: to give the borrower the full benefit of tax relief under the MIRAS system, such a facility has to operate as payment by the borrower of the *full* monthly instalment, immediately followed by a loan from the lender, back to the borrower, of the difference between the full payment and the amount to which it is to be reduced. At first sight, in either situation, the further advances to be made by the lender might seem to have their priority preserved by the Law of Property Act 1925, s. 94(1)(c) if the land is unregistered, or by the Land Registration Act 1925, s. 30(3) if the land is registered: both those provisions give further advances priority, if the lender is obliged to make them, even against subsequent mortgages of which he has notice. But the position is more complicated. First, it is common practice in such circumstances for the terms of the facility to entitle the lender to withhold further advances if in fact he receives notice of a subsequent incumbrance: if the lender has a choice whether or not to make an advance, it is not safe to assume that if he does make it he will be held to have acted pursuant to a binding obligation. (There appears to be no case law to show whether this analysis is correct, but it is put forward by Mr Lingard: see *Bank Security Documents*, 3rd Edn. para. 8.18.) Secondly, in the case of registered land, there appears to be a hiatus in the relevant statutory provisions. Section 30(3) of the Land Registration Act 1925 preserved the priority of obligatory further advances against "a subsequent registered charge", and *ibid.* subsection (1) also regulates priority in relation to entries on the register; but there is nothing in section 30 to protect further advances against incumbrances of which the lender has notice but which do not lead to an entry on the register—for example an overriding interest arising in favour of an occupier who pays for an extension to the property. Section 94(1) of the Law of Property Act 1925 at least confers protection against "subsequent mortgages (legal or equitable)", but by subsection (3) it does not apply to "charges registered under the Land Registration Act 1925". The result appears to be, somewhat oddly, that if a mortgagee of registered land receives notice of an unregistrable incumbrance or other disposition, the effect on an obligation to make further advances is still governed by the rules which applied before the law was changed in 1926; and the old rule was that, independently of anything in the lending documents, an obligation to make further advances was discharged by the lender obtaining such notice, because the borrower could no longer give the security he had contracted to provide: see *West* v. *Williams* [1899] 1 Ch. 132. (The same pre-1926 principles apply, it is thought, in relation to the priority of obligatory further advances so far as they are secured on an interest in proceeds of sale of land—if, for example, it is correct that a "*Boland* waiver" is a substantive security, as is suggested on page 141 above.) The conclusion to be drawn, it is submitted, is that the protection apparently given to obligations to make further advances is at best incomplete, and the safe course is (a) to include in the documentation a right to cease making further advances on receipt from any source of notice of a subsequent incumbrance or disposition, and (b) always to exercise that right on receiving such notice, unless and until satisfactory priority arrangements can be made with the other incumbrancer or disponee.

Charges with statutory priority

There are some statutory claims which rank as charges with absolute priority to every interest in land, including pre-existing mortgages. See, for example, *Paddington B.S.* v. *Finucane* [1928] Ch. 567, relating to a charge in favour of a local authority, under the Housing Acts, for work done to make premises fit for habitation. The works in question were said to have been beneficial to every interest in the land, and that was regarded as justifying the interpretation of the Act as giving the charge first priority. (A similar justification can be put forward in support of the paramountcy of maritime liens over ships for the cost of "necessaries", and of airport authorities' rights to detain and sell aircraft to recover landing charges, etc: everyone interested in the ship or aircraft benefits from it operating rather than lying idle, and the expenses in question are incurred to enable it to operate.) There does not seem to be any reliable way in which a mortgagee can protect himself against such incumbrances, though it will be of some help in the case of a commercial borrower to inspect the trading accounts periodically, to ensure that obligations are being discharged as they fall due.

Leases

Where the mortgaged property is agricultural land, it is not possible to exclude the mortgagor's statutory power to grant leases which will bind the mortgagee: see Agricultural Holdings Act 1986, s. 100 and Sched. 14, para. 12. It follows that even if such land is in hand when mortgaged, the lender should not rely on being able to realise it for more than its tenanted value.

Where the mortgaged property is itself leasehold, there is a risk that the security will be destroyed if the landlord successfully forfeits the lease on the ground of breach of covenant by the mortgagor tenant. A mortgagee is entitled to apply for relief against forfeiture: see Law of Property Act 1925, s. 146(4), operating in conjunction with *ibid*. s. 87(1) where the security is a legal charge rather than a mortgage by subdemise. The mortgagee must apply for relief whilst the landlord "is proceeding" for forfeiture, i.e., before the forfeiture has been completed by actual re-entry. (See *Official Custodian for Charities* v. *Parway Estates* [1985] Ch. 151, and associated authorities.) Since 1 October 1986, a landlord enforcing a forfeiture by court action, in the High Court or the County Court, has been required by Rules of Court to give notice of the proceedings to any mortgagee of whom he knows, so the risk of the mortgagee not hearing of a forfeiture in time will be greatly reduced if notice of the security is given to the landlord (and an acknowledgement of receipt of the notice is obtained), though there is a residual risk of a successor landlord saying that he knew nothing of such a notice given to his predecessor. There is also a slight risk of the landlord completing a forfeiture by peaceable re-entry; but that is normally only possible if the tenant has left the property vacant, and in that event the mortgagee will probably be considering taking steps to protect the security, and will be entitled even after the re-entry to apply for relief against forfeiture if the landlord has not obtained a judgment for possession, though the grant of relief is a matter of judicial discretion and may be refused if, for example, the application is made late and third parties have acquired rights which would be prejudiced if relief were granted: compare *Billson* v. *Residential Apartments Ltd.* [1992] 1 A.C. 494. A mortgagee who obtains relief against forfeiture will have to take a new lease from the landlord, and will be directly liable on the covenants it contains (*Re Good's Lease* [1954] 1 W.L.R. 309), but will hold it subject to the same right of redemption as the mortgagor had in respect of the old lease (*Chelsea Estates* v. *Marche* [1955] Ch. 328). The result is not one which a mortgagee is likely to find particularly attractive; but it is better than complete loss of the security if the lease is valuable in itself, or is essential for the continuation of a valuable business.

Perpetuity

It may be that a security over after-acquired land, given by a corporate borrower to a corporate lender, becomes void for perpetuity as regards land acquired more than 21 years after the date of the security, by virtue of section 10 of the Perpetuities and Accumulations Act 1964. If the point ever arises, it is likely that the terms on which loan facilities are made available will allow the lender to call in his money if the security ceases for any reason to be fully effective; so as a practical matter a new charge of future land, to which a new perpetuity period will apply, may well be granted (if requested) just before the first perpetuity period expires. It is not suggested that this problem will be a common one.

TAKING POSSESSION

Strict accountability to mortgagor

Although a mortgagee is entitled to take possession of the mortgaged property (unless the deed excludes or postpones the right) whether or not the mortgagor is in default, lenders have traditionally been reluctant to exercise that right unless it appears to be necessary to do so in order to protect or realise the security, because a mortgagee in possession is strictly accountable for all the income of the property he receives or might receive but for "wilful default". If he occupies the property for his own benefit, he must credit the mortgagor with an occupation rent; if he lets it for less than a full rent, or unnecessarily allows a tenant a rent reduction, he must credit the mortgagor with the whole rent he could have obtained; he is liable to the mortgagor for any negligent damage to the property or, if it is leasehold, for negligently allowing the landlord to forfeit the lease. The textbooks say that a mortgagor who takes "possession" of tenanted property by entering into receipt of the rents is safe if he collects the full amounts reserved under leases which bind him; but even in that situation, it is submitted that in modern conditions there is a potential liability, if such a lease contains a rent review clause and the mortgagee fails to operate it, or agrees the revised rent at an unnecessarily low figure. (Compare *Knight* v. *Lawrence* [1991] 1 E.G.L.R. 143, where mortgagors recovered damages against a receiver for failing to serve rent review "trigger" notices, which depressed the price received when the mortgagees later sold the property.) The usual course, therefore, where it is desired to manage the mortgaged property over a period without selling it, is to appoint a receiver or a receiver and manager, who will operate initially as the mortgagor's agent, and will not (necessarily) be treated as acting for the mortgagee even if the agency is determined by the bankruptcy or liquidation of the mortgagor. It is advisable to widen the power conferred on a receiver by the Law of Property Act 1925, s. 101(1)(iii): that is a power to appoint a receiver of "the income of" the mortgaged property, and it is therefore at least doubtful whether a receiver can be appointed, under that power, to manage and look after property which is not let and therefore does not produce income. It is submitted, however, that a mortgagee who takes possession with a view to selling need not fear an account "on the footing of wilful default", unless it would be possible to obtain some interim income without risking either delaying the sale or depreciating the price eventually obtained. It would arguably not be right for a mortgagee of an exhibition hall to cancel bookings for events which were scheduled to take place before a sale could be organised: that course would lose some income, and quite possibly would also damage any "goodwill" element in the value of the premises. But (as far as is known) it has not yet been contended that a mortgagee who obtains possession of residential property when the market is slack, and decides to wait for the next selling season, should create a "company let" or a shorthold tenancy over the interim period.

Liabilities to third parties

A mortgagee who takes possession of property, and as a result is in actual control of it, is potentially under the same obligations in respect of nuisance, or under the Occupiers' Liability Act 1957, as any other person in control of land. He may also be liable under various statutory provisions imposing obligations on the "owner", where the term is defined as "the person entitled to receive the rent or who would be so entitled if the property were let"—compare Highways Act 1980, ss. 152 *et seq.*, 305 and 329(1), relating to obstructions, fences, retaining walls, etc., or on near highways—or as "the person entitled to possession"—compare General Rate Act 1967, s. 17 and Sched. 1, para. 13, relating to empty rate. (Similar provisions apply for the purpose of the uniform business rate, under the Non-Domestic Rating (Empty Property) Regulations 1989, S.I. 1989 No. 2261.)

SALE

Duty of care

It is now established that a mortgagee exercising a power of sale owes the mortgagor a duty of care, on ordinary common-law principles, to take reasonable steps to obtain "the true market value" or "the proper price" of the property: *Cuckmere Brick* v. *Mutual Finance* [1971] Ch. 949, C.A.; *Tse Kwong Lam* v. *Wong Chit Sen* [1983] 1 W.L.R. 1349, P.C. (The duty of care in negligence relates only to the price obtained on the sale, and does not supersede the established equitable principles governing the realisation of securities: *China and South Sea Bank Ltd.* v. *Tan Soon Gin* [1990] 1 A.C. 536, also holding that the mortgagee may choose the time at which to sell, and is not under any *duty* to realise his security such as to give rise to a liability to the borrower, or to a surety for the debt, for a decline in the value of the property; *Downsview Nominees Ltd.* v. *First City Corporation Ltd.* [1993] A.C. 295.) A receiver exercising a power of sale is under a similar duty of care: *Standard Chartered Bank* v. *Walker* [1982] 1 W.L.R. 1410. (The latter case is also relevant to the definition of the class of persons to whom the duty is owed, considered further below, and as indicating that a mortgagee or debenture holder will be liable for a receiver's defaults if in fact it controls and directs the receiver's activities.) It is important, if the mortgagee or the receiver is to discharge his duty, to ensure that the sale is fully advertised, and the need for advertisement places a gloss on the established principle that if a mortgagee acts in good faith the court will not interfere with his decision to sell immediately rather than to delay in the hope that a depressed market will rise (see *Reliance P.B.S.* v. *Harwood-Stamper* [1944] Ch. 362): the duty of care must oblige the mortgagee not to fix the sale at so early a date that there is no time to advertise it appropriately. The duty also requires that features of the property tending to increase its value should be publicised, and that publicity should be directed to the whole range of potential buyers; it is not necessarily enough to sell by public auction rather than by private treaty. There are other points which may arise but (as far as is known) have not yet been decided. Is a mortgagee under the same duty as a trustee to "gazump" if he receives a better offer whilst a proposed sale is still "subject to contract"? (Compare *Buttle* v. *Saunders* [1950] 2 All E.R. 193.) It is suggested that there may be such an obligation, but that the mortgagee is entitled to consider that "a bird in the hand is worth two in the bush", particularly if the second offer involves delayed completion or is conditional on the new purchaser raising finance. Does the mortgagee's duty require him to incur expense not merely on advertising, but also on putting the property in a condition to fetch a better price? It seems arguable, though not certain, that in a clear case this may be necessary; but even if £1,000-worth of repairs would add £5,000 to the amount realised, without delaying the sale, and the mortgagee had a margin of security, it could be said with some force that the mortgagor ought to put up the money for work which was going to enure for his benefit; and if on any basis the security would be insufficient, it would be a strong thing to require the mortgagee to risk more of his own money.

The duty of care is owed to the mortgagor, and also to any third party who has guaranteed the mortgage debt and will therefore have to pay more if the primary security realises less than it should: see *Standard Chartered* v. *Walker*, already mentioned. A subsequent encumbrancer also has a right of action if a breach of a prior mortgagee's duty of care (or a breach of his equitable duties) causes him loss: *Downsview Nominees Ltd.* v. *First City Corporation Ltd.* [1993] A.C. 295. It is therefore submitted that if A has a first mortgage of Blackacre and Whiteacre, and B has a second mortgage of Blackacre alone, a negligent failure by A to realise the full value of Whiteacre will give B a cause of action if it creates or increases a deficiency on the second mortgage of Blackacre through A taking more of the proceeds of that property than he should have done. Allowing a cause of action to B on those facts would increase the range of possible plaintiffs, but would not increase the total potential liability: the result of so extending the scope of the duty would merely be to enable whoever in fact suffered by its breach to recover his loss.

"Self-dealing"

A purported "sale" by a mortgagee to himself is "no sale at all", and unless barred by lapse of time the mortgagor can subsequently redeem the property. A sale to an individual, firm or company with whom the mortgagee is closely connected is not absolutely void, but there is a heavy onus on the purchaser to show that the price was a proper one and the sale was fairly conducted. See the *Tse Kwong Lam* case, mentioned above, and the Australian decision in *Latec Investments* v. *Hotel Terrigal* (1965) 113 C.L.R. 265: in both cases a sale to a company associated with the mortgagee was held to have been liable to be set aside, notwithstanding that the sale was by auction.

CONCLUSIONS

As was said at the start of this chapter, there is no real common theme to the precautions which can be taken in relation to secured lending. The only general conclusions the writer feels able to draw are that security requires continual vigilance, and that taking precautions when the security is granted can prevent trouble arising later. Whether the risk of any particular form of trouble is worth the cost of taking precautions against it is not a question to which a general answer can be given.

GREGORY HILL

CHAPTER 5

DOMESTIC ENVIRONMENTAL LIABILITY

INTRODUCTION

The concept of "lender liability" for environmental harm is, at present, a concept unknown to English law. Indeed, it may be that the more it is taken seriously as a concept by lenders, and the more precautions are taken, the less likely it is that the concept will take root in English law. Put briefly, the essence of lender liability is that the lender, be it a bank or other financial institution, must take some responsibility for the acts and defaults of the borrower to which it lends.

The liability referred to could be criminal or civil. The lender could be fined for polluting a river, be found liable to pay clean-up costs or ordered to pay compensation to affected persons. There are also non-legal but commercially important risks of increased exposure or vulnerability to environmental harm, for example the risks of lending to a company which may go out of business because it failed to secure a particular licence or taking security over land which becomes worthless because of contamination.

Any discussion of lender liability should also include many non-legal factors such as the prospect of insurance for environmental damage, the impact of pollution on property valuation and importantly the effect of bad publicity on the lender's business.

The concept of lender liability originated in the United States and Canada. It is from an analysis of the way in which the concept has been developed in these jurisdictions that we can best foresee how it might develop in English law. The North American cases are also relevant for two other reasons. First, there is the international nature of much large lending and the possibility that part of the lending will be in North America. Secondly, many North American lenders and other financial institutions may have insured at Lloyd's of London against risks associated with environmental liabilities.

LESSONS FROM NORTH AMERICAN JURISDICTIONS

The framework of environmental protection in the United States is contained in what is known as the Superfund scheme. The scheme was enacted in the Comprehensive Environmental Response, Compensation and Liability Act

1980 and amended by the Superfund Amendments and Reauthorisation Act 1986. The Acts set up a large fund which can be used by the Environmental Protection Agency to clean up a contaminated site. Those costs are then recoverable from "potentially responsible parties". Liability is strict and there is no requirement of proof of fault. Although there is a defence provided for the "innocent landowner" who can show that the pollution was caused by a third party or a previous owner of the land, there is built into the defence a "due diligence" requirement which requires the landowner to show that he neither knew nor had reason to know that the land was being contaminated.

It is clear that the Superfund regime has the scope to turn into a classic "deeper pockets" refund scheme, in which the authorities would look to the wealthiest institution to refund their clean-up costs. It is noteworthy that when the regime was instituted it was not seen as heralding new risks for lenders. A series of important decisions has had that effect. Lenders should take heed that for financial institutions environmental legislation can be the legal equivalent of a wolf in sheep's clothing.

The reason why lenders were confident that the Superfund legislation would not affect them adversely was the "secured creditor" exception. The provision protected a person who was not an "owner or operator" who "without participating in the management of [the] facility, holds indicia of ownership primarily to protect his security interest in the ... facility". The effect of the provision, of course, depended upon the way the courts chose to interpret the crucial words "management of the facility".

The decision in United States v. Mirabile[1] had the effect of reassuring lenders that there was indeed nothing to fear from the legislation. A distinction was drawn between "participation in purely financial aspects of operations" and "participation in operation, production or waste disposal activities". The former did not invite liability; crossing the rubicon into the latter had the effect of voiding the secured creditor exemption.

The court rejected "mere financial ability to control waste disposal practices" as sufficient to impose liability. The court recognised that there were arguable policy considerations for placing liability on those most able to pay ("deeper pockets") but stated that the legislature had expressly excluded secured creditors from the legislation.

The Mirabile distinction was applied in the later case of Guidice v. BFG Electroplating & Manufacturing Co.[2] in which a bank was held not to be liable in respect of its pre-foreclosure activities. These had included attending meetings at which it was informed of the presence of raw materials, communicating with officials regarding discharges, inspecting the property after operations had ceased, restructuring the lending and communicating with a prospective purchaser regarding waste disposal. The court held that all these acts were

1. 15 E.L.R. 20994 (E.D. Pa 1985).
2. 732 F. Supp. 556 (W.D. Pa 1989).

undertaken in order to protect the bank's security interests, rather than to control the facility's operation. The bank was however held liable for the post-foreclosure period because it had purchased the site at the foreclosure sale.

Matters, so far as lenders were concerned, took a turn for the worse in the case of *United States* v. *Maryland Bank & Trust*.[3] On the face of it, the case was consistent with the earlier authorities in that a bank was held liable for an acquisition following foreclosure. The court held that the acquisition had been a step to protect the bank's investment rather than a step to protect its security.

It was the policy basis of the decision which was more worrying for the bank. The court held that too much emphasis should not be placed on the "grammar" of the "hastily conceived compromise statute". The court refused to "carve a judicially created loophole in the statutory structure" by putting a mortgagee in a better position than a purchaser and said that it intended by its decision to encourage "prudent lending". It stated that "mortgagees ... have the means to protect themselves by making prudent loans. Financial institutions are in a position to investigate and discover potential problems in their secured properties. For many lending institutions, such research is routine. [The legislation] will not absolve them from responsibility for their mistakes of judgment."[4]

The move away from the *Mirabile* test which was hinted at in *Maryland Bank & Trust* was evident in the landmark decision of *United States* v. *Fleet Factors Corporation*.[5] The initial hearing was an interlocutory application by the lender to strike out a claim for clean-up costs as failing to disclose a cause of action. The lender's application failed and the court rejected the *Mirabile* test. Instead the court proposed a test based on the lender's "capacity to influence" the borrower's treatment of waste. It was not necessary for a creditor to be involved in day to day operations nor to operate in management decisions. "A secured creditor will be liable if its involvement with the management of the facility is sufficiently broad to support the inference that it could affect hazardous waste disposal decisions if it so chose."

The creditor in this case was a lender under a factoring agreement. The lender had approved the goods shipped, set prices and controlled access to the facility, as well as supervised the office administration of the facility. The court held that this was sufficient to render the lender the "owner or operator" of the site. The *Mirabile* test was rejected as being too permissive.

Although the court in *Fleet Factors* emphasised the "overwhelming remedial" aim of the legislation, there were two holdings by the court which provided some comfort to lenders in what was otherwise a disappointing decision for them. First, the court rejected the submission that any manner of participation by the lender would take the lender out of the exemption and render it liable under the legislation. That submission would drive a coach and horses through the

---

3. 632 F. Supp. 573 (D.Md. 1986).
4. *Supra* at 580.
5. 901 F. 2d 1550 (11th Cir. 1990), cert denied, 111 S.Ct. 752 (1991).

exemption which Congress had specifically provided. Secondly, liability would not arise merely as a result of the creditor monitoring any aspect of the debtor's business or giving specific management advice to the debtor.

The *Fleet Factors* decision provides a difficult dilemma for lenders. On the one hand, a lender wishes to monitor the borrower in order to know when to support and when to bring to an end the borrower's activities. On the other hand, the closer the creditor gets to the borrower's activities the more likely it is that a court will find that the creditor is so involved in the borrower's activities as to render it liable for clean-up costs. The court also has a dilemma. It wishes to attach potential liability to lenders so that they will monitor their borrowers and prevent pollution. But instead of producing lenders who scrutinise their borrowers to minimise risks of liability, it may produce lenders who, for fear of being held liable for pollution costs, deliberately avoid any real involvement with or supervision of the borrower but will nonetheless lend to the unsupervised borrower.

There have recently been signs of a move away from *Fleet Factors*. In *Re Bergsoe Metal Corporation*[6] the capacity test was rejected. The court preferred to ask what the creditor actually did rather than what rights the creditor had. But in allowing *Fleet Factors* to stand without comment, the Supreme Court was seen as having endorsed the general approach of that case.[7] In the more recent case of *State of Wisconsin* v. *Better Brite Plating Inc.*[8] the trustees in bankruptcy escaped liability for pollution on the basis of the confused relationship between insolvency and environmental law. The court also emphasised the policy reasons why the law should not provide disincentives on insolvency practitioners to accept appointments.

The American Environmental Protection Agency has provided its own definition of the secured creditor exemption. It stated that all *bona fide* security interests fall within the secured creditor exemption. It also urged pre-lending environmental assessment for all loans secured on commercial or industrial properties. Most importantly, it has provided a list of instances when the creditor is taken to have participated in management decisions. Crucially for lenders, the fact that the lender has the capacity, the ability to influence or the unexercised right to control facility operations was held not to be sufficient to impose liability.

Interestingly, this was not enough to save the lender in *Fleet Factors* itself. The case was remitted back to the District Council which found that the lender's actions in foreclosure had gone beyond the EPA guidelines and accordingly held the lender liable.[9]

6. 910 F.2d 668 (9th Cir. 1990). This approach was followed in *In re: River Capital Corporation* 191 Bankr. LEXIS 2152 (Bankruptcy, 1991) and *Grantors to the Silresim Site Trust* v. *State Bank & Trust Company* 1992 US Dist. LEXIS 20612 (D.Mass, 24 November 1992).

7. 111 S.Ct. 752 (1991).

8. 466 NW 2d 239 (1991) and 1992 WL 105598.

9. 819 F.Supp. 1079 (S.D. 1993) and 821 F.Supp. 707 (S.D.Ga. 1993).

In Canada, there has been an important decision which illustrates the overlap between environmental law and insolvency law. The Canadian decisions are arguably of even greater importance than the American decisions because English courts will more readily take notice of Canadian decisions. The case of *Panamericana De Bienes Y Servicos* v. *Northern Badger Oil & Gas*[10] turned on whether an Order in Council obtained by the Energy Resources Conservation Board requiring the payment of clean-up costs ranked in a liquidation before or after the claims of the secured creditors. The Alberta Court of Appeal reversed MacPherson J. at first instance who had held that the clean-up costs were simply a claim provable in the bankruptcy.

The Court of Appeal did not characterise the issue as whether the Board was avoiding the statutory priority scheme but rather whether the agency had a duty to clean up the facility as part of the "general law". The court held that the agency was not simply a creditor with a provable debt but a public authority with a duty to enforce a public law. Since there was no creditor, there was no question of the statutory scheme being subverted. It is clear that the court was strongly influenced by policy considerations, stating that the creditor should not be allowed to take the benefit of the property while leaving the environmental liabilities for the public to bear. "If one of the wells which the Receiver has chosen to control should blow out of control or catch fire, it would be a remarkable rule of law which would permit him to walk away from the disaster saying simply that remedial action would diminish distribution to secured creditors."[11]

The case could be interpreted as simply stating that a receiver runs the risk of liability when he accepts appointment over a polluting facility. But the lesson may be of a more general nature—that all receivers should carefully consider the implications of accepting an appointment over a potentially polluting facility and should insist on both a full environmental audit and an appropriate and adequate indemnity.

CIVIL LIABILITY

It is important to appreciate that domestic civil law itself provides potential liability in a number of areas. The first is private nuisance. Liability in private nuisance may arise where an activity on the defendant's land represents an unlawful interference with the plaintiff's use or enjoyment of his own land or of some right over or in connection with that land. However, to succeed in private nuisance, the plaintiff must himself have an interest in land. It can be seen therefore that while private nuisance may be of use to an adjoining landowner, it

10. (1989) 75 Alta L.R. (2d) 185 per MacPherson J., revsd by Alberta Ct. of App. (1991) 81 D.L.R. (4th) 280.
11. Per Laycraft C.J.A., delivering the judgment of the Alberta Court of Appeal, at 297–298.

is of little use to groups of people, or perhaps specialist interest groups, who themselves have no interest in land but may be affected.

In public nuisance, however, the plaintiff need not show an interest in land. The test for public nuisance liability is whether the defendant has committed an actionable wrong which has materially affected the public, that is a sufficiently large class of people. In public nuisance there is, unlike private nuisance, no question that damages can be awarded in respect of personal injury and pure economic loss.

The third avenue of civil liability is the well-known rule in *Rylands* v. *Fletcher*.[12] There is strict liability for damage caused by the escape of hazardous substances kept on land. Although this is an obvious avenue for the imposition of liability for environmental damage, the courts have restricted rather than developed the use of this case, even to the extent of a suggestion in the authorities that liability under *Rylands* v. *Fletcher* requires fault.[13] In addition to this, the courts have interpreted "non-natural" user of the land in a very restricted manner. The courts have used a principle of public interest to characterise as "natural" land uses which are seen to have a public benefit.

In *Cambridge Water Company* v. *Eastern Counties Leather plc*[14] the House of Lords, contrary to the judge's finding, held that the use of solvent in the tanning process and its storage constituted a non-natural use of the defendant's land. However, the House of Lords held that foreseeability of harm of the relevant type was a prerequisite for the recovery of damages both in nuisance and under the rules in *Rylands* v. *Fletcher*. This limitation on the rule in *Rylands* v. *Fletcher* severely restricts its use as a means to establish liability for environmental damage.

The fourth and perhaps most obvious avenue of liability is that in negligence. Negligence of course requires both foreseeability and fault, although in environmental damage cases the plaintiff may be much assisted by the evidentiary doctrine *"res ipsa loquitur"*.

The fifth and final avenue of liability at common law is breach of statutory duty. Crucial questions in this area are to whom is the duty set out in the statute intended to be owed, and whether the statute intended to grant the individual the ability to sue. The second question is what kind of harm was the statute intended to prevent, because only that kind of harm will be actionable.

THE PRESENT LAW

Although the concept of lender liability for environmental harm is of recent origin, it should be set against existing and well-settled law which can impose

12. (1868) L.R. 3 H.L. 330.
13. *Read* v. *Lyons (J.) & Co. Ltd.* [1947] A.C. 156.
14. [1994] 2 W.L.R. 53.

similar liabilities on lenders in certain circumstances. In particular, the law has imposed various obligations on mortgagees in possession. In *Maguire* v. *Leigh-on-Sea UDC*[15] a mortgagee in possession was held liable for local authority works and in *Westminster CC* v. *Haymarket*[16] it was held that a mortgagee in possession was liable to pay a rating surcharge. There is also authority for imposing statutory liability as "occupier" on a local authority serving a compulsory purchase order[17] or a receiver accepting his appointment.[18]

The scope of liability may be far wider than mortgagees in possession and receivers. A bank will be held liable for the defaults of a receiver if it "gives him directions or interferes with his conduct of the realisation"[19] or by exercising a degree of control over the board of directors sufficient to characterise it as a "shadow director".[20]

In the seminal case of *Midland Bank* v. *Conway*[21] the bank was in regular receipt of rents paid by the tenant of a property owned by its customer. The bank paid the rents into the customer's account. The local council served a noise abatement notice on the bank because for the purposes of the notice,[22] the "owner" of the property was "the person for the time being receiving the rackrent of the premises ... whether on his own account or as agent or trustee for any other person".[23] The bank was held liable by the justices but succeeded on appeal by way of case stated.

The High Court, in quashing the conviction on the ground that, despite the wording of the Act, merely handling what the bank knew were rent cheques was not enough to constitute the bank the "owner" of the property. The bank was simply acting as a "conduit pipe"[24] or an "office boy".[25] However, all three judges emphasised that the case concerned only the normal relationship of bank and customer and that if there were "special circumstances"[26] the bank might be liable. No guidance was given on what those circumstances might be but they might well be analogous with factors resulting in the bank becoming a "shadow director".

The approach of this case can be compared with that of *Meigh* v. *Wickenden*[27] where a receiver was treated as "occupier" for the purposes of breach of statutory duty under the Factories Act 1937. The receiver was liable because

15. (1906) 95 L.T. 319.
16. [1981] 1 W.L.R. 677.
17. *Harris* v. *Birkenhead* [1981] 1 W.L.R. 1380.
18. [1942] 2 K.B. 160.
19. *Standard Chartered Bank* v. *Walker* [1982] 1 W.L.R. 1410.
20. *Re A Company No. 005009 of 1987 ex parte Copp* [1989] B.C.L.C. 13.
21. [1965] 1 W.L.R. 1165.
22. Served under the Public Health Act 1936.
23. *Ibid.*, section 343.
24. *Bottomley* v. *Harrison* [1952] 1 All E.R. 368.
25. *Watts* v. *Battersea Corporation* [1929] 2 K.B. 63.
26. At 1170B per Lord Parker C.J., at 1172E per Sachs. J. and at 1173D per Browne J.
27. [1942] 2 K.B. 160.

"the occupier's responsibility under the Act does not depend on proof of personal blame or even on knowledge of the contravention. The policy of the Act seems to be to fasten responsibility, in the first instance, on the occupier.[28] Thus the receiver was liable because of his potential power of management and control, rather than any need for the actual exercise of control.[29] This approach is not far from the "capacity to control" test of *Fleet Factors*.[30]

However, although these cases show that English law has the potential to impose lender liability without any requirement for a radical change of direction, to overemphasise the way in which courts have approached the definition of various terms in non-lender or non-environmental cases is dangerous. "No useful progress can be made ... by inquiring what meaning the courts have given [the word 'occupier'] in reported cases, for they draw their meaning entirely from the purpose for which and the context in which they are used.[31]

CRIMINAL LIABILITY

Criminal liability can have important civil liability implications. First, there is the civil liability which results from breach of statutory duty, in those cases in which such a breach can lead to an award of damages. Secondly, a criminal conviction can be adduced as evidence in a civil claim. Thirdly, criminal sanctions may be enforceable in civil courts. It is not, nor could it be, the purpose of this chapter to set out in full the many and varied legislative enactments with which a prudent lender should be familiar. However, there are certain themes running through the environmental regulation, and in particular the structure of the regimes governing the four most important areas, namely air pollution, water pollution, waste on land and statutory nuisance. These areas are dealt with in the Environmental Protection Act 1990 ("EPA 1990") Part 1, the Water Resources Act 1991 ("WRA 1991") Part 3, EPA 1990 Part 2 and EPA 1990 Part 3.

The first characteristic is that under each of the regimes, the polluter commits a criminal offence.[32] In most cases the maximum fine in a magistrates' court is £20,000 and an unlimited sum in a Crown Court. Each scheme also gives wide

---

28. Per Lord Caldecote at 164–165.

29. See also *Lord Advocate* v. *Aero Technologies* 1991 S.L.T. 134 where the same approach was used. Lord Sutherland said that provisions under the Explosives Act 1875 were "in the interests of public safety ... [which] should not be eluded on some highly technical ground" (at 136).

30. Cf. *Ratford* v. *North Avon DC* [1987] Q.B. 357 where under the General Rate Act 1967 the company and not the receiver was the occupier, the receiver being saved (unlike in *Meigh* v. *Wickenden*) by the usual "agent of the company" clause in the debenture and appointment.

31. *Southern Water Authority* v. *Nature Conservancy Council* [1992] 1 W.L.R. 775 at 781 per Lord Mustill quoting *Madrassa Anjuman Islamia* v. *Municipal Council of Johannesburg* [1922] 1 A.C. 500 at 504 per Viscount Cave.

32. Air pollution: EPA 1990, section 23, carrying on one of the activities designated a "prescribed process" in section 2;

powers to a policing authority,[33] and it is the existence of these authorities which provides the backbone of the environmental regulation. However, the powers of these authorities are both supplemented and circumscribed by regulations or objectives to be formulated from the Secretary of State. Behind every policeman there is the government, which is increasingly susceptible to pressures from the green lobby. The relevant policing authority is able to grant a permission, licence or authorisation (with the exception of statutory nuisance).[34]

Securing such a licence is of such fundamental importance that the forms have become extremely complex and specialist advice is now often taken on the completion of these forms. Broadly speaking, conduct covered by a licence, provided that there has been compliance with the conditions of the licence, is immune from prosecution. This can be seen either as a statutory defence of acting in accordance with a licence, or characterisation of the criminal offence as exceeding the powers granted in the licence or breaching its conditions.

The policing authority also has the important function of investigating and inspecting those to whom licences have been given, so as to ensure compliance with and enforcement of the schemes. The policing authority is given extremely wide powers which include entering premises for the purpose of investigating whether an offence has been or is being committed.[35] Because this legislation provides that obstructing the policing authority is an offence, mortgagees in possession, receivers and the like must take care. In each of these statutory

---

Water pollution: WRA 1991, section 85(1), causing or knowingly permitting noxious or polluting matter, solid waste, trade or sewage effluent etc. to enter "controlled waters", defined in section 104 as territorial, coastal, inland and ground waters;

Waste on land: EPA 1990, section 33(1), knowingly causing or permitting the deposit, treatment or storage of controlled waste on land;

Statutory nuisance: EPA 1990, section 79(1), an activity which is prejudicial to health or a nuisance after an abatement notice has been served under section 80.

33. Air pollution: a two-tier system (section 4, EPA 1990) of Integrated Pollution Control policed by Her Majesty's Inspectorate of Pollution and Local Authority Air Pollution Control policed by local authorities;

Water pollution: National Rivers Association (section 221(1), WRA 1991);

Waste on land: waste regulation authorities (section 30(1), EPA 1990) are broadly the same as the authorities under the Control of Pollution Act 1974;

Statutory nuisance: local authorities (section 80–81, EPA 1990). Section 82 provides that any "person aggrieved" can complain direct to the magistrates' court.

34. Air pollution: sections 6–12, EPA 1990 provides that an "authorisation" must be obtained;

Water pollution: section 88, WRA 1991 Schedule 10 provides for an application to the National Rivers Association for a "discharge consent";

Waste on land: sections 35–41, EPA 1990 provide for a "waste management licence";

Statutory nuisance: no licensing scheme.

35. Air pollution: enforcement notice under section 13, EPA 1990 or a prohibition notice to remove "an imminent risk of serious pollution of the environment" under section 14, EPA 1990;

Water pollution: prohibition notice banning discharges under section 86, WRA 1991;

Waste on land: waste removal notice served on occupier under section 59, EPA 1990;

Statutory nuisance: abatement notice under section 80(2), EPA 1990.

schemes the policing authority itself has the power to arrange and pay for the costs of any clean-up, and then recover them from the polluter.[36]

Each of the schemes also contains provisions for "third party liability".[37] This third party liability can attach to a director, manager, secretary or other similar officer of a corporate polluter or where the pollution offence was due to the act or default of some other person.

Those at risk from such liability include any administrative receiver, liquidator or administrator of the company. In R v. Boal[38] a company and its assistant general manager were prosecuted under section 23 of the Fire Precautions Act 1971, which is for practical purposes the same as section 157, EPA 1990. The Court of Appeal relieved Mr Boal of any liability for the accident, stating that the purpose of the statute was to fix with liability "only those who are in a position of real authority, the decision makers within the company who have both the power and responsibility to decide corporate policy and strategy. It is to capture those responsible for putting proper procedures in place; it is not meant to strike at underlings."[39]

SEIZED PROFITS?

At present there is no specific provision for the seizure of profits in relation to the environmental statutory schemes. However, the environmental policing authorities and the courts may prove bold enough to marry the contemporary statutory schemes for profit-seizing with the various measures to control environmental pollution.

The profit-seizing provisions of the Criminal Justice Act 1988 are of very general application and in principle there are appears to be no reason for excluding pollution offences. The concept of profit-seizing may be particularly attractive in the sphere of environmental pollution. The common law concepts of a victim, harm and causation do not easily fit into the environmental sphere where emissions can cause damage, as to which the victims and the causal link are almost impossible to identify, let alone prove.

There is also the concept at common law that a polluter will only be penalised to the extent that it crossed the permissible line of legality. In Andreae v. Selfridge[40] the court acknowledged that if the defendant's actions had produced a lesser degree of dust and noise the plaintiff would not have succeeded and therefore the court held that the defendant could be held liable only in respect of

36. Air pollution: section 27(1), EPA 1990.
Water pollution: section 161, WRA 1991.
Waste on land: sections 59–61, EPA 1990.
Statutory nuisance: section 81, EPA 1990.
37. Sections 157–8, EPA 1990 and section 217, WRA 1991.
38. [1992] 1 Q.B. 591.
39. Ibid., at 597–598.
40. [1938] Ch. 1.

matters in which it crossed the line of legality. Such a discount principle makes sense. However it may encourage a wrongdoer to take a risk, knowing that at worst his conduct will be penalised only insofar as it represents an excessive interference with the environment. With the common law adopting such a conservative approach, the attractiveness in policy terms of profit-seizing in the environmental sphere can be seen.

Environmental harm does not usually present an individual victim to whom profits can be awarded. When there are no direct or ascertainable victims of the pollution, it may be that seized profits could go into a central fund which will then be used for environmental protection and clean-up.

An alternative route through which seized profits may enter the environmental sphere may be that of "unjust enrichment". A court might be tempted to order payment of the defendant's profits, notwithstanding that there is no suggestion that it is the accurate measure of the plaintiff's loss or damage. The court may conclude that the only way to deter wrongdoing in this area is to confiscate profits.

It is perfectly possible, therefore, that the Criminal Justice Act 1988 is likely to appear in the environmental context, at least in cases concerning knowing or wilful pollution. It is conceivable that policing authorities will be bold enough to claim and courts bold enough to order profit-seizing orders against companies who have carefully calculated that the profits to be made from a particular transaction justify disregarding environmental law.

ISSUES FOR LENDERS

One of the most important issues for lenders will be the resolve and determination with which the new policing authorities pursue and enforce their aims and powers. The policing authorities are very powerful bodies, which are challengeable only by way of the limited grounds available in judicial review.[41] A further disadvantage of the judicial review procedure has been the judicial reluctance[42] to grant "pressure groups" *locus standi*, threatening to result in some administrative decisions which have major environmental implications being effectively unreviewable.

An important (if speculative) question is how "green" the domestic courts are. If magistrates are prepared to commit pollution prosecutions to the Crown Courts, then questions of environmental liability will be in the hands of juries, and the judges will have an unlimited power to fine, together with the prospect of profit-seizing.

41. In *Council of Civil Service Unions* v. *Minister for the Civil Service* [1985] A.C. 374 the grounds were labelled "illegality", "irrationality" and "procedural impropriety".
42. e.g. *R* v. *Secretary of State for the Environment ex parte Rose Theatre Trust* [1990] 1 Q.B. 504 per Schiemann J.; but see now *Greenpeace* [1993] *The Independent*, 30 September.

A further issue which will concern lenders is the relationship of an order for clean-up costs and secured and unsecured debts. The fact that there is no regime in the legislation to make clean-up costs registrable as a charge on the land suggests that clean-up costs are to be regarded as mere debts and that the policing authorities have only the status of unsecured creditors. However, as we have seen in the discussion of the Canadian case of *Panamericana* v. *Northern Badger*, this is also what creditors thought in Canada, only to be dismayed by the decision in that case.

Section 19(4) of the Insolvency Act 1986 provides that any expenses properly incurred by an administrator can be charged on and paid out of the property of the insolvent company. At the moment it is likely that enforcement agencies will prefer the administrator to perform the clean-up operations rather than do it themselves and then charge it to the company. Were the courts to adopt a *Northern Badger* approach or were statute to provide that clean-up costs were securable by a charge on the company's property, then the enforcement agencies may undertake the work themselves.

It could be that there is a distinction between clean-up debts and clean-up duties. The Alberta Court of Appeal rejected the judge's characterisation of the policing authority as a creditor seeking to have its claim preferred, because it said that the policing authority was seeking to enforce an order that the receiver carry out clean-up operations, not an order for recovery of clean-up costs already incurred by the policing authority. It could be argued therefore that the clean-up debt situation was left open in *Northern Badger* but it could be that the result would be different in such a context. Were such a distinction to appear in English law, the lesson is obvious. The policing authority would delay its own clean-up operations and rely instead on the public duty of clean-up. This would place policing authorities in a much stronger position in an insolvency.

There is an obvious dilemma for the lender in that on the one hand it wishes to obtain as much information as it is able about its borrower and on the other hand it wishes to avoid liability. This dilemma can arise both at the time of lending and at the time of debt collecting. The dilemma occurs because in scrutinising or monitoring the borrower, the lender may incur liability itself as directing or controlling the borrower's operations.

As regards the time of lending, the more actively the lender takes steps to know its borrower and the more carefully the lender monitors the borrower's activities, the more likely the lender is to become liable itself for the borrower's pollution. A lender will also wish not to become too closely involved with particular financial decisions made by its borrower, for fear that the courts will find that it put itself into a position where it owed a duty of care to its borrower. A problem can also arise at the time of debt collecting. The American and Canadian decisions show that courts may take the attitude that if a bank or receiver chooses to step into the polluter's shoes by enforcing a security, it must take the rough with the smooth. It cannot expect simply to sell off assets for its own benefit and ignore the environmental responsibilities.

SAFE LENDING

A lender when contemplating making any loan must have a full understanding of the risks involved. In particular the lender needs to be aware of both the nature and scale of any environmental liabilities which its borrower could face. These liabilities include the costs of obtaining any necessary licence, the expenditure incurred in complying with the conditions set out in that licence, the likely level of any fine in the event of an infringement and the scale of possible clean-up costs should there be a breach of the relevant legislation.

The lender will wish to know these things and in general to keep a close eye on its borrower, for more than purely commercial reasons. Inceasingly, the public takes an interest in which lenders take account of environmental considerations and lenders do not wish their public image to be tarnished by any association with environmental recklessness.

The American cases discussed above showed a distinction between those cases in which the court held that "the power to participate" was enough to fasten liability onto the lender, and those cases which held that only "actual participation" would be enough. It is unclear which side an English court would be likely to take. A lender therefore might be in danger even though it has not in fact exercised control. It might be enough that it had the power to exercise control even if it did not in fact do so. This would translate into a "duty" on the part of the lender to ensure that pollution does not take place in those cases where the lender had the power to prevent the pollution. It might not matter that the lender has not exercised the power which it had reserved to itself.

Lenders should also think very carefully before presenting their environmental awareness or expertise to their customers or prospective borrowers. If the court decides that the lender, whether through advertising or other assurances, put itself in the position of environmental adviser to its borrower, the court could well attach a tortious liability to the lender such that the lender could then be in breach of a duty to advise or warn its customer about environmental matters.

As regards the taking of security, a lender must of course be fully aware of what the security offered is actually worth. The lender must assess the likelihood of the value of any land decreasing as a result of environmental damage or becoming contaminated. The lender must also consider whether there is a prospect of a *Northern Badger*-type situation, where a court clean-up order might have the effect of depriving the lender of the value of its security. Most importantly, the lender when taking any security must be aware that should the time come when it wishes to enforce that security, environmental considerations may in fact prevent it from enforcing that security. The lender may, for example, be prevented from going into possession of mortgaged property because liabilities might attach to the lender exceeding the debts it is owed.

SAFE DEBT COLLECTION

The most important principle in this area could be characterised as "look before you leap". Before enforcing any security, the lender must be aware of all the risks involved. The lender must be careful not to enforce a security only then to find out that the liabilities it has taken on by enforcing that security substantially exceed the value of any security.

Unlike the United States, there is no "secured creditor exemption" in United Kingdom (or EU) law. There has been intensive lobbying from the banking community. Lord Alexander of Weedon Q.C., Chairman of the National Westminster Bank, exhorted the need for "a secured creditor exemption which holds the balance between requiring banks to do business on a responsible basis without imposing a liability which would be an active deterrent to the provision of finance".[43]

The UK government has indicated that it will not provide such an exemption in the near future, taking the view that "liability should follow responsibility, possibly even to bankers under some circumstances . . . No-one has the right to be regarded as a special case."[44] It is therefore possible that English law will reach even more wide-ranging decisions than American law. At common law a receiver who handles rent can be liable for breach of statutory duty and a mortgagee who takes possession is clearly at risk of liability whether as "owner" or "occupier". Neither is there any guidance, such as that contained in the American Environmental Protection Agency's rules, which provide some comfort for American lenders if they are able to bring themselves within the published guidelines.

Liquidators, receivers and secured creditors must also be aware that a court order for clean-up costs may be sought by the relevant policing authority, thus having the effect of reducing or even extinguishing the value of assets available for everyone else, as we have seen in the *Northern Badger* case.

CONCLUSION

We set out below some 10 principles of safe lending. In this rapidly changing and developing field of the law these principles can be seen only as guidelines. The numerical coincidence should not encourage readers to ascribe to these principles the immutability or infallibility claimed for the Ten Commandments.

1. The lender should carry out a thorough environmental investigation prior to lending including the past activities of the borrower and its future plans. Lenders could devise their own questionnaire for

43. Speech to the Chartered Institute of Banking in Bristol, 26 November 1991.
44. Speech by Mr Tim Yeo, Minister at the Dept. of Environment, to the British Bankers' Association, 13 October 1993.

completion by potential borrowers. Satisfactory answers to such a questionnaire could be a condition of any lending. A lender should impose an obligation on the borrower to notify the lender of any change in the answers after lending has taken place.

2. The lender should investigate any records of the appropriate policing authority and its policy as regards licences. Lenders may be able to communicate directly with the appropriate policing authority in order to seek information as to the nature of its borrower's activities and whether the borrower has complied with any conditions prescribed by the policing authority.

3. The lender should ensure that the borrower pays for such investigations. This minimises the prospect of the lender incurring liability on the basis that it participated or controlled the borrower.

4. The lender should ensure that there is a proper environmental audit undertaken by a suitably qualified person. It is also important that the environmental auditor owes direct duties to the lender should the report turn out to have been prepared negligently and the lender wishes to sue the auditor on it. The environmental auditor will therefore wish to have the appropriate and adequate professional indemnity insurance cover.

5. The lender should ensure that surveyors or valuers fully take into account environmental factors, including future risks, when ascribing a value to the property.

6. The lender should include environmental covenants and default figures in the loan terms. The lender should, for example, reserve to itself the right to demand the information relating to environmental and/or regulatory compliance. There should also be a provision that all clean-up costs and compliance costs should be borne by the borrower. A covenant could also be included to require the borrower to take out adequate environmental liability insurance. Environmental breach could also be one of the provisions which give rise to an accelerated demand on the borrower or a right to immediate repayment.

7. As a general point, the lender should insist on regular information to allow environmental monitoring during the period of lending. This is particularly important if the term of any lending is long. Such monitoring should also be introduced for old or current loans which involve environmental risk. If there is a provision for a regular review of the facility, that would be an appropriate time for introducing these new requirements.

8. The lender must tread a fine line between ensuring that it is fully aware of all the risks in respect of the lending and being very careful to avoid any acts which might be characterised as participation or control. Direct participation in the company's affairs or the right of veto as to a change of directors are examples of powers which could easily be

characterised as control. A lender should also make it clear both in the loan terms and also in correspondence, that investigations and monitoring are not intended to influence, control or advise the borrower.

9. The lender should be careful to include suitable terms in all of its security documentation. In particular, a receiver or manager should clearly be identified as the agent of the company. Such terms will also help to deflect the argument that prior to enforcement of security at least, the security-holder did not exercise control over the borrower.

10. The lender must keep good records of what it has done and why it had done it. This point is self-evident.

The paradox inherent in this area of law is clear. The more scrupulous lenders are in taking account of environmental risk, the less likely it is that they will be held liable by the courts. A more vigilant lending community is likely to mean fewer environmental accidents and a weaker judicial appetite for imposing liability on lenders. Paradoxically, then, the best way to ensure that the concept of direct lender liability for environmental damage never arrives in English law may be for lenders to behave as if it has already arrived.

JOHN JARVIS Q.C., MICHAEL FORDHAM AND DAVID WOLFSON*

---

* The subject-matter of this chapter is more fully explored in Jarvis and Fordham, *Lender Liability* (1993, Cameron May).

CHAPTER 6

LIABILITIES ON INSOLVENCY

This chapter is addressed to a single issue: in what circumstances may a bank advancing money to a company which goes into insolvent liquidation risk a claim by the liquidator as the result of its actions prior to winding up? We shall consider this first in the context of the general law and secondly in the light of the Insolvency Act 1986, with particular reference to the provisions relating to wrongful trading and voidable preferences.

I. LIABILITY UNDER THE GENERAL LAW

The liquidator can obviously pursue against the bank any claim which could have been asserted by the company itself prior to liquidation. Typically such a claim will lie in contract, tort, or both, but there are other sources of liability, in particular equity and trust. Forms of liability to which the bank may be exposed include the following:

(1) Breach of the loan agreement

Where the bank has agreed to advance money to the company and fails to do so in accordance with that agreement the consequences for the company can be serious. First, it may fail to secure an advantageous contract or property. Secondly, it may default on its obligations to another creditor, with potentially disastrous consequences, including termination of a contract, forfeiture of a lease and the triggering of an acceleration clause or cross-default clause. Similar consequences may attend a precipitate withdrawal by the bank, in breach of contract, of funds it has already advanced. These adverse events may be so severe in their impact as to force the company into winding up. In such a case the liquidator may sue in the company's name for all loss resulting from the breach so far as it falls within the rule in *Hadley* v. *Baxendale*.

Of course, banks do not generally break their contracts intentionally, but one can envisage circumstances where they might. The bank may, for example, withhold an advance or call for premature repayment because it has become concerned as to the borrower's solvency and fears that the borrower will be unable or unwilling to make repayment. In certain circumstances the bank may be able to justify its action on the basis of the borrower's anticipatory breach, but where the borrower has not evinced an intention to repudiate its future obligations, so that the case rests on the impossibility of its being able to repay on the due date, it may be hard to establish this defence. Another reason why a bank may break its contract, perhaps inadvertently, is because of an inconsistency in its contract documents, as where a standard mortgage provides for repayment on demand but the loan letter sets a term for repayment and the bank acts in reliance on the former when the latter is held to be the prevailing document.[1]

(2) Breach of a duty of care

A bank owes its customer a duty to exercise reasonable care and skill in the provision of its services and the execution of its instructions. This duty is owed in contract and is usually matched by a parallel duty in tort.[2] Any claim for breach of duty which could have been asserted by the company before winding up can be asserted by its liquidator after winding up. A likely source of liability under this head is the provision of negligent advice[3] and a common example is negligent investment advice which results in the total or partial loss of the customer's investment. This is perhaps less likely to occur in the case of a company than in the case of individual customers, who nowadays find banks considerably more cautious in their recommendations, to the point that the value of the advice is substantially diminished. A bank is liable for breach of a duty of care committed by itself or its agents. An administrative receiver appointed by the bank under a debenture holder is *prima facie* the agent of the borrower company, not of the bank,[4] up to the time the company goes into winding up,[5] and thereafter is *prima facie* the agent of neither but a principal considered to act on his own account.[6] Thus the bank as debenture holder is not in general liable for the acts or omissions of its receiver, whether before or after winding up.[7] The position is otherwise, however, where the bank makes the receiver its agent, whether expressly or by interfering in the conduct of the

1. For a case of inconsistency within the same document (the facility letter) see *Titford Property Co. Ltd.* v. *Cannon Street Acceptance Ltd.* (1975) 22 May, a decision of Goff J. which is unreported but summarised in *Encyclopaedia of Banking Law* (ed. Cresswell *et al.*), Volume 1, para. C183.

2. The court will not extend the scope of the contractual duty by reference to tort: *Tai Hing Ltd.* v. *Liu Chong Hing Bank* (P.C.) [1986] A.C. 80 at p. 107.

3. A bank is not generally liable for "failure to advise" where it has not been asked to proffer advice: *Redmond* v. *Allied Irish Bank plc* [1987] F.L.R. 307; *Schioler* v. *Westminster Bank Ltd.* [1970] 3 All E.R. 177; *Lloyds Bank plc* v. *Cobb* unreported, Court of Appeal, 18 December 1991. See Tony Shea, "Bankers and the Duty to Advise Customers" [1987] J.I.B.L. 181.

4. Insolvency Act 1986, s. 44(1).

5. *Ibid.*

6. *Gosling* v. *Gaskell* [1897] A.C. 575.

7. *Ibid.*

receivership.[8] Breach of the duty of care may preclude the bank from maintaining a debit to its customer's account, as where it honours a drawing by an officer of the company when it ought to have realised that the drawing was improper.

(3) Breach of mandate in the operation of a current account

This may take various forms: the failure to honour a cheque when the account is in funds or the drawing is within the limit of a credit facility; payment of a cheque after countermand of payment; payment of a cheque on which the signature has been forged or which lacks the signatures called for by the mandate.

(4) Breach of fiduciary duty

A bank may incur personal liability both in equity and under the Financial Services Act 1986[9] where, without the authority of its customer, it subordinates the customer's interests to its own or acts in a situation where there is a conflict of interest between the customer and another customer of the bank.[10]

(5) Liability as constructive trustee

A bank may incur a liability as constructive trustee where it receives for its own account money or property with notice of the fact that the transfer to it was a misapplication of the customer's assets or where it assists in such a misapplication and in so doing is guilty of want of probity.[11]

(6) Invalid appointment of an administrative receiver

A bank which appoints a receiver under an invalid debenture or when the conditions precedent to the right to appoint a receiver have not been fulfilled not

---

8. *Standard Chartered Bank Ltd.* v. *Walker* [1982] 1 W.L.R. 1410; *American Express International Banking Corp.* v. *Hurley* [1985] 3 All E.R. 564. For the possibility of a bank incurring a liability for misfeasance or wrongful trading in such circumstances see below.

9. Financial Services Act 1986, s. 62 and s. 62A; The Core Conduct of Business Rules, r. 2, and Financial Services (Conduct of Business) Rules 1990, r. 5.08(1). The Act gives a general civil remedy for breach of the Rules and of certain provisions of the Act itself. Since 1 April 1991 remedies for breach of statutory duty available to persons other than "private investors" have been restricted by s. 62A and the Financial Services Act 1986 (Restriction of Right of Action) Regulations 1991 (S.I. 1991/489).

10. See generally R.R. Pennington, *The Law of the Investment Markets*, pp. 112 *et seq.*

11. The case law on the degree of knowledge required for the "knowing assistance" head of liability is controversial. The better view is that only want of probity (because of actual knowledge or by deliberately turning a blind eye) suffices to fix the bank with liability. See *Lipkin Gorman* v. *Karpnale Ltd.* [1989] 1 W.L.R. 1340; *Agip (Africa) Ltd.* v. *Jackson* [1990] 1 Ch. 265 affirmed [1991] Ch. 547; *Eagle Trust plc* v. *SBC Securities Ltd.* [1991] B.C.L.C. 438.

only breaks its contract but may be ordered to indemnify the receiver[12] against his own liability for trespass and conversion in improperly taking possession of or otherwise dealing with the company's property or alternatively as constructive trustee of property coming into his hands.[13] Where the effect of the invalid appointment is to bring about a winding up which might otherwise have been avoided the bank's liability could be substantial.

Where a liquidator pursues a bank for a claim which could have been asserted by the company prior to liquidation, the company may have outstanding indebtedness to the bank incurred prior to liquidation. The effect of a winding up order by the court is that no proceedings may be commenced or proceeded with against the company save with the leave of the court.[14] However, the bank may counterclaim to recover the indebtedness by way of set-off against the company's claim to the extent of the sum claimed by the liquidator without requiring the leave of the court.[15]

II. WRONGFUL TRADING

Section 214 of the Insolvency Act 1986, re-enacting provisions introduced by the Insolvency Act 1985, contains provisions by which a person who was a director of a company at a time when he knew or ought to have concluded that there was no reasonable prospect of the company avoiding insolvent liquidation may, upon the company going into solvent liquidation, be declared liable to contribute to its assets unless he can show that he took every step with a view to minimising loss to creditors that he ought to have taken, having regard to his general knowledge, skill and experience and that reasonably to be expected of a person carrying out the same functions. For the purpose of section 214 "director" includes a shadow director,[16] that is to say, a person in accordance with whose directions or instructions the directors of the company are accustomed to act, other than a person whose advice is given in a professional capacity and is acted upon as such. It also includes a *de facto* director, that is, a person acting as director though not appointed (or validly appointed) as such.[17]

What is the position of a lending bank which is represented on the board of the company or which gives professional advice or intervenes in the management for the protection of its investment? Three things are clear. First, as I have pointed out elsewhere,[18] the professional adviser is excluded only from the

12. Either because of an express agreement between them for indemnity or under s. 34 of the Insolvency Act 1986.

13. *Rolled Steel Products (Holdings) Ltd.* v. *British Steel Corp.* [1986] Ch. 246.

14. Insolvency Act 1986, s. 130(2).

15. *Langley Constructions (Brixham) Ltd.* v. *Wells* [1969] 1 W.L.R. 503.

16. Insolvency Act 1986, s. 214(7), s. 251.

17. *Re Hydrodan (Corby) Ltd.* [1994] B.C.C. 161.

18. *Principles of Corporate Insolvency Law* (published by Sweet & Maxwell and the Centre for Commercial Law Studies, February 1990), p. 206.

definition of *shadow* director. A professional adviser who is a member of the board has all the normal liabilities of a director even if he restricts himself to the giving of professional advice; indeed, such a restriction would be an abnegation of his duties under general company law as well as under section 214 itself. It is not clear whether the appointing bank could be reached directly under section 214 as an employer responsible for the acts of its employees, but this is clearly a risk. Secondly, a bank which is an unsecured lender and which involves itself in management decisions is vulnerable to attack under section 214, for it has no special status in relation to the company's assets and thus no claim to take steps for their protection which would be detrimental to the general body of creditors. Thirdly, a bank which merely gives professional advice and is not represented on the board and does not intervene in the management of the company incurs no liability under section 214, though it may be liable to the company at common law if its advice was negligent and causes loss.

The grey area is the case of the bank which holds a secure debenture and intervenes for the protection of its security. How far can it go without attracting potential liability under section 214? In *Re A Company No. 005009 of 1987*,[19] which to the best of my knowledge is the only case where the point has so far arisen, the liquidator of a company in a creditors' voluntary winding up sought to attack the validity of a debenture taken by the bank as a preference under section 239 of the Insolvency Act or alternatively as a floating charge caught by section 245 and also sought to make the bank liable for wrongful trading as a shadow director. The bank applied to strike out the claims as unsustainable on the evidence then before the court. That evidence showed that the bank had commissioned a report into the company's affairs from its own financial services section which indicated that the company was in low financial water, that the report contained various recommendations, that the bank then took a debenture and that steps were taken to implement the various recommendations. The taking of those steps was the act relied on as constituting the bank a shadow director. The report furnishes no details of the steps in question. The application to strike out was dismissed by Knox J., who held that the claims could not be considered obviously unsustainable but declined to give his reasons for that conclusion on the ground that this would merely embarrass the trial judge.[20] In his judgment Knox J. made the point that the question whether the bank was a shadow director was also relevant to the preference claim, for if it were a shadow director then it would be a person connected with the company under section 249 and there would then be a presumption that the company, in giving the debenture, was influenced by the desire to produce the preference.

The case is interesting as it shows that banks have an exposure to wrongful trading but is of no assistance in answering the question I have posed, not merely

---

19. (1988) 4 B.C.C. 424.
20. The claim against the bank for liability as a shadow director under section 214 was withdrawn at trial after six days of oral evidence: *Re M.C. Bacon Ltd.* [1990] B.C.C. 78.

because it was an interlocutory order but also because, understandably enough, the learned judge declined to give reasons for his conclusion on the "obviously unsustainable" point. The status of a bank as a shadow director was considered by the Privy Council in *Kuwait Asia Bank EC* v. *National Mutual Life Nominees Ltd.*,[21] although not in the context of section 214. The bank had a shareholding in the parent of the company and had appointed two of the five directors of the company. Their Lordships noted that it was inherently unlikely that the directors were accustomed to act on the directions or instructions of the bank. It appears that the courts will require clear evidence that a company's directors have become accustomed to act on the directions or instructions of the bank.

It would not be appropriate to debate the facts of *Re A Company No. 005009 of 1987* (above). What I do want to raise in the abstract is the relevance of a valid security interest as an answer to an attack under section 214. It is settled law that a secured creditor is entitled to enforce his security and to give priority to his own interests above that of the debtor. It is also well established that the secured creditor, or his receiver on his behalf, may continue to exercise rights over the assets comprising the security even after the advent of an insolvent liquidation.[22] It is therefore reasonable to conclude that a bank whose intervention in the affairs of the company is limited to exercise of its rights *in rem* as a secured creditor cannot on that account alone be held liable for wrongful trading. What is less clear is the position of a bank which not merely takes steps in relation to its security but proceeds, directly or through a receiver acting in accordance with its instructions, to exercise a power to manage the company's business and, in so doing, to cause the company to incur further liabilities or otherwise cause its position to deteriorate, as by failing to get in or preserve assets outside the security or to take remedial steps to reduce loss-making parts of the business or ongoing liabilities. It may be that the position of the bank in this situation is not dissimilar from that of the receiver after winding up, in the sense that security rights continue to be exercisable but management functions of a purely *in personam* character are carried out at the bank's risk. The bank is entitled to protect and realise its security; beyond this its interventions in the running of the company would seem to enjoy no greater immunity than that of any other party. A key problem here is to distinguish acts that are purely managerial from those that are for the protection of the security. The bank might seek to argue that if the value of its security were not to be diminished it was essential for the company to continue trading and thus incur new debt.

The moral, of course, is for the bank to keep out of management altogether and to leave this to its receiver acting independently on his own initiative, or alternatively to an administrator.

---

21. [1990] B.C.C. 576.
22. *Sowman* v. *David Samuel Trust Ltd.* [1978] 1 All E.R. 616.

III. RESTORATION OF ASSETS RECEIVED UNDER A VOID OR VOIDABLE TRANSACTION

The Insolvency Act 1986 prescribes various grounds on which payments and transfers by a company prior to liquidation may be attacked and gives the court power to make such orders as it thinks fit for restoring the position to what it would have been if the company had not entered into the transaction. In particular, a payment or transfer may be vulnerable as a transaction at an undervalue,[23] a preference[24] or a floating charge given otherwise than for one of the specified forms of new value.[25] We do not propose to enter into a detailed analysis of the statutory provisions, which we have discussed elsewhere.[26] We should, however, like to focus attention on two points concerning the application of the preference provisions to payments made into a current account.

In essence, a payment to the bank is vulnerable as a preference at the suit of the office-holder where it is made at a relevant time,[27] the company was insolvent at that time, the effect of the payment was to put the bank in a better position on insolvent liquidation of the company[28] than it would have been if the payment had not been made, and in making the payment the company was influenced by a desire to produce that effect.[29] As under the previous law, the party whose state of mind is relevant is the company, not the recipient of the payment, a curious rule which produces the result, absurd in policy terms, that the more aggressive the creditor in pursuing his own interests by threat of proceedings the more readily he will be able to repel an attack on the ground of preference. In the case of a bank this is of particular relevance because the company's bank account is the natural repository of cheques and other payments to the company. What else should the company do with a cheque than pay it into its bank account? This makes it more difficult to attack as a preference, payments made into an overdrawn bank account than if the payments had been made to a different class of creditor.

That is the first problem which arises in applying the preference provisions to current account transactions. The second problem arises from the fact that, in contrast to the Australian insolvency legislation, the UK Insolvency Act 1986 contains no general exemption in respect of transactions entered into *bona fide*

---

23. Insolvency Act 1986, ss. 238, 240, 241. The creation of security over the company's assets does not deplete them and does not fall foul of s. 238(4)(b): *Re M.C. Bacon Ltd.* [1990] B.C.C. 78.

24. *Ibid.*, ss. 239–241.

25. *Ibid.*, s. 245.

26. See R.M. Goode, *Principles of Corporate Insolvency Law*, Chapter VIII.

27. I.e. normally within the period of six months ending with the onset of insolvency (Insolvency Act 1986, s. 240(1)).

28. It is thought that for this purpose the company must be assumed to have gone into insolvent liquidation immediately after the payment. Whether the company actually goes into liquidation and, if so, the actual time of liquidation are irrelevant.

29. *Re M.C. Bacon Ltd.* [1990] B.C.C. 78; *Re Fairway Magazines Ltd.* [1992] B.C.C. 924.

by the creditor in the ordinary course of business. Suppose that the company makes a payment into its overdrawn account which can be shown to be a preference but that subsequently, as part of the continued mutual dealings between banker and customer, the bank honours further drawings on that account. Can it be made to repay the preferential payment without credit being given for the later drawings? This would be both harsh and contrary to the policy of insolvency legislation, which is to prevent one creditor obtaining an unfair advantage over the others, not to penalise receipts matched by subsequent new value. There appear to be two routes by which this result can be avoided. The first is to look at the totality of the transactions on the account after the start of the relevant period in order to see whether at the end of that period the bank has been put into a preferential position.[30] The second is to accept the preferential character of the payment into the account but to treat subsequent payments from the account as *pro tanto* reversing the preference, on the basis that all items on a current account should be treated as connected by a mutual course of dealing.[31]

IV. OTHER SOURCES OF LIABILITY IN FOREIGN SYSTEMS

By way of conclusion we should mention two other interesting sources of liability that are to be found abroad, one under French law and the other under German law. Under French law a bank which continues to support a company when the bank knows or ought to know the company has reached the point of no return, and thereby enables the company to incur further credit from its suppliers, may be liable to those suppliers for the tort of *complicité de banqueroute*; whilst under German law a creditor taking security over the whole or substantially the whole of the debtor's assets becomes liable for payment of his debts!

ROY GOODE AND ANNIE HOCKADAY

30. This is the approach taken by the Australian courts. See, for example, *M. & R. Jones Shopfitting Co. Pty. Ltd.* v. *National Bank of Australasia Ltd.* (1983) 7 A.C.L.R. 445; *Re Weiss* (1970) A.L.R. 654.
31. Since each party impliedly extends credit to the other on the basis of their mutual dealings. The position would no doubt be different if the bank were to make a new advance by way of independent loan not connected in any way to the preceding credit to the account.

CHAPTER 7

BANK LIABILITY FOR IMPROPER CREDIT DECISIONS IN THE CIVIL LAW

INTRODUCTION

The number of bankruptcies or corporate reorganisations continues to increase in the aftermath of the recession that marked the early 1990s, while the reorganisation or liquidation of several of the businesses that failed in the 1970s still is underway. In their attempt to recover as much as possible for the creditors, bankruptcy receivers have diversified their attacks and increasingly have sued the directors, managers and auditors of the bankrupt entity. While this cause of action may not encounter insurmountable legal obstacles, the financial benefit it can realise for the creditors is relatively limited. This prompted the receivers to shift their focus to the banks that provided credit to the failed company, since these institutions have virtually unlimited resources.

Two kinds of actions should clearly be distinguished. On the one hand, there are actions based on an unwarranted or negligent withdrawal of credit by the bank which may have triggered the bankruptcy. On the other hand, third parties have often attempted to have the banks declared liable on the basis that they continued to support the failing company, thus creating an artificial creditworthiness which misled and hence damaged the other creditors. In one case liability will be bilateral and exist only *vis-à-vis* the beneficiary of the credit: liability will often be based on non-performance of the contract (e.g. undue withdrawal of the credit), more rarely on extra-contractual grounds (pre-contractual liability). Liability may also exist towards third parties, relying on the bank's credit assessment: co-creditors that have been misled. Here liability will usually be extra-contractual, although in some cases contractual relations between the bank and the third party will be affected (guarantors, or other beneficiaries of the bank's promises to pay).

If most legal systems subscribe to liability of the banks towards their clients, the beneficiaries of the credit, some systems also accept liability towards third parties. The conditions of applying the latter type of liability depend on the legal basis on which liability is based. Therefore the law governing the relationship is of prime importance.

This chapter gives a short overview of the criteria and cases in which such bank liability—more specifically third party liability—for improper credit decisions can attach. It mainly focuses on French and Belgian law, where numerous cases are found, but it also attempts a comparison with Dutch and German law.

As the overview will mainly deal with continental European systems, the terminology used will be more apt to reflect these legal systems. Therefore, credit institutions will invariably be designated as "banks", although they may have different regulatory status (including e.g. financial companies, leasing companies, factoring enterprises etc.). Also for the purpose of the present overview, the term "bankruptcy" ("faillite" in Belgium, "règlement judiciaire" and "liquidation de biens" in France) will be used to cover both bankruptcy of individuals as well as bankruptcy of companies or other legal entities. In continental systems, a "receiver" is appointed by the court. Conscious about the different uses of these words in English law, designating the procedure as "bankruptcy" seemed the more workable solution.

DIFFERENT ATTITUDES TOWARDS BANK LIABILITY

Published case law in the various Western European jurisdictions shows a varied approach to these actions. Three attitudes can be distinguished.[1]

In several countries, banks have frequently been declared liable for extending excessive, unwarranted or unjustified credit to ailing companies. These countries include France, where the doctrine of bank liability originated, Belgium, where it flourished, and Luxembourg, where a few decisions can be found.[2]

In other jurisdictions, the possible liability of banks for extending credit may be accepted as a principle, but the conditions for liability have been formulated in such a restrictive way that in practice few if any decisions can be found holding the bank liable. This category includes the Netherlands and the Federal Republic of Germany, where some cases exist. In Switzerland, Italy and probably Spain, the legal system would seem to permit such action, but no cases have been found.

---

1. For an extensive overview, see L. Simont and A. Bruyneel, *La responsabilité extracontractuelle du donneur de crédit en droit comparé*, Paris, Feduci, 1984, 256 pp. XXXV Travaux de l'Association Henri Capitant, *La responsabilité du banquier: Aspects nouveaux*, 1984, 662 pp.

2. See for Belgium: A. Zenner, "Rapport belge", in *La responsabilité du banquier: Aspects nouveaux*, *supra* n. 1, who adds the complete list of Belgian legal doctrine and case law on the subject; P. Van Ommeslaghe and L. Simont, "De aansprakelijkheid van de bankier-kredietverlener in het Belgisch recht", T.P.R., 1986, 1091; L. Cornelis, "De aansprakelijkheid van de bankier bij kredietverlening", T.P.R., 1986; 349; Van Rijn and Heenen, *Principes de droit commercial*, 2nd Edition, v.IV, nr. 663–673, pp. 531–542; For France, see: M. Vasseur, *La responsabilité civile du banquier dispensateur de crédit*, Banque, 3rd Ed., 1978, 100 pp., Ch. Gavalda (Ed.), *Responsabilité professionnelle du banquier*, Ed. Economica, Paris, 1978, 102 pp., G. Prat, *La responsabilité du banquier et la faillite de son client*, Ed. Lavoisier, 2nd Ed., 1983, 243 pp., J. Vezian, *La responsabilité du banquier en droit privé français*, Paris, Libr. Technique, 1972, 2nd Ed., 278 pp.; Gavalda and Stoufflet, *Droit bancaire*, 1992, n° 386 e.s., pp. 182–192; F. Rua, *Responsabilité civile du banquier en matière de crédit*, Fasc 151, Jurisclasseur "banque et crédit", loose leaf.

In the common law jurisdictions, including the United States, possible third party liability of banks—as opposed to liability to the creditor itself—is in principle, in these matters, excluded. Only in very specific circumstances, different from our subject, can statutory liability exist.[3]

Between the bank and the borrower, the possible liability is contractual and based on the credit agreement. It will not be dealt with in detail in the present overview.[3a] In exceptional circumstances, pre-contractual liability can arise between bank and beneficiary of the credit: banks have been held liable because, after having promised the credit, on which promise the debtor and third parties relied, the bank refused to effectively implement its promise.[4]

The action of third parties, suppliers, other creditors,[5] but also guarantors—the former most of the time represented by the bankruptcy receiver—however, is generally based on the rules of extra-contractual liability or tort. The conditions for the existence of this type of liability differ from country to country. As a consequence, the legal systems have developed different attitudes towards bank liability; these may be attributed not only to varying general conditions for liability, but to other, i.e. cultural factors related to the perceived position of the banking system in the economy.

Banks may be held liable to third parties on other grounds as well. Apart from liability arising out of specific transactions or relationships—such as on the basis of the services offered by the bank—overall liability has sometimes been attempted on the basis of the bank acting as the *de facto* director of the company, e.g. after the credit became worrisome. The French law on directors' liability for ailing companies[6] has been scaled down after the previous legislation led to rather extreme solutions. The Belgian law is based on similar ideas and has been invoked a few times in bankruptcy cases.[7] Banks therefore are very hesitant to exceed the limits of supervision and accounting control of the debtor and

3. For instance, when securities are issued, the underwriting or placement activity can create liabilities. See § 16 of the US Securities Act of 1933.

3a. See for the case: e.g. Cons. Etat, 26 March 1958, Pas., 1959, IV, 56.

4. Cass. Comm. Fr., 31 March 1992, Bull. Civ, IV, 145 (liability against the shareholder that committed itself irrevocably in the light of the bank's promise); comp. for Belgium: Comm. Brussels, 5 March 1991, R.D.C.B., 1992, 981, note; Comm. Liège, 7 March 1989, R.D.C.B., 1990, 1052.

5. See Comm. Brussels, 24 February 1983, R.D.C.B., 1983, 555, refusing a factoring company to sue the bank, being considered as well informed about the debtor as the bank.

6. See: art. 180, L. 85–98 of 25 January 1985 "relative au redressement et à la liquidation judiciaires des entreprises", J.O., 26 January 1985, JCP, 1985, Fd.G, Nr. 56711; see Gavalda and Stoufflet, fn. 2, nr. 403, p. 189.

7. See for France: art. 99, L. 13 July 1967, now replaced by the milder art. 180, L. 85–98, note 4; for Belgium: art. 63 ter, Companies Act. No liability: Comm. Brussels, 3 April 1984, R.P.S., 1984, nr. 6292, 184; Comm. Brussels, 24 October 1989, Rev. Not. belge, 1990, 196. The major case (*Bodart-Fittings*) declaring the State liable as a shadow director was overruled on appeal: Trib. Brussels, 22 October 1982, R.P.S., 1982, 244; annulled by Brussels, 14 September 1988, R.D.C.B., 1989, 171, nt.; TRV, 1989, 49, nte Lievens; For comments see: G. Laffineur, "La responsabilité des donneurs publics de crédit à la lumière de l'affaire Bodart-Fittings", Adm. Publique, 1984, 97; A. Haelterman, "De zaak Bodert-Fittings als toepassing van artikel 63 ter", Jura Falconis, 1982–1983, 373. Dony, "La responsabilité des pouvoirs publics en cas d'intervention dans une entreprise en difficulté", JT, 1990, 670.

intervene, or be seen to intervene, in the actual running of the debtor entity. In the UK, the question of liability of the bank as a shadow director has been raised, but obviously conditions are very strict and the risk of liability therefore quite remote.[8]

The main theory of bank liability developed first in France, and was later successfully introduced in Belgium. In both countries, this liability is based on the general rules of tort or negligence liability, that merely require negligence, damage and causation.

It is sufficient that the damage was caused by the conduct considered negligent, without any further requirement that the rule, the violation of which is alleged, was specifically designed to protect the interests of this victim. Negligence is defined in very broad terms: it is the violation of a specific rule of the law, or of the rule of behaviour that a normally prudent and diligent person would abide by in the same circumstances. It is also generally accepted that non-performance of a contractual obligation, such as the unwarranted withdrawal of an extended credit line, may in specific circumstances be the basis for extra-contractual or tort liability towards third parties,[9] provided the inexecution of the contract also included the violation of a general rule of conduct, to which all normally prudent and diligent persons can be expected to be held.[10] Considering the very broad character of these conditions, it should be no surprise that bank liability for extension of credit is primarily a French–Belgian theory.

In Germany, however, the criteria for torts are more restrictive. Most importantly, for the existence of a tort based on § 823 of the German Civil Code,[11] the breached duty should be aimed specifically at the protection of the interests of the victim, the creditors of the failing company.[12] Since no duty towards the interests of third parties, creditors of its clients, is imposed on the banks, bank liability cannot be based on this provision.

The cases imposing bank liability for extending credit are based on § 826 of the German Civil Code.[13] According to the strict conditions of this section, the

8. P. Fidler, "Banks as shadow directors", 1992, 3 J.I.B.L. 97.

9. As between contractual parties, liability will be governed by the rules of the contract (so called principle of "non-cumul de responsabilité"). Exceptions are admitted if criminal sanctions are attached to the obligation violated. See for details Mazeaud, Mazeaud and Chabas, *Leçons de droit civil, Obligations, théorie générale*, v.2(1) n° 403, p. 384; for Belgium: Vandenberghe and Van Quickenborne, "Overzicht van rechtspraak", T.P.R., 1987, nr 204 e.s. p. 1595 e.s.

10. For Belgium, see E. Dirix, *Obligatoire verhoudingen tussen contractanten en derden*, Maklu, Antwerpen, Nr. 243 e.s., p. 179, also referring to French and English case law on the subject.

11. "Wer vorsätzlich oder fahrlässig das Leben, den Körper, ... widerrechtlich verletzt, ist dem anderen zum Ersatze des daraus entstehenden Schadens verpflichtet. Die gleiche Verpflichtung trifft denjenigen, welcher gegen ein den Schutz eines anderen bezweckendes Gesetz verstösst."

12. This is called the Schutznorm theory. It has, for instance, been decided that public bank regulations may provide a civil cause of action to damaged clients of a bank, since part of these regulations are also aimed at the protection of the individual interests of a depositor. See BGH, 12 July 1979, III ZR 154/77, NJW, 1979, 1879 (Herstatt).

13. "Wer in einer gegen die guten Sitten verstossenden Weise einem anderen vorsätzlich Schaden zufugt, ist den anderen zum Ersatz des Schadens verpflichtet." See for details: K. J. Hopt and P. O. Mulbert, *Kreditrecht*, § 607, 291 e.s.

conduct of the wrongdoer should violate public morality (*Sittenwidrigkeit*). Through this criterion, contemporary technical, professional, but also moral and social evolutions may be taken into account.[14]

A number of cases have declared banks liable to the co-creditors of the bankrupt, provided that the bank wilfully caused the damage. Apart from the requirement that the wrongdoer acted knowingly and purposefully, it is also necessary that it acted intentionally. It must have wanted—or at least have known—that its actions would damage the creditors, even if this damage would not necessarily follow. Although some scholars have accepted a broader criterion, liability will not attach when the bank merely acted negligently knowing that creditors would be prejudiced.[15]

These conditions, although they do not exclude possible bank liability, limit its application to situations where it is proved that the bank actually tried to save its claim to the detriment of the other creditors. Thus, the standard for liability in Germany is much stricter than the one applied in French and Belgian law. The comparison between these legal systems is, therefore, limited to cases of misconduct, collusion or rather gross negligence by the bank.

In the Netherlands, the conditions necessary for bank liability for extending credit are also those formulated in general tort law.[16]

Several authors limit the possible liability to situations where the behaviour of the bank is a violation of its duties not only towards the debtor, but also towards the creditors of the borrower.[17] The credit decisions of the bank will only constitute a tort, requiring it to compensate the other creditors that suffered damages, if the bank's behaviour is to be considered negligent towards the interests of these other creditors which it has to take into account.[18]

It would seem that differences in general tort law cannot completely account for the different attitudes towards bank liability for extending credit. This can be shown by comparing Swiss and German law.

Article 41(1) of the Swiss *Code des Obligations*[19] is based on mere negligence and requires no intentional harm, but has not generated any case law in the area of bank liability. In Germany, on the other hand, there exists case law basing bank liability on § 826 of the German Civil Code, while this section is more restrictive and requires intention to harm.

Moreover, third party bank liability in these circumstances is ruled out in

14. H. J. Mertens, "Zur Bankenhaftung wegen Gläubigerbenachteiligung", 143 ZHR 174, 179 e.s. (1979); K. J. Hopt, *La responsabilité des banques en droit allemand*, Revue de la banque (belge), 1990, 383.

15. H. J. Mertens, *op. cit. supra* fn. 14.

16. See, apart from the articles cited in the footnotes, I. P. Michiels Van Kissenich-Hoogendam, *Aansprakelijkheid van banken*, Zwolle, 1987, 112 pp.; B. H. Croon and H. G. Van Everdinges, "De aansprakelijkheid van de bankier-kredietverlener in het Nederlands recht". T.P.R., 1988, 39.

17. See F. Molenaar, in L. Simont and A. Bruyneel, *op. cit. supra* fn. 1, p. 133 e.s.

18. See F. Molenaar, "De aansprakelijkheid van de kredietverlener", TVVS, 1984, 31.

19. "Celui qui cause, d'une manière illicite, un dommage à autrui, soit intentionnellement, soit par négligence ou imprudence, est tenu de le réparer."

common law jurisdictions. This is not due to more restrictive criteria of general tort law, since the relationship between the bank and the victim of its improper credit decision would seem to meet the general test for liability.[20] It is rather a consequence of the general sentiment that the credit business should only involve the bank and its client, and does not warrant the imposition of broader duties towards third parties on the banks.[21] The banks, according to this view, should not be forced to perform the function of protector of other interests than its own.

These diverging approaches towards bank liability can, however, be linked to differences in underlying philosophy towards the position of banks among the countries. The attitude of the judiciary seems to reflect the general perception of the banking system in each country.

In France, where the doctrine originates, the early case law was supported by the rationale that, given the importance of the banks for the monetary system, banking can be regarded as a "public service".[22] From this analysis flow broader duties of the banks to take into consideration other interests than those of the immediate concerned parties to the credit agreement, and in the view of some even the "general interest".[23]

This sensitivity for the duties of banks in these two countries is not unrelated to the dominant position, especially of public sector banks, in their domestic economies. With the increasing cross-border financial business and the ongoing privatisations, the assumption that banks have specific duties to the general interest no longer holds.

The analysis of the banking function as a public service, however, is no longer followed in France. It has been replaced by a more stringent duty of care to be observed by the banks in credit decisions, and in their other business as well. Hence banks try to capture their new responsibilities in "ethical codes". A comparable evolution can be traced in Belgium.

Another factor for the development of this philosophy is the deep-rooted tradition of suspicion towards bankers.[24] In the Netherlands, and even more in Germany, one can also find traces of concern over the powers of the banks.

---

20. M. Megrah in L. Simont and A. Bruyneel, *op. cit. supra* n. 1, p. 157 e.s.

21. Megrah, *op. cit. supra* fn. 20, p. 159. In the USA, third party liability can arise for underwriters of securities under section 16 of the Securities Act of 1933. This, however, will only apply if credit is extended in the form of the public offering of securities. For other types of liability see I. A. Aba, *Emerging theories of lender liability*, 3 vol. 1985.

22. For the first use of the idea of the bank performing a "public service", see R. Houin, Rev. Trim. Dr. Comm., 1955, 150; 1964, 161. Even today, some lawyers plead for banks having to respect the "public interest", which is clearly a confusion: J. P. Buyle, "Interventions nouvelles du juge en droit bancaire", D.A.O.R., 1989, 48.

23. See Aix-en-Provence, 31 July 1975, Gaz.Pal., 13 January 1976 (declaring the bank on this basis liable towards its client for not duly extending credit); Cf. Rouen, 8 April 1975, Banque, 1975, 872, note L. Martin.

24. See the reflections by a leading banker: P. E. Janssen, "Le banquier, mal aimé ou incompris?", Rev. Banque, 1983, 271.

The professional duty of the banks is rooted in the social responsibility that flows from their pivotal function in society. First, banks participate in the creation of money, a function traditionally surrounded by regal privileges. Secondly, banks almost exclusively perform functions essential for the functioning of the economic system, such as the collection of savings and the extension of credit, activities for which a limited monopoly has been granted by the legislator. Since its decisions in these areas have a direct effect on the interests of third parties, it is normal to expect the "reasonable professional banker" to take these interests into account.[25] They may even have to consider the general interest of the community, without, however, being held as a guardian of this general interest.[26]

On the other hand, banks being highly professionalised organisations, and presenting themselves as fully reliable and trustworthy partners in business, tend to be considered as being held to a "duty of excellence".[27] The latter basis for a general standard of liability constitutes certainly a firmer basis for holding banks to stricter rules of behaviour, and hence of liability. It also takes into account that banks are in the first place economic enterprises, pursuing their own profit, and not the general interest. The discussion about "financial ethics" therefore relates more to this way of thinking than to the qualification of the banks as a public service.

In those countries, but especially in France and Belgium, this reasoning has led to a strict standard of professional behaviour, requiring the banks to base their credit decisions on purely objective grounds, such as the economic situation of the borrower.[28] This liability is a specific application of rules of professional responsibility, taking into account the social and economic role of financial institutions. The applied test will be that of the "diligent behaviour of a normally

25. See e.g. Cass. Comm. Fr., 9 June 1980, JCP, 1980, IV, 319 ("En raison de son rôle économique et public de distributeur de crédit et de la foi qui s'attache à ses affirmations, elle est tenue envers les tiers à un certain devoir de renseignement et de prudence"); Gent, 25 April 1974, unreported, but reproduced in P. Van Ommeslaghe, "La responsabilité du banquier, dispensateur de crédit en droit belge", Société anonyme Suisse, 1979, ll e.s., also in Rev. Banque, 1980, Cahier Nr. 5; aff'd Cass. B., 19 March 1976, R.C.J.B., 1977, 38 note Merchiers. The decision, which especially stressed the importance of the banking function in society, was partially based on the memorandum of the then President of the Banking Commission E. De Barsy, published as A. Bruyneel, "Le 'Mémoire de Barsy' sur la responsabilité du donneur de crédit—Présentation et état de la question", Rev. Banque, 1977, 313; Gent, 4 October 1968, cited in A. Zenner, "Responsabilité du donneur de crédit", Rev. Banque, 1974, 707, 715; Cf. Comm. Brussels, 29 October 1976, J.T., 1977, 58; Comm. Brussels, 3 May 1976, J.T., 1977, 60; See also Liège, 1 February 1978, J.T., 1979, 181; Cf. Stoufflet, Note under Cass. Fr., 18 November 80, D., 1981, 210.

26. P. Van Ommeslaghe, op. cit. supra fn. 25 p. 114.

27. See for this evolution, K. J. Hopt, fn. 14, at 483 and 391.

28. One can compare this tendency towards a more objective standard to evaluate credit decisions with public banking regulations imposing a certain degree of autonomy on bank management, such as can be found in Belgium. Cf. the Protocols for "banking autonomy" the Belgian Banking Commission entered into with the Belgian banks. For the history of this practice, see Banking Commission, Annual Report, 1973–74, 15–32; 1975–76, 15 and 1976–77, 30–33; for their content see Annual Report, 1973–74, 32–40. See also Brussels, 10 May 1979, Rev. Banque, 1979, 583.

prudent bank under the same circumstances".[29] The legal basis is article 1382 Civil Code, that holds someone liable for the "*culpa levissima*".

In Switzerland, on the other land, where the banks for economic reasons obviously enjoy broad social acceptance, no similar evolution can be detected. Such theories also did not develop in the common law jurisdictions either. If the bank did not act dishonestly, its negligence in credit decisions cannot form the basis for an action by third parties because they lack a sufficiently direct relationship with the bank.[30] Thus, the banks have no duty to protect the interests of third parties and can limit their enquiry to their own interests. The larger awareness of the American legal system of the rules of proper conduct *vis-à-vis* creditors may constitute a footstep on the way to possible extension of liability to third parties.

THE BASIS FOR LIABILITY FOR IMPROPER CREDIT DECISIONS

The constitutive elements of the credit decision

Liability may flow from a decision to grant, to maintain or to discontinue a credit to an enterprise that was not creditworthy. Liability will be attached to improper decisions. This impropriety may be due either to the bank's insufficiently diligent preparation of its decision, or to its grossly mistaken appreciation of the chances of survival of the enterprise. The case law very often mixes these two elements, as the former often stands in a casual relationship with the latter.

The first part of the decision concerns the preparatory procedures the bank goes through prior to granting the credit. Before taking the actual credit decision, the diligent professional banker will gather the necessary information about the client to analyse its creditworthiness using methods of financial analysis.

With respect to this part of the decision, the law leaves the banker some room for discretion: liability attaches as soon as he or she has not proceeded in the way a reasonably diligent banker would have behaved. Negligence in this preparation will necessarily result in a credit decision being based on in-accurate or incomplete information, and will lead to a faulty credit decision if the firm later appears to be a greater risk than assumed. Some leeway, however, should be granted: the bank's decision could validly take account of the existence of signs of problems or risks, or of the amount of the credit involved in comparison to the size of the firm to adapt the thoroughness of its investigation.

29. L. Simont and A. Bruyneel, *op. cit. supra* fn. 1, p. 208.

30. M. Megrah, *op. cit. supra* fn. 20, p. 159 e.s.; Cf. for US law, P. Coogan, in L. Simont and A. Bruyneel, *op. cit. supra* fn. 1, p. 161 e.s.

Negligence at this preparatory stage will often lead the courts to conclude more readily to liability, although in practice it is difficult to establish causation: causation would require that, had the bank correctly prepared its decision, it would have discovered the borrower's weak position. Hence, by granting the credit the bank acted negligently.

The second and more crucial part of the credit decision consists of the bank's actual appreciation whether or not to grant credit, based on the elements of information gathered in the preparatory phase. Here, the bank enjoys considerable discretion with respect to its business judgement: each credit decision involves a risk and nobody can predict the future with certainty. Therefore the bank will not be liable if its risk assessment remains within the limits a normal, reasonable banker would respect.

If the bank nevertheless extends credit although the risk exceeds the level above which reasonable professional bankers would grant credit, it acts negligently and will be liable. As a consequence, it will have to compensate third parties for damages caused by their reliance on the artificial creditworthiness created by this unwarranted credit.

The distinction between these two elements of the credit decision can be found with respect to the granting, maintaining and withdrawing of the credit as well. The criteria for liability in each case are basically the same, taking into account the differences inherent to the circumstances in which these decisions are taken.

With respect to preparing its decision, the bank should act with due diligence in gathering the information and elements of evaluation of the firm's situation. With respect to the central core of the credit decision, the bank can freely decide to grant or to withdraw the loan, but by acting, it should not diverge from the standards a reasonable, professional bank would respect, or to put it more precisely, if it granted the credit or maintained the loan where normal diligent bankers would overwhelmingly have refused it. This will apply if the loan was granted to a borrower that manifestly had no ability to service the loan: the bank will thus commit a tort for which it will be liable to third parties, in particular to creditors.

In substance, the liability test applied in the area of bank liability does not seem to vary from similar tests applied in other areas, such as director's liability[31] and even invalidation of administrative acts.[32] In each case, the active party enjoys a large freedom of decision, and provided its decision is correctly prepared, the balancing of interests involved is beyond the judge's scrutiny, except if a manifestly unreasonable, unbalanced or disproportional decision had been struck. The congruency between public and private law in this respect has clearly been stressed by Van Gerven.[33]

31. See J. Ronse, *et al.*, "Overzicht van Rechtspraak (1978–1985) Vennootschappen", T.P.R., 1986, nr. 253 e.s., p. 1271 e.s.
32. E. Wymeersch, "De Quasi-jurisdictionele funktie", T.P.R., 1982, 841.
33. W. Van Gerven, *Hoe blauw is het bloed van de prins?* Antwerpen, Kluwer, 1984, 89 pp.

The duty to investigate the creditworthiness of the borrower

A bank, when deciding to grant credit, should analyse the creditworthiness of its prospective borrower. It has the professional duty to investigate the enterprise in a careful professional way. The bank could investigate itself, appoint experts, or use any other method. The choice of the adequacy of the investigation method once more will be appreciated according to the standard of the professional banker. The bank could validly rely on auditors' reports, except after the situation has thoroughly deteriorated, so that additional investigations are required.[34]

It should be noted that the fact the credit is agreed to on demand of the government and even that a government guarantee is obtained, does not in itself limit these duties of the banks.[35] The government's intervention may influence the appreciation as to whether the enterprise is irretrievably lost.

If several banks grant credit on a joint basis together, in principle each individual has this duty to investigate. However, if the individual bank is a member of a syndicate with the lead or managing bank assuming the responsibility to gather the necessary information to prepare the credit, the individual bank can rely on the lead bank's report, but remains responsible for assessing the borrower's creditworthiness independently.[36]

The investigative duty of the banks must be related to the specific circumstances of the case, such as the amount of the credit and the reputation of the borrower.[37] Hence, it is normal that in many cases less enquiry is needed for a renewal than for an initial decision to grant credit, and that a reputable, established commercial entity requires less enquiry than a small family business. With respect to this point, the bank has some freedom of judgement, which should be carefully weighed.

The bank should at least know the prospective borrower. If it turns out to be an inexperienced and dishonest person, who for instance has already been declared bankrupt or convicted of violations of rules protecting the public trust, the bank has not fulfilled its duty if it did not detect these serious shortcomings.[38]

---

34. See Paris, 6 January 1977, D., 1977, 144 note Vasseur, and the comments of M. Cabrillac and J.-L. Rives-Lange in Rev. Trim. Dr. Comm., 1977, 140–143.

35. Brussels, 14 September 1979, J.T., 1980, 133, aff'g Comm. Brussels, 3 May 1976, J.T., 1977, 64; Comm. Brussels, 8 June 1990, R.D.C.B., 1991, 241, note. For the liability of the subsidising government, see P. Charlier, "La responsabilité aquilienne des pouvoirs publics dans les dommages causés aux tiers par les aides publiques aux entreprises en difficultés" in C.D.V.A., *Les créanciers et le droit de la faillite*, Brussels, Bruylant, 1983, pp. 451 *et seq*.

36. Cf. Comm. Brussels, 25 February 1983, R.D.C.B., 1983, 555 and note (refusing the defence of a factoring company that invoked the fault of a bank that had extended credit to the bankrupt company, because it could have estimated that risks itself). See also Paris, 13 June 1985, D., 1986, Inf.R., 315, obs. Vasseur. For the liability of the lead bank in a syndicated credit for the information memorandum it gives to the prospective participant banks, see P. Wood, *Law and Practice of International Finance*, London, Sweet & Maxwell, 1980, p. 259 *et seq*.

37. Comm. Brussels, 3 May 1976, J.T., 1977, 60, aff'd Brussels, 14 September 1979, J.T., 1980, 133.

38. Comm. Brussels, 3 May 1976, J.T., 1977, 60, aff'd Brussels, 14 September 1979, J.T., 1980,

In the field of consumer credit, the legislation enacted in conformity with the EEC directive provides for a preliminary investigation by the bank, including the consultation of databases containing the lists of non-performing loans.[39]

With respect to commercial credits similar databases are organised, but their consultation has not been made compulsory.

Although there is no case law on this point yet, one can imagine that the significant progress business science has made these last years in predicting business failures through financial ratio analysis, extends the investigative duties of the banks. It seems reasonable to expect the banks—but also the firm's managers—to apply these methods of analysis which are readily available and the reliability of which has been sufficiently tested.

The bank has to analyse not only the financial situation of the borrower,[40] but also his acquaintance with the business activity. Special care is warranted when the credit is used for a new production process of which the borrower has no experience.[41] The bank should even verify the profitability of the proposed use of the borrowed funds.[42] If the credit is granted to establish a new business, the bank should investigate the chances of survival of this company, and check whether such credit is warranted.[43] The fact that other, especially commercial, creditors should reasonably be aware of the higher risk attached to starting enterprises does not necessarily rule out the bank's liability.[44]

An essential and often mentioned rationale for these strict duties is the bank's professional capacity to analyse the creditworthiness of prospective borrowers. Their central role in the credit market, their access to superior information, and the elaborate methods of financial analysis they can put to work, make banks especially privileged in the performance of this important monitoring function.[45] The risk of liability will induce the banks to be cautious, and to make sure they use their professional capacity to accurately assess creditworthiness. This financial guidance function is supposed to benefit the whole community, which will be able to rely on its bank's educated judgement.

133; Paris, 20 April 1982, Gaz.Pal., 13–15 June 1982; Paris, 4 February 1982, Gaz.Pal., 25–28 April 1982.

39. See for Belgium: art. 15 L. 12 June 1991 on consumer credit.

40. Comm. Brussels, 3 May 1976, J.T., 1977, 60, aff'd Brussels, 14 September 1979, J.T., 1980, 133.

41. Comm. Brussels, 3 May 1976, J.T., 1977, 60, aff'd Brussels, 14 September 1979, J.T., 1980, 133.

42. Paris, 4 February 1982, Gaz.Pal., 25–27 April 1982. If the internal technical credit committee of the bank has given a negative advice on the issue, the risk of liability is significantly increased. See Comm. Brussels, 3 May 1976, J.T., 1977, 60.

43. Aix-en-Provence, 5 May 1981, D., 1981, IR, 500, note Vasseur.

44. Paris, 10 June 1981, D., 1981, IR, 500, rev'g Trib. Comm. Paris, 21 April 1980, D., 1981, IR, 22, note Vasseur.

45. This is disputed by some bank lawyers, who allege that companies in the same sector as the borrower are usually better informed than outsiders, such as a bank. See L. M. Martin, "Où en est-on de la responsabilité du banquier?" Banque, 1985, 7; Vasseur, Note Paris, 6 January 1977, D., 1977, 150; cf., however, Stoufflet, Note Cass. Comm. Fr., 5 December 1978, J.C.P., 1979, II, 19132. See further our Conclusion, infra, p. 214.

The former reasoning raises the issue of to what extent the same liability should not be extended to other creditors, such as suppliers, the tax and social security administrations, the parent company and all bodies that in fact grant credit. The issue has received attention in legal writing and in case law: it is admitted that the same rationale does not apply to those other creditors, as they do not have the same financial and analytical capabilities as banks.[46] According to Belgian law at least, the question is also avoided by pointing at the causation rules that lead to bank liability, even if other creditors would have contributed to maintaining the firm's apparent creditworthiness.[47]

Other creditors should of course be equally prudent in allowing payment terms, and carefully assess their risks by using the customary methods. Commercial creditors should not close their eyes to manifest payment problems experienced by their debtors, and for example continue to supply although several invoices remained unpaid.[48] One decision held that commercial parties have contributed themselves to their damages if they "stupidly" relied on the decision of the bank to grant or maintain the credit.[49] But, as in general these are not specialised financiers, they are normally not held to comparable strict duties to investigate the debtor's financial situation.[50]

Commercial creditors, for instance, has been allowed to rely on the apparent solvency of a company that is supported by a bank or other financial institution.[51] Occasionally, a supplier has been held liable for providing unwarranted credit, but given the small amount, no consequences attached.[52]

The extent to which the supplier knows the business of the debtor, will have an effect on its liability. For instance, breweries in France and Belgium have contracts with bars, granting them the exclusive right to supply beverages. In return, they provide the equipment needed to install the bar. These contracts give them specific knowledge of the affairs of those bars. Therefore, they are well

---

46. e.g. in Civ. Huy, 15 December 1971, Jur.Liège, 1972–1973, 52.

47. See *infra* p. 206. With respect to parent companies see further p. 205.

48. Cass. Comm. Fr., 15 July 1982, J.C.P., 1982, IV, 337; cf. the note by Vasseur under Cass. Comm. Fr., 5 December 1978, D., 1978, IR, 138, referring to Nîmes, 5 December 1977, Banque, 1978, 1423 (raising the issue of the recourse of the bank against suppliers, but leaving it unanswered).

49. Comm. Brussels, 3 May 1976, J.T., 1977, 61, cited Comm. Brussels, 12 March 1973.

50. Paris, 2 December 1981, D., 1981, 483, note Derrida, aff'd Cass. Comm. Fr., 24 November 1983, D., 1984, 305.

51. See for example Comm. Brussels, 3 May 1976, J.T., 1977, 64 (approving the reliance of creditors on the solvency of a company that proposed a construction project that was financed for three quarters by a public credit institution), aff'd Brussels, 14 September 1979, J.T., 1980, 133; Brussels, 10 May 1979, Rev. Banque, 1979, 583 (allowing a supplier of a department store, who legitimately paid more attention to the trust the bank put in the company than to the rumours about possible problems that circulated, to recover its claim). But see Comm. Brussels, 3 May 1976, J.T., 1977, 61 cf. Brussels, 8 March 1983, J.T., 1983, 467.

52. Cass. Comm. Fr., 2 May 1983, D., 1984, IR, 89, note Vasseur.

placed to judge the creditworthiness of the bar, and will more easily than normal suppliers be held liable for their improper credit judgement.[53]

In a remarkable case, the owner-constructor of a shopping mall was held liable for the damages other creditors of one of the shops has suffered, relying on its misleading creditworthiness created by him. In order to attract more business to his mall, the constructor had convinced an apparently bankrupt trader to rent 12 shops for free, even financing the stock necessary to start up these businesses. By doing so, he created an appearance of reliability, and was held liable to the bankrupt trader's creditors.[54]

In these cases relating to the liability of commercial creditors for granting or maintaining credit to their clients, liability was only imposed if the supplier was grossly negligent or deliberately created a misleading image of financial health. These are merely applications of the general duty of care, imposed on every contractor.[55] In the cases on bank liability, however, a more strict standard of the reasonable, professional bank is applied. As specialised professional institutions, they are required to investigate the position of the prospective borrower more thoroughly.

Duties of the bank during the life of the credit

During the life of the credit, the bank has to monitor the performance of the agreement. First, this duty includes review of debtor's compliance with the conditions of the credit, such as the promised sureties.[56] Exceeding the credit limit is not in itself irregular, but can lead to liability in certain circumstances.[57] Unless otherwise stipulated, such as in the case of mortgage credits, the bank is not required to closely supervise the activities for which the loan proceeds are used.[58,59]

The extent of the necessary credit follow-up depends on the circumstances: if nothing happens which should alarm the bank, only normal communications, such as regular review of the accounts of the borrower, are required.[60] However,

---

53. Cass. Comm. Fr., 3 May 1983, D., 1984, IR, 112, note Derrida.

54. Brussels, 13 January 1981, R.D.C.B., 1981, 162.

55. See: Cass. Comm. Fr., 26 January 1993, RJDA, 1993, 6, n° 536.

56. Comm. Brussels, 3 May 1976, J.T., 1977, 60 (involving also a promised raise in capital), aff'd Brussels, 14 September 1979, J.T., 1980, 133.

57. Comm. Charleroi, 4 January 1984, R.D.C.B., 1985, 216 (accepting the overdraft, on the condition that they stopped in time and the situation is restored or extra guarantees or sureties are provided by the borrower); Liège, 1 February 1978, J.T., 1979, 181 (holding the bank liable for allowing transgression of the credit limit not covered by any guarantees or surety. However, specific circumstances contributed to this result, such as the fact that the bank handed the debtor uncovered cheques, which allowed him to flee the country).

58. Comm. Brussels, 29 October 1976, J.T., 1977, 58, at 60; see also Cass. Comm. Fr., 18 November 1980, D. 1981, J., 120 note Stoufflet; D., 1981, IR, 339, obs. Vasseur; see further Van Rijn and Heenen, fn. 2, nr. 668, p. 535.

59. Cass. Comm. Fr., 9 May 1978, D., 1979, 419, note Vasseur; cf. Comm. Charleroi, 18 December 1980, J.T., 1981, 119.

60. Cass. Comm. Fr., 22 May 1985, J.C.P., 1985, Ed.E., 14738; Montpellier, 13 October 1983, J.C.P., 1985, Ed.E., 14524 (requiring the accounts to be certified by an accountant, or especially

if there are warnings from third parties, the bank should investigate the situation.[61] Failure to investigate in cases where there are signs of problems may lead to liability if the bank could or should have ended the credit had it, after investigation, known the gravity of the situation.

The bank's duty to supervise the debtor has to be read with flexibility: if the bank had been defrauded along with all other creditors, no irregular act could be attributed.[62] It was decided that, while under normal circumstances the bank can rely on the company's accounts, it should verify these statements in the case of a debtor facing financial problems, given the risk of falsification.[63] If the bank was deceived by the debtor, who hid the financial problems of his business, the bank can use this argument to avoid liability.[64] But if the deceit was partially made possible because of the gross negligence of the bank in the initial investigation before granting the credit, the argument will be refuted.[65]

Normally, the borrower uses the same bank for its other financial transactions, such as its current payments. This bank, therefore, at least in principle, has the opportunity to monitor these transactions and trace irregular or questionable dealings. Does this create a duty for the bank to detect irregular events or financial problems that might lead to a later default? French and Belgian case law are very comparable on this point.[66]

In France, the bank in principle should not be concerned by the motives behind transactions done through its accounts.[67] It would even risk liability as a *de facto* director, if it were to interfere too much with the management of the debtor's affairs.[68] The mere fact that the bank had the opportunity to monitor the account of the borrower, is thus not a sufficient basis for liability.[69] But when certain transactions raise legitimate suspicion or depart from normal patterns,

---

verified by the bank); Cass. Crim. Fr., 25 February 1985, Rev. Trim. Dr. Comm., 1985, 544, note Cabrillac and Teyssie; Cass. Comm. Fr., 10 June 1986, J.C.P., 1986, Ed.E., 15694 (allowing the bank to rely on certified accounts); see also A. Viandier, "Compte rendu des travaux comptables effectués et responsabilité du banquier", J.C.P., 1984, Ed.E., 13257.

61. Aix-en-Provence, 8 July 1971, Banque, 1971, IR 45; Paris, 6 January 1977, D., 1977, 144, note Vasseur; Comm. Charleroi, 18 December 1980, J.T., 1981, 119; Comm. Gent, 1 March 1983, J.T., 1983, 396.

62. Comm. Grasse, 5 January 1981, R.J.C., 1981, note Deridder, cit. by G. Prat, *op. cit. supra* fn. 2, p. 32.

63. Paris, 6 January 1977, J.C.P., 1977, II, 18689, note Stoufflet.

64. Paris, 6 January 1977, D., 1977, IR, 217, note Vasseur, D., 1977, 144, note Vasseur.

65. Brussels, 14 September 1979, J.T., 1980, 132; Comm. Brussels, 19 November 1986, R.D.C.B., 1987, 786.

66. P. Van Ommeslaghe and L. Simont, *op. cit. supra* fn. 2, p. 1105.

67. Cass. Comm. Fr., 11 January 1983, Bull. Civ., IV, Nr. 11, p. 8, Cass. Comm. Fr., 12 April 1983, J.C.P., 1984, II, 20237; Cass. Comm. Fr., 8 February 1983, Bull. Civ., I, Nr. 51, p. 44; see Gavalda and Stoufflet, "Chronique de droit bancaire", J.C.P., 1986, nr. 14576, 588; Mons, 3 March 1992, J.L.M.B., 1992, 1102, R.D.C.B., 1993, 379, note Blommaert.

68. Paris, 17 March 1978, D., 1978, IR, 420, note Vasseur. Cf. the extreme case of Trib. Comm. Rouen, 10 March 1981, D., 981, IR, 337 (where the French State was held liable, based on the declaration of support for the company in difficulty the Prime Minister had pledged).

69. Moreover, such liability could only arise if the bank could have deduced the upcoming financial collapse of the borrower. Cass. Comm. Fr., 22 July 1980, J.C.P., 1980, IV, 379. One could also mention problems of insider dealings.

the bank should investigate the situation to avoid liability.[70] This duty of care can be relied upon by third parties and can result in liability towards third parties.[71]

It is sometimes accepted that the bank should be more vigilant if the transactions involved funds borrowed from the bank.[72] However, this specific duty should be restricted to credits, the proceeds of which are linked to a specific use.[73]

Belgian law is more hesitant on the subject and would, according to the circumstances, tend to a stricter standard of surveillance,[74] certainly when irregular dealings are apparent. The debtor could not invoke against his bank the protection afforded by the law on the protection of his privacy.

The actual judgement of the creditworthiness of the borrower

It is established case law, both in France and in Belgium that the bank will be liable towards third parties (co-creditors) if it has granted—or maintained—a credit to an enterprise that manifestly had no chance to survive, thus artificially extending this debtor's business life and creating an artificial appearance of solvency, which misleads the other creditors. The upper risk limit, above which reasonable professionals would not have differing opinions about the appropriateness of the credit, is transgressed if there are no chances for the borrower to survive, even taking the credit into account. In other words, the business is hopelessly lost, and the extension of credit can do no more than postpone the end. However, this limit is not yet reached if the bank reasonably believed that the borrower could be saved with the credit. If it afterwards turns out that the borrower fails, the bank cannot be blamed for having extended the life of the company.

The decisions the bank has to take relating to credit are thus necessarily

70. Cass. Comm. Fr., 11 January 1983, Bull. Civ., IV, Nr. 11, p. 8 (holding a bank liable because it failed to detect certain embezzlements, while they related to transactions between the corporation and its shareholders); Cass. Comm. Fr., 7 January 1976, J.C.P., 1976, 18327, note Gavalda and Stoufflet (holding a bank liable because it had not detected that the client had persistently received credit by discounting bills of exchange which were never paid by the drawee, but instead repurchased by the client itself, who had fictitiously drawn these bills); Cf. Comm. Draguignan, 27 April 1982, Banque, 1982, nr. 419, 945, note L. M. Martin, (where the fictitious bills of exchange were discounted with knowledge of the bank). Comm. Brussels, 20 September 1979, J.T., 1980, 45.

71. Cass. Civ. Fr., 8 February 1983, J.C.P., 1983, IV, 129 (investigation of ownership rights of bearer securities when delivered in suspect circumstances).

72. Cass. Comm. Fr., 9 May 1978, D., 1979, 419, note Vasseur; Cass Comm. Fr., 18 May 1993, D., 1993, 609: Rennes, 22 February 1977, D., 1978, IR, 227, note Vasseur, who refers to a contrary judgment in Castres, 27 October 1969, Banque 1970, 103, note Marin; Cf. Comm. Draguignan, 27 April 1982, Banque 1982, nr. 419, 945, note Martin (where the court reproached the bank for not limiting the personal expenses the borrower paid with the borrowed funds, but where the presence of other faults in the case make it difficult to appropriate the correct weight to this argument in the judgment).

73. Cass. Comm. Fr., 18 November 1980, D., 1981, p. 210, note Stoufflet.

74. Comm. Brussels, 3 May 1976, J.T., 1977, 60; aff'd Brussels, 14 September 1979, J.T., 1980, 133; Comm. Brussels, 29 October 1976, J.T., 1977, 59.

business judgements, implying a certain degree of discretion. The legal criteria for liability in such circumstances can be compared to the standards applied in other areas of discretionary powers, such as government liability for administrative decisions and liability of corporate directors.

The wrongful act of the bank could be further analysed as follows. The bank has granted or maintained credit to a borrower that, according to objective standards, was not or no longer creditworthy. This has created an appearance of trustworthiness, which has misled other creditors, because the creditors would not have contracted with the borrower if the credit had not been granted. Thus, if the creditors had been aware of the real situation, they would not have been caught in the bankruptcy, or if the business would already have failed, the later creditors would not have been creditors at all. Seen from another angle, the bank has artificially prolonged the life of the borrower, which has led to a further impairment of its assets. Therefore, the settlement of the bankruptcy takes place under less favourable circumstances.[75]

These viewpoints differ and could possibly lead to different results, for instance concerning the duty to remain an existing credit line, as opposed to the decision to grant the credit. However, they share the same central starting point, which is the bank's flawed judgement concerning the creditworthiness. The bank is held liable for overestimating the survival chances of the borrower, either by attaching new creditors or by diminishing the assets available for recovery to the old creditors. Its judgement is analysed in the light of the customary standards of the professional banker.

Estimating the chances for survival of a company facing financial difficulties is a delicate matter, about which professional and reasonable bankers can disagree. One has to take all relevant internal and external factors that can bear on the result into account, such as the personality of the entrepreneur, plans for reorganisation, even political support or subsidies. All of these elements can be found in the published cases.

At least two pitfalls should be avoided. The first one is hindsight: the bank's behaviour has to be assessed at the moment of its decisions, not in the light of the facts discovered afterwards. Therefore it is important that the bank thoroughly investigates the firm's situation.

On the other hand, a decision whether a firm is creditworthy will never be fully reliable. The law should only sanction lending to manifestly desperately lost enterprises, not to the one that can be salved. The courts should not intervene in the ultimate appreciation of creditworthiness, which belongs to the bank's business judgement. The same problem is regularly met in company law, where the jurisdictions have showed less restraint.[76]

Among the circumstances in which the bank's objective assessment of the

---

75. For this distinction, see L. M. Martin, *op. cit. supra* fn. 55, p. 8.

76. Comp. Liège, 24 October 1991, R.D.C.B., 1992, 993 about the business judgement exercised by the bank in relation to that of the debtor.

situation will be doubted, one can mention the following cases, all referring to judicial decisions:

(a) conflict of interest cases: the bank has pursued the credit in its own interest, e.g. to be able to recuperate more on its credit lines,[77] to be able to switch from one form of credit to another,[78] or when the pursuance of the loan contained no risk to the bank, the latter being fully secured[79];

(b) the bank effectively knew that the firm had already stopped its payments and therefore that it should have applied for liquidation[80];

(c) manifest disproportion between the volume of the credit, its conditions, including interest charges, or its form and the importance of the firm.[81]

The bank will also be liable if on granting the credit it acted in collusion with the firm or its managers, especially if the latter were infringing a rule enforced by criminal sanctions.

This hypothesis presents itself in cases in which the credit was granted merely to postpone the statutory obligation to declare bankruptcy, which is sanctioned by a criminal provision.[82] If the bank finances a new business that either is set up by a businessman excluded from trading,[83] or would constitute an irregular activity,[84] it would be liable as aiding a violation of the law. The use of illegal or

77. Cass. Comm. 5 December 1978, D., 1979, Inf. Rap., 138 obs Vasseur, Banque, 1979, 1109, obs Martin.

78. This argument was refuted in Comm. Brussels, 2 October 1974, J.T., 1975, 44, note Zenner, overruled on other grounds by Brussels, 10 May 1979, Pas., 1979, II, 97.

79. Chambéry, 21 January 1980, Banque, 1980, 638, obs Martin; Cass. Comm. Fr., 2 June 1982, JCP 1982, IV, 283.

80. Cass. Comm. Fr., 5 December 1978; Cass. Comm. Fr., 16 October 1979, JCP, 1980, II, 19279, note Gulphe.

81. Cass. Comm. Fr., 5 December 1978; Cass. Comm. Fr., 7 February 1983, JCP, 1983, CI, 11504; Mons, 4 October 1988, J.L.M.B., 1989, 1151.

82. See in France: Cass. Crim., 20 November 1978, D.S., 1979, 525 note Culioli et Derrida; Paris, 30 June 1983, Gaz. Pal., 1983, 2, 636 note Marchi. Some even thought of the bank aiding and abetting the firm's criminal action.

In Belgium a similar principle has been applied with respect to the liability of directors of a company: see for the lower jurisdictions: Comm. Liège, 7 December 1988, T.R.V., 1989, 441; Civ. Antwerp, 8 March 1982, R.D.C., 1983, 288 note J. Lievens. The Supreme Court stopped this evolution: Cass., 22 September 1988, R.C.J.B., 1990, 203, note Dalcq; R.P.S., 1989, 180, no. 6515 and Trib. Namur, 4 October 1986, R.P.S., 1989, no. 6516, 183. Also: Cass., 18 May 1990, Arr. Cass., 1989–1990, no. 550, 1196; Cass., 7 September 1990, T.R.V., 1991, 86, note M. Wyckaert. The lower courts have adopted the more refined standard: Antwerp, 13 February 1989, Pas., 1989, II, 205; R.D.C., 1990, 434; Trib. Turnhout, 15 March 1989, Turnhouts Rechtsleven, 1989, 169 and 26 March 1990, Turnhouts Rechtsleven, 1991, 111. Also legal writing approved the court's prudent attitude: Coppens and 't Kint, "Examen de jurisprudence", R.C.J.B., 1991, no. 90, p. 490; I. Verougstraete and C. Van Buggenhout, "Faillissement en continuïteit van de onderneming", T.P.R., 1990, 1750, note 51; more hesitant, K. Geens and H. Laga, "Overzicht van rechtspraak", T.P.R., 1993, no. 45, 1059; and very critical: R. Dalcq, "Appreciation de la faute en cas de violation d'une obligation déterminée", R.C.J.B., 1990, 207 e.s.

83. See in Belgium, but applied to the question of liability for the formation of a company: Comm. Brussels, 20 April 1983, R.D.C.B., 1984, 551.

84. See for France, Paris 26 May 1967, JCP, 1968, II, 15518, note Stoufflet.

irregular financing techniques would also result in bank liability: this might occur if the bank discounts bills that clearly are irregular,[85] fake, or constitute "kite flying",[86] but also if the bank grants credit at ruinous conditions, e.g. if the bank charged too high interest rates.[87]

It is widely accepted that the bank should not avoid all risks: it is sufficient for the bank to avoid liability that there be a reasonable chance of the debtor's survival.[88] The bank is allowed to provide credit to a company that in fact has already stopped payments, and, therefore, finds itself in the objective circumstances of bankruptcy, provided that the bank reasonably believed that the credit would provide real chances for recovery.[89] The good faith of the bank is, of course, to be presumed.

It is, therefore, the bankruptcy receiver who bears the burden of proof. The receiver will first have to prove that the bank knew that there were no chances for survival,[90] although negligent behaviour of the bank, such as failure to thoroughly investigate the matter in a timely manner, may be deemed equivalent to actual knowledge. The receiver will have to prove that the bank, in effect, artificially kept alive an entity that reasonable bankers would consider beyond salvation.[91]

What seems to be required, is a serious, grave error of judgement by the bank.[92] If reasonable doubt exists, the bank is not liable. This criterion, therefore, sometimes is referred to as a "marginal" test.[93]

---

85. See e.g. Brussels, 25 September 1986, J.T., 1987, 234.

86. Cass. Comm. 28 November 1960, Bull. Civ., 1960, III, 381.

87. See the bankruptcy laws expressly providing sanctions for the debtor taking out credit at ruinous conditions: art. 573, 3°, Belg. Bankr.L.

88. Comm. Charleroi, 4 January 1984, R.D.C.B., 216; Mons, 4 May 1983, R.D.C.B., 1984, 520; Brussels, 29 May 1980, J.T., 1980, 597; Trib. Comm. Lille, 14 October 1977, D., 1978, IR, 226; Trib. Liège, 22 September 1983, Jur. Liège, 1985, 561.

89. Nancy, 15 December 1977, J.C.P., 1977, 18912, note Stoufflet; Cass. Comm. Fr., 9 May 1978, D., 1979, 419, note Vasseur; Cass. Comm. Fr., 19 January 1983, D., 1984, IR, 90. For the older, now abandoned opinion that providing credit to a company that can be declared bankrupt is a tort, see Trib. Comm. Draguignan, 27 April 1982, Banque, 1982, nr. 419, 945, note Martin, referring to other cases; note of Stoufflet, under Paris, 6 January 1977, J.C.P., 1977, II, 18689; Cf. Comm. Brussels, 29 May 1980, J.T., 1980, 597; Comm. Brussels, 29 September 1983, R.D.C.B., 1985, 554.

90. Cass. Comm. Fr., 22 July 1980, J.C.P., 1980, IV, 379; Cass. Comm. Fr., 15 July 1982, J.C.P., 1982, IV, 337; Cass. Comm. Fr., 23 February 1982, J.C.P., 1982, IV, 167; Nancy, 15 December 1978, J.C.P., 1977, 18912, note Stoufflet.

91. Cass. Comm. Fr., 19 January 1983, J.C.P., 1983, IV, 100; Nancy, 15 December 1977, J.C.P., 1977, 18912, note Stoufflet; Trib. Comm. Lille, 14 October 1977, D., 1978, 226, note Derrida; Paris, 2 December 1981, D., 1981, IR, 483, note Vasseur; Nancy, 18 September 1981, J.C.P., 1983, 19937 note Vivant; Comm. Charleroi, 4 January 1984, R.D.C.B., 1985, 216; Brussels, 27 September 1978, R.D.C.B., 1979, 268; Comm. Charleroi, 18 December 1980, J.T., 1981, 119.

92. Comm. Brussels, 16 June 1975, R.D.C.B., 1976, 4; Rennes, 17 June 1977, D., 1977, IR, 449, note Vasseur; Comm. Charleroi, 4 January 1984, R.D.C.B., 1985, 216; Brussels, 27 September 1978, R.D.C.B., 1979, 268.

93. Mons, 4 May 1983 R.D.C.B., 1984, 520. Whether this method should be analysed as a "marginal test" (marginale toetsing), will not be commented on. As P. Van Ommeslaghe and L. Simont, op. cit. supra fn. 2, p. 1095, note 15, point out, it mainly appears to be a terminological matter.

The test is an objective one, making it irrelevant whether the decision was normal for this particular bank.[94] Hence the bank has to judge the creditworthiness of the borrower in a complete, independent manner. If the bank has an interest in the borrower, albeit indirectly, for example, through interlocking directorships, it cannot continue to support this borrower beyond the point an independent bank would consider reasonable.[95]

A special issue that has been dealt with by the courts is whether a mere disproportion between the amount of the credit and the financial size of the borrower renders the credit supplier liable. This question was raised in a case before the Court of Appeal of Paris, where the plaintiff alleged that the credit granted was completely out of proportion with the activity and the size of the borrower. The principle was accepted, but the claim was dismissed for lack of causation.[96] Thus, for example, a credit of FF 150,000 is not excessive if the borrower realises a turnover of FF 5 million,[97] but a credit of more than 11 times the net worth of the borrower is.[98] But special circumstances, such as the personal surety bond of directors or shareholders of the borrower, should be taken into account.[99]

The sureties the borrower offers the bank will necessarily influence the original credit decision. The right of the bank to require certain guarantees, pledges, mortgages or surety bond is undisputed. In deciding the extent of these surety interests, the size of the credit in proportion to the creditworthiness of the borrower should be taken into account. Clearly excessive requirements of the bank in this respect, however, could be deemed to be an abuse of rights.[100]

Can the bank in deciding to grant a credit solely rely on the fact that the repayment of the credit is adequately secured? The widespread opinion among scholars is that the bank cannot avoid its duty to independently assess the credit by stipulating ample sureties. As such, the economic gains the intended use of the proceeds of the loan will produce, must be weighed against the requested credit. Along these lines, the Belgian Banking and Finance Commission ascribes only a secondary role to the requirement of security interests by the banks,[101] and the

---

94. Antwerp, 5 October 1983, R.W., 1983–84, 1361, note J. De Lat.

95. Brussels, 10 May 1979, Rev. Banque, 1979, 583; *Cf.* Trib. Comm. Nice, 5 June 1979, D., 1979, 627, Note Honorat.

96. Paris, 21 May 1981, D., 1982, IR, 414, note Vasseur, Banque 1982, 389, note L. M. Martin, Rev. Trim. Dr. Comm., 1982, 596.

97. Paris, 6 January 1977, D., 1977, IR, 217, note Vasseur.

98. Paris, 10 June 1981, D., 1981, IR, 500; see also Paris, 12 April 1983, Banque, 1983, 1054, note Martin (proportion of 1/20, taking the future prospects and the personal surety bond of a director into account).

99. Comm. Brussels, 16 June 1975, R.D.C.B., 1976, 4.

100. BGH, 5 May 1956, WM, 1958, 756 (deciding that the bank abused its rights by demanding so much surety that it would not qualify anymore for further credit from competing banks); *Cf.* Nancy, 18 September 1981, J.C.P., 1983, 19937, note Vivant (mentioning the argument that by demanding excessive sureties, the risk is shifted to the other creditors); HR, 28 June 1957, N.J., 1957, 514; HR, 10 August 1983, N.J., 1984, 252 (challenging excessively secured credit on the basis of good faith).

101. Banking Commission, Annual Report, 1986, 34.

presence of adequate security interests does not release the banks from their duty to investigate and assess the creditworthiness of the prospective borrower.[102]

A related issue concerns bank's liability in case of back-to-back loans. The bank grants a loan to a company that has deposited sufficient cash or securities with the bank to guarantee the repayment. Sometimes, it is the parent company or the shareholders of the borrower that made the deposit. In that case, the bank might base its credit decision primarily on the possibility to enforce the guarantees, and care less about the creditworthiness of the borrower.

The French Cour de Cassation has declared a bank liable in comparable circumstances.[103] The court considered it unlawful to maintain the credit up to a maximum amount corresponding to the securities pledged by the borrower, while the bank knew that its situation was seriously jeopardised. The bank unsuccessfully argued that it had only reloaned the borrower's own funds: the ignorance of other creditors about the specific terms of the credit and the decay of the company were a sufficient basis for liability.[104]

The issue of bank liability for providing credit is usually raised under circumstances in which the proceeds of the credit were used to finance the business activity of the borrower in general. One can wonder whether the same criteria can lead to liability of the bank that granted an investment credit, the proceeds of which will be used to finance a specific asset. The argument that such credit does not artificially prolong the life of the borrower, and therefore does not mislead other creditors, is decisive. On this basis, among others, liability has been denied for such financing.[105] Moreover, the security interests the banks have in the assets financed with investment credits, are usually subject to disclosure requirements. Disclosure should at least alert the other creditors, shifting the risk of their future transactions with the borrower.

When the borrower is in reorganisation, the risks involved are different, and possibly greater. The bank will find itself in a delicate position. By refusing to cooperate and to provide credit without serious motives, it can be rendered liable.[106] But it can also incur liability when it participates in a plan that afterwards is found to be insufficient. Its decision will inevitably affect other interests, such as the possibility to attract other financiers, the employment prospects of the personnel, the future of suppliers and consumers, and the general or regional economic welfare as well. Does the bank have to take these

102. L. Simont and A. Bruyneel, op. cit. supra fn. 2, pp. 231–232.

103. Cass. Comm. Fr., 23 February 1982, J.C.P., 1982, IV, 167; D., 1982, IR, 414, note Vasseur.

104. Aix-en-Provence, 23 February 1979, D., 1980, IR, 287, note Derrida, aff'd Cass. Comm. Fr., 23 February 1982, J.C.P., 1982, IV, 167, D., 1982, IR, 414, note Vasseur (where this technique was held not to be illegal).

105. Note by Cabrillac and Teyssie, Rev. Trim. Dr. Comm., 1983, 583; but Cf. Cass. Comm. Fr., 2 May 1983, J.C.P., 1983, IV, 213 (reproaching the bank for having enhanced the increase of the deficit, by allowing the borrower to make investments that inevitably would fail).

106. Van Ommeslaghe and Simont, op. cit. supra fn. 2, p. 1115, nr. 34; see Nancy, 18 September 1981, J.C.P., 1983, 19937, note Vivant (declaring a bank liable that suddenly withdrew its credit during a voluntary reorganisation scheme, while negotiations for a takeover were taking place); Cf. Pres. Comm. Brussels, 30 October 1984, R.D.C.B., 1985, 572.

factors into consideration and can it invoke them as attenuating circumstances when its liability is alleged?[107]

The rule is that if the reorganisation plan is well conceived, well prepared and well balanced, the bank will not be liable for granting the agreed credit, even if later on the firm nevertheless fails.[108] Also, it has been decided that the bank will not be liable if it grants or maintains credit in favour of a firm that was irretrievably lost, but where serious takeover proposals had been submitted.[109]

The framework within which the reorganisation is taking place could have an effect on the bank's liability. If it is a voluntary reorganisation, one can reasonably expect the bank not to depart from its general attitude, judging the survival chances and the creditworthiness independently. However, the same standard also seems to apply if the procedure is supervised or led by a court or by the government, accentuating that even then it remains the first task of the banks to judge the reorganisation plan on its chances for success.[110] There may however be a presumption of seriousness if the court is involved.[111]

The participation of other public or private financial institutions is sometimes taken into account. Within the framework of a rescue plan, banks may rely on the attitude taken by other financiers, as well as on the attitude taken by shareholders.[112] According to part of the Belgian and French[113] case law and to Belgian doctrine,[114] a strict standard is applied, not allowing the bank to rely on the judgement of the public institution. Another point of view can be found in other French cases and in French writing[115]: it allows the bank to presume that the public financier has seriously investigated the borrower's chances of recovery. Exceptionally, the plaintiff creditors would be entitled to prove that the bank held information on the basis of which it should have denied its participation. This reasoning, however, is not convincing, as the presence of one financial institution does not relieve the other lenders, including the State, from their duty to assess the borrower's creditworthiness.[116] The outcome might be different if the bank could have assumed that the government would not let the borrower fail, as this assumption would be a sound basis for the bank to continue its lending. The latter, however, is a factual question, which will have to be examined in every case.

107. See Nancy, 18 September 1981, J.C.P., 1983, 19937, note Vivant (where the extent of liability was reduced because of such arguments).

108. Brussels, 22 September 1988, J.T., 1989, 694.

109. Cass. Comm., 15 June 1993, J.C.P., 1993, Ed.E, 1070; Bull. Civ., IV, N° 240; see also *supra* note 106.

110. Cf. Chambéry, 21 January 1980, Rev. Trim. Dr. Comm., 1980, 586, Banque, 1980, 683, note Martin.

111. See in general Gavalda and Stoufflet, fn. 2, nr. 409 e.s. p. 191. F. Rua, Fn. 2, nr. 13.

112. Brussels, 25 January 1990, J.L.M.B., 1990, 1272.

113. Aix, 4 July 1978, D., 1980, IR, 54; Comm. Brussels, 8 June 1990, R.D.C.B., 1991, 241 note.

114. Van Ommeslaghe, and Simont, *op. cit. supra* fn. 2, nr. 34, 1114 and Belgian cases cited there.

115. Chambéry, 21 January 1980, Banque, 1980, 638, note L. M. Martin; Rev. Trim. Dr. Comm. 1980, 586, note Cabrillac and Rives-Lange; Cass. Comm. Fr., 7 May 1978, Banque 1978, 899, aff'g Paris, 6 January 1977, Banque, 1977, 4.

116. See Brussels, 21 December 1983, Rev. Banque, 1984/3, 45.

Liability of the bank for unwarranted withdrawal of credit

A significant part of the case law on bank liability deals with the situation where the bank having provided credit, is actually confronted by the firm's serious financial problems. Fearing the loss of its money and possibly liability for continuing to support the borrower as well, the bank may decide to withdraw the credit line and to accelerate the outstanding loan.[117] This often causes the final collapse of the borrower's business. The bank thus finds itself with a dilemma: if it were to maintain the credit line, it would risk liability for unwarranted credit, while if it were to recall the credit, it would risk liability for unwarranted withdrawal.

First, the general conditions for ending credit agreements should be borne in mind. In most countries,[118] these conditions are spelled out in the loan documentation.[119] Sometimes, these contracts refer to the general conditions of the bank. These specific and general conditions define precisely the situations in which the bank can recall or accelerate the credit. The bank is bound by these stipulations and cannot arbitrarily withdraw the credit, as the borrower rightly relied on the performance of the agreement, or its termination according to the contractual clauses. If the bank nevertheless recalls the loan, in violation of the contract, it will be liable not only to the borrower, but also to third parties, who also could rely on the normal duration of the credit.[120]

A different problem arises if the debtor exceeds its credit ceiling, or, due to a simple toleration by the bank, if he overdrew his account.[121] In this case, the debtor has no right to the proceeds.[122] The bank can always recall the over-extension of the line of credit or the overdraft and the beneficiary cannot rely on their continuation, although in certain circumstances abuse of rights can limit the powers of the bank.[123] As a rule, the credit cannot be withdrawn at once but a reasonable notice must be served. Immediate withdrawal is allowed if the debtor has stopped his payments, or if the creditor's guarantees have been reduced.[124] Recent case law seems to go further and admits that continuous overdrafts correspond to a credit line, at least up to the average debit position;

---

117. For these rules in general see J. P. Buyle, "La dénonciation du crédit", Rev. Banque, 1988/9, 43.

118. In France, as opposed to Belgium, however, banks tend to grant credit without written conditions. Hence, most legal disputes relating to whether a withdrawal was a legitimate withdrawal or not, have been dealt with by French courts. See *infra* p. 203 about the effects of art. 60 of the Banking Act.

119. See P. Wood, *op. cit. supra* fn. 36, p. 164 *et seq.*

120. Brussels, 3 April 1984, R.P.S., 1984, Nr. 6292, p. 184.

121. As mentioned, such tolerances and formal credits are in France sometimes difficult to distinguish, because of the lack of written agreement for credits.

122. Comm. Brussels, 3 April 1984, R.P.S., 1984, Nr. 6292, p. 184; Comm. Liège, 2 June 1983, R.D.C.B., 1984, 70; B. Glansdorff, "La responsabilité du banquier qui refuse de consentir un dépassement de crédit", Rev. Banque, 1967, 669; P. Charlier, *op. cit. supra* fn. 35.

123. Comm. Brussels, 3 April 1984, R.P.S., 1984, Nr. 6292, p. 184; Comm. Liège, 2 June 1983, R.D.C.B., 1984, 76; *Cf.* Liège, 14 February 1964, R.C.J.B., 1969, 497, note De Bersaques.

124. Art. 1188 Civ.C.

therefore the bank cannot withdraw the credit except after having complied with the normal rules, as provided for in the French Banking Act.[125]

The bank should not use its right to cancel the credit, except in a diligent way. It would not act diligently, for example, if it withdrew the credit just before a major order is placed without bankruptcy being imminent.[126] In such case, the bank can be ordered to reopen the credit line, the courts annulling the bank's decision to suspend or stop the credit for violation of good faith,[127] if necessary under the imposition of damages in case of refusal.

In deciding to cancel the credit line on the basis of the borrower's financial problems—and in the absence of a formal bankruptcy—the bank not only has to weigh its own interests, but should also take into account the interests of other parties concerned such as the co-creditors.[128] In certain cases, however, no choice is left to the bank: if the creditworthiness of the borrower is ruined beyond any doubt, for example because it committed fraud, falsification, or used fictitious schemes with bills of exchange,[129] the bank would commit a tort if it continued to provide purchasing power to such an unreliable borrower.[130]

Even if the bank can legitimately regard the business of the debtor as lost, it has to weigh the interests involved in deciding to cancel or to reduce the credit. In that situation, the interests of the other creditors come to the foreground even more.

For these reasons, the borrower should be given advance notice of the bank's intention to withdraw the credit.[131] The length of this notice will depend on the circumstances, such as the possibility for the borrower to find financing with other banks.[132] During this transitional period, the bank has to live up to its contractual obligations under the credit agreement, including advancing funds as promised. If, however, the situation is extremely serious with no possible

125. See p. 203, *infra*. Paris, 31 January 1991, D., 1992, 298, obs. Tridi.

126. Comm. Liège, 2 June 1978, R.D.C.B., 1984, 76; *Cf.* Liège, 14 February 1964, R.C.J.B., 1969, 497, note De Bersaques; Comm. Brussels, 3 April 1984, R.P.S., 1984, Nr. 6292, p. 184.

127. Trib. Comm. Boulogne sur Mer, 24 September 1982, D., 1983, IR, 467, note Vasseur; Vezian, *op. cit. supra* fn. 2 p. 186. Cf. Pres. Comm. Brussels, 30 October 1984, R.D.C.B., 1985, 572; Comm. Charleroi, 27 December 1984, J.T., 1985, 370 (not ordering a continuation of the credit, because the financial position of the borrower was completely ruined). Comm. Gent, 31 January 1991 R.D.C.B., 1992, 984 note. Refusal of the reopening of the credit, allowing only damages: Comm. Kortrijk, 18 March 1993, R.D.C.B., 1993, 1048, note Buyle.

128. Comm. Brussels, 3 May 1976, J.T., 1977, 60 (referring to the Annual Reports of the Banking Commission); Comm. Brussels, 20 September 1979, J.T., 1980, 45 (where the bank was found to have breached its duty of good faith, by waiting to cancel the credit until it had taken all necessary real surety interests, without taking the position of third parties into account); Brussels, 12 February 1992, J.L.M.B., 1993, 155, R.P.S., 1993, nr. 6624, 256, note 't Kint; R.D.C.B., 1993, 1041, Pas., 1992, II, 23. As mentioned, some writers extend this balance of interest to the "general interest", see *supra*, note 22.

129. Comm. Liège, 2 June 1978, R.D.C.B., 1984, 70; Brussels, 11 September 1987, R.D.C.B., 1989, 7, note D. Devos.

130. See also Michiels Van Kessenich-Hoogendam, *op. cit. supra* fn. 16, p. 22.

131. Nîmes, 21 November 1971, Banque, 1972, 297, note Martin; Brussels, 4 December 1987, J.L.M.B., 1989, 394.

132. Arr. Rb. Arnhem, 20 October 1987, K.G., 1987, 505.

recovery, then the bank can, and in fact must, end the credit immediately. But it must state the reasons for its decision.[133]

The foregoing explains why cancellation or withdrawal of the credit can constitute a tort rendering the bank liable towards third parties: if the borrower's collapse, although he could still have recovered, is exclusively due to the unjustified action of the bank, the latter may be held liable.[134] Under Belgian law, the withdrawal normally cannot take effect immediately.[135] In order to safeguard the legitimate interests of the borrower, the bank should grant an accommodating procedure, containing not only advance notice, but also guidelines to repair the situation. Such an interim measure could be to freeze the credit, not advancing any additional funds, while waiting with the acceleration of the outstanding amounts.[136] Only after it appeared that these measures have not produced satisfactory results, can the bank effectively recall the credit. This intermediate period can take up to a couple of months.[137]

But if objectively the bank concludes that no recovery is possible, postponing the decision to stop the credit might mislead other creditors by creating an artificial creditworthiness. In this case, one could recommend the bank to cancel the credit with immediate effect.[138] If the bank will not do this and continues to support the borrower, it could be rendered liable for the damages suffered by other creditors.[139]

It is against this background that the question of liability for sudden cancellation of credit is raised. Most of the time, the bank has been negotiating and discussing with the borrower for months. The decision to finally withdraw the credit in such circumstances can be no surprise to the borrower and will, therefore, not constitute a tort.[140]

133. Vezian, *op. cit. supra* fn. 2 Nr. 236, p. 191. This renders it possible to verify the balancing of interests. See Comm. Gent 31 January 1991, R.D.C.B., 1992, 984 aff'd by Gent 17 May 1991 (unreported); see also Brussels, 12 February 1992, R.D.C.B., 1993, 1041, note Buyle and Thunis.

134. Cass. Comm. Fr., 22 April 1980, D., 1981, IR, 22, note Vasseur, J.C.P., 1980, IV, 245 (declaring liable the bank that had stopped the credit without taking into account new contracts the borrower was negotiating, and the fact that part of the credit was never used, while the bank itself had deferred the payment of certain cheques); Cass. Comm. Fr., 19 November 1985, J.C.P., 1986, Ed.E., Nr. 5149 (declaring the bank liable when it stopped and accelerated a credit, requiring repayment within 48 hours, while the borrower that had stopped payment expected important new orders); cf. Cass. Comm. Fr., 6 November 1984, J.C.P., 1985, Ed.E., 14032; Nancy, 18 September 1981, J.C.P., 1983, 19937, note Vivant.

135. Comm. Brussels, 12 May 1980, J.T., 1980, 693 (referring to the reliance of the borrower); Brussels, 12 February 1992, J.L.M.B., 1993, 155.

136. Comm. Brussels, 12 September 1980, J.T., 1980, 693; Comm. Charleroi, 4 January 1984, R.D.C.B., 1985, 216.

137. Comm. Liège, 2 June 1983, R.D.C.B., 1984, 70.

138. See Cass. Comm. Fr., 3 December 1991, Banque, 1992, 530; Comm. Brussels, 3 April 1984, R.P.S., 1984, Nr. 6292, p. 184; see also Arr. Rb. Arnhem, 20 October 1987, K.G., 1987, 505.

139. Comm. Liège, 2 June 1983, R.D.C.B., 1984, 70; Trib. Liège, 20 December 1983, R.P.S., 1984, Nr. 6291, p. 175; Comm. Brussels, 29 May 1980, J.T., 1980, 597; Paris, 16 May 1980, D., 1981, IR, 21, note Vasseur; Trib. Comm. Paris, 19 May 1980, D., 1981, IR, 21, note Vasseur; Cass. Comm. Fr., 6 March 1978, D., 1979, IR, 362, note Vasseur; Cass. Comm. Fr., 23 February 1982, D., 1982, IR, 414, note Vasseur; Canaris, *Bankvertragsrecht*, § 1246 e.s.

140. Comm. Liège, 2 June 1978, R.D.C.B., 1984, 70; Trib. Liège, 20 December 1983, R.P.S.,

The reform of the French Banking Law[141] and of the Law on Reorganisations[142] has considerably influenced the former set of rules.

According to article 60 of the Banking Act 1984 all loans to firms for an undetermined period of time may not be suspended until after a notice served in writing and after a time period as fixed in the credit agreement, has lapsed. The former rule is not applicable either if the debtor has behaved in a "gravely reprehensible" way or if his situation has become "irremediably lost".[143] The case law seems very strict in applying the two mentioned exceptions, and thus requiring due notice: only in cases in which false documents have been used, or other irregularities were committed,[144] or where the debtor refused to deliver the promised sureties[145] was immediate termination of the credit allowed. The mere fact that the debtor has virtually stopped payments is not by itself sufficient.[146]

The 1985 French Law on Reorganisations contains the provision according to which, notwithstanding the pending reorganisation, existing contractual relationships may be continued at the request of the "administrateur" at least during the "observation period", the initial orientation period in the reorganisation procedure. It was admitted that this rule also applies to loans granted to ailing firms submitted to the procedure.[147] The loan cannot be stopped except after having complied with the said article 60 of the Banking Act, i.e. after having given due notice, or for the reasons stated therein.[148]

Liability towards guarantors and drawers of bills of exchange

A specific case of liability arises when the bank enters into a contract with a third party, especially a guarantor, without disclosing the financial difficulties of the principal debtor.[149] If the debtor later defaults, the bank is sometimes held liable, either in contract or in tort. A similar setting is found when the bank agrees to discount a bill of exchange drawn on its client, the beneficiary of the credit by the drawer of the bill, who is paid in full by the bank.[150]

1984, Nr. 6291, p. 175; Paris, 16 May 1980, D., 1981, IR, 21, note Vasseur; Trib. Comm. Paris, 19 May 1980, D., 1981, IR, 21, note Vasseur; Cass. Comm. Fr., 6 March 1978, D., 1979, IR, 362, note Vasseur.

141. L. 84–46 of 24 January 1984, JCP, 1984, Ed.G., nr. 55250.

142. L. 85–98 of 25 January 1985, *supra*, note 6.

143. "En cas de comportement gravement répréhensible" or "au cas où la situation de ce dernier s'avérerait irrémédiablement compromise".

144. See Poitiers, 5 December 1990 and Trib. Comm. Paris, 11 February 1992, in Jurisclasseur, Banque et crédit, fasc 151, suppl. 1994.

145. Cass. Comm. Fr., 2 June 1992, Bul.civ., IV, n° 213.

146. Cass. Comm. Fr., 25 February 1992, Jurisclasseur, Banque et crédit, fasc 151, suppl. 1994.

147. Cass. Fr. 8 December 1987, D. 1988, 52, note Derrida— Cass. Comm. Fr., 10 October 1991, JCP, 1991, Ed. E, 236, obs Jeantin.

148. See for further details: Gavalda and Stoufflet, fn. 2, nr. 399, p. 188 e.s.

149. The bank is held to confidentiality about its client's financial situation. Rather than informing the third party, it should stop the credit: Brussels, 25 September 1986, J.T., 1987, 234; Brussels, 30 September 1986, J.L.M.B., 1987, 151.

150. This is the so-called "escompte-fournisseurs" which has been identified in French case law as

As a rule, the guarantor himself should investigate before promising to pay the debt of someone else. Reliance on the bank's analysis of the risk will not easily be accepted. Liability might be admitted if the bank knew that the situation of the debtor was hopeless at the moment the guarantee was delivered to the bank, and the bank made the guarantor believe that there was no substantial risk. This liability may be of a precontractual nature,[151] or may be based on fraud.[152] It also may be based on error in substance, the guarantor promising to be bound for the debt of somebody else, not as a principal debtor. On the basis of article 1382 Civil Code, the guarantor will be entitled to counterclaim, and to set off his claim against the bank's pursuit for specific performance. On the basis of fraud or error, the guarantee contract would be null and void, notwithstanding damages if fraud had been proved.

The same reasoning could be considered to apply if the financial situation of the debtor deteriorates after the guarantee had rightly been granted, and the bank decides to sever its relationship with the debtors. Once the guarantee has been granted, the bank should not inform the guarantor of the deterioration of the debtor's financial situation.[153] Here again the risk will essentially be borne by the guarantor, who should keep himself informed about the debtor's situation.[154] The position of the guarantor is essentially weaker, the guarantee having been contracted for with the debtor's non-performance specifically in mind. The liability of the bank would be limited to the cases in which the bank stopped the credit without due notice, or if it committed other irregularities, e.g. if the bank did not supervise the utilisation of the funds, as convened. Knowledge of the imminent collapse of the debtor is necessary: if the guarantor, as shareholder or director of the debtor company, knew or should have known about the threat to the firm's future, the bank could oppose this argument to stop the guarantor's claim.

The foregoing reasoning which relates to contractual guarantees will also apply if the credit, granted to the acceptor of a bill of exchange, is realised by having the drawer discount the bill at the drawee's bank. On the drawee's refusal to pay, the bank will have recourse against the drawer. In numerous cases, if the bank knew that the drawee was virtually insolvent at the moment

---

essentially based on a guarantee contract subscribed by the drawer in favour of the bank: see Cass. Comm. Fr. 23 June 1971, D. 1972, 175; Cf. Comm. Ghent, 10 January 1953, Rev. Banque, 1955, 704; the usual analysis in Belgian law is different due to differences in the way of transferring the bill, qualified a "contract for the discount of a bill": see Van Rijn and Heenen, fn. 2, nr. 565, p. 435; Winandy, "Les moyens de défense du tireur contre le recours du banquier escompteur d'un effet de commerce", Rev. Banque, 1983, 641.

151. Mons, 4 October 1988, J.L.M.B., 1989, 1151; Comm. Liège, 17 March 1989, R.D.C.B., 1990, 1052.

152. Brussels, 25 January 1990, J.L.M.B., 1990, 1272; see for a case involving a bill of exchange: Bruxelles, 22 November 1985, Rev. Banque, 1986, 6, 35.

153. Brussels, 25 November 1986, R.D.C.B., 1987, 430; Antwerp, 15 December 1992, R.W., 1992–1993, 1030 note Lanoye, Limb. rechtsl., 1993, 34; Brussels, 25 November 1986, J.L.M.B., 1987, 161; Civ. Namur, 1 April 1988, J.T., 1988, 410.

154. Antwerp, 17 December 1986, R.D.C.B., 1989, 3.

of discounting the bill, it has been held that the bank's recourse against the drawer would be off set by the drawer's right of action against the bank on the basis of precontractual negligence. The latter is not the lack of information to the drawer about the dangers inherent to this financing system,[155] but the continuance of the credit by the bank, notwithstanding the bank's knowledge of the hopeless situation of the drawee, its client.

Causation is especially important: the bank's fault should have directly caused the damage.[156] The plaintiff must prove that the damage would not have occurred had the bank not discounted the bill: often the plaintiff will already have sold to the drawee and therefore have taken his risk, so that no damage results from the later drawing of the bill.[157] Also he may have been aware of the drawee difficulties, and be estopped from suing the bank.[158]

A rather spectacular extension of the bank's liability was decided by the Court of Appeals of Brussels[159] in a case in which the bank was held liable for having accepted the personal guarantee of another bank, knowing or having had reasons to know that the latter bank had stipulated the guarantee in view of sureties given by the debtor's subsidiary, thereby appropriating the subsidiary's assets in order to allow the parent to acquire the subsidiary's shares. The decision implies that banks will be liable if they do not check whether the transactions on the basis of which guarantees are given are valid and do not constitute a violation of another party's rights.

Parent company liability for loans to subsidiaries

Whether a parent could be held liable on the mere basis of granting credit to an otherwise insolvent subsidiary has been discussed in connection with the general doctrine on bank's liability for granting credit.

The application of banker's liability to the parent's advances or guarantees has been argued by several writers, concluding to the parent's liability against creditors acting in reliance on the credit or possibly to a disqualification of the parent's loan in a subordinated debt. It was especially argued that the parent had a better knowledge of the subsidiary's difficult financial situation.[160]

---

155. See the argument on that point in Cass. b, 7 May 1953, Pas., 1953, I, 692.

156. See e.g. Brussels, 10 May 1979, Rev. Banque, 1979, 583; Brussels, 17 February 1983, R.D.C.B., 1983, 540.

157. Comm. Charleroi, 22 October 1986, R.D.C.B., 1987, 798.

158. See for further details Van Rijn and Heenen, fn. 2, nr. 671, p. 539.

159. Brussels, 15 September 1992, J.T. 1993, 312 (*Wiskemann* case), TRV, 1994, 275, note A. François; the decision has been submitted to the Cour de cassation (Cass., 14 October 1993, not yet published).

160. P. Van Ommeslaghe, "Rapport général", in: Study Centre on Enterprise Groups, *Droits et devoirs des sociétés mère et de leurs filiales*, 1985, 59–132, at 119; J. Ronse and J. Lievens, "De doorbraak-problematiek" in: Study Centre on Enterprise Groups, *Droits et devoirs des sociétés mère et de leurs filiales*, 1985, 133–189 at p. 189 plead for an even stricter liability; Y. Merchiers, in note to Cass., 19 March 1976, R.C.J.B., 1977, 38, comp. J. Ronse, a.o., "Overzicht van rechtspraak", T.P.R., 1978, no. 275, 881; T.P.R., 1986, no. 118, 967; Comm. Kortrijk, 20 October

However, the question is whether the parent acts contrary to normal prudent parental behaviour in supporting its subsidiary: the strategic nature of its investment in the subsidiary's business cannot mislead creditors who might expect the parent's loans not to meet the same strict, objective criteria as applicable to bank loans.[161] On the other hand, the continuous support of a noteworthy otherwise insolvent subsidiary would create a misleading appearance of solvency and shift the enterprise risk to the creditors. As a consequence one could refuse to rank the parent's loans *pari passu* with other debts.[162]

Causation and assessment of damages

The questions of causation and the assessment of damages are of immediate importance. Very often decisions that admit the liability of the bank, refrain from effectively declaring it liable on the basis that the requirement of causation has not been met, or that the damage alleged is only partially due to the bank's negligence.[163]

Causation

As a principle, only damages directly caused by the bank's negligence can be recovered. Very often, other factors, such as mismanagement by the company's directors or inefficient auditing practices will have contributed to the collapse. The Belgian courts seem to be stricter than their French counterparts.

If the damage is due to the creation of a false impression of creditworthiness, the plaintiff will have to prove that he has contracted with the enterprise in the light of his being misled by its apparent credit standing, and that the damage resulted as a consequence; hence if the damage existed before the bank is supposed to have acted negligently, there will be no recovery.[164]

In cases in which the bank's intervention merely postponed the declaration of bankruptcy, the plaintiff should prove that the enterprise would have been in bankruptcy if the credit had not been granted by the bank. The mere fact that the

---

1983, R.D.C.B., 1985, 213 relating the managing director's cash advances; see also: M. Ecker, "Het ontoereikend kapitaal in de concernverhouding", Jura Falconis, 1980, 437.

161. Also apart from loans, parents dispose of many other—open or covert—channels to support their subsidiaries. It was held that the mere existence of a group relationship did not result in the parent–subsidiary loan being fictitious or void: Gent, 28 May 1991, T.R.V., 1991, 292 (tax case).

162. The mere inclusion of the subsidiary with a negative net worth would not necessarily lead to parent liability: see for the accounting practice: E. Wymeersch, "Ondernemingsdiscontinuïteit in groepsperspectief", in H. Biron and C. Dauw (Eds.), Study Centre on Enterprise Groups, *Ondernemingsdiscontinuïteit*, 1984, p. 139.

163. See the concluding remarks made by Van Rijn and Heenen, fn. 2, nr. 669, p. 537 and nr. 673 p. 542.

164. See Van Rijn and Heenen, fn. 2, nr. 669, p. 538; Coppens and 't Kint, "Examen de jurisprudence", R.C.J.B., 1979, 378. But no such causation was admitted to exist if the subsidiary of the firm sued on the basis of having been misled by the bank's credit to the parent: Brussels, 5 April 1989, R.D.C.B., 1989, 795.

bank had not stopped the credit would not suffice as the enterprise might have found finance from other sources, e.g. at its subcontractors or suppliers, or even from the public authorities.[165]

The alleged negligence of the bank will in practice very often not be the only cause of damage: banks will defend themselves by pointing at other concurring causes of damages. Negligence by other creditors, especially by the plaintiff itself for having too readily or too naively relied on the apparent support by the bank, negligence on the part of the enterprise's management that should have applied for voluntary bankruptcy within a short statutory period, or inaction or carelessness on the part of the auditors who failed to report that the enterprise was no longer a going concern, in many cases are as material to the ultimate default of the firm.

If several causes have contributed to the damage, one will have to decide whether each of these result in full liability, or if liability can be mitigated: one of the causes having more heavily contributed to the ultimate damage. French and Belgian rules on causation differ without it being clear whether and to what extent these differences matter.[166] In shorthand one could state the Belgian position as rather strict, each cause being sufficient to lead to full liability ("théorie de l'équivalence") while the French opinion is less precisely defined, the prevailing opinion being that one has to search for the effective cause of the damage ("theorie de la cause efficiente").

According to Belgian law, in case of plurality of causes of damages, there will be liability as soon as it is proved that the defendant has contributed to the bundle of negligent acts.[167] Neither the presence of several causes of damages, nor the relative importance of the different torts will cut off the victim's right for damages against any of these. If the victim has himself contributed, this circumstance will not neutralise the action against the bank, but liability will be off set among victim and bank. The latter case could be applicable, and liability will be shared[168] if the victim had failed to adequately follow up the financial situation of the enterprise, had failed to check the annual accounts, easily available in Belgium, or had too greedily continued contracts notwithstanding the existence of undeniable signs of impending collapse.[169] Suppliers will not readily be rendered liable however, as they often will not have precise information on the actual status of the firm.[170]

165. Van Rijn and Heenen, fn. 2, nr. 669, p. 539.

166. See for an overview H. Bocken, "Actuele problemen inzake oorzakelijk verband", in *Recht halen uit aansprakelijkheid*, 1993, at 82.

167. Van Rijn and Heenen, fn. 2, nr. 671, p. 539.

168. On the basis of the general principle of liability: see Vandenberghe and Van Quickenborne, "Overzicht van rechtspraak", T.P.R., 1987, nr. 179 e.s. p. 1541 e.s. See however Van Rijn and Heenen, fn. 2, nr. 669, p. 536 who exclude the bank's liability if the victim knew, or had reason to believe, that the enterprise was on the verge of collapse, and the cases cited.

169. See Van Rijn and Heenen, fn. 2, nr. 668, p. 537 and further references.

170. Cass. Comm. Fr., 26 January 1993, RJDA, 1993, 6, n° 536; Cass. Comm. Fr. 18 May 1993, Quot. jur., 6 July 1993, nr. 53, 4; no right of action of the informed supplier was admitted in Brussels, 21 December 1983, Rev. Banque, 1984, 3, 45.

Under French law, if several torts have contributed, damages will be allocated according to each contribution. Therefore, if the management of the enterprise, or other victims of the enterprises's collapse have contributed to the damages, there will be proportional allocation of damages, and the bank will be partially exonerated.[171] The victim's own fault will as a consequence lead equally to a reduction of damages.

Damages

With respect to the amount of damages, there is a controversy as to whether one should take into account the full amount of the claim, or only the expenses lost, thus deducting the profits the plaintiff would not have realised if he had abstained from contracting. The former reasoning is more logical where the bank's negligence merely led to the continuous existence of the firm, while the latter is applicable where the bank's negligence would have avoided the plaintiff contracting.

Only damages caused after the moment the unjustified credit had been granted, or maintained, can be recovered. The victim will have to prove the causal link between the attacked credit decision and its damage. This will not be easy, especially when the plaintiff has to show that a higher rate of recovery would have been attained if the credit had not been maintained or had been more readily terminated. Moreover, it may also appear that the credit has contributed to avoiding even greater losses, without fully avoiding these.[172] The victim is also not entitled to damages if the loss would have occurred anyhow, even in the absence of the untimely termination of the loan. Finally the defendant bank sometimes successfully invokes the victim's own negligence, such as his deliberate assumption of the risk. The legal effect of the elaborate disclosure system of company accounts has not been tested in court, but one may expect its significance as not negligible.

In most cases recovery of damages is sought within the framework of a bankruptcy receivership. Under the French Act of 25 January 1985, however, the receiver, called "représentant des créanciers" is entitled to sue for collective damages; individual creditors are not barred from suing for their own individual damage, but they are not, as some pretend, also entitled to sue for the collective damage if the receiver refuses to act.[173]

171. Aix-en-Provence, 2 July 1970, JP, 1971, II, 16686 note Cabrillac; Cass. Comm. Fr., 15 July 1982, Bull. Civ. IV, n° 267 and 268; D., 1982, Inf. R., 486, obs Derrida. See Paris, 15 February 1982, D., 1982, Inf. R., 495 with respect to the partners of a partnership; T.G.I. Paris, 27 Jan. 1978, JCP, 1979, I, 2965.
172. See Riom, 18 January 1989, Rev. Banque, 1989, 449 cited by Gavalda and Stoufflet, fn. 2, n° 397, p. 187.
173. See for the controversy Gavalda and Stoufflet, fn. 2, nr. 395, p. 186. F. Grua, "Responsabilité civile du banquier en matière de crédit", Jurisclasseur, banque, fasc 151, nr. 24 *et seq*.

The Belgian[174] decision has been criticised on the basis that it did not differentiate between the reduction of the estate's value, a collective damage suffered by all creditors, and the increase in further losses, which are borne exclusively by the later creditors, and therefore could be reclaimed by the latter only. It also raises the difficulty if the receiver refuses to sue for damages: individual plaintiffs would be without effective remedy.

ELEMENTS OF COMPARISON WITH DUTCH AND GERMAN LAW

Dutch law

In Dutch law, the problem of liability of the credit supplier is mainly known from the leading Hoge Raad decisions *Erba* and *Osby*. The specific manner in which the question of liability arose in these cases has had an essential influence on Dutch thinking on this issue.[175]

In the *Erba* case,[176] an Italian supplier of a Dutch company, described as a "well known" established business, claimed damages from the bank that had extended credit to this company. Because of speculation, *inter alia*, during the Korean crisis, this company faced financial difficulties, which eventually led to the withdrawal of its bank credit. This credit had been extended twice, after additional security interests were granted to the bank, among which was a general transfer as surety, known in Holland as a "fiduciary surety transfer".[177]

The creditor Erba alleged that the bank, fully aware of the financial difficulties, had granted the company an emergency credit, and thus created a misleading appearance of creditworthiness. The bank had secured for itself plenty of surety interests, leaving no assets available for the other creditors. This attitude of the bank, by eliminating every recourse, would constitute a tort. In this way, all risks were shifted to the other parties, which is more objectionable, since they cannot obtain the same information.[178]

---

174. Cass., 12 February 1981, Pas., 1981, I, 639, note R. Declercq; J.T., 1091, 279; R.P.S., 1981, nr. 6133, 116, note P. Coppens; Arr. Cass., 1980–1981, 662, RCJB, 1983, 5, note Heenen; see also Heenen, "Préjudice collectif et action individuelle", Liber amicorum J Ronse, 227.

175. See Molenaar, *op. cit. supra* fn. 17.

176. Hoge Raad, 28 June 1957, N.J., 1957, Nr. 514, p. 1009; with brief of the Adv. Gen. Langemeijer, note L.E.H.R.

177. In France and Belgium, such transfer is not known, inasmuch as publicity is necessary. Cf. the Belgian Statute on General Pledge of a Business of 1919.

178. It was also alleged that the bank had in fact controlled the management of the borrower, but this issue was not further elaborated.

Of the interesting parts of the opinion of the court, the following especially seems important for the purposes of this enquiry:

"that it is in violation of one's duty towards the goods of others, that a bank, which provides credit against a stipulation of a surety of the extent assumed above, knowingly and deliberately or by lack of care for the interests of others ... is being paid at the expense of new suppliers ... while recovery for these suppliers from their debtor is rendered impossible from the outset."[179]

From this passage it can be deduced that, in the eyes of the Hoge Raad, the tort consisted not only in the providing of credit to a company that would necessarily fail, which had caused an appearance of creditworthiness, but also, as an aggravating circumstance, in the fact that the combination of the financial position of the borrower and the security interests of the bank deprived the other creditors of any possible effective recourse. This, the bank could have foreseen.

Such general fiduciary transfer of property as surety in itself, however, does not constitute a tort.[180] It is a necessary mechanism for debtors to obtain emergency financing when all other methods have been closed down. It can render the bank liable, however, if the bank is being paid "at the expense of the new suppliers, since it not only acquires the profit the debtor makes through the sale of the goods they deliver, but also the wholesale value or the property of the delivered goods that remained unpaid".[181] This shows that the tort requires not only the fact of the creation of a fictitious appearance of creditworthiness, but also that the bank thus acted in its own interests and consciously harmed the other creditors.

If this analysis is correct, the difference with the French–Belgian doctrine becomes clear: there, it is not required that the bank had any financial interest in supporting the company. As a rule, the bank is as much a victim of the collapse as its debtor. However, the interest of the credit supplier cannot be denied: by supporting the borrower, it hopes that the situation will clear up and that its loan will eventually be repaid.

Apart from this extra condition for bank liability under Dutch law, one can analyse how the criteria for judging the actual assessment of the creditworthiness and the credit decision itself differ from the French–Belgian test. When does the granting of credit render the bank liable?

The quoted passage from the *Erba* opinion seems to indicate that the granting of credit to a company in difficulty constitutes a tort when the loan cannot be serviced from the added value produced by the activity financed with the loan proceeds. If the company does not produce sufficient added value, the credit will only create an appearance of creditworthiness and in the long run the deficit will only widen. In that case, the other creditors alone bear the burden of the enterprise risk, while some of them can escape the *concursus creditorum* via secured transactions. The credit decision was wrongful, not because it was

179. H.R., 28 June 1957, N.J., 1957, 1079, 1015 (free translation by the author).
180. H.R., 13 March 1959, N.J., 1959, 579.
181. H.R., 28 June 1957, N.J., 1957, 1009, 1015 (free translation by the author).

accompanied by excessive security interests, but because it was fundamentally unhealthy in economic terms.[182] If this would be the final reading of the *Erba* decision, then the difference between French–Belgian and Dutch law is reduced to the nonetheless important additional condition mentioned before. On the other hand, this underlines the fundamental judgement criteria concerning business credit, in that creditworthiness is primarily based on earning capacity and to a lesser extent on solvency.[183]

In the *Osby* case,[184] the liability of a 100 per cent parent company that had negotiated the fiduciary transfer of the total assets of its Dutch subsidiary as surety for the credit it supplied, was examined. Upon bankruptcy of the subsidiary, its creditors found no assets left to attach. The Hoge Raad considered that a parent company can be declared liable for the damages suffered by the other creditors if it completely or almost completely acquires the assets, including the future assets, as surety, thus leaving no recourse for new creditors that provide credit later, without taking the interests of these new creditors into account. The knowledge of the prejudice, was formulated as follows:

"... this will be the case when the parent company had such insight in and control over the management of the subsidiary, that it, at the time of these actions, taking the size of its claim and of the surety transfer and the evolution of affairs in the subsidiary into account, knew or should have foreseen that new creditors would be prejudiced by their lack of recourse, and still neglects to secure their satisfaction."[185]

Thus, the essential tort the court withheld in the *Osby* decision was the action of the parent to trap other creditors, knowing the absence of any possible recovery. In this sense, the decision continues the line of reasoning of the *Erba* case. The element of apparent creditworthiness, however, is completely absent.[186]

In another Supreme Court case, elements of liability were developed. The *Albada Jelgersma* case concerned the liability of a parent company for the debts of its failing subsidiary.[187] The parent company had acquired the subsidiary only recently. Since it had serious financial problems, the parent had guaranteed the payments to the old suppliers in a letter. The claimant in this case, however, was not an addressee of that letter, since it only started delivering goods to the

---

182. See also Croon and Van Everdingen, "De aansprakelijkheid van de bankier-kredietverlener in het Nederlandse recht", T.P.R., 1986, 1172.

183. This is one of the essential lessons from the "Mémoire de Barsy", *op. cit. supra* n. 25.

184. H.R., 25 September 1981, N.J., 1982, 443, with brief of Adv. Gen. Ten Kate.

185. Free translation by the author.

186. Cf. the comments of Van Everdingen in Croon and Van Everdingen, *op. cit. supra* n. 4, 1173, n. 57.

187. H.R., 19 February 1988, R.V.D.W., 1988, 145, N.J., 1988, 487.

subsidiary after that date. The claim could thus not be based on this contractual guarantee. Instead, the court approved the reasoning of the lower court, holding the parent company liable in tort for not having warned the supplier in time about the financial position of the subsidiary which made bankruptcy inevitable. The parent had this duty because it was completely aware of the real situation and was in part managing the withdrawing. Under such circumstances, the parent should have taken all necessary steps to mitigate the damages of the supplier as soon as it foresaw or should have foreseen that this supplier would be prejudiced because no recovery was possible for the sizeable claims.

Of interest also is the line of reasoning followed in a few cases, which is that a creditor, also a parent[188] or able to exercise a dominant influence[189] on the debtor, behaves unlawfully if, directly or indirectly it obtained payment of its claim against the debtor, with the reasonable knowledge that upon the latter's liquidation, assets will not suffice to cover all liabilities. The circumstance that the creditor exercised a dominant influence is however to be considered essential, and the rule could not be extended to other creditors.

German law[190]

As noted earlier, under German law third party liability occurs only exceptionally. In the following cases liability has been accepted.

If the bank refuses to honour its promise to grant credit, it will be liable in *culpa in contrahendo*.[191]

On the basis of § 826 of the German Civil Code liability requires a specific intent to harm. Following a decision of the Reichsgericht of 9 April 1932,[192] German legal doctrine cites several cases of conscious or intentional violations of the rights of creditors (*Glaubigergefährdung*). Some cases are known as *Konkursverschleppung*, where the bank tries to postpone bankruptcy to recover its own claims at the expense of other, new creditors, thus knowingly and purposefully prejudicing the other creditors. Specific circumstances relate to the bank acting fraudulently in connection with the granting of the credit, or consciously acting to the detriment of the other creditors. Similar issues have been dealt with in the context of groups of companies.[193]

---

188. H.R., 8 November 1991, N.J., 1992, 174, note Ma. (liability of the dominant shareholder).
189. H.R., 9 May 1986, N.J., 1986, 792, note G.
190. See in particular K. Hopt, "Rechtspflichten der Kreditinstitute zur Kreditversorgung, Kreditbelassung und Sanierung von Unternehmen", 143 ZHR 139 e.s. (1979); K. J. Hopt, fn. 13, 383; K. J. Hopt in Baumbach-Duden-Hopt, BankGesch (7) IV, 5; C.-W. Canaris, "Kreditkundigung und Kreditverweigerung gegenüber sanierungsbedürftigen Bankkunden", 143 ZHR, 113 e.s. (1976); H.-J. Mertens, *op. cit. supra* fn. 14.
191. OLG Koblenz, 30 January 1992, BB, 1992, 2175.
192. RG, 9 April 1932, AcP, 136/247 e.s.
193. See e.g. BGH, 29 March 1993, 265/91, AG 1993, 371 (*TBB* case).

In cases of restructurings, the following rule applies: the bank will not be liable if it has thoroughly analysed the situation, such as it appears also from the auditors' reports, and, on the basis of the strict analysis of the chances of survival, has come to the conclusion that a reasonable chance to save the enterprise remains. However, if rescue efforts are undertaken while the chances of recovery are remote, liability may result, especially if the bank is acting out of a situation of conflict of interest, or is not sufficiently cautious in preparing its decisions, especially with respect to the restructuring procedure.[194]

Cases that are further classified under the same liability relate to the bank interfering with the management of the borrower, to such an extent that this company in fact becomes a mere front behind which the bank tries to recover its claims; or to where the bank agrees to the restructuring in such a way that it shifts the risk to the other, mostly unsecured creditors, which are fully exposed to the risk which the bank has fully secured for itself. Usually, these other creditors have no knowledge of these security interests.

In a fairly recent decision,[195] the Bundesgerichtshof applied these principles to a case involving bank liability towards shareholders of the borrower company. The bank had postponed the bankruptcy of its client, a company listed on the stock exchange. Just before closing its books, this company had issued new stock in an attempt to save it, which failed. A number of shareholders based their claim on alleged unwarranted extension of credit.

The claim of the shareholders which had purchased their shares on the stock exchange, failed. The protection of the violated rule was held to be limited to the shareholders which bought the new shares later. The fact that these shareholders also suffered damage which was effectively caused by the bank, is in itself not sufficient to find liability. This damage, as opposed to the damage suffered by the shareholders subscribing to the new issue, is not a direct, necessary consequence which the bank consciously pursued: their damage is not directly linked to the bank's financial advantage.

For the new shareholders, the artificial postponement of the bankruptcy could be a case of *Konkursverschleppung*, where the bank deliberately attracts new shareholders to bear the financial burden of the company failure, thus allowing the bank to escape financial harm. Whether this was the case, however, was a question of fact, which the court referred to the lower court. This court had to examine two questions: (1) could the bank reasonably believe recovery was possible, so that it did not have an intent to harm the other shareholders? and (2) what would have been the expected effect of the new issue of capital: was it sufficient to sustain a liable business or not?

194. See BGH, 12 July 1979 (III ZR 154/77), 75, 110; NJW, 1979, 1879; JZ, 1979, 683; WM, 1979, 932; BGH, 96, 213 (Beton-und Monierbau).
195. BGH, 11 November 1985, BB, 1986, 837.

The mere fact that the bank has refused credit in a way that could be considered not justified will as a rule not be considered a basis for liability. The reasoning behind this refusal is that contractual parties cannot validly rely on the continuance of contractual relationships of the debtor with all other commercial parties. However, liability may result from other parties relying on the granting of the credit.

It becomes clear that the limit of the discretionary judgement on the creditworthiness of a prospective borrower in German law is practically identical to the one in French–Belgian law: the complete absence of chances for survival. On the other hand, however, the conditions for liability in tort are essentially different, requiring the intent to purposefully harm the victim.

CONCLUSION

The subject of bank liability for negligent or tortious granting of credit has reached a definite stage of maturity, both in French and in Belgian law. Banks have learned to live with the new rules and have adapted their behaviour. Case law, after some early virulent developments, now seems to settle for a more mild approach, in which the banks and their powerful position are viewed in a more realistic perspective.

From the point of policy, several questions deserve further attention and study.

The first question relates to the economic nature of the function of the bank: under the cloak of liability, banks are imposed with the role of external crisis monitors of private business enterprises. This function of economic policy is designed to avoid banks financing businesses with manifestly no future, while it requires banks to trigger the clean-up of the consequences of mismanagement. This rule is formulated in the interest, not so much of the private parties involved, but of the well-functioning of the economic system, and therefore can be seen as belonging to the instruments of public policy. Seen from this angle, bank liability seems an instrument of private law enforcement of public order rules.

By requiring the bank to monitor private businesses in crisis, one can question if there is not a certain confusion in the role distribution: the first responsibility for a firm's functioning lies with its management and the internal mechanisms of the company. The ambiguity is the greater as preventive action, especially by a more heavy intervention at the level of management, is equally forbidden, under an even more menacing threat of the bank being treated as a shadow director. Therefore, and apart from the clear-cut cases in which the bank merely attempted to save its investment, the development of bank liability could also be seen as an illustration of the deficiencies in the normal mechanisms of detection and elimination of ailing enterprises.

Therefore a further issue arises: is not the bank, often the only remaining solvent party, called upon to be burdened by all liabilities, while several other parties that have more directly and often more substantially contributed to the firm's insolvency, are not, or are only rarely brought to reckoning. The directors, the managers, the auditors, the controlling shareholders, have often played a greater role in the firm's disappearance than the bank, but are rarely called to account for their action, or inaction.

This raises also the question of the costs: who bears ultimately the costs of this broadening of risks to the banks? Although no empirical evidence is available as of now, one can expect bank lending to be more expensive in countries where the risk factor is increased by this rather open-ended liability. One can presume that healthy firms bear the additional risk premium relating to these unhealthy firms' financing. As all firms could be considered to be virtually exposed to the same risk, there will be a net increase of costs charged to all firms whether these effectively present a risk of failure or not. Hence these firms will experience a competitive disadvantage in comparison to firms located in states where no such liability exists. Furthermore, the additional risk premium attaches to loans, not to other forms of financing, such as securities financing, where apart from the initial risk—which is considerable[196]—securities holders could not be held to any further liability.

Divergent patterns of liability, such as exist in the European Union, will normally lead to competition and arbitrage. Liability will normally be determined by the liability rules of the state where the debtor is located.[197] Hence banks may prefer to finance parent companies or headquarters that are located in states where no such liability exists, thereby taking advantage of the lower risk premium. Conversely, countries practising bank liability will be at a disadvantage: the smaller, locally operating firms will have to borrow at the first risk premium, while their internationally operating competitors will be able to finance themselves from abroad.

One could find in this reasoning an argument for harmonisation of the rules within the European Union. Two options could be envisaged: either to raise the liability level to the strictest, as practised in France and Belgium; or to remove the liability except for extreme cases of self-dealing. The first approach is largely impracticable: loans to multinational firms will tend to be granted outside the Union, while local firms will have to support the full risk burden.

Banks operating on a European scale should be aware of the consequences of these higher risks in certain transnational loans. Further, as loans are easily transferred from one bank to another, or will be securitised, some of these risks

---

196. See B. Wessels, "Eigen verantwoordelijkheid bank voor emissieprospectus", NV, 1993, 199, referring Amsterdam, 27 May 1993 (involving Co-op AG bonds).

197. In addition, contractual liability will also need to be taken account of. Third party liability is however mainly a question of extra-contractual nature.

will remain attached to the loan and follow in the hands of the assignee. Unexpected liabilities may result.[198]

EDDY WYMEERSCH

198. Abbreviations of law journals:
(a) Belgium
Adm. publique: Administration publique
DAOR: Droit des affaires -ondernemingsrecht
J.T.: Joural des tribunaux
J.L.M.B.: Jurisprudence de Liège, Mons, Bruxelles
Jura Falconis: Jura Falconis
Pas.: Pasicrisie
Limb. Rechtl.: Limburgs rechtsleven
R.C.J.B.: revue critique de jurisprudence belge
R.D.C.B.: Revue de droit commercial belge
Rev. Banque: Revue de la banque (belge)—Bank- en Financiewezen
Rev. not. belge: Revue du notaríat belge
R.P.S.: Revue pratique des sociétés
R.W.: Rechtskundig Weekblad
T.P.R.: Tijdschrift voor privaatrecht
TRV: Tijdschrift voor Rechtspersonen en Vennootschapsrecht
(b) France
Banque et Droit
Banque: Banque
Bull. civ.: bulletin civil de la Cour de cassation
D.: Dalloz
Gaz. Pal.: Gazette du Palais
JCP: Jurisclasseur périodique
(c) Netherlands
KG: Kortgeding
NV: de naamloze vennootschap
TVVS: Tijdschrift voor vennootschappen, verenigingen en stichtingen—Maandblad voor de Onderneming
(d) Germany
AG: Die Aktiengesellschaft
BB: Betriebs-Beraten
NJW: Neue Juristische Wochenschrift
WM: Wertpapier-Mitteilungen

CHAPTER 8

LENDER LIABILITY TOWARDS FINANCIALLY TROUBLED BORROWERS IN GERMAN LAW

INTRODUCTION

The traditional risks of lending money have been described by Shakespeare's famous words: "Neither a borrower nor a lender be; for loan oft loses both itself and friend."[1] Today's commercial lenders risk even more than losing their money and friends: they may also be held liable for damages suffered by their friends (clients) and for damages suffered by friends of their friends (third creditors). Commercial lenders are facing increased risks of doing business. In this situation, they are not alone. In Germany, recent developments in the law of professional liability,[2] the new Act on Product Liability and the new Act on Liability for Environmental Damages are indicators of a general tendency towards stricter standards for entrepreneurial conduct. Violations of these standards result in an increasing number of lawsuits. In the instance of commercial banks this development is most obviously reflected in the area of lending for investment purposes[3] and in the law of consumer credits.[4] Confronted with these developments some authors have pointed to the situation in the United States where juries are prone to award huge damages to alleged victims of lender misconduct. They warn that Germany, like the United States, is on its way to a "paradise for liability claims".[5] This study examines whether such an assessment holds true for a bank's dealing with its financially troubled commercial borrowers.

A financially troubled borrower who is working to overcome a crisis needs the support of its bank. There is an expectation that the lender will not leave the borrower in times of trouble, that the lender will not call in its loans, and maybe even that the lender will make available additional credit to master the

1. Shakespeare, *Hamlet, Prince of Denmark*, Act I Scene III 74–75.
2. See Hopt, "Nichtvertragliche Haftung außerhalb von Schadens-und Bereicherungsausgleich—Zur Theorie und Dogmatik des Berufsrechts und der Berufshaftung", AcP 183 (1983), 608.
3. See V. Heymann, "Die neuere Rechtsprechung zur Bankenhaftung bei Kapitalanlagen", NJW 1990, 1137; Immenga, "Bankenhaftung bei der Finanzierung steuerbegünstigter Anlagen", ZHR (151) 1987, 148.
4. See Westermann, "Verhaltenspflichten der Kreditinstitute bei der Vergabe von Verbraucherdarlehen", ZHR 153 (1989), 123.
5. Schilling, "Ein Anspruchsparadies für Haftungsschäden", FAZ 31 May 1990.

borrower's problems. The question is whether the banker's loyalty is merely a matter of morality or whether it is a matter of legal obligation. Once the law does require the lender to stick with its financially troubled borrower, entrepreneurial risks are shifted from the borrower to the lender.

Financially troubled borrowers are not bankrupt borrowers. Once a stage of virtual bankruptcy is reached the main focus is shifted to a lender's obligations towards third creditors and liability towards them. While a financially troubled borrower's difficulties may range from a short-term cash flow problem to a major reconstruction situation the issue of liability towards a financially troubled borrower implies that the borrower's business is economically viable. Often enough economic viability is not easy to determine and may only be the subject of an insecure prognosis. In these instances the burden of proof plays a pivotal role in the outcome of a lawsuit.

THE CONCEPT OF LENDER LIABILITY LAW

In German law[6] the term lender liability (*Kreditgeberhaftung*) does not refer to a specific theory of liability. In fact, even the very concept of a credit contract is not defined by the Civil Code (Bürgerliches Gesetzbuch, BGB) nor by the Commercial Code (Handelsgesetzbuch, HGB). It is true that § 607 of the Civil Code makes mention of "loans" (*Darlehen*) but this section only covers a small fraction of the wide variety of different credit arrangements. In order to fully fit credit agreements into the Civil Code contract provisions references need to be made to purchase contracts (*Kaufvertrag*. § 433 of the Civil Code), service contracts (*Dienstvertrag*, § 611 of the Civil Code), work contracts (*Werkvertrag*, § 631 of the Civil Code) and agency contracts (*Geschäftsbesorgungsvertrag*, § 675 of the Civil Code). One of the typical lending arrangements is the establishment of a line of credit (*Kreditlinie*) which offers the option to borrow a specified amount from time to time. As a rule, credit contracts are governed by the "General Terms and Conditions" of German lending institutions (*AGB Banken und Sparkassen*). These General Terms and Conditions were revised in 1993.

The theories on which lender liability is based are not contained in a specific section or set of sections of the Civil Code uniquely designed for the liability of bankers. On the contrary, the relevant liability theories do not differ from those which govern the liability of other professional groups. What makes lender liability a unique and tangible concept is the application of these general legal concepts to the specific instance of a lending case. Since this application is made

---

6. In Germany all commercial law is federal law. In first instance (Landgericht, Regional Court) and second instance (Oberlandesgericht, Court of Appeal) the law is administered by state courts, in third instance it is administered by the Federal Supreme Court (Bundesgerichtshof). Courts of first and second instance are bound by the jurisprudence of the Federal Supreme Court.

by the courts the authority to shape lender liability law rests with the courts rather than with the legislator. Thus, like judges in common law jurisdictions German courts are involved in making the law rather than merely being "la bouche qui prononce la loi". Since lender liability law is judge-made law its analysis requires a close look at the facts of each court decision.[7]

BREACH OF A LENDING CONTRACT

In theory, lender liability claims may be based on both contract and tort. In practice, however, borrowers have not been keen on suing their lenders on the basis of Civil Code tort provisions. The reason is that German law does not provide for punitive damages. On the other hand, contract theories offer a number of advantages to the plaintiff which make them the better choice for a borrower lawsuit. Contractual liability may be based on § 326 (1) 2 alt. 1 of the Civil Code. This subsection applies where a party to a contract refuses to deliver what it has promised under the contract. In the context of a lender liability case this means that a bank would refuse to make available the funds which it previously agreed to lend. § 326 of the Civil Code therefore covers a rather particular circumstance. In the majority of cases, the bank has made available the money; however, the complaint is that it called in the loan early or refused to grant an additional loan. In these cases the claim is based on the general doctrine of breach of contract (positive Vertragsverletzung).[8] In order to be successful in its lawsuit the borrower must establish that the bank breached its contractual obligations by prematurely calling in a loan or by refusing to extend additional credit. Furthermore, it is required that the bank's breach of contract was either wilful or negligent and that as a result the borrower suffered damage.

Calling a loan for cause

The first element of a lender liability claim alleging unjustified calling of a loan is the breach of contractual obligations. The question is whether the bank acted in accordance with the terms of the credit contract. A bank may terminate its lending relationship with a financially troubled borrower for cause. At times, the lending contract may also provide for a termination of the contract within the bank's discretion. The bank may then call in the loan without cause. The majority of the court decisions so far have dealt with the right to terminate a lending contract for cause.

---

7. At the same time, the role of legal scholars is rather important. The courts often enough borrow from ideas which were developed by legal writers especially when venturing into new territory.

8. Positive Vertragsverletzung is not explicitly mentioned in the Civil Code but has been developed under § 242 of the Civil Code which states the general obligation of good faith.

Grounds for calling a loan

The right to call a loan for cause is specifically provided for in virtually every commercial lending contract, and it is also part of the General Terms and Conditions of German lending institutions.[9] Furthermore, the right to call a loan for cause is part of a general principle of law derived from §§ 610, 626 of the Civil Code.[10] This principle says that continuous contracts may be terminated for cause. There are four different "important grounds" which enable a lender to call a loan for cause:

(1) the impairment of the loan in the view of the lender;
(2) the material deterioration or impairment of the borrower's assets;
(3) the borrower's refusal to offer additional collateral; and
(4) the borrower's breach of the credit contract.

The early cases of alleged lender liability mainly focused on "the impairment of the loan in the view of the bank". In two cases decided in 1957 and in 1960 the Federal Supreme Court established that it is not sufficient if the bank perceives the loan to be impaired. The impairment must rather exist as a matter of fact.[11] In a 1986 case the Supreme Court ruled once again that "the view of the bank" is an additional requirement to establish cause.[12]

During the trial a bank may, however, rely on additional facts establishing the impairment which it may not have been aware of initially.[13] There is no "impairment of a loan" if the lender is sufficiently secured.[14] More recent cases have mostly dealt with the "material deterioration or impairment of the borrower's assets". An important difference between the material deterioration clause and the impairment clause is that the material deterioration clause applies even if there is sufficient collateral.[15] Material deterioration of assets appears to be an obvious cause to call in a loan if a borrower runs into financial difficulties.

---

9. The Banks' General Terms and Conditions were revised in 1993. The new No. 19(3) reads as follows: "The bank may terminate all or parts of the business relationship without notice if there is such cause which makes it unreasonable for the bank to continue the business relationship even when taking into account the legitimate interests of the client. In particular, there is grounds to terminate if the client offered false information with regard to its financial situation, which was of material importance for the bank to grant a loan or to enter into any other business transaction involving a risk for the bank (e.g. granting of a credit card), or if a material deterioration of the client's financial situation occurs or threatens to occur which endangers the client's ability to meet its obligations towards the bank. The bank may also terminate without notice, if the client does not meet its obligation contained in No. 13(2) of these General Terms and Conditions or contained in any other agreement to offer collateral or additional collateral within reasonable notice as given by the bank."

10. Bundesgerichtshof (BGH) WM 1978, 234, 235; BGH WM 1981, 679, 680.

11. BGH WM 1957, 951; BGH WM 1960, 576, 577.

12. Decision of 6 March 1986, BGH WM 1986, 605, 606.

13. BGH WM 1960, 576; BGH WM 1979, 1176, 1178; BGH WM 1985, 1493; BGH WM 1986, 605, 606.

14. BGH WM 1986, 605, 606.

15. In the instance of sufficient collateral borrowers may introduce the argument of good faith and fair dealing. This does not, however, amount to a hard and fast rule, see below at fn. 40.

In fact, the material deterioration clause will most often justify calling in a loan to a financially troubled borrower. However, the courts have made some exceptions to this rule.

In a case decided by the Appeal Court of Düsseldorf the bank had called in a loan because of a low percentage of borrower equity capital. The court refused to accept this as a deterioration of assets. The reason was that the reduction of the equity capital percentage had been brought about by the loan itself.[16] In its 1986 decision the Supreme Court likewise dismissed low equity capital as grounds for termination. The Supreme Court held that the financial situation of an enterprise is not necessarily determined by its equity capital.[17] The Appeal Court of Hamm gave a rather narrow interpretation of material deterioration of assets in a 1985 decision.[18]

In this case a savings and loan institution (*Sparkasse*) had given a start-up loan to a young entrepreneur who had taken over a troubled metal-working shop. In spite of the loan the metal-working shop incurred additional losses. The savings bank called in the loan alleging that the borrower's assets were deteriorating. The entrepreneur contended that he had just acquired a new business licence and pointed to other signs of recovery. The court agreed with the borrower. It considered the negative balance sheet to be a mere technicality which under the circumstances did not represent a material deterioration of assets within the meaning of the credit contract.[19]

In order to reject a lender's allegation of material deterioration of assets borrowers have introduced the argument that the deterioration is not due to their fault. In a case before the Appeal Court of Zweibrücken[20] the plaintiff borrower was a mechanical engineering enterprise which ran into trouble when two of its lenders called in their loans. This caused a third bank to likewise call in its loan. This bank alleged that the borrower's financial situation deteriorated when the other two lenders demanded payment of their loans. The borrower maintained that the two lenders had no good reason to demand payment and was prepared to offer good evidence for that fact. The Appeal Court of Zweibrücken rejected the argument. Regardless of whether the other banks had good reason to call in their loans or not the third lender was entitled to call in its loan because of the ensuing deterioration.[21] The borrower further alleged a conspiracy of all three lenders. Such allegations had also been made in the Hamm metal-working shop case. In that case the young entrepreneur had argued that the savings bank called in the loan in order to bring relief to one of his competitors who was a more important borrower than himself.[22] In both

16. OLG Düsseldorf WM 1978, 1300, 1303.
17. BGH WM 1986, 605, 606.
18. OLG Hamm 1985, 1411.
19. OLG Hamm WM 1985, 1411, 1413–1414.
20. Decision of 21 September 1984, WM 1984, 1635.
21. OLG Zweibrücken WM 1984, 1635, 1638.
22. OLG Hamm WM 1985, 1411, 1412.

cases, however, the arguments of conspiracy did not prevail since the borrowers were unable to prove their allegations.

Implied waiver

Borrowers have often tried to counter the calling of a loan for material deterioration of assets or on other grounds by introducing the argument of an implied waiver. The point was first made in a 1957 Supreme Court decision.[23] In this case a pharmaceutical company which was based in the City of West Berlin experienced difficulties in selling its products. In order to boost sales the management decided to move the company to West Germany. The company's bank granted a loan to finance the transfer. Since the operation presented a risk the bank imposed restrictions on the borrower's management. Eventually the transfer of the business to West Germany failed and the bank called in the loan invoking the clause on "impairment of the loan". The borrower sued the bank for breach of contract. The Court of Appeal allowed the action holding that the termination of the lending contract was indeed unjustified. The bank granted the loan knowing that the borrower was facing a crisis and as a result imposed management restrictions. In the view of the Court of Appeal the bank knowingly assumed the risks of the business transfer to West Germany and was therefore prevented from invoking the clause on the impairment of the loan. The Federal Supreme Court, however, overturned the decision. According to the Supreme Court there was no implied waiver of the right to call the loan for impairment even though the bank knowingly financed a risky venture. The bank was well entitled to call in the loan for reasons which were foreseeable from the beginning.

More recently the argument of implied waiver has re-emerged. It was namely made in cases where the lender alleged borrower's breach of contract as grounds. A borrower's breach of contract often occurs if the borrower overdraws its line of credit. In such instances the bank is entitled to call in the loan.[24] In many cases, however, a bank may not call in the loan on the first or second occasion a borrower overdraws its line of credit. If this happens borrowers later argue that the bank increased the line of credit by way of implied contract and waived its right to call in the loan. While it is true that an implied contract may be derived from the conduct of the parties it also requires that both parties intend to assume a legal obligation to be bound by contract. The Düsseldorf Court of Appeal has held that a bank which tolerates the overdrawing of a line of credit does not intend to assume a legal obligation but is merely doing its borrower a favour.[25] In this respect the Düsseldorf Court of

23. Decision of 13 June 1957, WM 1957, 949.
24. BGH WM 1978, 234, 237.
25. OLG Düsseldorf WM 1989, 1838, 1842. The Court of Appeal quoted in this respect Hopt, "Rechtspflichten der Kreditinstitute zur Kreditversorgung und Sanierung von Unternehmen", ZHR 143 (1979) 139, 158.

Appeal agreed with the prevailing opinion in legal writing.[26] The Hamm Appeal Court, on the other hand, has been more inclined to recognise an implied contract without, however, deciding the issue in the particular case.[27] The Federal Supreme Court has not yet decided the issue.[28]

Another instance in which borrowers have argued implied waiver has been the banks' right to require additional collateral. The Banks' General Terms and Conditions provide for the right to call the loan if the borrower refuses to give additional collateral. The issue of implied waiver in this context was considered by a 1978 Düsseldorf Court of Appeal decision[29] which was later taken to the Federal Supreme Court.[30] In this case a bank financed the construction of warehouses which were later to be sold by the borrower. The loan agreement specifically mentioned the purpose of the loan and had specific terms on the amount of credit, interest and the duration of the loan. It also provided for specific collateral. At one point in the already ongoing business relationship the bank had its accountant audit the borrower's company and it was discovered that the borrower's financial situation was worse than originally thought. This revelation prompted the bank to demand additional collateral which the borrower refused. The bank subsequently called in the loan. The Court of Appeal allowed the borrower's lawsuit stating the bank had breached the loan agreement. The Court of Appeal held that the bank waived its right to demand additional collateral because it had agreed on specific collateral in the loan agreement. This decision was approved by legal scholars[31] but nonetheless the Federal Supreme Court did not accept the argument. The Supreme Court stated that commercial lending agreements often state the purpose of the loan and call for detailed terms and specific collateral. However, this does not mean that the bank intends to waive its rights contained in the Banks' General Terms and Conditions. The Supreme Court therefore dismissed the borrower's argument of implied waiver.[32] The Supreme Court did hold, however, that the banks behaviour was "contradictory" and therefore violated the principle of good faith and fair dealing.[33] This development is reflected in the new 1993 version of the Banks' General Terms and Conditions. According to the new No. 13(2) the bank is prevented from demanding additional collateral if it has been agreed that

---

26. Hopt, *loc. cit.*, fn. 25, ZHR 143 (1979) 139, 158; Rümker, "Verhaltenspflichten der Kreditinstitute in der Krise des Unternehmens", KTS 1981, 493, 502; Canaris, *Bankvertragsrecht*, 2nd edition, Berlin New York, 1981, Rn. 1208, 629.

27. OLG Hamm WM 1985, 1411, 1413.

28. The decision of 10 November 1977, BGH WM 1978, 234 leaves the issue of implied waiver open.

29. OLG Düsseldorf WM 1978, 1300.

30. BGH WM 1981, 150.

31. Grunewald, "Nachforderung von Sicherheiten bei der Kreditvergabe durch Banken", ZIP 1981, 586, 587; Schlenke, *Allgemeine Geschäftsbedingungen der Banken und AGB-Gesetz*, Berlin, 1984, 117.

32. BGH WM 1981, 150, 151.

33. Many of the arguments rejected under the doctrine of implied waiver re-emerge under the doctrine of "contradictory behaviour". The doctrine is discussed below at fn. 45.

the borrower does not have to give collateral at all or if specific collateral has been agreed upon.

Finally, some have suggested that in case of a reconstruction loan agreement the banks waive their right to invoke the General Terms and Conditions in order to call a loan for cause.[34] Since a reconstruction loan is granted for the specific purpose of recovery it expressly acknowledges the borrower's financial difficulties. In addition, there are often specific clauses supervising the borrower's management which according to this opinion compensate for the restriction of the right to terminate. In a recent decision, however, the Hamm Court of Appeal rejected the argument.[35] The court held that absence of any express waiver of the right to terminate a reconstruction loan agreement does not represent an obstacle to calling in the loan. This decision confirmed the general reluctance of the courts to derive restrictions of the right to call a loan for cause from the doctrine of implied waiver or implied contract.

Good faith and fair dealing

The principle of good faith and fair dealing plays an important role in German contract law, and the specific instance of loan agreements is no exception to this rule. The obligation of the parties to a contract to act in good faith is as a matter of law enshrined in § 242 of the Civil Code. The courts have derived various principles from § 242 of the Civil Code, and there are two which are of particular importance in the context of lender liability law: the principle of reasonableness (*Zumutbarkeit*) and the prohibition of contradictory behaviour (*venire contra factum proprium*).

The principle of reasonableness as part of lender liability law can be traced back to a 1955 Supreme Court decision.[36] It emerged prominently in the Federal Supreme Court's landmark decision of 10 November 1977.[37] In this case a banking association had been extending credit over decades to a linen factory. A life insurance policy, securities and a mortgage served as collateral. The borrower overdrew the credit limit on various occasions. When matters got worse the bank politely advised the factory managers to refrain from overdrawing the account. Nonetheless the bank honoured yet another overdraft of DM 150,000. The bank once again asked its customer to stay within its line of credit and also demanded additional collateral. None was given and the bank called in the loan on the grounds of the borrower's breach of contract. Two months later the bank started foreclosure proceedings. The borrower sued the bank for breach of contract. In its decision, the Supreme Court established that as a matter of principle a bank may only prematurely call in a loan if "after

---

34. Staudinger/Mülbert/Hopt, *Kommentar zum BGB*, 12th edition, Berlin 1988, § 610 BGB Rn. 22.
35. OLG Hamm, decision of 22 January 1990, WM 1991, 1116, 1118.
36. Decision of 20 December 1955, BGH WM 1956, 217.
37. BGH WM 1978, 234.

considering all the circumstances of the particular case and after balancing the interests of the other party it is unreasonable for the terminating party to continue the agreement for the duration contemplated by the agreement."[38]

In the case at hand, the borrower argued that it was unreasonable to call in the loan since the bank was sufficiently secured. The borrower's argument won the approval of the Court of Appeal. The Supreme Court, however, refuted the argument. Even if the lender is fully secured the borrower does not have the right to permanently overdraw its line of credit.[39] A further issue was whether it was unreasonable for the bank to call in the loan without prior notice. The Supreme Court stated that there is no general duty to give notice but that such a duty may exist under specific circumstances. In the case at hand the bank had no reason to expect that the borrower would meet its obligations and stay within the line of credit. It was therefore not unreasonable to call in the loan without warning.[40] Even though the Supreme Court rejected the borrower's claim and overturned the Appeal Court decision the case still marks an important development since it expressly introduced the element of reasonableness. This development is also reflected in No. 19(3) of the 1993 General Terms and Conditions.

In the aftermath of the linen factory case it was Canaris who strongly argued that it is unreasonable for a bank to call in a loan if there is sufficient collateral.[41] This is especially so if the bank intends to call in the loan on the grounds of deterioration of the borrower's assets. Canaris's opinion does not directly contradict the Supreme Court's decision in the linen factory case since in that case the borrower breached the credit contract by overdrawing its credit limit. There has been some support in legal writing for Canaris's proposal.[42]

The issue was under subsequent judicial consideration in two cases. In a 1982 case of the Celle Court of Appeal[43] a savings bank had granted an operating loan to a chemical plant. When financial difficulties occurred the savings bank called the loan for deterioration of the borrower's assets. Since the loan was protected by a government guarantee it was an undisputed fact that the savings bank was fully secured. The Court of Appeal did not reject the borrower's argument that as a matter of principle it is unreasonable to call a loan for deterioration of assets if there is sufficient collateral. However, in the case at hand it was also clear that rehabilitation of the enterprise was impossible. Given that the borrower's enterprise was not economically viable the savings bank was entitled to call in the loan regardless of sufficient collateral. In the above-mentioned case of the mechancial engineering enterprise the Zweibrücken Court of Appeal also

38. BGH WM 1978, 234, 236.
39. BGH WM 1978, 234, 237.
40. BGH WM 1978, 234, 236.
41. Canaris, "Kreditkündigung und Kreditverweigerung gegenüber sanierungsbedürftigen Bankkunden", ZHR 143 (1979), 113, 120.
42. See e.g. Karsten Schmidt, "Das Insolvenzrisiko der Banken zwischen Vernunft und Rechtssicherheit—Bemerkungen zu einem Zielkonflikt in der bankrechtlichen Judikatur", WM 1983, 490, 491.
43. Decision of 30 June 1982, ZIP 1982, 942.

considered the issue of collateral.[44] In this case the bank had arranged for a transaction whereby the owners of the enterprise would surrender their shares in order not to be held liable for the loan. The bank provided the new owners with credit and the enterprise soon enough posted substantial gains. It was thus obvious that the enterprise was economically viable. The borrower argued that the bank had not right to call in the loan because of "more than sufficient collateral". The Court of Appeal, however, did not agree. In its view the bank had every right to call in the loan, and it was not obliged to give the borrower advance warning.[45]

In its linen factory case the Federal Supreme Court had further noted that a bank may not act contradictorily (*venire contra factum proprium*) when calling a loan.[46] The doctrine of *venire contra factum proprium* generally says that a person must not act counter to any reasonable legal expectation which it has created through its own conduct. In the linen factory case the Supreme Court stated that the bank was not entitled to call in the loan if it previously created the impression it would approve its borrower's behaviour. By this, however, the Supreme Court only meant that the bank might have been required to give the borrower advanced warning. The Supreme Court did not envisage that the bank was completely prohibited from calling in the loan. The Supreme Court held that in the case at hand the bank did not act contradictorily. The court stated that the borrower should have taken the first polite warning seriously. Since the bank also waited another two months before starting foreclosure proceedings the borrower was left with sufficient time to obtain a loan from a different bank.

Also in a 1979 decision the Supreme Court[47] merely considered an obligation to give a warning. In this case a bank extended credit to a furniture wholesale company which did business with eastern Europe. Some of the company's warehouses served as collateral. When financial difficulties occurred the bank granted an overall line of credit of DM 3,000,000 and the company gave another warehouse as collateral. Nonetheless the bank subsequently allowed the company to overdraw the line of credit and further gave another loan of DM 300,000 against a personal guarantee by one of the directors. A week later, however, the bank was no longer prepared to honour overdrafts and also demanded additional collateral. In a meeting with bank representatives the director did not offer additional security. He flatly stated that a withdrawal of the bank's credit would force his company into bankruptcy. The bank subsequently called in the loan on the grounds of the borrower's refusal to give additional security. The borrower sued the bank alleging contradictory behaviour and claiming that the bank knew about its financial difficulties when it extended yet another DM 300,000 loan. In this situation it was contradictory

44. OLG Zweibrücken WM 1984, 1635, cf. fn. 20 above.
45. OLG Zweibrücken WM 1984, 1635, 1639.
46. BGH WM 1978, 234, 236.
47. Decision of 19 September 1979, BGH WM 1979, 1176.

behaviour to later demand additional security. The Supreme Court rejected the claim. The court stated that there was no implied waiver of the right to demand additional security. In the absence of such an agreement, the borrowers also could not reasonably expect that as a matter of good faith the bank would not call in the loan when it refused additional security. The impact of good faith and the prohibition of contradictory behaviour was limited to an obligation to give a warning. In the case at hand, the bank was not required to give a warning since the borrower flatly refused to give additional collateral.

While in these two cases the Supreme Court only considered an obligation to give advanced notice it changed its jurisprudence in its 1980 case concerning the financing of the construction and sale of warehouses.[48] In this case the bank had called in the loan because of the borrower's refusal to give additional collateral. The borrower had argued that this was unjustified since the loan agreement provided for specific collateral and the bank was involved in the financing of a specific project. While rejecting the idea of an implied waiver the Supreme Court did hold that the borrower could reasonably rely on the bank not to call in the loan without a specific reason, and thus jeopardise or even thwart the financing of the project.[49] Apparently, the refusal to give additional collateral was no such specific reason. From this decision it follows that the prohibition of contradictory behaviour may result in a prohibition to call a loan.

The Supreme Court took the same stand in a 1986 case.[50] In this case a bank had granted a loan to a bull breeding farm which it later called on the grounds of deterioration of assets. The bank argued that there had been idle capacity and that the borrower's financial situation was unsound because of a high percentage of borrowed capital. The borrower maintained that the bank had known about the situation for quite some time and had tolerated it. The Supreme Court held that the bank should have given the borrower a warning to express its concerns about idle capacity. With regard to the high proportion of borrowed capital the Supreme Court examined whether the bank had lost its right to call in the loan for that reason. In that regard the borrower argued that the bank had disapproved of the intended sale of a residential home in order to raise more equity. The Supreme Court held that this behaviour, if proven, would indeed have prevented the bank from calling in the loan.[51] The court therefore remitted the case for a new trial.

The bull breeding case was a second case in which the Supreme Court considered a prohibition to call a loan on the basis of contradictory behaviour. The change in jurisprudence becomes very obvious especially when looking at the 1957 pharmaceutical plant case.[52] In that case the bank was entitled to call in the loan even though it knew about the borrower's difficulties right from the

---

48. Decision of 18 December 1980, BGH WM 1981, 150, cf. fn. 30 above.
49. BGH WM 1981, 150, 151.
50. Decision of 6 March 1986, BGH WM 1986, 605.
51. BGH WM 1986, 605, 606.
52. Cf. above fn. 23.

beginning. One should be careful in generalising about the Supreme Court decisions. Both decisions were not final but only called for a new trial. With regard to the bull breeding case it must be emphasised that the borrower alleged a very specific contradiction. The bank itself prevented the borrower from taking action, i.e. selling the residential home, which the borrower intended in order to redress the situation which the bank later used as grounds.

Calling a loan at lender's discretion

According to No. 19(2) of the Banks' General Terms and Conditions lenders are entitled to call a loan "at any time without giving advanced notice" if no other specific term has been agreed upon. Some legal scholars have argued that this stipulation contravenes the Act on General Terms and Conditions (*AGB Gesetz*) because it is unfair towards borrowers who depend on long-term planning of their financing.[53] The courts and the majority of legal scholars, however, do not share this view.[54] Borrowers who need long-term financial planning have the option to negotiate long-term credit agreements. Absent such an agreement, it is legitimate for a bank to keep its freedom of action rather than being obliged "until kingdom come".[55] According to a decision of the Cologne Court of Appeal the discretionary termination clause continues to apply even if the bank and its borrower have been engaged in a long-standing business relationship.[56]

Acknowledging the validity of the discretionary termination clause, however, does not mean that a bank is free to terminate a lending contract wantonly. In a 1964 decision of the Hamburg Court of Appeal and a 1977 decision of the Federal Supreme Court it was said that the bank must "take into account the borrower's legitimate interests".[57] The context of these decisions were low interest loans financing housing projects for modest income private individuals. One could therefore say that the rationale does not necessarily apply to commercial loans involving business people. Nevertheless, the 1993 version of the Banks' General Terms and Conditions incorporates the above-mentioned court decisions by stating that "the bank shall take into account its client's legitimate interests when exercising the right to terminate" (No. 19(2) 2 of the Banks' General Terms and Conditions). Naturally, the question is what it means for a bank to take into account its client's legitimate interests. First and foremost, it means that a bank must give its client sufficient advanced warning if it plans on invoking the discretionary termination clause. However, it is the borrower's responsibility to secure alternative financing within a reasonable time. An already financially troubled borrower will find it difficult to find a

---

53. Stauder, *Der bankgeschäftliche Krediteröffnungsvertrag*, Geneva 1967, 150.
54. BGH WM 1985, 1136; BGH WM 1985, 769; Canaris, *loc. cit.* fn. 26, Rn. 1239, 637.
55. OLG Köln WM 1985, 1128, 1136.
56. Decision of 16 March 1984, OLG Köln WM 1985, 1128, 1132.
57. BGH, decision of 28 June 1977, WM 1977, 834, 835; OLG Hamburg, decision of 22 October 1964, MDR 1965, 294, 295.

lender who is willing to take over from a bank who is pulling out. The main interest of a troubled borrower is therefore that the bank is completely prevented from invoking the discretionary termination clause.

In defence of financially troubled borrowers legal scholars have been looking for ways to expand the concept of "taking into account the borrower's legitimate interests". In doing so, Canaris[58] has been most vocal and has received much attention albeit not unanimous consent. Canaris maintains that it is "uncivilised behaviour" if a bank calls in a loan without having a compelling reason to do so. A bank does not have a compelling reason if it is fully secured. Even if a bank is not fully secured it may be "uncivilised" to call in a loan given the devastating effect for the borrower. Canaris argues that in these cases the bank does not greatly benefit and must therefore yield the borrower's vital interest.[59] Canaris's arguments have been widely criticised.[60] In fact, the doctrine of "uncivilised behaviour" only applies as a last resort in rather extreme cases of an abuse of legal rights. There seems to be no case in which it was applied by the courts in a lender liability context. We would therefore agree with those who reject Canaris's propositions.

In a second line of argument Canaris invokes the doctrine of contradictory behaviour. Canaris maintains that discretionary termination of a lending agreement is contradictory and thus in violation of § 242 of the Civil Code in three instances:

(1) It is contradictory behaviour for a bank to invoke the discretionary termination clause if the bank is financing a specific project. The "project" may namely be the reconstruction of a troubled business under a reconstruction loan agreement.

(2) A bank acts in a contradictory manner if calling in the loan of a borrower who is totally dependent on this particular bank for its financing. A bank may not create or encourage such a dependency and then suddenly leave the borrower to its own devices.

(3) It is contradictory behaviour if the bank tolerates a certain behaviour of its client (short of cause) for some time and then later decides to call in the loan because of that behaviour.

The prevailing opinion in legal writing is that Canaris's categories of contradictory behaviour deserve approval at least in principle.[61] Canaris himself emphasises that none of his categories makes a compelling case held alone but they merely represent factors to be taken into account when examining the merits of each particular case.

---

58. Canaris, *loc. cit.*, fn. 41, ZHR 143 (1979), 113.
59. Canaris, *loc. cit.*, fn. 41, ZHR 143 (1979), 113, 135.
60. See e.g. Rümker, *loc. cit.*, fn. 26, KTS 1981, 493, 497–498.
61. See e.g. Karsten Schmidt, *loc. cit.*, fn. 42, WM 1983, 490, 491–492; Pleyer, "Zur Frage der Kündigungsschranken und der Kreditgewährungspflicht für eine Bank in der Krise des Kunden", *Gedächtnisschrift für Dietrich Schulz*, Köln *et al.*, 1987, 271, 281–284.

It was the Hamm Court of Appeal who put Canaris's theories to the test in its 1985 metal-working shop case.[62] In this case the lender had given a business start-up loan and was thus financing a specific project. The borrower had also received a government investment grant which was contingent on the loan from that particular lender. Hence, the borrower had to depend totally on its lender. And finally the lender was fully secured. Under these circumstances the Hamm Appeal Court ruled that the lender violated principles of good faith and fair dealing by calling in the loan based on the discretionary termination clause. The court also mentioned that the lender was aware of the devastating effect that the withdrawal of the loan would have on the borrower's business.[63]

Refusal to grant additional financing

The risks of doing business with a financially troubled borrower are not limited to the observance of certain rules when it comes to calling a loan be it for cause or be it based on a discretionary termination clause. It has also been proposed that lenders should be obliged to grant additional credit in order to keep the borrower's business afloat. In the context of a lender liability lawsuit the issue is whether a bank breaches its loan agreement by denying its borrower additional credit. The idea that a bank might be obliged to help its borrower out by giving additional credit was first discussed in a 1937 decision of the Imperial Court of the German Reich (Reichsgericht)[64] and a 1955 decision of the Federal Supreme Court.[65] In both cases it was said that the lenders had become involved to a degree where they owed a "certain obligation of loyalty" to their borrowers. However, in neither case was there a final decision on the issue. In a 1959 decision the Federal Supreme Court rejected the idea that a bank should give additional credit in order to support a financially troubled borrower.[66] In this case the loan agreement specifically stated that the bank would not give any credit beyond what had been agreed upon.

More recently the obligation to give additional credit was considered in several Appeal Court decisions. In a 1983 case before the Düsseldorf Court of Appeal[67] a bank agreed to increase a long-time business client's credit limit on a short-term basis. The bank did, however, refuse a long-term commitment to help the client overcome financial difficulties. The borrower sued the bank for breach of contract. The Düsseldorf Appeal Court rejected the claim stating that the borrower was not in a position to give additional collateral corresponding to an increase in the credit limit. In a 1989 Düsseldorf Appeal Court case[68] the

---

62. OLG Hamm WM 1985, 1411; cf. fn. 18 above.
63. OLG Hamm WM 1985, 1411, 1413.
64. Decision of 23 July 1937, RG Bankarchiv 1937/1938, 311.
65. Decision of 20 December 1955, BGH WM 1956, 217.
66. Decision of 12 February 1959, WM 1959, 626.
67. Decision of 30 June 1983, OLG Düsseldorf WM 1983, 873.
68. Decision of 9 February 1989, OLG Düsseldorf WM 1989, 1838.

plaintiff borrower had likewise needed additional credit on a long-term basis. The court stated that there might have been an obligation on the part of the lender to help the borrower out of short-term difficulties. A long-term commitment, however, was once again ruled out because of lacking collateral. The issue was also considered in the above-mentioned Zweibrücken Court of Appeal case.[69] In this case the borrower offered full collateral and presented a detailed work out plan. The borrower needed an additional DM 581,000. The Zweibrücken Court of Appeal rejected any obligation to grant additional credit regardless of the availability of collateral. According to the court it is unacceptable to burden lenders with the borrower's entrepreneurial risk. Thus the Zweibrücken court took a more restricted stand than the Düsseldorf court.

It has also been suggested that under a reconstruction loan agreement a lender is obliged to give additional credit if that is what it takes to make the reconstruction work.[70] One of the reasons for this added obligation is that the bank's risks are compensated by supervisory and control powers which are usually part of a reconstruction loan agreement. It is doubtful, however, that this is indeed the nature of a reconstruction agreement. Also, according to a decision of the Hamm Court of Appeal a reconstruction agreement does not imply that the bank surrendered its right to call the loan.[71] Hence, if a bank may still call a loan it should, all the more, be entitled to refuse additional credit.

CAUSATION

Besides the lender's breach of contract, causation is another important element which needs to be established in a lender liability lawsuit. A borrower who claims damages for the loss of its business must prove that the bank's breach of contract caused that business to collapse. In fact, banks have often successfully argued that the borrower's business would have collapsed even if the bank had met its contractual obligations.[72] In order to evaluate the defence of lack of causation one has to distinguish three different types of situations:

(1) In the first, the borrower's business was already insolvent when the bank's breach of contract occurred. The bank therefore breached its obligations towards a business which was already "clinically dead".[73] In these cases there is no causation. The borrower must prove that its business was alive at the time when the breach of contract occurred.

(2) In the second situation the borrower has established that its business was indeed alive. In these cases the banks have, however, maintained

69. OLG Zweibrücken WM 1984, 1635, 1638; cf. fn. 20 and 44 above.
70. Hopt, *loc. cit.* fn. 25, ZHR 143 (1979) 139, 169.
71. OLG Hamm WM 1991, 1116, 1118; cf. above fn. 35.
72. See e.g. BGH WM 1956, 217; OLG Düsseldorf WM 1989, 1838; OLG Celle ZIP 1982, 942; OLG Hamm WM 1991, 1118.
73. BGH WM 1957, 949, 952.

that the borrower's business was in severe difficulties. The argument is that the breach of contract would not have caused the business to collapse if it had been perfectly healthy. Such an allegation does not remove causation in the legal sense. It suffices that the breach of contract was one factor causing the collapse. The bank may not argue that its particular borrower was more likely to collapse than others.[74]

(3) The third situation likewise involves a business which was alive at the time of the breach of contract. The bank would, however, argue that the collapse would in any event have occurred at a later date. The borrower's business was, so to speak, already "poised with destruction".[75] It is part of the general doctrine of causation that hypothetical developments may be taken into account. A borrower whose business would have collapsed sooner or later may not claim the damages which it would have suffered in any event.[76] However, in this instance it is the lender who makes a factual allegation in its favour. Therefore the lender bears the burden of proof for the hypothetical course of events.

CONCLUSION

German law imposes relatively tough standards for lender behaviour and borrower protection. Those standards are being developed by the courts on a case by case basis and are derived from the general obligation of good faith and fair dealing. A lender can rarely be sure that the calling of a loan is merely determined by the terms of the loan agreement or by the General Terms and Conditions. Moreover, a lender may even be obliged to provide its borrower with additional credit in order to help it overcome a financial crisis. The point has been made that the imposition of stricter standards is counterproductive.[77] It leads to a reluctance to give credit in the first place and encourages costly lawsuits. In Germany there is a lively debate on the overall economic impact of recent developments in lender liability law and there have been warnings of an increasingly litigious environment. However, it would be wrong to assume that Germany is a borrower's paradise for lender liability lawsuits. There are a number of circumstances which hold excessive lawsuits in check:

(1) The most important is the strict application of the requirement of causation. Since insolvent borrowers are barred from recovering damages a lawsuit is hardly a means to recover "windfall damages".

(2) In Germany there is no trial by jury. Borrowers therefore have a hard time introducing emotional arguments in order to present themselves

74. BGH WM 1968, 1214, 1215.
75. Cf. BGH WM 1968, 1214, 1215.
76. BGH WM 1968, 1214, 1215.
77. For an analysis see Ebke/Griffin, "Lender Liability to Debtors: A Conceptual Framework", (1986) 40 Sw.L.J. 775, 800–816.

as victims of powerful and callous banks. Also, there are no punitive damages which means that awards are a far cry from those which borrowers have obtained in the United States.

(3) The losing party in a lawsuit is fully liable for court fees and the legal fees of the other party. This reduces the likelihood of frivolous borrower–lender lawsuits. It is also illegal to hire a lawyer on a contingent fee.

For these reasons recent developments in lender liability law have not caused the same alarm in Germany as they may have caused overseas especially in the United States. There have been no lender liability cases as spectacular as the US cases in *Farah*[78] or *KMC*[79] Thus, it becomes obvious that the impact of lender liability law cannot be measured solely on how strict standards of lender behaviour are, but to a large extent, depend on procedural and other aspects of the respective legal system.

DIRK SCHLIMM

---

78. *State Nat. Bank* v. *Farah MFG Co.*, 678 S.W.2d 661 (Tex.App. El Paso 1984), writ dism'd by agr.

79. *KMC Co.* v. *Irving Trust Company*, 757 F.2d 752 (6th Cir. 1985).

CHAPTER 9

LENDER LIABILITY IN THE NORDIC COUNTRIES

INTRODUCTION

Lender liability is a legal concept developed in the courtrooms of the United States. As a social phenomenon the acts and omissions demonstrated by lending institutions in their behaviour towards their borrowers are universally alike. In other words, banking, its practices and problems are, in many respects, the same in every country, yet the solutions to the problems are not. The Scandinavian countries represent legal systems deeply tied into the German–Scandinavian legal tradition that the Anglo-American lawyers call a civil law system. Common law legal tradition offers, at least to some degree, different remedies to lender liability issues. While the wave of lender liability swept over the North American continent during the 1980s the concept remained more or less unknown in the Nordic region until the 1990s. First seminars about the subject were arranged in 1990 by American law firms. Even among legal scholars lender liability is more or less a newcomer. First articles about the subject were written by the authors of this chapter in 1991 and 1992.[1] Apart from recent books and articles by the authors the subject is still little discussed by the academic writers. Since the late 1980s, however, distinct signs of emerging awareness of lender liability related case law can be found in Finland, Sweden, Norway and Denmark. In this contribution the writers will illustrate the problems that have emerged in the Nordic countries and how they have been dealt with. Because of our nationalities the main focus will be on Finnish and Swedish law.

Lender liability exists primarily in contractual relationships between lenders and borrowers. Guarantors and pledgors are at least by Scandinavian interpretation also parties to a contract with the lender. Action against them is a very common cause for lender liability related litigation in the Nordic region. Other creditors to the same borrower comprise a third source of lender liability even if there is no contractual relationship between the creditors. All these relationships will be discussed in the following. In the first part a chronological approach has been chosen. Initially, we will concentrate on the problems arising

---

1. Huhtamäki, 72 *Defensor Legis* 695 (1991); Kleineman, 4 *Juridisk Tidskrift vid Stockholms Universitet* 289 (2/1992–1993).

from breach of promises to lend, commitment letters and formation of a contract between the parties prior to funding a loan. Some of the lenders' potential breaches of contract will be discussed thereafter. The final part of the lender–borrower presentation includes collection and foreclosure problems.

The non-contractual liability towards other creditors of the same borrower represents a very common dilemma in everyday business life. The lack of effective remedies—such as equitable subordination—and the rocky road to any award in damages makes attempts to improve one creditor's position against the others common. Litigation geared to cancelling such attempts is very usual in the Scandinavian countries.

Since much lender liability doctrine can be traced to US law, comparative aspects between civil law and common law systems are of interest. Comparison is not easy, though. The main difficulty is that the legal tools and concepts do not always match. This is particularly true in tort law related issues. The main points of interest will be pointed out.

THE DIMENSIONS OF LENDER LIABILITY

As a social phenomenon lender liability involves exercise of economic power, which by its nature is more immediate than political or administrative power. Reluctance to deal with difficult or unpopular issues in political or administrative decision making forces the economic decision makers to find ways to solve the aspects necessary for their business interests on their own.[2] Economic power concentrates in investors with plenty of money. Thus, banks and other financial institutions represent significant decision making powers in societies. On the other hand financial institutions are subject to political and administrative control. The purpose of the surveillance is primarily protection of the depositors.

A rapid relaxation of the control network was a typical feature in the banking business in many countries during the 1980s. Deregulation was usually induced in these countries after repeated requests by the banking institutions themselves. Growth driven banks desired more freedom to enter into new business areas and markets. In the United States deregulation was mainly related to opening new markets to American financial institutions.[3] In Sweden interest rate regulation was gradually abolished in 1978–1985. Restrictions on upper limits on lending were set aside in 1985.[4] In Finland the main deregulatory issue was free access to foreign money and capital markets. Finnish banks had previously been forced to

---

2. For further reading on the subject see John K. Galbraith, *The Anatomy of Power*, 1980, *passim*.

3. The American deregulation process is well described by Pauline B. Heller, 43 *Consumer Finance Law Quarterly Report* 227 (1989) and Marcela Davison Avilés, 44 *Consumer Finance Law Quarterly Report* 115 (1990).

4. L. Jonung, "Financial deregulation in Sweden", 4/1986 *S-E Banken Quarterly Review* 109.

seek their funding primarily from domestic depositors. All this was changed during the 1980s.

In the United States deregulation led to the notorious savings and loan association crisis which affected the rest of the American banking industry, too. In the Nordic countries, deregulation followed by a credit expansion unseen prior to the 1980s, contributed to a banking catastrophe in many respects worse than the one experienced in the 1930s. The governments were forced to grant subsidies to the major banks and banking groups one way or another.

The Norwegian banks were hit a couple of years earlier than the rest of the Scandinavian banks—already in the mid-1980s. By 1990 the losses of three major banks were reduced to US$ 1 billion while the Danish banks still lost that year over US$ 3 billion.[5] Two of the Finnish[6] and one of the Swedish[7] banks were taken over by the regulators. Additionally, the smallest of the Finnish banks was merged into one of the others. The operations of Swedish Gotabank were merged after the takeover into another large but troubled Swedish institution, Nordbanken, which was government owned from the beginning. Skopbank and Nordbanken were granted massive subsidies in fresh equity contributions.

One explanation for the severity of the banking crisis in the Nordic region is probably the fact that the financial institutions are very big compared to the relatively small national economies. Many of the Scandinavian banks ranked within the top 500 largest financial institutions worldwide. In nations with combined populations of 23.5 million this may have stood out of proportion but it also gives a perspective to the seriousness of the collapse.

The Swedish débâcle was initiated by the default of one of the finance companies that was predominantly active in the real estate market. Its collapse caused a chain reaction due to its funding linkage to some of the major banks. In Finland the downfall started by failure to manage the interest rate risk involved in Finnish currency (markka) denominated domestic lending. It was accelerated by the banks' consequent inability to continue keeping the stock and real estate markets afloat. Their diminishing ability to lend had the same effect. For this reason the market values dropped sharply. Non-performing loans accumulated in the banks. The plunging asset values affected the banks' net worth and capital ratios. The more immediate problem leaving the government no other choice but to intervene was, however, the melting liquidity.

The banks' turnaround from powerhouses into subjects of government aid and public scorn happened so fast that panic reactions towards the borrowers

---

5. Udo Reifner, *Sicherheit und soziale Verantwortung—Finanzdienstleistungen*, Hamburg, 1992, 8, 9.

6. Skopbank and Savingsbank of Finland. The latter is a consolidated group of savings banks that once owned Skopbank. The two groupings had a combined asset base of more than US$ 40 billion in the late 1980s.

7. Gotabank of Sweden was formally taken over as opposed to Nordbanken (which was already owned by the government) and a group of savings banks that were otherwise issued government aid. The equity contributions were by no means lesser compared with the cost related to Gotabank, however.

were inevitable. When the banks started losing money their lending policies, collection activities and foreclosure procedures changed dramatically. Loan commitments were not always honoured, loans were accelerated, additional collateral was requested, foreclosures were stepped up and borrowers' interests in foreclosure sales occasionally ignored. Attacking the borrowers supposedly helped protect the depositors.

One could ask, however, why is it allowed and moreover even commendable to protect depositors at the expense of the borrowers? Yet, this is how priorities are set by banking authorities in most countries. The depositors and the borrowers are in many instances the same citizens. Due to this bias borrowers have been treated badly for a long time. Depositors and borrowers usually play a third role, too. The ultimate payer, the lender of last resort suffering the cost of a collapsing banking system, is the taxpayer. Depositors seem to be protected. Increasing awareness of lender liability will eventually improve the protection of borrowers as well. The question remaining to be tackled is who would protect the taxpayers?

A CIVIL LAW VIEW OF LENDER LIABILITY

One of the basic categorisations in civil law is to make a difference between private and public areas of law. Legal problems without governmental or municipal interests are considered private. This makes most of family, contract, corporate and trade law and tort law private. The areas mainly affected by lender liability are the law of contract and the law of torts. In civil law systems these two combined together are called the law of obligations. Among other things, this area covers breaches of contract and the duty to compensate damage caused to third parties.

The fundamental difference between the American common law and civil law approaches to lender liability is the availability of punitive damages in the USA. The concept is unknown in all of the continental European countries.[8] In the Nordic region punitive damages do not exist and they cannot be had—no matter what the tort might be.[9] Another dilemma, that of consequential damages, has to be faced in both common law and civil law systems. The instruments for solving the problem are not in all respects the same.

In the Nordic region punitive damages do not create incentives to plaintiffs. The same applies to other civil law countries. Therefore, there is no reason to seek combinations of contracts and torts (contorts) in the same way as in the United States. The most characteristic features of American lender liability have

8. Even in the UK punitive damages have in most cases been abolished years ago.
9. Compensation for the counterparty's reasonable (as found by the court) legal fees is awarded as a rule in most Scandinavian cases against the losing party. This is considered compensation of costs to the winning party without any penal purpose.

been the emerging theories of liability which accumulate torts with contractual liability. The quest for punitive damages seems to have encouraged innovative attorneys to successfully bridge the gap between the two areas of law. In civil law countries nothing can be gained by shifting from a contractual relationship into the realm of torts. Because compensation for pure economic loss cannot be obtained in the same way as under Anglo-American law, opposite endeavours are, in fact, often to be recommended.

LIABILITY THEORIES IN NORDIC COUNTRIES

Contractual liability

A contract is—*prima facie*—considered to be the expression of the will of the contracting parties. This is equally true in civil and common law environments. The binding nature of a contract (*pacta sunt servanda*) and the freedom from any outside influence have been cherished in both legal traditions for centuries. A contract has carried a prestigious position as the sign of the autonomy of wills. Non-compliance with the contract is seen as default and a cause of action for damages. In Scandinavia the flexibility of contract doctrine has facilitated the widening of responsibilities of the parties into a realm that in common law countries is treated as non-contractual liability. The Nordic countries share the German tradition of developing contractual liability into relations similar to contractual relationships. The principle of consideration is not regarded as a necessary prerequisite of a contract.

The party suffering from the breach of contract is entitled to have the value of his contract compensated. The value is often called the positive performance (bargaining) interest in Scandinavian law.[10] It equals the concept of lost expectation in common law.[11] Some variations occur in determining how far the consequential expectations can be stretched.[12]

In situations where a contract has not yet been reached, one negotiating party may still have caused damage to the other by giving a false impression of the probability of the contract being consummated. Furthermore, it is possible that a party negotiates in bad faith. These situations are called *culpa in contrahendo* (negotiation liability) even in the Nordic countries, in accordance with the German doctrine.[13] Under Scandinavian law the suffering party is not entitled to

---

10. Joseph M. Lookofsky, *Consequential Damages in Comparative Context*, 114, a dissertation by a Danish lawyer, Copenhagen, 1989. Also, Knut Rodhe, *Obligationsrätt*, Lund 1984, 479.

11. Lookofsky, *supra*.

12. Jan Hellner, 4 *Canadian Business L.J.* 480 (1979–1980) and Jan Kleineman, *Ren Förmögenhetsskada* (Pure Economic Loss), a Swedish dissertation, Stockholm 1987 with a summary in English, 579.

13. Hannu von Herzen, *Contract Negotiations*, a Finnish dissertation with English summary, Helsinki, 1983, 280.

the loss expectation if the contract has not been established. He may still have the right to compensation for his cost of negotiating. This, in turn, resembles the reliance interest in the common law.[14]

In the lending context the tricky situation of whether the contract was already reached or whether it was still in formation, is fairly common. Claims can be made of oral and written loan commitments. Compensating the consequential economic damage presents a special problem with regard to liability in the negotiating stages. It is a lesser problem in a breach of contract situation. According to Scandinavian law compensation for economic damage in non-contractual situations can be awarded only if special circumstances apply.[15] Such circumstances are difficult to prove in negotiation situations.[16] Outside contractual liability criminal offences, abuse of public authority or other special conditions are often a prerequisite for economic damage.

The principle of the binding nature of contracts has been gradually eroding on occasions where there have been disturbances in consummation of a contract or where the contract itself (or its content) is proven to be unconscionable. A contract can be declared void from its inception (*ab initio*) if a party was fraudulently or usuriously induced to enter into it. Signing the contract under duress has the same effect. Coercion and a more lenient form of duress equalling economic duress are distinguished even in the Scandinavian contract law. In every Nordic country the Contract Code[17] also recognises nullification of a contract if one of the contracting parties signed in bad faith (§ 33). In section 33 lack of good faith is described as an inability to execute contracts that were consummated under dishonourable or dubious circumstances if the one pleading to the contract was or should have been aware of such circumstances.

There are, in fact, two separate general clauses in the Nordic Contract Codes. Section 33 ("the small general clause") allows the courts to set aside contracts tainted by lack of good faith and dishonesty. It has close links to the older provision in the German Civil Code BGB (Bürgerliches Gesetzbuch) § 242.[18] The other Nordic general clause is of later origin and does not have a direct counterpart at least in the German Code even if the principle of adjusting unconscionable contracts is accepted also in Germany.[19] In the Nordic region the courts are also allowed to adjust a contract without setting it aside entirely. Section 36 in the Nordic Contract Codes ("the large general clause") enables

---

14. Lookofsky, *supra*.

15. Kleineman, *Pure Economic Loss, supra*.

16. The problem was recently raised in a Swedish precedent—NJA 1990, 745—where the court left little doubt that the right to compensation especially in negotiation situations is limited. See Kleineman, 3 *Juridisk Tidskrift vid Stockholms Universitet* 125 (1/1991–1992).

17. Common Codes for Contracts were drafted as a joint effort in the Scandinavian countries in early twentieth century. In Sweden the Code entered into force in 1915 and in Finland in 1929.

18. The German BGB section 242 has had significant impact elsewhere too. Traces of it can be found even in the American UCC § 1–203.

19. The German Code for Standard Terms contains provisions to that effect (Gesetz zur Regelung des Rechts der Allgemeinen Geschäftsbedingungen, AGB-Gesetz § 6).

judges to alter or modify a contract or its individual provision(s) if the contract as a whole or some of its parts are unconscionable. When assessing unconscionability consideration must be given to the entire content of the contract, the position and negotiating power of the parties at the time the contract was made and afterwards, and also to other relevant factors.[20]

Credit agreements are often made between banks with professional knowledge about finance and private individuals (consumers) with limited or no knowledge of the same. In the Scandinavian countries legal and financial counsel are used by the borrowers only on rare occasions even in a corporate lending context. Separate documents called credit agreements are used seldom. However, the custom of using such an agreement has been spreading in foreign currency denominated corporate loans. Usually the note (promissory note) still remains the sole evidence of debt, not only as to the debtor's obligation to repay, but also as the sole source of written terms and conditions for the loan.

Unequal bargaining power combined with the habit of using standard terms in lending contracts (notes)[21] almost without exception create a favourable environment for claims based on unconscionability. Avoiding bad faith is not always an easy endeavour in these circumstances. The general obligation of good faith expressed in § 33 of the Scandinavian Contract Codes is of significant importance in cases related to unconscionable terms in credit or security agreements. In the Nordic countries the good faith obligation is reduced to a specific doctrine of loyalty that binds the parties to a contract. Loyalty means an obligation—especially for the dominating party—to take care of the weaker party's reasonable interests. Loyalty plays a vital part in closing financial transactions, following the contractual provisions, and mitigation of damage (avoiding unnecessary escalation of damage) when a contract has been defaulted.

A German scholar specialising in banking law, Professor C.W. Canaris has introduced a theory called *Vertrauenshaftung*—reliance liability—whereby he suggests that borrowers are entitled to place more trust on their bankers as contract partners than on others in everyday contractual relationships. The banks are supposed to be in a quasi-public position in society and therefore subject to higher moral standards. Also, the borrowers who share more than just a lending relationship with their bankers are entitled to increased loyalty.[22] At the very least where the banker wears several hats *vis-à-vis* his client,[23] he loses

20. See Juha Pöyhönen, *The System of Contract Law and the Adjustment of Contracts*, a Finnish dissertation on the subject (§ 36) with a summary in English, Helsinki 1988, 379.

21. Scandinavian lending institutions use almost exclusively standard lending terms listed on the verse side of their promissory note forms.

22. Claus-Wilhelm Canaris, *Bankvertragsrecht* (Gross-kommentar), Berlin, 1981, and *idem*, 143 *Zeitschrift für Handelsrecht* 113 (1979).

23. Occasionally there are good examples of banks wearing a multitude of "hats" simultaneously: mutual funds were introduced as investment devices in Finland in 1987. They were heavily advertised to consumers and even to those consumers who did not have the means or knowledge to invest. They were made a loan against the fund shares instead. The funds were managed by the banks

the independence of a normal contract party dealing at arm's-length and becomes a fiduciary to the client.[24] The closer the relationship between the lender and the borrower gets and the more dimensions that relationship contains, the larger the demand of loyalty grows.[25]

Liability towards guarantors and pledgors

Collateral issues are important in the Scandinavian lending context. Lending based on cash flow has never had too many supporters. In this respect the market differs from US or Japanese markets. The main lender liability issues involving collateral are blanket (general) pledges and guarantees. In a typical case an entrepreneur or rather his spouse signs a personal guarantee or pledge agreement for a loan that appears to be harmless, say, a domestic mortgage loan. By the same token the unwitting spouse may have signed also for corporate debt without realising that the security interest will cover "all debt *whatsoever* that either one of the signee(s) will now *or in the future* be responsible". Blanket pledge agreements have been voided in recent Scandinavian case law on several occasions.[26] A guarantor's responsibility for "every current and future obligation of the borrower" "is an even greater commitment". In Finland its feasibility as a binding contract has recently been restricted to special occasions only.

On the other hand, the guarantor or the pledgor may have been persuaded to sign without proper prior knowledge of the financial condition of the borrower. Lender's obligation to inform the guarantor/pledgor has been debated for quite some time by Norwegian scholars.[27] In Norway the issue has been decided in favour of the lender throughout the twentieth century until 1984 when presumably due to the strong opinions of the Norwegian scholars—the development reached a turning point. This was demonstrated in a ruling by the Supreme Court of Norway.[28]

It is worth emphasising that according to Scandinavian law there is a contractual relationship between a lender and a guarantor/pledgor and

---

and a good part was invested in stocks of related companies. Allegedly, the banks sold some of their own portfolios to the funds too. The funds were first introduced in September 1987. On Black Monday (19 October 1987) the Scandinavian markets crashed along with the others. Demands for additional collateral and threats to accelerate the loans in case of non-compliance with those demands would have sounded hollow under the circumstances.

24. This is, in essence, also the core of breach of fiduciary duty as one of the so-called emerging lender liability theories in the United States.

25. The principle of loyalty has been discussed at length twice in recent Swedish Supreme Court cases, see NJA 1987, 697 and a Supreme Court decision from 7 April 1994 (# not issued yet) concerning letters of credit. According to a Finnish Professor L-E Taxell, various grades of loyalty can be separated from one another, *Köplagen*, Turku 1991, 52.

26. In Finland spouses (wives) have been exonerated by the Supreme Court from responsibility with regard to the other spouse's (husband's) business debts. KKO 1989:106, 1990:73, 1991:75.

27. Carsten Smith, *Garantirett* III, Oslo 1981, 174 and Kai Krüger, *Norsk kontraktsrett*, Bergen 1984, 642.

28. Rt 1984:28.

therefore lenders have a duty to inform guarantors and pledgors which is based on the doctrine of loyalty discussed above. Lenders' good faith notice of issues central to the guarantor's/pledgor's risk is usually required. The duty to inform does not cover every aspect of the financial condition of the borrower but it certainly does cover specific facts. Such facts may include a lien on real property already pledged for other debt, additional debt being granted against such lien on a coinciding lien on real property once a guarantee is put in place, the debt being already due at the time a guarantee or pledge is required and other circumstances that obviously add to the guarantor's/pledgor's risk. Where there are facts which are significant to the risk that the one submitting collateral is assuming and evidently unaware of and of which the lender *is* aware, the lender has a good faith duty to inform. According to new Swedish case law even commercial lenders are obliged—*uberrimae fidei*—to inform guarantors about the financial condition of the debtor and any development thereof.

Tort liability

Fraudulent conduct and wilful misrepresentation may constitute criminal acts. Breach of contract and a criminal act can be committed simultaneously. In Anglo-American law it appears to be natural that even tortious acts can be added to other liability grounds. That, in turn, does not sit very well in the Nordic legal systems. There is, in fact, no single concept that would even correspond to the concept of "tort" in any of the Scandinavian languages. Liability for tortious acts is covered in the Codes regarding Compensation of Damage.[29] The Codes do not cover contractual liability, however. The concept of tort is not defined in the Code. It only states that those who wilfully or negligently cause damage to others, must compensate them by paying damages.

Consequently, tortious acts which are not crimes seldom provide grounds of liability between the lender and the borrower. Therefore, Finnish lenders especially have been horrified by multimillion dollar punitive damage awards against some of their US subsidiaries in consumer loan cases handed down lately by Alabama courts.[30]

In the Nordic countries tortious claims are for third parties. Co-creditors' demands are usually expressed in bankruptcy proceedings after the discovery of a lender's previous workout measures that may have violated the rights of other creditors. The Scandinavian remedies for correcting such events are relatively weak. For all practical purposes the only remedy available is *actio pauliania*—a type of civil suit. Even though creditors in Finland and Sweden can go back further in order to find preferential or fraudulent transfers than they could

---

29. This central piece of legislation has been drafted together by the Danes, Norwegians, Swedes and the Finns.

30. *Union Mortgage Company Inc.* v. *Barlow*, Ala. Sup. Ct. 10 January 1992, no. 1901350, *Baker* v. *Harper*, Ala. Cir. Ct. Barbour City, no. 48, 24 July 1991. Also *Lender Liability News* (Buraff Publications) 6/1991, 1, 9, 16/1992, 1, 3.

previously,[31] they lack other effective remedies, such as equitable subordination.[32] The only result of a successful Scandinavian lawsuit is that the lender getting caught must return the payment, security interest or other advantage it has gained. At least compared with American remedies there is little deterrence in Scandinavian law.

Actions for damages based on tortious behaviour are plausible in third party violations. They have so far been rare, although there are signs of a turnaround in the recent Swedish case law.

Strict liability

Strict liability is interesting in the lender liability context only as to the risk of environmental hazards caused or condoned by borrowers. The reason for concern stems from the USA. The introduction of CERCLA and SARA[33] in the United States as a response to dramatic environmental catastrophies[34] and the significant authority granted to the Environmental Protection Agency (EPA) meant a turning point in American environmental law. EPA has the right to order a clean-up of the polluted properties first and then to look to the responsible persons for the clean-up cost. CERCLA is based on strict liability. No proof of negligence or intent to harm is necessary. All the owners and operators of polluted property are liable. Financial institutions are normally excused by the innocent lien holder exception. The exception will apply to banks which have not interfered with the decision-making process of the borrower nor influenced the borrower's decisions regarding the property. American case law illustrates that even a slight participation in the borrower's activities will put the applicability of the exception in jeopardy.[35]

Of the Nordic countries, Sweden already has legislation concerning compensation for environmental damage. The Swedish law is based on strict liability too. In Finland, the legislative organs are working on a proposal for similar legislation. The corresponding statutes in the other Nordic countries are under preparation. It seems that no attention has been paid by any of the Scandinavian legislators to the possibility of lenders becoming the ones found liable for the damages. One of the authors has recently suggested that potential lender liability for environmental damage should be investigated before the

31. The relevant statutes have been recently revised in the two countries.

32. In American bankruptcy law equitable subordination involves downgrading the claims of any party involved in unlawful attempts to improve its position against others.

33. Comprehensive Environmental Response, Compensation and Liability Act, 42 U.S.C. §§ 9601–9657 (1982 & Sup. IV 1986). Superfund Amendments and Reauthorisation Act, 42 U.S.C. § 9607 (1) (Supp. IV 1986).

34. For *Love Canal*, *The Times Beach* or *The Valley of Drums* etc. see Ann M. Burkhart, 25 *Harvard Journal on Legislation* 317, 319 (1988).

35. Of the American case law see *United States* v. *Mirabile*, 15 Environmental L. Rep. (Envtl. L. Inst.) 20, 994, 20, 996 (E.D. Pa. 1985); *United States* v. *Maryland Bank & Trust Co.*, 632 F.Supp. 573, 577–578 (D. Md. 1986), *In re T. P. Long Chemicals Inc.*, 45 Bankr. 278 (Bankr. N.D. Ohio 1985) and *United States* v. *Fleet Factors Corp.*, 901 F.2d 1550 (11th Cir. 1990).

legislation is passed in Finland.[36] The objective of the legislators may not be to address financial institutions' liability regarding environmental damages, but the issue should be addressed while the law is being drafted.

Combining grounds for liability

In a typical lender liability case a Scandinavian borrower would be well advised to stay with a contract claim where there is one, the most important reason being the burden of proof. Where the plaintiff can show a contract and a breach of it, the defendant has the duty to show that he is not culpable for the breach (exculpation). This is in many instances an advantage for the plaintiff.

The other contributing factor is the easier access to economic and consequential damages. Outside contractual relationships, the availability of compensation for economic damage that is not linked to damaged goods—such as lost profits on other deals—is very limited. In Finland the Code for Compensating Damage requires the damage to be caused by government officials while engaged in exercising public power (an authority),[37] by criminal acts or proof of special circumstances in order to make such damage eligible for compensation. In Sweden the corresponding code only mentions criminal acts but exceptions similar to the ones listed in the Finnish code have been recognised in the Swedish case law.[38] The Scandinavian (and German) division of damages into damage caused to persons, to goods and economic damage not linked to damage to persons or goods ("pure economic damage", *reine Vermögensschaden*) is not completely compatible with the Anglo-American theory of damages.[39]

Within a contractual relationship in the Scandinavian context, a person breaching the contract is always *assumed* to be responsible even for pure economic loss especially where negligence can be proven. Therefore, it makes sense to stay within the contractual framework and collect the highest compensation for the plaintiff.

The question of consequential damages arises often in situations where the damage would fall into the category of pure economic loss. Since the availability of economic damages is limited it also affects the availability of consequential damages. Otherwise the question of consequential damages is treated the same way both within and outside contractual relationships. In the Nordic jurisdictions the question of "where shall we stop?" relating to consequential damages is answered by applying an adequacy measurement to each individual case. The relevant doctrine is called the *adekvans-theory*.[40]

---

36. Ari Huhtamäki, 129 JFT, 95 (1993).
37. Such as measures taken by the police resulting in damages to third parties or their property.
38. Jan Kleineman, *Ren Förmögenhetsskada*, Stockholm 1987, 579.
39. Lookofsky, *supra*, 11 and Kleineman, 5 *Juridisk Tidskrift vid Stockholms Universitet* 718 (1993–1994) and *idem*, *Scandinavian Studies in Law*, 1992, 312.
40. *Ibid.*

INDIVIDUAL BANKER'S LIABILITY

Individual bankers representing lending institutions are occasionally sued personally along with the institutions. Usually there is no contract between the borrower and the banker. Thus, civil liability must be allocated among the defendants.[41] This has a definite impact in the Nordic countries.[42] Criminal liability may exist with respect to individual bankers. While discussing lender liability, however, criminal liability cannot be ruled out. Outside borrowers or co-creditors have seldom any reason to suggest criminal liability of individual bankers. Guarantors and pledgors sometimes have. Usually criminal charges are brought by the financial institutions themselves, though. In fact, according to fresh case law substantial recent losses in Finnish and Swedish banks have been caused intentionally by bankers abusing their fiduciary positions.[43] For the most part criminal liability falls outside the scope of this chapter.

THE LENDING PROCESS

General remarks

In the Scandinavian countries lending arrangements are documented with very few and rather brief documents. Credit agreements are commonly perceived as being like promissory notes. Lenders rarely sign any documents. Commitment letters[44] are issued rarely and credit agreements[45] are used seldom. The borrower must sign the note. Until 1989 the Finnish banks did not even give a copy of the note to the borrower. In the Anglo-American legal environment the lack of a Contract Code has probably resulted in a better comprehension of the nature of lending arrangements and that credit agreements are contracts.[46]

Even in a straightforward case of consumer credit there is more involved than just signing a note. In many instances consumers receive marketing information. Misleading information at that stage or in subsequent negotiations, if not corrected at a later point of time, can lead to liability (e.g. misrepresentation).[47]

---

41. See Huhtamäki, 74 *Defensor Legis* 101 (1993).

42. Should both the bank and the bankers be found liable, joint and several liability would not allow double recovery for the plaintiff. Under Scandinavian law he could choose which one to turn to primarily. Other rules define the relationships among the ones found to be liable.

43. There are plenty of appellate court rulings from both countries but especially from the Finnish courts. See Huhtamäki, *Pankkirikokset* (Crime in the Banks), Helsinki 1994.

44. Written offers to extend credit.

45. Agreements signed by both parties.

46. This has also meant a proliferation of documents and forms, which have grown thicker and thicker as lenders and borrowers develop new defences, claims and counterclaims.

47. In some of the Nordic countries contract law has been influenced by a doctrine called social contract law over the past two decades. The underlying objective is to protect the weaker party to a contract by letting the binding effect of the contract be judicially eroded. The erosion is caused by adjusting unconscionable contracts. Most areas of contract law—especially the ones relating to

Credit applications must be treated without prejudice. Notifying a credit decision to the borrower constitutes a commitment to lend which cannot be unilaterally withdrawn unless the right to do so is specifically withheld. Accepting the offer constitutes a contract.[48] Even the borrower may become bound to take the loan. The content of this agreement is usually transferred into a credit agreement. In simple cases credit agreements consist of a note, a security agreement (or combination note and security agreement) or a mortgage, pledge agreement, guarantee or some combination of these documents. Final agreement upon and execution of these documents is generally a condition precedent to the consummation of the loan. The primary function of the note is to serve as evidence of the borrower having received the funds and the borrower's obligation to repay. At least in the Scandinavian countries the holder of a note also enjoys the *prima facie* privilege of not having to prove the cause of the debt. In the Nordic region note holders enjoy benefits related to litigation too. In other words, the note facilities collection.

Lending gets more complicated with business borrowers. The larger the institutions involved, the more complex the arrangements tend to be. The contractual process is sometimes enhanced by further phases. Letters of intent can be drafted. Financing instruments grow in number and features too.

The point to be made is that lending involves a series of phases bringing the parties closer to one another, thus adding to their mutual responsibilities towards one another.

The Nordic jurisdictions are free from formal rules regarding assessment of evidence. Every piece of evidence is allowed while the material truth is being sought. Therefore no equivalent to the parol evidence rule exists.[49] Representations and promises etc. made at some point of the lending process all count. Should they be contrary to what is stated in the written contract document, the common meaning of the parties, as determined by the court, will prevail. If no such intent can be detected, the court will go to the rules of contract interpretation. In a lending context it becomes valuable for the borrowers that standard terms[50] will be interpreted in favour of the party who did not draft the

---

consumers—have been affected. Banking, however, has not been particularly affected. The standard terms remained essentially intact for a number of years. The value of the doctrine is being debated. Critical views of the essence of it have been published (in Swedish) recently by Claes Sandgren, 4 *Juridisk Tidskrift vid Stockholms Universitet* 456, 480, 482 (1992–1993). A response has been presented by Finnish Professor Thomas Wilhelmsson in the following issue of the same periodical.

48. Finnish case KKO 1991:42 (acceptance of oral promise).

49. In the USA statements of complete agreement are commonly used at the time of signing the credit agreement. The purpose of such statements is to ensure that promises and representations made prior to signing the written and finalised contract will lose any binding effect they might have had. This concept bolsters the parol evidence rule when applied to contracts in the USA. The impact of the rule on Scandinavian law has been discussed by Prof. Hellner in 1993 (*Festskrift till prof. Bengtsson*).

50. Especially contracts with standard terms. However in Finland this particular interpretation rule has wider acceptance.

document (*contra proferentem*), that the actual text will prevail over the headings, that hand-written text will prevail over printed and so forth.

The credit agreement in the broad sense of the word is to be understood as a series of contractual phases increasing the responsibilities and the rights of the contracting parties step by step. The true nature of the credit agreement has been demonstrated in Finnish case law.[51] For this reason credit applications, oral promises to lend money, loan commitment letters, credit agreements, security agreements, notes and other loan documents are often kept apart from one another when deciding the scope of liability at any phase of the lending process. In Nordic civil law there is no reason for responsibilities created in each previous phase to be deleted in the next phase. It is possible to let the liability producing components gradually accumulate.

Commitment to lend

In Scandinavian contract law much emphasis is placed on binding offers and acceptances. For this reason it is valuable to define what is meant by an offer. Credit applications are sometimes said to be offers. If that was the case, borrowers could not simultaneously solicit bids from various lenders without risking significant liability themselves. In everyday life, exactly the opposite is commonplace. Even for practical purposes credit applications cannot be considered binding offers. The borrower receiving a notification of approved credit, on the other hand, must have the right to rely on such promise.

Scandinavian law does not require contracts to be drafted in a written form except for wills, purchase agreements concerning real estate and a few other types of contracts. Credit agreements can be made orally. As a rule, a note is signed by the borrower when the money is to be received. Yet the Supreme Court of Finland confirmed scholars' opinions by ruling that an oral promise to make a mortgage loan for a family changing homes could not be cancelled unilaterally by the bank.[52]

Consumer lending is an area where views of credit analysis and lender's due diligence differ substantially. A fundamental difference between the attitudes towards credit reports is easily observed. A common feature in the Scandinavian countries is that keeping records on citizens is a delicate area. Overly active tracking is contrary to the right of privacy and a reluctance to allow records is therefore understandable. In the Nordic area this has led to legislation forbidding, among other things, most useful credit information. Oftentimes credit institutions are allowed to record only judgments against debtors. No positive credit information can be gathered. No delinquencies or charge-offs can be recorded. The best credit report is a blank sheet. One might question how

51. KKO 1991:42, KKO 1992:50.
52. KKO 1991:42.

consumer lending is feasible under these circumstances at all. Traditionally Scandinavian consumers were known as very reliable debtors and they defaulted seldom. That unfortunately changed in the 1980s.

Statistical methods in granting loans such as credit scoring have been criticised as immoral by the Swedes in new consumer credit legislation.[53] Without ample data of accurate consumer credit histories lenders should act cautiously. This was, however, not the point made in Swedish legislation. Instead, much was said about the lenders' duty to prove whether the consumer would be able to repay the loan or not. Consequently, the Swedish law obligates lenders to determine this with respect to each individual consumer. The other Nordic countries have not followed suit.

Honouring the terms and conditions of a loan

Living up to the expectations documented in the credit agreement is normally more of a borrower's than a lender's problem. Yet, in many instances lenders step over the boundaries defined or implied in credit agreements. Bankers do not always recognise the ongoing performance that is required from the lender after the funds have been advanced. The lender is still expected to perform. The financier's end of the bargain after the borrower has received the money is to allow the borrower an undisturbed possession of the funds in accordance with the credit agreement as long as the borrower follows the payment schedules and other conditions set forth in the credit agreement.

As part of allowing the borrower to operate undisturbed, the lender may not unilaterally alter the terms and conditions agreed upon. Judging from cases decided it seems that lending institutions are at times tempted to take advantage of borrowers' ignorance when calculating interest rates and other charges. The largest lender liability case ever tried in Finland was based on facts like that.[54]

"Long term refinancing for the average Finnish 10-year mortgage loans and other long-term commitments was not obtainable. For this reason the banks were accustomed to lending long and funding short. They did not change their habits even after having gained access to the global capital markets, although it led to a mismatch situation where the cost of funds could in an unfavourable interest rate environment exceed the interest earned on loans outstanding.

In 1989 the Finnish currency (markka) denominated interest rates, which by that time were freely determined[55] in the markets, rose rapidly. The banks were suddenly paying double digit interest and the domestic lending portfolios were yielding only single digits. The banks suffering most tried to solve the problem by relying on an ambiguous rate clause in notes of their customers. The standard term only stated a frame within which the rate could fluctuate. In the negotiations the customers had been told the exact rate of interest which would only be altered if and when the stable administrative Finnish base rate was raised or lowered. Subsequently, borrowers were informed by the lenders that

53. Swedish Ministry of Justice, Committee Proposal, Ds 1990:84, 41.
54. KKO 1992:50.
55. As opposed to being administratively regulated.

the rates had been raised unilaterally. This resulted in hundreds of lawsuits. The increases were banned by the courts."[56]

Accelerating a loan

Collecting a loan is sometimes a problem to lenders. Where the borrower shows inability or unwillingness to repay, lenders must act in order to recover their money. Of the myriad of issues relating to loan collection procedures only some are covered here.

Lenders often discover that further repayments of principal are endangered because the interest payments or amortisations are delayed. In those instances it is natural to demand immediate payment of the entire principal and accrued interest owing. Accelerating a loan is a heavy weapon and it ought to be used sparingly. Clear monetary defaults do not usually present much problem. The same cannot be said about other causes of default. In the Nordic countries they are usually included in the general terms and conditions printed on the reverse side of the standard note documents.

The problem with the terms is that they contain several contradictory provisions concerning repayment. The borrower may be told in the negotiations that the loan will be repaid in periodic increments, with the final payment being due at a particular point in time. This is sometimes confirmed with a separate document called a "payment plan". Simultaneously, a general condition on the note may allow the creditor to call the loan due any time or in 30 or 60 days without cause (at will). Another general clause always states that the creditor has the right to call in the loan immediately if the debtor has given misleading information, misses a payment or disposes of property securing the loan. Yet another general clause entitles acceleration in 30 or 60 days unless the borrower, at the creditor's request, offers additional collateral when the value of creditor's security interest has decreased or the creditor otherwise deems itself insecure.

According to contract interpretation rules a lender cannot call in a loan at will if the dates for repayment have been set. Simultaneous use of acceleration clauses based on just causes is possible. A default caused by delinquency must be clearly manifested. Delinquency must be established to be relevant both in terms of amount and elapsed time/frequency. Both Swedish and Finnish consumer credit legislation gives specific guidelines on this issue.[57] The creditor carries the burden of proof concerning misleading information and disposal of property.

The falling value of properties and collateral for secured loans has been a common phenomenon recently. The same could be said about demands for additional collateral. Because the lender accepted the collateral offered, any

---

56. KKO 1992:50.
57. Statute on Consumer Protection, 385/23 May 1986, § 7:16, Swedish Ministry of Justice, Committee Proposal on Consumer Credit Legislation, Ds 1990:84, 101.

devaluation resulting from pure market fluctuations could be seen as a risk that the lender must bear at least if the lender did not specifically make other arrangements with the borrower.

A Finnish standard clause authorises the lender to call a loan (based on a standard contract term) in six months if the liquidity or the solidity of the bank so requires. No regard is given to whether the borrower has lived up to his end of the bargain or not. The Finnish banking authorities have indicated that this particular clause should be used on occasions other than mass accelerations when a bank is about to fail. In spite of the directive, it is doubtful whether courts would allow accelerations based on such—at least from the borrower's point of view—an unconscionable standard term. In Sweden, the banking laws provide that a bank must retain the right to accelerate any loans with maturity over one year without cause.[58] Unpleasant things can be imposed on citizens by legislation, as in this statute, but not by sneaking provisions into standard terms of Finnish notes.

Foreclosing on security

Problems related to security agreements are very common lender liability matters. Two specific issues are overwhelmingly dominating: first, until recently property was usually pledged to the creditor not just for any specific debt but for all of the debtor's current and future obligations (general pledge).[59] The subject has already been discussed under the section on tort liability. The other point has also been made in the same section: a lender has a duty to inform the guarantor or a pledgor about the financial situation of the debtor. A bank can no longer take cover behind the veil of confidentiality nor claim in good faith that no reason existed to inform the guarantor about facts relevant to his risk.

A number of cases involving foreclosure on property and disposal of the foreclosed property have also been decided by the Scandinavian courts. In the seminal Finnish case (KKO 1985 II 29), damages were awarded to an owner of a condominium who lost the property for less than a quarter of its lowest plausible market value. The bank auctioned the collateral to the highest bidder but the bid only covered the receivables of the bank. Under the circumstances the bank should have refused to sell and arranged a new auction or disposed of the collateral in another way.

An interesting comparison to American law is provided by *Durrett* v. *Washington National Insurance Co.*[60] In the United States the courts have followed the rule presented in *Durrett*. The court stated that 70 per cent of the market value was the lowest acceptable price for a foreclosure sale of this nature.[61] The Supreme Court of Finland could have set a precedent at 66.6 per

58. Swedish Statute on Banking Activities, § 2:19.
59. In the USA this is often called the "drag-net" for all obligations.
60. 621 F.2d 201 (5th Cir. 1980).
61. Where the foreclosure is subsequently challenged in a bankruptcy proceeding.

cent in a case[62] decided only a few weeks after KKO 1985 II 29. Yet damages were awarded in this unpublished case under circumstances similar to those in KKO 1985 II 29.

Workout liability

Because of the monetary interest involved workout situations for major corporations represent probably one of the most important areas of lender liability. Only a couple of interesting features can be brought up in this chapter. The most illustrative Finnish case involves forestry which is natural for the Scandinavian scene.

"An industrialist and an owner of a sawmill were hit by the recession in 1957. Heavy investments had been made for new production facilities which were getting close to completion at that time. Even though equity on the books represented 50 per cent of the total assets of the corporation, the mill suffered from tight liquidity. The sole financier threatened to accelerate all financing unless the bank was granted seats on the board and all of the corporate stock as collateral.[63] Additionally, the bank demanded a power of attorney allowing its representatives to vote the way they wanted with the owner's shares in shareholders' meetings. The owner was compelled to consent. Later one of the mill's short-term credits defaulted and the bank foreclosed immediately on the stock and sold it for a nominal price to a subsidiary of the bank. The stock was resold a few years later for millions of marks. In the meantime, the new production facilities has already earned significant profits for the corporation. The District Court of Helsinki awarded 3 million marks in damages based on bad faith in disposing of the security; the Appellate Court of Helsinki reduced them to 0.5 million, but the Finnish Supreme Court reversed the award completely. The outcome today could be different."[64]

Finding other lenders to step into the workout financier's shoes has always been an attractive alternative. In the United States a multitude of cases have shown that attempts to attract money from the public in order to repay the lenders of ailing corporations is forbidden.[65] Securities trading was first covered by statutes much later in the Nordic countries. Prior to that no specific rules regulating securities issues, insider trading or other securities issues existed. The Stock Exchanges had ethic codes, but they did not contain any effective sanctions. Case law has evolved after the statutes have been passed.

One of the authors recently tried a case in Finland against the investment bank of a bond issue.

"Senior bond issues had usually been covered by bank guarantees. In this case the issue was the second ever without a guarantee. The issue was sold through 1,100 bank outlets. Five thousand prospectuses were printed. A vast majority of the 1,544 investors who

---

62. KKO, 21 May 1985, T:1279.

63. Up to that moment the bank's collateral position was fully covered by liens on the mill's real property.

64. No lender liability doctrine to speak of existed in those days. The "large" Scandinavian general clause (section 36) of the Contract Codes had not been passed either.

65. Both section 12(2) of the Securities Act of 1933 and section 10b–5 of the Securities Exchange Act of 1934 prohibit such conduct in the United States.

bought FIM 50 million worth of bonds were handed one of the 88,000 look-alikes of the prospectus without disclosure of the lack of guarantee. The financial data presented was outdated and the interim financial statements were not disclosed. The issuer stopped most of its payments and the bonds were no longer traded six months after the issue. The issuer filed bankruptcy four months after that. The case was decided in favour of 55 plaintiffs by the Helsinki District Court. The bank did not appeal but paid off all the 1,544 investors, with interest."[66]

ARI M. HUHTAMÄKI AND JAN KLEINEMAN

---

66. District Court of Helsinki, 23 March 1994, S 92/8267.

CHAPTER 10

CANADIAN BANK LENDER LIABILITY: CAVEAT LENDOR

1. INTRODUCTION

Lending has, for the past decade or so, become a risky business for bankers in Canada. Losses from Third World loans, agricultural failures and commercial real estate collapses have been reflected in some of the least profitable years on record, even for the Big Five.[1] A significant minority of the smaller Schedule II banks, mostly regional or foreign banks, have either become insolvent or have wound down their business in Canada, and the spectre of insolvency has stalked and continues to stalk the near banks, including some major trust companies, which have actively sought mergers with the largest banks, to avoid the fate of their smaller competitors over the past decade.

While changes within the domestic and international environments within which banks must operate made the 1980s an exhilarating period for Canadian banks, the courts and the legislatures have compounded the frisson of danger in lending by importing an increasing number of legal duties into the loan relationship in addition to those for which express agreement is made. "Lender liability" is not yet as widely referred to as such in Canada as in the United States, but the growing use of the phrase as an umbrella to cover all of the particular events in the life of a loan transaction, from negotiation to repayment or judgment enforcement, in relation to which legal liability might accrue, implicitly acknowledges the evolution of a coherent judicial approach to bank lending issues.

This coherence is found in the willingness of both the judiciary and the legislators to impose higher standards of care in contract, tort, trust and restitution than those traditionally expressed within the four corners of the agreement. Thus, it is now accepted that in relation to the negotiation of a loan, banks owe fiduciary duties besides being subject to a wide-ranging concept of negligent misrepresentation and a variety of other legal doctrines including unconscionability, undue influence and unequal bargaining power. Canadian courts have also imposed liability for fraudulent misrepresentation, despite its evidentiary difficulties. The implication of terms based on "reasonableness" is

---

1. Royal Bank of Canada, Canadian Imperial Bank of Commerce, Bank of Montreal, Bank of Nova Scotia and Toronto-Dominion Bank.

255

also characteristic of recent judicial pronouncements as is the willingness of the courts to enforce oral collateral representations in preference to the written agreement. Although Canadian courts appear not yet to have considered in detail the legal standards of care required during the life of a loan, there can be little doubt that the high standards expected during loan negotiation and subsequently during the enforcement of the obligation to repay would be equally expected of banks during the life of a loan.

The duties of the lending banker in the enforcement of the obligation to repay have come under particular judicial and legislative scrutiny in the past decade, resulting in a standard requirement of reasonable notice prior to enforcement of a security, and the imposition of a constructive trust on bankers in favour of competing third party claimants, so as to thwart, in a significant number of cases, the common law right of set-off. In addition, both federal and provincial legislatures have increasingly created special statutory priorities in relation to both judgment enforcement and insolvency, which have resulted in delaying the repayment of the bank loan until other prior statutory claims have been discharged, if then. Finally, threats of the imposition of lender liability in relation to such non-lending issues as environmental clean-ups, currently suggest that lending will become an ever more hazardous and costly activity for Canadian banks. As banking law increasingly seems to be thought of as a tool of social engineering in Canada, it is not difficult to understand why bankers express exasperation about even being in the lending business at all today.

2. GENERAL THEORIES OR GENERAL THEORY?

Although expressed in traditional legal categories such as fiduciary duty, misrepresentation, unconscionability, reasonableness and constructive trust, it appears that a fundamental paradigm shift is occurring in judicial and legislative attitudes to lender liability similar to that occurring to a greater extent in the United States[2] and to a much lesser extent in Australia[3] and England.[4] Bank lender liability law appears to be undergoing conflation with the apparently emerging private obligations law in relation to commercial matters generally, following trends first visible in the 1970s in relation to consumer transactions, and resulting ultimately, perhaps, in the re-merger of both commercial and consumer law, subject to the same general standards of moral conduct.

2. J.J. Norton and W.M. Baggett, "American Lender Liability: Common Law, Statutes and Contorts", in Ross Cranston (ed.), *Banks—Liability and Risk* (London, Lloyd's of London Press Ltd., 1990), 203.
3. Kathryn Jane Smith, "The Liability of Banks and Lending Institutions: An Australian Perspective", in Cranston, *supra*, n. 2, at 117.
4. See generally, Cranston, *supra*, n. 2.

Explicit public acknowledgement by the judiciary that the moral underpinnings of commercial transactions are to be patent rather than implicit has been made recently by several members of the judiciary. In *Harvey* v. *Kreutziger*,[5] in which an Indian of low intelligence and poor education sought the rescission of a contract for the sale of a boat to which a valuable fishing licence was attached on grounds of unconscionability, Lambert J.A. of the British Columbia Court of Appeal stated that the real issue in such cases, "is whether the transaction, seen as a whole, is sufficiently divergent from community standards of commercial morality that it should be rescinded."[6] While in *Lac Minerals Ltd.* v. *International Corona Resources Ltd.*,[7] LaForest J. of the Supreme Court of Canada asserted, "It is simply not the case that business and accepted morality are mutually exclusive domains",[8] and references to business morality are peppered throughout the case.

The assumption implicit in LaForest J.'s opinion that business has been immoral and must be made moral through law is arguably mistaken. Rather, the renewed concern to infuse morality into commercial law may be more accurately characterised as the replacement of one moral view with another. A system of commercial law based on promise-keeping, bargains, individualism, independence and self-sufficiency is being replaced by a system of commercial law based on values as yet undefined, but definitively collectivist in orientation. Whatever one may think of this trend towards an externally imposed collectivist morality in relation to commercial transactions, should it be sustained, the challenge for the judiciary is, as McLachlin J. has observed, "to define legal rules which, while providing the certainty so critical to commercial relations, reflect to borrow Justice Lambert's words, the prevailing moral standards of our community".[9] Whether there are even prevailing moral standards, or any at all, or even a coherent Canadian community any more is another matter.

For two reasons, it is unclear that the importation of this new judicial morality into commercial law can be characterised as a principled development or even as demonstrating judicial concern for honesty, predictability and certainty as protected values in commercial law. First, the courts continue to use the traditional categories of contract, tort and fiduciary law but often with changed substantive contents beneath the classical terminology. Nor are the new meanings unambiguous. It is difficult to know from reading the cases whether this is deliberate or merely a sad reflection of the intellectual quality of the Canadian judiciary (with few exceptions). The net result, however, is increased uncertainty for commercial parties and a growing perception among

---

5. (1979) 95 D.L.R. (3d) 231 (B.C.C.A.).
6. *Ibid.*, at 241.
7. (1989) 61 D.L.R. (4th) 14 (S.C.C.).
8. *Ibid.*, at 44.
9. Beverley M. McLachlin, "A New Morality in Business Law?" (1990) 16 Can. Bus. L.J. 319 at 327.

commercial people that the courts are more in touch with the spiteful and jealous attitudes of the anti-business special interest groups than with the principled requirements of a business community struggling to sustain the economic infrastructure of the country in the face of global marketplace changes.

Secondly, the approach of the courts to commercial transactions generally is fragmented. The various categories of private law are frequently flung concurrently at a dispute without visible appreciation of their respective functions or substantive contents in relation to the chronology and impugned conduct in the transaction under judicial scrutiny. Indeed, it might sometimes be wondered if the courts either know or care about their respective distinctions. A good example of this confusion is the definition of unconscionability offered by McIntyre J.A. (as he then was) in *Harvey* v. *Kreutziger*:

"Where a claim is made that a bargain is unconscionable, it must be shown for success that there was inequality in the position of the parties due to the ignorance, need or distress of the weaker, which would leave him in the power of the stronger, coupled with proof of substantial unfairness in the bargain. When this has been shown a presumption of fraud is raised and the stronger must show, in order to preserve his bargain, that it was fair and reasonable.

Like many principles of law, it is much easier to state than to apply in any given case."[10]

This "principle" mingles elements of unconscionability, unequal bargaining power, unfair bargains, undue influence, fraud and reasonableness, besides reversing the onus of proof. And all to protect a commercially inept Indian who had received the fishing licence in the first place simply because he was a member of a statutorily privileged special interest group!

A few Canadian courts[11] have openly flirted with a notion of good faith along the lines of the UCC, sections 1–203 and 1–208, but the explicit adoption of a general principle under whose guise a duty of fair dealing as defined by the courts could be imposed on commercial parties has not occurred. Rather, Canadian jurisprudence remains fragmented and apparently variously unprincipled, responding on a case by case basis in no evidently pragmatic manner to commercial disputes, including bank lender disputes. It may be wondered whether the real underlying principle is simply the "deep pockets" theory of bank liability as expressed by LaForest J. of the Supreme Court of Canada in *CP Hotels* v. *Bank of Montreal*,[12] when he quoted with approval the notorious statement of Bray J. in *Kepitigalla Rubber Estates Ltd.* v. *Bank of India Ltd.*[13]

10. *Supra*, n. 5.

11. See generally: Philip Girard, "Good Faith in Contract Performance: Principle or Placebo" (1983) 5 S.C. Law Rev. 309; Michael G. Bridge *et al*; "Does Anglo-Canadian Contract Law Need a Doctrine of Good Faith?" (1984) 9 Can. Bus. L.J. 385; Edward P. Belobaba, "Good Faith in Canadian Contract Law" (1985) *Special Lectures of the Law Society of Upper Canada*, (Toronto), 73.

12. (1987) 40 D.L.R. (4th) 385 (S.C.C.).

13. *Ibid.*, at p. 434. Bray J. stated: "To the individual customer the loss would often be serious; to the banker, it is negligible." [1909] 2 K.B. 1010 at p. 1026.

The following discussion will analyse the current state of bank lender liability at various stages in the life of a loan. As stated earlier, judicial and legislative activists have increased the legal duties owed by bankers at virtually all stages of the transaction so that the absence of any unique doctrinal developments at one or more stages argues against special focus on particular stages only. If there is any noteworthy change in Canadian law in relation to bank lender liability over the past decade or so, it is the widely fronted attack on the lending banker by the courts.

3. THE OBLIGATION TO GRANT A LOAN

The potential for lender liability accrues the moment a prospective borrower makes known to a bank its interest in a loan, even if the bank refuses a loan application where the applicant is a natural person. Although it has not yet been so interpreted by any court or human rights tribunal in Canada, it is widely thought that the net effect of provincial and federal human rights legislation is to restrict the grounds for the rejection of a loan application to a proven absence of creditworthiness on the part of the applicant. Two provisions in the Ontario Human Rights Code[14] may be taken as typical of such legislation in relation to the provision of banking services:

"s.1 Every person has a right to equal treatment with respect to services, goods and facilities, without discrimination because of race, ancestry, place of origin, colour, ethnic origin, citizenship, creed, sex, sexual orientation, age, marital status, family status or handicap.
. . .
s.3 Every person having legal capacity has a right to contract on equal terms without discrimination because of race, ancestry, place of origin, colour, ethnic origin, citizenship, creed, sex, sexual orientation, age, marital status, family status or handicap."

The net effect of such legislation is to place a positive legal duty on all bankers to give consideration only to the economic characteristics of the applicant and the application in the lending decision. This duty to investigate the creditworthiness of the prospective borrower and to appraise the business plan for which the loan is sought is likely to attract the same legal standards of care already expressly required of the banker at other stages of the life of the loan. In one older case, *Wheatley* v. *Provincial Bank*,[15] the Supreme Court of Canada found that the bank's duty to provide loans within the reasonable limits of sound banking practice was satisfied when a bank refused to confirm interim financing to a log exporter when a required letter of credit as a security was not forthcoming.

To assist this assessment, the prospective borrower must make voluntary disclosures of information, creating simultaneously a potential duty of

14. R.S.O., 1990, c. H. 19.
15. (1970) 12 D.L.R. (3d) 1 (S.C.C.).

confidentiality on the part of the bank in relation to that information. The prospective borrower must also forego privacy rights to permit the lending banker to make enquiries beyond the matters voluntarily disclosed in the application process. This latter relinquishment of privacy is accomplished by a written consent.

The legal power to regulate the use of information acquired by banks about customers is vested by the Bank Act[16] in the Governor in Council, who has yet to publish the regulations stipulated for by the Act in this regard.[17] The only statutorily permissible breach of confidentiality in relation to customer information is information requested by the Superintendent of Financial Institutions, but that too is required to be treated by the Superintendent with confidence, except where the Superintendent decides to pass information along to any government agency, body or person who is also required to treat it with confidence.[18]

However, the Bank Act also requires the directors of each bank to establish procedures restricting the use of confidential information,[19] and in partial compliance with that statutory mandate, the Canadian Bankers Association has produced a model privacy code,[20] which is currently being implemented by Canadian banks. While the code is an internal industry document, there is reason to believe that the courts would, by analogy, regard it as an appropriate minimum standard for the banks in relation to their duties of confidentiality to customers[21] or even prospective customers.[22]

In one case to date, in which a bank manager disclosed loan application information from a customer to his wife, who took advantage of the business opportunity, while the customer's application was rejected, the court found such conduct to be not only a breach of the banker's duty of secrecy[23] but also breach of a fiduciary duty, although no punitive damages were awarded despite the dishonesty and high-handedness of the manager.[24] Why a prospective borrower was regarded as having entered a fiduciary relationship with a bank was not elucidated by the court, which appears to have resorted to the use of the word "fiduciary" to characterise its moral outrage at the manager's conduct.

Whether or not a decision to reject an application is reviewable by the courts at the instigation of an applicant on grounds of an alleged improper assessment of creditworthiness by the bank, has not yet been considered. Judges are not

16. S.C., 1991, c. 46.
17. Section 459.
18. Section 531.
19. Section 157(2).
20. Reproduced in Consolidated Bank Act and Regulations 1994 (Toronto: Carswell, 1994) at 538–542.
21. *Stanley Works of Canada Ltd.* v. *B.C.N.* (1981) 20 B.L.R. 282 (Que. C.A.) and *National Slag* v. *C.I.B.C.* (1985) 19 D.L.R. (4th) 383 (Ont. C.A.) regarded the inter-bank clearing rules as an appropriate analogy for an individual bank's duties to a customer.
22. *Woods* v. *Martin's Bank* [1959] 1 Q.B. 55 (Leeds Assizes).
23. *Tournier* v. *National Provincial and Union Bank of England* [1924] 1 K.B. 461 (C.A.).
24. *Guertin* v. *Royal Bank* (1983) 43 O.R. (2d) 363; aff'd. (1984) 47 O.R. (2d) 794 (C.A.).

bankers, and it may be expected that reversals of negative decisions would be rare, although little ingenuity need be applied to plead arguments based on negligence or fiduciary duty or reasonableness for a successful review.

4. THE AUTHORITY TO GRANT A LOAN

When the creditworthiness of the applicant and the commercial viability of the business plan are required to be assessed, the standard of care expected of the lending banker is the statutory standard set out in the Bank Act for all directors and officers in their conduct of all banking business. Thus, section 158 requires that directors and officers shall perform all duties "honestly and in good faith with a view to the best interests of the bank, and exercise the care, diligence and skill that a reasonably prudent person would exercise in comparable circumstances". This section has never been judicially interpreted, but it is clearly a codification of common law standards of care for directors and officers, and balances, on the bank's side, the *prima facie* right to credit which the Human Rights Code would otherwise seem to promote.[25] The Bank Act further provides for high standards of disclosure for directors and officers where potential conflicts of interest may occur in relation to loans.[26] It remains to be seen whether the courts will regard section 158 as promoting an industry standard test against which to judge lending decisions or some higher standard.

The 1980 Bank Act[27] effectively abolished the *ultra vires* doctrine and the constructive notice doctrine in relation to the liability of a bank for the conduct of its directors and officers, and codified the indoor management rule. These provisions were continued in the 1992 Act,[28] so that effectively, potential borrowers need not concern themselves about the possibility of a successful denial of liability on the older common law grounds of absence of authority or internal control failures in relation to lender liability problems. In the only reported case to date on these sections, the Ontario High Court found that where a bank's accounts manager had instructed solicitors to commence actions in relation to loans and to enforce guarantees, the absence of an express resolution by the board of directors authorising the manager to make such decisions was irrelevant in relation to the solicitors.[29] It may be expected that an identical interpretation will be made in relation to borrowers.

A novel question arose recently in relation to liability for decisions about a borrower's creditworthiness in the context of loan participation agreements. *Canadian Deposit Insurance Corporation* v. *Canadian Commercial Bank*[30]

25. For a general discussion of these principles in relation specifically to s. 158 and its predecessor sections, see: M.H. Ogilvie, *Canadian Banking Law* (Toronto: Carswell, 1991) at pp. 62–70.
26. Sections 202–206.
27. R.S.C., 1985, c. B–1, ss. 18–21.
28. Sections 15–20.
29. *Bank of Montreal* v. *Vola* (1980) 31 O.R. (2d) 60 (Ont. H.C.).
30. (1986) 27 D.L.R. (4th) 229 (Alta. Q.B.); (1987) 46 D.L.R. (4th) 518 (Alta. Q.B.); (1990) 69 D.L.R. (4th) 1 (Alta. C.A.); leave to appeal to S.C.C. granted (1991) 77 D.L.R. (4th) vi (note).

concerned the insolvency of the defendant Alberta bank which was the lead bank in the participation agreement. CCB entered into various agreements whereby it would lend money and then farm out participations to other entities which had signed the loan agreement, agreeing to lend up to their respective stated obligations. CCB either assigned an interest in the loan to other lenders or directly syndicated the loan to be granted directly to a borrower by a number of lenders. Trust mechanisms facilitated the transfers and the participation agreements contained provisions by which CCB disclaimed liability for the creditworthiness of the borrowers. After placing CCB in receivership, the CDIC challenged the validity of the participation agreements, as did the unsecured creditors. CCB sought to avoid liability by arguing that it was *ultra vires* the bank to engage in lending through such agreements. The Alberta Queen's Bench and Court of Appeal upheld the agreements as valid within the statutory authorisation of section 173(1) of the 1980 Bank Act, to engage in all business generally appertaining to the business of banking, and as within section 18 of the Act which empowered a bank with the capacity of a natural person, subject to the Act. It would appear, then, that whether banks act alone or in a syndicate the legislative authority to grant a loan is so comprehensive as to render virtually impossible evading liability in relation to the loan, regardless of who made the decision in relation to creditworthiness.

5. DISCLOSURE OF THE COST OF A LOAN

The remaining statutory duty required of a lending banker is disclosure of both the interest rate and the entire cost of the loan in accordance with the relevant legislation and regulations pursuant thereto. Whether the relevant legislation is the federal Bank Act alone, or concurrently with provincial legislation, is the prior constitutional issue. Originally, disclosure regulation for loans was first implemented by most of the provinces in the 1960s as a response to the rise of consumerism, and on the assumption that provincial jurisdiction over "property and civil rights" pursuant to section 92(13) of the Constitution Act 1867 encompassed contracts of loan. The 1980 Bank Act, and subsequently the 1992 Bank Act, provided for the first time for interest and charges disclosure regulation, pursuant to federal jurisdiction under section 91(15) over "banking". The constitutional question of which jurisdiction has prior authority over the issue remains unresolved.

However, in some provinces,[31] the practical solution of ensuring that federal and provincial legislation are identical through federal–provincial negotiation, has neutralised the constitutional issue and restored the proper focus to the nature of the required regulation. Again, in cases of direct conflict, the constitutional paramountary doctrine formulated in *Multiple Access* v.

---

31. Alberta is a good example.

McCutcheon[32] should result in the enforcement of the federal legislation in cases of express direct conflict, and peaceful co-existence in all other cases.

The Bank Act requires all banks operating in Canada to disclose the interest or discount applicable to a loan and all other charges in connection with the loan to the borrower or to any other person from whom the bank receives any such charges directly or indirectly.[33] The details of this statutory requirement are set out in full in two sets of regulations, the Cost of Borrowing Regulations[34] and the Disclosure of Charges (Banks) Regulations.[35] These regulations provide detailed lists of what is to be disclosed and how disclosure is to be made, besides showing how the calculation of the cost of the loan is to be done mathematically. The disclosures are to be made on a written "Disclosure Statement" and delivered to the prospective borrower prior to the execution of the lending agreement. Banks in Canada routinely comply with the provisions of the Bank Act and the regulations pursuant thereto, and there have been no cases to date in relation to them.

Only two other pieces of legislation, both federal, appear to be potentially applicable to bank lending practices, the Interest Act,[36] and the Criminal Code.[37] The former is of general application in relation to loans and overtaken in relation to bank lending by the greater detail of the Bank Act. However, the 60 per cent ceiling for which the latter provides as the annual total cost of a loan beyond which the rate is criminal, clearly sets the top limit on the amount banks may charge in relation to loans.[38] Again, no banking cases have considered how this amount is calculated in relation to banks.

6. DUTIES OWED TO THE BORROWER IN THE COURSE OF LOAN NEGOTIATION

The three legal categories to which Canadian courts most frequently resort in relation to the lending banker's legal duties to the borrower outside the four corners of the contract are unequal bargaining power, negligent misrepresentation and fiduciary duty. Undue influence, breach of confidence and fraudulent misrepresentation have also been called upon to provide redress more frequently than in the past but the first trilogy is most favoured by the judiciary. Liability while negotiating a loan usually arises in relation to giving financial or investment advice, providing credit references and joining a co-signee to a loan (usually a wife or aged parents), either as a joint borrower or to provide security. A single or similar factual situation will sometimes attract

32. [1982] 2 S.C.R. 161.
33. Sections 499–553.
34. SOR/92–320 (21 May 1992).
35. SOR/92–324 (21 May 1992).
36. R.S.C., 1985, c. I–15.
37. R.S.C., 1985, c. C–46.
38. *Ibid.*, s. 347.

judicial application of one or more of negligent misrepresentation, unequal bargaining power or fiduciary obligation concurrently.

Despite frequent application of these principles by the courts in lender liability litigation, the leading cases, considered from the perspective of significant doctrinal development, are still *Hedley Byrne & Co. Ltd.* v. *Heller and Partners Ltd.*[39] for negligent misrepresentation, *Lloyds Bank Ltd.* v. *Bundy*[40] for unequal bargaining power, and *Standard Investments Ltd.* v. *C.I.B.C.*[41] for fiduciary obligation, although *Standard Investments* itself relies substantially on Sir Eric Sachs' decision in *Bundy*. *National Westminster Bank plc* v. *Morgan*[42] has not been followed by Canadian courts in overruling Lord Denning M.R.'s unequal bargaining power doctrine, and *Standard Investments* has been supplemented by *Lac Minerals*,[43] a company law case, in relation to further elucidation of fiduciary obligation in Canada. As stated earlier, the notable feature of Canadian jurisprudence in recent years is neither novelty nor ingenuity in judicial reasoning but rather the stolid application of legal doctrines to an expanding range of fact situations.

(a) Giving financial or investment advice

At one time Canadian courts took the position that where officers or employees of a bank had given advice in the course of negotiating a loan, the bank could not be liable because banks had no statutory authority pursuant to earlier Bank Acts to engage in investment advice as part of the "business of banking".[44] Such cases were construed within the context of the law of agency and on the implicit assumption that banks would never tread on the territory statutorily set aside for trust companies or investment brokers. However, not only has recent financial institutions legislation[45] generally moved towards the assimilation of the traditional four pillars (banks, trust companies, insurance companies and securities companies) resulting in statutory authority for banks to engage in advice giving,[46] but judicial realism about the role of the lending banker in facilitating investments through bank loans has seriously taken hold of the courts, so that the previous fiction has now been abandoned. It had contrasted unfavourably with the reality of Lord Finlay in *Banbury* v. *Bank of Montreal*[47]

39. [1964] A.C. 465 (H.L.).

40. [1975] Q.B. 326 (C.A.).

41. (1986) 22 D.L.R. (4th) 410 (Ont. C.A.). Application for leave to appeal to the S.C.C. dismissed 3 February 1986 53 O.R. (2d) 663.

42. [1985] A.C. 686 (H.L.).

43. *Supra*, n. 7.

44. *Royal Bank* v. *Mack* [1932] 1 D.L.R. 753 (S.C.C.); *McIntyre* v. *Bank of Montreal* (1957) 10 D.L.R. (2d) 288 (Man. Q.B.); *Mutual Mortgage Corp.* v. *Bank of Montreal* (1965) 55 D.L.R. (2d) 64 (B.C.C.A.); *Young* v. *Bank of Montreal* (1970) 9 D.L.R. (3d) 588 (S.C.C.).

45. In addition to the Bank Act, *supra*, n. 16, the recent package consisted of the Trust and Loans Companies Act, S.C., 1991, c. 45; The Insurance Companies Act, S.C., 1991, c. 47 and the Cooperative Credit Associations Act, S.C., 1991, c. 48.

46. Bank Act, Part VIII generally.

47. [1918] A.C. 626; (1918) 44 D.L.R. 234 (H.L.).

and Salmon J. in *Woods* v. *Martins Bank*.[48] Recently, Canadian banks have been found liable in relation to financial advice during loan negotiation for both fraudulent and negligent misrepresentation and for breach of a fiduciary obligation.

(i) Fraudulent misrepresentation

Fraudulent misrepresentation cases are rare in contract law because the evidentiary standard of proving subjective intention to lie or defraud is difficult to discharge.[49] Such cases are even rarer in banking law and the case of *Sugar* v. *Peat Marwick Ltd.* appears to be the first such case in Canada. There appears to be no English case. However, in an earlier Canadian case, involving a credit union, fraudulent misrepresentation on the part of the near-bank was also found.

Fraser Valley Credit Union v. *Canorama Development Corp.*[50] concerned loans officers who induced three corporations to execute a promissory note and mortgage as security by false representations. The three corporate respondents were engaged in the complementary businesses of acquiring raw land, supplying building materials and residential construction. They sought umbrella financing for several projects and were assured by the commercial loans officer that financing would be forthcoming. After several months, approval had still not been granted but under acute pressure for credit, the officer agreed to a loan on the security of three mortgages granted by the respondents. It was understood that these mortgages would be revised once the major financing was approved. The loan officer continued to reassure the respondents that the financing would be forthcoming, but in the meantime granted additional loans, taking as security four promissory notes. Subsequently, a further mortgage was taken from two of the respondents on the promise of additional financing. The money was not forthcoming, and without telling the respondents, the loan officer used the mortgage to replace three promissory notes.

The credit union then petitioned for foreclosure on all four mortgages and the fourth promissory note. It succeeded in relation to the first three mortgages because the court found that the loan officer's representations were enthusiastic expressions of optimism in which the respondents should have known better than to place any store. However, the court also found that the execution of the fourth promissory note and the final mortgage had been induced by false representations by the loan officer that approval of the original loan application was now assured. The court further found that the final mortgage was unsupported by consideration, and that neither the fourth promissory note nor the mortgage was enforceable.

---

48. *Supra*, n. 22 at 70.
49. (1989) 66 O.R. (2d) 766 (H.C.). See also: M.H. Ogilvie, "How Banks Engage in Fraudulent Misrepresentation: *Sugar* v. *Peat Marwick Ltd.*" (1990) 5 B.F.L. Rev. 88.
50. (1984) 56 B.C.L.R. 145 (S.C.).

It may be asked whether the first three mortgages should have been enforced against the respondents since the credit union appeared to be engaged in a course of conduct to get as much security as it could in exchange for as little financing as possible and as little legal commitment to the respondents.

In *Sugar*, the fraudulent misrepresentation of the bank was more clearly asserted by the Ontario High Court. Although lengthy, the facts were straightforward, and their essentials may be briefly stated. The plaintiffs decided to purchase a company, assisted by a loan from C.I.B.C. However, the bank, to which the company was seriously indebted, knew that the company's accounts receivable were fraudulently overstated but did not inform the plaintiffs of its knowledge. The bank appointed receivers through whom it negotiated the sale of the company to the plaintiffs. The plaintiffs examined some of the company books prior to the closing but they were incomplete; the receivers were also unaware of the problems with the books, although the bank was not. The company failed and the plaintiffs sought to avoid repaying the loan as well as damages for their own additional investment.

Southey J. found that C.I.B.C. was aware of the falsifications, failed to inform both the receiver and the plaintiffs and that the plaintiffs relied on the books, but for which they would not have secured the loan or purchased the company. Not surprisingly, the court further found C.I.B.C. liable for fraudulent misrepresentation and that the plaintiffs' negligence in not making a fuller examination or enquiry was irrelevant in the light of the bank's fraudulent silence.

In so concluding, the court cited no earlier cases, but the constituent elements of fraudulent misrepresentation as stated in the small body of cases in contract and the tort of deceit are present in *Sugar*: wilful and knowing falsity which induced reliance as intended and subsequent damage. Since the bank negotiated through its agent Peats, its absolute silence, which might otherwise have relieved it from liability, since there is no absolute duty of disclosure in contractual negotiations, was, in fact partial, because Peats provided accounts which were only as accurate as far as they went. *Suppressio veri est suggestio falsi.*

The position of the plaintiffs in *Sugar* was not unlike that of the purchasing solicitor in *Redgrave* v. *Hurd*,[51] in which the court found that the failure of the purchaser to take full opportunity to examine books that were too confused to be likely to yield accurate information did not preclude a finding of what was at the time characterised as innocent misrepresentation, since no wilful deceit was proven. It may be, therefore, that *Sugar* indirectly requires a duty of full disclosure of banks who seek to solve an indebtedness problem in respect of one customer by making a fully secured loan to another who wishes to invest in it.

On the other hand, Southey J. declined to find for the plaintiffs on the ground that a fiduciary duty had been breached. No "special relationship" ever existed

51. (1881) 20 Ch. D. 1 (C.A.).

between the bank and the plaintiffs, in his view, because the plaintiffs were sufficiently experienced in business, received independent advice to check the books thoroughly and were not subjected to duress or undue influence. The mere fact of being a customer is not sufficient to create a special relationship. Since reliance and confidence have been found to be the benchmarks of fiduciary obligation by both *Bundy* and *Standard Investments*, and since both were found to be present in the plaintiffs' relationship with the bank for the purposes of fraudulent misrepresentation, it may be wondered why breach of a fiduciary duty was not also found by Southey J. on the same facts. The bank's conflict of interest in relation to both customers, the indebted company and the plaintiffs, which was not disclosed fully, underlines this doubt about the trial judge's finding of no special relationship. Since fraudulent misrepresentation requires an additional finding of wilful deceit, the conclusion is even more doubtful.

(ii) Negligent misrepresentation

Negligent misrepresentation has been the more frequent conclusion of Canadian courts in relation to advice-giving during the course of loan negotiation in the past decade. Since *McBean* v. *Bank of Nova Scotia*[52] in 1981, the courts have found banks to be liable in negligent misrepresentation in relation to various kinds of financial advice given in the course of negotiating a loan.

   McBean is an example of a most common fact situation, where a bank advises a customer to borrow money to invest in a company which is also a customer and which the bank knows to be in financial difficulty. *Sugar* was another case although construed as one of fraudulent misrepresentation by the courts. The companion case to *McBean*, *Hayward* v. *Bank of Nova Scotia*[53] was another, but there, the court found breach of a fiduciary duty.

   Although McBean and Hayward were separate plaintiffs, the facts of their respective cases were virtually identical. In both of these "exotic cow" cases, the plaintiffs were widows with meagre financial resources who were persuaded by the branch manager of a small rural branch of the defendant bank to invest in a business breeding rare European cattle. The manager did not inform either lady that the bank regarded the business to be extremely risky and financially unsound, and was concerned about its large overdraft. Loans were made, secured against real property which was the respective plaintiffs' largest asset; the business failed; the bank sought to seize the security. In *McBean*, Carruthers J. in the Ontario High Court found the bank liable for negligent misrepresentation and was upheld in a brief decision by the Court of Appeal. In *Hayward*, Potts J. of the Ontario High Court found breach of a fiduciary duty

52. (1981) 15 B.L.R. 296 (Ont. H.C.); aff'd 17 A.C.W.S. (2d) 154 (Ont. C.A.).
53. (1984) 7 D.L.R. (4th) 135 (Ont. H.C.); aff'd (1985) 19 D.L.R. (4th) 758 (Ont. C.A.).

but declined to decide whether or not there was any negligent misrepresentation. This decision will be considered below.

Since the manager in *McBean* knew that the company in which he was advising investment was failing, it is difficult to understand why a finding of fraudulent misrepresentation or breach of a fiduciary obligation was not made, although the latter was certainly argued by counsel. Nevertheless, several other recent cases have also found banks liable for negligent advice in relation to their own indebted customers. In *Royal Bank* v. *Aleman*,[54] the bank was found liable to customers who had purchased shares in and given the bank a guarantee in relation to a company which was also a customer and in financial difficulty. In *Dartbord Holdings Ltd.* v. *Royal Bank*,[55] liability was found in relation to a pub which the bank subsequently petitioned into receivership.

A second fact situation in which a bank has been found liable in negligent misrepresentation in relation to investment advice occurred in *Dixon* v. *Bank of Nova Scotia*[56] in which the advice consisted of representations to a potential investor that the bank was providing financial support for the company. The shares subsequently diminished in value and it transpired that the bank had never provided support. The manager who had made the statements was found personally liable to the plaintiffs in fraudulent misrepresentation and the bank was found to be liable to the plaintiffs in negligent misrepresentation for employing the manager. This divided finding by a county court judge may be as unique as it is incomprehensible!

Thirdly, banks have been found liable in negligent misrepresentation where interim financing or credit has been promised but the actual loan never approved. In *V. K. Mason Construction Ltd.* v. *Bank of Nova Scotia*[57] a contractor was advised by his bank prior to submitting a tender that interim financing was available to the owner and that it would be sufficient for the project. The contractor won the tender, which was subject to adequate financing being arranged by the owner. The financing proved to be inadequate and the contractor sued the bank for the sum still owed to it by the owner. The contractor succeeded against the bank in negligent misrepresentation. Again, a bank was found liable in negligent misrepresentation when a company transferred its accounts to the bank on the representation by an employee that substantial credit would be made available to it, in *Billings Mechanical Ltd.* v. *Lloyd's Bank of Canada*.[58]

Fourthly, a bank has been found liable in negligent misrepresentation where it advised a borrower that a car for which the loan was granted was free of liens when it was in fact stolen.[59] Fifthly, a bank was found liable when it advised the

54. [1988] 3 W.W.R. 461 (Alta. Q.B.).
55. (1991) 12 C.B.R. (3d) 88 (B.C.S.C.).
56. (1979) 13 B.C.L.R. 269 (Co. Ct.).
57. (1985) 116 D.L.R. (4th) 598 (S.C.C.). See also: *Streamside Engineering and Development Ltd.* v. *C.I.B.C.* (1990) 266 A.P.R. 220 (Nfld. T.D.).
58. (1987) 82 N.B.R. (2d) 54 (Q.B.).
59. *Zahara* v. *Hood* [1977] 1 W.W.R. 359 (Alta. Dist. Ct.).

seller of a mobile home that the deposit had been received, when in fact it had not, and the buyer to whom it had made a loan subsequently went into bankruptcy.[60]

In only two reported cases, have recent actions against a bank in negligent misrepresentation failed. In *Heller* v. *Royal Bank*,[61] a bank's advice that the customer had sufficient assets to purchase a ranch was found not to be negligent because the customer did not realise the assets sufficiently quickly after the advice had been given. In *Bank of Nova Scotia* v. *Lienaux*[62] the bank was not found liable in relation to a loan to a solicitor to start up a practice insofar as the cash flow financial projections prepared by the bank were based on a hastily prepared and optimistic loan application by the lawyer, who did not rely on the bank's projections in any case, in deciding to open a law office.

Only three of the 10 cases described in which the courts found banks to be negligent in giving advice while negotiating a loan were appealed. This may be an indication that the defendant banks, not normally known for declining to appeal in order to protect their turf, accepted the correctness of the trial judge's findings of fact, that the banks had made statements carelessly on which their customers detrimentally relied so as to suffer loss. In the three cases appealed, the appellate courts sustained the trial judge's findings. In some of the cases, where the bank's actual or constructive knowledge of the true facts could be evidence of wilful intention to deceive, it is somewhat difficult to understand why the courts did not find these to be fraudulent misrepresentation.

Such a finding would have been easier to justify legally since it is most likely that virtually all of the lending contracts contained some type of whole contract clause. Thus, findings of negligent misrepresentation would contradict the written agreement and amount either to enforcing an oral collateral contract or to the implication of higher standards of care into the contract than those for which the contract likely provided.

This *de facto* creation of higher duties in tort than those for which the contracts provided has been frowned upon in two banking cases. In a decision in 1977, the British Columbia Supreme Court clearly stated that the existence of a contractual relationship between a banker and customer precluded an action for negligent misrepresentation.[63] While LaForest J. stated in *CP Hotels*,[64] which concerned the question of implying a common law duty of account verification on the part of a customer, that a higher duty in tort was precluded where there was an express agreement between the parties. However, it may be that the recent Supreme Court decision in *B.C. Hydro and Power Authority* v. *BG*

60. *Teahan's Mobile Home Sales Ltd.* v. *National Bank of Canada* (1993) 333 A.P.R. 264 (N.B.Q.B.).
61. (1990) 76 Alta. L.R. (2d) 280 (C.A.).
62. (1982) 109 A.P.R. 541 (N.S.T.D.).
63. *Guest* v. *Toronto Dominion Bank* (1979) 105 D.L.R. (3d) 347 (B.C.S.C.).
64. *Supra*, n. 12 at pp. 433–444.

Checo International Ltd.[65] in which the court decided that an action in tort may only be brought where the express terms of the contract do not so preclude, may be taken more seriously in future banking cases.

(iii) Fiduciary obligation

The leading case on the nature of the fiduciary obligation owed by a bank to a customer in the context of giving financial or investment advice is still the 1986 decision of the Ontario Court of Appeal, *Standard Investments Ltd.* v. *C.I.B.C.*[66] Although *Standard* may be distinguished from other cases by virtue of the fact that it was concerned with a failure to give advice rather than with giving advice which proved costly for the plaintiff, the distinction between commission and omission has proven irrelevant in the case law since.[67]

The complex facts of *Standard* which transpired over almost a decade, may be stated essentially as follows. C.I.B.C. allowed itself to become caught between two competing long-term customers in relation to a takeover by share purchase of Crown Trust Company. Standard was a company owned by two highly successful businessmen, who sought the advice and assistance of their bank, the C.I.B.C., in relation to their takeover bid and received a loan from the bank to purchase shares in the market. The bank's president assured Standard of the bank's assistance; however, unknown to him, the bank's chairman was aware that a director of the bank and former director but still influential *eminence grise* of Crown Trust was opposed to the takeover, and therefore instructed the bank to purchase in the market 10 per cent of Crown Trust's shares, so as to be in a position to thwart a takeover. Ten per cent is the maximum ownership share statutorily permitted to banks. The bank completed this purchase in 1972, and over the next six years the plaintiffs steadily built up their equity in Crown Trust. In 1978, after the death of the director, his successor on the bank board and also a customer of the bank, Conrad Black, built up a 44 per cent equity holding in the company, partly financed by the bank. Subsequently, Black sold his block and the bank's block to a third party with the result than the 32 per cent block owed by the plaintiff left it in a minority position. The takeover bid had failed. The market price of the shares fell and the plaintiff sued the bank for breach of a fiduciary duty by placing itself in a conflict of interest by favouring one customer over another.

---

65. *B.C. Hydro and Power Authority* v. *BG Checo International Ltd.* (1992) 99 D.L.R. (4th) 577 (S.C.C.).

66. *Supra*, n. 41.

67. See generally in relation to *Standard Investments*: M.H. Ogilvie, "Banks, Advice-giving and Fiduciary Obligation" (1985) 7 Ottawa L. Rev. 263; Donovan Waters, "Banks, Fiduciary Obligations and Unconscionable Transactions" (1986) 65 Can. Bar Rev. 65; Bradley Crawford, "Bankers' Fiduciary Duties and Negligence" (1986) 12 Can. Bus. L.J. 145; R.P. Austin, "The Corporate Fiduciary" (1986) 12 Can. Bus. L.J. 96; Jacob S. Ziegel, "Bankers' Fiduciary Obligations and Chinese Walls: A Further Comment on *Standard* v. *C.I.B.C.*" (1986) 12 Can. Bus. L.J. 211; John D. Marshall, "The Relationship between Bank and Customer: Fiduciary Duties and Confidentiality" (1986) 1 B.F.L. Rev. 33.

The trial judge found that there was a fiduciary relationship between the bank and the plaintiffs until 1972 when the plaintiffs first learned of the real role of the bank in relation to their takeover. However, there was no breach of the fiduciary duty thereafter because the plaintiffs were not discouraged in their plans by this knowledge. The Ontario Court of Appeal decided that the bank had been a fiduciary throughout and until the sale of its equity holding in 1979. It was always in a conflict of interest position and it took no positive steps to inform the plaintiffs. Speaking for a unanimous court, Goodman J.A. stated that while the bank need not disclose the precise nature of its conflict, it ought to have disclosed that it had a conflict and that it was unwilling to advise or assist the plaintiffs further in the matter. The bank could not rely on a defence of confidentiality in relation to its other customer. Rather, it had to choose to assist one or other customer and suffer whatever loss of business might result. Substantial damages were awarded against the bank and the Supreme Court refused leave to appeal.

In reaching its decision, the Court of Appeal relied upon the definition of a fiduciary relationship stated by Sir Eric Sachs in *Bundy*. A "confidential relationship" arose when the plaintiffs sought the advice and assistance of the bank. Once established, the bank had a duty to disclose conflicts of interest and to advise with reasonable skill and care. The bank had to choose between its customers for the purposes of this particular transaction, and failure to disclose its conflict was a breach of its fiduciary duty.[68]

It is doubtful that Sir Eric Sachs meant that a fiduciary relationship arose every time a customer approaches a bank in relation to a potential investment. Moreover, while *Standard Investments* remains the most comprehensive statement by a Canadian court of a bank's fiduciary duties to a customer, it may be contrasted with the slightly earlier decision of a differently constituted bench of the Ontario Court of Appeal in *Hayward*, the second of the two exotic cow cases to which reference was made earlier.

In *Hayward*, the trial judge found that the unequal bargaining power between the bank manager and the customer in relation to their respective knowledge of the exotic cow breeding business, placed the bank under a duty to advise independent advice and a duty to advise with reasonable care, failing which, the bank was in breach of a fiduciary duty. The Court of Appeal agreed, but it expressly disapproved reliance on unequal bargaining power to establish the fiduciary relationship, expressing instead a preference for the two-fold test of a dominating influence and a manifestly disadvantageous bargain enumerated in *Morgan*. There is some evidence in the subsequent case law that the courts favour the stricter approach of *Hayward*, which paradoxically, concerned a small loan to an inexperienced borrower in contrast to the large sophisticated customers with which *Standard Investments* was concerned. However, the courts do not expressly find either *Morgan* requirement, preferring instead to

---

68. The court did not refer to *Natwest* v. *Morgan, supra*, n. 42 which had already been reported by the time of the appeal.

run through the facts, drop the appropriate case names and find breach or no breach of a fiduciary duty. Legal readers searching for novel doctrinal development or even explicit doctrinal application are sorely disappointed in such cases.

Lending in which other family members are legally implicated might be thought to be the most likely context within which courts would prefer *Standard Investments* to *Hayward*. In *Bertolo* v. *Bank of Montreal*,[69] a widow of meagre means borrowed a sum of money from the bank to permit her son to purchase a Chinese restaurant for conversion into an Italian restaurant. Another bank had already rejected the son's own application for a loan. Mrs Bertolo was in her seventies, poorly educated, spoke only Italian and took no part in negotiating the loan. At the bank's insistence, she visited a lawyer with her son for independent advice. The lawyer was acting for both the bank and her son, and both the lawyer and the bank assured her there would be no problems. She executed a mortgage on her sole asset, her house, and a promissory note. The business failed within a year, and the bank sought to enforce the security. The Court of Appeal found the lawyer to be in conflict of interest and the bank to be in breach of a duty to obtain legal advice for Mrs Bertolo. The court further found that it was unconscionable to permit the bank to take advantage of the security and stated that it was invoking "equitable intervention" to set it aside.

The court also found that a fiduciary relationship was not created for four reasons:

    (i) no advice was ever given by the bank to the plaintiff on matters germane to the transaction;
    (ii) there was no duty on the bank to provide financial information about the transaction;
    (iii) there was no evidence of trust and confidence such as that required by *Standard Investments*;
    (iv) there was no evidence that the bank manager had exercised a dominating influence over Mrs Bertolo.

Bertolo is an example of an earlier observation about the doctrinally imprecise way in which Canadian courts tend to throw about loosely words like "unconscionable", "inequitable" and "fiduciary". Ironically, on the facts, it is difficult not to find a fiduciary relationship satisfying the two-fold test in *Morgan*: the bank and the lawyer must surely have been a dominating force and a transaction in which the loan was secured by Mrs Bertolo's only asset for a venture likely to fail is surely manifestly disadvantageous to a person in Mrs Bertolo's position. Certainly, the liberal definition of fiduciary obligation in *Standard Investment* is more than satisfied.

Judicial reluctance to impose a fiduciary obligation on banks in relation to commercial loans to commercially experienced customers is demonstrated in a

---

69. (1986) 57 O.R. (2d) 577 (C.A.). See also: M.H. Ogilvie, "To Be or Not To Be (A Fiduciary)" (1987) 2 B.F.L. Rev. 256.

handful of cases since 1986, in a variety of fact situations in which financial or other investment advice was either given or ought to have been given. A bank which loaned money to a borrower, who had extensive knowledge and experience of joint ventures of the kind for which the money was borrowed, was found not to be in a fiduciary relationship when the trustees of the joint venture absconded with the money, since the bank had no dominating influence over the borrower and was not subject to a duty to investigate the joint venture, given the borrower's experience. The bank had discharged its duty once it conveyed any information it may have had.[70]

Where a borrower is a sophisticated businessman who borrows money secured by mortgages and a guarantee to invest in a mortgage investment company on the advice of his solicitor, the bank owes no duty to suggest independent legal advice and may enforce the loan.[71] Where a bank lends money to a customer for the purpose of purchasing a truck, taking back a chattel mortgage, no fiduciary relationship is created whereby the bank is encumbered with a duty to either search the title or advise the borrower to do so.[72]

Nor is one branch of a bank deemed to know the business of another,[73] so that, where a farm equipment distributor who was a customer at one branch was misinformed of the financial difficulties of a dealer who was a customer at another branch, no fiduciary obligation arose between the distributor and its branch in relation to failure to disclose the dealer's difficulties.[74]

The reluctance of Canadian courts to exploit the liberal scope of *Standard Investments* so as to incline towards finding most banker and customer relationships to be fiduciary in nature in relation to advice-giving is mirrored in the Supreme Court of Canada's decision in *Lac Minerals*,[75] in which the court explained the doctrinal content of fiduciary obligation in a company law case. The plaintiff, Corona, owned mining rights on land in northern Ontario on which it was drilling exploratory holes. The defendant, Lac, suggested a possible partnership or joint venture, and during subsequent negotiations, Corona revealed the results of its drilling. No joint venture materialised, but on the basis of the information revealed, Lac realised that an adjacent property was likely to be as rich in gold-bearing ore. Both Lac and Corona bid for this property and Lac's bid was successful. Lac developed the site on its own account, spending $204m building a mine and a mill. The trial judge found that an industry practice imposed an obligation on seriously negotiating parties not to act to the detriment of each other. He further found that the information was confidential and revealed only for the purpose of the joint venture. Corona succeeded at trial

70. *Continental Bank of Canada* v. *Hunter* (1986) 49 Alta. L.R. (2d) 358 (Q.B.).
71. *Weitzman* v. *Hendon* (1989) 69 O.R. (2d) 678 (C.A.). See also: *Wildfang* v. *Royal Bank* (1989) 78 Sask. R. 250 (Q.B.).
72. *Thibert* v. *Royal Bank* (1990) 103 A.R. 279 (Master).
73. *Royal Bank* v. *Hein Real Estate Corp.* [1977] 3 W.W.R. 298 (Alta. C.A.).
74. *C.I.B.C.* v. *Otto Timm Enterprises Ltd.* (1991) 79 D.L.R. (4th) 67 (Ont. Gen. Div.).
75. *Supra*, n. 7.

and in the Ontario Court of Appeal on the grounds of breach of confidentiality and breach of a fiduciary duty. The Supreme Court unanimously found a breach of confidentiality, but on the issue of fiduciary duty three judges found no fiduciary relationship between the parties, while two found that a fiduciary obligation not to misuse the information had been breached.

Speaking for the majority,[76] Sopinka J. indicated increasing alarm over the burden fiduciary obligation was being required to bear in relation to business disputes. He opined that "equity's" blunt tool must be reserved for situations that are truly in need of the special protection that equity offers."[77] Both Sopinka J. and one of the minority judges, LaForest J., thought that three characteristics of a relationship were required to find a fiduciary relationship:

  (i) the fiduciary has scope for the exercise of some discretion or power;
  (ii) the fiduciary can unilaterally exercise that power or discretion for its beneficiary; and
  (iii) the beneficiary is peculiarly vulnerable to or at the mercy of the fiduciary.[78]

Sopinka J. thought vulnerability to be indispensable to the existence of a fiduciary relationship but that it was not present in *Lac* since Corona had voluntarily placed itself in a vulnerable position by its gratuitous revelation of information to Lac. Wilson J., the other minority judge, took exactly the opposite position: Corona's disclosure to Lac created the necessary degree of vulnerability at the time of the disclosure. LaForest J. denied that vulnerability is a *sine qua non* of a fiduciary relationship and further asserted that Lac's acquisition of the adjacent property permitted it to harm Corona on the basis of Corona's own disclosures and that a remedy should not be denied because Corona might have protected itself by contract. Both Wilson J. and LaForest J. sought to establish a fiduciary relationship because they regarded it as necessary for the creation of a duty of confidentiality, while the majority thought a duty of confidentiality to be a separate cause of action, eliminating the need to establish a fiduciary relationship.

Once a duty not to disclose confidential information in commercial dealings is hived off, fiduciary obligation is left to perform its traditional function of protecting the truly vulnerable. But how it does so and where it sought to arise is meaning "at the mercy of", fiduciary obligations are unlikely to be found by the courts to be as widespread as the test in *Standard Investments* originally suggested. Although *Standard Investments* remains the leading Canadian banking case on the issue, it is being ignored or got around by lower or less persuasive courts in the spirit of *Lac Minerals* instead.[79]

76. McIntyre and Lamer JJ.
77. *Supra*, n. 7 at p. 61.
78. *Frame* v. *Smith* (1987) 42 D.L.R. (4th) 81 (S.C.C.) per Wilson J. at pp. 98–99.
79. I am aware of only one unreported case since, in which a fiduciary obligation between banker and customer has been found in relation to advice; see: M.H. Ogilvie, "Moral Obligation and the Lending Banker as Fiduciary: *Roy Pape* v. *Royal Bank*" (1991) 7 B.F.L. Rev. 141.

(iv) Unequal bargaining power

The reluctance of Canadian courts explicitly to find fiduciary relationships between banker and customer in relation to advice during loan negotiation may be explained in the light of judicial utilisation of other legal doctrines to achieve the same final goal of redress for the borrower. Negligent misrepresentation is one. Unequal bargaining power is the other.

It is somewhat artificial to separate cases based on unequal bargaining power from cases in which fiduciary obligation, undue influence and unconscionability are not also argued by counsel and relied upon to a greater or lesser extent by the courts in reaching a decision. It is also largely artificial to separate unequal bargaining power cases about advice-giving only from cases about taking security either from the borrower or from a guarantor. Virtually all of the cases in the various fact situations show the same doctrinal approach, confused or not, in relation to giving advice prior to taking security, to either the main borrower, a "co-signee" or a guarantor. Thus, it is simpler to deal with these issues concurrently through the relevant cases.

Despite *Morgan* and its judicial approval in *Hayward*, Canadian courts continue to rest decisions on findings of disparity of bargaining power *per se*, or more typically, in conjunction with undue influence and/or unconscionability as sufficient grounds for relieving borrowers, co-signees and guarantors from obligations to the lending bank. That most of the cases concern wives or aged parents brought in to pledge their sole assets, often their houses, to the bank as security for loans to failing businesses, suggests that courts have primarily responded emotionally and not challenged themselves to examine the facts or to rethink the applicable law dispassionately. That the same judicial approach is found in cases before *Morgan, Standard* and *Hayward* as well as after underlines this possibility. In these cases, the failure by a bank to advise that independent advice be sought is regarded as raising the presumption of unequal bargaining power exercised against the customer.

If there is a discernible bias in the unequal bargaining power cases, it favours such findings in relation to spouses but not non-family members. Thus, a wife who signed a promissory note for a loan to cover her husband's business overdrafts without being so advised by the bank or advised to seek independent advice was relieved from liability on the ground of unequal bargaining power.[80] Again, where a wife knowingly signed a guarantee in relation to loans to her husband's corporation for his personal use, the failure of the bank to inform her that subsequent loans had also been made was found to be a breach of its duty to inform her and to advise her to seek independent advice.[81]

---

80. *Bank of Montreal* v. *Hancock* (1982) 137 D.L.R. (3d) 648 (Ont. H.C.). In *MacKenzie* v. *Bank of Montreal* (1975) 7 O.R. (2d) 521 (H.C.); aff'd (1976) 12 O.R. (2d) 719 (C.A.), a woman in a common law relationship was also relieved from a guarantee on the same basis.

81. *C.I.B.C.* v. *Hardy* (1985) 34 Man. R. (2d) 310 (Q.B.) See also: *Bank of Nova Scotia* v. *Organ Fisheries* (1984) 150 A.P.R. 322 (Nfld. Dist. Ct.).

On the other hand, the presence of knowledge or experience on the part of wives may result in an opposite finding. Where three men purchased the assets of an insolvent company and both they and their respective wives were required to give guarantees to the bank as security for the loan two of the wives were found to be liable to the bank although the other wife was not. An argument that no independent advice had been recommended failed in the absence of proof of *non est factum*, unconscionability, fraud, misrepresentation or undue influence.[82] Nor will a bank be liable where a daughter and son-in-law sign a guarantee under the influence of the daughter's father's representations as to its purpose, although the bank failed to advise independent advice.[83]

Where the guarantor is another businessman,[84] an employee guaranteeing a loan to an employer,[85] or directors and shareholders,[86] the courts have assumed in the absence of evidence to the contrary that the guarantors are capable of protecting themselves and that there is no duty to suggest independent advice, breach of which causes unequal bargaining power.

Canadian cases where a bank takes security without making full disclosure or ensuring that independent advice is procured so as to create bargaining power disparity have also been found to be instances of unconscionability,[87] and of undue influence.[88] In the cases here categorised under the rubric "unequal bargaining power", the courts typically recite the facts as found, then characterise the relationship as lacking bargaining equality, and the resulting loan or security transaction as void for unconscionability, undue influence, breach of a fiduciary duty, and so on. Doctrinal analysis is largely lacking from the reported decisions, thus it is difficult to do more then draw several broad conclusions about the current state of bank lender liability in relation to advice during negotiation of both loan and security.

First, Canadian courts have resorted to the entire panoply of contemporary fashionable doctrines in order to determine lender liability during negotiation. Secondly, while some courts show appreciation for the doctrinal distinctions among these, many do not, thereby suggesting that, thirdly, they are increasingly focused on the underlying "morality" of the relationship and regard any one or more of these theories as appropriate to "doing justice". Fourthly, their greater willingness to afford relief for family members may suggest some paternalism in approach, but this is unclear. Fifthly, whether this apparent disintegration in

---

82. *Bank of Montreal* v. *Featherstone* (1989) 68 O.R. (2d) 541 (C.A.).

83. *Beaulieu* v. *National Bank of Canada* (1984) 144 A.P.R. 154 (N.B.C.A.). For family law cases involving parents, see: *Buchanan* v. *C.I.B.C.* (1980) 125 D.L.R. (3d) 394 (B.C.C.A.); *Bank of Nova Scotia* v. *MacLellan* (1980) 70 A.P.R. 596 (N.B.C.A.); *Bomek* v. *Bomek* (1983) 21 B.L.R. 205 (Man. C.A.); leave to appeal to S.C.C. refused (1983) 27 Man. R. (2d) 239n.

84. *Bank of Nova Scotia* v. *Forest F. Ross & Son Ltd.* (1982) 105 A.P.R. 563 (N.B.Q.B.).

85. *Bank of Montreal* v. *Winter* (1981) 101 A.P.R. 305 (Nfld. T.D.).

86. *Royal Bank* v. *Starko* (1993) 9 Alta. L.R. (3d) 339 (Alta. Q.B.).

87. *MacKenzie, supra,* n. 80; *Royal Bank* v. *Hinds* (1978) 20 O.R. (2d) 613 (H.C.); *Buchanan, supra,* n. 83; *MacLellan, supra,* n. 83; *Bomek, supra,* n. 83.

88. *Featherstone, supra,* n. 82, although no actual undue influence found on the facts.

judicial reasoning indicates intellectual sloppiness or poverty or a deliberate disdain for doctrine is also uncertain. From the perspective of lending institutions, however, the uncertainty introduced into the negotiation process is disconcerting.

(b) Taking security

The discussion in section 6 (a) (iv), *supra*, dealt with the current law.

(c) Giving credit references

Although not a potential source of liability in relation to its own loans, giving inaccurate credit references is a potential source of liability in relation to third parties, in the view of several recent Canadian courts, in which the issue has been parsed as one either of fiduciary obligation or negligent misrepresentation. Of course, the leading case, if in *obiter dicta*, is *Hedley Byrne* v. *Heller*[89] Considered overall, the cases to date demonstrate that in appropriate fact situations, the courts will find banks to be liable in negligent misrepresentation for inaccurate credit advice; however, arguments based on breach of a fiduciary obligation have failed. This reluctance may stem from the same reluctance to find fiduciary obligation in relation to negotiating loans with customers, that is, judicial disinclination to import fiduciary obligations into bank dealings with business persons despite the authorisation to do so in *Standard Investments*. An apparent double standard in commercial as opposed to consumer or domestic loans may underline curial reluctance in this regard.

In the earliest case, *Kuruyo Trading Ltd*. v. *Acme Garment Co. (1975) Ltd.*,[90] the plaintiff sought credit information from its bank, which was also the bank of a customer with an unpaid account against which it wished to start an action. The bank told the plaintiff that the customer was good for the amount outstanding on a standard reply form which limited the bank's liability for incorrect information. However, the bank did not inform the plaintiff of its registered personal property security pursuant to the Bank Act secured against the customer's assets, and when the plaintiff got a judgment against the customer, the bank claimed the funds. In an action for a declaration that the bank was estopped from claiming the moneys, the plaintiff argued that the bank was in breach of a fiduciary duty in not disclosing the existence of the security. The Manitoba Court of Appeal found that no fiduciary relationship had arisen in relation to giving credit information, but if it had, the bank had not breached it because the plaintiff ought to have known that the bank would likely hold security over the customer's assets. No doctrinal justification was offered in the court's support for this dishonest conduct by the bank.

The unwillingness of some Canadian courts to create a fiduciary obligation in

89. *Supra*, n. 39.
90. (1988) 51 D.L.R. (4th) 334 (Man. C.A.).

relation to credit advice is demonstrated in two other recent cases. In one case,[91] where a bank had provided a loan to a manufacturer, secured by a debenture and floating charge over all the manufacturer's assets, the plaintiff was advised by the bank that the manufacturer had some cash flow difficulties. The bank did not inform the plaintiff of the manufacturer's large operating losses prior to approval of the loan and the plaintiff granted a loan. Shortly thereafter, the bank appointed a receiver under the debenture. The court found, on the facts, that the bank's failure to advise of previous loans did not affect the plaintiff's decision to grant the credit, and that in any case, the plaintiff had been told enough to put it on guard. In the other case,[92] the defendants asked the plaintiff bank for credit advice prior to buying shares in a company and executing a guarantee in respect of the company's indebtedness to the bank. The manager replied that the company was viable and that it consistently met its obligations to the bank, when in fact it had received extended financing recently. The bank placed the company in receivership and sued on the guarantee. The court found that no fiduciary relationship had come into existence and that while a duty of care existed, the bank had discharged this duty adequately.

These cases suggest that the duty of full disclosure expected in a fiduciary relationship is not required of banks giving credit references, rather a considerably lower duty, even than that for negligent misrepresentation, which is discharged by giving some information, is sufficient. *Suppressio veri est suggestio falsi?*

Canadian judicial response has not been entirely uniform, however. In two cases to date, courts have found banks liable for inadequate credit advice. In one case, *Les Fenêtres St-Jean Inc.* v. *B.C.N.*,[93] the Quebec Civil Code was relied upon to find a bank guilty of gross negligence within article 1056c. In *Fenêtres*, the bank knew at the time of its report that the company in relation to which the credit reference was given was in a poor financial situation, nevertheless there were some grounds for hope of a recovery. The Quebec Court of Appeal upheld an appeal against the bank because its report suggested that the company was in excellent financial health and the non-responsibility clause was inapplicable where there was gross negligence. The court appears to have regarded the bank's failure to disclose the full details of the company's position as little short of dishonest.

That *Fenêtres* may not be a case dependent in its result on the Quebec Civil Code is suggested by the most recent reported case, *Vita Health Co.* v. *Toronto-Dominion Bank*.[94] There, a plaintiff supplier, a long-time customer of the bank who used the bank to do credit checks on persons to whom it supplied products, continued to supply products on credit to a customer on the strength of regular credit reports from the bank which omitted to report that the

91. *Excellon Ltd.* v. *Dunwoody Ltd.* (1985) 33 Man. R. (2d) 117 (Q.B.).
92. *Royal Bank* v. *Aleman* [1988] 3 W.W.R. 461 (Alta. Q.B.).
93. (1990) 69 D.L.R. (4th) 384 (Que. C.A.).
94. [1993] 7 W.W.R. 242 (Man. Q.B.).

customer had exceeded its overdraft, frequently had to stop payment on cheques and was generally in poor financial condition. On the bankruptcy of the customer, the supplier sued the bank for negligent misrepresentation. The court found that the bank had misrepresented the true state of the customer's affairs and awarded damages to the supplier. Although not directly about an advance of credit or receipt of a credit reference, another recent case, *Streamside* v. *C.I.B.C.*[95] adopted a similar approach where a contractor relied upon advice from a bank that financing was in place to the project owner for the project and proceeded to work on that assumption. The financing was not in place and the bank was liable for the unpaid amounts as well as the additional amounts incurred in mitigation for a negligent misrepresentation.

Misrepresentation, whether negligent or even fraudulent, may be becoming the preferred way to construe such cases in preference to fiduciary obligation which requires full disclosure of the bank's position. Where the line between them is to be drawn with respect to the degree of disclosure required in giving credit references may be difficult to state, even impossible. Such criteria as disclosure or not of prior bank securities, previous financial difficulties, or banker's fears and/or hopes in relation to the customer, fade into insignificance when the net result is insufficient disclosure to permit the plaintiff to make a considered and informed business judgement in relation to extending credit. In *Fenêtres, Vita* and *Streamside*, the courts effectively required a full disclosure by the banks, sufficient to satisfy a finding of breach of fiduciary obligation. Should this trend continue, negligent misrepresentation will essentially be doing the job fiduciary obligation is designed to do.

7. COMMITMENT LETTERS

Lender liability may accrue at the next stage of a loan, after its initial negotiation, when a commitment letter is drawn up by the lender to set out the essential "business deal" between lender and borrower.[96] A commitment letter records the offer to provide a loan and the fundamental terms of the agreement and is the paper basis on which the loan agreement will be drafted. On the assumption that the offer is accepted, the commitment letter may be regarded as a binding contract, if it satisfies the normal legal requirements for a binding contract.

Thus, several Canadian cases have found commitment letters to be binding provided certain essential terms are present, including the parties, the principal amount, interest rate and property to be given as security.[97] Courts will imply

95. *Supra*, n. 57.

96. See generally: Trevor W. Bell, "Commitment Letters and Loan Agreements" (1987) 2 B.F.L. Rev. 1 and Ian C. MacLeod, "Commitment Letters, Their Use and Some Specific Considerations" (1992) 7 B.F.L. Rev. 63.

97. *First City Investments Ltd.* v. *Fraser Arms Hotel Ltd.* [1979] 6 W.W.R. 125 (B.C.C.A.); *Dot Developments Ltd.* v. *Fowler* (1980) 118 D.L.R. (3d) 371 (B.C.S.C.); *Accord Holdings Ltd.* v.

terms to give contractual substance on the same principles as for other contracts,[98] and will require that conditions precedent required prior to the making of advances be performed or satisfied before concluding that the letter is a binding agreement.[99] Canadian courts are divided on whether or not references in commitment letters to additional terms and covenants in other security agreements are sufficient to incorporate these into the loan contract based on the commitment letter.[100]

Most standard form commitment letters contain a clause whereby the lender reserves the absolute right to decide whether or not to advance the loan. The presence of such a clause has resulted in a finding that the commitment letter was an offer unsupported by consideration so that the lender was not obliged to make an advance.[101] And in respect to mortgages on the security of realty, several courts have found that where such a clause is present, a failure to make an advance on the basis of a commitment letter is not a breach of contract since no contract came into existence in the first place.[102]

Where no advance is made in breach of a commitment letter, damages have been held to be an adequate remedy.[103] The measure will be the cost of the replacement loan to the borrower which may well be higher than the cost of the original promised loan. In addition, the fee normally stipulated for to cover expenditures in preparing the commitment letter will also be forfeited when the advances are not made. Otherwise, when the borrower does not accept a loan, the commitment fee is still nevertheless payable except where it is found to be a penalty clause[104] or where it raises the total cost above the 60 per cent ceiling on the cost of borrowing in the Criminal Code.[105]

8. DUTIES OWED DURING THE LIFE OF THE LOAN

The increasing willingness of Canadian courts to consider and occasionally find banks liable in misrepresentation, fiduciary obligation and implied contract in relation to loan negotiation is mirrored in relation to lender–borrower–third

---

Exclusive Life Insurance Co. (1982) 44 A.R. 368 (Alta. Q.B.); revs'd. in part (1985) 62 A.R. 234 (Alta. C.A.).

98. *Marquest Industries Ltd.* v. *Willows Poultry Farm Ltd.* (1968) 66 W.W.R. 477 (B.C.C.A.).

99. *Equitable Life Assurance Society of the United States* v. *British Pacific Building Ltd.* (1980) 33 B.C.L.R. 68 (B.C.S.C.).

100. Compare *First City, supra,* n. 97 and *Accord Holdings, supra,* n. 97.

101. *Equitable Life, supra,* n. 99.

102. *Frankel Structural Steel Ltd.* v. *Golden Holdings Ltd.* [1969] 2 O.R. 221 (C.A.); *First National Mortgage Co. Ltd.* v. *Grouse Nest Resorts Ltd.* (1977) 2 B.C.L.R. 300 (B.C.C.A.); *Adriatic Development Ltd.* v. *Canada Trustco Mortgage Co.* (1983) 2 D.L.R. (4th) 183 (B.C.C.A.).

103. *Grouse Nest Resorts, supra,* n. 102; *F.B.D.B.* v. *F.B. Holdings Ltd.* [1979] 2 W.W.R. 455 (Sask. Dist. Ct.); *Frankel Structural Steel, supra,* n. 102.

104. *Cumberland Realty Group Ltd.* v. *B.L.T. Holdings Ltd.* (1984) 32 R.P.R. 9 (Alta. Q.B.).

105. *Nelson, Nelson and Nationwide Auto Leasing Ltd.* v. *C.T.C. Mortgage Corporation* (1984) 59 B.C.L.R. 221 (B.C.C.A.); *William E. Thompson Associates Inc.* v. *Carpenter Developments Inc.* (1989) 69 O.R. (2d) 545 (Ont. C.A.); *B.C. Corp. Financial Inc.* v. *Baseline Resorts Developments* (1990) 46 B.C.L.R. (2d) 89 (B.C.S.C.).

party dealings during the life of the loan and beyond, after the decision to seize is made. This section will focus on the cases dealing with lender liability during the life of the loan and the next section will focus on the cases dealing with lender liability once the decision to enforce the loan is made. Not surprisingly, the lending banker has been found in the past decade or so liable in fraud, fiduciary obligation and for breach of a duty of reasonable care in private obligation as measured by a judicial perception of an industry standard.

Claiborne Industries Ltd. v. *National Bank of Canada*[106] is a somewhat unusual case in which the sixth largest Canadian chartered bank based primarily in Quebec, was found liable for conspiracy, fraud and breach of trust, and where punitive damages were awarded by the Ontario Court of Appeal. The facts were quite complex, involving a large number of transactions in and out of a multiplicity of bank accounts, but may be simplified as follows. An entrepreneur, Black,[107] was both chairman of Claiborne, a prosperous public company, and the controlling owner of a group of private companies, referred to as the "Black Connection". Black opened various accounts for his companies and for Claiborne and the Unity Bank, a small bank, subsequently bought by National. At that time these accounts constituted most of the business of the Unity Bank, and Black developed a close relationship with the senior officers, particularly the assistant general manager who was also a personal friend. Essentially, a series of transactions occurred whereby money, including bank loans to Claiborne, were siphoned from Claiborne to the heavily overdrawn accounts of the Black Connection. The bank condoned these because it wished to reduce the overdrafts and keep the money within its own bank. About one-half of the *c.* $3m siphoned, ended in Black's personal bank account. In addition, the bank engaged in a series of doubtful transactions in relation to shares given up as security for the overdraft, such as releasing these without taking any equivalent security. The subsequent owner of Claiborne sued Black, his corporations and the bank for conspiracy and breach of trust.

The trial judge found the bank liable for breach of trust in failing to enquire about or stop these transactions and would have found the bank liable for conspiracy but for the view that the conspiratorial acts caused no financial injury to the plaintiff. The Court of Appeal found the bank to be liable as well in the tort of conspiracy because the plaintiff company did suffer financial injury in that it had suffered a reduction in working capital, fewer opportunities and only partial repayment of the interest charges. The Court of Appeal did not have to consider the breach of trust issue, however McKinlay J.A. stated in *obiter dicta* that while the debtor–creditor relationship of banker and customer had recently been overlaid by obligations in tort, contract and trust, whether or not such findings should be made depended on the "specific facts of individual cases."[108]

---

106. (1989) 59 D.L.R. (4th) 533 (Ont. C.A.).
107. *Not* Conrad Black!
108. *Supra*, n. 106 at 538.

The learned judge further opined that she knew of no case where such an onerous duty was imposed on banks as to monitor all the Claiborne transactions, only cases where banks were found to fail in monitoring a single transaction. One has to assume the learned judge did not mean to condone large-scale fraud while condemning a single oversight!

Claiborne established that banks may be liable to third parties who suffer loss when they condone the fraudulent use of loans and overdrafts made to customers. Despite McKinlay J.A.'s odd remarks, it also suggests that banks owe a legal duty to monitor closely the use of a loan, or at least to make enquiry into any suspicious circumstances of which it becomes aware, especially those in its own ledgers.

A second area in which the lending banker has recently been said to have potential liability for the first time in Canada is in relation to confidentiality during the life of a loan (as opposed to during negotiation.)[109] In a recent lower court case,[110] a bank extended credit to a debtor corporation based on its receivables and guaranteed by the debtor related corporation which had the same directors as the debtor. The borrower failed to collect significant receivables and caused the related corporation to grant a debenture to the debtor's largest creditor and transfer related corporation property to the borrower so as to render the guarantee worthless, all without the bank's knowledge. The creditor suggested that it purchase property from the borrower, but the creditor was also a customer of the same bank and the bank counselled it not to proceed. The bank put the borrower into receivership and the borrower sued the bank for, *inter alia*, breach of confidentiality. The trial judge held that by counselling the borrower's largest creditor, the bank was in breach of confidentiality, but that in view of the actions of the borrower and its related company, the bank acted properly to protect its interests. It remains for a future court to carry out the threat contained in this case.

The remaining cases in relation to duties owed during the life of a loan are, despite their varied facts, essentially about the "contort" standard of care required in carrying out the ongoing duties pursuant to a loan agreement. Except for a typical reluctance to articulate the doctrinal basis on which decisions are arrived at, the cases appear to be determined in accordance with the courts' perception of the industry standards and to be a copse of single factual instances.

Thus, where a loan agreement required that a bank pay the fire insurance premium on a property and the bank failed to do so, and where the building was subsequently burnt, the bank was liable in damages for failure to perform a contractual undertaking, although on the facts only nominal damages were awarded because the borrower had not arranged a renewal policy.[111] Again,

---

109. See: *Guertin, supra*, n. 24.

110. *Polar Heating Ltd.* v. *Banque nationale de Paris (Canada) Ltd.* (1991) 114 A.R. 229 (Alta. Q.B.).

111. *Caines* v. *Bank of Nova Scotia* (1978) 39 A.P.R. 631 (N.B.C.A.).

where a bank promised a third party supplier of a customer, whose financial situation it was closely monitoring, that it would honour cheques made payable to the third party supplier, and when it failed to do so, the Newfoundland Court of Appeal found both negligent misrepresentation and breach of a constructive trust in relation to the third party.[112]

On the other hand, when a line of credit was arranged at a floating interest rate and an action brought to recover an alleged overpayment of interest, a court found on the facts that the bank had informed the customer, as it was bound to do, of the changing rates as they occurred.[113]

Finally, recent courts have also considered whether or not a bank may decline further extensions of credit where the loan agreement places no such express obligation on it and where it is particularly concerned about the borrower's solvency. Again, the courts have found that banks may decline to increase a customer's indebtedness provided the decision is made with reasonable skill and care in the circumstances.[114]

9. DUTIES OWED IN THE ENFORCEMENT OF A LOAN

At one time, the lending banker had virtually complete discretion to decide when a lending agreement was to be terminated and the loan called and receiver sent in, without warning so as to protect the bank's security from further dissipation. After the landmark case, *Ronald Elwyn Lister Ltd.* v. *Dunlop Canada Ltd.*,[115] in 1982 in which the Supreme Court of Canada found that the debtor must be given a reasonable period of time within which to meet a demand for repayment of the loan, whether or not the loan is expressed as payable on demand, the decision to seize has become fraught with uncertainty as to whether or not a court *ex post facto* will agree with the lending banker's decision. In the past decade or so a series of cases have revisited the *Lister* decision, with the result that the notice issue at the time when seizure is made is one of the two major areas of difficulty for the lending banker.

The other issue is the right of set-off and constructive trust in favour of a third party. At one time banks were virtually free to call a loan, appropriate and set-off any assets of the borrower to discharge that loan. However, the growth of conflicting claimants with the bank to the borrower's assets has resulted in constructive trusts frequently being imposed on banks in respect of those assets in favour of some third party other than the bank. The potential for conflict, and the attack on the traditional common law right of set-off, is largely the result of the creation by both Parliament and the provincial legislatures of prior

112. *Taran Furs* v. *C.I.B.C.* (1986) 181 A.P.R. 132 (Nfld. C.A.).
113. *Palachek* v. *C.I.B.C.* (1991) 79 Alta. L.R. (2d) 159 (C.A.).
114. *CIP Inc.* v. *Toronto-Dominion Bank* (1988) 55 D.L.R. (4th) 308 (B.C.C.A.); *Barclay Construction Corp.* v. *Bank of Montreal* (1989) 65 D.L.R. (4th) 213 (B.C.C.A.); *Bank of Montreal* v. *Bond* (1988) 24 B.C.L.R. (2d) 80 (C.A.).
115. [1982] 1 S.C.R. 726. See also: M.H. Ogilvie, "Comment" (1982) 60 Can. Bar Rev. 733.

statutorily based claims. As the cases to be discussed show, the net effect has often been to leave a bank empty-handed after it has done the work of collecting the assets.

(a) Reasonable notice of repayment and seizure

What is a reasonable period within which repayment must be made after demand is a vexed question.[116] In *Lister*, a representative of Dunlop simply arrived at Lister's premises, presented a demand for repayment and then gave notice of a receiver-manager under a debenture security. The Supreme Court found that a clause in the debenture which provided that repayment was to be made immediately on demand should be interpreted to mean "within a reasonable time" of demand being made. What was reasonable depended on the circumstances, provided sufficient time was given to the debtor to take some action such as to arrange refinancing. No guidance was given as to what was reasonable notice even to Lister whose indebtedness was so long-standing and serious that it seemed unlikely refinancing would be forthcoming.

In the subsequent Ontario Court of Appeal case, *Mr Broadloom Corp. (1968) Ltd.* v. *Bank of Montreal*,[117] the issue was again considered, where the debtor had been called to a meeting at the bank at which the repayment was demanded, followed an hour later by the arrival at the debtor's premises of the receiver to take possession. The trial judge found that the debtor could have arranged refinancing within three or four days, and that there was no evidence that the debtor was likely to abscond if given time to refinance. The appellate court found the bank to be liable for a wrongful seizure of the assets because insufficient time was given. In view of the findings that the debtor would have benefited from being given time, it may be that the net effect of the decision is that no time need be given at all when the debtor had no other options to receivership. Thus, no time may be a reasonable period of time. The Ontario Court of Appeal also found that if time is granted, it need not be requested by the debtor.

Reconsideration of the requirement of reasonable notice by the Ontario Court of Appeal in *Kavcar Investments Ltd.* v. *Aetna Financial Services Ltd.*,[118] led one senior authoritative practitioner to refer to the rule as the "elusive shrinking concept",[119] so difficult has it become to comprehend and apply. In

---

116. See generally: R. Gordon Marantz, "Tactics For Survival: What to do When the Borrower is in Trouble" (1986) 1 B.F.L. Rev. 1 and "Reasonable Notice: The Elusive Shrinking Concept" (1990) 6 B.F.L. Rev. 1063.

117. (1983) 49 C.B.R. (N.S.) 1 (Ont. C.A.).

118. (1989) 70 O.R. (2d) 225 (C.A.).

119. *Supra*, n. 116.

Kavcar, the lender demanded repayment and made an immediate appointment of a receiver who took possession three hours after the demand had been made. The borrower was then given six weeks to satisfy the debt. The trial judge found the seizure to have been unlawful but on appeal the issue was whether giving no time to meet the demand was reasonable in the circumstances. Speaking for the court, McKinley J.A. noted the rejection of the *Lister* principle by courts in England, Australia and New Zealand and their restriction of "reasonable time" to time to obtain funds already available to the debtor rather than to arrange refinancing.[120] She further stated that a debtor ought to be allowed a reasonable time to refinance, despite the incongruities that the creditor's loss is increasing daily during that time and that if the debtor's assets are shrinking, reasonable time will avail him nothing.[121] The court suggested that any period of notice of less than one day would be, *prima facie*, unreasonable. It further decided that, in view of the trial judge's finding of fact that there was no evidence that Kavcar could not have arranged the refinancing if given time, the seizure here was unreasonable and wrongful, and awarded damages.

The net result of these cases is that while reasonable notice is to be given prior to seizure by a bank, no precise term has been established to constitute reasonable notice. However, the more hopeless the debtor's position, the less time appears to be required, and, in any case, reasonable notice is likely to be a very short period of time, perhaps a few days. *Kavcar* also confirmed the position of an earlier case, *McLachlan* v. *C.I.B.C*,[122] that the damages awardable against the bank are in the tort of conversion, are to be determined by a valuation of the business on a going concern basis or an asset valuation basis, and are awarded on the basis producing the higher recovery.

The Supreme Court of Canada subsequently reconfirmed the requirement of reasonable notice in a civil law case which is authority only in Quebec and on the basis of provisions in the Quebec Civil Code, in *National Bank of Canada* v. *Houle*.[123] There, a bank, acting on a recommendation of an accounting firm that loans be immediately recalled, gave one hour to find refinancing, after which the line of credit was rescinded. The Supreme Court found that one hour was unreasonable and that there was no evidence to justify it, although the bank was ultimately found not liable for unlawful seizure since it had been granted a release by the company. In coming to this decision, the court stated that reasonable time to refinance must be given and that the length of time was a question of fact in each case. Regrettably, the court did not use this rare opportunity afforded to it to consider the issue fully.

What, then, is a reasonable period of time, in the view of lower courts, since

---

120. *Supra*, n. 118 at p. 235.
121. *Ibid*.
122. (1987) 13 B.C.L.R. (2d) 300 (B.C.S.C.). See also: R. Gordon Marantz, "A Measure of Damages: *McLachlan* v. *C.I.B.C.*" (1987) 2 B.F.L. Rev. 384.
123. [1990] 3 S.C.R. 122. See also: Louise LaLonde, "Reasonable Notice and Abuse of Contractual Rights: *National Bank of Canada* v. *Houle*" (1992) 8 B.F.L. Rev. 105.

Lister? In one case, 24 hours was regarded as reasonable, given the financial condition of the corporation and the absence of refinancing prospects.[124] In another case, 18 days was regarded as more than reasonable.[125] On the other hand, where a bank gave one month to a borrower to remove all loans from the bank's books, forcing the customer into liquidation, a court found that guarantors were not liable on the loans because the bank had acted "intemperately".[126] Moreover, another court recently decided that the only duties owed by a bank in respect of reasonable notice to seize were those for which the contract expressly provided, or the legislation, so that no notice was required at all.[127] Yet, five days has also been found to be reasonable.[128]

Each case is not decided on its facts and on the judicial digestive system to which it has been assigned. A certain level of chaos appears to have been introduced into the process of seizure by *Lister* and there is no sign that the resulting uncertainty for banks, who see assets diminishing daily, will be resolved in their favour in the immediate future.

It should be noted that the same test (and associated problems) is used by the courts in relation to overdrafts, which are also regarded as loans.[129] In *Thermo King Corp.* v. *Provincial Bank of Canada*,[130] the Ontario Court of Appeal so decided, and other courts have followed suit.[131]

The issue of calculating damages has recently been addressed by the British Columbia Court of Appeal in *Bradshaw Construction Ltd.* v. *Bank of Nova Scotia*,[132] in which the bank agreed not to call its security pursuant to a floating charge over the plaintiff's holdings, until the proceeds from an agreement for the sale of a motel fell in. The bank breached this agreement, called the loan and appointed a receiver. After liquidation, the bank was left with a deficiency including the receiver's fees and disbursements. The plaintiff sued for wrongful seizure and won. In assessing the compensation, the court stated the onus was on the bank to prove that the award should be anything less than the book value of the property sold and awarded the plaintiff the value of the net equity in its properties when the receiver was appointed. In addition, the plaintiff was awarded the amount due to its other creditors and a sum of $500,000.00 for its loss of opportunity to preserve its assets and accumulate greater equity.

This approach has been followed in a very recent unreported decision from

124. *Royal Bank* v. *Starr* (1987) 41 D.L.R. (4th) 715 (Ont. H.C.).
125. *Atlantic Sporting Distributors Ltd.* v. *Bank of Montreal* (1988) 222 A.P.R. 376 and additional reasons at (1989) 233 A.P.R. 181 (N.S.T.D.).
126. *Bank of Nova Scotia* v. *Raymond Contractors Ltd.* (1988) 25 B.C.L.R. (2d) 54 (B.C.S.C.).
127. *Caton Cattle Co.* v. *Bank of Montreal*, unreported decision of 10 September 1990 (Sask. C.A.). See also: *Royal Bank* v. *Starko*, *supra*, n. 86.
128. *Barclay Construction Corp.* v. *Bank of Montreal* (1989) 65 D.L.R. (4th) 213 (B.C.C.A.).
129. See generally: Ogilvie, *supra*, n. 25 at pp. 464–467.
130. (1981) 34 O.R. (2d) 369 (Ont. C.A.); leave to appeal to S.C.C. refused (1982) 130 D.L.R. (3d) 256n.
131. *CIP Inc.* v. *Toronto-Dominion Bank* (1988) 55 D.L.R. (4th) 308 (B.C.C.A.); *Barclay Construction Corp.* v. *Bank of Montreal*, *supra*, n. 128.
132. [1993] 1 W.W.R. 596 (B.C.C.A.).

Alberta in *Royal Bank of Canada* v. *W. Got and Associates Electric Ltd.*,[133] in which the court also stated that the onus was on the bank to prove an entitlement to less than the net value of the assets, the outstanding liabilities, lost accounts and the lost opportunity of accumulating greater equity. In addition—and most unusually in a banking case—the court awarded exemplary damages against the bank since the bank had appointed a receiver without giving notice to the debtor of its intention to do so. The court stated that the $100,000.00 exemplary damage award, a considerable sum in exemplary damages in Canada, was to emphasise that the court does not condone the clear violation of the law that reasonable notice is required when appointing a receiver.[134]

Recent legislation, in particular, the 1992 Bank Act and the Bankruptcy and Insolvency Act,[135] has mirrored the requirement of reasonable notice in relation to seizure but has yet to be considered by the courts. Since these provisions are linked to priority issues in situations of insolvency, for which further provision is made in both federal and provincial legislation, their discussion will be continued in Section 10 below. Priority issues concern competitions by a bank with other third parties who also claim an interest in the debtor's assets, and Canadian courts have been particularly busy in relation to the issue of the bank's common law right of set-off and its common law duty of constructive trusteeship in cases of conflicting claims.

(b) Set-off and constructive trust

The collision between the banker's common law right of set-off and the marked preference of recent Canadian courts to deem the banker to be a constructive trustee for a third party in relation to funds which have come into the banker's hands has been a significant and troublesome development in Canadian law in the past decade or so. In this, Canadian courts appear to have diverged considerably from the current English doctrine on constructive trust. The absence of a theoretical framework capable of predicting when a constructive trust will be imposed on a bank means that the law seems at best simplistic or at worst confused.[136] The Canadian cases are generally poorly reasoned,[137] if enthusiastic about promoting the doctrine in a more expansive manner than the English courts.

In England, the seemingly innocuous principle stated by Lord Selborne in *Barnes* v. *Addy*,[138] that strangers were only liable for knowing receipt or

---

133. [1994] 5 W.W.R. 337 (Alta. Q.B.).
134. See also a Quebec case: *B.C.N.* v. *Couture* (1991) 38 Q.A.C. 23.
135. S.C. 1992, c. 27.
136. Ruth Sullivan, "Strangers to the Trust" (1986) 8 Est. & Tr. Q. 217 at pp. 222–223.
137. Kathy Kalinowsky, "The Constructive Trustee: A Stranger's Knowing Participation in the Breach of Trust" (1991) 7 B.F.L. Rev. 383 at pp. 387–388.
138. (1874) L.R. 9 Ch. App. 244 at 251.

knowing assistance in a dishonest or fradulent design, was subsequently transposed to include a stranger who not only knew but also ought to have known that disposing of the property or otherwise dealing with it was in breach of trust. The requirement of objective as well as subjective knowledge was added by Ungoed Thomas J. in *Selangor United Rubber Estates* v. *Cradock (No. 3)*,[139] in relation to knowing assistance in the disposition of trust property. Thus, whereas previously liability as a constructive trustee was based on active participation in the disposition, after *Selangor* it was based on a failure to infer. In the subsequent case, *Karak Rubber Co.* v. *Burden (No. 2)*,[140] the court confirmed that constructive knowledge was sufficient to impose liability in relation to assistance in the disposition of trust property as well as in its receipt.[141]

Although the later case, *Baden Delvaux*,[142] codified this development into five levels of knowledge which would bring liability, the bulk of the English case law has pulled back from imputing constructive trusteeship where there may be constructive knowledge. In *Baden Delvaux*, Gibson J. suggested that the five levels of knowledge bringing potential liability were:

(i) actual knowledge;

(ii) wilfully shutting one's eyes to the obvious;

(iii) wilfully and recklessly failing to make such enquiry as an honest and reasonable man would make;

(iv) knowledge of circumstances that would indicate the facts to an honest and reasonable man; and

(v) knowledge of circumstances that would put an honest and reasonable man on enquiry.

However, this approach has been rejected in recent cases[143] where liability as a constructive trustee has been limited to situations where there is a want of probity, and actual knowledge in knowing assistance in the disposition of trust property.

In contrast, recent Canadian cases have adopted the *Selangor* approach, at first without knowingly doing so and after 1975,[144] expressly, to impose

---

139. [1968] 2 All E.R. 1073 (Ch. D.).

140. [1972] 1 W.L.R. 602 (Ch. D.).

141. *Rowlandson* v. *National Westminster Bank* [1978] 3 All E.R. 370 (Ch. D.).

142. *Baden Delvaux and Lecuit* v. *Société Generale pour Favoriser le Développement du Commerce et de l'Industrie en France S.A.* [1983] B.C.L.C. 325 (Ch. D.).

143. *Carl Zeiss Stiftung* v. *Herbert Smith & Co. (No. 2)* [1969] 2 Ch. 276 (C.A.); *Competitive Insurance Co. Ltd.* v. *Davies Investment Ltd.* [1975] 1 W.L.R. 1240 (Ch. D.); *Consul Development Property Ltd.* v. *D.P.C. Estates Property Ltd.* (1975) 132 C.L.R. 373 (Aust. H.C.); *Belmont Finance Corp. Ltd.* v. *Williams Furniture Ltd.* [1979] 1 Ch. 250 (C.A.); *Feuer Leather Corp.* v. *Frank Johnstone & Sons* [1981] Com. L.R. 251 (Ch. D.); *International Sales and Agencies Ltd.* v. *Marcus* [1982] 3 All E.R. 551 (Q.B.); *Re Montagu's S.T.* [1987] Ch. 264; *Lipkin Gorman* v. *Karpnale Ltd.* [1991] 3 W.L.R. 10; *Agip (Africa) Ltd.* v. *Jackson* [1989] 3 W.L.R. 1367 (Ch. D.); *Barclays Bank* v. *Quincecare Ltd.* [1992] 4 All E.R. 363 (Ch. D.).

144. The first reported case to cite *Selangor* was *Groves-Raffin Construction Ltd.* v. *C.I.B.C.* [1976] 2 W.W.R. 673 (B.C.C.A.).

constructive trusteeship on banks and others where there is deemed to be constructive knowledge. Two cases pre-dating *Selangor* set the tone for all subsequent Canadian courts. In *Fonthill Lumber* v. *Bank of Montreal*[145] and *John M.M. Troup Ltd.* v. *Royal Bank*,[146] the Ontario Court of Appeal and Supreme Court of Canada, respectively, found that banks were liable as constructive trustees in respect of funds deposited by contractors which were subject to statutory liens. The bank ought to have known from their customer's business that the funds were possibly for the benefit of a third party and ought not to have set them off against the customer's concurrent indebtedness to the bank. In *Carl B. Potter* v. *Mercantile Bank*,[147] although the court found the bank not liable on the facts, it stated that constructive knowledge of the *Baden Delvaux* type (iv) kind, that is, knowledge of circumstances that would indicate the facts to an honest and reasonable man, was sufficient to impose a constructive trusteeship on a bank.

This approach has been applied in close to 100 reported decisions to date in Canada in relation to banks and near-banks.[148] Perusal of these cases[149] indicates that Canadian courts have collapsed actual and constructive knowledge, wilful wrongdoing and inadvertence, and receiving and assisting. The net effect is that, in Canada, a bank faces potential liability where a court deems it to have had constructive notice of another claim to funds in its possession and whether or not it has either merely received or actually assisted in their disposition.

Whether or not a bank is found liable depends entirely on whether or not a court finds evidence which it deems sufficient to place it on notice. Several of the most recent cases exemplify the uncertainty for the lending banker anxious to secure the pay down of an outstanding loan.[150] In *Ansell* v. *Laprairie*,[151] the defendant owned land subject to foreclosure proceedings and the plaintiff put up funds for the defendant in exchange for a one-half interest in the land, on the understanding that the sale proceeds would be split evenly after payment to the creditors. The defendant was also indebted to his bank and after the sale deposited the funds with the bank. The plaintiff sued both defendant and bank for breach of trust and the court found that the bank was liable to the plaintiff as constructive trustee on the ground that constructive knowledge was sufficient to create the trust. The bank was said to be reckless in not making enquiry as to other potential interests in the funds.

145. (1959) 19 D.L.R. (2d) 618 (Ont. C.A.).
146. [1962] S.C.R. 487.
147. [1980] 2 S.C.R. 343.
148. See a partial list in Ogilvie, *supra*, n. 25 at pp. 450–457.
149. Not really recommended!
150. For discussions of cases from the 1980s see: Catherine A. Walsh, "Breach of Trust by Bank as to Proceeds of Joint Venture Contract and Estoppel" (1986) 1 B.F.L. Rev. 255; Robert P. Stark, "Bank's Liability for Assurances to Third Parties" (1987) 2 B.F.L. Rev. 250; M.H. Ogilvie, "When is a Bank a Constructive Trustee? Three Recent Cases" (1988) 3 B.F.L. Rev. 77; James J. Reynolds, "Registration and Constructive Notice" (1988) 3 B.F.L. Rev. 369; John R. Braun, "Financial Institution as Constructive Trustee" (1990) 6 B.F.L. Rev. 95.
151. (1989) 65 Alta. L.R. (2d) 233 (Q.B.).

On the other hand, in *Wonsch Construction Co. Ltd.* v. *National Bank of Canada*,[152] the plaintiff construction company and the defendant entered into a joint venture agreement financed by the defendant to construct a building. The agreement promised that on the completion of the construction, there would be an equalisation of the parties' respective contributions. It was further provided that if, at a certain date, the plaintiff owed money to the bank, the two parties would pay equally such amounts as required. On that date, the plaintiff owed $2.65m, which was subsequently reduced to $1.06m. The defendant purchased the debt from the bank for $860.000 after notification to the plaintiff, and received an assignment of all the security held by the bank. Subsequently, the defendant demanded payment from the plaintiff and seized the assets. The plaintiff sued both for trespass and breach of fiduciary duty, arguing on the basis of *Carl B. Potter* that the bank was a constructive trustee. The Ontario Court of Appeal found that the defendant had wrongfully seized the assets and ought to have looked to the agreement for settlement, but that the bank had no reason to doubt that the transaction would be for the plaintiff's benefit and was under no duty to enquire into the circumstances.

This case was undoubtedly correctly decided; yet, a bank has been found to be a constructive trustee where it had also given notice to and been granted approval from a plaintiff to deal with funds in a particular way. In *Arthur Anderson, Inc.* v. *Toronto Dominion Bank*,[153] the bank was the banker for a group of almost 60 companies involved in the construction industry, each originally with its own bank account. By agreement with the plaintiff, the bank implemented a mirror accounting system which eliminated the need for a separate account balance for each company, instead offering only a daily net balance for all the companies. As long as the net balance was positive, individual company overdrafts were regarded as unimportant. The group ran into financial difficulty as a result of the collapse in the real estate market and the bank terminated the system and seized most of the money in the accounts. The court found this system to have been inappropriate for construction companies since they were frequently in receipt of trust funds and that the bank ought to have known that breach of trust would occur and to make reasonable enquiries. Mere knowledge that the borrower was a construction company was sufficient to fix the bank with constructive notice of alleged breaches of trust. Such a case, like many of the others, place banks in the very difficult position of protector of the interests of persons unknown and as insurer of last resort in respect of those persons wronged by their customers.

(c) Lender priority wars

The final threat to recovery by a lending banker from a defaulting borrower is that, when all is said and done, other creditors with claims against the borrower

---

152. (1990) 75 D.L.R. (4th) 732 (Ont. C.A.).
153. Unreported decision of 16 July 1992 (Ont. Gen. Div.).

may enjoy first discharge of their indebtedness on the basis of a statutorily based prior claim. Indeed, the cases on constructive trust often concern such claims, as did those to which reference was made above in relation to mechanics' or construction liens.

The proliferation of statutorily based prior claims has increased over the past three or four decades in response to social and economic changes, and range from the traditional claimants such as other secured interest holders, to employees, spouses, and children in respect of whom legislation has been enacted to protect their interests in insolvencies. The complexity of competing claims is exacerbated by the fact that both federal and provincial governments have been active in attempting to protect other claimants, so that conflicting legislation abounds and constitutional issues have first to be addressed in priority disputes.

A large book rather than a short chapter is required to do full justice to the priority battles which banks are obliged to wage in order to secure perhaps only a small portion of their original investment. The legislation and the resulting case law is both voluminous and confused. Non-Canadian readers should be aware that the potential for banks to lose out at the end of the day to other claimants is considerable, so that being fully apprised of the potential problems should insolvency ensue, is a factor in making the loan decision in the first place, and in ensuring that as many legal safeguards as possible are in place at the time. Therefore, the following discussion will simply survey some of the major areas of difficulty, and also suggest the variety of claimants with whom a lending banker must contend in attempting to recover on a soured loan.

In addition to the usual forms of security which a bank may take in relation to a loan, such as promissory notes, guarantees, accounts receivable, debentures and floating charges, since 1890[154] banks in Canada have also been able to take a "special security" pursuant to successive Bank Acts. This security was formerly known as a section 88 and a section 178 security, those being the sections of previous Bank Acts where provision was so made. The 1992 Act now refers to a "special security".[155] Since banks as a normal practice, take a special security in relation to loans, most priority conflicts concern the special security and some other statutory priority.

This security may be taken over a wide variety of property from natural resources to future crops and manufactured products as well as their instruments of production.[156] Documentation and registration are required to protect the security,[157] and provisions are further made for its enforcement.[158] Banks are entitled to seize the security and use the proceeds of a sale to pay down

154. Bank Act, S.C, 1890, c. 31.
155. Sections 425–436.
156. Sections 425–427.
157. Sections 427–429.
158. *Ibid.*

indebtedness, and may do so without a court order.[159] Although the Act makes no express provision for procedures to be employed in seizure, there is some indication in the case law that reasonable procedures are to be followed including giving reasonable notice,[160] and following any relevant provincial statutory procedures which do not directly conflict with the federal Bank Act.[161] The sale is by public auction[162] and the Bank Act expressly provides that a bank is to act honestly and in good faith and in a timely and appropriate manner in relation to the sale.[163]

The 1992 Bank Act contains an incomplete code in relation to the priority of the bank's rights in the security or its sale proceeds. The Act provides that the bank's rights and powers take priority over all subsequently acquired rights and also over the claim of a mechanics' lien holder or unpaid vendor who has a lien at the time of the bank's acquisition, unless the bank had knowledge of the lien,[164] which it will be deemed to have if it is registered—as it normally is. In addition to the priority of prior registered liens, the Act further provides for the priority of prior registered interests in land[165]; claims for wages, salaries or other renumeration for up to three months where either a receiving order or an assignment is made under the Bankruptcy and Insolvency Act[166]; and claims of a grower or producer of agricultural products for money owing by a manufacturer to the grower or producer for such products from the producer and delivered to the manufacturer within six months of the making of an order or assignment in bankruptcy. [167]

These express statutory priorities are only some of those for which accommodation has to be made, whether derived from other federal or provincial legislation. Since each case is a "single instance" whose ultimate outcome is dependent on the particular statutory priorities in question and the fact finding of the trial judge as to their documentation, timing, registration and the like, it is only useful here to list some of the most important priority issues.

Undoubtedly, the most difficult priority disputes are those between the bank special security and secured interests protected by the various provincial Personal Property Security Acts.[168] These Acts provide for a scheme of protection of "secured interests", which replaced the older interests such as chattel mortgages, debentures, conditional sales, floating charges and so on. In the hope of avoiding priority disputes, banks usually register their special

159. Section 426(3). B.N.C. v. *Atomic Shipper Co.* (1991) 80 D.L.R. (4th) 134 (S.C.C.).
160. *Waldron* v. *Royal Bank of Canada* (1991) 78 D.L.R. (4th) 1 (B.C.C.A.).
161. *Bank of Montreal* v. *Hall* (1990) 65 D.L.R. (4th) 361 (S.C.C.).
162. Section 426(6).
163. Section 428(10), (11). *Les Équipements Lorac Ltée* v. *National Bank of Canada* (1991) 77 D.L.R. (4th) 523 (S.C.C.).
164. Section 426(7).
165. Section 426(8).
166. Section 428(7)(a).
167. Section 428(7)(b).
168. See, for example, the Ontario Act: R.S.O., 1990, C.P. 10.

security in a provincial P.P.S.A. registry as well as the Bank Act registry and some appellate courts have concluded that this is a proper way to defeat another claimant.[169] Nevertheless, significant problems remain,[170] and leading scholars and practitioners in the area advocate a national integrated security registration system as the only means of eliminating these disputes.[171] The legislators have yet to regard this as a significant issue, or at least, are remarkably reluctant to stir up the constitutional muddy waters on a matter remote from the everyday concerns of the electorate, so that no resolution is on the immediate horizon.[172]

Federal legislation has been the subject of priority disputes in relation to the special security and the federal income tax,[173] excise taxes,[174] grain,[175] fisheries,[176] and shipping.[177] Provincial legislation has been the subject of priority disputes in relation to wages,[178] workers' compensation,[179] crop

169. *City of Moose Jaw* v. *Pulsar Ventures Inc.* (1987) 42 D.L.R. (4th) 385 (Sask. C.A.); *Birch Hills Credit Union Ltd.* v. *C.I.B.C.* (1989) 52 D.L.R. (4th) 113 (Sask. C.A.); *Bank of Nova Scotia* v. *International Harvester Credit Corp.* (1990) 74 O.R. (2d) 738 (Ont. C.A.).

170. See generally: Jacob S. Ziegel, "The Interaction of Section 178 Security Interests and Provincial PPSA Security Interests: Once More into the Black Hole" (1990) 6 B.F.L. Rev. 342; Bradley Crawford, "Interaction Between the PPSA and Section 178 of the Bank Act" (1992) 8 B.F.L. Rev. 1.

171. See generally: R.C.C. Cuming and Roderick J. Wood, "Compatibility of Federal and Provincial Personal Property Security Law" (1986) 65 Can. Bar Rev. 267; R.C.C. Cuming, "The Relationship Between Personal Property Security Acts and Section 178 of the Bank Act: Federal Paramountcy and Provincial Legislative Policy" (1988) 14 Can. Bus. L.J. 315; R.C.C. Cuming, "Security Interests in Accounts and the Right of Set-Off" (1990) 6 B.F.L. Rev. 299; R.C.C. Cuming, "P.P.S.A.—Section 178 Bank Act Overlap: No Closer to Situations" (1991) 18 Can. Bus. L.J. 135; Jacob S. Ziegel, "The Future of Canadian Commercial Law" [1986] 20 U.B.C. Law Rev. 1; Jacob S. Ziegel, "The Intervention of PPSA Legislation and Security Interests Under the Bank Act" (1986) 12 Can. Bus. L.J. 73; Jacob S. Ziegel, "Protecting the Integrity of the Ontario PPSA" (1987) 13 Can. Bus. L.J. 359; Jacob S. Ziegel, *supra*, n. 170; Bradley Crawford, *supra*, n. 170.

172. For the provincial view see: Roderick A. Macdonald, "Provincial Law and Federal Commercial Law: Is 'Atomic Slipper' a New Beginning?" (1991) 7 B.F.L. Rev. 437.

173. *R.* v. *Banque d'Hochelaga* [1926] 3 D.L.R. 91 (Que K.B.); *384238 Ontario Ltd.* v. *R.* (1981) 81 D.T.C. 5215 (F.C.T.D.).

174. *Re International Metal Works Ltd.; ex parte The King* [1929] 1 D.L.R. 309 (Ont. S.C. in Bkcy.); *A.G. Can.* v. *Gordon* [1925] 1 D.L.R. 654 (Ont. S.C.); *A.G. Can.* v. *C.I.B.C.* (1973) 41 D.L.R. (3d) 749 (Alta. S.C.-T.D.); *R.* v. *Nest Mfg. Ltd.* [1978] 1 F.C.R. 624 (T.D.); *MacCulloch & Co. Ltd.* v. *A.G. Can* (1978) 89 D.L.R. (3d) 369 (N.S.S.C.—App. Div.) rev'd 105 D.L.R. (3d) 266 (S.C.C.); *Re Swaan* (1980) 37 C.B.R. (N.S.) 1 (B.C.S.C.); *C.I.B.C.* v. *R.* (1984) 52 C.B.R. (N.S.) 145 (F.C.T.D.).

175. *Re Swaan, supra,* n. 174. Cf. *Indust. Rel. Bd.* v. *Avco Financial Services Realty Ltd.* (1979) 98 D.L.R. (3d) 695 (S.C.C.); *Dauphin Plains Credit Union Ltd.* v. *Xyloid Indust. Ltd.* (1980) 108 D.L.R. (3d) 257 (S.C.C.); *Min. of Natural Resources for Ont.* v. *Bank of N.S.* (1980) 34 C.B.R. (N.S.) 262 (Ont. S.C.); *C.I.B.C.* v. *Klymchuk* (1990) 70 D.L.R. (4th) 340 (Alta. C.A.).

176. *Re C.I.B.C. and Min. of Fisheries* (1966) 59 D.L.R. (2d) 403 (P.E.I.C.A.).

177. *Royal Bank* v. *Queen Charlotte Fisheries Ltd.* (1981) 13 B.L.R. 306 (B.C.S.C.); aff'd (1983) 50 B.C.L.R. 128 (C.A.).

178. *Royal Bank* v. *W.C.B.N.S.* [1936] 4 D.L.R. 9 (S.C.C.); *Armstrong* v. *Coopers and Lybrand Ltd.* (1986) 5 P.P.S.A.C. 296 (Ont. H.C.); aff'd (1987) 65 C.B.R. (N.S.) 258 (Ont. C.A.); *Royal Bank* v. *Canadian Aero-Marine Industries Inc.* (1989) 67 Alta. L.R. (2d) 17 (Q.B.). Cf. *Royal Bank* v. *Government of Manitoba* [1978] 1 W.W.R. 712 (Man. Q.B.); *Abraham* v. *Canadian Admiral Corp.* (1993) 48 C.C.E.L. 58 (Ont. Gen. Div.).

179. *Ibid.*

insurance,[180] insurance proceeds,[181] distress,[182] exemptions,[183] workers' liens,[184] provincial tax,[185] and landlords.[186] In addition, it has been recently held[187] that the Bank Act is entirely subordinate to the federal Companies' Creditors Arrangement Act.[188] Finally, it is important to note the question of whether or not environmental legislation, which is either now enacted[189] or in the legislative process at both the federal and provincial levels, and which will create a super-priority similar to that of the American CERCLA, is currently threatening to render lending an even more uncertain activity in relation to the legal rights or ability of a lending bank to recover when a loan must be enforced.[190]

10. CONCLUSION

A propensity for sophisticated doctrinal analysis has never been a notable characteristic of the Canadian judiciary, with few exceptions. Rather, enthusiastic adoption of principles, rules and judicial trends from England or the United States is typical of the judiciary. The move towards increasing bank lender liability is an example. As the foregoing has attempted to demonstrate, the legal grounds for increasing the risk and uncertainty in lending to banks have accelerated in number and in standards of proof over the past decade. Whether

---

180. *Oliver Chem. Co.* v. *Fischer* (1963) 42 W.W.R. 269 (Alta. Dist. Ct.).

181. *R.* v. *Bank of N.S.* [1962] 1 D.L.R. 666 (Ont. C.A.).

182. *C.I.B.C.* v. *Heppner* (1965) 51 D.L.R. 254 (Sask. Q.B.); *C.I.B.C.* v. *Sledz* [1991] 1 W.W.R. 42 (Alta., Master).

183. *C.I.B.C.* v. *Surkan* (1978) 5 Alta. L.R. (2d) 323 (Dist. Ct.); *Royal Bank* v. *Riehl* [1978] 6 W.W.R. 481 (Alta. Dist. Ct.); *Thomas* v. *Royal Bank* (1985) 42 Sask. R. 303 (Q.B.); revs'd. (1986) 49 Sask. R. 161 (C.A.); *Rodger* v. *Bank of Montreal* (1986) 47 Sask. R. 213 (Q.B.); *Johnson* v. *Bank of Nova Scotia* (1985) 41 Sask. R. 292 (Q.B.); *Re LeBlanc and Bank of Montreal* (1987) 46 D.L.R. (4th) 15 (Sask. Q.B.); (1988) 54 D.L.R. (4th) 89 (Sask. C.A.); *Sharp* v. *Bank of Montreal* (1988) 67 Sask. R. 129 (Q.B.).

184. *Bank of Nova Scotia* v. *McLaughlin* (1980) 63 A.P.R. 688 (N.B.Q.B.); *C.T.C.* v. *Cenex Ltd.* [1982] 2 W.W.R. 361 (Sask. C.A.); *Re Woodley* (1983) 47 B.C.L.R. 227 (S.C.).

185. *Brantford* v. *Imperial Bank of Canada* (1930) 65 O.L.R. 625 (C.A.).

186. *Re Newmarket Lumber Co.* [1951] 4 D.L.R. 710 (Ont. H.C.); *Re Alfandri Inc.* [1975] Que. S.C. 448 (Que. S.C. in Bkcy.); *Re Fermo's Creations Ltd.* (1969) 10 D.L.R. (3d) 560 (Que. C.A.).

187. *Hong Kong Bank of Canada* v. *Chef Ready Foods Ltd.* [1991] 2 W.W.R. 136 (B.C.C.A.).

188. R.S.C., 1985, c. C–36. See: M.H. Ogilvie, "Rehabilitation, Equity and Efficiency: The New Bankruptcy Law in Canada" [1994] J.B.L. forthcoming.

189. Many provinces now have draconian environmental legislation in the legislative process.

190. Of the burgeoning Canadian literature in this area, see, in particular relation to banks: Jodene D. Baker, "Lender's Environmental Liability" (1990) 6 B.F.L. Rev. 189; Jimmy Y. Levy, "Landlord and Lender Liability for Hazardous Waste Clean-Up: A Review of the Evolving Canadian and American Case Law" (1992) 20 Can. Bus. L.J. 269; M.H. Ogilvie, "The Constitutionality of Provincial Regulation of the Environmental Liability of Banks as Secured Lenders in Canada" (1993) 21 Can. Bus. L.J. 429; M.H. Ogilvie, "The Environmental Liability of Banks as Secured Lenders in Canada" (1992) 8 B.F.L. Rev. 363.

or not this is a rational or necessary development either from a moral or marketplace perspective is uncertain. What is certain is that lending has become so risky a business for banks in Canada that the watchword for doing business today must surely be: *Caveat lendor!*

M . H . OGILVIE

CHAPTER 11

THE LIABILITY OF AUSTRALIAN BANKS FOR SWISS FRANC LOANS

"There is no sphere of human thought in which it is easier to show superficial cleverness and the appearance of superior wisdom than in discussing questions of currency and exchange."[1]

The disastrous experience of the foreign currency borrowers and their subsequent battles in the courts for recovery of losses incurred can be traced back to the deregulation of the Australian financial markets that occurred in the early 1980s. The reforms undertaken included the abolition of exchange controls on foreign currency borrowings, the flotation of the Australian dollar and the granting of a number of new bank licences. This meant that for the first time Australian residents could be offered, by banks carrying on business in Australia, loans that were denominated in currencies other than Australian dollars. It was also the first time that the Australian dollar was subject to the vagaries of the world money markets without Reserve bank intervention. Similarly, for the domestic Australian banks, it was the first time that they perceived they would be subject to such direct competition for their customer base. On that basis they felt a need to innovate and internationalise the financial services that were on offer so as to be able to compete with one another and the new banks.

The Australian borrower in the early 1980s was incurring interest rates on borrowings that were substantially higher than their foreign counterparts. The differential between Australian dollar interest rates and the Swiss franc, deutschmark and yen rates was on occasion as high as 9 per cent. The availability of overseas funds at a lower rate was therefore superficially very attractive to both the domestic borrower and the Australian banks who, in promoting such a loan, would be able to write new business.

The mechanics of the transaction involved the intervention of the domestic bank (or a non-bank financier) prepared to offer the facility engaging in a borrowing transaction with an overseas lender. The liability of the Australian borrower would therefore be to his or its bank with whom an agreement would be entered into and for whom security would be provided. The majority of borrowers who entered this market were ignorant of its intricacies and relied upon what they were told by the banks. Critically, the borrowers failed to appreciate and the banks failed to explain the reasons for the interest rate differential, i.e., the domestic and international, political, social and economic

---

1. Sir Winston Churchill, 28 September 1949.

influences that determine how and why interest and exchange rates differ between countries. In *Lloyd* v. *Citicorp*, Rogers J. described the foreign currency market as follows,[1a]

"Ultimately it is a gamble. It is a gamble because unpredictable factors may have immediate and violent repercussions. A rumour of the death of the President of the United States, the MX missile crisis, dismissal of an oil minister cannot be predicted or guarded against ... deregulation has brought in its train volatility of proportions previously unknown."

Borrowers were not aware of the crucial distinction between the nominal rate of interest (being the foreign currency interest rate) and the real rate of interest, that could only be calculated after accounting for variations in the exchange rate during the course of the loan.

The banks were able to allay the fears of prospective borrowers as to possible movements in the exchange rates by showing tables and graphs that plotted the Australian dollar against the Swiss franc and often other currencies (usually for a period of five years). These graphs revealed an apparent exchange rate stability, particularly between the Swiss franc and the Australian dollar, which, when combined with the lowest nominal interest rate, made it the most "attractive" currency to borrow in. In other instances the bank undertook to advise the borrower regularly as to what currency to be in and to monitor and manage the facility. Most borrowers were ignorant as to the range of risk minimisation techniques that were available when the loans were drawn down. The whole of the foreign currency risk could be eliminated by a forward hedge, which locked the borrower into a fixed forward position eliminating currency risk. Other risk minimisation techniques included drawing the loan down in a basket of currencies and the putting of a stop loss in place.[2]

On the basis of information provided by the four major banks and two of the state banks it is estimated that up to 1986 there were between 2,180 and 2,420 foreign currency borrowers.[3] The loans were drawn down by a wide range of borrowers that included farmers, professionals, businessmen, small scale

---

1a. *Lloyd* v. *Citicorp* (1986) 11 N.S.W.L.R. 286.

2. *Hedge.* A technique whereby a buyer of foreign currency is matched with a seller of foreign currency to eliminate the exchange risk on an equal and opposite amount of foreign currency. The disadvantage is that the cost of hedging eliminates the interest rate differential between the currency borrowed and the currency that is being protected. Ideally they are used selectively during periods of exchange rate volatility.

Basket of Currencies—Involves drawing down the loan in several foreign currencies so as to reduce the risk.

Stop Loss. Is a mechanism that is put in place by the borrower in consultation with the bank and enables the borrower to terminate the loan once a threshold loss has been incurred. Borrowers' experts universally recommend a stop loss of 15 per cent, i.e., after a 15 per cent drop in the value of the dollar against the currency borrowed the loan is brought onshore.

3. The banks provided the information to the House of Representatives Standing Committee on Finance and Public Administration–Australian Banking Industry Inquiry. The report of the Committee is titled "A Pocket Full of Change—Banking and Deregulation", November 1991, AGPS, p. 295.

property developers and family trust companies. The loans were provided both for new projects and to refinance existing domestic commitments, with the amounts loaned varying between $250,000 and three to four million dollars.[4] Estimates of the overall losses suffered by borrowers have been put at between one[5] and five[6] billion dollars. Those that borrowed in Swiss francs prior to 1985 saw their liability increase over 100 per cent during the term of the loan. The typical loan agreement was entered into for a period of five years with interest payable each six months in arrears when the loan would be rolled over. The losses on the loans were crystallised either when the loan expired and was brought onshore, when the bank declared the borrowers in default for failing to comply with security ratios, or when the borrower elected to bring the loan onshore during the term of the loan.

A number of borrowers have both commenced and completed proceedings against the bank claiming that the banks breached their contractual duties, gave negligent advice, were in breach of fiduciary duties and in breach of their statutory duties under the Commonwealth Trade Practices Act 1974 and analogous state-based consumer legislation. Some borrowers have also claimed the banks have breached the Income Tax Assessment Act (Cth) 1936 by contractually obliging the borrower to pay withholding tax.[7] Whilst there are many common threads between the borrowers' cases, given the semi-standard presentation by the banks in promoting the facility, each case has to be examined individually. The borrowers have been successful in approximately half the decided cases; in all the cases it is apparent from the judgments that they are predominantly witness actions, with the credibility of the respective parties and their experts of paramount importance.

The losses incurred by borrowers and the subsequent litigation have attracted a lot of media attention in Australia and have featured prominently in the Federal Government Inquiry into the Banking System. Given the banks' aversion to detrimental publicity it would appear that only a small percentage of those cases where writs are issued actually proceed to trial and still less to a judicial determination.

CONCURRENT LIABILITY

The High Court of Australia has expressly adopted the principle that concurrent liability in contract and tort may exist between parties that are in a contractual

---

4. *Ibid.*, p. 296.
5. *The Bulletin*, 2 May 1989, p. 49.
6. *The Courier Mail*, Brisbane, 18 October 1986.
7. *Withholding tax*—a tax of 10 per cent of the interest paid by the borrower to the bank was payable to the Australian Taxation Office.

or commercial relationship.[8] In *Hawkins* v. *Clayton*[9] the issue was whether a solicitor who held a will for safe keeping had a duty to seek out the executor named in the will and inform him of the will's contents upon becoming aware of the death of the testatrix. Mason C.J. and Wilson J. agreed with the observation of Deane J. that: "There are no acceptable grounds for refusing to recognise the liability of a solicitor in tort for negligence in the performance of professional work for a client."[10]

After quoting the aforementioned passage, Hill J., in the Federal Court case of *David Securities Pty. Ltd. and Ors.* v. *Commonwealth Bank of Australia and Ors.*,[11] stated:

"The same is true of the duty of care owed by a banker to a customer assuming that the bank as part of its contractual relationship with its client accepts an obligation to advise. Thus, leaving aside questions of different periods of limitations or cases where the measure of damages in contract or tort might differ, the liability of an adviser, who is in a contractual relationship to give advice to a client in tort will be conterminous with his liability in contract."[12]

In this section of the chapter the borrowers' causes of action will be examined in the context of the decided cases and with reference to their efficacy.

CONTRACT

The contractual relationship between banker and customer consists of a general contract which is basic to all transactions between the parties and special contracts which come into being through the express acts or implied intentions of the parties.[13] In a contract to borrow in a foreign currency there are three possible "special contracts". There is the contractual provision to borrow and there may also be contractual provisions to advise or manage the borrowing. In claiming against the banks in contract the borrowers have sought to establish that the representations of the bank officers as to the stability of the exchange rate and low interest rate should be categorised as either express terms of or collateral warranties to the main agreements to borrow, the breach of which has caused the borrowers' loss. The borrowers have also pleaded that terms to advise or manage the facility were expressly stated by the bank officers or should be implied into the contract to borrow.

---

8. This is despite the Privy Council decision in *Tai Hing Cotton Mill Ltd.* v. *Liu Chong Hing Bank Ltd.* [1986] A.C. 80 where Lord Scarman delivering judgment stated that concurrent liability was inapplicable where a commercial relationship existed between the parties. The English Court of Appeal has held that an action against a professional (which may be defined as a commercial relationship) may be brought in tort or contract. *Forster* v. *Outred and Co.* [1982] 1 W.L.R. 86.
    9. (1988) 164 C.L.R. 539.
    10. *Ibid.*, p. 575.
    11. (Unreported), Federal Court of Australia, New South Wales Registry, 11 May 1989.
    12. *Ibid.*, p. 57.
    13. Hapgood M., *Paget's Law of Banking*, 10th Edn., Butterworths, London, p. 159.

(a) Express terms

The loan agreement and any management agreement entered into by the borrower, have, from the bank's point of view, been the vehicle to declare the loan in default, demand repayment or extra security and exclude themselves from any liability.[14] The bank's technical breach of the loan agreement was the only claim in which the plaintiff was successful in *McEvoy* v. *Australia and New Zealand Banking Group Ltd.*[15] In that case the bank witnesses conceded at the trial that an express term of the loan agreement had been breached, by charging the borrower a less favourable exchange rate for foreign currency transactions undertaken on his behalf. The bank loan agreement provided that the "spot rate" of exchange was to be the applicable rate, i.e., the actual rate existing at the time of the transaction in the foreign currency market. The bank conceded that the "carded rate" had been used, which is the rate commonly charged for foreign currency transactions, such as the buying or selling of travellers' cheques and small amounts of foreign currency. This rate includes an inbuilt commission for the bank and in *McEvoy*'s case the ANZ was obliged to refund $39,000.[16]

The principal claim of the borrower in that case was that the bank had a contractual duty to advise him and to take some action to prevent him losing money when the Australian dollar fell in February 1985. McEvoy claimed that there was a collateral contract arising out of a conversation with the bank manager in October 1982 when the main part of the loan was drawn down. The bank's defence was that on a number of occasions it had told McEvoy that it would not manage the loan whether for a fee or not.

On the facts it was found that the borrower had retained a range of other parties to advise him, and that the initial advisers' services had been terminated after disagreements with the plaintiff. After examination of the facts Brownie J. concluded:

"The terms of the contract which I find that the parties entered into, did not include the terms relied upon, that the defendant would provide the plaintiff with a managing or monitoring service, or that it would volunteer advice, or that it would provide advice of the type alleged upon request. The defendant did no more than agree to respond to the plaintiff's request for advice by which I think the parties intended that the defendant would provide oral advice, if and when requested, of the nature of information about current market rates, and the provisions of the expressions of opinion as to market trends and being advice different from and falling short of a service such as managing or monitoring the plaintiffs loan indebtedness. I do not accept that there was an oral collateral contract."[17]

14. In the decided cases little reliance has been placed by the banks on the exclusion clauses and disclaimers.

15. (Unreported), New South Wales, Supreme Court, 1 October 1987. A headnote and extract from the judgment of Brownie J. are reported at (1988) Aust. Torts Reports 67,351. The following reference is to the page number of the unreported decision.

16. To ascertain whether a borrower has been charged the spot or carded rate it is necessary to obtain the bank dealing slip applicable to each transaction. The dealing slip notes the time, date and precise exchange rate.

17. *McEvoy*, p. 26.

In the Supreme Court of South Australia decision of *Foti and Ors.* v. *Banque Nationale de Paris*,[18] although the plaintiffs were successful, Legoe J. dismissed their argument that there was an oral agreement partly reduced to writing. The borrowers maintained that in discussions with the bank prior to the loan agreement being entered into, the bank had represented that the loan would be for seven years and not two, and that the defendant bank would manage the borrowing. Although he found in favour of the borrowers that there was a common law duty of care that had been breached, Legoe J. stated that: "It is not possible on the evidence and material in this case to identify any particular act by one party which constitutes an offer to one party or by the other which amounts to an acceptance. The contract was entered into when the agreement was signed."[19]

The courts have been reluctant to find that collateral warranties or promises are given in consideration of the making of a contract. This is particularly the case when the collateral warranty is one that could reasonably be in the principal contract.[20]

The difficulty faced by the borrowers in rebutting the parol evidence rule and establishing that the contract was partly written and partly oral, is due in part to the nature of the representations which they have sought to introduce as terms or warranties. Counsel for the banks have successfully argued that representations as to the stability of the dollar and the minimal risk in borrowing were merely the opinions of the bank officers and therefore not actionable as terms of the contract.

(b) Implied terms

According to Professor Allan, "it is doubtful whether the mere relationship of banker and customer gives rise to an implied duty to advise the customer on financial matters".[21] In *David Securities* v. *Commonwealth Bank of Australia*, Hill J. found on the facts before him that the contract between the bank and the borrowers did not contain an implied term that the bank would advise on risk management techniques:

"first, the implication of such a term was not necessary to give business efficacy to the contract between the Bank and the applicants; second, if it be a different matter, such a term would not be so obvious that it would go without saying; and third, the term would be inconsistent with the express refusal by the Bank Manager to involve the Bank in

18. (Unreported), Supreme Court of South Australia, 17 March 1989. The decision of Legoe J. was upheld by the Full Court of the Supreme Court of South Australia (1990) Aust. Torts Reports 67, 835.

19. *Ibid.*, p. 117.

20. *Shepperd* v. *Municipality of Ryde* (1952) 85 C.L.R. 1 at 13.

21. Allan, D. "Bankers Liability for Financial Advice", (1987) 16 *Melbourne University Law Review* 213, at 216.

advising the borrowers which in any case could have involved the Bank in a position of conflict of interest."[22]

Further to the third factor, where a borrower seeks to imply a term that the bank should have managed the facility, that will in many cases be inconsistent with an express term of the loan agreement that any changes in currency will only be made on the borrower's instructions. In *Ferneyhough* v. *Westpac Banking Corporation*,[23] Lee J. distinguished David Securities on the facts and, in addition to finding that the bank had been negligent and breached section 52 of the Trade Practices Act, found that there had been a breach of the implied term of the banker–customer relationship to give adequate information and assistance to an unsophisticated borrower who sought advice.[24]

In *Hawkins* v. *Clayton*, Deane J. stated that where a contract is partly written and partly oral, implied terms may be established by mercantile usage, professional practice or a past course of dealing between the parties.[25] In the context of foreign currency borrowing, if a long standing customer of the bank entered into such a borrowing and the previous course of dealings between the parties indicate the customer's reliance on the bank, and the bank actively involved itself in the management and supervision of its customers' affairs, a term to monitor or manage could be implied. It is fair to say that this would only occur in exceptional circumstances.

(c) Standard of care

The standard of care applicable to a contractual obligation will depend on the construction of the contract. The courts will not normally construe the contract to guarantee the outcome of any service provided by the bank as adviser or manager.[26] If a borrower was able to prove on the facts that the adviser or manager had clearly guaranteed a particular result, e.g., nominated a net cost of funds for a particular period, and that was not attained, the standard of care would be irrelevant where the terms of the contract are ambiguous. A relevant factor for the court to consider would be the state of knowledge of the customer in the circumstances. In the aforementioned example, the more familiar the borrower is with the risks involved, the more likely he is to know the result cannot be guaranteed, and accordingly it is less likely that the court would make such a finding.

In *Lloyd* v. *Citicorp*, Rogers J. examined the standard of care applicable

---

22. *David Securities*, p. 55.

23. (Unreported), Federal Court of Australia, Queensland Registry, 18 November 1991.

24. Weaver and Craigie, *The Law Relating to Banker and Customer in Australia* (2nd edn, Law Book Company) at p. 2737 question "the correctness of the basis upon which the trial judge considered it appropriate to base his decision in part upon an implied contractual term."

25. *Hawkins* v. *Clayton*, at 554.

26. *Stafford* v. *Conti Commodity Services* [1981] 1 All E.R. 691.

where the bank had admitted a contractual duty to advise. He stated that where the market is speculative, incorrect advice may be given to a client but not represent a breach of the contractual duty to advise so long as it is given in good faith. Accordingly the contractual duty imposed upon the bank required the "exercise of skill and diligence which a reasonably competent careful foreign exchange adviser would exercise ... I would take leave to doubt that the content of the duty would be very high."[27]

The contractual duties owed to a borrower who entered into a separate management agreement were examined by the Supreme Court of New South Wales in *Davcot and Ors* v. *Custom Credit and Ors*.[28] The borrowers were exposed to a foreign currency risk by way of a simulated foreign currency loan. That loan was procured by Custom Credit and was to be managed by First National Limited (FNL). A simulated loan involves a borrowing of Australian dollars at domestic interest rates, accompanied by an entry into non-deliverable foreign currency transactions which are supposed to be vigorously managed to close out and reopen those transactions during the period of the loan, having regard to exchange rate movements. The borrowers and FNL entered into an agreement which contained a wide discretion as to the form of management to be adopted. The management letter authorised FNL to act "as and when it saw fit to attempt to minimise any currency risks existing under the loan facility or to do anything it considered necessary or appropriate to further the interest of the borrower". It was submitted on behalf of FNL that it was entitled to adopt a range of open positions and hedge those positions as seemed appropriate, enter into day trades, and from time to time place the loan in full simulation or bring it fully back onshore. Wood J. found this submission to be incorrect: "Properly construed I do not consider that the loan documents and management authority as originally executed went so far as to permit such form of unrestricted speculative dealing in the foreign exchange market."[29]

This finding did not assist the plaintiffs because his Honour found that during the rollover in which substantial losses were sustained, they were sustained as a result of transactions that were authorised and encouraged by them. The plaintiffs could not assert that the losses arising from the wider forms of transaction which they participated in or approved were causally connected to any breach on the part of FNL.

The fact that the borrower had in this case participated in and encouraged speculative transactions can be contrasted with the typical physical currency borrowings where the borrower was unaware of the risks involved in transactions being undertaken or what was meant by a transaction which was undertaken or recommended by a bank. The plaintiffs also argued that their

27. *Lloyd*, p. 288.
28. (Unreported), New South Wales, Supreme Court, 27 May 1988.
29. *Ibid.*, p. 151.

instructions were not always complied with. Wood J. held that management must be coupled with the realities of the foreign exchange market, and that:

"in managing the foreign exchange exposures under forward contracts taken in this wider form of dealing it became necessary for F.N.L. to make decisions as to the timing of the entry into a fully simulated position, the taking of separate legs at different times and hedging and trading (from day to day). The use of these management tools depended on the state of the market at any given time and dealers' perception of it".[30]

His Honour found there was no evidence that the failure on the part of the defendants to carry out dealing transactions other than those which would have been carried out by a careful and prudent advisor did cause the borrower loss. Accordingly, he rejected as impracticable and of any unduly high standard, the proposition that careful management should have protected the borrower against all adverse currency movements.

TORT

To be successful in an action in tort against the bank, a borrower must prove to the court that it was owed a duty of care that has been breached either by negligent acts, omissions or misrepresentations and that as a consequence a loss has been suffered. Negligent acts may include a claim by a borrower that the bank has mismanaged the loan or failed to manage when it had undertaken to do so. Negligent omissions include claims that the bank failed to warn the borrower of the risks associated with the loan and failed to take action to protect the borrower from losses that would be sustained during the period of rapid deterioration of the dollar. Negligent misrepresentations would include claims that bank officers misled the borrowers as to the stability of the relationship between the Swiss franc and the Australian dollar. It is on the facts of each individual case that the courts have had to decide whether any of the aforementioned claims can be sustained.

(a) The duty of care

To establish whether a duty of care exists between banker and customer in the circumstances it is necessary to demonstrate that there exists between the parties the requisite degree of proximity which is used as a limitation on the test of reasonable foreseeability. Where a claim is for economic loss, reliance will be the key factor in determining whether there is a duty of care between the giver and the recipient of the advice. The High Court's rationalisation of this area of law is

---

30. *Ibid.*, p. 153.

evident in cases such as *Jaensch* v. *Coffey*,[31] *Sutherland Shire Council* v. *Heyman*,[32] *Stevens* v. *Brodribb Sawmilling Co. Pty. Ltd.*,[33] *San Sebastian Pty. Ltd.* v. *The Minister*[34] and is summarised by Messrs Quinlan and Gardiner in their article "New developments with respect to the duty of care in tort"[35] as follows:

"Proximity in its broad sense as a general conception is now firmly established in Australia as a tool of analysis to be used as an anterior control device, particularly in new and developing categories involving non physical damage and even in exceptional cases of physical damage.

Proximity involves more than a factual assessment of the closeness of a relationship between parties in a particular category of case, it involves also a judgment of the legal consequences.

Proximity includes physical circumstantial and causal proximity, but the recognition and relative importance of particular factors will vary from category to category."

The correct statement of principle to determine whether a duty of care exists in this context was laid down by Barwick C.J. in *M.L.C.* v. *Evatt*[36] as follows:

"1.   ... the circumstances must be such as to have caused the speaker or to be calculated to cause a reasonable person in the position of the speaker to realise that he is being trusted by the recipient of the information or advice to give information which the recipient believes the speaker to possess or to which the recipient believes the speaker to have access or to give advice, about a matter upon or in receipt of which the recipient believes the speaker to possess a capacity or opportunity for judgment, in either case the subject matter of the information or advice being of a serious or business nature. It seems to me that it is this element of trust which the one has on the other which is at the heart of the relevant relationship.

2.   ... the speaker must realise or the circumstances be such that he ought to have realised that the recipient intends to act upon the information or advice in respect of his property or of himself in connection with some matter of business or serious consequence.

3.   ... the circumstances must be such that it is reasonable in all the circumstances for the recipient to seek or accept, and to rely upon the utterance of the speaker."

This statement of principle was accepted by Foster J. in *Chiarabaglio and Anor* v. *Westpac Banking Corporation*[37] as the law in Australia in determining the existence of a duty of care between the bank and the customer.

31. (1984) 155 C.L.R. 549.
32. (1985) 157 C.L.R. 424.
33. (1986) 160 C.L.R. 16.
34. (1986) 51 A.L.J.R. 41.
35. 62 *Australian Law Journal* 347, at 361.
36. (1968) 122 C.L.R. 556, at 571.
37. (1989) 11 A.T.P.R. 50,602 at p. 50, 622: an appeal to the Full Federal Court was dismissed (1991) A.T.P.R. (Digest) 46–067.

(b) The standard of care

The standard of care required to discharge the duty once established has been summarised by the English courts as follows: "A professional will not be held liable for mere slips, errors of lapses of judgment although if an error of judgment is well below proper standards applicable and not in accordance with the standards of a reasonably competent professional of a particular calling, negligence will be made out."[38]

The courts have demanded clear evidence before determining that the professional has been negligent in discharging his duties. In the foreign currency cases expert evidence has been used extensively and will be discussed shortly. In the decisions to date, the speculative nature of the market, the commercial sophistication of the borrower, the novelty of the facility and the relationship between the lender and borrower have all been relevant factors in determining the appropriate standard of care owed by the bank to its customer and whether it has been breached.

The standard of care applicable between adviser and client when both parties were already in the speculative market was examined by Rogers J. In *Lloyd*'s case. His Honour adopted as the appropriate standard that identified by Mocatta J. in *Stafford* v. *Conti Commodity Services*. In that case the defendants were brokers on the London commodities futures market. The plaintiff entered into a number of transactions and lost heavily, and brought an action for damages for allegedly negligent advice. After making reference to the fact that the commodities futures market was a notoriously wayward and erratic market, His Honour stated:

"The duty of the defendants was not in dispute between the parties. Counsel on both sides were prepared to accept what was said in Charlesworth on Negligence (6th Edition 1977, para. 1021) in relation to the liability of stockbrokers who in this respect, it was agreed, did not differ from commodity brokers: with regard to the customer a stockbroker's duty lies in contract and not in tort and stockbrokers are liable for failing to use that skill and diligence which a reasonably competent and careful stockbroker would exercise ... Counsel for the defendants submitted, plainly rightly in my judgment, that a broker cannot always be right in the advice that he gives in relation to so wayward and rapidly changing market as the commodities futures market."[39]

Although Mocatta J. expressed the duty in a contractual context, Wood J., in *Davcot*, stated: "I see no reason in a case where no express duty was spelled out in the contractual documents, why a dual duty should not arise in tort. Nothing however turns on this."[40]

Thus it would appear that where an adviser or manager has been retained the standard of care in both contract and tort will be identical.

In *Chiarabaglio and Anor* v. *Westpac Banking Corporation* and *Spice* v.

---

38. *Whitehouse* v. *Jordan* [1981] 1 W.L.R. 246.
39. [1981] 1 All E.R. 691, at p. 696.
40. *Davcot*, p. 121.

Westpac Banking Corporation,[41] Foster J. distinguished *Lloyd*'s case on the basis that in the aforementioned cases the decision which the borrowers had to make on the basis of information and advice supplied by the bank was whether or not to enter into the loan in the first place. The duty owed by the bank in those circumstances was to provide a full and fair explanation of the loan facility, including all the advantages and disadvantages of that particular market. The court in both cases accepted the borrower's assertion that if they had been made aware of the substantial complexity in managing or monitoring the facility they would not have entered into the borrowing. The court found on the facts that the bank had consciously adopted the role of the adviser and had failed to achieve the standard that could be expected from a reasonably prudent financial adviser in the circumstances.

The suggestion that the nature and extent of the advice required from a foreign currency adviser would vary with the known commercial experience of the client was raised by Rogers J. in *Lloyd*'s case. He stated:

"It seems to me likely that the advice to be given to a treasurer of a multinational incorporation in relation to dealing in foreign currencies will be minimal compared to that required to be given to a farmer in western New South Wales who, to the knowledge of the adviser, is entering the foreign exchange market for the first time.

Accordingly, it seems to be that one of the matters to which attention needs to be paid is the commercial and financial background of the borrower and lender at the time of the transaction."[42]

In the light of this statement, pleadings sought to portray the plaintiff as lacking commercial sophistry and unfamiliar with business matters. It would appear from a number of subsequent judgments that the ambit as to the nature and extent of advice to be given has been widened considerably. In *Davcot* the directors of the borrower had considerable assets and commercial expertise but none had any prior experience with foreign currency borrowings. Further, the son of one of the directors had claimed expertise as a consultant in foreign currency transactions. In that case it was held that the financier owed the plaintiffs a duty to exercise the skill and diligence of a prudent financier in respect of the transactions undertaken and to supply information which was both accurate and sufficient to enable the borrower as an intending borrower to make a decision whether to take it up or not. Legoe J., in *Foti*, found that the plaintiff's commercial experience as a tax agent gave him no specialist knowledge about foreign exchange rates, loans in foreign currency, hedging or forward exchange rates and would not limit the duty owed to him. The duty on the adviser would be limited only where the borrower had previous experience in foreign currency borrowings. This approach was also accepted by Foster J. in *Chiarabaglio* and *Spice*. In the former case, the borrower was a successful businessman with extensive experience as a property developer. However, he

---

41. (Unreported), Federal Court of Australia, New South Wales Registry, 1 September 1989: an appeal to the Full Federal Court of Australia was dismissed (1990) 12 A.T.P.R. 51,386.
42. *Lloyd*, p. 8.

had never previously borrowed in a foreign currency. It was held that he was owed a duty which extended to an adequate explanation of exchange risk, a recommendation that he take independent advice, an explanation of the importance of monitoring foreign currency fluctuations and a full explanation of recognised loss limiting mechanisms. In *Spice*'s case the borrower was a retired solicitor who had travelled extensively abroad and had been involved in the importation of goods. Although he was credited with a knowledge of how exchange rates worked, he was not aware of the intricacies of foreign currency borrowing or the risk minimisation strategies available.

The novelty of foreign currency borrowing as a financing technique was considered by Wood J. in *Davcot* (in the context of a simulated foreign currency loan) to be one of the factors to be taken into account in considering the extent of the duty of care. He stated:

"I am satisfied that as packager of a new and complex facility, Custom Credit did owe the plaintiffs a duty to exercise the skill and diligence of a prudent financier in respect of the transaction extending to the supply of information which was both accurate and sufficient to enable Davcot, as an intending borrower, to make an informed decision whether to take it up or not."[43]

Hill J., in *David Securities*, in response to the plaintiff's argument that the bank had a duty to advise because it was marketing a new and complex product found that:

"Even if it could be said that the making available of a foreign currency loan is a matter of such inherent danger that it should be seen as involving strict liability along the lines of the principles discussed in *Rylands* v *Fletcher* (1866) LR 1 Ex 265 (which I doubt) the content of the duty of the bank would be to do no more than warn of the dangerous quality inherent in the product. There is no requirement that a purveyor of dangerous substances who has warned of the dangers inherent in them go further and instruct the user as to the safeguards that may be employed in the use of such substances: *Norton Australia Pty. Ltd.* v. *Streets Ice Cream Pty. Ltd.* (1970) 120 C.L.R. 635, p. 644 per Barwick. C.J."[44]

Foster J., in *Chiarabaglio* and *Spice*, in contrast found that the duty to be imposed upon the bank extended to explaining to the borrower both the importance of monitoring currency fluctuations and recognised loss limiting techniques, but does not appear to have addressed the product liability issue.

This aspect of the loans received considerable media attention and was the main grievance of the Foreign Currency Borrowers Association (F.C.B.A.) which was formed in August 1988. The argument of the F.C.B.A. was that despite the newness and unavailability of such loans to borrowers of less than $500,000 before 1982, little or no research was done by the banks. Rogers J.[45]

---

43. *Davcot*, p. 117.
44. *David Securities*, p. 55.
45. Rogers J. after hearing expert evidence in the matter of *Perciballi* v. *Westpac*, invited counsel to amend their pleadings to take up the product liability issue. That case was settled in November 1988. *Sydney Morning Herald*, Saturday 10 December 1988.

was sympathetic to this argument and in addressing counsel in *Perciballi* v. *Westpac* stated that:

"Having heard a few of these cases now it seems to me that one ought to consider whether there is not a real problem in the formulation of the duty of care that has not really been explored. What I was wondering about was, if it is true to say that the banks and financial intermediaries were presented with a new opportunity at this time, in the middle of 1984, and that there was some enthusiasm for promoting loans denominated in foreign currencies, then it might be said that there was a duty on the banks to fully explore the risk inherent in these loans being taken up by customers, before promoting them—a bit like the US Surgeon-General's warning on the financial packages: If you take one of these loans you may be in real financial danger ...

Here is a bank in a competitive market place pushing a new product, and it should jolly well research it and find out its dangers before it markets. It is almost a *Rylands* v. *Fletcher* situation where you are unleashing on unsophisticted borrowers a dangerous product."

In the borrower's unsuccessful appeal to the Full Federal Court in *David Securities*,[46] the Full Court rejected the analogy between a foreign currency loan and a dangerous product. The court stated:

"It may be accepted that there will always be a risk of an adverse movement in the rate of exchange. But it does not follow that a foreign loan transaction is something 'dangerous' let alone dangerous in itself ... all that can be said is that it is possible that such a transaction may result in some economic gain in certain events or in some economic loss if other contingencies occur. A foreign borrowing is not of itself dangerous merely because opportunities for profit or loss may exist."[47]

Mr Justice Rogers in a paper reported in the *Journal of Banking and Finance Law and Practice*[48] suggested that another factor in measuring the duty of care should be the recognition by the bank's senior management of the potential problems of a foreign currency borrowing. The problems included the lack of trained staff and the inability to manage the foreign currency exposure. Of crucial importance in determining the extent of the duty of care will be the relationship of the parties. In *Foti* it was held that the relationship between the parties was not confined to the traditional banker/customer relationship and that it will be the facts of the particular case that determine the extent of the duty. Legoe, J. found that:

"... because of the banks involvement with the plaintiff by negotiating a loan of this particular kind and by arranging the drawdown of the Swiss francs, and by submitting the facility offers which were accepted by the plaintiffs, and by opening and operating the Torrensville Shopping Plaza rental account with the relevant charges and financial benefits to the banks, I am of the opinion that the defendant bank involved itself far more closely with the plaintiffs than a mere arm's length agreement to lend a sum of money. Furthermore, the relationship was not just that of acting on behalf of its customer. There was both the professional banking element in the transaction and the personal rights and

46. *David Securities Pty. Ltd.* v. *Commonwealth Bank of Australia* (1990) 93 A.L.R. 271.
47. *Ibid.*, p. 291.
48. (1990) 1 J.B.F.L.P. 201.

duties of a bank lending money to a group of people in the particular way in which this transaction was set up. The proximity of the parties to each other and their respective rights and duties arising from the negotiations was as to the actual performance of several transactions clearly giving rise to a duty of care in the circumstances."[49]

It was held that placing a hedge required specialist knowledge which the bank had and which the plaintiffs relied upon. After hearing expert evidence his Honour held that a hedge should have been put in place between March 1985 and May 1986. It is worth noting that in this case B.N.P. were not the usual bankers of the plaintiffs, therefore his Honour's emphasis that the relationship was closer than that of simply borrower and lender. This can be contrasted with the position in most cases where the lender was in fact the usual banker of the borrower. Foster J., in *Chiarabaglio*, identified the relationship as a "local banker–customer relationship of the best possible kind".[50] The mutual regard and trust that existed between the parties readily enabled the court to establish the total reliance of the borrower on the bank. According to Wood J. in *Davcot* "the interposition of a financial adviser or solicitor retained by the potential borrower would limit the extent of the disclosure necessary".[51] Although this was not the position in *Davcot*, both Brownie J. at first instance and Rogers J. on appeal identified McEvoy's retention of other foreign currency advisers as a significant factor in refuting his alleged reliance on the bank.

In his appeal, McEvoy claimed that the bank had voluntarily assumed a responsibility to give him advice as and when he requested it, in relation to the foreign currency borrowing. It was alleged that the bank's failure promptly or immediately to tender such advice over the course of a five-day period of extreme exchange rate volatility in February 1985 caused him a foreseeable economic loss. Drawing heavily on the findings of fact of Brownie J., Rogers J., giving judgment on behalf of the New South Wales Court of Appeal,[52] dismissed the appeal. His Honour acknowledged that whilst there was confusion amongst the bank witnesses as to what advice, if any, would be provided, McEvoy had failed to prove that the bank agreed to provide the type of advice service that he alleged it would. In reviewing the evidence, Rogers J. gave considerable cognisance to the conclusion of Brownie J. that McEvoy was not a reliable witness. In holding that the bank had not breached its limited obligation to give advice, his Honour emphasised that the bank had at all times eschewed the task of loan management.

In *Parton* v. *Australia and New Zealand Banking Group Ltd.*,[53] the plaintiff was a finance broker who was found to have undertaken his own independent enquiries as to the feasibility of borrowing in a foreign currency. Giles J. in the

---

49. *Foti*, p. 123.
50. *Chiarabaglio*, p. 50,605.
51. *Davcot*, p. 118.
52. *McEvoy* v. *Australia and New Zealand Banking Group Ltd.* (1990) Aust. Torts Reports 67,690.
53. (Unreported) New South Wales Supreme Court December 1991.

Supreme Court of New South Wales found that the plaintiff had not relied on anything said by the bank.

Ultimately the content of the duty of care will depend on the circumstances and the extent to which the lender is acting in the capacity of an adviser. Where the court finds that the bank was acting as an adviser the bank has a duty to give a full and fair explanation.

THE TRADE PRACTICES ACT

The Commonwealth Trade Practices Act 1974 creates an independent cause of action relevant to cases based on negligent advice. Section 52 provides that a corporation shall not in trade or commerce engage in conduct that is misleading or deceptive or likely to mislead or deceive.

The advent of the Cross Vesting Scheme[54] has meant that the Trade Practices Act is being used to an increasing degree in State Supreme Court cases involving allegations of negligent financial advice as alternative pleas to those in contract and tort. Whether particular conduct is misleading or deceptive is a question of fact to be determined in the context of the relevant circumstances of the case. Those circumstances do not require an intent on the part of the party giving the advice to mislead or deceive.[55] A bank which acted honestly or reasonably in advising its customer to borrow offshore may nonetheless have engaged in misleading or deceptive conduct. To be eligible for relief it will be necessary for the applicant[56] to show that the bank's conduct in fact caused his loss. Where the misrepresentation alleged relates to the entry into the loan facility, causation will usually be readily established.[57] Section 82 provides that a person suffering loss or damage as a result of a contravention of Parts IV or V of the Act may recover the amount of loss or damage against that person. Ancillary remedies available under the Act will be discussed shortly.

In *Kullack* v. *Australian and New Zealand Banking Group Ltd.*[58] Pincus J., in the Federal Court (Queensland Registry), found that the applicant failed to prove any of the factual allegations she made against the bank and he therefore had no cause to consider the application of section 52. In *Chiarabaglio* and *Spice* Foster J.'s finding of negligence obviated any discussion of, or the need for, reliance on this section. His Honour simply stated that the causes of action under section 52 were made out within the meaning of the authorities. The

---

54. Jurisdiction of Courts (Miscellaneous Amendments) Act 1987 Commonwealth and the Jurisdiction of Courts (Cross Vesting) Act 1987 Commonwealth provide that causes of action previously the domain of the Commonwealth Federal Courts are to be pleaded in the various State Supreme Courts.

55. *Hornsby Building Information Centre* v. *Sydney Building Information Centre* (1978) 140 C.L.R. 216.

56. Applicant instead of Plaintiff is used in Federal Court pleadings.

57. *Spice* and *Chiarabaglio*. This issue will be discussed in more detail.

58. (1988) A.T.P.R. 40–861.

borrower's section 52 claim was examined in *David Securities* where Hill J. considered that claim first (it was conceded by the applicant's counsel that unless they were successful under this cause of action it was unlikely they would succeed against the bank on the other counts). The borrowers claimed that:

1. It was misleading and deceptive for the bank manager to say it would be advantageous to borrow in a foreign currency.
2. The bank's failure to advise of risk minimisation techniques was misleading and deceptive.

On the facts Hill J. found that the first claim could not be made out:

"... it is not possible to select a phrase used at one meeting which is admittedly misleading and to rely upon that phrase as constituting misleading or deceptive conduct giving rise to loss when the phrase, seen in the context of the whole advice given over the proper period can be seen to have been put in its proper context so that it is no longer able to be seen as misleading or deceptive."

In respect of the applicant's second argument, he simply found that:

"failure to advise on a particular matter can only constitute misleading or deceptive conduct if the person remaining silent had a duty to so advise. See *Rhone Poulenc Agrochemie SA and Anor* v. *U.I.M. Chemical Services and Anor* (1986) 68 ALR 77; *Henjo Investments Pty. Ltd.* v. *Collins Marrickville Pty. Ltd.* (1988) A.T.P.R. 40–850 at p. 49 153 per Lockhart, J. with whose reasons Burchett, J. agreed ..."[59]

His Honour concluded that there was no express or implied term that the bank should advise on risk minimisation techniques and the applicant's second claim should also fail. The rationale of Hill J. is important as he imposed a common law test as to whether there was a positive duty on the bank to advise. The borrowers appealed to the Full Court of the Federal Court who unanimously dismissed the appeal.[60] The Full Court stated that it was "now well established that silence, that is the failure to advise on a significant matter when the task of advising has been embraced or undertaken or there is a duty to advise, may demonstrate a breach of section 52 in the right circumstances".[61]

The circumstances where a bank could be liable for engaging in misleading and deceptive conduct were critically examined by the New South Wales Court of Appeal in *Commonwealth Bank of Australia* v. *Mehta*.[62] The bank appealed Rogers C.J.'s decision at first instance[63] where it was held to be misleading and deceptive for the bank not to complete a presentation, thereby giving the borrower a false sense of security. In allowing the appeal the Full Court found that the borrower had not relied upon the bank's presentation. The Full Court identified the following factors in reaching that conclusion:

59. *David Securities*, p. 52.
60. (1990) 23 F.C.R. 1.
61. *Ibid.*, p. 24.
62. (1991) 23 N.S.W.L.R. 84.
63. (1990) Aust. Tort Reports 68,119.

(1) the borrower did not seek advice from the bank as to the merits or otherwise of a foreign currency loan;

(2) the borrower continued with the loan despite the express reservations of his accountant; and

(3) despite the invitation by the bank, the bank's foreign currency managers were not consulted.

These factors together with the failure by the borrower to give evidence of relying upon a complete explanation by the bank meant that it was not possible to conclude that the explanation was a complete exposition of the risks in borrowing in a foreign currency and as such was not misleading or deceptive.

On the issue of whether tort liability is a necessary prerequisite for liability under section 52 Weaver and Craigie conclude that:

"the majority of judges (*Foti, Chiarabaglio, Spice, David Securities*) appear to be disposed to approach the matter from the point of view of a duty of care in tort, with resultant questions relating to reliance and causation, and to assume the existence or non-existence of a liability under section 52 ... will depend on whether or not a liability exists in tort."[64]

Rogers C.J. in *Mehta* v. *Commonwealth Bank of Australia* suggested that "questions of liability in tort may have been superseded by statute".[65]

Samuels J.A. in the New South Wales Court of Appeal expressly agreed with the view that it is inappropriate for a claim under section 52 to stand or fall with a claim under the general law. This approach was adopted by Beaumont J. in *Donkin and Anor* v. *AGC (Advances) Ltd.*[66] who found that although the lender had not engaged in conduct that was misleading or deceptive in relation to its own expertise or the explaining of the risk of loss there was a common law duty of care to advise the borrower of the steps available to minimise the risk of loss.

FIDUCIARY DUTIES

Fiduciary relationships arise between parties that exhibit the special qualities of trust reliance and confidence between one another. Such relationships are therefore presumed to exist between solicitor and client, parent and child the trustee and beneficiary. The law of equity will impose strict duties on the "trusted party" not to take advantage of that position of trust by competing against the other party and to fully disclose the nature and circumstances of the relationship where there is a potential for conflict of interest.

The relationship as between banker and customer does not of itself give rise to a fiduciary relationship between the parties. The onus is therefore on the plaintiff to prove that the bank was in a special relationship of trust, reliance and

---

64. Weaver and Craigie, *op. cit.*, p. 2740.
65. *Ibid.*, p. 2741.
66. 103 A.L.R. 95.

confidence as against the borrower. In *Woods* v. *Martins Bank*,[67] the bank advertised its managers as investment advisers and recommended, as an investment to its customer, shares in a company which the bank knew to be in a precarious financial position. It was held that a fiduciary relationship existed between the parties. Hill J. in *David Securities* observed that:

"this finding which seems to depend rather on the character of the manager as an adviser than as a banker, hardly seems necessary for the resolution of the case ... it will be noted that the Martins Bank Case was decided before the House of Lords in *Hedley Byrne and Co. Ltd.* v. *Heller and Partners Ltd.* [1964] AC 465 had decided that a liability for negligent advice lay in negligence, and the discussion of the duty arising out of a fiduciary relationship should be seen in that light."[68]

His Honour went on to distinguish the New South Wales Supreme Court case of *Catt* v. *Marac Australia Limited*[69] where Rogers J. held that fiduciary duties were owed by an investment adviser, a merchant bank and an air freight company to a number of partnerships of doctors and dentists in relationship to a tax minimisation scheme. The scheme involved the partnerships' borrowing through the merchant bank and investing in jet aircraft which were then leased to the freight company. The freight company went into liquidation and it was revealed that the purchase price of the jet aircraft had been inflated and the investment adviser had received secret commissions. The borrowers alleged they were owed fiduciary duties by the aforementioned parties and that they had been breached. The bank (which was the most viable of the defendants) claimed that it was only the supplier of finance and in that context did not owe a fiduciary duty. It was held that such a duty was owed albeit indirectly to the plaintiffs because the bank had, along with the adviser, assumed the role of promoter and had actively participated in the arrangement.

Although unsuccessful in *David Securities* the principle enunciated in *Catt* v. *Marac Australia Ltd.* could be applied to a foreign currency loan contract where the borrower enters into the loan with the bank via an intermediary finance broker/adviser. This would necessitate the borrower proving that the bank actively participated in the activities of the intermediary in terms of promoting the loans and inducing people to enter into the facility through promotional material calculated to mislead or deceive, together with the payment of secret commissions. Whilst many foreign currency loans were arranged through loan brokers, this aspect has yet to be judicially considered.

In the decided cases the courts have demonstrated their traditional reluctance to find fiduciary relationships in commercial transactions as no borrowers have been successful in pleading such a duty. The consequences of findings such as in *Catt* v. *Marac* according to Professor Allan are to place very onerous duties on suppliers of finance and a heavy responsibility on advisers and promoters.

67. [1959] 1 Q.B. 55.
68. *David Securities*, p. 63.
69. (1986) 9 N.S.W.L.R. 639.

"It may be that responsibilities of this nature are not reasonable and would jeopardize many financing and commercial transactions, if the responsibilities are imposed without any reference to the character experience wisdom and motives of the client investor. The investor may well be a person of some experience and education who is speculating for high and possible tax free profits and who could legitimately be said to be taking some risks."[70]

An alternative equitable claim for undue influence may be available to those borrowers who were forced to bring their loans on shore without having the opportunity to obtain independent financial and legal advice. Where a borrower was threatened with the sale of secured properties or bankruptcy, unless refinancing the loan was done on the bank's terms (such terms including releasing the bank from liability) undue influence may be made out. To succeed, the borrower will have to established that the new arrangement was "manifestly disadvantageous".[71] Although this test is a subjective one, there is no clear authority as to what is meant by it.[72]

In the Supreme Court of New South Wales Mr and Mrs Rahme (who were co-applicants in the *David Securities* litigation) applied to have the guarantees and mortgages they had given set aside on the grounds that they were obtained by unconscionable conduct by the bank and alleged injustice within the meaning of the Contracts Review Act 1980 (NSW). The New South Wales Court of Appeal[73] upheld the decision of Brysdon J. that the plaintiffs had already had the opportunity in the Federal Court proceedings to have these claims determined.

The appellants in *David Securities* also appealed to the High Court of Australia on the issue of whether withholding tax paid had been paid under mistake of law. The liability to pay the withholding taxes were imposed on the borrower in the security documentation and were paid by the borrower in ignorance of the prohibition of such payments by a borrower under section 261 of the Income Tax Assessment Act (Cth). The High Court in a landmark decision found that the rule preventing the recovery of money paid under mistake of law was not part of the law of Australia.

THE EVIDENCE

In litigation the demeanour and credibility of witnesses in the manner of their giving evidence will be crucial to the outcome of the case. Peculiar to the foreign currency cases is the fact that the representations alleged to have been made were some years before the litigation and in the intervening years the parties, both plaintiff and defendant, have become far more expert in the subject matter of the

70. Alan D.E. *op. cit.* at p. 222.
71. *National Westminster Bank Plc* v. *Morgan* [1983] 3 All E.R. 85.
72. Penn, Shea and Arora, *The Law Relating to Domestic Banking*, 1987, p. 303.
73. (1991) A.T.P.R. 52,426.

litigation. Some commentators take the view that it is the banks who are disadvantaged evidentially, as it is the borrower rather than the banker who will have a better recollection of a particular set of circumstances. It is necessary for bank officers to "rely on diaries and other internal memoranda and the courts seem prone to attach little weight to these as a comprehensive record of what took place at what relevant time".[74] In attempting to establish whether the bank was negligent in its acts, omissions or representations the court must decide without the benefit of hindsight, on the basis of the knowledge of the parties when the loan was drawn down.

The courts are assisted in this by expert testimony provided by both parties. A "team" of experts including a "banking" expert, a foreign currency dealer and an applied economist are necessary to convey both a practical and theoretical appreciation of the foreign currency markets both at the time the loan was drawn and at selected stages over the history of the loan. On the basis of the expert evidence in the *Foti* case Legoe J. was able to ascertain when a reasonable and prudent foreign currency adviser/manager would have hedged the loan. In *Chiarabaglio* the evidence called on behalf of the applicants satisfied Foster J. that, at the time the borrowers were engaged in initial discussions with bank representatives, there were known and substantial risks involved in the offshore borrowing, and that a person such as the plaintiff should have been advised not to enter the loan at all. The applicant's experts were of the opinion that such a facility was singularly inappropriate for a domestic property developer and should only have been available to: "sophisticated borrowers financially able to absorb losses and with management skills of a high order necessary to engage in the involved procedures of monitoring and hedging which would be required to control losses in the event of adverse movements in the exchange rates".[75]

His Honour preferred the applicant's expert evidence to the bank's and was satisfied that they had a far better appreciation of the practical situation in 1981 and 1982.

Where the management of the loan is in dispute, a foreign currency dealer will be retained to reconstruct from the internal working documents discovered from the bank the particular transactions in dispute and to summarise for the court's benefit the nature and effect of the transactions. In recent cases the ambit of discovery has been extended beyond those documents relating directly to the borrower's loan to include internal bank policy documents which are discovered with the assistance of specially retained bank experts. Such documents as the ones that came to light in *Chiarabaglio* reveal how much the bank's senior management knew about the pitfalls for borrowers in such facilities and how the foreign currency loans were marketed aggressively.

"It is plain that at high management level there was a full appreciation of the fact that there were significant risks involved in offshore borrowing both from the point of view of

74. Weaver and Craigie, *op. cit.*, p. 2740.
75. *Chiarabaglio*, p. 50,626.

the customer borrower and the bank as lender ... it is clear that it was bank policy that risks should be fully explained and that the borrower himself should be considered in relation to his suitability to handle such a loan."[76]

These documents and others which suggested *intra* bank competition between various managers as to the marketing of a loan, led Foster J. to his conclusion that the enthusiasm to sell the loans may have led to the breaches of which the applicants complained. The existence of these documents has become common knowledge among potential litigants, as the Foreign Currency Borrowers Association has, in addition in its more legitimate functions, acted as a clearing house for discovered documents for the major banks between its borrower members. Such activities have justifiably raised the ire of the banks and necessitated judicial intervention.

The consequences for a bank of failing to make full and complete discovery were examined by the Full Court of the Federal Court in *Quade* v. *Commonwealth Bank of Australia*.[77] The Full Court held that the failure by the bank to give proper discovery meant that the initial proceedings had not been regularly conducted. The documents that had come to light suggested that the bank at the time of the loan in question had actually promoted foreign currency loans as a matter of policy which meant that the bank officers involved may have played down the risks associated with a foreign currency loan. The failure of the bank to discover this material entitled the borrower to a new trial.

In *D.F. Lyons* v. *Commonwealth Bank of Australia*[78] the applicants tried to adduce similar fact evidence in an attempt to infer that the same representations had been made to them by a particular bank employee as had been made to other customers. Despite the fact that the representations and presentations were similar Gummow J. took the view that the characteristics were not so similar as to render their evidence relevant.

LIMITATION PERIOD

The time available to a borrower to commence an action will depend upon how the action is framed. All states in Australia have limitation statutes[79] which prescribe the period within which proceedings to enforce a right must be taken, after which the right of action will be forever barred. In contract, where it is alleged that an agreement to manage a foreign currency loan was breached by the bank, or that the bank had agreed to take a course of action and has failed to

76. *Ibid.*, p. 50,626.
77. 27 F.C.R. 569.
78. (1991) A.T.P.R. 41,102.
79. Limitation Act 1969 (NSW); Limitation of Actions Act 1958 (Victoria); Limitation of Actions Act 1974 (Qld); Limitation Act 1974 (Tasmania). ACT has a six year limitation period as per s. 39 NSW Supreme Court Act; Limitation Act 1981 (NT) (three years).

do so, the right of action will be barred six years from the date of breach. Similarly with an implied term to act with due skill, care and diligence, time will run from the date of breach, which in practical terms is recognised as the date on which the contract was signed.

In the case of a failure to advise or where it is alleged that the bank acted negligently, a similar six-year limitation period applies. In negligence the cause of action will not arise until the actual loss and damage is suffered. Section 82(2) of the Trade Practices Act 1974 prescribes a three-year limitation period from when the actual loss or damage is incurred.

In *Potts* v. *Westpac Banking Corporation*[80] the borrower's claim under section 52 was dismissed as being outside the time limit. MacKenzie J. at first instance adopted the reasoning of Cole J. in *Ralik Pty. Ltd.* v. *Commonwealth Bank of Australia*[81] and held that the borrower incurred a loss not later than the date of the first rollover. Notwithstanding this his Honour concluded that the factual circumstances were such that a duty of care arose. The issue was further considered in *Ferneyhough* where the decision of the Full Court of the Federal Court in *State of Western Australia* v. *Wardley Australia Limited* was applied.[82] Lee J. held that a cause of action could only arise for the purposes of a section 52 claim after the loss had been crystallised and this would happen only after the loan was paid out. The *Wardley* case did not involve a foreign currency loan but an indemnity which was held to have been induced by a misrepresentation more than three years before the proceedings were commenced but which crystallised within the three-year period. The High Court[83] considered the issue, with a majority finding that the common law concept of causation should be applied and that loss or damage in section 82 includes economic and financial loss. The majority also held that a risk of loss is not of itself a category of loss.

REMEDIES

The basis for a damages calculation, where a court finds an express or implied term of the contract has been breached is to put the party in the same position as if the contract has been performed. In the context of a foreign currency loan, if a court found that a borrower has been guaranteed an interest rate for the life of the loan, a calculation could be undertaken to work out the effective interest rate incurred by the borrower with the damages being the dollar difference between that rate and the guaranteed rate. (This calculation would account for the

80. (Unreported) Supreme Court of Queensland, 10 December 1990, the bank's appeal was allowed by the Full Court of the Supreme Court of Queensland [1993] 1 Qd. R. 135. The limitation question was not in issue on appeal.
81. (Unreported) Supreme Court of New South Wales, 14 August 1990.
82. (1991) 102 A.L.R. 213.
83. (1992) 175 C.L.R. 514.

interest advantages (if any) that had accrued to the borrower and the principal loss due to the devaluation of the currency.)

It is unlikely that even if a court did deem misrepresentations as to the stability of the Australian dollar and minimal risk to be terms of the contract, such a contract to borrower would be voidable. The banks would be able to argue that the borrowers have taken the benefit and impliedly affirmed the contract by having the Australian dollar equivalent of the foreign currency borrowed for the term of the borrowing, which may in the circumstances be an unreasonably long period in which to allow rescission.

In tort, the borrower will seek to recover for the economic loss incurred as a result of the negligent acts, omissions or representations of the bank. In general terms, where the loan is still offshore or where the borrower has refinanced onshore, this will involve estimating the domestic cost of borrowing the Australian dollar equivalent of the foreign currency borrowed and comparing that against the actual cost of borrowing the foreign currency. In *Foti*, Legoe J. found as a matter of fact based on the expert evidence of money market dealers, that a prudent investment adviser would have recommended in May 1984 the taking out of a Swiss currency loan. The consequence of this finding was that as far as the capital loss was concerned, i.e., the difference between the amount borrowed in May 1984 and the amount repayable in May 1986, that was not the borrower's loss and damage. The expert evidence tendered for the plaintiff and accepted by the judge was that a hedge should have been put in place in March 1985 until May 1986 when the loan was to be repaid and it was on that basis that he referred the matter to a Master for assessment. A similar principle was applied by the Supreme Court of New South Wales in *Cappers Holdings Pty. Ltd.* v. *Deutsche Capital Markets Australia Ltd.*[84] In *Cappers* the court acknowledged that whilst there was not a duty on a lender to provide the borrower with commercial advice, in this case the lender had made representations as to the type of risk management strategies it would provide, so the lender had assumed a duty of care. The loss and damage suffered by the borrower was that caused by the breach of the duty of care and was the amount in excess of the loss that the borrower would have suffered if a stop loss procedure had been implemented.

In *Chiarabaglio*, damages were awarded to the applicants on the basis that misrepresentations induced them to enter the facility. The borrowers' submission was that if they had not been induced they would have maintained their April 1982 indebtedness to the bank, i.e., $100,000. The bank's submission was that the borrowers would have borrowed the $500,000 in Australian dollars in any event, so that a calculation of any loss must account for the Australian dollar interest rate that would have been payable on this amount from July 1982; in the alternative they would have borrowed $130,000 to discharge an associated company's debt. Foster J. preferred the borrowers'

---

84. Unreported Supreme Court of New South Wales 12 August 1991.

submission and the damages calculation assumed a continuation of their original indebtedness. It is worth noting that after drawing the funds down, the borrowers, due to a downturn in the Queensland property market, elected not to continue with the proposed development. The funds drawn down were placed in an interest-bearing account with the bank. This approach may be distinguished from that adopted in *Spice* where the loan was still offshore and the funds had been applied to a property development. Foster J. stated that an award of damages was unsuitable because it would require the court to estimate what would happen in the future. The injunctive relief granted by the court meant that Mr Spice was liable to pay to the bank in March 1990 (when the loan fell due) the original $800,000 drawn down and not the expanded liability. Interest for the five years was to be calculated by reference to the commercial bill interest rate applicable at each six-monthly roll over and not the Swiss franc rate. The net effect was to place him in the same position as if he had originally borrowed onshore. In those cases where the borrower has been successful the courts have, in the absence of special factual circumstances such as in *Chiarabaglio*, attempted to place the parties in the position they would have been in had the loan been drawn in Australian dollars at Australian interest rates. This has the effect of substantially defraying from the bank's perspective the capital loss between the amount borrowed and the amount the borrower was obliged to repay.

The Trade Practices Act 1974 (Commonwealth) provides a range of remedies broader and more flexible than those available in common law. As previously stated section 82 provides that a person who suffers loss or damage due to the conduct of another in breach of Parts IV or V of the Act may recover that amount. For breaches of section 52 the High Court has held that the appropriate measure of damages is tortious. In the context of the foreign currency borrowed, it would be to put the borrower back in the position he would have been in had the misleading or deceptive conduct not occurred. This may also be achieved through the wide range of remedies in section 87(2) which provides that a court may declare contracts and collateral agreements void in whole or in part, or vary or refuse to enforce any contract, or order the refund of money or return of property, and that any instrument effecting a transfer of land may be varied or terminated. This range of remedies is more analogous with those available in equity.

Foreign currency borrowers pursuing actions in the Federal Courts have also been successful in obtaining interim interlocutory injunctions preventing the realisation of securities pending the trial of the action. In *Westpac Banking Corporation* v. *Eltran Pty. Ltd.*[85] Fox J., giving judgment for the Full Court of the Federal Court, stated that part of the function of a interlocutory injunction was to maintain the status quo pending a judicial determination of the principal proceedings. As one of the remedies sought was under section 87 of the Trade

85. (1987) 14 F.C.R. 541.

Practices Act varying the terms of the mortgage, declining the application would have allowed the bank to exercise the rights that were being challenged and that would have altered the status quo. The preconditions for the granting of the relief were the service of a fully particularised writ and the fact that the assets were appreciating. In *Graham and Ors.* v. *Commonwealth Bank of Australia*,[86] although the applicants had not demonstrated a strong case, they had demonstrated a serious case under section 52. The main factors to be considered were the marked balance of convenience in the borrowers' favour, given the disastrous consequences of a sale and the lack of evidence from which the court could infer that the bank faced an acute risk of devaluation of the security. Accordingly, the court granted an injunction conditional upon interest being paid. These cases are a significant departure from the normal attitude taken by the State Supreme Courts in respect of applications to prevent mortgagee sales.

CAUSATION

Where a borrower suffers loss or damage, the onus will be on him to prove that such loss or damage was caused by the bank's negligence or breach of contractual or statutory duties owed. In pleading their defences so as to avoid or reduce any potential liability, the banks have argued that any loss to the borrower was caused independently of any breach on their part; the borrower has a contractual duty to mitigate his loss or damage; and the borrower contributed by his own negligence to the loss or damage.

(a) Contract and tort

The test for causation in actions in contract and tort is identical[87] and is a question of fact to be decided in each case. In the "management" cases of *Lloyd* and *McEvoy* neither plaintiffs were able to establish that they were owed tortious, contractual or statutory duties that had been breached. Both Rogers J. and Brownie J. expressed doubt as to whether reasonable care in such a volatile and erratic market would have had any effect in minimising the losses incurred. The question of fact (e.g. whether a particular strategy should have been undertaken) will be a difficult one for the borrower to prove. In addition to the market itself being seen as an independent cause of the borrower's loss, findings of fact in respect of the borrower's behaviour may also break the chain of causation. In *Davcot*, Wood J. held that "even had the plaintiffs been fully informed at the outset of the way the facility operated and of the risks, they would have acted in the same way they did",[88] and accordingly the plaintiffs'

---

86. 10 A.T.P.R. 49–753.
87. David J. Partlett, *Professional Negligence*, Law Book Company, 1985.
88. *Davcot*, p. 186.

claim failed on the grounds of causation. On the facts he found that before any loss was suffered the borrowers had come to "a clear realisation and appreciation of what was involved yet they elected to continue with the facility".[89] In *Ralik* the court held that the loss suffered by the borrower was not related to any breach of a duty to warn as the court was of the view that no warning would have deterred the borrower from proceeding with the loan.

When the borrower has relied upon negligent representations and entered into the loan, without becoming aware of the risks involved, and has suffered a loss, it is unlikely that causation will be in issue. In *David Securities*, Hill J. stated:

"In cases where the breach of duty alleged consists of the giving of negligence advice, the issue of causation will seldom arise. It will readily be inferred that the plaintiff relied upon the negligently wrong advice with the consequence that damage was suffered. Provided the damage is reasonably foreseeable the plaintiff will be entitled to succeed."[90]

His Honour went on to consider the claim against the co-respondent accountants who had been retained by the applicants, on the bank's recommendation, to advise in respect of the loan.

His Honour found that where the breach of duty alleged is a failure to advise, the onus of showing a causal relationship between the duty owed and damage suffered will lie on the applicants to show that they would have relied upon the advice if it was given. Where there is a failure to advise, the applicants submitted the causation should be decided on an objective basis in terms of what a prudent person in the applicants' position would have decided.[91] His Honour preferred the dicta of Cole J. of the Supreme Court of New South Wales in *Ellis* v. *Wallsend District Hospital*,[92] in supporting the proposition that the correct test was a subjective one. "The causative link critical to success of a plaintiff is what the plaintiff who suffered the change would have done, not a hypothetical reasonable man."[93]

It should be noted that Hill J. was critical of the applicants' witnesses and clearly preferred the respondents' in reaching his conclusion that the applicants had not proved that they would have relied upon the advice.

(b) Trade Practices Act

In an action for breach of section 52 and recovery of damages under section 82 of the Trade Practices Act 1974, the loss or damage must be caused by the conduct of another person. The test that will apply where a party was induced to enter into a contract was stated by the Full Court of the Federal Court in

89. *Ibid.*
90. *David Securities*, p. 87.
91. *Ibid.*, p. 91 US authority cited *Canterbury* v. *Spence*, 464 F.2d 772 (1972) (Circuit Court of Appeals for the District of Columbia).
92. (1989) N.S.W.L.R. 553.
93. *David Securities*, p. 91.

Kabwand Pty. Ltd. v. *National Australia Bank Ltd.*[94] The applicant "must show that he has been induced to do something or to refrain from doing something which gives rise to damage or has been influenced to do or refrain from doing something giving rise to damage by contravening section 52".[95]

In *David Securities* the court considered the subsequent explanations of the bank manager put the representation as to "cheap money" in its proper context and held that the initial representation in isolation would not be adequate to show inducement or influence arising from the original and unqualified representation leading to damage suffered.

There is a duty on a party to a contract that has been breached to mitigate his loss and damage. In the decided cases there is little discussion in a contractual context as to whether borrowers should have undertaken their own risk minimisation strategies, upon being informed by the bank that it would not be managing the facility. Rather, the banks have sought to argue in tort that the failure of a borrower to take action to avoid loss and damage occurring was contributory negligence and any damages awarded should be reduced to the extent that the borrower caused his own loss.

The argument of the banks is that the borrowers could have, at a very early stage of the loan, remitted it back onshore as per the terms of the loan agreement or could have used the mechanism of hedging to reduce the losses. In *Chiarabaglio*, Foster J. stated that the right to bring the loan back onshore did not dispose of the causation issue, but rather, "the circumstances obtaining at any relevant rollover date must be examined to determine whether the failure on behalf of the applicants to exercise the right of repayment amounted to fault on their part sufficient to break the chain of causation".[96]

After discussing the events and circumstances pertaining to each rollover since 1982, his Honour concluded that it was reasonable for the applicants to "hang on" in the hope that the exchange rate would improve. It should be noted that the bank in crucial stages of volatility was not encouraging the applicants to bring the loan back onshore. I would argue that any consideration as to whether it was reasonable for a borrower to bring the loan back onshore must be examined from the borrower's perspective. Accordingly, the individual borrower's financial position must be considered, to determine whether it was possible to service the expanded domestic commitment without realising income producing securities. If it was not feasible "commercially" for the borrower to bring the loan back onshore, the failure to do so should not be deemed to be negligent.

In *Chiarabaglio* the bank also argued that the borrower's complaints as to misrepresentation and negligence were stale and should be "scrutinised very closely". His Honour was not prepared to attribute any substantial significance

94. (1989) A.T.P.R. 50,369 at p. 50,378.
95. *Ibid.*, p. 30. As cited in *David Securities*, at p. 52.
96. *Chiarabaglio*, p. 50,620.

to the fact that Mr Chiarabaglio had not complained in 1983, 1984 or 1985. He reached this conclusion after being satisfied that the bank encouraged him to take an optimistic view and: "It was not in his interests as a major debtor to make serious allegations against bank officers when he was in effect looking to the bank for assistance and believing that the bank would assist him in the difficult problem that had arisen."[97] In unanimously dismissing the bank's appeal the Full Court of the Federal Court confirmed the conclusions of the trial judge in finding that the reasonableness or otherwise of the borrower's decision not to repay the loan six or 12 months after draw-down was relevant to the question of causation and that on the facts of the case the borrower's decision was reasonable.

LESSONS FOR THE BANKS

The foreign currency loan debacle has introduced to the Australian banking community the principle of lender liability. Such a liability has existed in the United States for many years and afforded borrowers causes of action and remedies that were unknown in Australia. As a consequence of the claims against the United States' banks and their directors there was a sharp increase in professional indemnity insurance. The same has now occurred in Australia. Prior to the deregulation of the financial markets, the domestic banks had never had any significant professional negligence claims. As a direct consequence of the Swiss franc cases, professional indemnity insurance for banks increased by 100 per cent in 1986.[98] Whilst these costs are invariably passed on to the customer in the form of higher bank charges, they reflect the need for banks to be more careful in and accountable for the wider range of products and services they provide. It is significant that after 1986 very few foreign currency loans were made available by the banks to their "domestic customers".

The outcome of the cases and the criticism that has been levelled against the banks may mean that the new or novel financing techniques or investment opportunities that are relatively sophisticated may not be available outside the business sector. This would avoid a repeat of the situation where country and suburban bank managers, whose only experience in international banking was the issue of travellers' cheques, were offering such a dangerous financial facility in the form of a foreign currency loan to customers at large.

This issue was noted in the Banking Inquiry report which concluded:

"It is possible that bank staff in the general competitive atmosphere prevailing at the time of the writing of foreign currency loans and lacking sound knowledge of the product may have glossed over the risk. This would have been less likely where it was the policy and practice to involve a person with extensive experience in foreign currency risk in the

97. *Ibid.*, p. 50,618.
98. A. Davies, The *Australian Financial Review*, 2 December 1986.

interviews with clients. The facts of individual cases are crucial in this area of advice to borrowers."[99]

Where a bank holds itself out as an investment or financial adviser, there is a duty to explain fully both the advantages and disadvantages and risks inherent in the facility. Depending on the nature of the facility this duty may best be discharged by suggesting that the customer takes independent advice. It is the writer's experience that at the time these loans were being promoted many independent advisers such as accountants and lawyers were extremely wary about permitting their clients to borrow offshore. For banks to recommend that their customers take independent advice is contrary to the image they seek to portray to the public at large. They promote themselves through large advertising campaigns as offering a wide range of quality financial services. In *Foti*, Legoe J. placed considerable emphasis on the fact that the lender was the internationally experienced Banque National de Paris and arguably bestowed a more onerous responsibility on them "to control" the borrower's loan. This is despite the fact that the judge had accepted that the bank had not agreed to manage the loan. Advertising by banks that boasts the prowess of its money market dealers, the round-the-clock monitoring of economic trends, market movements and currency fluctuations does not fit neatly with the experience of the "small scale foreign currency borrower" who in many cases found the bank less than helpful.

In addition to becoming liable to customers directly, a bank may be exposed indirectly through loan brokers and financial intermediaries who market the bank's financial products. Professor Allan, in summarising the recent Australian cases on fiduciary duties, stated that a provider of finance, "will become a fiduciary if he knowingly participates in the activities of the advisers or promoters so as to make breaches of duty possible and to become privy to them".[100]

Many of the foreign currency loans were promoted by loan brokers advertising in the daily newspapers and potential borrowers were provided with bank charts, graphs and promotional materials. It would therefore be prudent for banks to review the operational marketing of new facilities and to carefully screen and review the activities of brokers to avoid becoming potentially liable. Allied to this is the need for banks to explain to the customer the costs and charges involved in any facility they promote. Professor Allan also states that a financier "will become a fiduciary if he does more than provide the finance and becomes a promoter of the scheme—especially if he personally stands to gain from it".[101]

A bank may be able to avoid liability in foreign currency cases and many other potential instances of lender liability if it can demonstrate that it has adhered to

99. Australian Banking Industry Inquiry, *op. cit.*, p. 321.
100. Allan D., *op. cit.*, 222.
101. *Ibid.*

all and any codes of conduct or lending procedures that are reasonable in the circumstances. Guidelines released by the Trade Practices Commission relate particularly to loans and deposits and provide that the bank shall fully disclose interest rates payable, security required, the availability of investment advisory services and any penalties for prepayment. Adherence to these would support any defence to a section 52 claim that a bank had been misleading or deceptive. In the New South Wales Supreme Court case of *Corpers Pty. Ltd.* v. *NZI Securities Australia*,[102] after discussing the importance of compliance with internal lending procedures, the court held that liability would not be diminished if the lender's employee exceeded his authority when making representations. In *Chiarabaglio* the Advance Policy Committee minutes of Westpac that were discovered by the applicants and exhibited in the action detailed guidelines and lending procedures. Significantly it was found on the facts that these initial guidelines had not been adhered to by the bank's officers. That these guidelines were adequate is however questionable, since in an interview in the *Sydney Morning Herald* a former Westpac internal auditor said: "When these loans were launched there were no procedures, policy safeguards or contingency in place. Nevertheless teams went out on the roads touting the loans."[103]

There are important lessons to be learnt for banks in how they should respond to such crises when they occur so as to limit their liability. Whilst there is anecdotal evidence of banks approaching particular groups of borrowers en masse (e.g., farmers in a particular region where the loans were heavily marketed) and seeking to conciliate rather than litigate, this appears to be the exception rather than the rule. Instead banks have sought to stretch borrower litigants to their absolute financial limits by prolonging hearings so that borrowers cannot afford to continue. Whilst tactically commendable, in that many borrowers shied away or withdrew from the litigation, such strategies have attracted almost as much adverse publicity as the loans themselves. The Banking Inquiry[104] in its recommendations suggested that the banks should fund an independent mediator in an attempt to resolve the disputes without resort to protracted litigation. The banks have not formally committed themselves to such a procedure. The Westpac Banking Corporation did invite those customers who had managed foreign currency loans with Partnership Pacific Limited (PPL) (Westpac's former merchant banking subsidiary) to contact the bank with a view to mediation of any disputes. This occurred only after a series of damaging legal advices known as the "Westpac letters" were published revealing that among other activities PPL had taken points exceeding its entitlements and undertaken switching transactions.

The complexity and novelty of these facilities means that extra care must be

102. (1989) 20 A.T.R. and [1989] A.S.C. 58,402.
103. *Sydney Morning Herald*, Saturday 10 December 1988.
104. Australian Banking Industry Inquiry *op. cit.* p. 385.

taken in the preparation of loan and security documentation and the keeping of full and complete records. As has already been discussed in *McEvoy* the bank was found liable for the difference between the carded and the spot rate of exchange charged to the borrower.

The courts have not imposed a liability upon the Australian trading banks for introducing and promoting foreign currency borrowing *per se*. In the decided cases where banks have contracted with customers to lend foreign currency or advise or manage an exposure, the courts have been reluctant to impose excessively onerous duties on the banks by either implying terms or setting "unrealistic" thresholds for the standard of loan management. Similarly the courts have been reluctant to interfere in the ostensibly commercial relationship between foreign currency lender or manager and customer, and to impose fiduciary duties upon the former. In the judicial consideration of section 52 the courts have been reluctant to impose a positive duty on the bank to explain "risk" minimisation techniques.

Rather, the application of general negligence principles indicates that where the borrower has requested an explanation or the bank has embarked on one, the explanation must be sufficient to enable the borrower to make an informed decision whether to borrow or not. Where the bank has engaged in management on behalf of the borrower, the question to be determined is whether the management has been conducted in the manner that would have been conducted by a prudent foreign currency manager. This is not an easy question and without substantial proof is unlikely to be answered in the borrower's favour. The speculative nature of the foreign currency market, the relationship between borrower and lender, adviser or manager, and their familiarity or otherwise with the facility all contribute to the physical, circumstantial and causal components which make up the touchstone of proximity. The foreign currency cases to date serve to broaden further the categories in which the giver of advice will be liable to the recipient for negligent misrepresentations.

PETER NANKIVELL

CHAPTER 12

LENDER LIABILITY IN THE UNITED STATES: A DECADE IN PERSPECTIVE

I. INTRODUCTION

This past decade brought worrisome times for institutional commercial lenders in the United States. First, there was the catastrophe with international lending; then energy lending; next agricultural lending; and finally, in the midst of all this, loomed a foreboding picture for commercial real estate lending. For institutional lenders in the US, all this created an environment that translated into troubled loan portfolios, diminishing lending opportunities, increased loan loss reserves and earning losses and a significant rise in regulatory enforcement actions. The affrontery came, however, not only from this deteriorating business environment, but from the rise of less pliant, more uncooperative, and more litigious borrowers (and their other creditors).

The first highly publicised awards began a decade ago with the 1984 landmark $19 million award (finally settled for approximately $12–13 million) in *State National Bank of El Paso* v. *Farah Manufacturing Company*.[1] The case involved an action against a group of financial institutions as a result of an alleged course of tortious conduct characterised by fraud, duress and intentional interference with the borrower's corporate governance process. The second landmark case, *KMC Company* v. *Irving Trust Company*,[2] in 1985 resulted in a $7.5 million award against the defendant for breach of an implied covenant of good faith and fair dealing under the Uniform Commercial Code resulting from the lender's refusal to advance funds up to the credit limit under a pre-existing secured financing agreement. These cases forebode a trend toward increased findings of lender liability. In fact, these multi-million dollar jury awards became more frequent (although many, but not all, began to be reversed or reduced on appeal) against institutional lenders and became indicative of an era of lender liability litigation.[3]

---

1. 678 S.W.2d 661 (Tex. Civ. App. 1984), *writ granted and dismissed by agreement.*
2. 757 F.2d 752 (6th Cir. 1985).
3. See generally, J.J. Norton and W.M. Baggett, *Lender Liability: Law and Litigation* (Matthew Bender, 1994); see also Blanchard, Gerald L., *Lender Liability: Law, Practice, and Prevention*, rev. ed., Deerfield, Ill. (Callaghan 1994); Budnitz, Mark E., *The Law of Lender Liability*, Boston (Warren, Gorham & Lamont 1991); Cappello, A. Barry, *Lender Liability*, 2nd ed., Salem, N.H.

Lender-liability theories came to be used by borrowers (who were becoming more sophisticated, imaginative, and assertive in their lending relationships) to draw the line between a lender's legitimate rights to oversee and to protect its loan and any collateral and a borrower's right not to have undue interference in the management of its business and management structure and otherwise to change the traditional (and often "one-sided") balance of power between lender and borrower.[4] These theories also began to be employed by creditors of borrowers seeking a "deep pocket" and by regulators of troubled or failed financial institutions seeking to recoup mounting federal deposit insurance losses.[5]

Although in the past, most US courts had a tendency to provide the lender with broad latitude in this area of exercising lender control,[6] today a prudent lender and its counsel no longer presumes that unbridled discretion will be permitted. Thus, while the legal theories employed in such cases are often fundamental legal notions known to all first-year US law students, the aggressive and innovative usage of such theories in the US by borrowers, their other creditors, and regulators of troubled financial institutions can only send shivers through institutional commercial lenders and their counsel.

For the borrower, the common law and statutory theories of lender liability represented a legal arsenal to help balance what often, traditionally, had been a "one-sided" playing field. Under these theories, a borrower had a far greater chance than in the past to right excessive, unnecessary, or unreasonable lender conduct, or attempt to minimise the adverse impact of such conduct. For the borrower and its counsel an understanding of lender liability theories proved helpful in establishing acceptable parameters in negotiating a loan, in restructuring a loan, in pursuing a plaintiff's cause of action or an affirmative defence in a civil suit or bankruptcy proceeding, or in devising a suitable bankruptcy plan.

Perhaps, more constructively, these theories created a "two-sided" field within which mutually beneficial negotiations could be conducted by lender and borrower and within which a more balanced "leverage" between the parties would exist.

This chapter, in emphasising the past decade of lender liability litigation in the

---

(Butterworth Legal Publishers, 1993); Mannino, Edward F., *Lender Liability in the 1990's*, New York, N.Y. (Law Journal Seminars-Press, 1990). Also see the following newsletters: Chaitman, Helen D., ed., *Lender Liability Law Report* (Warren, Gorham & Lamont), published monthly; *Lender Liability Litigation Reporter* (Andrews Publications), published 24 times per year; *Lender Liability News* (Buraff Publications), published 24 times per year. Unless otherwise indicated, this chapter speaks as of 1 June 1994.

4. See, *inter alia*, Lundgren, "Liability of a Creditor in a Control Relationship With Its Debtor", 67 Marq. L. Rev. 523 (1984).

5. Norton and Baggett, *supra*, fn. 3, explores in depth the various common law and statutory theories of lender liability, certain special circumstances in which such liability claims may arise, and the litigation aspects of such claims.

6. E.g. *Harris Trust & Savings Bank* v. *Keiz* (*Re Prima Co.*), 98 F.2d 952, at 964–966 (7th Cir. 1903). 4–108.

US, will attempt to take a balanced perspective (from a lender and borrower point of view) in discussing in Part II factual indiciæ and situations often leading to or involving lender liability; in Part III the basic common law theories being utilised in lender liability litigation; and in Part IV the emerging statutory theories. However, in Part V, the author admits to taking a pro-lender posture in setting forth the proposition that uncritical approaches taken by some US courts in blurring legal lines and policy distinctions between contract and tort causes of action have led to an unwarranted and undesirable expansion of lender liability in the US. In Part VI a brief discussion of certain lender protective devices is made, and in Part VII the author offers certain practical suggestions for lenders in avoiding or minimising liability exposure.

II. BACKGROUND: FACTUAL INDICIÆ OF LIABILITY AND THE LITIGATION IMPLICATIONS

In sifting through the diversity and complexity of the lender liability theories, one can decipher certain indiciæ or signposts as significantly influencing the proof of liability and damages against a lender.

A. Inordinate control

Factual bases for many of the common law and statutory liability theories now being employed against lenders centre around the alleged exercise of inordinate control over the borrower and its affairs by the lender.[7] These "badges of control" have included:

— the lender's direct interference into the day-to-day operations of the debtor;
— lender conduct that causes a change in the debtor's management and replacement with management suggested by or favourable to the lender;
— lender fraud that directly injures the borrower or its other creditors;
— the lender's direct ownership or control over the voting stock of a debtor; and
— the lender's coupling traditional lending objectives with other business objectives.

In all events, the exercise of actual control over the business affairs and operations of a borrower should give the lender pause for concern and careful assessment of the possible legal implications, inasmuch as the determination of

---

7. E.g. see sections III.D., F., & G. *infra*. See also Hynes, J. Dennis, "Lender Liability: the dilemma of the controlling creditor" (1991) 58 Tenn. L. Rev. 635–668.

direct lender liability is highly "fact sensitive". Moreover, in determining liability, a trier-of-fact will consider not one factor as determinative, but will view all control factors in light of the overall relationship between the lender and the borrower. As such, the legal standards for liability may be viewed fairly subjectively at the trial level. Further, through the inordinate exercise of control over a borrower, a lender may become liable not only to a borrower but also to affected creditors of the borrower.

The practical problem for the lender is often one of the "degree" of control being exercised. As such, a trier-of-fact may have considerable latitude in determining the legal significance of the degree of control. In addition, assuming the court gave the jury legally proper instructions, findings of fact adverse to a lender are most difficult (if not impossible) to overturn on appeal.

B. Course of conduct

Many of the lender liability theories permit a plaintiff, in pursuit of its claim, to go beyond the "four corners" of the loan documentation. Often, important in the judicial determination that this is permissible will be the lender's "course of conduct" with respect to the borrower. "Course of conduct" may become a critical factor for extrinsically amending the terms of the loan arrangement, for demonstrating the existence of fraud, for establishing a "special relationship" giving rise to an implied duty of "good faith", or otherwise for conditioning the jury towards sympathising with the plaintiff's claims. For example, if the documents indicate one course of action, but the lender has consistently taken another course of action, then a plaintiff will most probably argue that the lender's "course of conduct" has amended the expressed contrary terms of the loan documents.[8] Also, a course of conduct may give rise to a fact situation where questions of lender misrepresentational fraud could be inferred.[9] Further, a course of conduct between borrower and lender that goes beyond a straightforward lender-borrower relationship may give rise to what the courts are beginning to label a "special relationship", which in turn gives rise to an implied duty of good faith (and not simply to contractual duties under the loan documents).[10] In addition, although it cannot be scientifically demonstrated, most good plaintiff's and defendant's attorneys will agree that a factual showing of a certain course of conduct by a lender may well influence (i) a tier-of-fact's analysis of the specific legal issues presented for determination at the trial court level, and (ii) whether (upon what amounts) punitive (exemplary) damages may be sustained.[11] Accordingly, it becomes increasingly important for a lender not only to know what is in the loan documents but what in fact has been the

8. E.g. see discussion of *KMC* case (note 2, *supra*) in section IV.B. *infra*.
9. E.g. see discussion of *Farah* case (note 1, *supra*) in section III.C. *infra*.
10. E.g. see discussion in sections III.B., IV.B. and V A.3. and 4 *infra*.
11. For discussion of litigation aspects, see generally *Norton & Baggett, supra*, fn. 3, Part IV.

lender's course of conduct with respect to that specific borrower and with respect to other borrowers similarly situated.

C. Atypical lending practices

A straightforward lender-borrower relationship will mostly always *not* give rise to lender liability. However, once a lender begins to deviate from normal prudent lending practices, then concern should arise as to whether the potential or actuality of lender liability is being created. This does not mean that a lender, in protecting its interest, has to adhere to basic forms of lending arrangements. To the contrary, it may well be prudent and in the best interests of the lender (and sometimes even of borrower) to deviate from the standard practices. But where the lender's conduct and actions, directly or indirectly, begin to indicate that the relationship is something more than a creditor/debtor situation, then the legal implications have to be carefully reanalysed. For example, the issues of inordinate control, discussed above in this chapter, provide numerous factual examples where the conduct of the lender went beyond normal practices to the point that the court recharacterised the relationship or otherwise recharacterised the legal liability theories.

D. Lack of professionalism

Related to the issue of course of conduct and normal prudent lending practices is the notion of professionalism by the lender (or the lack thereof). In many of the cases, there exists (at least by implication) the sense that at some point in the lender-borrower relationship the representatives of the lender lost sight of their professional positions and responsibilities. This is most understandable, as most of the lender liability situations result from a protracted relationship with a troubled borrower or otherwise in a workout situation.[12] In such pressured and stressful environments, it is easy for one to engage in subjective and personalised approaches to the lending relationship. The danger, though, is that this often will result in something being said or done that could lead to or otherwise could serve as evidence of a claim of lender liability.

E. Abuse of a special relationship

As indicated above and as will be discussed elsewhere in this chapter, fact situations surrounding the lender-borrower relationship can give rise to a "special relationship" and conceivably (in extreme cases) to a fiduciary relationship.[13] If facts are proven to trigger such re-characterisation of the

---

12. E.g. see discussion in section IV.F. *infra*.
13. E.g. see discussion in sections III.D. and V.3. *infra*.

relationship, then the duties and liabilities of the lender will go beyond simple contractual duties. In a "special relationship" situation, the courts will imply a common law or statutory duty of "good faith". In a fiduciary relationship, then, the whole spectrum of fiduciary duties of care and loyalty will be present. In both cases, the cause of action will be in tort and punitive damages may be available.

F. Conflicts of interest

The specific legal notion of conflicts of interest ordinarily arises only in a fiduciary situation; and normally a lender-borrower relationship does not give rise to a fiduciary duty. However, as will be elaborated upon elsewhere in this chapter, factual circumstances can give rise to a fiduciary duty by the lender. For example, if a lender has one of its officers (or other persons under its control) on the board of directors of a borrower or otherwise the lender or an affiliate is a controlling shareholder or person of the borrower, then a duty of loyalty may arise, whereby the lender has placed itself in the dilemma of having to protect its own interests without violating this duty. Also, in various situations, a lender may be standing on both sides of a particular transaction. Cases have existed where a lender in trying to bail itself out of one lending situation involves another borrower. Also, in tender offer situations, a bank may find itself on both sides of a transaction as adviser and as lender. In these instances, inevitable conflicts of interest may arise.[14]

G. Implications for litigation strategy

While the above indiciæ of liability may not by themselves give rise to a viable cause of action, they are elements that can (as discovery evolves) be developed into sustainable specific causes of action. The primary implications of these indiciæ and causes of action is that they will permit a plaintiff to go beyond basic contract law theories and to bring in circumstantial and extraneous evidence outside of the specific loan documents. This, in turn, makes a very dangerous situation in defending a lender liability suit, as summary judgment will invariably be precluded (if plaintiff's attorney properly develops the theories, facts and causes of action), and undesirable (from a defendant's perspective) issues of fact will often get into the hands of a jury. Frequently, if plaintiff's strategy in selecting forum and venue has been successful, a jury in the United States may well find itself more sympathetic (as a general proposition) to a borrower or other third party plaintiff than to an institutional lender defendant.[15]

---

14. E.g. see discussion in *Norton & Baggett, supra* fn. 3, § 6.06.

15. *Ibid.*, Part IV. See also Lodge, Kenneth M., and Cunningham, Thomas J., "Reducing excessive and unjustified awards in lender liability cases", (1993) 98 Dick. L. Rev. 25–65; Overby, A. Brooke, "Bondage, domination, and the art of the deal: an assessment of judicial strategies in lender liability good faith litigation" (1993) 61 Fordham L. Rev. 963–1032.

H. Specific areas of lender liability concerns

Many of the lender liability cases centre around loan negotiations, alleged commitments and troubled loan situations. Special areas of lender liability concerns include regulatory actions, misuse of borrower's collateral, and loan participation arrangements.

1. The loan-cycle: commitment, negotiation and workout stages

The cases indicate several periods in a loan's cycle from creation to final pay off that appear to be especially susceptible to lender liability concerns. The first concerns informal contacts between lender and borrower that are subsequently alleged by borrower to have created a binding commitment to lend initially or to lend additional funds. Though, as will be discussed below, courts and certain legislatures now are taking a more restrictive view of alleged oral commitment situations, both formal and informal borrower contact that conceivably could lead to misplaced borrower expectations of funding needs to be guarded against by lenders.[16]

A second possible problem area is in the actual negotiation of the loan arrangement and related security arrangements as to what actually has been agreed, and whether the "four corners" of the document control or are somehow altered or avoided by a contrary lender course of conduct or representations.[17] Perhaps the most dangerous stage is the workout stage, at which point the loan is actually in or near a default status. Often, it is in the best interest of borrower and lender to effect a constructive workout arrangement; but, in such tensed and troubled situations, dangerous factual indiciæ can occur easily and (in the hindsight of a trier-of-fact) can form the basis of a lender liability claim.[18]

2. Bank regulatory actions

Certain institutional lenders, such as finance and mortgage companies, are largely unregulated entities. However, other institutions, such as banking institutions (commercial banks and thrift institutions) and insurance companies, are highly regulated under state and/or federal laws. These institutional lenders may be subject to examination and enforcement proceedings by the regulators. Through these administrative processes, liability can arise for the institution and its management. For example, a bank that has demonstrated imprudent management or has violated certain statutes (such as statutory lending limits) may find itself and its management subject to

---

16. See discussion in Part VI.A. *infra*.
17. See discussion in Part III.A. *infra*.
18. See guides to dealing with workout situations in Part VII *infra*.

administrative action or suit seeking a whole series of liabilities (ranging from civil money penalties for the institution and its members, to revocation of authority to conduct banking business, to industry-wide bans on culpable management, to criminal actions).[19]

3. Lender's misuse of borrower's collateral

A lender takes a security interest in a borrower's collateral in order to protect itself against the possibility of the borrower's default. In the past, lenders and other secured parties have been allowed a rather free hand in foreclosing upon and disposing of the borrower's collateral. This has constituted another realm in which a lender could exercise "control" over its borrower—by disposing of (or not disposing of) the borrower's collateral in ways that are to the lender's advantage. However, recent cases indicate that the secured party may incur liability for misconduct. Thus, certain issues as to the lender's liability remain open even after the borrower has defaulted and the lender has foreclosed. Two of these issues need special attention: notice of disposition, and retention of collateral. Both issues arise in the context of obtaining or losing a deficiency against the debtor and preserving one's rights against other security or other lenders. As they are matters of state law, these matters need to be examined on a state-by-state basis.[20]

4. Liability of lead bank in a loan participation

One issue respecting loan participation is the scope of the lead lender's duty to keep the participants informed. When there is the possibility of insolvency, either of the borrower or of the lead, the scope of the lead's powers, duties and responsibilities comes even more sharply into issue. Resolution of these problems may call for decisions on issues that simply were never contemplated in the execution of the participation agreement.

Another specific problem for the participant is that if the lead becomes insolvent, the FDIC as receiver for the lead may offset the borrower's deposit accounts against the loan balance, without passing any funds through to the participants.

Fiduciary duty, "good faith", and regulatory concerns may arise in a lender liability situation respecting loan participations. An obvious source of liability for the lead is a failure to perform its contractual obligations to the participants and situations involving an express or implied covenant of good faith.[21]

19. See generally, *Norton and Baggett, supra* fn. 3, Ch. 19 (Federal Bank Regulatory Enforcement Actions).

20. See generally, W.M. Baggett, *Texas Foreclosure: Law and Practice* (1984; as updated periodically).

21. See generally, *Norton and Baggett, supra* fn. 3, Ch. 20 ("Loan Participations").

5. *Leveraged buyouts (LBOs)*

US lenders have also experienced liability exposure resulting from lender involvement in highly leveraged acquisitions and buyout transactions and more generally from lenders' increasing emphasis upon fee-generating, investment banking-type activities.[22]

III. FUNDAMENTAL LEGAL THEORIES INNOVATIVELY USED

Various fundamental legal theories, rooted in case law development, have been utilised innovatively to create lender liability by borrowers and other persons (e.g., creditors of a borrower). A lender should not forget that other creditors of a borrower or regulators of troubled financial institutions may employ these theories in trying to make a lender responsible for a borrower's obligations to such creditors or other parties.

A. Contract theories

Although the greatest danger of a lender liability theory is that it permits a plaintiff to go beyond the loan documentation by raising non-contract theories and causes of action, basic contract causes of action still remain important in the lender liability area. The lending relationship is, at its heart, a contractual relationship giving rise to a host of duties and liabilities for both borrower and lender. Particularly important in the area of contractual claims on lender liability is when a loan commitment or promise of a lender becomes legally binding. Also questions of interpretation and integration of the various loan documents will often be key elements in a lender liability suit. Moreover, from the lender's point of view the attempt to keep the litigation within the context of what the contractual relationship says and permits remain a first priority for lender's counsel[23] The contract doctrine of consequential damages (e.g., as embracing economic loss such as lost profits) is proving nearly as dangerous as tort notions of damages.[24]

Contractual lender liability is usually based on one of the following concepts:

— *anticipatory repudiation* (usually involving instances in which a lender has required additional performance by the borrower not called for in the initial contract)[25];

---

22. *Ibid.*, Ch. 1. See also Rehon, Peter M., "The law of equitable subordination: new risks for LBO and non-LBO lenders" (1991) 108 Banking L.J. 536–544.

23. *Ibid.*, Ch. 3 ("Contract Theories"), from which portions of this section are derived.

24. E.g. *Shaughnessy* v. *Mark Twain State Bank*, 715 S.W.2d 944 (Mot. Ct. App. 1986).

25. E.g. *Davis* v. *Nevada National Bank*, 737 P.2d 503 (Nev. 1987). For an excellent review of case law in this area, see *DeBry* v. *Valley Mortgage Co.*, 835 P.2d 1000 (Utah 1992).

— *promissory estoppel* (generally involving situations in which a borrower has reasonably relied upon promises of a lender to extend credit and has, as a result, suffered damage);

— *condition precedent* (normally involving the issue of whether a condition which the borrower failed to meet was material or whether the borrower had substantially performed the obligation required);

— *wrongful acceleration* (a difficult area, in light of the differences in the interpretation and treatment of acceleration clauses under the laws of the various states);

— *duty to inspect* (an area in which the traditional rule—that lenders have no duty to inspect the construction projects they fund—has come under challenge); and

— *breach of good faith* (this last topic is discussed in other parts of this chapter).

Without diminishing the importance of the other mentioned contract liability theories, anticipatory repudiation and promissory estoppel have been selected for more detailed discussion.

1. Anticipatory repudiation

Anticipatory repudiation occurs when a promisor (lender) without justification and before any breach has been committed by it unequivocally indicates by statement to the promisee (borrower) or by its conduct that it is no longer willing or able to perform substantially his contractual obligations.[26] The repudiating statement or conduct must be positive and unequivocal; a mere implication of repudiation is not sufficient.[27]

Anticipatory repudiation by lenders often takes the form of an insistence by the lender that the borrower perform conditions not required by the original contract.[28] Lenders commonly attempt to justify their alleged anticipatory repudiation on grounds of "prospective default", maintaining that the borrower would have been unable to meet stipulated conditions.[29] Indeed, a lender's obligation to pay damages for anticipatory repudiation will be excused if the

---

26. *Glatt* v. *Bank of Kirkwood Plaza*, 383 N.W.2d 473, 477 (N.D. 1986); see 4 *Corbin on Contracts* section 959 (1962).

27. *United Cal. Bank* v. *Prudential Ins. Co.*, 140 Ariz. 238, 681 P.2d 390, 429 (App. 1983). See 4 *Corbin on Contracts* section 973 (1962).

28. See *United Cal. Bank* v. *Prudential Ins. Co.*, fn. 20 *supra*; *Penthouse Int'l, Ltd.* v. *Dominion Fed. Sav & Loan Ass'n*, 665 F. Supp. 301 (*rev'd in part and aff'd in part*, 855 F.2d 963 (2d Cir. 1988) (S.D.N.Y. 1987); 4 *Corbin on Contracts* section 973 (1951); Restatement (Second) of Contracts section 250(b) (1981).

29. See *Glatt* v. *Bank of Kirkwood Plaza*, fn. 26 *supra*, 383 N.W.2d 473; *F.D.I.C.* v. *Scharenberg*, 49 BNA Banking Rptr. 349 (US Dist. Ct. S.D. Fla. 1987).

evidence shows that the borrower would have failed to perform specified conditions precedent.[30]

For a borrower to recover on a theory of anticipatory repudiation, the following elements must be established:

— the lender made a loan commitment to the borrower;
— the lender withdrew the commitment before the expiration of the time allotted the borrower to comply with the required conditions, or the lender insisted that the borrower perform conditions not contained in the original commitment agreement; and
— the borrower was damage as a result of the withdrawal of the commitment.[31]

A repudiating party may unilaterally withdraw or retract its repudiation.[32] To be effective, a retraction must come to the attention of the aggrieved party before he materially changes his position in reliance on the repudiation and before he signals to the repudiating party that he deems the repudiation to be final.[33] The filing of suit by the aggrieved party conclusively signals unequivocal acceptance of the repudiation and terminates the power of the repudiating party to retract.[34]

A typical anticipatory repudiation case illustrating the above principles is *Glatt v. Bank of Kirkwood Plaza*[35] In *Glatt*, the bank committed to lend the plaintiff developers $1,700,000 for the purchase of condominiums and the building of a restaurant, bar and racquetball club. The commitment was to be held open, subject to 23 conditions, for six months. However, within one month of the commitment the majority stockholder of the bank's holding company orally indicated to the developers that the bank was no longer interested in funding the loan. The reasons given for not honouring the loan commitment were that the development would be unsuccessful and that the developers would not be able to satisfy the required conditions. Approximately three weeks later, the repudiation was unequivocally confirmed by telephone conversation and by follow-up letter to the legal counsel for the developers. The developers proceeded to sue the bank for specific performance of the commitment or damages.[36]

The court held for the developers on the issue of anticipatory repudiation and placed the burden of proof on the bank to show that the developers would have been unable to meet the required conditions precedent. The court rejected the bank's contention that any repudiation had been retracted because the alleged

---

30. *Native Alaskan Reclamation & Pest Control, Inc. v. United Bank Alaska*, 685 P.2d 1211, 1216 (Alaska 1984).

31. See *Glatt v. Bank of Kirkwood Plaza*, fn. 26 *supra*, 383 N.W.2d at 477–478.

32. *Ibid.*, at 479.

33. *Ibid.*

34. *Ibid.*

35. *Ibid.*, at 473 (for full case citation see fn. 26 *supra*).

36. See specific performance and the various damage remedies discussed in section 3.06 of Chapter 3 in *Norton & Baggett*, *supra* fn. 3. See also section V.C.2. *infra*.

retraction did not take place until after suit had been filed by the developers. Any retraction was, therefore, ineffective. The court remanded the case for a decision on the issue of damages only. The developers had sought at trial a last-minute increase in damages, and the bank being thus surprised had not been allowed sufficient time to respond.

Damages for anticipatory repudiation can be extremely large. A good example is *Federal Deposit Insurance Corp.* v. *Scharenberg*,[37] a recent case arising from a construction loan default. Although the borrower had complied with all loan conditions, the lender declared the loan to be in default and turned the loan over to the FDIC. The lender alleged that the borrower would have been unable to meet certain conditions. The FDIC sued the borrower for this alleged default and recovered a $55,000,000 judgment. A week later, the borrower won a $105,000,000 jury verdict against the lender for breaching the loan contract. The borrower is currently appealing the judgment in favour of the FDIC and has asked the federal district court to order the lender to indemnify him for any amounts he is obligated to pay the FDIC.

Two relatively recent cases illustrate anticipatory repudiation by lenders who insisted on performance of conditions not required by the original loan commitment. In *United California Bank* v. *Prudential Insurance Company*,[38] the permanent lender refused to honour its loan commitment unless the developer agreed to place a first lien on the property, a condition not set forth in the commitment agreement. The court held that the lender's insistence upon the unspecified condition constituted an anticipatory repudiation of its contract to lend.

A similar repudiation was the basis of the favourable borrower's trial award (later reversed) in *Penthouse International Limited* v. *Dominion Federal Savings & Loan Association*.[39] The decision resulted in an award to the borrower of over $129 million, one of the highest trial awards against lenders to date on any theory, contract or tort. The defendant Dominion was a third party participant which had refused to honour its commitment to lend Penthouse $60 million. When Dominion made its commitment, it accepted the conditions set forth in the loan commitment of the lead lender. When Dominion learned that one of its underwriters intended to back out of the commitment, Dominion began demanding new conditions of the borrower. First, Dominion required that numerous documents be rewritten by its legal counsel at the borrower's expense. Dominion then required that the borrower replace its legal counsel and began making seemingly unending requests for additional information. Dominion also insisted that it be made lead lender. The trial court concluded, based on these numerous unjustified demands, that Dominion was guilty of anticipatory repudiation of its loan commitment.

37. 49 *BNA Banking Rptr.* 349 (US Dist. Ct. S.D. Fla. 1987).
38. Fn. 27 *supra*, 140 Ariz. 238, 681 P.2d 390.
39. Fn. 28 *supra*, 665 F. Supp. 301 (S.D.N.Y. 1987), rev'd in part and aff'd in part, 855 F.2d 963 (2d Cir. 1988).

The Second Circuit reversed in *Penthouse*, holding there was not sufficient evidence to support the trial finding that Dominion and its counsel had intentionally attempted to sabotage the transaction, that the lender-imposed conditions precedent were reasonable and customary and that the reason the transaction failed was due to Penthouse's failure to satisfy such conditions. Thus, when the commitment expired, the lenders were held by the appeals court to be under no further obligation to continue the negotiations.[40]

In defence of an allegation of anticipatory repudiation, the lender should consider whether the borrower has concealed material changes in its financial status in violation of the loan application or financial statement. Also, when possible, the lender should reserve in its loan commitment the right to alter the loan terms or to require new conditions when the borrower's financial condition changes. Further, when possible, any new conditions being sought by the lender should be agreed to in writing by the borrower.

2. Promissory estoppel

Even though the lender has not made a binding loan commitment, liability may attach for promises made by the lender during the loan negotiation process. If the proposed borrower (the promisee) has reasonably acted to its detriment in reliance upon such promises, it may have a successful action against the lender (the promisor) under the doctrine of promissory estoppel.[41] This doctrine is codified in the new *Restatement of Contracts*.[42]

The general rule is that a cause of action for promissory estoppel involves four essential elements:

— an unequivocal promise by the promisor to the promisee;
— a reasonable expectation that the promise will influence the conduct of the promisee;
— reasonable reliance on the promise by the promisee; and
— detriment to the promisee which would make it unjust for the promise not to be enforced.[43]

The promisee's remedy under promissory estoppel may be limited as justice

---

40. *Ibid.* On 3 April 1989, the US Supreme Court denied the petition for *certiorari* (US Sup. Ct. No. 88–1339).

41. See, e.g., *Zimmerman* v. *First Fed. Savings & Loan Ass'n of Rapid City, S.D.*, 848 F.2d 1047 (10th Cir. 1988); *Wheeler* v. *White*, 398 S.W.2d 93 (Tex. 1965).

42. Restatement (Second) of Contracts section 90(1) (1981) provides: "A promise which the promisor should reasonably expect to induce action or forbearance on the part of the promisee or a third person and which does induce such action or forbearance is binding if injustice can be avoided only by enforcement of the promise. The remedy granted for breach may be limited as justice requires."

43. *Malaker Corp. Stockholders Protective Committee* v. *First Jersey Nat'l Bank*, 163 N.J. Super. 463, 395 A.2d 222 (1978); *Varela* v. *Wells Fargo Bank*, 15 Cal. App. 3d 741, 93 Cal. Rptr. 428 (1971).

requires; the courts usually deny recovery for lost expectation damages and limit recovery solely to reliance damages.[44]

For example, in the well-known case of *Wheeler* v. *White*,[45] Wheeler owned a three-lot tract of land upon which he desired to construct a commercial building or shopping centre. White promised to obtain the necessary funds for this construction from a third-party or to provide funding himself within six months. The parties signed a formal written "contract". White then assured Wheeler that the funds would be available and encouraged him to proceed with the demolition of the buildings currently on the site to make way for the construction. Accordingly, Wheeler razed the buildings. Thereafter, White informed Wheeler that no loan would be forthcoming. Wheeler was unsuccessful in securing other financing.

In his suit against White, Wheeler alleged breach of commitment to lend and, alternatively, promissory estoppel. The contract was found to be legally insufficient because it failed to provide such critical terms as the amount of interest due, the method of calculating interest, and the time of paying interest. The case was ultimately resolved by the Supreme Court of Texas, which "overruled" the courts below and found that the facts supported the essential elements of a recovery based upon promissory estoppel. The case was remanded for trial on that theory. However, the court made clear that damages based upon expected profits should not be allowed even though such a loss could be proved with certainty. The court stated that any recovery must be limited to damages based upon the detriment sustained by Wheeler in reliance upon White's promise that the loan would be forthcoming. It seems likely that for liability to attach under this theory, the promise must be definite and unequivocal to the effect of assuring the promisee that an agreement will be consummated, thereby making reasonable any reliance by the promisee.[46]

In an interesting application of the doctrine, a bank was allowed recovery against a contractor on the theory of promissory estoppel. In *First State Bank in Archer City* v. *Schwarz Co.*,[47] Schwarz was the general contractor for the construction of apartments. Schwarz executed a subcontract with Holman to do painting and dry wall work on the project. At Holman's request, Schwarz wrote a letter to its bank for the purpose of assisting the subcontractor in arranging financing. On the basis of Schwarz's assurances in the letter, which later proved to be false, the bank extended a $300,000 line of credit to Holman. After drawing on the line of credit, Holman failed to repay the loan. The court held that the evidence was sufficient to support a *prima facie* case of promissory estoppel for the bank against Schwarz.

---

44. See Restatement (Second) of Contracts section 90(1) (1981), and further discussion in section V.A.3.(d) *infra*.
45. Fn. 41 *supra*, 398 S.W.2d 93.
46. See *Hoffman* v. *Red Owl Stores, Inc.*, 26 Wis. 2d 683, 133 N.W.2d 267 (1965).
47. 687 S.W.2d 453 (Tex. Ct. App. 1985).

The estoppel doctrine was also used successfully in *Griswold* v. *Haven*,[48] a nineteenth-century case. In that case, the court used the doctrine of estoppel *in pais*, sometimes called equitable estoppel, rather than promissory estoppel. The basic difference between the two doctrines is that promissory estoppel is based on a promise whereas estoppel *in pais* is based on a misrepresentation of fact.

The bank brought action for the conversion of grain against a warehouseman. The warehouseman had misrepresented to the bank the existence of grain that it alleged that it held for the borrower. In reliance on the grain as a collateral, the bank loaned the borrower money. Upon default by the borrower, the lender moved to recover on its collateral against the warehouseman. The warehouseman took the sensible position in defence that the grain did not exist, and thus it could not be sued for conversion of it. The court held that the warehouseman's misrepresentation estopped it from denying the existence of the grain. Since the warehouseman could not produce the grain, he was found guilty of conversion.

As a practical hint, the commitment to lend should be in writing whenever possible, and the lender should avoid giving advice during the negotiation process regarding use of the loan money or as to how the borrower should proceed on the contemplated project beyond what is agreed to in the contract.

B. "Good Faith" outside the UCC

In the mid 1980s, two California cases[49] (albeit one a bank-depositor case and one a lender-borrower case) about the "good faith and fair dealing" covenant outside the UCC received early national attention.[50]

48. 25 N.Y. 595 (1862).
49. See *Commercial Cotton Co.* v. *United California Bank*, 163 Cal. App. 3d 511, 209 Cal. Rptr. 551 (1985); and *Kruse/Jewell* v. *Bank of America* trial decision Sonoma County Superior Court, Case No. 112439; *rev'd* 201 Cal. App. 3d 354, 248 (Cal. Rptr. 217 (1988), review refused by Cal. Sup. Ct. For brief discussion of early development of case see, Cappello, "Banking Malpractice?," 91 *Case & Comment No. 5*, at 3 (Sept.–Oct. 1986). However, the appellate court reversal of all counts signifies a tightening of the legal standards for proving tortious "bad faith." With respect to the breach of the alleged agreement to make long-term financing, the court held that the alleged oral statements lacked the essential terms of an agreement to make a loan (i.e., amount, interest rate, repayment terms, loan fees and charges, etc.). Thus, at least in California now, denial of the existence of a contract no longer appears to be available as a basis for bad faith. Proof of a valid enforceable contract is a prerequisite to recovery. 201 Cal. App. 3d 354.
50. Note also that another tort, the tort of "bad faith" denial of contract (breach of a contract combined with bad faith denial that a contract even exists) also arose under California law during this time. See e.g. *Price* v. *Wells Fargo Bank*, 213 Cal. App. 3d 465, 261 Cal. Rptr. 735, 739 (1989); *Kruse* v. *Bank of Am.*, 202 Cal. App. 3d 38, 248 Cal. Rptr. 217, 228–29 (1988), *cert. denied*, 488 US 1043 (1989). The elements of this tort were (1) an underlying contract, (2) which is breached by the defendant, (3) who then denies liability by asserting that the contract does not exist, (4) in bad faith and (5) without probable cause for such denial. *Careau & Co.* v. *Security Pacific Business Credit, Inc.*, 222 Cal. App. 3d 1371, 272 Cal. Rptr. 387 (1990). The continuing viability of this tort in the lender context could also be questioned in light of the overall judicial retreat from *Commercial*

Today, however, the availability of this tort cause of action in the ordinary debtor-creditor context has been substantially curtailed. In *Copesky* v. *Superior Court*,[51] the California Court of Appeals, in a thoughtful and well-reasoned analysis, recognised that its prior decision in *Commercial Cotton* is no longer viable as a basis for lender liability, holding that banks are not fiduciaries for their depositors, and that the bank-depositor relationship is not a "special relationship" such as to give rise to tort damages when an implied contractual covenant of good faith is broken.[52]

Similarly, in *F.D.I.C.* v. *Coleman*,[53] the Texas Supreme Court held that a common law duty of good faith is not imposed in every contract, only in special relationships marked by a shared trust or an imbalance of power.[54] Absent such a special relationship, the duty to act in good faith is contractual in nature and does not amount to an independent tort.[55] Consequently, the relationships between mortgagors and mortgagees, creditors and guarantors, lenders and borrowers, and letter of credit issuers and beneficiaries, do not ordinarily involve such a duty of good faith.[56] Other States are in accord.[57]

The duty of good faith arises not because of the contractual relationship itself, but because of the relationship existing between the parties. While courts traditionally are reluctant to impose fiduciary duties upon a lender solely by virtue of the creditor-debtor relationship, the existence of excessive control by

---

Cotton. See *Copesky* v. *Superior Court*, 229 Cal. App. 3d 678, 280 Cal. Rptr. 338, 348 (1991) ("ordinary bank-customer relationship [is] not a special relationship giving rise to tort remedies when the bank unreasonably, and even in bad faith, denies liability on a contract or interposes spurious defenses"). But cf. *DuBarry Int'l* v. *Southwest Forest Ind.*, 231 Cal. App. 3d 552, 282 Cal. Rptr. 181 (1991) (recognising and applying this tort in non-lending context). Bad faith denial of contract does not appear to have emerged as a significant basis for lender liability in other jurisdictions.

51. *Copesky* v. *Superior Court*, *supra* fn. 50.

52. *Copesky* v. *Superior Court*, *supra* fn. 50. *Mitsui Mfrs. Bank* v. *Superior Court*, 212 Cal. App. 3d 726, 260 Cal. Rptr. 793 (1989) (tort doctrine of breach of duty of good faith and fair dealing did not extend to normal commercial banking transactions); *Price* v. *Wells Fargo Bank*, *supra* fn. 50 (no fiduciary relationship existed between bank and its customers to support claim of tortious breach of implied duty of good faith).

53. 795 S.W.2d 706 (1990).

54. *Ibid.*, at 708–09.

55. *Central Sav. & Loan Ass'n* v. *Stemmons Northwest Bank*, 848 S.W.2d 232, 239 (Tex. App.—Dallas 1992, *no writ*).

56. E.g., *Hall* v. *RTC*, 958 F.2d 75 (5th Cir. 1992); *FDIC* v. *Condo Group Apartments*, 812 F. Supp. 694 (N.D. Tex. 1992); *FDIC* v. *Coleman*, 795 S.W.2d 706, 709 (Tex. 1990); *Central Sav. & Loan Ass'n* v. *Stemmons Northwest Bank*, 848 S.W.2d 232 (Tex. App.—Dallas 1992, *no writ*). *Baskin* v. *Mortgage and Trust, Inc.*, 837 S.W.2d 743 (Tex. App.—Houston 1992, *writ denied*); *Security Bank* v. *Dalton*, 803 S.W.2d 443 (Tex. App.—Fort Worth 1991, *writ denied*).

57. See e.g. *Bachmeier* v. *Bank of Ravenswood*, 663 F. Supp. 1207, 1225 (N.D. Ill. 1987) (principle of covenant of good faith does not create an independent cause of action); *First Nat'l Bank and Trust Co. of Vinita* v. *Kissee*, 859 P.2d 502 (Okla. 1993) (without gross recklessness or wanton negligence on behalf of party to commercial contract, breach of implied duty of good faith and fair dealing, except in insurance context, merely results in breach of contract, and not independent tort); *Rogers* v. *Tecumseh Bank*, 756 P.2d 1223 (Okla. 1988) (refusing to extend the implied-in-law duty of good faith and fair dealing imposed in insurance contracts to commercial loans in order to support a cause of action for "tortious breach of contract").

the lender could in and of itself give rise to a special relationship that, in turn, would create a duty of good faith outside the UCC.

C. Basic tort theories

Lenders may incur liability based on various tort theories. These theories often come into play where the lender engages in conduct that is not documented, is outside the context of the terms of existing documents, or involves improper exercise, or threat to exercise, rights and remedies provided under the loan documents.

1. Fraud

Lenders may incur liability based on fraud. Ordinarily, to recover against a lender for fraud, a borrower must prove:

— that a material misrepresentation was made by the lender;
— that the lender made the misrepresentation with knowledge of its falsity or recklessly, as a positive assertion without any knowledge of the truth;
— that the lender made it with the intention that it would be acted upon by the borrower;
— that the borrower acted in reliance upon it; and
— that the borrower suffered some damage as a result.[58]

If the lender's representation involves a promise to do an act in the future, the borrower must prove that, at the time the bank's representative made the promise, the bank had no intention of performing the act.[59] An intent not to perform an act in the future as promised may be proven by circumstantial evidence.[60] Finally, a representation that is literally true is actionable as fraud if it is used to create an impression that is substantially false.[61]

Fraudulent practice typically is asserted in connection with a lender's

---

58. *T.O. Stanley Boot Co. v. Bank of El Paso*, 847 S.W.2d 218, 222 (Tex. 1992); *State Nat'l Bank of El Paso v. Farah Mfg. Co.*, 678 S.W.2d 661, 681 (Tex. App.—El Paso 1984, *writ dism'd by agrmt*). See also *Banco Do Brasil, S.A. v. Latian, Inc.*, 234 Cal. App. 3d 973, 285 Cal. Rptr. 870, 896 (Cal. Ct. App. 1991), *cert. denied*, 112 S. Ct. 2967 (1992) (in order to recover for fraud against lender under California law, borrower must prove that (1) lender made a representation including a promise made without the intent to perform; (2) knowledge of the representation's falsity; (3) an intent to defraud; i.e., to induce reliance; (4) justifiable reliance on borrower's part; and (5) resulting damage).

59. *T.O. Stanley Boot Co. v. Bank of El Paso, supra*, fn. 58.

60. See *Farah Mfg. Co., supra*, fn. 58.

61. *Commonwealth Mortgage Corp. v. First Nationwide Bank*, 873 F.2d 859 (5th Cir. 1989); *Farah Mfg. Co., supra*, fn. 58.

promises of benefits in exchange for security,[62] groundless threats,[63] misrepresentation concerning the effect of loan documents,[64] failure to disclose information in order to protect its own interests,[65] giving improper advice to a borrower[66] and falsely representing that it has done or will do something for the borrower.[67]

For example, in *State National Bank of El Paso* v. *Farah Manufacturing Company*,[68] allegations of fraud focused on the lenders' representations that a default would be declared and the borrower bankrupted and padlocked if William Farah, rather than the lenders' preferred candidate, were elected CED of the borrower. The failure of the lenders to explain their intention when they knew it was capable of two interpretations, one false (the declaration of default upon William Farah's election), was actionable fraudulent conduct: "[W]here a promise regarding future action is made with the intent that it will not be performed and is made to deceive a person, then it is actionable as a fraudulent representation."[69]

The *Farah* case involved a form of promissory misrepresentation by the lender. A lender's conduct also may give rise to a form of fraud known as constructive fraud. Constructive fraud is the breach of some legal or equitable duty which, irrespective of moral guilt, the law declares fraudulent because of its tendency to deceive others, to violate confidence, or to injure public interests.[70]

Constructive fraud most commonly arises in lender liability where a confidential or fiduciary duty has arisen between the lender and borrower, and the lender either fails to disclose material facts to the borrower or engages in some self-dealing or overreaching. Ordinarily, however, such a special relationship does not exist between a borrower and a lender, and where one has

---

62. See, e.g., *Dean W. Knight & Sons, Inc.* v. *First W. Bank & Trust* Co., Cal. App. 2d 148 Cal. Rptr. 767 (Cal. Ct. App. 1978). But see *Centerre Bank* v. *Distributors, Inc.*, 705 S.W.2d 42 (Mo. Ct. App. 1985).

63. See, e.g., *Loyola Fed. Sav. & Loan Ass'n* v. *Galanes*, 365 A.2d 580 (Md. Ct. Spec. App. 1976); *Farah Mfg. Co., supra* fn. 58.

64. See, e.g., *Holm* v. *Sun Bank/Broward*, 423 So.2d 1007 (Fla. Dist. Ct. App. 1982); *Lee* v. *Heights Bank*, 446 N.E.2d 248 (Ill. App. Ct. 1983). But cf. *Farmer City State Bank* v. *Guingrich*, 487 N.E.2d 758 (Ill. App. Ct. 1985).

65. See, e.g., *Merrill Lynch, Pierce Fenner & Smith* v. *First Nat'l Bank*, 774 F.2d 909 (8th Cir. 1985); *General Motors Acceptance Corp.* v. *Central Nat'l Bank*, 773 F.2d 771 (7th Cir. 1985); *Central States Stamping Co.* v. *Terminal Equip. Co., Inc.*, 727 F.2d 1405 (6th Cir. 1984).

66. *Banco Totta e Acores* v. *Fleet Nat'l Bank*, 768 F. Supp. 943 (D.R.I. 1991); *United Cos. Fin. Corp.* v. *Brown*, 584 So. 2d 470 (Ala. 1991); *Rainsville Bank* v. *Willingham*, 485 So. 2d 319 (Ala. 1986); *Nie* v. *Galena State Bank & Trust Co.*, 387 N.W.2d 373 (Iowa Ct. App. 1986); *Shogyo Int'l Corp.* v. *First Nat'l Bank of Clarksdale*, 475 So. 2d 425 (Miss. 1985).

67. See, e.g., *Richter* v. *Bank of America*, 939 F.2d 1176 (5th Cir. 1991); *General Motors Acceptance Corp.* v. *Covington*, 586 So.2d 178 (Ala. 1991); *First Fed. Sav. & Loan Ass'n* v. *Caudle*, 425 So.2d 1050 (Ala. 1982); *Frame* v. *Boatmen's Bank*, 782 S.W.2d 117 (Mo. Ct. App. 1989); *Commerce Sav. Scottsbluff* v. *F.H. Schafer Elevator, Inc.*, 436 N.W.2d 151 (Neb. 1989).

68. See *Farah Mfg. Co., supra* fn. 58.

69. *Ibid.*, at 682.

70. *Great Southwest Office Park, Ltd.* v. *Texas Commerce Bank Nat'l Ass'n*, 786 S.W.2d 386, 391 (Tex. App.—Houston 1990, *writ denied*).

been found it has rested on extraneous facts and conduct, such as excessive lender control over or influence in the borrower's activities.[71]

2. Economic duress

Lenders also may incur liability for conduct constituting duress. Generally, there can be no duress unless:

— there is a threat to do some act that the threatening party has no legal right to do;
— the threat is of such character as to destroy the free agency of the party to whom it is directed;
— the restraint caused by the threat is imminent; and
— the threatened person has no present means of protection.[72]

In essence, economic duress is present where one is induced by wrongful act of another to make a contract under circumstances which deprive him or her of the exercise of free will. A contract executed under duress is voidable.[73] To establish duress, one must demonstrate that the threat has left the individual bereft of the quality of mind essential to the making of a contract.[74] It is a defence to obligations to which a party would not otherwise agree, were it not for the other party's wrongful and oppressive demands, and is recognised as an affirmative defence to an action on a contract or note.[75]

The general rule is that while threats to enforce legal rights may constitute duress under certain circumstances, they do not constitute duress when made to enforce *existent legal rights*.[76] Duress does not exist where consent to an agreement is secured by hard bargaining or the pressure of the financial circumstances.[77] Duress would only occur when the threatened enforcement is to enforce rights that in fact are non-existent, such as when a contract sought to be enforced is illegal.[78]

71. *Cara Corp.* v. *Continental Bank (In re Cara. Corp.)*, 148 B.R. 760 (Bankr. E.D. Pa. 1992); *Great Southwest Office Park, Ltd.* v. *Texas Commerce Bank Nat'l Ass'n*, 786 S.W.2d 386, 391 (Tex. App.—Houston 1990, *writ denied*).

72. See, e.g., *Mirax Chem. Prod. Corp.* v. *First Interstate Commercial Corp.*, 950 F.2d 566, 570 (8th Cir. 1991); *Bank of El Paso* v. *T.O. Stanley Boot Co.*, *supra* fn. 58, modified, 847 S.W.2d 218 (Tex. 1992).

73. See *FDIC* v. *Linn*, 671 F. Supp. 547, 556 (N.D. Ill. 1987).

74. See *ibid.*, at 556.

75. *Ibid.*

76. See *Spillers* v. *Five Points Guaranty Bank*, 335 So. 2d 851 (Fal. Dist. Ct. App. 1976).

77. See *Mirax Chem. Prod. Corp.* v. *First Interstate Commercial Corp.*, *supra* fn. 72; *FDIC* v. *Linn*, *supra* fn. 73.

78. See *Spillers* v. *Five Points Guaranty Bank*, *supra* fn. 76. See also *State Nat'l Bank of El Paso* v. *Farah Mfg. Co.*, *supra* fn. 58. In response to the defendant's assertion that no legal right for duress could exist where the parties in fact have a legal right of enforcement, the court found that the lenders' threat was in fact not lawful in that it violated section 1.208 of the Texas Business and Commerce Code (the Texas version of the Uniform Commercial Code), which legally obligated the

3. Tortious interference

Lenders may incur liability for tortious interference in certain circumstances. Tortious interference typically encompasses two torts: tortious interference with contract and tortious interference with prospective business relations.[79] Both torts recognise that a person's business relationships constitute a property interest and as such are entitled to protection from unjustified tampering.[80]

The traditional common law elements of tortious interference with contract vary from state to state, but typically include:

(1) existence of a valid contract subject to interference;
(2) an interference that was wilful and intentional;
(3) proof that the intentional act was a proximate cause of plaintiff's damage; and
(4) resulting actual damage.[81]

Similarly, under the tort of interference with a business relationship or prospective advantage in business, the same elements apply except that no

---

parties to the loan agreement to deal in "good faith" with one another.

Section 1–208 provides in part: "A term providing that one party may accelerate payment on performance 'at will' or 'when he deems himself insecure' or in words of similar import shall be construed to mean that he shall have power to do so only if he in good faith believes that the Prospect of payment or performance is impaired."

The specific objective behind this particular statutory "good faith" requirement is the avoidance of the use of an acceleration clause as an offensive method of enforcement in order to place the creditor in a commercially advantageous position. As noted by the *Farah* court: "Even where an insecurity clause is drafted in the broadest possible terms, the primary question is whether the creditors' attempts to accelerate stemmed from a reasonable, good faith belief that its security was about to become impaired. Acceleration clauses are not to be used offensively such as for the commercial advantage of the creditor. They do not permit acceleration when the facts makes its use unjust or oppressive."

Ibid., at 685. The *Farah* court further found that the lenders in fact were advancing their own economic interests to the detriment of Farah Manufacturing Company, that the threats and intimidations of the lenders caused the corporation's board of directors to accede to the lenders' demand, and that the lenders' actions were done to ensure management of the corporation by persons they approved of and specifically to exclude William Farah from management. But see, *FDIC* v. *Linn*, supra fn. 73.

79. *State Nat'l Bank* v. *Academia*, 802 S.W.2d 282, 295 (Tex. App.—Corpus Christi 1990, *writ denied*).

80. *Ibid.*

81. See *Victoria Bank & Trust Co.* v. *Brady*, 811 S.W.2d 931, 939 (Tex. 1991). See also *Flintridge Station Assocs.* v. *American Fletcher Mortgage Co.*, 761 F.2d 434, 440 (7th Cir. 1985) (under Indiana law, five elements must be proven to recover for tort for interference with the contractual relations of another: "(1) existence of a valid and enforceable contract; (2) defendant's knowledge of the existence of this contract; (3) defendant's intentional inducement of a breach of contract; (4) the absence of justification; and (5) damages resulting from defendant's wrongful inducement of the breach"); *State Nat'l Bank* v. *Academia*, supra fn. 79; *Lachenmaier* v. *First Bank Sys.*, 803 P.2d 614, 619 (Mont. 1990) (under Montana law, to make out a claim for tortious interference with a contractual relationship, the complaint must allege: "(1) that a contract was entered into, (2) that its performance was refused, (3) that such refusal was induced by unlawful and malicious acts of the defendant, and (4) that damages have resulted").

contractual relationship need be shown.[82] The elements of the tort of interference with prospective business relations typically include:

(1) the existence of a valid business relationship or plaintiff's reasonable expectancy of entering into a valid business relationship;
(2) defendant's knowledge of this relationship or expectancy;
(3) intentional interference by defendant inducing termination of the relationship or preventing the expectancy from ripening into a valid business relationship; and
(4) damage to plaintiff as a result of the interference.[83]

Proof of these elements establishes a *prima facie* case for interference—in response, the defendant must show that its acts were either justified or privileged.[84] In all cases, the act of interference must be without legal right or justifiable cause on the part of the defendant.[85]

The privilege of legal justification or excuse is an affirmative defence to the claim of tortious interference with contractual relations.[86] Under this defence, one is privileged to interfere with another's contractual relations (1) if such interference constitutes a *bona fide* exercise of one's own rights, or (2) of one has an equal or superior right in the subject matter to that of another party.[87] However, this defence only protects good faith assertions of legal rights.[88] For example, a lender's failure to release a security interest after the indebtedness has been paid, combined with continued assertion of a lien during an attempted sale of the collateral, can evidence that the lender did not act in good faith and thus could not establish the defence of legal justification or excuse for its tortious interference with the business relationship.[89]

Notably, an agent is privileged, when acting on behalf of its principal, to interfere with a contract between its principal and a third party.[90] Consequently, an agent's acts, if motivated and taken in furtherance of the purposes and interests of its principal, will not give rise to a cause of action for tortious interference by the third party.[91]

---

82. See also *Flintridge Station Assocs.* v. *American Fletcher Mortgage Co., supra* fn. 81.
83. *State Nat'l Bank* v. *Academia, supra* fn. 79.
84. See *State Nat'l Bank of El Paso* v. *Farah Mfg. Co., supra* fn. 58.
85. *Ibid.*
86. See *Victoria Bank and Trust Co.* v. *Brady, supra* fn. 81.
87. *Ibid.*
88. *Ibid.*
89. *Ibid.*
90. See *Lachenmaier* v. *First Bank Syst., supra* fn. 81.
91. *Ibid.* The court's decision in *State Nat'l Bank of El Paso* v. *Farah Mfg. Co. (supra* fn. 58) is perhaps the leading national lender liability case on tortious interference. In the second alternative holding in that case, the court found that the plaintiff had properly stated a cause of action entitling it to "foreseeable damages" resulting from the lenders' interference with Farah's right to lawful management and proper corporate governance. Such interference included the lender's installation of a certain individual as CEO, the forcing out of another individual, the installation of a bank-affiliated person as chairman of the board, the prevention of the election of two persons to the

A case upholding a theory of lender liability based on tortious interference was *Melamed* v. *Lake County National Bank*.[92] In that case, the lender replaced the debtor's accountant with one selected by the lender, retained final approval of all payments made by the debtor, developed a "13–point" programme to help savage the debtor, and forced the president of the debtor to take a 50 per cent reduction of pay.[93]

4. Infliction of emotional distress

Lenders also may incur liability for intentional infliction of emotional distress.[94] The elements of this tort are:

(1) outrageous conduct by the lender;

(2) intentional causing or reckless disregard of the probability of causing distress by the lender;

(3) suffering of severe or extreme emotional distress by the borrower; and

(4) actual or proximate causation of the emotional distress by the lender's outrageous conduct.[95]

To be considered outrageous, a lender's conduct must be so extreme in degree as to go beyond all possible bounds of decency, and to be regarded as atrocious and utterly intolerable in a civilised community.[96] Factors to consider in assessing whether particular conduct is outrageous include the degree of power or authority a lender exerts over a borrower, whether the borrower reasonably believed that a lender's threats would be carried out, whether the lender reasonably believed that its objection was legitimate, and whether the lender was aware that a borrower was peculiarly susceptible to emotional distress by reason of some physical or mental condition.[97] This tort generally cannot be

---

board, the replacement of these individuals with individuals favoured by the lenders, and the interference with another person's efforts to use the proxy system to regain control. *Ibid.* at 688–690.

The *Farah* court (noting the strong public policy in favour of maintaining the corporate governance structure) chose to expand this cause of action to situations in which a specific contract interference did not exist but where there existed interference through the corporate governance rights of a borrower corporation and its shareholders. *Ibid.*, at 690. Although it was not argued, perhaps this deviation is not so radical if the corporate governance structure is viewed as a series of contracts between the corporate and its owners and managers. Also of note is the conclusion of the court that actual malice was not required, only that the acts were done wilfully, intentionally, and without just cause. No intent to harm need be proven as long as actual harm resulted. *Ibid.*, at 690.

92. 727 F.2d 1399 (6th Cir. 1984).

93. *Ibid.*

94. See, e.g., *Citicorp Credit Serv.*, 686 F. Supp. 330 (S.D. Ga. 1988); *Ricci* v. *Key Bancshares of Maine*, 662 F. Supp. 1132 (D. Me. 1987); *Sanchez-Corea* v. *Bank of America*, 38 Cal. 3d 892, 701 P.2d 826, 215 Cal. Rptr. 679 (1985); *Meads* v. *McGrath* v. *Fahey*, 533 N.E.2d 806 (Ill. 1988). But cf. *Commercial Cotton Co.* v. *United California Bank*, 163 Cal. App. 3d 511, 209 Cal. Rptr. 551 (1985); *Harsha* v. *State Sav. Bank*, 346 N.W.2d 791 (Iowa 1984).

95. See *Harsha* v. *State Sav. Bank*, supra fn. 94.

96. *Ibid.*

97. *McGrath* v. *Fahey*, 533 N.E.2d 806 (Ill. 1988).

established by mere rudeness or lack of consideration by the lender,[98] nor does it extend to mere insults, indignities, threats, annoyances, petty oppression or other trivialities.[99] Whether particular conduct is outrageous is ultimately a question of fact, and resolution by summary judgment is inappropriate.[100]

Finally, the tort of intentional infliction of emotional distress should be distinguished from lender liability for damages based on emotional distress arising from some other tort, such as wrongful dishonour of a cheque.[101]

5. Negligence

The existence of a duty of care is a prerequisite to establishing a claim of negligence against a lender.[102] As a general rule, a financial institution owes no duty of care to a borrower when the institution's involvement in a loan transaction does not exceed the scope of its conventional role as a mere lender of money.[103] Liability to a borrower for negligence arises only when the lender actively participates in the financial enterprise beyond the domain of the usual lender.[104] Ordinarily, normal supervision of the enterprise financed by the lender for the protection of its security interest in the collateral is not active participation beyond that of the ordinary role of a lender in a loan transaction.[105]

The general rule notwithstanding, lenders have incurred liability based on negligence in many instances, including negligent processing of a loan application.[106] negligent appraisal,[107] negligent inspection,[108] negligent failure to obtain insurance related to the loan,[109] negligent administration of a loan,[110]

---

98. See *Spillers* v. *Five Points Guaranty Bank*, *supra* fn. 78.

99. *McGrath* v. *Fahey*, *supra* fn. 97.

100. *Meads* v. *Citicorp Credit Serv.*, 686 F. Supp. 330 (S.D. Ga. 1988).

101. *Kendall Yacht Corp.* v. *United California Bank*, 50 Cal. App. 3d 949, 123 Cal. Rptr. 848 (1975).

102. See, e.g., *Nymark* v. *Heart Fed. Sav. & Loan Ass'n*, 231 Cal. App. 3d 1089, 283 Cal. Rptr. 53 (1991); *Larsen* v. *United Fed. Sav. and Loan Ass'n*, 300 N.W.2d 281 (Iowa 1981).

103. *Nymark* v. *Heart Fed. Sav. & Loan Ass'n*, *supra* fn. 102.

104. *Ibid.*

105. *Ibid.*

106. See, e.g., *High* v. *McLean Fin. Corp.*, 659 F. Supp. 1561 (D.D.C. 1987); *First Fed. Sav. & Loan Ass'n of Hamilton* v. *Caudle*, 425 So. 2d 1050 (Ala. 1982); *Jacques* v. *First Nat'l Bank of Maryland*, 515 A.2d 756 (Md. App. 1986). But cf. *Howard Oaks* v. *Maryland Nat'l Bank*, 810 F. Supp. 674 (D. Md. 1993); *G & M Oil Co.* v. *Glenfed Fin'l Corp.*, 782 F. Supp. 1078 (D. Md. 1989).

107. Compare *Larsen* v. *United Fed. Sav. and Loan Ass'n*, *supra* fn. 102, with *Nymark* v. *Heart Fed. Sav. Ass'n*, *supra* fn. 102, with *Hughes* v. *Holt*, 435 A.2d 687 (Vt. 1981).

108. See, e.g., *Williamson* v. *Reality Champion*, 551 So. 2d 1000 (Ala. 1989). Cf. *Rudolph* v. *First S. Fed. Sav. & Loan Ass'n*, 414 So. 2d 64 (Ala. 1982) (no duty is imposed on lender of construction loan to exercise reasonable care in inspection of borrower's premises unless lender voluntarily undertakes to perform such inspection on behalf of and for the benefit of the borrower).

109. See, e.g., *Hancock Bank* v. *Travis*, 580 So. 2d 727 (Miss. 1991); *Walters* v. *First Nat'l Bank of Newark*, 433 N.E.2d 608 (Ohio 1982); *Stone* v. *Davis*, 419 N.E.2d 1094 (Ohio), *cert. denied*, 459 US 1081 (1981).

110. See, e.g., *Brunswick Bank & Trust Co.* v. *United States*, 707 F.2d 1355 (Fed. Cir. 1983); *First Nat'l City Bank of New York* v. *Gonzales*, 293 F.2d 919 (1st Cir. 1961).

negligent supervision of construction,[111] negligent loan disbursement,[112] and negligent response to credit enquiries.[113] To date, however, lenders typically have not been held liable for negligent loan approval,[114] and a lender owes no duty to enquire of or inform one joint depositor of the actions of another.[115]

6. Conversion

Lenders also may incur liability based on conversion. Conversion is the unauthorised and wrongful assumption of dominion and control over the personal property of another, to the exclusion of or inconsistent with the owner's rights.[116] Conversion requires ownership of the property, a right of possession and unauthorised dominion over the property by another resulting in damages.[117] Conversion claims against lenders typically arise in cases involving wrongful repossession.[118] Without ownership, however, no claim for conversion exists.[119] Further, there can be no conversion when a lender properly takes action pursuant to the terms of a valid security agreement.[120] Finally, an action for conversion requires specific and identifiable property; consequently, funds in an account cannot be converted.[121] In extreme circumstances, lender conversion may support an award of punitive damages.[122]

111. See, e.g., *Connor* v. *Great W. Sav. & Loan Ass'n*, 69 Cal. 2d 850, 447 P.2d 209, 73 Cal. Rptr. 369 (Cal. 1968).

112. See, e.g., *Commercial Standard Ins. Co.* v. *Bank of America*, 57 Cal. App. 3d 241, 129 Cal. Rptr. 91 (1976); *English* v. *Ford*, 17 Cal. App. 3d 1038, 95 Cal. Rptr. 501 (1971); *Davis* v. *Nevada Nat'l Bank*, 737 P.2d 503 (Nev. 1987). Cf. *Columbia Plaza Corp.* v. *Security Nat'l Bank*, 676 F.2d 780 (D.C. Cir. 1982) (while lender was not found negligent, loan officer was). But see *Boyd & Lovesee Lumber Co.* v. *Modular Mktg. Corp.*, 44 Cal. App. 3d 460, 118 Cal. Rptr. 699 (1975); *Daniels* v. *Army Nat'l Bank*, 822 P.2d 39 (Kan. 1991); *Thormahlen* v. *Citizens Sav. & Loan*, 698 P.2d 512 (Or. App. 1985).

113. See, e.g., *MSA Tubular Prod.* v. *First Bank & Trust Co.*, 869 F.2d 1422 (10th Cir. 1989); *Central States Stamping Co.* v. *Terminal Equip. Co.*, 727 F.2d 1405 (6th Cir. 1984); *Brayton Chem.* v. *First Farmers State Bank*, 671 F.2d 1047 (7th Cir. 1982); *Berkline Corp.* v. *Bank of Mississippi*, 453 So. 2d 699 (Miss. 1984); *Bank of Nevada* v. *Butler Aviation-O'Hare*, 616 P.2d 398 (Nev. 1980); *Ostlund Chem. Co.* v. *Norwest Bank*, 417 N.W.2d 833 (N.D. 1988).

114. See, e.g., *Nelson* v. *Production Credit Ass'n*, 930 F.2d 599 (8th Cir.), *cert. denied*, 112 S. Ct. 417 (1991) (state law imposed no duty on lender to use reasonable care in making a loan); *FDIC* v. *Fordham*, 130 B.R. 632 (Bankr. D. Mass. 1991); *Wagner* v. *Benson*, 101 Cal. App. 3d 37, 161 Cal. Rptr. 516 (1980); *Gries* v. *First Wisconsin Nat'l Bank of Milwaukee*, 264 N.W.2d 254 (Wis. 1978).

115. *Pulliam* v. *Pulliam*, 738 S.W.2d 846 (Ky. Ct. App. 1987).

116. *Richter* v. *Bank of Am. Nat'l Trust & Sav. Ass'n*, 939 F.2d 1176, 1191 (5th Cir. 1991).

117. See, e.g., *Farmers State Bank of Victor* v. *Imperial Cattle Co.*, 708 P.2d 223 (Mont. 1985).

118. See, e.g., *Betterton* v. *First Interstate Bank of Arizona, NA*, 800 F.2d 732 (8th Cir. 1986); *Varela* v. *Wells Fargo Bank*, 15 Cal. App. 3d 741, 93 Cal. Rptr. 428 (1971); *Henderson* v. *Maryland Nat'l Bank*, 336 A.2d 1 (Md. 1976); *Mitchell* v. *Ford Motor Credit Co.*, 688 P.2d 42 (Okla. 1984); *Lee* v. *Wood Prod. Credit Union*, 551 P.2d 445 (Or. 1976); *Ford Motor Credit Co.* v. *Washington*, 573 S.W.2d 616 (Tex. Civ. App.—Austin 1978, *writ ref'd*).

119. *Farmers State Bank of Victor* v. *Imperial Cattle Co.*, 708 P.2d 223 (Mon. 1985).

120. See *Richter* v. *Bank of Am. Nat'l Trust & Sav. Ass'n*, 939 F.2d 1176 (5th Cir. 1991).

121. See, e.g., *Geller* v. *National Westminster Bank*, 770 F. Supp. 210 (S.D.N.Y. 1991); *Spencer Co.* v. *Chase Manhattan Bank*, 81 B.R. 194 (D. Mass. 1987); *Luxonomy Cars* v. *Citibank, NA*, 65 A.D.2d 549, 408 N.Y.S.2d 951 (1978); *Feder* v. *Fortunoff, Inc.*, 123 Misc. 2d 857, 474 N.Y.S.2d 937 (1984). But cf. *Rainsville Bank* v. *Willingham*, 485 So. 2d 319 (Ala. 1986).

122. See, e.g., *Rainsville Bank* v. *Willingham*, *supra* fn. 121; *Ford Motor Credit Co.* v. *Waters*,

7. Defamation

Lenders may also incur liability for defamation.[123] For instance, improper repossession of collateral can constitute a statement concerning a borrower's failure to honour its financial obligations, which may be injurious to the plaintiff's business reputation and defamatory *per se*.[124]

8. "Prima facie" tort theory

Under this theory a lawful act unjustifiably performed with intent to harm another is on its face unlawful. This theory is derived from the assumption that a residue of tort liability exists apart from the tort law forms of action.[125] As indicated by the Restatement (Second) of Torts section 870:

"One who intentionally causes injury to another is subject to liability to the other for that injury, if his conduct is generally culpable and not justifiable under the circumstances. This liability may be imposed although the actor's conduct does not come within a traditional category of tort liability."

The scope of *prima facie* tort theory, however, is essentially left to judicial application.

One modern case indicating the possible use of the *prima facie* tort theory to impose lender liability is *Bronfman* v. *Centerre Bank of Kansas City*,[126] wherein the lender was held liable by the trial court under this theory for wrongfully calling a demand note. On 21 August 1981, the lender had notified the borrower that the outstanding demand note would continue for only 60 days. Contrary to his representation, the lender continued to advance funds and to co-operate with the borrower well into December of 1981. On 15 December 1981, however, the lender made formal demand on the note. Shortly after the demand, the assets and accounts receivable of the borrower were voluntarily turned over to the lender for liquidation. The borrower filed suit against the lender, alleging that the lender's conduct, although lawful, was performed with the intent to injure the borrower. The jury returned its verdict against the lender in the amount of $1,480,000, consisting of $480,000 in actual damages and $1,000,000 punitive damages.

Under the local state law (which did not recognise a cause of action for tortious interference), the elements of the cause of action for a *prima facie* tort are: (i) an unlawful act by the defendant, (ii) an intent to cause injury to the

---

273 So. 2d 96 (Fla. Dist. Ct. App. 1973); *Mitchell* v. *Ford Motor Credit Co.*, *supra* fn. 118; *Lee* v. *Wood Prod. Credit Union*, 551 P.2d 446 (Ord. 1976).

123. See, e.g., *Alaska State Bank* v. *Fairco*, 674 P.2d 288 (Alaska 1983). But see *Sun First Nat'l Bank of Lake Wales* v. *Stegall*, 395 So. 2d 1248 (Fla. Dist. Ct. App. 1981).

124. See, e.g., *Alaska State Bank* v. *Fairco*, 674 P.2d 288 (Alaska 1983). But see *Sun First Nat'l Bank of Lake Wales* v. *Stegall*, *supra* fn. 123 (borrower failed to show that statements caused him any damage).

125. For an analysis of the legal foundations of this theory, see *Porter* v. *Crawford & Co.*, 611 S.W.2d 265 (Mo. Ct. App. 1980).

126. *Rev'd on appeal*, 705 S.W. 2d 42 (Mo. App. 1985).

plaintiff, (iii) injury to the plaintiff, and (iv) absence of any justification or an insufficient justification for the defendant's action.[127] This decision, however, was reversed on appeal. The key legal issue on appeal concerning the *prima facie* tort theory was the standard of "intent to injure" that will be applied by the court.

In reviewing the evidence, the appeals court concluded that there was sufficient business justification (i.e., "valid business interests to protect") to call the demand loans, inasmuch as borrower was in a negative cash position and was already suffering losses and the borrower's inventory figures were questionable and the borrower's late receivables were high. As such, a cause of *prima facie* tort could not be proven *in this case*. In so deciding, the court utilised the "balancing test" in section 870 of the Restatement (Second) of Torts as a guide for the development of this new form of tort action. This test calls for a balancing of four factors: (i) the nature and seriousness of the harm; (ii) the interests promoted by the actor's conduct; (iii) the character of the means used by the actor; and (iv) the actor's motive.

Also on related causes of action, the appellate court found there was not a confidential or fiduciary relationship arising from this lending arrangement and that the maker and guarantors of demand instruments could not refuse to honour obligations for the bank's failure to act in good faith.

However, what can be missed in this reversal is the appellate court's apparent acceptance of the possible existence (under different facts, of course) of a *prima facie* tort claim against a lender.[128] Although *Centerre* was reversed on appeal, the appeals court left open the possibility that under another set of facts, a *prima facie* tort might be sustained.

The *prima facie* tort theory, if adopted by a jurisdiction, could perhaps be the broadest theory of lender liability. Again, the lender's course of dealing with the borrower, notwithstanding the terms of the loan documents, is critical to the liability issue. However, the validity doctrine has been challenged.[129]

9. Misrepresentation of borrower's financial condition

By the very nature of a workout situation, the lender will have information about the borrower's troubled financial condition. The lender's dilemma is that revelation of the borrower's financial difficulties may accelerate or exacerbate such financial difficulties, while concealment of such information may mislead

127. 611 S.W.2d at 268.
128. 705 S.W.2d 42 (1985).
129. See *Castello* v. *Shelter Mut. Ins. Co.*, 697 S.W.2d 237 (Mo. Ct. App. 1985) (noting that "recent decisions have left doubt as to the validity of the *prima facie* tort theory". See also *Shaughnessy* v. *Mark Twain State Bank*, 715 S.W.2d 944, 948 (Mo. Ct. App. 1986). But in addition to Missouri, New York and New Mexico recognise the possibility of a *prima facie* tort claim. See, e.g., *Schmitz* v. *Smentowski*, 785 P.2d 726, 735 36 (N.W. 1990); *Luxonomy Cars, Inc.* v. *Citibank, NA*, 65 A.D.2d 549, 408 N.Y.S.2d 951 (1978).

other creditors of the borrower and may lead to litigation by such creditors against the lender.

A modern case under Ohio law arose from a dispute between a heavy equipment manufacturer's lender and a company that has contracted to purchase a $200,000 machine from the manufacturer.[130] Although the prospective purchaser was satisfied with the manufacturer's engineering ability, it had some concern about its financial strength and accordingly the purchaser quizzed the manufacturer's lender at some length about the manufacturer's financial strength and about its integrity.[131] Citing the Ohio Supreme Court's adoption of the Restatement (Second) of Torts section 551, the Sixth Circuit held that "once Martin [president of Central States, the prospective purchaser] undertook to advise Scheer [president of Central States] with respect to Terminal's [the manufacturer's] financial condition he had a duty to disclose information in his possession which would reasonably be considered material to the decision he knew Scheer was in the process of making. Martin knew that Scheer had confidence in his knowledge about Terminal. His positive answers were likely to induce Central States to accept Terminal's proposal. Failure to disclose Terminal's true financial position made his previous positive responses misleading at least."[132] The court upheld the jury's award of damages equal to the two payments that the purchaser had made to the manufacturer before the manufacturer, having failed to deliver the requested machine, filed for bankruptcy protection.[133]

More recently, the Illinois Court of Appeals held a bank liable for negligently supplying false information to a second bank that relied on the information to make an unsecured loan on which the borrower subsequently defaulted.[134] In addition, a federal court has found a bank liable for negligent misrepresentation with respect to a credit request regardless of whether a duty to provide the information existed.[135]

D. Fiduciary duty notions

The general state of the law is that a lender, solely by virtue of the lending relationship, is not in a fudiciary position with the borrower, but is in a contractual, creditor-debtor relationship.[136] Notwithstanding movements of the

---

130. See *Central States Stamping Co.* v. *Terminal Equip. Co., Inc.*, 727 F.2d 1405 (6th Cir. 1984). This was a companion case to *Melamed* v. *Lake County Nat'l Bank*, 727 F.2d 1399 (6th Cir. 1984), in which the same lender was held liable for tortious interference with the same manufacturer. Cf. *MSA Tubular Prods. Inc.* v. *First Bank and Trust Co.*, 869 F.2d 1422 (10th Cir. 1989) holding liability regardless of duty to provide information.

131. *Ibid.*, at 1406–07.

132. *Ibid.*, at 1409.

133. *Ibid.*, at 1409–11.

134. *DeQuoin State Bank* v. *Norris City State Bank*, 595 N.E.2d 678 (Ill. App. Ct. 1992).

135. See *MSA Tubular Prods. Inc.* v. *First Bank and Trust Co.*, 869 F.2d 1422 (10th Cir. 1989).

136. See *Okura & Co. (America), Inc.* v. *Careau Group*, 783 F. Supp. 482, 494 (C.D. Cal. 1991);

case law in the bank-depositor area to create a quasi fiduciary-like relationship between a bank and its customers under special situations,[137] such cases should (in the author's view) not be applied to commercial, arm's length lending situations.[138] This being said, however, additional facts and circumstances (including the nature of a pre-existing lending relationship, prior course of conduct, reasonable expectations of the borrowers, inordinate lender control, and ongoing rendering of advice to a borrower who relies on such advice)[139] may give rise to a "quasi-fiducial" or "special relationship" between lender and borrower, which at minimum would create an implied lender duty of good faith and fair dealing and possibly even a fiduciary duty.[140] In addition, under either the agency or inadvertent partnership theories discussed above, a fiduciary relationship may arise from the very nature of the theories themselves.[141]

Obviously, if a fiduciary relationship exists then the lender will be deemed to have far greater duties than those arising under a loan contract (e.g., due care, undivided loyalty, confidentiality, fair dealing, material disclosure) and may be charged with the burden to show the fairness of the lender's conduct, and may have its claim subordinated in a bankruptcy proceeding.

E. Wrongful set-off

The common law is clear that a lender, with respect to a matured obligation of a creditor, has a right to set-off or to reduce the indebtedness by charging the debt to the borrower's deposit accounts.[142] To exercise lawfully the right of set-off, the following requirements must be met[143]:

Van Arnem Co. v. *Mfrs. Hanover Leasing*, 776 F. Supp. 1220, 1223 (E.D. Mich. 1991); *Price* v. *Wells Fargo Bank*, 213 Cal. App. 3d 465, 261 Cal. Rptr. 735 (1989).

137. See generally "The Bank-Customer Relationship: Evolution of a Modern Form?" Okla. City U.L. Rev. (Winter 1987). See also *Young* v. *United States Dept. of Justice*, 882 F.2d 633 (2d Cir. 1989); *Barnett Bank of W. Fla.* v. *Hooper*, 498 So. 2d 923 (Fla. 1986); *Crystal Springs Trout Co.* v. *First State Bank of Froid*, No. 85–342 (Sup. Ct. Mont. 15 Jan. 1987) (wherein bank president and bank held liable to borrower in part because of existence of a fiduciary duty derived from the existing circumstances).

138. *Lanz* v. *Resolution Trust Corp.*, 764 F. Supp. 176, 179 (S.D. Fla. 1991); *Bankest Imports, Inc.* v. *ISCA Corp.*, 717 F. Supp. 1537, 1541 (S.D. Fla. 1989).

139. Such additional facts and circumstances may include: the nature of a pre-existing lending relationship, prior course of conduct, reasonable expectations of the borrowers, inordinate lender control, and ongoing rendering of advice to borrower who relies on such advice.

140. See *Federal Land Bank of Spokane* v. *Stiles*, 700 F. Supp. 1060 (D. Mont. 1988); see also, *Barrett* v. *Bank of Am.*, 178 Cal. App. 3d 960, 224 Cal. Rptr. 76 (1986); *American Spacers, Ltd.* v. *Ross*, 269 S.E.2d 176 (Ga. 1982); *Deist* v. *Wachholz*, 678 P.2d 188 (Mont. 1984).

141. See § 28.03[3] of J. Norton, T. Gillespie and D. Rice, *Commercial Finance Guide* (1994).

142. See generally, on right of set-off, J. Norton & S. Whitley, *Banking Law Manual*, Ch. 11 (1994); and Te Selle, "Banker's Right of Set-off—Banker Beware," 34 Okla L. Rev. 40 (1981); and Travalio, "Now you have it, now you don't: the Depositary Bank's Rights of Charge-back and Set-off", 30 Ariz. L. Rev. 719 (1988).

143. On lender liability aspects, see *Norton and Baggett*, *supra* fn. 3 Ch. 18 ("Set-off"), at section 18.02.

— the debtor/creditor relationship must exist;
— the funds must be owned by the debtor;
— the indebtedness must be an existing one;
— the debt must have been matured;
— a mutuality of obligation must exist; and
— there must be an absence of deposit restrictions.

Various legal theories that might sustain such a claim are[144]:

— breach of the deposit contract, which also may entitle a successful plaintiff to reasonable attorney's fees;
— wrongful set-off;
— wrongful dishonour, if the set-off results in the wrongful dishonour of the depositor's cheques, which is often the case;
— intentional interference with contractual relations;
— intentional infliction of mental anguish and emotional stress;
— conversion, which may be best pleaded if a special account is involved;
— breach of a duty of good faith, if a special relationship or a prior contrary or mitigating course of conduct existed between the banking institution and the debtor;
— negligence, but this may give rise to the application of the comparative negligence doctrine, which would not be available otherwise; and
— a claim under a state Deceptive Trade Practices Act (assuming the plaintiff can prove he or she was a consumer), which might allow special damages and reasonable attorney's fees.

If a wrongful set-off case is properly pleaded, then it is conceivable that a banking institution could be liable for damages well in excess of the amount of the funds set-off.[145] Depending upon the specific cause of action, a plaintiff could recover damages which include not only the return of the set-off funds, but also consequential injuries such as other out-of-pocket expenses incurred in the depositor's efforts to recover the funds, emotional distress, lost employment time, damage to credit standing, damage to business relationships, damage to business reputation, and lost profits. Additionally, punitive damages may be recovered if oppression, fraud, or malice (or their legal equivalents) can be proven. For example, in the situation where a wrongful set-off triggers the wrongful dishonour of a depositor's cheque, the Uniform Commercial Code ("UCC") provides for the following measure of damages[146]:

"When the dishonour occurs through mistake, liability is limited to actual damages proved. If so proximately caused and proved damages may include damage for an arrest or prosecution of the customer or other consequential damages. Whether any

144. *Ibid.*, at section 18.05.
145. See TeSelle, *supra* fn. 142, at 74–75. For a modern punitive damages-set-off case, see *Bottrell* v. *American Bank*, 773 P.2d 694 (Mont. 1989).
146. UCC, section 4–402.

consequential damages are proximately caused by the wrongful dishonour is a question of fact to be determined in each case."

Set-off damages are viewed more in a tort context than as strict contract damages. As such, it appears that if the dishonour is not simply through mistake, then the common law "trader rule" would permit a debtor to recover "substantial damages" without having to prove actual loss for wrongful dishonour of the cheque.[146a]

Also, consider the possible scenario that a plaintiff debtor proves it had a "special relationship" with a banking institution as a result of its lending and other dealings and that the institution had established a course of conduct whereby it was willing to work out past debt problems (or in any event was to give prior notice to the debtor before exercising any of its security rights). Although it might be well argued that the right of set off can be separated and viewed independently of this relationship and course of conduct, a distinct possibility exists that a court or trier-of-fact may integrate the rights and conduct of the banking institution so as to require "good faith" efforts and prior notice on behalf of the institution. If such legal duties exist, and the set-off results in the debtor's business and business relationships being destroyed or impaired by virtue of bankruptcy or otherwise, then the resulting damages of this wrongful set-off can, depending upon the circumstances, be most substantial. Naturally, the applicable limitations period will depend on the applicable cause of action.[147]

F. Instrumentality theory

The instrumentality theory for creating lender liability may prove successful in situations where the creditor control and dominance over the borrower is so substantial as to indicate that the effective control of the borrower's operations and affairs rests with the creditor.[148] A leading case that discusses the theory is *Krivo Industrial Supply* v. *National Distillers and Chemical Company*.[149] In this case the plaintiffs (trade creditors of a bankrupt corporation) sued the primary creditor of the bankrupt. In addition to the collateral taken for its financing, the primary creditor placed one of its employees with the bankrupt for the purpose of overseeing the use of the new financing. In analysing the facts of the situation, the Fifth Circuit court delineated the "instrumentality" theory.[150]

"When one corporation controls and dominates another corporation to the extent that the second corporation becomes the 'mere instrumentality' of the first, the dominant

---

146a. See generally, *Norton and Baggett, supra* fn. 3 at section 18.05.

147. For further discussion on concept of special relationship, see section V.A.3. *infra*.

148. For discussion of this theory, see, *inter alia,* Lundgren, *supra* fn. 4 at 525–534; and De Natale and Abram, "Equitable Subordination as Applied to Nonmanagement Creditors," 40 Bus. Law. 417, at 443–445 (1985).

149. 483 F.2d 1098 (5th Cir. 1973), *modified* 490 F.2d 916 (1974).

150. 483 F.2d at 1101.

corporation becomes liable for those debts of the subservient corporation attributable to the abuse of that control."

In effect, the circuit court expounded two elements necessary to constitute an actionable instrumentality allegation: (i) dominant control of the creditor over the borrower, and (ii) such dominance that proximately causes harm to the borrower or its other creditors through a misuse of this control. As further noted by the court[151]: "If a lender becomes so involved with its debtor that it is in fact actively managing the debtor's affairs, then the quantum necessary to support liability under the 'instrumentality' theory may be achieved."

However, the court in *Krivo* was cautious to note that merely taking part in the active management of the debtor in and of itself did not constitute the requisite control. As summarised by the court[152]:

"The control required for liability under the 'instrumentality' rule amounts to total domination of the subservient corporation, to the extent that the subservient corporation manifests no separate corporate interest of its own and functions solely to achieve the purpose of the dominant corporation."

The control factors found present in *Krivo* were: (i) creditor's employee acting as borrower's internal auditor; (ii) creditor's employee acting as production consultant; (iii) existence of veto power by creditor over debtor's disbursements and repayments; and (iv) creditor authority to provide advice and to monitor production (albeit without a veto power). Yet, reviewing such factors cumulatively, the court determined that there did not exist "total actual control" of the debtor for liability purposes.

While *Krivo* provides a creditor with considerable latitude in overseeing a loan credit (e.g., rendering advice, obtainment of information, and exercise of contractual veto power over borrower's financial transactions), the case should be read prospectively to caution creditors that at some point a creditor's actual exercise of control over the business and affairs of a borrower may give rise to liability. Though the facts situation in *Krivo* did not create direct lender liability under the "instrumentality" theory, the existence of such a fact situation, if cast under a different cause of action (as discussed immediately below), may well form the basis of a successful borrower's suit and give rise to lender liability.[153]

---

151. *Ibid.*, at 1105.

152. *Ibid.*, at 1106. On instrumentality theory, see also *James E. McFadden, Inc.* v. *Baltimore Contractors, Inc.*, 609 F. Supp. 1102 (E.D. Penn), 1985).

153. Cases in which a lender was found liable based on the instrumentality or *alter ego* theory include: *Second Serv. Sys.* v. *St. Joseph Bank & Trust Co.*, 855 F.2d 406 (7th Cir. 1988); and *Riquelme Valdes* v. *Leisure Resource Group Inc.*, 810 F.2d 1345 (5th Cir. 1987).

G. Principal–agent and inadvertent partnership theories

1. Principal–agent

A relatively recent case commonly cited for the principal–agency theory of lender liability is *A.G. Jensen Farms Co.* v. *Cargill, Inc.*[154] In this case, the primary creditor and supply purchaser of a bankrupt grain elevator company was sued by a group of farmer-creditors under the theory that the elevator company was in fact the agent of its primary creditor and therefore this creditor was liable for the debts owed them by the company. Unlike in *Krivo*, where "total actual control" by the creditor was required for direct liability, the Minnesota Supreme Court indicated that creditor liability, under a principal-agency theory, could arise if the creditor exercised "substantial control" over the debtor's affairs: liability, thus, may hinge upon the degree of control required under the particular underlying legal theory.

In *Cargill*, the court relied heavily upon the Restatement (Second) of Agency 14.01 (1958):

"A security owner who *merely exercises a veto power* over the business acts of his debtor by preventing purchases or sales as specified amounts does not thereby become a principal. *However, if he takes over the management of the debtor's business, either in person or through an agent, and directs what contracts may or may not be made, he becomes a principal for the obligations incurred thereafter in the normal course of business by the debtor who has now become his general agent. This point at which a creditor becomes a principal is that at which he assumes de facto control over the conduct of his debtor,* whatever the terms of the formal contract with his debtor may be." (emphasis added.)

In *Cargill* the court therefore acknowledged that if the creditor had merely exercised its contractual veto power, it would not have been deemed a principal of the debtor. Also, the court recognised that a number of the elements of conduct in the instant case could be found in most normal debtor-creditor relationships. However, the court stated that such factors cannot be considered in isolation, but must be viewed in light of all of the circumstances surrounding the creditor's "aggressive financing" and "control" of the borrower. The factors that existed in *Cargill*, when considered in their totality in light of the given circumstances, that gave rise to lender liability were: (i) financing arrangements covering all of the debtor's grain purchases and operating expenses; (ii) creditor's power and discretion to discontinue the financing; (iii) creditor's right of first refusal on grain to be sold; (iv) creditor's restrictions on debtor's ability to enter into mortgages, purchase stock, or to pay dividends without creditor's approval; (v) creditor's actual entry onto the debtor's premises to carry on periodic checks and audits; (vi) creditor's constant recommendations to the debtor by telephone; (vii) creditor's correspondence and criticism regarding the

---

154. 309 N.W.2d 285 (Minn. 1981). Cf. *Buck* v. *Nash Finch Co.*, 102 N.W.2d 84 (S.D. 1960), refusing to find an agency relationship.

borrower's finances, officers' salaries, and inventory; (viii) creditor's conclusion that the debtor needed "strong paternal guidance"; (ix) provision of drafts and forms to borrower upon which creditor's name was imprinted.[155]

From *Cargill*, one begins to appreciate that the exercise of actual control over the business affairs and operations of a borrower should always give the lender pause for concern and careful assessment of the possible legal implications, inasmuch as the determination of direct lender liability is highly "fact sensitive". For instance in determining liability, a trier-of-fact will consider not one factor as determinative, but will view all control factors in light of the overall relationship between the lender and the borrower. As such, the legal standards for liability may be viewed fairly subjectively. Thus, a trier-of-fact may have considerable latitude in determining the legal significance of the degree of control. Assuming the court gave the jury legally proper instructions, findings of fact adverse to a lender will be most difficult (if not impossible) to overturn on appeal.

If a lender comes to the point where to protect the credit it deems it necessary to take significant active participation in the business affairs of the borrower, then (in trying to do so) the lender and its counsel should carefully consider whether it would in fact be better to call the debt and proceed legally to collect the debt and realise upon any security. In all events, a lender that combines customary lenders' objectives (e.g., as in *Cargill*, access to a supply of grain) will increase its liability exposure. Extending this notion to situations where a lender takes an equity position in the borrower in addition to extending the credit, this exposure would also appear to be heightened under the principal–agency theory.

For the borrower, internal and external efforts should be made to document or otherwise substantiate lender's efforts at control, whether with respect to conversations, meetings, telephone calls, etc. This will facilitate the borrower's position in any subsequent litigation, settlement negotiations, or bankruptcy proceedings.

2. Inadvertent or informal partnership

The definition of a partnership can become important in the litigation context, when courts are required to decide whether two or more persons or entities are, in reality, partners or co-venturers, so as to require imposition of partnership disadvantages (e.g., joint and several liability) upon the one denying that he is a partner. Numerous examples exist where the parties did not subjectively intend a partnership, but the courts inferred an inadvertent partnership.[156]

As rightly indicated by one commentator, the general factors that may

155. *Ibid.*, at 291.
156. E.g. *Fate* v. *Saratoga Savings & Loan Assoc.*, 216 Cal. App. 3d 843, 265 Cal. Rptr. 440 (1989); and *Rosenberger* v. *Herbert*, 232 A.2d 634 (Pa. 1967).

influence a court in finding an inadvertent or informal partnership are: (i) the intent of the parties as determined by objective standards; (ii) the presence and degree of control over the business; and (iii) the existence of profit sharing in some form. More specifically, a court may consider[157]:

— Who makes the management decisions of the business entity?
— Did the conduct of parties or surrounding circumstances indicate an "objective intent" to be partners?
— The existence of a written agreement either affirmatively indicating an objective intent to be partners, or alternatively denying such intent and affirming a contrary intent, such as a desire to be an independent contractor;
— Amount of services contributed by each of the alleged partners;
— Record title of real property or personal property;
— Existence of alternative motives other than partnership to explain the transaction;
— Whether partnership tax returns were filed;
— Any purpose to evade a regulatory or taxing statute; and/or
— Any purpose to avoid tort liability.

Application of the Uniform Partnership Act (UPA) rules for determining the existence of a partnership has been the subject of much litigation, especially with regard to the concept of a lender as a partner with a borrower. For example, a partnership was found to exist in one case when a company loaned funds to a person, enabling that person to purchase inventory from the company, when the company and the person also agreed to share resale profits and to receive warehouse charges.[158] As a general proposition, excessive control over the business of the borrowing entity by a lender may well expose the lender to allegations that it is a partner of the borrower, especially if the loan contains profit-making aspects for the lender.[159]

Although, absent agreement to the contrary, sharing of losses is implicit in a partnership arrangement, the definition of partnership contains no such explicit requirement (cf. sections 6(1) and 18(a) of UPA). Some courts may, however, consider a sharing in losses essential to find a partnership, particularly in a "joint venture" claim. The existence of profit sharing, coupled with co-ownership and management rights, is (in most instances) certain indication of a partnership. Whether or not a failure to show factually the existence of a sharing of loss

---

157. H. Reuschlein & W. Gregory, *Agency and Partnership*, at 250–251 (1979), as updated). See generally, A. Bromberg and L. Ribstein, *Brombery and Ribstein on Partnership* (1988, as updated).

158. See *Minute Maid Corporation* v. *United Food, Inc.*, 291 F.2d 577 (5th Cir. 1961), *cert. denied*, 386 U.S. 928 (1961); but, cf. with majority view in *Martin* v. *Peyton*, 158 N.E. 77 (N.Y. 1927).

159. E.g. *Connor* v. *Great Western Savings and Loan Ass'n*, 447 P.2d 209 (1968); and *Dunson* v. *Stockton, Whatley, Davin & Co.*, 346 So. 2d 603 (Fla. 1977).

arrangement would preclude the application of an inadvertent partnership in a particular jurisdiction is uncertain.[160]

The obvious potency of a partnership finding is the lender acquires joint and several liability for the obligations of the borrower and will lose its outside creditor status and priority.[161]

IV. THE STATUTORY THEORIES

Various state and federal statutory theories have been utilised to create lender liability.

A. Usury claims

One of the most prevalent and traditional claims by a borrower against a lender in applicable jurisdictions having strict usury laws is that of usury (i.e., charging in excess of the lawful interest rate). A claim of usury is an affirmative cause of action or (more often) an affirmative defence. As such, the borrower has the burden of proof respecting the existence of each legal element of usury. These legal elements are: (i) a loan, forbearance or detention of money; (ii) an absolute obligation to repay; (iii) an objective intent to exact usurious interest; and (iv) an exaction of usurious interest. The legal consequences of usury differ significantly from jurisdiction to jurisdiction; but, such consequences can range from a voiding of the tainted transaction *ab initio*, to forfeitures of interest and/or principal, and to payment of other significant monetary penalties. Criminal, as well as civil, penalties may exist.[162] Judicial principles of public policy are also very important in the usury area.[163]

In the United States, usury is largely a matter of state law, although there exist a federal statute for national banks and a number of important pre-emptive federal usury statutes.[164] Yet, even where federal law applies, state usury laws

---

160. Consider *Coastal Plains Development Corp.* v. *Micrea, Inc.*, 572 S.W.2d 285 (Tex. 1978), wherein sharing of losses was held essential in a "joint venture" situation. This holding has been followed in *U.S.A.* v. *$47,875.00 in United States Currency*, 746 F.2d 291 (5th Cir. 1984).

161. See generally A. Bromberg and L. Ribstein, *supra,* fn. 157, particularly Ch. 2 and section 2.14 thereof (1988), as updated.

162. See generally *Norton & Baggett, supra* fn. 3, Ch. 10 ("Usury Claims", particularly section 10.02. See also *Finance America Corp.* v. *Moyler*, 494 A.2d 926 (D.C. App. 1985). The fact that borrower had prior knowledge of usury is not a bar to suit. See *Sun Bank of Tampa Bay* v. *Spirgin Prop. Ltd.*, 469 So. 240 (Fla. App. 1985). Also, see generally, Am. Jur. 2d, "Interest and Usury" section 238.

163. See, e.g., *Carboni* v. *Arrospede*, 2 Cal. Rptr. Id. 845 (Cal. App. 1991), in which a California Court of Appeal, applying the California civil statute on unconscionability, determined that even absent a usury statute violation, collection of a 200 per cent interest rate was legally unconscionable.

164. E.g. 12 U.S.C. section 85 (respecting national banks) and Monetary Control Act of 1980, section 501 on first lien residential real estate mortgages.

may still be applicable for determining what constitutes interest and how the amount of usury will be calculated.[165]

A preliminary determination of the existence of usury includes numerous considerations, such as (i) a proper characterisation of the loan (e.g., as business or consumer, or as secured or unsecured), (ii) an assessment of the total direct economic benefits (i.e., interest) to be derived by the lender, (iii) calculation of the real principal amount and interest calculation method, (iv) identification of the applicable law(s), and (v) analysis of related legal concerns.[166]

Rarely is the exaction of usurious interest apparent on the face of the loan document. Usury issues are most often more subtle and complex, involving such matters as the legal status and consequences of various lender fees and expenses borne by the borrower,[167] of compensating balances,[168] pre-payment charges,[169] late charges,[170] contingent interest and profit-sharing arrangements,[171] collateral advantage situations,[172] tying arrangements,[173] and disguised loan transactions.[174]

A lender may wish to utilise a number of protective provisions in a loan agreement to guard against usury. These provisions can include appropriately drafted "savings" and "speading" clauses[175] and requests for satisfactory "no-usury" opinions from borrower's counsel. Although it is extremely difficult, as a legal and practical matter, to "purge" a usurious transaction, in some jurisdictions this may be possible—assuming strict compliance with criteria established in applicable case law (e.g., existence of a genuine dispute, new and independent consideration, timing of settlement, full intent of borrower to agree, and coverage of only past events).[176]

165. See Norton & Baggett, supra fn. 3, at 10–5.

166. Ibid., at section 10.04.

167. E.g. Stedman v. Georgetown Sav. & Loan Ass'n, 595 S.W.2d 486 (Tex. 1980); see also, Tony's Tortilla Factory, Inc. v. First Bank, 857 S.W.2d 580 (Tex. Cir. App. 1993); Norris v. Sigler Dairy Corp., 392 S.E.2d 242 (Ga. 1990), and Najarvo v. SASI Int'l Ltd., 904 F.2d 1002 (5th Cir. 1990), cert. denied, 498 US 1048 (1991).

168. E.g. American Timber & Trading v. First Nat'l Bank of Oregon, 690 F.2d 781 (9th Cir. 1982).

169. See Norton & Baggett, supra fn. 3, section 10.03[3][d]; see also Parker Plaza West Partners v. UNUM Pension and Ins. Co., 941 F.2d 349 (5th Cir. 1991).

170. See Annot. 28 A.L.R. 3d 449 (1969); see also Beasley v. Wells Fargo Banks, 1 Cal. Rptr. 2d 446 (Cal. App. 1991).

171. See Norton & Baggett, supra fn. 3, section 10.04[3][f].

172. Ibid., at section 10.04[3][g]; see also Alamo Lumber v. Isold, 661 S.W.2d 926 (Tex. 1983), and Victoria Bank and Trust Co. v. Brady, 811 S.W.2d 931 (Tex. 1991).

173. E.g. Alamo Lumber Co. v. Gold, 661 S.W.2d 926 (Tex., 1983).

174. Norton & Baggett, supra fn. 3, at section 10.04[5][a].

175. E.g. American Century Mortgage Investors v. Regional Center, Ltd., 529 S.W.2d 578 (Tex. App. 1975); and Smith v. Miller, 995 F.2d 883 (9th Cir. 1993).

176. E.g. Helms v. First Alabama Bank of Gadsden, N.A., 386 So.2d 450 (Ala. App. 1980).

B. UCC: implied covenant of "good faith"

In addition to the specialised provision of "good faith" in section 1–208 concerning acceleration of payment, the Uniform Commercial Code contains the following provisions: Sec. 1–203. Every contract or duty within this title implies an obligation of good faith in its performance or enforcement. Sec. 1–201(19): "Good faith" means honesty in the conduct or transaction concerned.

It is important (for damages and other purposes) to note that UCC bad faith claims are contractual (and not tort) claims.

A significant decision in the areas of creditor liability resulting from a "good faith" test is the Sixth Circuit Court of Appeals in *KMC Co., Inc.* v. *Irving Trust Co.*[177] In this case Irving Trust had extended KMC a line of credit, taking a security interest in the company's inventories and accounts. In a period of time when the borrower experienced severe financial difficulty, but was not in default under its loan agreement, the borrower requested the bank to advance an additional $800,000 that was undrawn on its line of credit and to increase the line of credit from $3.5 million to $4 million. The bank, while not agreeing to the increase, did initially agree to advance the remaining $800,000. Subsequently, however, Irving reneged on this informal agreement to advance, and KMC went into bankruptcy.

Basing its decision squarely on principles of good faith under the UCC, the Sixth Circuit concluded that Irving Trust owed KMC an implied obligation to give a period of notice to the company in order to allow it to obtain alternative financing, at least in the absence of valid business reasons. As such, the court affirmed the $7.5 million judgment against the bank, based on a finding that the lender's refusal without prior notice of refusal to advance the requested funds under the loan agreement breached the bank's implied duty of good faith performance.

The facts in *KMC* indicated that the loan was at all times adequately secured, that a pattern of bank conduct had developed in which the bank covered KMC's overdrafts, the existence of a general bank policy to give notice of acceleration if the loan was adequately secured, and indications that considerable personal tension had arisen between the bank's loan officer and the president of KMC. Evidence also tended to indicate that the bank loan officer knew the importance of continuing the business and the resulting difficulties if the business was closed. Also, the officer acknowledged that delaying the calling of the loan for a period of a few days would not have injured the bank. Furthermore, the officer had indicated he would continue to honour KMC cheques by making advances,

---

177. 757 F.2d 752 (6th Cir. 1985). Cf. *Layne* v. *Fort Carson Nat. Bank*, 655 P.2d 856 (Colo. App. 1982) applying test to enforcement of a security interest. See also *Quality Automotive* Co. v. *Signet Bank/Maryland*, 775 F. Supp. 849, 851 (D. Md, 1991) (citing *KMC* Co. v. *Irving Trust* Co. as authority for its discussion of the adequacy of good faith notice); *Reid* v. *Key Bank of Southern Maine, Inc.*, 821 F.2d 9, 13 (1st Cir. 1987) (citing *KMC* Co. v. *Irving Trust* Co.).

but changed his mind and refused to make advances to cover outstanding cheques.

The court held that Irving Trust had acted arbitrarily and capriciously in contravention of the implied requirement of good faith and fair dealing implicit in all contracts covered by UCC section 1–203. The court indicated that even where a demand note exists and a lender has a discretionary right to make advances, the lender was, nevertheless, under an obligation of "good faith". As such, if a change were to occur in the pattern of prior creditor-debtor dealings, notice was required. As indicated by the court[178]:

"Whether or not the $800,000 requested would have been sufficient to cover all of KMC's outstanding cheques, [the bank loan officer's] abrupt refusal to advance funds to KMC on 1 March amounted to a unilateral decision on his part to wind up the company. If [the officer] had agreed to advance the $800,000 but no more, and cheques still had bounced, we would have a different case. But, given that [the officer] knew and should have known that the bank was adequately secured, and that if adequately secured it was Irving's policy that some period of notice would be due before financing was denied, [the officer's action could only be justified if in some way he reasonably believed that it was necessary to protect the bank's interest. There was ample evidence—in particular, the conclusion of Irving's auditors that no losses would be sustained by the bank in the absence of liquidation, and [the officer's decision on March 4 to advance almost the full amount requested just three days earlier despite the fact that KMC was in much worse condition because of the intervening damage to its credit standing—from which the jury could have concluded that [the officer] had no such reason in mind and hence that his action was arbitrary and capricious."

As the foregoing court statement indicates, the bank's "good faith" was tested by a standard that is more "objective" than "subjective".

As mentioned above, the *Farah* decision was partially based upon an application of the "good faith" principles to the applicable transaction. The facts in *Farah* would have met either a subjective or an objective test of good faith. Also, it must be remembered that the plea of good faith arises not because of the contractual relationship itself, but because of the relationship existing between the parties. While courts traditionally have been reluctant to impose fiduciary duties upon a lender solely by virtue of the creditor–debtor relationship,[179] the existence of control to the extent actually shown in *Farah* could in and of itself give rise to a special relationship that, in turn, would create a duty of good faith.

KMC teaches the lender and its counsel a number of lessons:

— Demand notes are looked upon suspiciously by many courts.
— A loan officer should not let personal tension with a borrower affect his or her lending judgement.
— Notwithstanding the terms of loan documents, a loan officer should

178. *Ibid.*, at 763.
179. E.g. *Re W.T. Grant Co.*, 699 F.2d 599 (2nd Cir. 1983).

consider the actual course of conduct and bank procedure and policy in similar circumstances.

— If a prior course of conduct is to be changed, adequate notice should be given.

— In terms of the quantum of jury proof, the line between an "objective" or "subjective" test for good faith is a most important one. To prove objectively something to be "reasonable" or "unreasonable" is an easier task than to show subjectively dishonesty or the lack of an actual belief. In a practical context, meeting an objective standard is similar to proving a negligence case, while proving dishonesty and no actual belief is similar to proving a fraud case.

From a borrower's perspective, a prudent borrower should keep careful note of a lender's course of conduct and any changes therein in the event the lender develops an intransigent position or litigation or bankruptcy proceedings become necessary.

C. Federal tax liabilities

A lender who "controls" a debtor's ability to pay its creditors may also be liable for federal withholding tax penalties if the debtor fails to pay the withheld portion of the tax to the IRS. Under section 6672 of the Internal Revenue Code (IRC),[180] liability arises if (i) the individual or entity involved is a "responsible person", and (ii) the failure to pay the tax was "wilful".[181]

The courts have developed a functional test for determining a "responsible person" by examining the degree of control the person exercises over the withholding tax collection and payment process. A person is responsible if that person has significant, though not necessarily exclusive, control over corporate funds. Such a person is considered to have significant control if he or she has a strong say about which bills or creditors get paid.[182] A bank officer as well as the lending institution who has a part in the final determination concerning what bills the debtor should pay are "responsible persons". Also, bankers who control the debtor's purse strings through a lock-box arrangement for receivables, veto rights over the cheques to be honoured, or who loan only enough funds to keep a debtor alive, arguably have sufficient control over the bills to be paid and therefore could face liability if the debtor's withholding taxes are not paid. The element of "wilfulness" does not require a finding of intent to

---

180. 26 U.S.C. section 6672. See, *inter alia*, *Wollman* v. *U.S.*, 571 F. Supp. 824 (S.D. Fla. 1983), for discussion of "responsible person" and "wilful"; see generally, *O'Hare* v. *U.S.*, 878 F.2d 953 (6th Cir. 1989).

181. See generally, *Wetzel* v. *U.S.*, 802 F. Supp. 1451 (S.D. Mass. 1992); and Kaye, "A Primer on the Defence of Banks Against Liability for Unpaid Withholding Taxes", 2 *Complete Law*, No. 1 at 37 (Winter, 1985).

182. See *Quattrone Accountants, Inc.* v. *IRS*, 895 F.2d 921 (3rd Cir. 1991).

defraud or to deprive the United States of tax revenue. Rather, what is required is a finding of a "voluntary, conscious and intentional act" to prefer other creditors over the United States. Once both legal elements of "responsible person" and "wilfulness" are found, all responsible persons are jointly liable for the taxes and penalties.[183]

Section 3505 of the IRC also would impose liability on a lender who directly or indirectly finances the "net payroll" of a borrower without causing payment or the withholding tax portion of the payroll to the IRS.[184] More specifically under section 3505(a), liability may arise for withholding taxes when a lender pays the employee directly. Even in situations where a lender has had only a veto power over borrower's payroll account or honours overdrawn payroll cheques, liability has been held.[185] Also, specific liability under section 3505(b) could occur in the situation where (i) the lender provides funds to a borrower to pay wages[186] with (ii) actual knowledge or notice[187] that (iii) the borrower does not intend or will not be able to pay the withholding tax.[188] In proving liability under section 3505(b), the IRS must first establish that the lender knowingly advanced funds for payroll purposes. Such knowledge has been established when a lender honours overdrafts on a payroll account or other account from which wages have been previously paid.[189] As to the "actual knowledge" element, constructive notice has been held sufficient. For example, the courts have imputed knowledge that a borrower is unable to pay withholding tax to a lender having knowledge of the borrower's deteriorating position.[190]

In a workout situation, a lender having actual or apparent control over a debtor's payment to his creditors should ensure that the withholding taxes are paid to the IRS. Further, a lender having knowledge that a borrower is in financial difficulty should avoid advancing funds for payroll, or even honouring overdrafts for wages. If the lender does so advance or honour cheques, it should affirmatively assure itself that the IRS has been paid.

D. Federal securities laws liabilities

The primary federal securities laws that may concern a lender in a workout period are the Securities Act of 1933 (1933 Act) and the Securities Exchange Act of 1934 (1934 Act),[191] both as subsequently amended on various occasions. The

---

183. E.g., see *Commonwealth National Bank of Dallas* v. *U.S.A.*, 665 F.2d 743 (5th Cir. 1982).
184. 26 U.S.C. section 3505.
185. E.g. *Abrams* v. *U.S.A.*, 333 F. Supp. 1134 (S.D. W.Va. 1971).
186. See *U.S.A.* v. *Park Cities Bank & Trust Co.*, 481 F.2d 738 (5th Cir. 1973).
187. See *Kaye, supra* fn. 181, at 39.
188. See 26 U.S.C. 6323(i)(1). See also, *O'Hare* v. *United States*, 878 F.2d 953 (6th Cir. 1989).
189. E.g. *Taubman* v. *U.S.A.*, 499 F. Supp. 1133 (E.D. Mich. 1978).
190. *Park Cities, supra* fn. 186.
191. 15 U.S.C. section 77a, *et seq.* (1933 Act); and 15 U.S.C. section 78a *et seq.* (1934 Act.) For detailed discussion of securities law aspects of lender liability see *Norton and Baggett, supra* fn. 3, Ch. 6 ("Securities Law Bases for Lender Liability").

1933 Act is designed to achieve truth in the "public distribution" of securities by providing full and fair disclosure to the investing public. The basis requirement of this Act is that every offer of sale or sale of a security must meet the formal registration requirements of the 1933 Act unless specifically exempt from registration under the Act or under regulations of the Securities Exchange Commission (SEC).[192] An unregistered distribution of securities that does not qualify for a statutory exemption may trigger civil and criminal sanctions and liabilities. Moreover, even if a distribution is registered or is exempt, this fact will not necessarily preclude the applicability of antifraud provisions of the federal securities laws.[193] The 1934 Act addresses the various aspects of trading securities subsequent to an initial distribution and ongoing registration and reporting of publicly held entities. The primary areas of concern for a lender under this Act (aside from "margin requirements")[194] would be respecting the broker-dealer requirements[195] and possible securities fraud liabilities in connection with the "purchase or sale" of a security.[196]

1. Collateral liability

Only in rare instances should direct securities liability arise for a lender and its officers and directors. However, under the federal securities laws numerous bases exist for such parties to incur collateral or derivative liability, pursuant to the following legal theories[197]:

> (i) *Aiding and abetting.* Generally, a person aids and abets another in breaching the federal securities laws when he knows or should have known that a violation is occurring, and he renders substantial assistance either by an affirmative act, or by remaining silent or inactive when he has a duty to speak or to act.[198] If a borrower has violated the federal securities laws in a workout arrangement (e.g., through an issurance of stock or a recapitalisation), then a lender or its involved management officer (if "aiding and abetting" can be shown) could be held liable under the antifraud provisions of the federal securities laws.

192. Section 5 of 1933 Act; 15 U.S.C. section 77e.

193. See generally J. Norton and S. Whitley, *Banking Law Manual*, Ch. 16 ("Securities Laws and Activities") (1994). On securities antifraud liabilities, see A. Bromberg & L. Lowenfels, *Securities Fraud and Commodities Fraud*, 5 vols. (1984, as updated).

194. 15 U.S.C. section 78g, and Federal Reserve Board of Governors Regulation "U", 12 C.F.R. section 221.

195. Ss. 7–11 of the 1934 Act; 15 U.S.C. Ss. 78f–78k.

196. S. 10 of the 1934 Act; 15 U.S.C. section 78j and SEC Rule 10b–5, 17 C.F.R. 240.10b–5. See also, *Bromberg*, fn. 193 *supra*.

197. See *Norton & Whitley*, *supra* fn. 193, section 16.07[3].

198. See, *inter alia*, *Woodward* v. *Metro Bank of Dallas*, 522 F.2d 84 (5th Cir. 1975). See also, *Norton & Whitley*, *supra* fn. 193, section 16.07[3][a].

(ii) *Controlling person.* Liability under the 1933 and 1934 Acts may be incurred by persons who "control" another person or entity subject to these Acts.[199] Although both Acts contain comparable provisions on this matter, the determination of a "control" person is a factual issue.[200] A "control" person may be liable under sections 11 and 12 of the 1933 Act, under SEC rule 10b–5 under the 1934 Act (if he engaged in the "purchase or sale" of securities), under section 18(a) of the 1934 Act (with respect of filing of false or misleading public documents), or under section 16 of the 1934 Act (with respect to short-swing profits).

A most significant recent case on "aiding and abetting" is the 1994 US Supreme Court decision in *Central Bank of Denver* v. *First Interstate Bank of Denver.*[201] In this case the Supreme Court held that section 10(b) of the Securities Exchange Act does *not* provide for the imposition of aiding and abetting liability in private litigation.[202] The court made clear that its construction was based on "a strict statutory construction"[203] and that the issue before it was one involving "the scope of conduct prohibited by s. 10(b)".[204] Importantly, the court's rationale extends to preclude aiding and abetting liability from being imposed by private plaintiffs for alleged violations of other federal securities law provisions.[205] Moreover, the court's restrictive approach should extend to the SEC, thereby precluding the Commission from bringing enforcement actions

---

199. See section 20(a) of the 1934 Act (15 U.S.C. section 78r); and section 15 of the 1933 Act (15 U.S.C. section 77o).

200. See e.g., *Zweig* v. *Hearst Corporation*, 521 F.2d 1129 (9th Cir. 1975). Also see, *Norton & Whitley, supra* fn. 193, section 16.07[3][b].

201. 1994 US LEXIS 3120, 62 U.S.L.W. 4230, ____ U.S. ____, ____ S.Ct. ____, ____ L.Ed.2d ____ (1994) (cites not yet available). For law review commentary prior to *Central Bank of Denver*, see Branson, "Collateral Participant Liability Under the Securities Laws—Charting the Proper Course", 65 Oregon L. Rev. 327 (1986); Bromberg & Lowenfels, "Aiding and Abetting Securities Fraud: A Critical Examination", 52 Albany L. Rev. 637 (1988); Kuehnle, "Secondary Liability Under the Federal Securities Laws—Aiding and Abetting, Conspiracy, Controlling Person and Agency: Common-Law Principles and the Statutory Scheme", 14 J. Corp. L. 313 (1988); Ruder, "Multiple Defendants in Securities Law Fraud Cases: Aiding and Abetting, Conspiracy, *In Pari Delicto*, Indemnification and Contribution", 120 U. Pa. L. Rev. 597 (1972). The information and materials for this portion regarding the *Central Bank of Denver* case have been furnished by Professor Mark Steinberg (SMU School of Law and author of *Securities Regulation* (2nd edn. 1993)).

202. ____ S.Ct. at ____ (cite not yet available).

203. *Ibid.*

204. *Ibid.*

205. After examining sections 11 and 12 of the Securities Act and sections 9, 16, 18 and 20A of the Exchange Act, the court concluded that none of these express causes of actions provided for aider and abettor liability. *Ibid.* Moreover, the court's analysis in *Central Bank of Denver* certainly should extend to other implied causes of action, such as section 14(a) of the Exchange Act. Indeed, the

premised on aider and abettor liability (except where a statute provides for such liability).[206]

Nonetheless, discussion of aider and abettor liability principles should continue to be undertaken for a number of reasons. For example, the SEC has express authority to proceed administratively against brokers and dealers (and associated persons) who aid and abet securities law violations.[207] Rule 2(e) of the Commission's Rules of Practice[208] also provides the SEC with such authority to proceed against professionals, including accountants and attorneys.[209] Moreover, although the Commission's cease and desist power against those who are a "cause" of an alleged violation evidently is more expansive than aider and abettor liability principles,[210] the Commission still may draw on some of these principles to ascertain the parameters of the liability net.[211] And, as a last example, a number of state securities statutes provide for aiding and abetting liability.[212]

Prior to the Supreme Court's decision in *Central Bank of Denver*, the lower federal courts overwhelmingly held that aiding and abetting liability was

---

statutory language of section 14(a), like that of section 10(b), "controls" and "bodes ill" for litigants who seek to hold collateral parties liable as aiders and abettors. *Ibid.* The same holds true for SEC enforcement actions based on violation of section 17(a) of the Securities Act.

The court's decision also should signify that the common law theories of conspiracy and *respondeat superior* should be precluded. As Justice Stevens pointed out in his dissent, lower court decisions recognising these theories of liability "appear unlikely to survive the Court's decision". See generally Comment, "Causation Concerns in Civil Conspiracy to Violate Rule 10b–5", 66 N.Y.U. L. Rev. 1505 (1991); sources cited fn. 201 *supra*.

206. See Gorman, "Who's Afraid of 10b–5? The Scope of a Section 10(b) Cause of Action After *Central Bank of Denver*", ____ Sec. Reg. L.J. ____ (1994). See generally Grundfest, "Desimplifying Private Rights of Action Under the Federal Securities Laws: The Commission's Authority", 107 Harv. L. Rev. 961 (1994).

207. See section 15(b)(4)(E), 15(b)(6)(A)(i), 15 U.S.C. s. 78o(b)(4)(E), 78o(b)(6)(A)(i). See also, 15 U.S.C. s. 78u–2 (civil penalty may be assessed against broker-dealer aiding and abetting certain violations of Exchange Act).

208. 17 C.F.R. s. 201.2(e).

209. *Ibid.* (providing, *inter alia*, that the SEC may suspend or bar any person from practising before it if such person is found by the Commission to have wilfully aided and abetted a violation of any federal securities statute, rule or regulation). Under this provision, SEC case law has developed with respect to the requirements for finding aider and abettor liability. See *In the Matter of Carter and Johnson*, [1981 Transfer Binder] CCH Fed. Sec. L. Rep. para. 82,847 (SEC 1981). After *Central Bank of Denver*, challenges may be made that the SEC has no authority to discipline aiders and abettors under Rule 2(e). Cf. Rule 1.2(d), Model Rules of Professional Conduct (prohibiting an attorney from aiding and abetting his or her client's fraudulent conduct). For further discussion, see § 12.06[2] *infra*.

210. See Martin, Mirvis & Herlihy, "SEC Enforcement Powers and Remedies Are Greatly Expanded", 19 Sec. Reg. L.J. 19, 23 (1991) (stating that the concept of a "cause" of a violation in relation to the SEC's cease and desist authority "would appear to go far beyond traditional concepts of aiding and abetting violations").

211. See §§ 12.02, 12.05[1], 12.06 *infra*.

212. See, e.g., Texas Securities Act, Art. 581–33(f)(2); J. Long, *Blue Sky Law* § 7.08 (1993); discussion § 9.06 *supra*.

appropriate under section 10(b) of the Exchange Act.[213] Although courts differed on the precise content of the various elements giving rise to aiding and abetting liability,[214] three basic prerequisites emerged: (1) a primary securities law violation by another, (2) substantial assistance by the alleged aider and abettor in the commission of the primary violation, and (3) requisite "knowledge" on the part of such alleged aider and abettor that his or her conduct was improper.[215]

In determining whether the requisite knowledge has been shown,[216] reckless conduct[217] sufficed if a fudiciary relationship existed between the complainant and the alleged aider and abettor.[218] Absent a fiduciary relationship, a number of courts required conscious intent,[219] particularly if the alleged violator's role constituted "the daily grist of the mill".[220] Disagreeing, other courts found recklessness to suffice where the alleged aider and abettor had reason to foresee that third parties would be relying on his conduct[221] or where he derived financial benefit from the wrongdoing.[222] Still other courts as a general principle deemed reckless conduct to satisfy the "knowledge" requirement.[223]

In view of the Supreme Court's decision in *Central Bank of Denver*, private parties and the SEC increasingly will assert theories of liability based on primary violations. Hence, where a party makes an affirmative statement, such as an

---

213. See, e.g., *Cleary* v. *Perfectune, Inc.*, 700 F.2d 774. See also Fischel, "Secondary Liability Under Section 10(b) of the Securities Act of 1934", 69 Calif. L. Rev. 80 (1981).

214. Compare *Rolf* v. *Blyth, Eastman Dillon & Co. Inc.*, 570 F.2d 38 (2d Cir. 1978) with *Schatz* v. *Rosenberg*, 943 F.2d 485 (4th Cir. 1991). Note, moreover, that the Seventh Circuit required the plaintiff to "show that each person alleged to be an aider, abettor or conspirator himself committed one of the 'manipulative or deceptive' acts or otherwise met the standards of direct liability". *Barker* v. *Henderson, Franklin, Starnes & Holt*, 797 F.2d 490, 495 (7th Cir. 1986).

215. See, e.g., cases cited 114 S.Ct. at 1456 n. 1 (Stevens J., dissenting) and in fn. 213 *supra*.

216. Questions also arose as to whether the defendant's conduct constituted "substantial assistance". For a narrow view, see *Schatz* v. *Rosenberg, supra*, fn. 214 (lawyer drafting of key documents not substantial assistance. This view largely was rejected, even by those courts which otherwise adhered to a restrictive approach. See, e.g., *Abell* v. *Potomac Insurance Co.*, 858 F.2d 1104 (5th Cir. 1988), *vacated on other grounds* 492 U.S. 914 (1989). For a case dealing with whether a bank's participation constituted substantial assistance, see *K&S Partnership* v. *Continental Bank, NA*, [1991–1992 Transfer Binder] CCH Fed. Sec. L. Rep. para. 96,414 (8th Cir. 1991).

217. Courts generally have adopted the "highly" reckless standard.

218. See, e.g., *Abell* v. *Potomac Insurance Co.*, *supra* fn. 216.

219. See, e.g., *Schatz* v. *Rosenberg, supra* fn. 214.

220. See, e.g. *Abell* v. *Potomac Insurance Co.*, *supra* fn. 216.

221. See, e.g., *Breard* v. *Sachnoff*, 941 F.2d 142 (2d Cir. 1991); *SEC* v. *Electronics Warehouse, Inc.*, 689 F. Supp. 53 (D. Conn.), *aff'd* 891 F.2d 457 (2d Cir. 1989); *Andreo* v. *Friedlander, Gaines, Cohen, Rosenthal & Rosenberg*, 660 F. Supp. 1362 (D. Conn. 1987).

222. See, e.g., *Walck* v. *American Stock Exchange, Inc.*, 687 F.2d 778, 791 n. 18 (3d Cir. 1992); *Gould* v. *American-Hawaiian S.S. Co.*, 535 F.2d 761, 780 (3d Cir. 1976).

223. See, e.g., *Stern* v. *American Bankshares, Inc.*, 429 F. Supp. 818 (E.D. Wis. 977).

attorney rendering an opinion letter,[224] primary liability exposure is clear.[225] When one solicits the purchase for the financial benefit of the securities owner or one's own financial benefit, then liability under section 12 of the Securities Act may be incurred.[226] In addition, because executive officers "make policy or generally carry authority to bind the corporation [t]heir action in behalf of the corporation is therfore primary, and holding a corporation liable for their action does not require *respondeat superior*".[227] Similarly, under the "group published" theory, those officers who are actively involved in a corporation's affairs may be subject to primary liability for disclosure deficiencies contained in such entity's prospectuses, press releases and SEC filed documents.[228] The Sixth Circuit's "direct contacts" test also will provide complainants with an opportunity to assert that those who are deemed to have "furnished" documents to investors are subject to liability as primary participants.[229] This rationale encompasses attorneys who draft documents with the anticipation that such documents will be provided to investors.[230] While at this time it appears unlikely that many courts will embrace the Sixth Circuit's rationale, the fact remains that private litigants and the SEC will devise alternative strategies in their efforts to emerge victorious.[231]

2. *Covered activities*

It is conceivable (given the proper fact situation) that the following lender activities in a workout situation could give rise to potential liability concerns under the federal securities laws:

(i) If the structuring of a workout plan involves the issuance of a "security" to third parties and such issuance did not satisfy a statutory exemption from registration and was in fact not registered as required by the 1933 Act, then possible liability could arise.[232] Further, even if

---

224. See, e.g., *Kline* v. *First Western Government Securities, Inc.*, [1993–1994 Transfer Binder] CCH Fed. Sec. L. Rep. para. 98,185 (3d Cir. 1994). See generally FitzGibbon & Glazer, *Legal Opinions* (1992); M. Steinberg, *Corporate and Securities Malpractice* (1992); Rice & Steinberg, "Legal Opinions in Securites Transactions", 16 J. Corp. L. 375 (1991).

225. See, e.g., *Abell* v. *Potomac Insurance* Co., *supra* fn. 216 (stating that "an attorney is rarely liable to any third party for his or her legal work unless the attorney has prepared a signed 'opinion' letter designed for the use of a third party").

226. See, e.g., *Morse* v. *Abbott Laboratories*, [1993–1994 Transfer Binder] CCH Fed. Sec. L. Rep. para. 98,139 (N.D. Ill. 1994).

227. *SEC* v. *Washington County Utility District*, 676 F.2d 218 (6th Cir. 1982).

228. See, e.g., *Molecular Technology Corp.* v. *Valentine*, 925 F.2d 910 (6th Cir. 1991); *In re Rospatch Securities Litigation*, [1992 Transfer Binder] CCH Fed. Sec. L. Rep. para. 96,939 (W.D. Mich. 1992).

229. See Coffee, "Securities Law", Nat.L.J., 11 July 1994, at B4, B7.

230. See Steinberg, "The Ramifications of *Central Bank of Denver* on Federal and State Securities Litigation" (paper presented to the Centre for Commercial Law Studies (London, 1994)).

231. *Ibid.*

232. See *Norton and Whitley*, *supra* fn. 193, section 16.03[2][a] and section 16.07[1].

exempt or registered, if there was deemed to be a false or misleading material statement or omission made in connection with the issuance, and the lender had actual or constructive knowledge of this and otherwise participated in the dissemination of the misstatement or omission, then lender liability could arise.[233]

(ii) If the workout situation involves the lender acquiring an equity position in the borrower, then (even if an exempt transaction) it could be subject to antifraud claims under rule 10b–5.[234]

(iii) If in a workout situation a lender facilitates the distribution and sale of any securities, it could incur "underwriter" liability and/or "broker-dealer" liability under federal and state securities laws.[235]

(iv) If as a result of a workout situation a lending institution obtained nonpublic information of a public reporting borrower under the 1934 Act, the lender could incur securities liabilities with respect to an improper disclosure of such inside, non-public information, or for trading in the securities of the borrower based upon such insider information.[236]

(v) Even if a lender does not have direct or derivative liability under the federal securities law in a workout situation involving the issuance of the securities, if the borrower in fact has such liability, this may raise special credit-risk considerations for the lender. For example, if in a workout loan situation, the lender is relying upon others (e.g., limited partners or investors) as a source of additional ("gap") funding,[237] it is important that these "securities" or federal securities have been properly registered or are exempt under securities laws and that otherwise proper disclosure has been made to the investors. If a violation of the securities laws does occur, then the obligations of the investors may be unenforceable or may otherwise create significant liability for the borrower, thus creating a serious lender financing risk in completing a project.[238]

E. RICO liability

Title IX of the Organised Crime Control Act is the Racketeering Influenced and Corrupt Organisations Statute, commonly referred to as RICO.[239] RICO prohibits the following four activities:

---

233. *Ibid.* section 16.03[2][b] and section 16.07[1].
234. *Ibid.* section 16.03[2][c] and section 16.07[2][a].
235. *Ibid.* section 16.03[f].
236. *Ibid.* section 16.03[d] and section 16.07[2][c] and [d].
237. *Ibid.* section 16.03[3].
238. E.g. the rescission rights under section 12(1) of the 1933 Act.
239. Pub. L. No. 91–452, 84 Stat. Title 9, 18 U.S.C. section 1961 *et seq.* (1970). On RICO and lender liability, see *Norton & Baggett, supra* fn. 3, Ch. 9 ("Lender Liability Under the Racketeer Influenced and Corrupt Practices Organizations Act").

(a) If a business or person receives income from a "pattern of racketeering activity" or from a collection of an unlawful debt, it is illegal to use this money, directly or indirectly, to operate or to acquire an interest in any "enterprise"[240];

(b) A "pattern of racketeering activity" or a collection of an unlawful debt cannot be used to acquire or to maintain, directly or indirectly, any interest or control in any enterprise[241];

(c) A person who is employed in any enterprise cannot conduct or participate in the conduct of that enterprise's affairs through a "pattern of racketeering activity" or collection of an unlawful debt[242]; and

(d) It is unlawful for any person to conspire to do any of the above prohibited activities.[243] The embrace of these prohibitions may result in a criminal or civil action and may go well beyond the realm of organised crime and into the traditional business and commercial world.[244]

A "pattern of racketeering activity", as defined by RICO, requires at least two *acts* of racketeering activity within 10 years of one another.[245] "Racketeering activity" includes any act or threat of murder, kidnapping, gambling, arson, robbery, bribery, extortion, or dealing in dangerous drugs, which is chargeable under state law and punishable by more than one year's imprisonment. Even more significantly for financial institutions, "racketeering activity" also includes many other specific acts such as counterfeiting, embezzlement, mail fraud, wire fraud, and fraud in the sale of securities.[246]

It is important to note that the two offences necessary to establish the pattern apparently need not be related, although the predicate criminal acts must be connected to the enterprise.[247] For instance, an individual or business could engage in a "pattern of racketeering" by a fraudulent sale of securities in 1976

240. 18 U.S.C. section 1962(a).

241. 18 U.S.C. section 1962(b).

242. 18 U.S.C. section 1962(c).

243. 18 U.S.C. section 1962(d).

244. E.g. see, Comment, "Civil RICO Actions in Commercial Litigation: Racketeer or Businessman?", 36 Sw. L.J. 925 (1982).

245. See 18 U.S.C. section 1961(5).

246. 18 U.S.C. section 1961(1).

247. It is important to note that it appears that the two offences necessary to establish the pattern need not be related, although the predicate criminal acts must be connected to the enterprise. See, e.g., *United States* v. *Weisman*, 624 F.2d 1118 (2d Cir.), *cert. denied* 449 U.S. 871 (1980). For instance, an individual or business could engage in a "pattern of racketeering" by a fraudulent sale of securities in 1976 and mail fraud in 1985. Additionally, two repetitive acts in the same scheme, such as two sales of securities in one fraudulent securities scheme, have been held by courts to constitute a "pattern of racketeering activity" even if they occur on the same day. See generally *H.J. Inc.* v. *Northwestern Bell Tel. Co.*, 492 U.S. 229, 109 S. Ct. 2893, 106 L. Ed. 2d 195 (1989), which reversed an Eighth Circuit Court holding that required multiple criminal schemes as proof of a "pattern of racketeering activity" under RICO.

and mail fraud in 1985. Also, two repetitive acts in the same scheme, such as two sales of securities in one fraudulent security scheme, have been held by certain federal circuit courts to constitute a "pattern of racketeering activity" even if they occur on the same day.[248]

The US Supreme Court has resolved, in its recent *Sedima* decision, a conflict between the Second and Seventh Circuit Courts of Appeals regarding certain restrictive standing requirements under RICO inferred by the Second Circuit.[249] The Supreme Court has overruled the Second Circuit by holding that it was not necessary in a RICO civil action for the plaintiff to show that injury was caused by an activity RICO was designed to deter and not simply by the "predicate acts", or that the two "predicate acts" had to consist of actual prior criminal convictions against the RICO defendant before the bringing of the civil RICO action. The effect of the court's decision will be a broadened civil access to RICO, and to leave to Congress any future (if any) limitations on RICO's availability.[250]

Federal prosecutors almost routinely, now, add RICO counts to indictments in business cases. The bank regulators are now also using RICO in certain bank failure cases.[251]

Congress provided for criminal sanctions of RICO violation and for civil action.[252] More importantly, the statute provides a private right of action for any person injured in his business or property because of RICO violation.[253] Most significantly to the private litigant is the authorisation of treble damages, plus costs and reasonable attorney's fees.[254]

RICO concerns involving financial institutions have arisen recently with respect to the various "prime rate" litigation, stock fraud, mail fraud, antitrust violations, and financing retail purchases of mobile homes.[255] Absent restricting RICO legislation from the Congress, however, it would appear that there will be an increase of RICO causes of actions against lending institutions. For example, in a pre-*Sedima* case of *Banowitz* v. *State Exchange Bank* (which is consistent with *Sedima*),[256] an investor sued a national bank and certain of its officers, directors and owners for securities laws and RICO violations, along with various state law claims. With respect to the RICO claim, the plaintiff alleged that the defendants engaged in a "pattern of racketeering activity" by their recommendations to the plaintiffs that the purchase of investment notes in

248. See *Norton & Whitley, supra* fn. 193, section 8.06[8], 8–29.

249. *Sedima, S.P.R.L.* v. *Imrex Co., Inc.*, 105 S. Ct. 3275, 87 L. Ed. 2d 346 (1985). Also see, *Am. Nat. Bank and Trust Co.* v. *Haraco, Inc.*, 105 S. Ct. 3291 (1985).

250. See Greenberg, "The Application of Civil RICO (Racketeer Influenced and Corrupt Organisations Act) to Lender Activities", in *Chaitman*, fn. 3 *supra*, at 299.

251. E.g. see *Norton & Baggett*, Ch. 9, *supra* fn. 239.

252. 18 U.S.C. section 1964.

253. 18 U.S.C. section 1963(c).

254. *Ibid.*

255. See *Norton & Whitley, supra* fn. 193, section 8.06[8], at 8–29.

256. 600 F. Supp. 1466 (N.D. Ill. 1985).

affiliated corporation were safe, high quality investments, and that the issuer corporation was a financially sound and profitable company, facts that allegedly were not true. Refusing to dismiss the RICO claims, the district court determined that the securities fraud and mail fraud activities were sufficiently pleaded for RICO purposes.

It should be noted that the principle of *respondeat superior* can be linked to a RICO claim against a bank.[257]

Conceivably, RICO may become used, if the fact situations permit, by private litigants and the bank regulators to address serious cases of bank fraud or mismanagement and (by the bank regulators) for wilful (i.e., criminal) violations of the banking laws.[258]

F. Federal bankruptcy law concerns

In most troubled loan situations, the borrower's goal is to continue in business and the lender's goal is for the loan to be repaid and perhaps for additional credit to be extended to the borrower that survives and continues in business. Nevertheless, the economic uncertainties of the 1980s and 1990s require both the prudent lender and the prudent borrower to recognise that the borrower may enter bankruptcy proceedings, whether on a voluntary or involuntary basis. They almost must recognise that the borrower's entry into bankruptcy proceedings may be only temporary, or may be permanent. This economic reality means that the Federal Bankruptcy Code[259] may well be brought to bear upon the lender's conduct. Thus, lenders and borrowers both need to "think about the unthinkable" in order to conduct a reasonable amount to pre-bankruptcy planning. The realm of bankruptcy proceedings is intricate, and it is the subject of many institutes, publications, and other resources for lenders, borrowers, and their counsel. The bankruptcy realm is beyond the scope of the present article but nevertheless pre-bankruptcy issues are so closely interrelated with the other legal issues in the workout realm that a brief review of pre-bankruptcy issues is necessary and appropriate.

1. Insider status: control

A significant issue in bankruptcy proceedings is that a lender may find that its conduct causes it to be deemed an "insider", a status that can have serious consequences for the lender.[259a] The term "affiliate" is defined to include any

---

257. See *Quick* v. *People's Bank of Cullman City*, 993 F.2d 793 (11th Cir. 1993).

258. *Norton & Whitley, supra* fn. 193, section 8.06[8], at 8–30.

259. See generally, Bankruptcy Reform Act of 1978, Pub. L. No. 95–598, 92 Stat. 2549 (certified and amended in scattered sections of 11 U.S.C.). See also, *Norton & Whitley, supra* fn. 193, Ch. 13 ("Bankruptcy; A Practical Analysis"). On specific lender liability aspects, see *Norton & Baggett, supra* fn. 3, Ch. 8 ("Bankruptcy Concerns") by Franklin.

259a. 11 U.S.C. section 101(31).

entity that "directly or indirectly owns, controls, or holds with power to vote, 20 per cent or more of the outstanding voting securities of the debtor."[260] Thus, if the lender has accepted 20 per cent or more of the borrower's voting stock, or holds such stock with the right to vote it, the lender would be an "affiliate" of the debtor and thus would be an "insider" under the Bankruptcy Code. Additionally, the term "insider" of a corporate or partnership debtor includes any individual, partnership, or corporation that is in control of the debtor.[261] Thus, if the lender is in control of the debtor corporation or partnership, the lender is an "insider". The Bankruptcy Code does not define the conduct that constitutes "control" for purposes of "insider" status, but presumably some of the activities that cause "control" problems for tort law, instrumentality, and agency purposes discussed above may also cause the lender to be deemed an insider if the debtor enters bankruptcy proceedings.[262]

One consequence of "insider" status under the Bankruptcy Code is that the 90-day preference period is extended beyond 90 days to one year prior to the filing of the bankruptcy petition. This means that if the debtor enters bankruptcy proceedings, and the lender is deemed to have been an insider, the court will scrutinise the debtor's transfers of interests in property during a one-year period, rather than during only a 90-day period, prior to the filing of the petition. Any such transfers that were made to the lender or for the lender's benefit, for or on account of any debt owed by the debtor before the making of the transfer, and that were made while the debtor was insolvent, are voidable by or for the benefit of the debtor if the transfer enabled the lender to receive more than it would have received under a Chapter 7 liquidation. As an example, if the lender took a lien on additional collateral without advancing new loan proceeds, and this creation of a lien occurred six months prior to the debtor's entry into bankruptcy proceedings, the transfer could not be challenged as preferential unless the lender was an insider.

Another consequence of "insider" status is loss of voting rights. Specifically, a lender who is an insider cannot vote for the selection of a trustee in a Chapter 7 proceeding.[263] Similarly, a lender who is deemed to be an insider cannot vote for (or against) a proposed plan of reorganisation in a Chapter 11 proceeding.[264]

---

260. *Ibid.* section 101(31)(E).

261. *Ibid.* ss. 101(28)(B) and (C).

262. See Kornberg, "Who is an 'Insider'? What does it Mean?", 1 Bankr. Strat. No. 12, at 2 (Oct. 1984). See also controversial decision of *Levit* v. *Ingersoll-Rand Fin. Corp.*, 874 F.2d 1186 (7th Cir. 1989), requiring creditors to give up payments from debtor for entire year if those payments benefited insiders and as guarantors.

263. 11 U.S.C. section 702(a)(3).

264. *Ibid.* section 1129(a)(10).

2. Equitable subordination

A powerful tool in the hands of the bankruptcy court is its authority to subordinate a creditor's claim or lien to all or parts of other claims or liens, or to order that the lien that secures the lender's claim must be transferred to the bankrupt party's estate.[265] The Code indicates that such action is to be performed "under principles of equitable subordination", but does not define the term "equitable subordination". Thus, the development of this important doctrine is left to the courts. The doctrine of equitable subordination should play an important role in the guidance of a lender's conduct, because the results of such subordination can be catastrophic. As an example, a lender who has a first lien upon all of the debtor's assets could lose its lien, in whole or in part, and could find that its claim is to be paid, if at all, behind a claim or claims that otherwise would not have been paid until after the lender had been paid in full.

The Fifth Circuit has stated three conditions that must be satisfied before a bankruptcy court may appropriately exercise the power of equitable subordination: "(i) The claimant must have engaged in some type of inequitable conduct; (ii) The misconduct must have resulted in injury to the creditors of the bankruptcy or conferred an unfair advantage on the claimant; (iii) Equitable subordination of the claim must not be inconsistent with the provisions of the Bankruptcy Act."[266] The court also indicated that three principles are applicable to the determination of whether such three conditions have been satisfied[267]:

"The first is that inequitable conduct directed against the bankrupt or its creditors may be sufficient to warrant subordination of a claim irrespective of whether it was related to the acquisition or assertion of that claim ... The second principle is that a claim or claims should be subordinated only to the extent necessary to offset the harm which the bankrupt and its creditors suffered on account of the inequitable conduct ... The third guiding principle relates to allocation of the burden of proof ... the proper rule is that the claimant's verified proof of claim obliges the objecting trustee to come forward with enough substantiations to overcome the claimant's *prima facie* case and thus compel him to actually prove the validity and honesty of his claim."

The application of these concise principles to a particular lender/debtor relationship can be intricate, and a concise definition of what constitutes "inequitable conduct" or of what constitutes an "unfair" advantage is difficult. A few examples are that a creditor's claim can be equitably subordinated if the creditor misrepresents the debtor's financial condition[268]; if the lender exercises such complete control over the debtor as to overwhelm the debtor's corporate management (e.g., the right to have one of the lender's employees exercise

---

265. *Ibid.* section 510(c).

266. See *Re Mobil Steel Co.*, 563 F.2d 691, 699–700 (5th Cir. 1977). See also *Smith* v. *Assocs. Commercial Corp.*, 870 F.2d 1022 (5th Cir. 1989), where a lender's lien was subordinated due to lender misconduct in keeping debtor afloat for its own benefit and to the detriment of other creditors, *aff'd in part, rev'd in part and remanded* 693 F.2d 693 (5th Cir. 1990).

267. *Ibid.* at 700–01.

268. See *Re Just For The Fun of It of Tennessee, Inc.*, 7 B.R. 166 (Bankr. E.D. Tenn. 1980).

complete veto power over the debtor's day-to-day operations), even if such measure of control is authorised by the loan documents[269]; or if the lender advances funds to an insolvent debtor only in order to complete projects in progress and thus improve accounts receivable, while also taking a lien on inventory and equipment to collateralise such advances and damage the unsecured creditors, and commences liquidation of the debtor while simultaneously advising a local credit association that the lender is doing everything possible to protect the unsecured creditors.[270]

This very brief reference to a few of the equitable subordination cases should alert lenders and borrowers that the issue of "control" remains open long after the loan has been closed. This is important if the debtor survives the period of financial difficulty and of lender control, as in the *Farah* case discussed above. It is also important even if the debtor does not survive the difficulty period and arrives in bankruptcy proceedings.

3. Fraudulent transfers

Borrowers in bankruptcy proceedings also may seek to avoid transfers made prior to bankruptcy on the basis that they were fraudulent. Such actions may be asserted directly under the Bankruptcy Code,[271] or under the Bankruptcy Code provision permitting a trustee or debtor in possession to bring actions under state law, which include state fraudulent conveyance law.[272] Often fraudulent conveyance actions against lenders take one of two forms: when a lender makes a loan to a distressed borrower and, as part of the loan agreement, gains an advantage over the borrower's other creditors; and when the amount of debt reduced as a result of lender's taking of collateral is significantly less than the collateral's market value.

During the process of renegotiating and perhaps extending an existing loan, the lender may decide to demand additional collateral. Although the lender may well have contractual authority to make this demand, there are two circumstances under which the taking of additional collateral may constitute a fraudulent transfer if the debtor later enters bankruptcy proceedings. First, if the value of the collateral exceeds the loan balance as of the date the additional collateral is taken, then unless new loan proceeds of reasonable equal value to the additional collateral are extended, the transfer of the additional collateral to the lender may later be set aside as having been a fraudulent transfer.[273] Secondly, at the time of the taking of additional collateral, if the lender knows or has good reason to know that the debtor is insolvent, and that any new funds

---

269. See *Re T.E. Mercer Trucking Co.*, 16 B.R. 176, 189–190 (Bankr. N.D. Tex. 1981).
270. See *Re American Lumber Co.*, 5 B.R. 470 (D. Minn. 1980), *aff'g* 7 B.R. 519 (Bankr. D. Minn. 1979).
271. 11 U.S.C. section 548.
272. *Ibid.* section 544.
273. *Ibid.* section 548(a)(2).

advanced will be used to prefer one or more creditors over other creditors, then any new collateral obtained as collateral for the new advance can be set aside as a fraudulent transfer.[274]

A lender also may be subject to fraudulent transfer claims when it forecloses on collateral and fails to credit the debtor's loan balance by an amount adjudged reasonably equivalent to the collateral's value. Some courts have prescribed a bright-line rule requiring lenders to apply a certain percentage of the collateral's market value to the underlying indebtedness to meet fraudulent transfer prohibitions.[275]

G. Bank anti-tying statutes

For present purposes, the primary bank anti-tying statute that may be applicable to workout negotiations between a lender and borrower is section 106 of the Bank Holding Company Act Amendments of 1970.[276] This is the anti-tying provision of such Amendments, and it prohibits banks, bank holding companies, and their subsidiaries from making agreements to extend credit, or to sell one product or service, only on the condition that the bank's customer also obtain additional credit, or purchase a different product or service, or at least agree that he will not purchase that product or service from any other supplier. The statute also prohibits any reciprocal arrangement whereby a bank conditions its extension of credit or furnishing of other service on the requirement that the bank's customer provide the bank with something of value in exchange for the bank's product or service. Significantly, the statute exempts any transaction that exclusively involves any of four traditional banking services: loans, discounts, deposits, and trust services.[277]

The anti-tying provision does not prohibit a bank from requiring additional protection for credit that it extends. For example, in *Palermo* v. *First National Bank & Trust Company*,[278] the Tenth Circuit saw nothing wrong with a bank's conditioning renewal of plaintiff's credit upon obtaining a guarantee of the debtor corporation's indebtedness. The plaintiff in *Palermo* owned part of the

---

274. See *Porter* v. *Yokon Nat'l Bank*, 866 F.2d 355 (10th Cir. 1989), wherein lender's taking of additional security as collateral for a pre-existing debt was deemed a voidable transfer. For use of this doctrine in a leveraged situation, see *Wiebolt Stones Inc.* v. *Schottenstein*, 725 F.2d 71 (1988). But cf. *Ohio Corrugating Co.* v. *O.P.P.A.C., Inc.*, 74 B.R. 488 (Bankr. N.D. Ill. 1988).

275. See *Durrett* v. *Washington Nat'l Ins. Co.*, 621 F.2d 201 (5th Cir. 1980) (no fraudulent transfer occurs when a lender credits a minimum of 70 per cent of the collateral's market value to the loan balance).

276. 12 U.S.C. section 1971 *et seq.* (West Supp. 1993). For detailed discussion, see *Norton & Baggett, supra* fn. 3, Ch. 14 ("Antitrust Aspects of Lender Liability").

277. *Ibid.* section 1972(b). For a bank to come under the statute, it need not have actually made a loan. See *AmerFirst Properties Inc.* v. *FDIC*, 880 F.2d 821 (5th Cir. 1989).

278. 894 F.2d 363 (10th Cir. 1990); see also *Alpine Elec. Co.* v. *Union Bank*, 979 F.2d 133 (8th Cir. 1992) (bank did not violate anti-tying provisions of Bank Holding Company Act by using money from depositor's chequing account to reduce debt of related corporation and by conditioning renewal of depositor's loan on its agreement to assume loan of the corporation).

debtor corporation and was an officer and employee of a family corporation. The family corporation defaulted on one of its loans, and the bank agreed to renew the plaintiff's personal loan only if the plaintiff would guarantee the corporation's loan. After unsuccessfully attempting to get other financing, the plaintiff guaranteed the corporation's debt and then claimed that the bank violated the anti-tying provisions of the Bank Holding Company Act by attaching the condition to renewal of the loan. The Tenth Circuit rejected the plaintiff's argument, reasoning that the bank did no more than evaluate its entire existing relationship with the plaintiff when it attached a condition to renewal. The court emphasised that the case was not about a bank requiring one customer to guarantee the debt of another unrelated or incidentally related customer.[278a]

As one court has stated, the anti-tying provision is not "designed to insure fair interest rates, collateral requirements, and other loan agreement terms. It has a narrow target; it is intended to provide specific statutory assurance that the use of the economic power of a bank will not lead to a lessening of competition or unfair competitive practices."[279] A significant feature of the anti-tying provision is that if the plaintiff is successful, treble damages are mandatory.[280]

In the years since the enactment of the anti-tying provision rather few reported cases have been decided under the statute.[281] Nevertheless, the anti-tying provision does raise issues that are relevant to the workout of troubled credits, and lenders and borrowers need to be aware of the restrictions it imposes on workout arrangements.

H. CERCLA environmental liabilities

A lender may incur strict as well as joint and several liability under the federal Comprehensive Environmental Response, Compensation and Liability Act ("CERCLA").[281a] CERCLA liability attaches if each of the following elements are established: (1) there is a release or threatened release of a hazardous substance; (2) at a facility; (3) causing the plaintiff to incur response costs; and

---

278a. 894 F.2d at 370.

279. *Freidco of Wilmington, Delaware, Ltd.* v. *Farmers Bank*, 499 F. Supp. 995, 1001 (D. Del.80).

280. 12 U.S.C. section 1975. See also *Tri-Crown Inc.* v. *American Fed. Sav. & Loan Ass'n*, 908 F.2d 578 (10th Cir. 1990) (borrowers who lost financing when they refused to assume bad loans or assumed bad loans in order to get financing sought treble damages).

281. See generally, Nicoll, Federick A. and Delventhal, Robert W., "The antitying provisions of the Bank Holding Company Act: lenders beware" (1991) 109 Banking L.J. 4–27; see Cotham & Cotham, "The Bank Tying Act: An Underutilized Tool in Seeking Redress against Abuse by Financial Institution", 49 Texas B.J. 110, 119 (1986); and Naegle, "The Anti-Tying Provision; Its Potential Is Still There", (1983) 100 Bank. L.J. 138, 144.

281a. 42 U.S.C. sections 9601 *et seq.* (1993). See, e.g., *New York* v. *Shore Realty Corp.*, 759 F.2d 1032, 1044 (2d Cir. 1985).

(4) the defendant is a responsible party as defined in the statute.[282] A responsible party is defined to include an owner or operator of a facility.[283] Consequently, a lender may be liable as an "owner or operator" of a contaminated property by virtue of its security interest in that property unless the lender fits within a "secured creditor" exemption set forth in the statute: the lender (1) holds indiciæ of ownership; (2) primarily to protect its security interest in the property; and (3) it does not participate in the management of the property.[284]

Because these vague phrases are not defined in CERCLA, many reported court decisions on CERCLA lender liability have attempted to define the nature and scope of these elements of the secured creditor exemption.[285] Certain of these decisions, notably the Eleventh Circuit's 1990 *Fleet Factors*[286] decision, left the status of this exemption in doubt. In 1992, however, the federal Environmental Protection Agency (the "EPA") adopted a new regulation (the "Rule") defining the key elements of CERCLA's secured creditor exemption.[287]

The major goal and purpose of the Rule was that it purported to replace the general judicial principles interpreting the secured creditor exemption with the certainty of a "substantive" regulation that, in effect, had the force of a statute.[288] Moreover, this regulation was to apply not just in actions brought by the EPA, but in third party actions as well.[289] The EPA took the position in promulgating the Rule that the Rule was a "legislative" or "substantive" rule that has undergone notice-and-comment pursuant to the Administrative Procedures Act and thus "defines the liability of holders [of security interests] for CERCLA response costs in both the United States and private party litigation".[290] Alternatively, the EPA states that, in any event, even if the Rule was considered a mere interpretation of the secured creditor exemption, it anticipated that the Rule would be followed by the courts because of the

---

282. 42 U.S.C. section 9607(a); *United States* v. *Aceto Agricultural Chemical Corp.*, 872 F.2d 1373 (8th Cir. 1989).

283. 42 U.S.C. sections 9607(a)(a), (2).

284. *Ibid.* section 9601(20)(A). See generally Billauer, Barbara Pfeffer, *The Lender's Guide to Environmental Law: Risk and Liability*, New York, N.Y. (M. Bender, 1993).

285. See, e.g., *In re Bergsoe Metal Corp.*, 910 F.2d 668 (9th Cir. 1990) (holding that lender does not lose exemption merely by having the power to become involved in the borrower's management; the lender must exercise actual management authority before liability attaches); *United States* v. *Fleet Factors Corp.* 901 F.2d 1550 (11th Cir. 1990), *cert. denied*, 498 U.S. 1046 (1991); *United States* v. *Nicolet Inc.*, 712 F. Supp. 1193 (E.D. Pa. 1989); *United States* v. *Maryland Bank & Trust Co.*, 632 F. Supp. 573 (D. Md. 1986) (holding that foreclosure followed by a rapid divestiture would not cause a loss of the exemption).

286. *United States* v. *Fleet Factors Corp.* (*supra*, fn. 285) (lender must be actively involved in the management of a facility before it loses the exemption but does not require actual involvement in management decisions concerning hazardous waste; the exemption may be lost if the lender's involvement in management is sufficiently broad to support the inference that it could, if it so chose, affect the borrower's hazardous waste disposal decisions).

287. "National Oil and Hazardous Substances Pollution Contingency Plan; Lender Liability Under CERCLA", 40 C.F.R. s. 300.1100 (1992).

288. Fed. Reg. 18,344–18,346 (1992).

289. Fed. Reg. 18,346 (1992).

290. *Ibid.*

traditional "substantial deference" courts give to agency interpretations of laws that it administers.[291]

The EPA's authority to adopt the Rule was challenged in two separate petitions filed in the United States Court of Appeals for the D.C. Circuit, *Kelley v. Environmental Protection Agency*,[292] and *Chemical Manufacturers Association v. Environmental Protection Agency*.[293] In its opinion issued on 4 February 1994, the Court of Appeals agreed that the EPA has exceeded its authority in issuing the Rule, and accordingly, vacated the Rule.[294]

To understand what was lost in the vacating of the Rule in *Kelley*, it is necessary to understand the actual advantages of the Rule over existing case law.[295] As noted by the court in *Kelley*, the purpose of the Rule was to provide "an overall standard for judging when a lender's 'participation in management' causes the lender to forfeit its exemption".[296] The four phrases are: pre-loan, the loan term, which includes workout negotiations and activities, foreclosure, and post-foreclosure.[297] For the "pre-loan" period, the Rule essentially states the obvious that it is very difficult for a lender to "participate in management" of a borrower before a loan is even placed.[298]

For the "loan term and workout" period, the Rule gave several specific and very helpful examples of what does *not* constitute "participation in management": lenders could make loans on contaminated properties, require post-closing remediation, place environmental covenants in the loan documents, and monitor environmental compliance.[299] Moreover, during workout negotiations, the lenders could, essentially, exercise their full array of restructuring options.[300] These specific examples provided a limited "safe harbour" for certain activities during the "loan term and workout" period. The Rule's three-prong test, however, for what *does* constitute "participation in management" was not particularly illuminating. The test was not significantly different in substance from the general principle developed by courts prior to the promulgation of the Rule: a lender loses the exemption if it takes over direct responsibility for hazardous waste management; if it takes over overall management of the borrower's affairs, including environmental compliance; or if it takes over overall management of the borrower's affairs, except for environmental compliance.[301]

291. *Ibid.*

292. No. 92–1312, D.C. Court of Appeals (filed 28 July 1992).

293. No. 92–1314, D.C. Court of Appeals (filed 28 July 1992).

294. See *Kelley v. Environmental Protection Agency*, 1994 U.S. App. LEXIS 1715 (D.C. Cir. 1994). (*Kelley* and *Chemical Manufacturers* were consolidated for purposes of the court's opinion).

295. See *Kelley v. Environmental Protection Agency*, *supra* fn. 294, at 4 (D.C. Cir. 1994) (citing 40 C.F.R. s. 300.1100(c)(1)).

296. 40 C.F.R. s. 300.1100(c), (d).

297. *Ibid.*

298. *Ibid.*

299. 40 C.F.R. s. 300.1100(c).

300. *Ibid.*

301. *Ibid.*

The Rule's most significant improvement over judicial developments prior to the Rule was in the "foreclosure and post-foreclosure" periods. The Rule emphatically stated that the exemption is not lost by foreclosure or by post-foreclosure operation of the property as long as the lender actively attempts to resell the property and does not itself create or exacerbate environmental problems.[302] This "safe harbour" for foreclosure and post-foreclosure activity is not firmly established in the pre-Rule case law.

Because the Rule did not add a great deal of clarity to the analysis of the secured creditor exemption in the "pre-loan" period, the loss of the authority of the Rule should not have a significant impact on a lender's activities prior to the making of a loan. The Rule did, however, state that several activities during the "loan term" period, including workouts, would be "safe harbours" and would not constitute "participation in management". These "safe harbours" will be missed; however, these same activities can still be analysed with a certain degree of clarity under the general principles that predated and, according to the EPA, were consistent with the Rule.

The most serious impact of the loss of the Rule will be in the "foreclosure and post-foreclosure" periods. Before the Rule, notwithstanding the decision in *Maryland Bank*,[303] many commentators recognised the possibility that a lender foreclosing on collateral could immediately become an "owner or operator" of the foreclosed property, and consequently could be liable for the costs of any required environmental clean-up.[304] With the loss of the Rule, lenders must once again be aware that, if they foreclose, they could lose the exemption and become liable as an owner or operator of the foreclosed property.[305]

I. Criminal liability

There are numerous federal and state statutes, the wilful violation of which by a lender can result in criminal liability.[306]

302. 40 C.F.R. s. 300.1100(d).

303. *United States* v. *Maryland Bank & Trust* Co., 632 F. Supp. 573 (D. Md. 1986).

304. See, e.g., *Norton & Baggett, supra* fn. 3, "Lender Liability Law and Litigation", Ch. 11.

305. The judgment of the court in the *Kelley* case is not final until on or about 4 April 1994. Moreover, if the EPA appeals the decision, the judgment could be stayed indefinitely until the issue is decided by the United States Supreme Court. Lenders, however, should nevertheless assume that the rule has been vacated. Lenders should analyse their activities during the "pre-loan" and "loan term" periods utilising the judicial principles that predated the Rule. The "pre-loan" and "loan term" activities may also be compared to the tests set forth in the vacated Rule; to the extent the analysis of the pre-Rule case law and the vacated Rule agree, a lender can take some limited and cautious comfort in this concurrence. Lenders should note, however, that at the end of its opinion, the *Kelley* court observed that the Rule "could be sustained as a policy statement that would guide EPA's enforcement proceedings across the country, but EPA has not asked that its regulation be so regarded." *Kelley*, 1994 U.S. App. LEXIS 1715, at 11 (D.C. Cir. 1994).

306. E.g. 18 U.S.C. section 215 (bank bribery), 18 U.S.C. ss. 656–657 (misapplication of funds), ss. 1001, 1005, 1006 (false entries), 18 U.S.C. section 1014 (wilful overvaluation of assets), 18 U.S.C. ss. 1341 & 1343 (mail and wire fraud), 18 U.S.C. section 1344 (financial institution fraud), 18 U.S.C. section 2113(b) (larceny), 18 U.S.C. sections 371 (criminal conspiracy), 18 U.S.C. s. 1956 (money laundering) as well as criminal liability under RICO and the securities laws.

V. THE CRUX OF THE LIABILITY EXPANSION PROBLEM: OF CONTORTS AND SPECIAL RELATIONSHIPS

Traditionally, law has striven to reflect a balance between contract and tort bodies of law. However, as business becomes more complex and as social demands increase, tort duties and damage compensation have been applied to or engrafted upon contract matters (as is the case in the lender liability area). The legal distinctions between social compensation and tort concepts and business voluntary risk and profit negotiations and, if agreed, duties and rewards or penalties have been blurred and a non-discriminate area of "contorts" in the lender liability area raises its head. Yet, the duties and rewards or compensation should be decided by consciously developed legal concepts and policies and not by random views of what twelve jurors think is fair (as is most often the case in a US lender liability trial). A properly functioning economic and social system demands predictability and certainty for planning and voluntary compliance with legal standards. This, in the author's view, is the crux of the dilemma facing the US legal system in the lender liability area.

A. Liability—duties

Any legally recognised cause of action includes liability, causation, and damage components. The liability component must begin with a legal duty—whether tort or contract. Once a legal duty is recognised, it must be breached in order to sustain a recovery.

1. Tort

Tort duties arise from common law recognition that certain obligations are owed by people to the world at large. These duties are not dependent upon an agreement between parties, but rather, reflect obligations or conduct between parties as their actions affect each other—by negligence or otherwise.

Tort duties arise from involuntary relationships among parties. No voluntary privity of contract exists. Rather, one party acts in such a manner that the law will recognise a wrong by a party interfering with personal health or property of another party—whether intentionally or negligently. Examples of these tort duties include the duty to drive a car with reasonable care, the duty to manufacture goods free of unreasonably dangerous defects, and the duty not to assault or unreasonably interfere with the physical well-being of another.

These common law obligations, among citizens at large, are governed by an objective standard—how the ubiquitous "reasonable person" would act in the same or similar circumstances. This standard or duty of performance is not founded upon a voluntary bargain negotiated and agreed between parties—there are no subjective agreed obligations between parties. Tort duties compare the actions of the accused with those of a reasonably prudent person.

Tort law, as discussed above, recognises recoveries where parties unreasonably interfere with contractual relationships. For example, tort law recognises a legal cause of action for wilful and intentional interference with a contract, which interference proximately causes damage.[307] However, one cannot have tortious interference with a contractual relationship to which one is a party.[308] Also the law recognises the action for duress, which is threatening to do something that the threatening party has no legal right to do, there is some illegal exaction or fraud or deception, and the restraint is imminent and such as to destroy free agency without present means of protection.[309] If a party's action is in accordance with contractual duties it is not actionable.[310]

2. Contract

Contract causes of action arise from duties defined by parties who voluntarily seek a mutual agreement. Parties may present whatever terms and conditions they desire—but, if they do not agree—no duties arise.

Contract duties arise when parties, seeking profit or other benefits, voluntarily negotiate duties of performance. The parties to the contract generally write down what each expects from the other. Neither party normally receives everything they wanted and, generally, the parties may agree to whatever they wanted—agree to whatever each expected to be his or her "benefit of the bargain". These expectations may be right or wrong—but in either event, the parties will be held to the agreed bargain. The bargain is not to be rewritten by judges and juries many months after the agreement, based upon changing economic conditions or what may later be perceived as "fair".

To govern the establishment of legally enforceable duties, the law of contract developed well defined elements—offer, acceptance and consideration. Each party offered performance and/or promises in exchange for requested performance and/or promises. The offer must be accepted as given, to be enforceable; and, the offer and acceptance must be supported by consideration flowing between the parties.

If an offer is accepted as given and consideration is exchanged, the parties have established their agreed performance duties. These voluntarily negotiated duties, sought for reasons unique to both parties, should and will be enforced by judges and juries—enforced as agreed—not as what parties, not involved in the negotiations, later consider to be "fair".

A contract law reflection of the voluntary, negotiated and agreed duties of performance is privity of contract. Many contract cases, dealing with business

---

307. *State Nat'l. Bank* v. *Farah Mfg. Co., Inc.*, 678 S.W.2d 661 (Tex. App. 1984, *writ dism'd by agr.*).
308. *Baker* v. *Welch*, 735 S.W.2d 548 (Tex. App.—Houston [1st Dist] 1987, no writ).
309. *Simpson* v. *MBank Dallas*, 724 S.W.2d 102 (Tex. App.—Dallas 1987, *writ ref'd n.r.e.*).
310. *Spillers* v. *Five Points Guaranty Bank*, 335 So. 2d 851 (Fla. 1976).

disputes, have limited contract duties to those parties in privity of contract—those parties who actually negotiate and agree upon standards of performance. One who is not a party to a contract has no rights under a contract and does not have legal standing to rely upon a duty established in a contract between others.

The existence of a legal duty is a question of law for the court.[311] Standards of conduct must be consistently recognised by courts and not left to random and inconsistent views of 12 jurors. Once a legal standard is recognised, that standard may be submitted to a jury to determine factual compliance or breach of duty; but juries should not decide the legal question of the existence of a legal duty.[312]

3. The dividing lines between contract and tort

The basic distinction between tort and contract duties—tort duties are founded upon a reasonable man's standard of conduct to the world at large, whereas contract duties are founded upon agreed voluntary performance standards—is recognised in common law development. Courts, however, struggle with "voluntary" relationships where the parties do not have equal bargaining positions that permit arm's-length negotiations. Because of special circumstances between contracting parties, courts have tended to impose implied or objective good faith or reasonable standards beyond the specific agreed contractual duties negotiated as a part of the contract promises and consideration. The common law has carved out categories of party relationships where legal duties may be more than the contractual agreed duties of performance.

In defining contractual duties, the legal distinction between the recognition of an agreed duty and the implication of a duty beyond the agreed promise or consideration must be remembered. Furthermore, the distinction between the existence of a duty and standards of "performance" and "execution" of recognised legal duties *must* also be recognised. The first issue is the circumstances of expansion of legal duties beyond those mutually agreed upon pursuant to contract law principles. The second issue—implication of performance or execution standards for recognised legal duties—arises only after establishment of a legal duty and relates to the analysis of breach of duty rather than existence of a duty.

Circumstances where the common law considers extension of contract duties beyond those specifically agreed in the contract include:

(a) *Consumer protection* Many common law and, ultimately, statutory struggles focus upon duties of suppliers of goods and services to consumers.

---

311. See *Massey* v. *Armco Steel*, 652 S.W.2d 932 (Tex. 1983); *Stowers Furniture Co.* v. *American Indemnity Co.*, 15 S.W.2d 544 (Tex. Comm'n. App. 1929, opinion adopted); *Jackson* v. *Assoc. Dev. of Lubbock*, 581 S.W.2d 208 (Tex. Civ. App.—Amarillo 1979, *writ ref'd n.r.e.*).

312. *Anderson* v. *Griffith*, 501 S.W.2d 695 (Tex. Civ. App.—Fort Worth 1973, *writ ref'd n.r.e.*).

While consumer contracts to purchase goods and services may not include broad duties of performance upon the suppliers, common law and legislation struggles to supply implied duties to balance the unequal bargaining positions of the parties and the lack of arm's-length negotiations. An example of statutory protection of consumers would be a Deceptive Trade Practices Act ("DTPA") that specifically enumerates duties owed to a consumer.[313]

(b) Fiduciary relationships General contractual settings are inconsistent with an increased duty of utmost care, disclosure, and acting in the best interest of the opposing contracting party, such as are found in fiduciary relationships. In most contractual circumstances, each party voluntarily enters into a relationship whereby both parties negotiate and agree upon consideration and promises they believe will produce profits and maximise the benefit of their bargains. Contracting parties are negotiating for their best business interest and if the negotiations are not satisfactory, either party may refuse the offer or acceptance of contract considerations and promises. In a business relationship, including borrower/lender, where both parties are negotiating for a profitable contract, justifiable trust and confidence in the fiduciary duty of the opposing contractual party is difficult to prove.[314]

A confidential or fiduciary relationship may exist where one party is in fact accustomed to being guided by the judgement or advice of the other party, or is justified in placing confidence in the belief that the other party will act in its interest.[315] A fiduciary relationship may also exist in those cases in which one party has acquired influence over another and has abused that influence.[316] A fiduciary relationship generally arises over a long period of time when parties have worked together towards a mutual goal.[317] Subjective trust alone, however, is not sufficient to transform an arm's-length business dealing into a fiduciary relationship.[318] Extensive prior dealings alone are also insufficient to establish a fiduciary relationship.[319] Further, as a general rule, as discussed above, a lender is not a fiduciary either of the debtor or other creditors.[320]

(c) Special relationship: the new battleground Some courts refer to a "special

---

313. E.g. Tex. Bus. & Com. Code Ann. section 17–41 *et seq.* (Vernon 1987).

314. *Winston* v. *Lake Jackson Bank*, 574 S.W.2d 628 (Tex. Civ. App.—Houston [14th Dist.] 1978, no writ).

315. *Texas Bank and Trust Co.* v. *Moore*, 595 S.W.2d 502, 507 (Tex. 1980); *Thames* v. *Johnson*, 614 S.W.2d 612, 614 (Tex. Civ. App.—Texarkana 1981, no writ).

316. *Texas Bank and Trust*, 595 S.W.2d at 507.

317. *O'Shea* v. *Coronodo Transmission Co.*, 656 S.W.2d 557, 563 (Tex. App.—Corpus Christi 1983, *writ ref'd n.r.e.*).

318. *Thigpen* v. *Locke*, 363 S.W.2d 247, 253 (Tex. 1962); *Thomson* v. *Norton*, 604 S.W.2d 473, 476 (Tex. Civ. App.—Dallas 1980, no writ).

319. *Re Letterman Bros. Energy Securities Litigation*, 799 F.2d 967, 975 (5th Cir. 1986) (applying Texas law), *cert. denied*, 107 S. Ct. 1373 (1987); *Thigpen*, 363 S.W.2d at 253.

320. *Re Letterman*, 799 F.2d at 975; *Weinberger* v. *Kendrick*, 698 F.2d 61, 78–79 (2d Cir. 1982), *cert. denied*, 464 U.S. 818 (1983); *Re W.T. Grant Co.*, 4 Bankr. Rptr. 53, 78–79 (Bankr. S.D.N.Y. 1980), *aff'd*, 20 Bankr. Rptr. 186 (Bankr. S.D.N.Y. 1982), *aff'd*, 699 F.2d 599 (2d Cir.), *cert. denied*, 464 U.S. 822 (1983); *Thigpen*, 363 S.W.2d at 253.

relationship", arising out of a contract, creating an implied covenant of good faith and fair dealing. While some courts may imply a covenant of good faith and fair dealing in special relationships—particularly insurer/insured—the adoption of an implied covenant will not normally arise contrary to an expressly negotiated contractual duty or add a general undefined duty which was not negotiated by the parties agreeing to a voluntary contractual relationship.[321]

As a predicate to a "special relationship", arising out of contract, there must be a contract with the traditional elements of offer, acceptance and consideration. Understandably, there is no duty of good faith and fair dealing to negotiate a contract or arising out of circumstances that do not fulfil the basic contract elements.[322] Without a contract, no special relationship, arising out of contract, and no implied covenant of good faith and fair dealing exist.

Further, many courts confuse an implied duty of good faith and fair dealing and a distinct obligation of good faith and fair dealing only in performance and execution of contractually agreed upon duties.[323]

Thus, there is a clear distinction between establishing an implied general duty of "good faith and fair dealing" and applying good faith and fair dealing only to determine if there is a breach of an expressly agreed performance duty. Good faith and fair dealing will not generally be used as the basis of a contract duty not expressly negotiated, but may be applied to determine if expressly agreed upon duties have been breached.

In *Standard Wire and Cable Company* v. *Ameritrust Corporation*,[324] the court found that a plaintiff in California could allege a tortious breach of the covenant of good faith and fair dealing under any one of three theories: bad faith denial of the existence of a contract; bad faith breach of an agreement between parties who have a "special relationship"; or bad faith denial of liability.[325]

The court further set forth five elements that must be shown in order for a court to determine that a special relationship exists:

— the contract must be such that the parties are in inherently unequal bargaining positions;
— there must be a non-profit motivation for the contract;
— contract damages must not adequately compensate the plaintiff for the breach;
— the plaintiff must be vulnerable because of the defendant's position of trust; and

---

321. *English* v. *Fischer*, 660 S.W.2d 521 (Tex. 1983).

322. *Bank of America* v. *Kruse*, 202 Cal. App. 3d 38, 248 Cal. Rptr. 217 (1988).

323. Section 205 of the Restatement (Second) of Contracts applies good faith and fair dealing only to "performance" and "enforcement", *Black Lake Pipeline Co.* v. *Union Constr. Co.*, 538 S.W.2d 80 (Tex. 1976). Likewise section 1–203 of the UCC applies only to performance and enforcement of contracts and not formation of a contract. Summers, " 'Good Faith' in General Contract Law and the Sales Provision of the Uniform Commercial Code", 54 Va. L. Rev. 195, 218 (1968).

324. 697 F. Supp. 368 (C.D. Cal. 1988).

325. *Ibid.*, at 373.

— the defendant must have knowledge of the plaintiff's vulnerability.

The California Supreme Court recently has refused to permit tort damages in a bad faith claim in an employment context, limiting the "special relationship" concept to the insurer–insured context.[326]

Applying the elements of a "special relationship" in *Standard Wire and Cable Company* v. *Ameritrust*,[327] it seems that a borrower/lender is not a "special relationship". The parties are not inherently in an unequal bargaining position, lender/borrower loans are not non-profit motivated, the borrower is not necessarily vulnerable because of a position of trust, and the lender does not normally have knowledge of the borrower's vulnerability.

These elements will vary in particular borrower/lender relationships, but generally, in a profit-oriented economy, both the borrower and lender believe the borrower's use of loan proceeds will result in a profit that will pay the lender's interest return and generate excess return for the borrower. Both borrower and lender are free to negotiate the most advantageous business agreement; or if they believe the business opportunity does not justify the risk or can be structured more favourably with others, they are free to improve their proposed business deals or decline them and go to other opportunities. A borrower/lender relationship is not a circumstance where both are obligated to act for the economic benefit of the opposing party. Both borrower and lender are fully aware of both parties' desire to reduce their risks and generate profits. The borrower presents the lender with his or her proposal for a profitable use of loan proceeds. The borrower anticipates profits beyond capital costs. The lender evaluates the borrower's proposal and determines if the borrower's plan is likely to generate income necessary to pay the lender's principal and generate an interest return. The borrower is obligated to return the principal and interest loaned and anticipates profit return above costs. If the borrower is successful, he or she pays the principal and interest and retains the entire profits. If the borrower is unsuccessful, he or she must return the principal and pay interest, even though the business venture may have incurred a loss.

In *Rodgers* v. *Tecumseh Bank*,[328] the Oklahoma Supreme Court faced the issue of whether an obligation of good faith and fair dealing should be extended beyond insurance contracts to commercial loans to support an action for "tortious breach of contract". *Rodgers* reasoned:

---

326. See *Foley* v. *Interactive Data Corp.*, 765 P.2d 373 (Cal. 1988). But see *Lanouette* v. *Ciba-Geigy Corp.*, 272 Cal. Rptr. 428 (Cal. App. 1990), *petition for review granted*, 275 Cal. Rptr. 420 (Cal. 1990), in which a California appeals court permitted a claimant in a wrongful employment termination suit to collect tort and punitive damages resulting from a claim of intentional infliction of emotional distress. Whether this case erodes the more restrictive *Foley* approach remains to be seen. Other California cases dealing with specific commercial situations, however, suggest that the "special relationship" notion is not readily transferable to the commercial arena. See, e.g., *Copesky* v. *Superior Court of San Diego*, 280 Cal. Rptr. 338 (1991).

327. 697 F. Supp. 368 (C.D. Cal. 1988).

328. 756 P.2d 1223 (Okla. 1988).

"An insurance policy, by its very nature, is an adhesion contract ... The definitive characteristic of an adhesion contract is the weaker party has no realistic choice as to its terms.

The facts of the instant case belie that this commercial loan agreement was an adhesion contract. The borrowers shopped around and came to the bank because it offered the most favourable interest rates, and in negotiating the contract, the borrowers were successful in having a favourable term inserted into the printed form. Here we have arms-length negotiating, a relatively equal bargaining capacity and no snares or traps for the unwary, quite unlike the circumstances surrounding the instance of an insurance policy.

Furthermore, the purpose of an insurance policy is the elimination of risk, an aspect wholly absent in the contract now before us ... The purpose of a commercial loan, on the other hand, is to provide the funds to facilitate the taking of a business risk. Where, as here, there is no special relationship, the parties should be free to contract for any lawful purpose and upon such terms as they believe to be in their mutual interest. To impose tort liability on a bank for every breach of contract would only serve to chill commercial transactions."[329]

The purpose of an insurance contract is to eliminate risk, whereas the purpose of a commercial loan is to give the borrower an opportunity to take a business risk in hopes of profit. Further, in insurance controversies the insurer holds the money and the insured must take action to require payment of the money, whereas a lender typically has loaned money to the borrower and is attempting to get the money back.

(d) Tort causes of action arising out of attempts at a voluntary contractual relationship A business relationship is a voluntary attempt to contract for the agreed promises and considerations from both parties. An enforceable contract traditionally includes elements of offer, acceptance, and consideration reflecting a meeting of minds between contracting parties on the material terms of the agreement. Some attempted contracts are not consummated because of improper actions by one of the contracting parties. Where one contracting party unfairly represents facts, promises, or prevents finalisation of a contract, tort law will balance the relationship by recognising a duty providing for recovery to the damaged contracting party.

   (i) *Fraud*—As discussed earlier in this chapter, here one contracting party misrepresents a material fact or makes a promise with an intent not to perform, the opposing party, reasonably relying upon the representations, may recover for injuries.[330] The representation must be a material fact as opposed to a mere matter of opinion, judgement,

---

329. *Ibid.*, at 1226–1227.

330. *Custom Leasing, Inc.* v. *Texas Bank and Trust Co.*, 516 S.W.2d 138 (Tex. 1974), lists the elements of fraud: (1) that a material representation was made; (2) that it was false; (3) that, when the speaker made it, he knew it was false or made it recklessly without any knowledge of its truth and as a positive assertion; (4) that he made it with the intention that it should be acted upon by the party; (5) that the party acted in reliance upon it; and (6) that he thereby suffered injury.

probability, or expectation[331] and the reliance on the representation must be reasonable.[332] These elements required for tort fraud recovery recognise the business reality that prospective contracting parties do not have an enforceable legal obligation without a voluntary mutual meeting of the minds, but that a party improperly deceived by reliance upon an untruthful fact or promise may recover for injuries. However, the reliance on the opposing party must be reasonable in the business environment recognising that neither party is obligated to contract and both parties are attempting to maximise profits from the agreement. Further, the representation must be more than an opinion, judgement, probability, or expectation advanced in the course of negotiations.

As will be mentioned in Part VI, some states have statutorily recognised the need to reduce a business contractual agreement to writing to be enforced. For example, in Texas, effective 1 September 1989, a loan, with required disclosures, is not enforceable for amounts in excess of $50,000.00 unless it is in writing and all rights shall be determined solely from the written loan agreement and any prior agreements are superseded and merged into the loan agreement.[333]

(ii) *Promissory estoppel*—Also as discussed earlier, promissory estoppel is an action similar to fraud. If a contracting party reasonably relies upon the promise of another to its detriment, he or she may recover under promissory estoppel.[334] As with fraud, the promise and reliance, in the proposed business arrangement, must be reasonable, taking into consideration that neither party has a duty to agree to a contract and that expectations and reliance must recognise that both parties are acting in their own best interest to maximise their profits.[335] Further, in the promise of a loan, statutory provisions in certain states may now require a loan commitment above a certain amount to be reduced to writing to be enforced.[336]

---

331. *Hicks* v. *Wright*, 564 S.W.2d 785 (Tex. Civ. App.—Tyler 1978, *writ ref'd n.r.e.*).

332. *Simpson* v. *MBank Dallas*, 724 S.W.2d 102 (Tex. App.—Dallas 1987, *writ ref'd n.r.e.*).

333. Act of 14 June, 1989, ch. 831, section 1 (to be codified at Tex. Bus. & Com. Code Ann. section 26–02 (Vernon Supp. 1989–1990)).

334. The elements of promissory estoppel are: (1) an unequivocal promise by the promisor to the promisee; (2) a reasonable expectation that the promise will influence the conduct of the promisee; (3) reasonable reliance on the promise by the promisee; and (4) detriment to the promisee which would make it unjust for the promise not to be enforced. *Wheeler* v. *White*, 398 S.W.2d 93 (Tex. 1965). Restatement (Second) of Contracts section 90(1) (1981) provides: "A promise which the promisor should reasonably expect to induce action or forbearance on the part of the promisee or a third person and which does induce such action or forbearance is binding if injustice can be avoided only by enforcement of the promise. The remedy granted for breach may be limited as justice requires." *Malaker Corp. Stockholders Protective Committee* v. *First Jersey Nat'l Bank*, 163 N.J. Super. 463, 395 A.2d 222 (1978); *Varela* v. *Wells Fargo Bank*, 15 Cal. App. 3d 741, 93 Cal. Rptr. 428 (1971). See discussion of promissory estoppel in section III.A.2. *supra*.

335. See generally *English* v. *Fischer*, 660 S.W.2d 521 (Tex. 1983), finding no contractual duty to release insurance proceeds and therefore no detrimental reliance to support promissory estoppel.

336. Act of 14 June 1989, ch. 831, 51 (to be codified at Tex. Bus. & Com. Code Ann. section 26.02 (Vernon Supp. 1989–1990).

4. Breach of duty

Once a duty (whether under contract or tort) is established, it must be breached for recovery. However, care needs to be taken to distinguish between the circumstances that create a duty and those that must be considered in determining whether there has been a breach of the recognised duty.

As previously discussed, tort law generally recognises duties arising out of an obligation to act in a reasonable, prudent manner or not to intentionally injure parties in the world at large. Contract law, on the other hand, generally recognises duties between contracting parties who voluntarily exchange promises and consideration pursuant to mutually agreed terms and conditions.[337] In contract circumstances—where parties voluntarily assume only those duties which are bargained for—courts sometimes *assume* general tort duties and simply consider only whether the contracting parties have breached some general obligation of reasonable prudence or good faith and fair dealing or good and workmanlike performance. This analysis disregards the initial issue—what duties do voluntarily negotiating parties owe to each other?[338] Once a duty is recognised in tort law or as a bargained for promise or consideration under contract law, then, and only then, is it appropriate to determine whether there is a breach of the recognised duty.[339] The distinction between existence of a legally recognised duty and breach of that duty must always be considered in determining legally recognised recovery.

(a) Exercise of agreed voluntary contract duties Obviously, the exercise of agreed voluntary contract duties does not constitute a breach of duty—whether tort or contract. Further, a failure to breach an agreed contractual duty cannot be turned into a tort duty and breach.[340] Even where the legislature statutorily creates duties between voluntarily contracting parties pursuant to the Deceptive Trade Practices Act (DTPA), the Texas Supreme Court, facing an

---

337. *Rodriguez* v. *Dipp*, 546 S.W.2d 655, 659 (Tex. Civ. App.—El Paso 1977), states: "The action of tort has for its foundation the negligence of the defendant, and this means more than a mere breach of promise. Otherwise the failure to meet a note or any other promise to pay money could sustain a suit in tort for negligence, and thus the promisor be made liable for all the consequential damages arising from such failure. As a general rule, there must be some breach of duty distinct from breach of contract."

338. In *Simpson* v. *MBank Dallas*, 724 S.W.2d 102 (Tex. App.—Dallas 1987, *writ ref'd n.r.e.*), the borrower argued that the lender's failure to obtain a waiver of a landlord's lien was a DTPA violation. The *Simpson* court held that: "MBank had no duty to obtain the waiver of the landlord's lien. Hence, failure to obtain the waiver cannot constitute a deceptive practice." *Simpson* affirmed summary judgment for the lender denying a factual issue for DTPA recovery.

339. Even *Montgomery Ward & Co.* v. *Scharrenbeck*, 204 S.W.2d 508 (Tex. 1947), which is cited as the basis of finding tort duties arising out of contract circumstances, applied a duty of care, skill, reasonable expedience and faithfulness to "the thing agreed to be done". Thus, the general tort obligations of performance apply only to "the thing agreed to be done" in agreed voluntary contract circumstances.

340. *Abilene National Bank* v. *Humble Exploration Co.*, No. 05–87–01167–CV (Tex. App.—Dallas, 17 March 1989) (removed to federal court after issuance of opinion).

unconscionable jury finding under the DTPA, found the lender. "had the right under the contract lien to start foreclosure proceedings for the amount due under the partial performance lien provision. Therefore, there is no DTPA violation for commencing foreclosure."[341]

(b) Good faith and fair dealing in performance and execution of agreed duties Much debate has argued whether a party has a general obligation of good faith and fair dealing with others. While recognising that our society approves voluntary freedom of contract in our economic system, courts have struggled with "special relationships" that arguably create obligations of duty of good faith and fair dealing even in voluntary contractual relationships. The struggle is misfocused. Voluntary contracting parties, in "special relationships", have an obligation of good faith and fair dealing in performance and execution of agreed duties of performance and execution. However, courts do not rewrite or add duties not agreed to by parties. Parties agreed to contracts attempting to maximise the benefits of their bargains under common law requirements for recognition of an enforceable contract. This clarification of the obligations of good faith and fair dealing does not deny their existence—it recognises only the obligations arising out of performance or execution of agreed duties. Thus, good faith and fair dealing does exist as a legal obligation, but it does not create duties not agreed between parties voluntarily; rather, it requires good faith and fair dealing in performance and execution of agreed contractual duties.[342]

In *Bank of America* v. *Kruse*,[343] as discussed above and hereafter, a California appellate court found there was no duty of good faith and fair dealing arising out of unsuccessful negotiations that never resulted in a legally recognised contract. Without consummation of a legally recognised contract and a resulting duty, there is no legal duty of good faith and fair dealing.

Consistent with the nonexistence of a non-agreed duty of good faith and fair dealing: "There can be no implied covenant as to a matter specifically covered by the written terms of a contract."[344] Further, the agreement made by the parties and embodied in the contract cannot be varied by an implied good faith and fair dealing covenant.[345]

Factual contractual circumstances also lead to confusion and misfocus as to obligations of good faith and fair dealing. Contractual agreements may involve exchanges of properties and promises of future performance. Exchange of

---

341. *Ogden* v. *Dickinson State Bank*, 662 S.W.2d 330 (Tex. 1983).

342. Good faith and fair dealing under section 1–203 of the UCC is limited to performance and enforcement of contracts. Noting that UCC 1–203 and the Restatement of Contract have limited applications, a commentator noted that neither the Restatement nor section 1–203 of the UCC apply to good faith in formation of a contract. See Summers, " 'Good Faith' in General Contract Law and the Sales Provision of the Uniform Commercial Code", 54 Va. L. Rev., 195, 218 (1968). See also discussion in section IV.B. *supra*.

343. 202 Cal. App. 3d 38, 248 Cal. Rptr. 217 (1988).

344. *Cluck* v. *First Nat'l. Bank of San Antonio*, 714 S.W.2d 408 (Tex. App.—San Antonio 1986, no writ).

345. *Centerre Bank of Kansas City* v. *Distributors, Inc.*, 705 S.W.2d 42 (Mo. App. 1985).

properties at the time of execution of the contract does not suggest imposition of any additional duties between the contracting parties. However, promises of future performance may carry obligations of such performance in good faith and fair dealing. This appears reasonable—it does not add or vary agreed contractual duties; but it does require performance of promises for future performance in good faith and fair dealing. Thus, if a lender funds a loan as contractually agreed, it has no further good faith and fair dealing duty to the borrower; and, the borrower, in exchange, has the duty to perform its promise to repay the loan with interest.

In indicating a shift to a restrictive approach to the expansion of tort damage claims to contractual situations, the recently reconstituted California Supreme Court, rejecting a line of appellate cases and data in the *Seaman's* case,[346] refused to hold the employment relationship a "special relationship" permitting bad faith tort damages. In *Foley* v. *Interactive Data Corporation*,[347] the court's narrow view of the "special relationship" concept was rooted in a comprehensive analysis of the role of tort liability in contractual settings. The court opted for what it saw as sound economic policy and the need for stability and predictability in commercial relationships.[348]

(c) Negligent breach of agreed contract performance duty Like the duty of good faith and fair dealing, when evaluating the duty to use care of a reasonably prudent person in a contract relationship, the distinction between a general duty of reasonable care in addition to or modification of mutually agreed duties and a duty of reasonable care in performance of agreed duties must be remembered and recognised. In the often cited case of *Montgomery Ward & Co.* v. *Scharrenbeck*,[349] the Texas Supreme Court affirmed recovery for negligent performance of a contract which included, as voluntarily negotiated consideration, a promise to repair a kerosene hot-water heater. In affirming recovery for loss resulting from the house burning down, the court stated: "Accompanying every contract is a common-law *duty to perform* with care, skill, reasonable expedience and faithfulness *the thing agreed to be done,* and a negligent failure to observe any of these conditions is a tort, as well as breach of the contract" (emphasis added).[350] The duty of care referred to in *Montgomery Ward & Co.* v. *Scharrenbeck* is not in addition to other agreed contractual duties, it is only an obligation to perform" "the thing agreed to be done" in a reasonably prudent manner. While a court may imply an obligation to use reasonable care in performance of an agreed obligation and allow recovery for negligent performance of the promised obligation, that same court should not imply a general undefined duty of reasonable care for promises not mutually

---

346. See *Seaman's Direct Buying Service, Inc.* v. *Standard Oil Company of California*, 686 P.2d 1158 (Cal. 1984).
347. 765 P.2d 373 (Cal. 1988).
348. *Ibid.* at 389–401.
349. 204 S.W.2d 508 (Tex. 1947).
350. *Montgomery Ward & Co.* v. *Scharrenbeck*, 204 S.W.2d 508 (Tex. 1947).

negotiated and agreed by the parties. Tort law recognises general obligations of reasonable care in involuntary relationships between the tortfeasor and the world at large, generally for unreasonable or intentional interference with the physical well-being of a person or property damage; whereas contract law recognises only those promises and considerations voluntarily negotiated and agreed between contracting parties. In determination of breach of a mutually agreed contractual promise to perform in the future, contract law will impose an obligation to use reasonable care in performance of the agreed promise.

B. Causation

Most discussions of duties focus primarily upon liability issues. However, causation and damages must be coupled with liability to support recovery.[351]

Causation may be a particularly important issue in an economic dispute. In many circumstances, damages may be caused by the complaining party as well as the party breaching a contractual duty. In discussing economic duress, *Simpson* v. *MBank Dallas*[352] stated: "economic duress may be claimed only when the party against whom it is claimed was responsible for claimant's financial distress." Thus, even with a liability finding, the breaching party must have caused or be responsible for resulting damages.

C. Remedies—tort and contract

Even if liability and causation are found to be legally and factually supportable, the party seeking recovery must sustain and properly prove damages. Historically, potentially recoverable damages have been different in tort and contract law. Additionally, some courts have looked to the nature of the injury to determine which duties are breached—tort or contract. While it seems backward and illogical to determine duties by looking at injuries, it may be reasonable to limit recoveries to contract damages if the injury is only the economic loss under the contract itself.[353]

1. Tort damages

Traditionally, characterising the claimant's cause of action in tort provides a broader range of damages than actions viewed solely as contract. Tort actions allow recovery for actual damages, pain and suffering, mental anguish, and

---

351. *MacDonald* v. *Texaco, Inc.*, 713 S.W.2d 203 (Tex. App.—Corpus Christi 1986, *no writ*) (no DTPA recovery without evidence of causation); *Rodriguez* v. *Carson*, 519 S.W.2d 214 (Tex. Civ. App.—Amarillo 1975, *writ ref'd n.r.e.*) (no recovery where plaintiff cannot establish liability and causation); *Watson* v. *Brazelton*, 176 S.W.2d 216 (Tex. Civ. App.—Waco 1943, *no writ*) (no fraud recovery where plaintiff fails to establish liability, causation and damages).

352. 724 S.W.2d 102 (Tex. App.—Dallas 1987, *writ ref'd n.r.e.*).

353. *Jim Walter Homes, Inc.* v. *Reed*, 711 S.W.2d 617 (Tex. 1986).

punitive or exemplary damages and any other damages reasonably resulting from breach of the tort duties.

(a) Actual damages All personal injuries or property damage reasonably foreseeable and caused by breach of tort liability duties are recoverable.[354]

(b) Punitive damages In tort actions, punitive damages are recoverable for malicious actions by the defaulting party. In *Pacific Mutual Life Insurance Co. v. Haslip*,[355] the United States Supreme Court held that the Alabama common law system of awarding punitive damages was not unconstitutional on due process grounds, as the Alabama system provided adequate guidance to the jury and meaningful judicial review of jury awards.

354. Restatement (Second) of Torts, section 522B expressly precludes benefit-of-the-bargain contract damages in situations of negligent supply of false information, limiting the damages to pecuniary losses resulting from reliance on such misinformation. There is a basic distinction between damages available for fraud and those for negligent misrepresentation. See *Frame* v. *Boatmen's Bank of Concord Village*, 824 S.W.2d 491 (Mo. App. 1992). The award of "reliance" damages to one set of plaintiffs and "benefit of the bargain" damages to another set are mutually exclusive and impermissible. See *Pathway Fin.* v. *Miami Int'l Realty Co.*, 588 So.2d 1000 (Fla. Dist. App. 1991).

355. 499 U.S. 1 (1991). Cf. *Mattison* v. *Dallas Carrier Corp.*, 947 F.2d 95 (4th Cir. 1991), which held the South Carolina system unconstitutional as it had no meaningful review of awards (i.e., all federal trial courts could do so to reduce an excessive award). For some interesting developments in this area:

— A bankruptcy company won an award against a lender for failure to fund a line of credit and for refusal to honour cheques drawn on the line of credit. The bankruptcy court awarded both compensatory and punitive damages. Compensatory damages were determined by a comparison of the value of the borrower entity immediately prior to the filing of a Chapter 7 petition to the value after liquidation. Using prior statutory law (U.C.C. s. 4–402), the court concludes the award of punitive damages was appropriate as the lender was "morally culpable" under Florida law. See *Govaert* v. *First Am. Bank and Trust Co. (In re Geri Sahn, Inc.)*, 135 B.R. 912 (Bankr. S.D. Fla. 1991).

— The Supreme Court has held that a $10 million punitive damage award (in light of a $19 million actual damage award) did not violate the due process clause of the United States Constitution as the award "was not so 'grossly excessive' ". The court noted that the award was large on a relative basis, but the countervailing factors were the total millions of dollars that were ultimately at stake in the case, the defendant's bad faith, the wealth of the defendant, and the fact that the acts in question were part of a broader scheme to defraud. See *TXO Production Corp.* v. *Alliance Resources Corp.*, ___ U.S. ___, 113 S.Ct. 2711, 125 L.Ed. 2d 366 (1993).

— A California appellate court reduced aggregate punitive damages against a lender from $8.5 million to $2.8 million to avoid a disparity in the manner in which certain of the multiple punitive damages compared to corresponding awards of compensatory damages. The court, relying on *Pacific Mut. Life Ins. Co. v. Haslip*, 111 S.Ct. 1032 (1991), chose the lowest ratio as the appropriate standard. See *Hilgedick* v. *Koehring Fin. Corp.*, 5 Cal. App. 4th 1118, 8 Cal. Reptr. 2d 76 (1992).

— The Kentucky Supreme Court reversed an appellate court's order to remand a $5.7 million punitive damage award, based on a $1 million compensatory damage award, inasmuch as the jury instructions were consistent with the standards set forth in the *Haslip* case. See *Hanson* v. *American Nat'l Bank & Trust Co.*, 844 S.W.2d 408 (Ky. 1992), *vacated and remanded*, ___ U.S. ___, 113 S.Ct. 3029, 125 L.Ed. 717 (1993).

— A Maryland state court has held that jury instructions on punitive damages need to include a finding of actual or implied malice. *Fairfax Savings, F.S.B.* v. *Ellerin*, 619 A.2d 141 (Md. Ct. Spec. App.), *cert. granted*, 621 A.2d 897 (Md. 1993) relying on *Owens-Illinois, Inc.* v. *Zenoiba*, 601 A.2d 633 (1992).

2. Contract damages

As a general rule, damages for breach of contract are measured by the aggrieved party's lost expectations. This measurement, which includes incidental and consequential damages, is designed to put the aggrieved party in the position it would have occupied had the contract been performed or to receive the benefit of the bargain.[356] In reviewing contract damages, the nature of the remedy requested must also be considered—whether equitable remedies or legal damages.

(a) Equitable remedies Generally, equitable remedies are not available if there is an adequate remedy at law.[357]

Further, even if an equitable remedy may be available, claimants are generally put to an election between equitable and legal remedies. Equitable relief, which generally requests retention of properties, is inconsistent with legal damages at law compensating the claimant for monetary damages to the property sustained as the result of liability and causation findings.

> (i) *Specific performance*—Generally, the specific performance remedy requires a greater degree of specificity of terms for enforcement than necessary for damages for breach of contract.[358] Further, courts are hesitant to order future performance because it is difficult for the court to supervise and enforce.[359]

> (ii) *Recission*—If there are liability and causation findings, the claimant may seek the equitable remedy of recission. Rescission returns the parties to their respective positions prior to the wrongful acts. As a

356. See Restatement (Second) of Contracts, section 347 (1981) and UCC s. 1–106.

357. *First Nat'l. Bank of N.J.* v. *Commonwealth Fed. Sav. & Loan of Norristown*, 610 F.2d 171 (3rd Cir. 1979). The ancient writ of injunction is deraigned to us through the exercise of equitable powers vested in the chancery courts of England. By long usage and custom the principle has become deeply anchored in equity jurisprudence that the injunctive relief ought not to be granted in any proceeding unless it is made to appear that the complainant has no adequate remedy at law for the prevention or redress of the wrongs, injuries, and grievances of which the complaint is made. The granting of an injunction in violation of this time honoured principle constitutes an erroneous abuse of the discretionary powers vested in the chancellor. *Burdette* v. *Bell*, 218 S.W.2d 904, 905 (Tex. Civ. App.—Waco 1949, *no writ*).

358. See Annot. 82 A.L.R. 3d 121–1128 (1978); *Vandeventa* v. *Dale Constr. Co.*, 271 Or. 691, 534 P.2d 183 (1975).

359. *Houston Electric Co.* v. *Glen Park Co.*, 155 S.W. 965, 968 (Tex. Civ. App.—Galveston 1913, *writ ref'd*). See also *Texas & Pacific Railway Co.* v. *Marshall*, 10 S.Ct. 846, 849 (1890); *Canteen Corp.* v. *Republic of Texas Properties, Inc.*, No. 05–88–01397, slip op. at 6 (D. Ct. Dallas 8 June 1989) ("A court will generally not decree a party to perform a continuous series of acts which extend through a long period of time and require constant supervision by the court.") *Rodriguez* v. *Via Metropolitan Transit System*, 802 F.2d 126, 132 (5th Cir. 1986) (applying Texas law) ("A decree of specific performance should be readily enforceable and should not require long continued court supervision."); *American Housing Resources, Inc.* v. *Slaughter*, 597 S.W.2d 13, 15 (Tex. Civ. App.—Dallas 1980, *writ ref'd n.r.e.*) ("Thus, the comparative advantages of the equitable remedy must be shown to outweigh those of the legal remedy. Among the factors to be considered are whether long continued supervision by the court will be required, whether complete relief can be rendered by the remedy sought, and whether if the remedy sought is granted it can be adequately enforced.")

prerequisite to rescission, the claimant must do equity. As an example, in a wrongful foreclosure setting, the complaining mortgagor must tender the debt in order to obtain rescission.[360]

(b) Damages at law Traditionally, tort damages have been much broader than contract damages. Tort recoveries include all reasonably forseeable damages, whereas contract damages generally include those that return the benefit of the bargain to the complaining party.[361] Thus, characterisation of the cause of action as tort or contract may have considerable influence on the categories and extent of damages recoverable. For example, characterisation of the breach of a duty of good faith and fair dealing, as tort or contract, may determine whether punitive damages are recoverable. If the obligation of good faith and fair dealing does not create, in a voluntary contract relationship, a new and independent duty, beyond the agreed promises and consideration, but rather, simply requires good faith and fair dealing performance of agreed contractual promises, then the action should be considered contractual and recovery should be limited to those necessary to give the complaining party the benefit of the bargain.

The Texas Supreme Court, looking to the nature of the injuries proved, rather than the duties, held: "When the injury is only the economic loss to the subject of the contract itself, the action sounds in contract alone."[362] The court, after determining there were no damages other than loss of the benefit of the bargain, refused to uphold an award of punitive damages even though the jury found gross negligence in supervision of construction.[363] The court reasoned: "Gross negligence in the breach of contract will not entitle an injured party to exemplary damages because even an intentional breach will not."[364]

(i) *Actual damages*—As has been stated previously, actual damages, for breach of contract duties, is the benefit of the bargain lost.[365] Although the benefit of the bargain damage standard is consistently referenced and followed, complaining parties must be sure that they plead and prove the particular measures of damage recognised for the breach of contract at issue. In *Farrell* v. *Hunt*,[366] the Texas Supreme Court found that the borrower, in a wrongful foreclosure action, had not proved the correct measure of common law damages—the difference between the value of the property at the date of the foreclosure and the remaining balance of the indebtedness. *Farrell* denied recovery despite

360. See generally, Baggett, *Texas Foreclosure: Law and Practice*, section 2.89 (1984, as updated).

361. See Restatement (Second) of Contracts, section 347 (1981) and UCC s. 1–106.

362. *Jim Walters Homes, Inc.* v. *Reed*, 711 S.W.2d 617 (Tex. 1986).

363. *Ibid.* It does seem strange to discuss the range of available damages by looking at the injuries sustained, but reference to benefit of the bargain damages is consistent with a review of the foundation of the duty as one of contract and not tort.

364. *Ibid.*

365. See Restatement (Second) of Contracts, section 247 (1981) and UCC s. 1–106.

366. 714 S.W.2d 298 (Tex. 1986).

jury findings that the note was not in default, the conduct was unconscionable (DTPA finding), that the unconscionable act was the producing cause of damage, and that the act was committed knowingly. Even though the jury also found the fair market value of the property at the time of the foreclosure, recovery was denied because the mortgagor/borrower, suing for wrongful foreclosure, did not request a special issue or otherwise establish the balance of the indebtedness remaining against the property. Because common law damages for wrongful foreclosure were not properly proved, the mortgagor/borrower did not recover for common law wrongful foreclosure or under the Texas Deceptive Trade Practices Act. Likewise, recovery was denied, despite jury findings of liability, causation and damages, in *Re Letterman Bros. Energy Securities Litigation*[367] because the proper measure of damages was not proved and found.

(ii) *Consequential damages*—In addition to general contract damages, claimants may recover for consequential damages that are foreseeable.[368] In order to prove foreseeability of consequential damages, the loss must have been within the contemplation of the parties at the time of the making of the contract.[369] However, the complaining party must mitigate or reduce its loss[370] and only when there is certainty of proof will consequential damages be recoverable.[371]

(iii) *Lost profits*—The most controversial form of consequential damages is lost profits.[372] For recovery to be allowed, consequential damages must be capable of reasonable ascertainment.[373] Certainty problems often are presented in attempting to prove lost profits. Little difficulty

---

367. 799 F.2d 967 (5th Cir. 1986).

368. *Hadley* v. *Baxendale* (1854) 9 Exch. 341, 156 E.R. 145, *Investors* v. *Hadley*, 738 S.W.2d (Tex. App. 1987).

369. *National Bank of Cleburne* v. *MM Pittman Roller Mill*, 265 S.W. 1024 (Tex. Ct. of App. 1924).

370. *Davis* v. *Small Business Inv. Co. of Houston*, 535 S.W.2d 740 (Tex. Civ. App. 1976).

371. *Pipkin* v. *Thomas & Hill, Inc.*, 33 N.C. App. 710, 236 S.E.2d 725 (Ct. App. 1977); *Harsha State Sav. Bank*, 346 N.W.2d 791 (Iowa 1984). In *In re Ginther*, 884 F.2d 575 (5th Cir. 1989), the borrowers alleged that the bank wrongfully terminated their credit line and, as a result, many of their ventures failed, resulting in millions of dollars in losses. The borrowers contested the lower court award of $7.5 million, asserting it was insufficient to meet the estimated $105 million in damages. However, the US Court of Appeals for the Fifth Circuit approved the settlement based on the difficulties the borrower would have in convincing the jury of their lender liability claims.

Relying on Restatement of Contracts s. 205, the US District Court for the District of New Jersey expanded a plaintiff liability for bringing a wrongful suit under Fed. R. Civ. P. 11 by awarding legal costs for "bad faith" litigation based on implied covenant of good faith in instituting litigation. See *Riveredge Assoc.* v. *Metropolitan Life Ins. Co.*, 774 F. Supp. 897 (D.N.J. 1991).

372. *Coastland Corp.* v. *Third Nat'l. Mortgage Co.*, 611 F.2d 969 (4th Cir. 1979) (lost profits allowed), *Harsha* v. *State Sav. Bank*, 346 N.W.2d 791 (Iowa 1984) (lost profits allowed).

373. *Coastland Corp.* v. *Third Nat'l. Mortgage Co.*, 611 F.2d at 977, fn. 12.

is presented by cases involving established businesses with proven earnings records.[374] However, new businesses frequently present serious difficulties in proving anticipated profits with a reasonable degree of certainty.[375] Many courts have found the profits of such businesses to be too remote and speculative for recovery to be allowed.[376] Nevertheless, recovery in such cases depends on the individual facts of the case, and numerous cases have allowed recovery for the lost profits of new businesses.[377]

(iv) *Punitive damages*—There must be actual damages before punitive damages are recoverable.[378] Further, "[g]ross negligence in the breach of contract will not entitle an injured party to exemplary damages because even an intentional breach will not."[379] However, punitive damages may be available to a complaining party who proves an independent tort resulting in actual damages.[380]

In considering whether tort damages were available for breach of a UCC duty of good faith, a Missouri Court of Appeals concluded that tort damages are not recoverable by virtue of UCC s. 1–106(1), which provides that "neither consequential or special or penal damages may be had except as specifically provided in this Act or by other rule of law".[381]

---

374. *Ibid.*

375. *Ibid.*

376. *Ibid. Harsha* v. *State Sav. Bank*, 346 N.W.2d at 797, fn. 8.

377. *Welch* v. *U.S. Bancorp Realty & Mortgage Trust*, 596 P.2d at 963, fn. 12; *Penthouse Int'l, Ltd.* v. *Dominion Fed. Save & Loan Ass'n.*, 665 F. Supp. 312, fn. 10, *rev'd in part and aff'd in part*, 5 F.2d 963 (2d Cir. 1988). Applying New York contract law, the Second Circuit Court of Appeals held that, in a breach of contract claim involving loss of "an item with a determinable market value", the market value at the time of the breach is the measure of damages. In this case, the value of the collateral turned out to be less than the amount of the debt required by the bank as a result of the sale of the collateral. As a result, the court held that the borrower could not claim damages for lost profits. See *Sharma* v. *Skaarup Ship Mgt. Corp.*, 916 F.2d 820 (2d Cir. 1990), *cert. denied*, ____ U.S. ____, 111 S. Ct. 1109, 113 L.Ed. 2d 218 (1991). The Texas Supreme Court held that a borrower in a negligent misrepresentation suit against a lender is not entitled to damages for lost profits or mental anguish, but only to actual pecuniary loss. See *Federal Land Bank Ass'n* v. *Sloane*, 825 S.W.2d 439 (Tex. 1991).

378. *Nabours* v. *Longview Savings & Loan Assn.*, 700 S.W.2d 901 (Tex. 1985).

379. *Jim Walter Homes, Inc.* v. *Reed*, 711 S.W.2d 617 (Tex. 1986) citing *Amoco Production Co.* v. *Alexander*, 622 S.W.2d 563 (Tex. 1981) and *City Products Corp.* v. *Berman*, 610 S.W.2d 446 (Tex. 1980) as authority.

380. *Texas Nat'l. Bank* v. *Karnes*, 717 S.W.2d 901 (Tex. 1986); see also Restatement (Second) of Contracts, s. 355 (1981), which states: "Punitive damages are not recoverable for a breach of contract unless the conduct constituting the breach is also a tort for which punitive damages are recoverable."

381. *Rigby Corp.* v. *Boatman's Bank and Trust Co.*, 713 S.W.2d 536 (Mo. Ct. App. 1986).

VI. CERTAIN PROTECTIVE DEVICES

Major developments respecting lender protective devices includes statutory protection in the form of revised state statute of frauds to cover oral commitment situations, use of arbitration clauses in loan documentation, and inclusion of jury waiver provisions.

A. Statute of frauds—oral commitments

A loan commitment case that caught the attention of a number of state legislatures involved the Royal Bank of Canada, which found itself in serious straits respecting a California loan "commitment". In the case of *Landes Construction Co., Inc.* v. *Royal Bank of Canada*,[382] the Ninth Circuit Court of Appeals affirmed an $18.5 million jury verdict based upon a finding that the Royal Bank of Canada breached an oral commitment to make a loan. The Ninth Circuit rejected contentions that there was insufficient evidence in the record to establish the existence of a contract, that the contract was unenforceable under the statute of frauds, and that there was insufficient proof of damages.

The case involved an oral agreement to finance, to purchase and to renovate a commercial building in Los Angeles. According to the testimony, the Royal Bank of Canada promised to provide a total of $10 million of financing. This was primarily based upon a dinner conversation by a vice president of the Bank and a statement at that dinner to the effect that "we are going to lend you the $10 million".

A purchase agreement was signed between the buyer and seller and the first $3 million down payment was made through an existing line of credit established by an associate of Mr Landes with the bank. The $7 million balance was to come from the "promised" $10 million financing. When the loan proposal was sent to Canada for approval, the bank refused to provide the financing. Landes Construction sued the bank for breach of its oral contract. The jury found that a promise had been made and the Ninth Circuit held that the promise was not covered by California's statute of frauds.

Although the appellate courts recently appear less willing to find oral "commitments" to loan,[383] various state legislatures (e.g., California, Texas, Illinois and Oklahoma) have also attempted to restrict alleged oral loan commitment liability by enacting revisions to their statutes of fraud. For instance, the California legislature amended its general purpose, civil statute of frauds to provide that in non-consumer transactions a commercial lender's promise or commitment to loan money or to grant or extend credit in an amount greater than $100,000 is not enforceable unless it is in writing and signed by the

---

382. 833 F.2d 1365 (9th Cir. 1987).

383. E.g. *Penthouse Int'l Ltd.* v. *Dominion Federal Savings and Loan Association*, 855 F.2d 963 (2d Cir. 1989), *cert. denied*; and *Kruse* v. *Bank of America*, 202 Cal. App. 3d 38 (1988).

person to be charged.[384] Lenders should be cautioned, however, because the general exceptions to the statute of frauds will apply to this revision as well. In particular, the doctrine of equitable or promissory estoppel has, under existing case law, been successfully asserted to avoid the statute of frauds. Generally, equitable estoppel is available when (a) one party suffers an unconscionable injury based on a serious change in position in reliance on the oral promise or (b) when necessary to prevent the unjust enrichment of the party denying the validity of the contract. These notions of estoppel have been discussed earlier in this chapter.

Notwithstanding changing judicial attitudes and legislative responses to oral commitments, the writing of a conditional commitment or proposal by a lender should be done with great care. The following are factors that should be taken into consideration so as to minimise the risks in connection with loan commitments or proposals.[385]

If it is a proposal and the lender specifically does *not* want to be viewed as having made a commitment:

— clearly state that the letter is a proposal and is not a commitment;
— do not charge a large fee. The fee should be reasonable and related to the costs of the lender in its review and credit appraisal. If any portion is to be non-refundable, make sure that portion relates to costs and expenditures of the lender such as appraisals, searches, legal fees, etc.;
— do not issue press releases or inform third parties that you are in the process of preparing to extend credit;
— insert a confidentiality provision to avoid reliance by third parties;
— make sure your other credit documents, including the credit file, do not evidence a "commitment" to make a loan.

If the lender *does intend to commit* to making a loan, describe in detail the transaction, including the parties involved, the structure and the purpose:

— make a detailed list of conditions precedent to the consummation of the transaction;
— describe in detail the amount of the loan, interest rate, fees, penalties and other monetary terms;
— describe key negative and affirmative covenants. Describe collateral, security agreements and guaranties;
— insert a protective provision relating to a change in circumstances, e.g., a material adverse change in the debtor's business, increase in the interest rates, etc.;

---

384. Cal. Civ. Code section 1624 (1989). See also Pearson, Todd C., "Limiting lender liability: the trend toward written credit agreement statutes" (1991) 76 Minn. L. Rev. 295–325.

385. See *Norton & Baggett, supra* fn. 3, Ch. 22 ("Use of Arbitration and Jury Waiver Clauses in the Context of Lender Liability"), section 22.03[1], from which this Part VI is based.

— require that all documentation and the structuring of the transaction has to be acceptable to lender's legal counsel;
— insert a costs and expenses clause, including reasonable attorneys' fees, in the event of any action taken with respect to the enforcement of the commitment letter;
— describe any unusual aspect to the transaction which would not normally be found in a standard loan agreement, e.g., unusual events of default based on the unique character of the debtor's business, etc.

B. Arbitration clauses in loan documentation

Typically, the very nature of a loan arrangement and the desire of a lender for prompt and effective enforcement when needed cuts against arguments for use of arbitration clauses in commercial loan arrangements. However, with the rise of lender liability awards, arbitration proponents now cite many reasons why arbitration is a desirable dispute resolution technique[386]:

— Avoidance of excessive jury awards;
— Minimisation of threatened lender liability claims in workout situations;
— Savings in time and expense;
— Arbitrators' special knowledge and expertise;
— Less adversarial nature and privacy of proceedings.

However, some of the problems inherent to arbitration may include:

— Recently court created possibility of punitive damages[387];
— No written opinion supporting the arbitration award;
— Tendency of arbitrator to compromise;
— Absence of appeal from award and limited judicial review.[388]

If an all-inclusive arbitration clause is used (e.g., all claims or disputes arising under or in connection with the loan shall be subject to arbitration), the lender may be precluding the availability of pre-trial remedies traditionally available to lenders, such as claim and delivery and attachment. Consequently, when drafting an arbitration clause in loan documentation, the lender must carefully and specifically state what disputes are subject to arbitration.

Parties may identify certain types of claims arising out of a particular transaction as being arbitrable and certain others as not. In order to preserve quick access to court to obtain desirable pre-trial remedies, it may be advisable to split the proceedings by excluding from a general arbitration clause the

---

386. *Ibid.* section 22.03[2] and section 22.04.
387. E.g. *Willoughby Roofing & Supply Co., Inc.* v. *Kajima Int'l*, 598 F. Supp. 353 (N.D. Ala. 1984).
388. E.g. *I/S Starborg* v. *Nat'l Metal Converters, Inc.*, 500 F.2d 424 (2d Cir. 1974). See also 9 U.S.C. section 10 on grounds for vacating an award.

determination of whether the loan is in default and the subsequent proceedings including entry of judgment on the debt.[389]

Under most arbitration statutes, strong preference is given to enforcing the agreement to arbitrate. Even ambiguous or unclear arbitration agreements will be enforced.[390] There are, however, certain circumstances in which a court will decline to enforce arbitration, such as failure to comply with statutory formalities,[391] contracts of adhesion,[392] fraud in the inducement,[393] waiver[394] and conflict with fundamental public policy.[395]

Statutory law in some states (e.g., California) may make the inclusion of arbitration clauses risky or undesirable in loan transactions where real property collateral is involved. For example, under California's "single-action" rule,[396] it is arguable that an arbitration proceeding would be an "action".

Neither arbitration agreements nor arbitration decisions are binding on third parties. The variety of third parties who may have an interest in the transaction giving rise to the arbitrable dispute is vast. Such parties would include junior secured creditors, guarantors or sureties, and affiliates of the debtor who may have been "harmed" by the lender's alleged wrongdoing. By proceeding with arbitration with the debtor, the lender still could conceivably be facing a myriad of claims by or against others in separate litigation.

Since debtors' attorneys can be expected to use various means to side-step arbitration, it is plausible (even likely) that they may arrange for one or more third parties not bound by the arbitration agreement to file suit against the lender for any number of possible claims. This, obviously, would lead to quite undesirable results for the lender who truly desired to arbitrate all disputes relating to a given transaction.[397]

C. Jury waiver provisions

In reviewing the recent lender liability cases in which tremendous punitive damage awards were granted, it is apparent that it is the jury which normally sides with the plaintiff in imposing damages against the lender. Consequently, it is often in the lender's interest to keep the case away from a jury, if possible. As discussed, arbitration is one recognised method for keeping a civil case away from the jury. A second method is the incorporation of a jury waiver provision in the contract out of which the dispute arises.

---

389. See *Dean Witter Reynolds, Inc.* v. *Byrd*, 470 U.S. 213 (1985).
390. E.g. *Morgan* v. *Smith Barney, Harris Upham & Co.*, 729 F.2d 1163.
391. E.g. agreement be in writing or contain certain conspicuous legends.
392. E.g. *Shearson/American Express, Inc.* v. *McMahon*, 107 S. Ct. 2332 (1987).
393. E.g. *Prima Paint Corp.* v. *Flood & Conklen Mfg. Co.*, 388 U.S. 395 (1967).
394. E.g. *American Locomotive Co.* v. *Chemical Research Corp.* 171 F.2d 115 (6th Cir. 1948), *cert. denied*.
395. E.g. *Mitsubishi Motors Corp.* v. *Soler Chrysler-Plymouth*, 105 S. Ct. (1989).
396. Cal. Code of Civ. Proc. section 726.
397. See *Norton & Baggett*, *supra* fn. 3, section 22.04[4].

Case law has established that the constitutional or statutory right to a jury trial may be waived by a contractual provision in advance of litigation.[398] Under this general rule, it follows that a provision in a loan agreement waiving the right to a jury trial in any dispute arising out of that agreement should be enforceable.

There are a number of limitations, however, on the enforceability of jury waivers. Specific state statutory or constitutional law may impose special requirements on such provisions. For instance, in some states, an enforceable waiver may be required to be in conspicuous type. Further, there may be certain transactions in which such waivers are prohibited, such as in consumer loan transactions. In some jurisdictions, a jury trial waiver may not be enforceable in personal injury or direct property loss cases as a matter of public policy.[399] Cases involving pure economic loss have been distinguished.

Language in the jury waiver must be appropriately broad to encompass all possible permutations of the debtor-creditor dispute. For instance, the language should be sufficiently broad to cover disputes arising in connection with a refinanced note.

When documenting a transaction, remember that a jury waiver will not apply to those who are not a party to the waiver provision. For example, if a guarantor or surety is involved in the transaction, they will not be bound by a jury waiver unless a specific waiver is also put into the guaranty or surety documentation.

Contracts of adhesion or unconscionable provisions are particularly susceptible to attack in the jury waiver context.[400] A recent federal court decision has found a jury waiver to be enforceable against attacks of unconscionability when there was a basic equality of bargaining power between the lender and the borrower.[401] The court found that relative bargaining positions of the parties was equal and that therefore the borrower had knowingly and voluntarily consented to the waiver provision. This conclusion was evidenced by the fact that the borrower had been represented by counsel during the documentation phase of the transaction and the documentation had been negotiated by the borrower. Presumably an inequality in bargaining power would be evidence that a contractual jury waiver was not knowingly or intentionally made.

To protect against attacks of unconscionability, or that the waiver is unenforceable as a contract of adhesion, the following guidelines are suggested:

— print the waiver in boldface type, perhaps conspicuously on the front of the contract if it is a preprinted form;
— have the borrower initial the provision;

398. See Annot., "Validity and Effect of Contractual Waiver of Trial by Jury," 73 A.L.R. 2d 1332 (1960). See also Rusoff, David T., "Contractual jury waivers: their use in reducing lender liability" (1992) 110 Banking L.J. 4–29.

399. See *Avenue Assocs., Inc.* v. *Buxbaum*, 373 N.Y.S. 2d 814 (Sup. Ct. 1975).

400. E.g. *Department Stores, Inc.* v. *Stephens*, 404 So. 2d 586 (Ala. 1981).

401. *Re Reggie Packing Co.* v. *Lazare Financial Corp.*, 671 F. Supp. 571 (N.D. Ill. 1987).

— in the interest of fairness as well as assisting in enforceability, the waiver should apply to both the lender and the borrower.

To further bolster the argument, it would be helpful if the borrower was represented by counsel at the documentation phase and if the documents were negotiated by the borrower.

As with agreements to submit disputes to arbitration, jury waiver provisions can be waived by a party's conduct. For example, as discussed above, the Sixth Circuit in *KMC* v. *Irving Trust Co.*[402] invalidated a jury waiver on the grounds that evidence indicated that the loan officer represented to the borrower, prior to closing the loan, that the jury waiver would not be enforced if the parties proceeded to litigation. This action was deemed to constitute a waiver of the jury waiver provision.

VII. BASIC RULES AND GUIDEPOSTS FOR LENDERS

As readily discerned from the discussions above, the legal implications of the exercise of inordinate control and other misconduct by a lender can have broad adverse practical significance for a lender. While the issues present broad policy considerations concerning fundamental economic and social matters that should ultimately be resolved in a thoughtful (and not inadvertent and unthinking) fashion by the courts and legislature, the issues also raise numerous practical considerations for lenders that ought to be incorporated into their planning processes. The planning dilemmas for a lender and its counsel are most often to determine the line between the proper exercise of control pursuant to normal and prudent lending practices and the inordinate exercise of control creating legal liability for the lender, and otherwise to ensure professional conduct of its officers, employees and agents. As with much of business litigation, the results are highly "fact sensitive", with hindsight often being a slayer of giants. With this in mind, the authors make the following "basic rules" for a lender prior to developing a "workout plan" for a borrower:

Basic rules for lender

1. Know the borrower.
2. Know the borrower's assets.
3. Know the existing loan documents.
4. Know the interrelationship of loan documents with other loan documents, indentures, and other material agreements of the borrower.
5. Understand the entire lender relationship with the borrower.
6. Understand the lender's general policy in loan and workout situations.

---

402. 757 F.2d 752 (6th Cir. 1985).

7. Be aware of the existence of any prior course of lender conduct with the borrower.
8. Know the true objectives of the workout and the realistic likelihood of achieving them.
9. Know your professional role as a lender and loan officer.

Many of the problems in the lender "control" cases appear to stem from a loss of perspective by the lender and its loan officers as to their roles. By having a sound initial perspective as to what is, in fact, the intended role of the lender in the workout situation, many lender-liability problems can be avoided. Clearly, a lender is permitted to have tough, arm's-length negotiated lending arrangements, to require significant information and reporting by the borrower, to seek additional collateral, etc. However, at the point that the lender begins (directly or indirectly) to interfere with the day-to-day operations and business affairs of the borrower or with the management structure of the borrower or to exact unfair advantage, then the "danger zone" has been entered. Also, by understanding one's role as a lender, a sense of professionalism will result in the relationship with the troubled borrower. High-handed tactics, table pounding, threats and intimidations, and ambiguous and misleading statements designed to force a certain borrower reaction can all lead to the detriment of the lender. In addition, sloppy and ill-conceived internal memoranda concerning the lender's assessment of the situation, or concerning various meetings among a group of lenders or between the lender and the borrower, can also prove fatal upon discovery in the litigation context. As such, a loan officer should know the proper role of the lender, should know his or her professional role in the transaction, and should be sensitive to the fact that what is said or written (or not said or left unwritten) prior to or during the course of a workout situation can either prove helpful or harmful to the bank depending upon the lender's and loan officer's professionalism and sound judgement employed in such matters. It should be remembered that lender liability does not arise by one dramatic event but mostly evolves over a period of time through a course of conduct engaged in by the lender.

In a workout situation, a lender should consider also some of the following specific *guideposts*:

Guideposts for lender

1. A lender should avoid threatening a borrower with default in a workout situation (or otherwise), unless the lender then intends and has the legal right to carry out the threat. For example, if in *Farah*, the lenders had, prior to the 22 March lender's letter, determined, in fact, to declare a default if Willie Farah were elected, the letter (and comments of counsel), albeit overly harsh, would probably have been legal.

2. A lender should avoid requiring (or even urging) specific changes in the

management of a borrower, even if there is an explicit clause in the loan document allowing it. If a lender has a change in a management clause, it should be as objective and as comprehensive as possible. For example, in *Farah*, any two of the banks could declare default under the clause and the clause did not include any changes covering the board of directors. Also if a lender has a change of management clause in a loan document, and if there is a borrower-originated management change to the lender's dislike, the lender should not declare a default unless it has a "reasonable, good faith belief" that the security or collateral of its loan is materially and directly impaired by the management change. Otherwise, the default may be found to be in bad faith and unjustified.

3. It is the conduct of the lender between the time it discovers the financial difficulty of its borrower and the time of default and foreclosure that normally causes the problem. That is why it is important for the lender to have a firm grasp of the situation prior to the "workout" period and then to monitor carefully the lender's and its loan officer's conduct during the "workout".

4. While a lender can enforce its loan rights, declare default, and foreclose upon its collateral, before doing so a careful review should be made of the lender's actual prior course of conduct with the borrower, the actual financial conditions of the borrower, and the lender's "security" status under the loan.

5. While nothing is wrong with requiring tough financial ratios, positive and negative covenants, and financial reports in a loan arrangement or with requiring the financial stability of your borrower, a lender should be careful to avoid actual involvement in the day-to-day business of the borrower.

6. While a lender can protect its loan and collateral through loan documents freely negotiated, the more onerous the restriction on the borrower, the worse off the lender may become when loan rights are initiated during the workout.

7. A lender engaging in the following activities towards its borrower runs significant risks of being deemed to have so dominated its borrower's daily operations as, in effect, to control it, and to be responsible for the borrower's losses and also possibly of being deemed to be in a "conflict of interest" situation when exercising what otherwise would be legitimate lender rights and practices:

> (i) having officers, directors, employees, or agents of the lender or its affiliates serve as directors, officers, or managers of the borrower;
> (ii) directing (directly or indirectly) who serves as an officer, director, or stockholder of the borrower;
> (iii) having direct or indirect involvement through an agent in the day-to-day management decisions of the borrower, including, but not limited to, decisions concerning: (1) the hiring or firing of employees or officers; (2) the specific purchase and sale of goods and assets; and (3) the bills (creditors that it should pay or when it should pay them);
> (iv) having lender employees on the borrower's payroll;
> (v) having lender employees or agents on the borrower's premises, except

under clear written agreement with the borrower detailing the activities in which such agents are to engage;

(vi) paying the salary or wages of the borrower's officers or employees;

(vii) paying or indemnifying any person to serve as a director of the borrower;

(viii) participating directly or indirectly in the borrower's financial decisions;

(ix) threatening any action without both the legal right to take the action and the present intent to take the action if the threat is not heeded;

(x) lending sums for wages without assurance that the trust fund portion of withholding taxes are paid to the IRS;

(xi) preventing the payment of withholding taxes;

(xii) preventing the payment of dividends when the borrower is financially able to pay them;

(xiii) owning or possessing (e.g., voting trust) a significant block of voting stock of the borrower can give rise to serious risks, such as:

(a) A lender which (alone or through collective action) has control over a borrower through voting stock or otherwise may be deemed to be a fiduciary for state law purposes, an "insider" for federal bankruptcy purposes, and a "control" person for federal securities laws purposes. In such cases, the lender should exercise very careful precautions to be certain that its conduct does not harm the borrower or its creditors, or (if securities are involved) its investors. Further, the lender should consider divesting itself of the equity on the loan as soon as possible.

(b) In the workout context, if equity is offered, the lender should avoid taking voting stock, but instead (unless the lender is willing contractually to subordinate itself to the unsecured creditors) take preferred stock, convertible debt, or warrants exercisable upon default.

VIII. CONCLUDING OBSERVATIONS

Expansion of lender liability in the United States over the past decade has, in fact, had a therapeutic effect upon untoward lender conduct. However, it must be remembered that profits and increased property ownership are produced through negotiated contracts, hopefully mutually benefiting both parties and thereby leading to increased production for all citizens. Freedom of contract provides all citizens with the opportunity to participate in economic growth and the reward of the benefits of their bargains. Though not all contracts will prove economically beneficial to both parties, the legal system should allow all parties the opportunity to benefit from their negotiated bargain. Likewise, freedom of contract discourages the unwise and inefficient. Even negative contractual consequences push society towards progress and productivity. A sound economic system rewards efficient and effective productivity and redirects inefficient and ineffective production to new or alternative opportunities.

To encourage profit motivation, private ownership, and freedom of contract, the law should provide understandable and predictable permissible standards of conduct. The law should allow parties to negotiate contracts for profits and reasonably to expect voluntary performance of the carefully crafted business arrangements. Judges and juries that seek to restructure profit-motivated agreements, after time, change economics, alter justifiably anticipated profits, and discourage private risk assumption and voluntary compliance with negotiated performance, even though the performance later proves less than desired and potentially detrimental. An appropriate legal approach to lender liability should encourage all parties to enter into and perform agreed bargains, and if not beneficial, redirect their bargains and performance in future agreed contracts.

One major danger of undefined lender liability theories is that they will create an overly cautious lending system. In that event, companies and individuals will likely be heard to complain that lenders are refusing to grant loans or to engage in constructive workouts. The lenders' refusal will not be premised on their belief that the loans or restructure are unreasonably risky credits, but rather on the lenders' choice to minimise the risk getting caught in an expensive liability theory lottery. Defensive lending practices will hinder entrepreneurship. Law should create and enforce legal rules with proper incentives for lenders, rather than to take away incentives.

The current trend of the US courts appears to be to go back to a more classic approach to "line drawing" between contract and tort claims. However, most likely some expansion of lender liability will continue, particularly in such areas as environmental claims, leveraged buyout arrangements and other business arrangements involving lender conflict of interest, loan participations (and other *bank* v. *bank* situations) and claims against management of financial institutions. All will not be contained within the "four corners" of a commercial contract as innovative plaintiffs' lawyers will continue to show tenacity and imagination in structuring their claims. At the end of the day the US's famous or infamous "love affair" with lay juries will (most likely) continue in the commercial areas (e.g. contrasted with the limited jury uses in such matters in England or the absence of juries in commercial affairs in "civil law" jurisdictions).

JOSEPH JUDE NORTON*

* The author acknowledges the contribution of W.M. Baggett to this chapter.

INDEX

Administrative receiver
  environmental liability, 164
  invalid appointment of, 173–174
Administrator
  clean-up operations by, 166
  environmental liability, 164
Advertising
  home loan services, of, 115
Agency
  actual or apparent authority, 2
  principal-agent theory of lender liability,
    359–361
Agricultural land
  mortgagor, leases binding, 149–150
Arbitration clause
  loan documentation, in, 405–406
Australian banks
  Cross Vesting Scheme, 312
  fiduciary duties,
    banker and customer, relationship of, 314
    exposure to, 326
    foreign currency loan contract, principles
      applied to, 315–316
    trust, reliance and confidence, arising on,
      314–315
    undue influence, claim of, 316
    where owed, 315
  foreign currency adviser, nature and extent
    of advice from, 308
  foreign currency borrowings, 297–299
  foreign currency borrowings, standard of
    care as to, 309–313
  lender liability, introduction of concept, 325
  misleading and deceptive conduct, 313
  negligent advice, cause of action, 312
  risk minimisation techniques, advice on,
    313
  Swiss franc loans, liability for,
    avoidance of, 326
    background to, 297–299
    causation, 322–325
    concurrent, 299–300
    conduct of another person, damage
      caused by, 323–325

Australian banks—*cont.*
  Swiss franc loans, liability for—*cont.*
    contract, in, 300–305
    contractual obligation, standard of care,
      303–305
    damages calculation, 319
    duty of care, 305–306
    duty to advise, 301–302
    economic loss, recovery of, 320
    evidence, 316–318
    exchange rates, movement in, 298
    express terms of contract, 301–302
    fiduciary duties, 314–316
    general negligence principles, application
      of, 328
    implied terms of contract, 302–303
    interim interlocutory injunction,
      obtaining, 321
    lessons of, 325–328
    limitation of, 327
    limitation period, 318–319
    litigation, course of, 316–317
    misrepresentation, basis of, 320
    remedies, 319–322
    statutory remedies, 321
    tort, in, 305–314
    tortious standard of care, 307–314
  Trade Practices Act, 312–314, 321, 323
    Cross Vesting Scheme, 312
    misleading and deceptive conduct,
      313
    negligent advice, cause of action, 312
    risk minimisation techniques, advice
      on, 313

Bank
  customer, relationship with. *See* Customer
  standards of conduct, expectations about,
    116
Bank syndicates
  arrangers of, 3
Banker's references
  Canadian lender liability, 277–279
  duty of confidentiality, 19–21

413

Parker Hood